SOCIOLOGY
for a NEW CENTURY

Also from Pine Forge Press

Sociology for a New Century: A Pine Forge Press Series

Edited by Charles Ragin, Wendy Griswold, and Walter W. Powell

An Invitation to Environmental Sociology by Michael M. Bell
Global Inequalities by York W. Bradshaw and Michael Wallace
Schools and Societies by Steven Brint
Economy/Society by Bruce Carruthers and Sarah Babb
How Societies Change by Daniel Chirot
Ethnicity and Race: Making Identities in a Changing World by Stephen Cornell and
    Doug Hartmann
The Sociology of Childhood by William A. Corsaro
Cultures and Societies in a Changing World by Wendy Griswold
Crime and Disrepute by John Hagan
Gods in the Global Village: The World's Religions in Sociological Perspective by Lester R. Kurtz
Waves of Democracy: Social Movements and Political Change by John Markoff
Development and Social Change: A Global Perspective, Second Edition, by Philip McMichael
Aging, Social Inequality, and Public Policy by Fred C. Pampel
Constructing Social Research by Charles C. Ragin
Women and Men at Work by Barbara Reskin and Irene Padavic
Making Societies: The Historical Construction of Our World by William A. Roy
Cities in a World Economy, Second Edition, by Saskia Sassen
Gender, Family, and Social Movements by Suzanne Staggenborg
Law/Society: Origins, Interactions, and Change by John Sutton

Titles of Related Interest from Pine Forge Press

Sociological Theory by Bert N. Adams and R. A. Sydie
Taking It Big: Developing Sociological Consciousness in Postmodern Times by Steven Dandaneau
Sociology in Action: Cases for Critical and Sociological Thinking by David Hachen
Illuminating Social Life: Classical and Contemporary Theories Revisited, Second Edition,
    by Peter Kivisto
Sociology Through Active Learning: Student Exercises for Exploring by Kathleen McKinney,
    Frank D. Beck, and Barbara S. Heyl
The Production of Reality, Third Edition, by Jodi O'Brien and Peter Kollock
This Book Is Not Required, Revised Edition, by Inge Bell and Bernard McGrane
Sociology: Exploring the Architecture of Everyday Life, Third Edition, by David Newman
Sociology: Exploring the Architecture of Everyday Life (Readings), Third Edition,
    by David Newman
The McDonaldization of Society, New Century Edition, by George Ritzer
Worlds Apart: Social Inequalities in a New Century by Scott Sernau

About the Authors

York W. Bradshaw is Professor and Chair of Sociology at the University of Memphis. Prior to this position, he was Director of African Studies and Professor of Sociology at Indiana University, Bloomington. He has also taught and lectured at a number of African universities in Kenya, Zambia, and South Africa. Professor Bradshaw has written and taught on a number of topics, including education and health in developing countries, debt and economic adjustment in poor regions, and African and Asian development. His most recent book is *The Uncertain Promise of Southern Africa* (edited with Stephen Ndegwa).

Joseph F. Healey is Professor of Sociology at Christopher Newport University. His research interests include American minority group relations, immigration, and the sociology of sport. He has written several textbooks, including *Statistics: A Tool for Social Research* (5th edition, Wadsworth) and *Race, Ethnicity, Gender, and Class* (2nd edition, Pine Forge Press).

Rebecca Smith is a freelance writer and editor who has worked on many Pine Forge Press publications, as well as textbooks and journals on psychology, business, and communication. She has a master of science degree in communication and teaches written, oral, and interpersonal communication skills to working adults through the University of California, San Diego.

About the Publisher

Pine Forge Press is a new educational publisher, dedicated to publishing innovative books and software throughout the social sciences. On this and any other of our publications, we welcome your comments. Please call or write us at

Pine Forge Press
A Sage Publications Company
Editorial Offices
31 St. James Avenue, Suite 510
Boston, MA 02116
(617) 753-7512
E-mail: info@pfp.sagepub.com

Visit *www.sagepub.com/pineforge,* your direct link to a multitude of on-line resources.

SOCIOLOGY

for a NEW CENTURY

York W. Bradshaw
University of Memphis

Joseph F. Healey
Christopher Newport University

Rebecca Smith

PINE FORGE PRESS
Boston • Thousand Oaks, California • London • New Delhi

For information, address:

 Pine Forge Press
A Sage Publications Company
2455 Teller Road
Thousand Oaks, California 91320
E-mail: sales@pfp.sagepub.com

Sage Publications Ltd.
6 Bonhill Street
London EC2A 4PU
United Kingdom

Sage Publications India Pvt. Ltd.
M-32 Market
Greater Kailash I
New Delhi 110 048 India

Publisher: Stephen Rutter
Assistant to the Publisher: Kirsten Stoller
Copy Editor: Nancy Campbell Wirtes
Project Management, Design, and Typesetting: Books By Design, Inc.

Printed in the United States of America

00 01 02 03 04 05 06 7 6 5 4 3 2 1

Library of Congress Cataloging-in-Publication Data

Bradshaw, York W., 1960–
    Sociology for a new century / by York W. Bradshaw, Joseph F. Healey,
and Rebecca Smith.
        p. cm.
Includes bibliographical references and index.
ISBN 0-8039-9082-0 (alk. paper)
1. Sociology. 2. International relations—Social aspects. 3. Cultural relations.
4. Globalization. I. Healey, Joseph F., 1945–   II. Smith, Rebecca. III. Title.
HM447 .B7 2000
301—dc21

                                                        00–012774

Contents in Brief

1 A Global View of Society • *How can sociology help us understand global trends?* • BRADSHAW **1**

Topical Essay • *My Personal Journey to a Global Perspective* • DAWSON **35**

2 Sociology and Society • *How does sociological theory help us interpret the world?* • HEALEY **41**

Topical Essay • *The Globalization of Taste* • HART **75**

3 Sociology and Science • *How do sociologists investigate questions about society?* • HEALEY **85**

4 Culture and Society • *Can local culture coexist with global culture?* • HEALEY **117**

Topical Essay • *How Culture Shapes Schooling* • BRINT **149**

Topical Essay • *Local Gods and Universal Faiths* • KURTZ **155**

5 Inequality • *Are the rich getting richer and the poor getting poorer?* • HEALEY **161**

Topical Essay • *Biopiracy and Gene Theft* • McMICHAEL **197**

6 Assimilation and Pluralism • *Will racial and ethnic groups persist?* • HEALEY **205**

7 Gender • *How is globalization affecting inequalities between women and men?* • FERNANDEZ-KELLY AND FALLON **239**

Topical Essay • *Sex as a Global Commodity* • NAGEL **275**

8 Families • *What is happening to families in a changing world?* • LYE AND BRADSHAW **281**

9 Crime and Punishment • *Can crime be controlled?* • HEALEY **319**

10 Economics and Politics • *Does democracy have a future?* • MARKOFF **353**

Topical Essay • *Activists Crusade against Sweatshops* • SEIDMAN **393**

At Issue SOCIOLOGY EXAMINES A NEW CENTURY 401

11 The Changing Face of War / BRADSHAW **403**

12 The Future of Work / LEICHT **421**

13 Can the World Develop and Sustain Its Environment? / BELL **441**

14 How Many People Is Too Many People? / LYE **461**

15 The Global Healthcare Challenge / MBUGUA **483**

16 Creating Positive Social Change / BRADSHAW **503**

Appendix A Sociologist's Atlas / FALLON **A1**

Contents

Graphics xix

Preface xxiii

1   A Global View of Society • *How can sociology help us understand global trends?* • YORK W. BRADSHAW   **1**

The Interconnected World   **3**

Sociology's Contribution to Understanding Global Issues   **6**

A Global Perspective   **7**

The Book's Themes: Global Trends   **9**

The Spread of Technology Is Both Blessing and Curse   10

Economic Ties Strengthen as Political Structures Fracture   14

Culture Is at the Center of Globalization   18

Ethnicity Shapes People's Lives   21

Modernity and Progress Depend on Perspective   24

Internal and External Forces Interact to Change Societies   25

Inequality Grows within Societies and across Societies   28

A Look Forward   **31**

Key Concepts   **32**

Active Learning   **32**

Topical Essay • *My Personal Journey to a Global Perspective* • TRACEY JANE DAWSON   **35**

2   Sociology and Society • *How does sociological theory help us interpret the world?* • JOSEPH F. HEALEY   **41**

The Origins of Sociology   **42**

Karl Marx (1818–1883)   45

Max Weber (1864–1920)   48

Emile Durkheim (1858–1917)   51

The Sociological Perspective 55

The Continuing Relevance of Marx, Weber, and Durkheim 57

Marxism and Modern Capitalism 58
World Systems Theory 58
The Limits of World Systems Theory 61
Rationalization in Modern Society 63
Bureaucracy 63
McDonaldization 64
Suicide in the Modern World 67
Suicide around the Globe 67
Teenage Suicide in the United States 68

Conclusion 71

Key Concepts 71

Active Learning 72

Topical Essay • *The Globalization of Taste* • NICKY HART **75**

3   Sociology and Science • *How do sociologists investigate questions about society?* • JOSEPH F. HEALEY **85**

**Using Science to Examine a Social Problem:
Is American Society Disintegrating? 86**

Approaching the Problem: The Scientific Method 87

Description, Explanation, and Causation 88
Interaction between Theory and Research 90
Scientific Inquiry 92
Skepticism and Critical Thinking 92
Evaluation of Evidence 95
Probabilistic Relationships 96
Correlation and Causation 97
Traditions of Research 98
Communities of Scholars: The Loyal Opposition 99
Issues of Definition and Measurement 99
The Effects of Changing Age Distribution 103
The Importance of Comparison Points 103
Alternative Causes 104
The Value of Debate 106

Gathering Data 107

Experiments 108
Field Experiments 110
Surveys 110
Observation (Field Research) 112
Analyses of Existing Data 113

Conclusion   113

Key Concepts   114

Active Learning   114

4   Culture and Society • *Can local culture coexist with global culture?* • JOSEPH F. HEALEY   **117**

A Sociological Perspective on Culture   119

Culture and Community   122

Elements of Culture   123

Material Culture   123

Nonmaterial Culture   125

Beliefs   125

Values   126

Norms   127

Rituals   128

Technology   130

Communication   131

The Construction of Culture   132

The Transmission of Culture to Individuals   133

Socialization   134

Acculturation   136

The Social Production of Culture   137

Culture Change   139

The Globalization of Culture   141

Conclusion   144

Key Concepts   145

Active Learning   146

Topical Essay • *How Culture Shapes Schooling* • STEVEN BRINT   **149**
Topical Essay • *Local Gods and Universal Faiths* • LESTER R. KURTZ   **155**

5   Inequality • *Are the rich getting richer and the poor getting poorer?* • JOSEPH F. HEALEY   **161**

Sociological Perspectives on Inequality   162

Class Interests and Inequality   165

Three Dimensions of Stratification   166

The Functions of Inequality   168

The Evolution of Inequality 169

    Hunting and Gathering Societies 170
    Agricultural Societies 171
    Industrial Societies 172
        The Kuznets Curve 174
        Labor Sectors 175

Increasing Inequality in the United States 177

    The Great U-Turn 178
    Deindustrialization 180

Inequality around the Globe 183

    Inequality among Nations and the Effects of Globalization 183
    Inequality within Nations 186
        High-Income Nations: The European Welfare States 187
        Middle-Income Nations: Newly Industrializing Countries 189
        Low-Income Countries: Africa 190

Conclusion 192

Key Concepts 193

Active Learning 194

Topical Essay • *Biopiracy and Gene Theft* **•** PHILIP McMICHAEL **197**

6 **Assimilation and Pluralism •** *Will racial and ethnic groups persist?* **•** JOSEPH F. HEALEY **205**

    Global Species Consolidation: Analyzing Race and Ethnicity 207

        Dispersion and Differentiation: The Origins of Ethnicity and Race 207
        Contact and Consolidation: Evolution of a Global Species 209

    Social Relations in a Differentiated World 210

        Minority Groups and Dominant Groups 210
        Prejudice and Discrimination 211
        Assimilation and Pluralism 212
        Contact Situations 214

    Contact Situations: Conquest and Colonization 215

        The European Colonization and Conquest of Africa 215
            Rwanda 215
            South Africa 218
        Involuntary Americans: Slavery and Segregation 220
        Contemporary Race Relations in the United States 222
            The Impact of Deindustrialization 222

Residential Segregation 225
The Persistence of Racial Inequality 226

Contact Situations: Immigration 227

Immigration and Assimilation Then 228
Immigration and Assimilation Now 230
Racial and Cultural Differences 230
Permanent Immigration 230
Economic Trends 231
Segmented Assimilation 232
Prospects for Consolidation 233

Conclusion 233

Key Concepts 235

Active Learning 235

7 Gender • *How is globalization affecting inequalities between women and men?* • PATRICIA FERNANDEZ-KELLY AND KATHLEEN M. FALLON **239**

Sociological Perspectives on Gender Relations 241

Gender Roles and Subsistence Technology 243
Hunter-Gatherer Societies 243
Agricultural Societies 244
Industrial Societies 246
The Social Construction of Gender: The U.S. Women's Movement 247
Early 1900s 247
Mid- to Late 1900s 249

Gender Inequality Today: A Global Concern 252

Low-Wage Factories in Mexico 252
Structural Adjustment in Ghana 254

Gender in Comparative Perspective 256

Work and Gender 257
Schooling and Gender 262
Politics and Gender 267

Conclusion 269

Key Concepts 270

Active Learning 270

Topical Essay • *Sex as a Global Commodity* • JOANE NAGEL **275**

8 Families • *What is happening to families in a changing world?* • DIANE LYE AND YORK W. BRADSHAW **281**

A Sociological Approach to the Family   282

Recent Trends in Family Life   284

Marriage and Cohabitation   286
Childbearing   290
Number of Children   290
Timing of Childbearing   293
Childbearing and Marriage   294
Divorce and Remarriage   295

The Causes of Family Change   298

Weakened Family Values   299
Increased Women's Employment   303
Economic Adjustments   306
Social Crises   308

The Consequences of Family Change   309

Conclusion   312

Key Concepts   313

Active Learning   314

9 Crime and Punishment • *Can crime be controlled?* • JOSEPH F. HEALEY **319**

Defining and Measuring Crime   320

How Can the Crime Rate Be Measured?   323
"Official" Crime Rates   323
Victimization Surveys   324
Self-Reports   325
Who Commits Street Crime?   325
How Is Globalization Affecting Crime?   328

Theorizing about the Causes of Crime   330

Structural Strain and Anomie   331
Differential Association   333
Deviant Subcultures   335
Social Control Theory   336

Controlling Crime   338

Proposition 1: Criminals Must Be Punished More Harshly   339
Proposition 2: Social Control Mechanisms Must Be Strengthened   344
Proposition 3: Social Inequality Must Be Reduced   345
Implications of the Propositions   346

Conclusion   348

Key Concepts   349

Active Learning   350

10   Economics and Politics • *Does democracy have a future?* •

JOHN MARKOFF   **353**

The Rise of the Modern State   **355**

Politics in the National States   356
Economics in the National States   359

Globalization and the State, Yesterday and Today   **360**

The Great Global Mobility of Trade and Investment   361
The Considerable but Lesser Global Mobility of People   363

Challenges to the Economic and Political Status Quo   **365**

Reconstitution of State Power   366
  Upward Reorganization   366
  Downward Reorganization   366
  Outward Reorganization   369
Weakened Labor Movement   370
New Politics of Ethnic Identity   372
State Management of Economic Life   376

Threatened Democracy   **378**

Attempts by States (and Their Citizens) to Control Globalization   **381**

Government Organizations   381
Citizen Organizations   385

Conclusion   **388**

Key Concepts   **389**

Active Learning   **389**

Topical Essay • *Activists Crusade against Sweatshops* • GAY W. SEIDMAN   **393**

At Issue

SOCIOLOGY EXAMINES A NEW CENTURY 401

11   The Changing Face of War / YORK W. BRADSHAW   **403**

Yugoslavia, 1990s: Lessons Unlearned   406

Ethnic Cleansing and the "Little Hitlers"   407
Turning Point: Intervention in Kosovo   409

Voices of War   411

The Responsibility to Stop Someone Else's War   413

The Limitations of Peacekeeping   414

Five Recommendations for Ending War   416

Thinking about the Topic of War   419

12   The Future of Work / KEVIN T. LEICHT   **421**

Workplace Change and Your Labor Market Prospects   422

The Rise of the Disorderly Work Career   424
Downsizing: Drastic Reductions in the Labor Force   426
Temporary Workers: Here Today, Gone Tomorrow   427
Outsourcing and Subcontracting: Why Make It If We Can Buy It?   429
Flatter Organizational Hierarchies: Who Needs the Pyramid?   430
The Postunionized Workplace: Can Unions Shoot at Moving Targets?   431

The Social Consequences of the Changing Workplace   432

The Cycle of Work and Spend   434
Fraying Community Ties   437

The Hopes and Fears of the New Workplace   439

Thinking about the Topic of Work   439

13   Can the World Develop and Sustain Its Environment? / MICHAEL MAYERFELD BELL   **441**

We Consuming Humans   443

Owning Up to What We Own   447

The Sociology of Environmental Inaction   449

The Social Organization of Consumption   452

Social Power and the Social Organization of Consumption   455

Virtual Environmentalism and the Social Reorganization of Consumption 457

Thinking about the Topic of Sustainable Development 459

14 How Many People Is Too Many People? / DIANE LYE 461

How Does Population Grow? 462

Causes of Population Growth 464
Population Growth in Developed Countries 465
Population Growth in Developing Countries 467

How Many People Can Earth Support? 471

Famine 472
Environmental Degradation 475
Economic Underdevelopment 476

Can We Slow Population Growth? 477

A Reality Check 480

Thinking about the Topic of Population Growth 481

15 The Global Healthcare Challenge / NJERI MBUGUA 483

The Grim Reality of Healthcare in Lower-Income Countries 485

Healthcare in the Era of Economic Development Programs 485
Healthcare in the Era of Political Turmoil 487
Healthcare in the Era of Drug Resistance 489
Healthcare in the Era of International Trade and Travel 491
Healthcare in the Era of HIV/AIDS 494

The Great Divide: Haves versus Have-nots 495

What Constitutes Quality? 496
Why Are the Poor Denied the Healthcare They Need? 498

The Healthcare Challenge of the Twenty-First Century 500

Thinking about the Topic of Healthcare 501

16 Creating Positive Social Change / YORK W. BRADSHAW 503

What Solutions Does Sociology Suggest? 504

Solutions at the Global Level 505
Reducing Poor Countries' Debt Burdens 506
More Foreign Aid 506
Cooperation between Public and Private Sectors 508
Solutions at the Regional Level 508

Solutions at the National Level   509
Solutions at the Community Level   510

What Can Individuals Do?   511

Thinking about the Topic of Positive Social Change   512

Authors and Contributors   515

References   519

Photo Credits   547

Glossary/Index   551

Appendix   **A Sociologist's Atlas /** KATHLEEN M. FALLON   **Color insert**

Using Technology to Find Information   A1
Interpreting Data Carefully   A2
Reporting Data Responsibly   A3

Maps Included in This Atlas   A4

Regions of the World   A5
Population and Culture   A13
Economic Development   A16
Human Development   A19
International Trade   A23
Environment   A27
Health   A30

Graphics

1.1   Selected Corporate Downsizings in the 1990s   **2**
1.2   Top Ten Occupations Expecting Growth, 1992–2005   **3**
1.3   Performance of U.S. Stock Market during Asian Crash and Recovery   **4**
1.4   Two Maps of the World   **8**
1.5   Technological Inequality, 1996–1997   **11**
1.6   The Expanding Roster of Nations   **17**
1.7   Racial Composition of the United States, 1990   **19**
1.8   Poverty among U.S. Children   **28**
1.9   Gap between Rich and Poor Children in the Developed World, 1991   **29**
1.10   Child Death Rates by Country's Economic Status, 1996   **30**

2.1   European Colonization in the Early Twentieth Century   **60**
2.2   Fifty Richest Entities in the World (Excluding High-Income Nations)   **62**
2.3   Suicide Rates for Developed Nations, 1999   **68**
2.4   Suicide Rates for U.S. Teenagers and Young Adults   **69**

Topical Essay   The Global Spread of McDonald's   **77**

3.1   Interaction of Theory and Research   **92**
3.2   Measures of Social Capital in Twenty-One Industrial Nations   **102**
3.3   Voter Turnout in U.S. Presidential Elections   **104**
3.4   Televisions, Computers, and Internet Hosts by National Income Level, 1999   **107**

4.1   Status of Women in India and Sweden   **121**
4.2   Traditional American Values   **126**
4.3   Culture Industry System   **138**
4.4   China's Changing Culture   **142**

Topical Essay 1   Teachers' Judgments about the Most Important Attributes of a Good Teacher   **151**
Topical Essay 2   Social Class and Evaluation of Twenty-Three Students in a Private Girls' School in Paris   **152**

Topical Essay   Abraham's Journey through Ancient Lands   **157**

5.1   Growing Inequality of World Income   **163**
5.2   Kuznets Curve   **175**
5.3   The Changing Labor Market in the United States   **176**
5.4   Gap between Rich and Poor in the United States   **179**
5.5   Share of Income for the U.S. Middle Class   **181**
5.6   Key Characteristics of the Four "Little Dragons," Japan, and the United States   **185**
5.7   Income Distribution for Ninety-Seven Nations   **187**
5.8   Income Inequality in Industrialized Nations   **188**
5.9   Government Expenditures in the European "Welfare States" and the United States   **189**

5.10   Income Inequality in the Four Asian Dragons, the United States, and Brazil **190**
5.11   Indicators of African Economic Development **191**
5.12   Class Structure and Economic Development **192**
5.13   Social Class, Values, and Lifestyle **196**

Topical Essay   Countries That Have Filed the Most Biological Patents **203**

6.1   A Model of Global Species Consolidation **208**
6.2   Effects of European Colonization of Africa, 1950 **216**
      Effects of European Colonization of Africa, 2000 **217**
6.3   Black-White Inequality in the United States **223**
6.4   Patterns of Residential Segregation, 1999 **225**
6.5   Rates of Legal Immigration to the United States **227**
6.6   Ethnic and Racial Groups in the United States **231**
6.7   Latino Acculturation Survey **237**

7.1   Progress in the Professions for American Women **257**
7.2   Rising Labor Force Participation among U.S. Women **258**
7.3   "Female Professions" and the Wage Gap in the United States, 1997 **259**
7.4   Working Women around the World **261**
7.5   College Enrollments in the United States since Passage of Title IX **263**
7.6   Bachelor's Degrees Earned by American Women **265**
7.7   Gender and Schooling in Developing Countries, 1997 **266**
7.8   Women in National Legislatures **268**

8.1   Age at First Marriage **287**
8.2   Single U.S. Women Ages 20–24 **288**
8.3   Total Fertility Rates Worldwide **291**
8.4   U.S. Total Fertility Rates **293**
8.5   U.S. Nonmarital Births **295**
8.6   Divorce Rates **296**
8.7   U.S. Family Values **316**

9.1   Rates of Serious Crime in the United States **321**
9.2   Homicide Rates for Selected Industrialized Nations, Mid-1990s **322**
9.3   Major Felonies Included as Part I Offenses in the *Uniform Crime Reports* **324**
9.4   Ages of Those Arrested for Three Types of Crime, 1998 **326**
9.5   Number of Arrests by Age and Sex, 1998 **327**
9.6   U.S. Federal and State Prison Inmates per 100,000 Population **340**
9.7   Rates of Incarceration for Selected Nations, 1994 **341**
9.8   U.S. Clearance Rates for Selected U.S. Crimes **342**

10.1   Countries That Have Become More Democratic in the Late Twentieth Century **358**
10.2   Refugees in Europe, 1999 **364**
10.3   Foreign-Born Persons in the United States **365**
10.4   Reconfiguration of State Power at the Turn of the Twenty-First Century **367**
10.5   New National States since 1989 **368**
10.6   U.S. Union Membership **371**
10.7   Lack of Confidence in Labor Unions, 1990 **373**
10.8   Dissatisfaction with National Legislatures, 1990 **380**

At Issue: Sociology Examines a New Century

11.1 Conflicts around the World, 2000 405
11.2 Yugoslavia, 1990 406
11.3 Major Peacekeeping Missions in 2000 415

12.1 Implied Contract between Employers and Employees, 1950–1985 422
12.2 U.S. Job Cut Announcements 426
12.3 Average Daily Value of Transactions on Stock Exchanges 427
12.4 Organizations' Use of Contingent Workers 429
12.5 Hypothetical Employee Stock Ownership Plan 431
12.6 Working More but Not Earning More 433
12.7 Revolving Credit in the 1990s 434
12.8 Community Activities among Threatened Employees in the 1990s 438

13.1 Increase in Gross World Product per Person 443
13.2 Increasing Demands on World Ecosystems 444
13.3 Loss of Leisure Time in the United States 446
13.4 Worldwide Motor Vehicle Use 450
13.5 Disappearing Farmland and Wildlife Habitat in the United States 454
13.6 Declining World CFC Production 458

14.1 Human Population Growth Throughout History 463
14.2 Countries with Projected Populations over 100 Million in 2050 464
14.3 Birth and Death Rates in Developed and Developing Countries 465
14.4 The Demographic Transition 469

15.1 Prioritizing Military and Healthcare Spending 488
15.2 Increases in Air Travel 492
15.3 The Threat of Infectious Disease 493
15.4 Americans without Health Insurance, 1998 498
15.5 The Global Burden of Infectious Disease 500

16.1 The Burden of External Debt in Developing Nations 507

Appendix: A Sociologist's Atlas

Map 1 Regions of the World: The World A5
Map 2 Regions of the World: Africa A6
Map 3 Regions of the World: Asia A7
Map 4 Regions of the World: Europe A8
Map 5 Regions of the World: Middle East A9
Map 6 Regions of the World: North America A10
Map 7 Regions of the World: South America A11
Map 8 Regions of the World: Oceania A12
Map 9 Population and Culture: Population Density A13
Map 10 Population and Culture: Urbanization A14
Map 11 Population and Culture: Ethnic Diversity A15
Map 12 Economic Development: Purchasing Power A16
Map 13 Economic Development: Poverty A17
Map 14 Economic Development: Service Workers A18
Map 15 Economic Development: Women's Earnings A19
Map 16 Human Development: Relative Human Development A20

Map 17   Human Development: Gender-Related Human Development   **A21**

Map 18   Human Development: Education Expenditures   **A22**

Map 19   International Trade: Growth in Global Trade   **A23**

Map 20   International Trade: Foreign Investment Magnets   **A24**

Map 21   International Trade: High-Tech Exports   **A25**

Map 22   International Trade: Film Imports   **A26**

Map 23   Environment: Deforestation   **A27**

Map 24   Environment: Carbon Dioxide Emissions   **A28**

Map 25   Environment: Access to Safe Water   **A29**

Map 26   Health: Life Expectancy   **A30**

Map 27   Health: Health Expenditures   **A31**

Map 28   Health: Nutrition   **A32**

Preface

College students today need to be prepared to live in the world, not just in their hometown or native land. The world grows more interconnected every day, and human affairs—business, politics, the arts, personal biographies—are increasingly played out on a global scale. Even as globalization and technological change shrink the world, civil wars and other conflicts threaten to tear it apart, and issues and problems as diverse as crime, immigration, gender relations, racism, justice, AIDS, divorce, inequality, and acid rain clamor for attention everywhere. The wonders of space travel and the miracles of modern medicine coexist with the horrors of genocide and famine, and a world with enough resources to feed and educate everyone faces the continuing possibility of total destruction and annihilation.

We wrote this textbook because we are convinced that sociology can play a major role (perhaps *the* major role) in helping you understand how your life is shaped by such complexities. We use the methods and concepts of sociology to analyze major issues and trends, place them in historical context, compare their effects on various societies around the world, examine the consequences for everyday life, and provide the information and ideas you need to reach your full potential as a global citizen. We want to help you develop an approach to thinking about social issues and evaluating claims and arguments about society that you can use long after the course has ended.

This book stresses some of the greatest strengths of sociology: a well-developed tradition of critical and self-reflective thinking, a commitment to the principles of scientific investigation, a deep concern for social problems and human welfare, and a macro approach that takes account of history, geography, and relations among the societies and regions of the globe. Our goal is to convince you that sociology matters and that the sociological perspective can help you understand the world around you and the trajectory of your own life.

The Book's Themes and Principles

Sociology is a dynamic and complex field of study, and it is a considerable challenge to introduce students to the discipline. Most textbooks approach the task by attempting to incorporate all the diverse subjects and viewpoints in the field, an approach that often produces little more than chaotic collections of definitions, disparate insights, and disconnected factoids. We have followed a different course. Our goal is not so much to introduce the discipline of sociology but rather to demonstrate the power of thinking sociologically and to present a version of the discipline that is coherent, consistent, useful, and accessible. We accomplish that goal primarily in two ways.

First, the book is organized around a limited number of themes and principles, which are introduced in Chapter 1 and used throughout the other fifteen chapters. We rely on those themes to bring a consistent perspective and build a cohesive analysis. Second, our approach is uniformly macro, comparative, and global. It focuses on the larger elements of society and social structure (for example, inequality, the family institution, culture, and ethnic group relations) and on the relationships between societies and regions of the globe. The text does not address individual-level phenomena such as personality development.

We are primarily concerned with the United States, but we are also sensitive to the global context in which U.S. society exists and the emerging global social system itself. Now more than ever, the dynamics of any society—even the wealthiest and most powerful—cannot be understood in isolation. Every aspect of social life—crime, global warming, the future of the family, job markets—must be analyzed in the context of the growing interconnectedness of societies everywhere.

This textbook will introduce you to an analytically powerful version of sociology that you will find meaningful, coherent, and valuable. You will emerge from this course with much more than memorized definitions and a collection of unconnected research results. You will be more aware of the issues facing modern society, better able to analyze them for yourself, and more convinced of the potential for sociology to provide answers to important questions.

The Book's Organization

This book consists of sixteen chapters divided into two sections, supplemented by seven topical essays and an appendix. The elements work together to integrate the book's themes and link them to the important questions that dominate social life at the turn of the new century. We focus on the crucial issues that are shaping social life today and use them to illustrate the value of thinking sociologically.

Foundations: Chapters 1–10

The first ten chapters are the core of the book. Chapter 1 introduces the sociological perspective and the seven themes that are the analytical framework for the remainder of the book. Chapters 2 and 3 discuss major sociological theoretical perspectives, social research, and critical thinking. Chapters 4 through 10 examine the foundations of sociological thought and the basic principles in the major subareas within sociology. For example, Chapters 5 through 7 present an integrated treatment of inequality, one of the continuing issues that affect every contemporary society. Chapter 5 focuses on social class, Chapter 6 on race and ethnicity, and Chapter 7 on gender inequalities; each chapter examines the myriad ways in which those forces interact with each other to shape our lives and the societies in which we live.

Each of the first ten chapters is organized around a specific question or problem. The question is stated at the beginning of the chapter, examined from multiple perspectives, used as a vehicle to introduce relevant sociological theory and research, and addressed throughout the chapter. The chapters stress the process of investigation, the sociological craft of "finding out," critical thinking, and careful analysis rather than simply presenting answers. For example, Chapter 3 examines whether civic participation, sense of community, and mutual trust are declining in the United States and other advanced industrial societies, an issue that has far-reaching consequences for social life. If people are less involved with each other, the everyday "work" of the community (coaching Little League, joining the PTA, helping neighbors, voting, raising money for civic projects) will not get done, and the ability of society to continue functioning eventually will be compromised. Chapter 3 stresses the process by which sociologists address such issues and examines the issue from several points of view. The techniques and principles of the scientific method (theory versus research, the experimental method, correlation versus causation) are introduced as they become useful to the discussion, an approach that avoids the tendency of many textbooks to present laundry lists of unconnected terms that need to be memorized.

Topical Essays. Interspersed throughout the first ten chapters are seven topical essays, brief analyses of global issues that broaden the coverage of the book. Most are written by leading scholars and researchers, but one essayist, Tracey Jane Dawson, is a recent graduate of the College of Charleston. The essays cover diverse issues (for example, sex, sweatshops, schooling) and display various analytical approaches found in modern sociology. Some essays are in the tradition of the scientific, data-driven analysis that informs the book as a whole, but others use more pointed—and more personal—approaches to their topics.

At Issue: Chapters 11–16

The second part of the book is distinctly different from the first part in both appearance and tone. We think of it as a "magazine" of thoughtful articles about significant global issues. That's why we call it "At Issue: Sociology Examines a New Century."

Chapters 11 through 15 apply sociological thinking to the topics of war, careers, the environment, population growth, and healthcare. These chapters combine cutting-edge, timely analysis by respected scholars with passionate calls for change where change is needed. They are intended to stimulate thought and discussion about the state of the world at the beginning of the twenty-first century and to shed light on and suggest solutions for some important problems facing the globe.

Chapter 16 brings the book to a close with a discussion of how individuals and organizations can create positive change in the world. We would be remiss if we raised your concern about the dilemmas facing the globe and failed to point out that there are realistic actions—actions available to ordinary citizens of every sort, including students—by which the world can be made a better place.

Appendix: A Sociologist's Atlas

A potential problem with a global approach to sociological issues is that it involves places that most of us have never visited. Some of us would be hard-pressed to find certain countries on the map. The full-color appendix inserted at the end of the book presents a world map and seven regional maps to make it easier to locate the places referred to in the text and to understand the context in which societies exist.

The appendix also presents twenty thematic maps of the world that visually represent statistical data on important indicators of countries' well-being and relative standing. These maps round out the discussions in the chapters and the topical essays, which often have a narrower focus, and may help you better understand the issues underlying globalization.

The appendix begins with a brief overview of ways to find information using electronic technology and guidelines for interpreting data and presenting it in reports.

The Book's Learning Tools

◆ *Graphics.* Some of the graphics in this book present detailed data that support and elaborate on points made in the text. Others represent data visually to make sociological models easier to understand or to highlight essential trends and relationships. We hope you'll find both types of graphics useful in coming to grips with the many facets of contemporary society and in formulating informed opinions about social issues.

◆ *Cartoons.* The cartoons are meant not to be funny but rather to be a form of thought-provoking social commentary. Nick Rutter, a student at Brown University, has illustrated numerous concepts in the "At Issue" section. He has also provided his own perspective on sweatshops, one of his main social concerns, in the topical essay on that topic.

◆ *Photographs.* The photographs have been carefully selected to put a human face on concepts and data. Many of the photographs are grouped in "essays" to demonstrate the similarities and differences among societies around the world.

◆ *Chapter pedagogy.* Included at the ends of Chapters 1 through 10 are point-by-point chapter summaries. At the end of the book are a glossary (incorporated into the index) and a list of references.

◆ *Active Learning exercises.* To help you become actively engaged in the learning process, Chapters 1 through 10 include assignments that will help you use sociological methods to understand the world around you. Many types of activities are included: doing research in the library and on the Internet, making observations in the field, discussing your findings and opinions with other students, reporting to your instructor, and simply taking time for some personal reflection and thought. We hope the exercises will serve as practice for a life-long dedication to sociology's methods of inquiry.

◆ *Thinking about. . . .* Chapters 11 through 16 each end with a set of questions that can be used as essay questions or topics for in-class discussion. The questions have two purposes: to suggest how the concepts presented in Chapters 1 through 10 can be applied to the issue of the current chapter and to encourage you to think critically about the topic.

◆ *Web site.* Bookmark this web address: www.pineforge.com/snc. It includes a number of helpful features for students of sociology: supplementary information and updated data, all the book's graphics, forms for some of the Active Learning exercises, guidelines for writing term papers, resources for traveling abroad to study other societies, self-tests to help you review each chapter, and links to other useful web sites. Use the site as a resource while you are taking this course as well as afterward.

Teaching Resources

A comprehensive instructor's manual, available in print and on CD-ROM for both Macintosh and Windows platforms, accompanies this textbook. The manual includes these features:

◆ Forty to fifty multiple-choice test items per chapter plus additional short-answer and essay questions

◆ Defined learning outcomes, with suggestions for using the textbook, web site, and test items to achieve them

◆ Chapter summaries and annotated lists of relevant films, videos, and web sites

◆ Extensive annotated bibliography of resources on the art and craft of teaching

Acknowledgments

The development of this textbook was guided and facilitated by a multitude of people. First and foremost, we thank our colleagues who wrote chapters or topical essays. They contributed a depth and expertise to this book that would be impossible to match in any other way. We also thank our students, most of whom never realized the importance of the role they played in helping us organize and present our ideas. And we thank our departmental colleagues for their support and advice, freely given and greatly appreciated. In particular, we thank Dr. Shahid Shahidullah of Christopher Newport University for his assistance with Chapter 9, "Crime and Punishment." We also thank Professor Daniel Chirot at the University of Washington for his assistance in the early stages of this project.

We would also like to thank Liezell Bradshaw for assisting us with the data collection and organization for several chapters; Jocelyn Viterna (Indiana University) for providing us with useful articles, books, and reports on topics related to technology and society; Katy Fallon (Indiana University), who not only wrote for the book but also provided valuable research assistance; Nancy Wirtes for her thorough and very professional copy editing; Dianne Schaefer for her assistance with design, photos, and many other issues; Kirsten Stoller, a recent graduate of Colby College in Maine, who scoured the Internet for sociologically relevant photographs; and Jillaine Tyson, who skillfully and efficiently converted a great diversity of materials into the visually coherent graphics and maps that extend the impact of the words in this book. The authors also greatly appreciate the assistance of Betty Wiley and the entire sociology office staff at the University of Memphis in helping research, coordinate, and manage a myriad of details.

We owe a special debt to Steve Rutter, founder and president of Pine Forge Press. He was the inspiration for this textbook and throughout the project provided invaluable guidance. Steve was intimately involved in its design and organization and in the selection and recruitment of contributing authors, and he read and analyzed every chapter and essay. This is as much his book as anyone else's, and we thank him for his support, his encouragement, his gentle prodding, and his inspiration.

The staff of Pine Forge Press (Ann Makarias, Kirsten Stoller, Sherith Pankratz, and Paul O'Connell) were extremely helpful and supportive throughout the project, and we gratefully acknowledge their assistance. We also thank our production partners at Books By Design for their help in shepherding a complex manuscript into print.

Finally, we also owe a great debt to our colleagues who served as anonymous reviewers during development of *Sociology for a New Century*. It has been immeasurably improved by their suggestions and criticisms; whatever failings remain are our own. We are especially grateful to three reviewers who provided extensive feedback on every part and at every stage of the manuscript: Tracy Burkett, College of Charleston; Peter Landstreet, York University; and Kristin Park, Westminster College. In addition, we thank the following:

Joan Alway, University of Miami

Peter S. Bearman, Columbia University

Daniel Brook, University of California, Davis

Steven Caldwell, Cornell University

Douglas Constance, Sam Houston State University

Richard Coon, Carroll College

Ione Y. DeOllos, Ball State University

Susan Eckstein, Boston University

Valerie Gunter, University of New Orleans

Thomas Hirschl, Cornell University

Gary Hytrek, Georgia State University

Louise Jezierski, Brown University

Cheryl Joseph, College of Notre Dame

Edward Kain, Southwestern University

Fred Kniss, Loyola University, Chicago

Roberto Korzeniewicz, University of Maryland

David Kyle, University of California, Davis

Hugh Lautard, University of New Brunswick

Peter Lehman, University of Southern Maine

Peggy Lovell, University of Pittsburgh

Neil McLaughlin, McMaster University

Christopher Mele, State University of New York at Buffalo

Kelly Moore, Barnard College

Joane Nagel, University of Kansas

Lea Pellett, Christopher Newport University

Ted Sasson, Middlebury College

Allen Scarboro, Augusta State University

Thomas Schott, University of Pittsburgh

William J. Staudenmeier Jr., Eureka College

Boris Stremlin, State University of New York, Binghamton

Vegavahini Subramaniam, Western Washington University

Henry A. Walker, Cornell University

Adam Weinberg, Colgate University

Robert E. Wood, Rutgers State University

Cynthia A. Woolever, formerly of Midway College

To Chrystal and Autymn Bradshaw,

Benjamin and Caroline Healey,

and all the children

of the twenty-first century

SOCIOLOGY

for a NEW CENTURY

1 A Global View of Society

*How can sociology help us
understand global trends?*

On February 13, 1997, workers at the largest television assembly plant in the world were called together for a surprise announcement: they would all lose their jobs over the next fourteen months. Their employer, Thomson Consumer Electronics (formerly RCA), told the 1,100 employees in the Bloomington, Indiana, factory that global competition had forced it to move its manufacturing operations to Ciudad Juarez, Mexico. The Bloomington workers were earning an average of $18 an hour in wages and benefits, whereas Thomson could pay Mexican workers an average of only $2.10 an hour in wages and benefits. With the close of the Thomson factory, televisions are no longer manufactured in the United States.

Understandably, the Bloomington workers felt betrayed. The average Thomson worker was fifty years old, had worked at the factory for twenty-seven years, and had little work experience outside of assembling televisions. What would they do? How would they support their families? How would they obtain health insurance? One worker, Wendell Sullivan, stated, "I was thinking, damn, I'm going to be fifty-three years old. Where am I going to find a job?" When asked whether he is bitter about the experience, Bill Cook, the local union leader for the Thomson hourly employees, replied, "I am. It's a raw deal. People have spent half their lives here" (*Herald-Times,* July 1, 1997, p. A1).

If the workers hoped to apply for a job across town at the giant General Electric (GE) factory, which made over 200 different types of refrigerators, they would have to think again. In 1999 that plant would announce that it, too, was moving to Mexico in search of cheaper wages.

GRAPHIC 1.1 SELECTED CORPORATE DOWNSIZINGS IN THE 1990S		
Company	**Year**	**Number of Layoffs**
McDonnell Douglas	1990	17,000
General Motors	1991	74,000
Boeing	1993	28,000
Sears Roebuck	1993	50,000
IBM	1993	63,000
Phillip Morris	1993	14,000
Xerox	1993	10,000
Eastman Kodak	1993	16,800
Delta	1994	15,000
GTE	1994	17,000
Digital Equipment	1994	20,000
Nynex	1994	16,800
Lockheed–Martin Marietta merger	1995	30,000
Tenneco	since 1990	11,000
United Technologies	since 1990	33,000
AT&T	1990–1995	83,000
AT&T	1996	40,000

Source: Derived from Wallace, 1998, p. 25.

Thomson's and GE's moves, though difficult for Bloomington workers, were part of a nationwide trend that started in the 1970s, in which millions of blue-collar jobs were sent to developing countries as American companies sought cheaper wages and less restrictive working conditions (for example, fewer safety regulations). Downsizing the work force was a way to save money and become more competitive in the global economy (Bluestone and Harrison, 1979). Televisions, radios, computers, shoes, refrigerators, clothing, automobile components, and many other products are now manufactured abroad and imported into the United States. Downsizing continued during the 1980s and 1990s, with the further loss of blue-collar jobs and then the elimination of many white-collar, professional positions (Wallace, 1998). Graphic 1.1 lists some of the largest corporate downsizers in the 1990s.

From a corporate perspective, downsizing is a good idea. It increases efficiency, cuts costs, and enhances profits. U.S. corporations posted large profits during the 1990s, fueling a stock market that nearly tripled in value during the 1990s. After AT&T laid off 40,000 workers in 1996, its stock value increased immediately by $6 billion (Wallace, 1998). AT&T stated that although it regretted the layoffs, they were necessary because of global competition in the telecommunications industry.

Indeed, the increasingly global economy has forced many Americans to change jobs. However, their new jobs often pay much less and provide fewer benefits than their old jobs. Only 24% of downsized workers are able to find employment in the

GRAPHIC 1.2 TOP TEN OCCUPATIONS EXPECTING GROWTH, 1992–2005

Occupation	1992 Jobs (in thousands)	2005 Jobs (in thousands)	Number of New Jobs (in thousands)	Average Weekly Earnings (in 1995 dollars)
Retail salespersons	3,660	4,446	786	$252
Registered nurses	1,835	2,601	766	$643
Cashiers	2,747	3,417	670	$195
General office clerks	2,688	3,342	654	$333
Truck drivers	2,391	3,039	648	$489
Waiters and waitresses	1,756	2,394	638	$262
Nursing aides, orderlies, and attendants	1,308	1,903	595	$275
Janitors and cleaners	2,862	3,410	548	$263
Food preparation workers	1,223	1,748	525	$181
Systems analysts	455	956	501	$931

Source: Derived from Wallace, 1998, p. 26.

same line of work; about 42% of workers who find new employment are paid less than they were paid in their old jobs (Wallace, 1998). Graphic 1.2 shows the ten occupations projected to experience the greatest growth through 2005. Most of the occupations are in the service sector and pay low wages, offer few benefits, and provide little or no job security. Only three occupations—registered nurses, systems analysts, and truck drivers—earn incomes above $20,000 (in 1995 dollars). The United States is turning into a nation of service workers. The largest private employer is Manpower Temporary Services, an agency that provides temporary (primarily clerical) workers to a wide variety of businesses.

The first chapter of this book looks at economic and other changes facing society in the United States and other societies around the world. We want you to understand that virtually no country exists in isolation. Chapter 1 also introduces you to the special perspective that sociology offers and explains how this book uses sociological concepts to provide insight into economic and cultural developments around the world.

The Interconnected World

Although the chief executive officers (CEOs) of large corporations and unemployed factory workers may have different views on the changing world economy, they probably would agree on one point: the United States is only one piece of a dynamic global puzzle. Jobs move from one country to another; money crosses national borders with ease; trade patterns change quickly; and events that occur in one country can have vast effects on other countries. In 1997, for instance, the once-booming Asian economies suddenly stagnated and then declined. The Asian stock markets reached their lowest values in the middle of 1998. The U.S. stock market also plummeted in 1998, falling over 1,000 points between July and September (Graphic 1.3). Prior to that time, some investors thought the bullish U.S. stock market was immune to harmful foreign influences, but the Asian economic crisis was a reminder that we live in an interconnected world. As the Asian economy began to recover in late 1998, the U.S. stock market also surged, setting records throughout 1999.

Coinciding economic trends remind us that we live in a global village, but they are only one reminder. E-mail and fax machines link people across oceans, new diseases ignore national boundaries, wars and environmental destruction in one region profoundly affect events in other regions—the list goes on and on. People are paying increased attention to the way the world is shrinking, for three reasons in particular.

✦ *To increase their employability.* Millions of U.S. citizens now work for foreign companies and institutions in both the United States and other countries. In this new global environment, employers place a premium on people who speak at least two languages and are knowledgeable about other cultures. Moreover, the U.S. workforce is becoming increasingly diverse and multicultural. Workers who do not understand the experiences and cultures of a diverse population will not function well. Effective managers and executives will be those with the knowledge and skills to build bridges among different groups in a changing world.

✦ *To understand global events.* There is a growing realization that what happens in one area of the world affects other regions. For example, the United States and

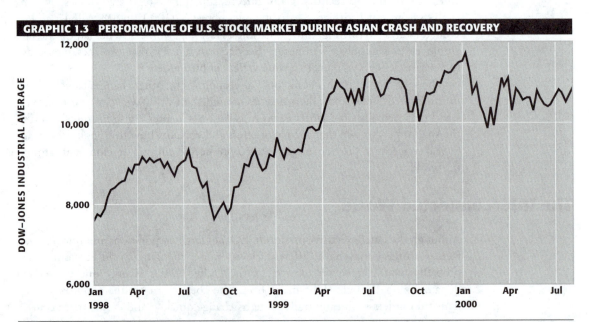

GRAPHIC 1.3   PERFORMANCE OF U.S. STOCK MARKET DURING ASIAN CRASH AND RECOVERY

Source: Derived from *The Wall Street Journal,* 1998–2000 (various issues).

Seeing the beauty of another country can be fun and exhilarating. At the same time, learning the customs, values, and lifestyles of a new place can lead to "culture shock" and confusion. These Asian visitors to Arizona's Grand Canyon have undoubtedly encountered new experiences and ways of viewing the world.

other countries in the North Atlantic Treaty Organization (NATO) increasingly are called on to act as global peacekeepers in cases of ethnic conflict, as in Bosnia, Kosovo, and Rwanda. For humanitarian as well as national security reasons, the United States and its allies feel obligated to become involved in conflicts around the world. Disease is another example of how events in one place affect other regions. The Ebola virus, the Marburg virus, even HIV may have emerged from deforested regions in the tropics and made their way into broader segments of animal and human populations (Preston, 1994). Most frightening of all, some scientists and doctors believe that a few of those viruses (though not HIV) can mutate and become airborne, meaning that large populations could risk dying terrible deaths just by breathing the air. Not everyone agrees with that view (Gladwell, 1995), but it points to the way global events can render national boundaries irrelevant.

♦ *To enjoy travel.* More people than ever are traveling internationally. Many people travel on business; an even larger number travel abroad to learn, vacation, and relax. The international travel and tourism industry is booming, airplanes are becoming bigger and faster, and some airport hubs have all the amenities of upscale shopping malls (Cole, 1995). Incredibly, nearly 11% of the international labor force works in the travel or tourism industry (Naisbitt, 1994, p. 104). One popular travel opportunity is "ecotourism": travelers visit some of the world's most beautiful spots—the Galapagos Islands, the Ecuadoran cloud forests, Mount Kenya, the South African coasts, wild game preserves—and learn about their environmental and cultural significance. Portions of the fees go to protect the region visited.

All the economic, political, medical, and other phenomena alluded to so far are signs of **globalization,** the process by which people all over the world are exposed to and affected by ideas, issues, and cultures from other places. This book examines the interconnectedness of the world, with a particular focus on how the United States fits into the system. In a global age, what happens in one area of the world clearly has implications for what happens in other regions. Learning about global issues, therefore, is important for those who want to participate in and shape the world in the twenty-first century.

Sociology's Contribution to Understanding Global Issues

Sociology is the study of human society. Sociologists use theories and research methods to understand, explain, and analyze events in society. For example, sociologists are interested in why companies like Thomson move to Mexico. The focus is not on the companies themselves, but on the social, economic, and political conditions that cause the companies to move. Likewise, sociologists are interested in why there is war in the former Yugoslavia. The focus is not on individual politicians or warlords but on the social conditions, economic inequality, and ethnic divisions that help to explain why wars have been fought in that region for centuries. Sociologists are always interested in the social context in which an event occurs, whether the event affects only a small group or an entire country.

Sociologists are particularly interested in building and refining theoretical models of society. For example, sociologists have different theories about why wars are fought in different societies. Some theories argue that ethnic conflict is the primary cause, others claim it is economic inequality, and still others assert that ideology is to blame. Sociologists examine the evidence and then discuss how it supports, contradicts, or is irrelevant to existing theories. Theories often go beyond conventional explanations of reality and require citizens to think deeply about social problems. Such an approach helps us understand the conflict in the former Yugoslavia; more important, it may enable us to predict future conflicts and perhaps stop some of them.

Let us examine the sociological approach in greater detail by looking at the war in the Balkans, which is not easily explained. Most people have some notion that the conflict there is caused by ethnic hatred, which is certainly part of the problem. But two other issues are important in explaining the conflict.

✦ There was severe inequality in the former Yugoslavia in the early 1990s. The wealthiest and most productive regions, Slovenia and Croatia, were dominated by ethnic minorities. When Slovenia and Croatia declared political independence from the larger Yugoslavia, they threatened the national economy and prompted the national government in Serbia (the dominant political region of Yugoslavia) to act against them.

✦ Before the breakup of Eastern Europe in 1989, the Soviet Union provided support to Yugoslavia and thereby artificially held the country together. Ethnic regions benefited from Soviet support and also feared what would happen if they broke away from Yugoslavia. After the Soviet Union fell, however, ethnic regions had little reason to stay within Yugoslavia and therefore declared independence.

Sociologists explain the conflict in the former Yugoslavia, then, by focusing on at least three factors: ethnic hatred, economic and regional inequality, and the changing political power structure. Without focusing on all those factors, we would have an incomplete explanation of the situation in the Balkans.

Theories are useful because they transcend particular situations and normally can be generalized, with some restrictions, to more than one situation. The war in the Balkans can help us explain conflicts in other world regions, and vice versa. However, not all conflicts are explained by the same set of circumstances—far from it. But certain conditions in the former Yugoslavia (for example, ethnic conflict and the absence of a strong outside power) also may exist in, say, East Africa, where war erupted in 1994 and killed close to 1 million people. Sociologists compare and contrast countries and situations in this way to build new theories and refine existing ones.

A good sociologist must have knowledge of the discipline's substantive topics, relevant theories, and favored methodological approaches. The first three chapters examine each of those areas. This chapter presents some important substantive issues and introduces concepts and ideas that are used throughout the book. Chapter 2 attaches those ideas to the main theoretical traditions that guide sociology, and Chapter 3 introduces a variety of methodological techniques available to sociologists. The remainder of the book examines the primary substantive issues that concern sociologists, with frequent reference to sociological traditions and techniques.

A Global Perspective

The world is full of different perspectives and values. We are all products of a variety of phenomena that shape our view of reality: family, culture, life experiences, school, friends, church, media—the list of influences is endless. It is not easy to set aside the assumptions and biases, many of which are subconscious, that shape our view of the world, but that is exactly what we must do if we are to understand the dynamic global system in which we live.

Consider the two maps of the world in Graphic 1.4. You will no doubt recognize the first one, still the most popular wall map in the United States. Most people assume that this map, based on the so-called Mercator projection, is a reasonably accurate representation of the world. But take a closer look. It splits Asia (and the former Soviet Union) in half to ensure that the United States fits in the middle of

GRAPHIC 1.4 TWO MAPS OF THE WORLD

Mercator Projection

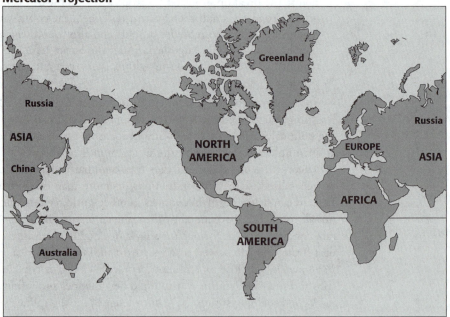

Peters Projection

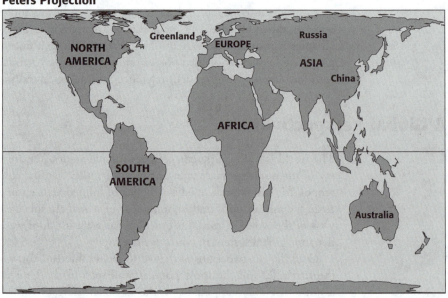

the map. (How would you feel if the United States were cut in half to highlight another country?) Even more important, this projection encourages us to define everything according to the placement of the United States: "north" is Canada and above; "south" is Mexico and below. The "Middle East," a widely accepted term, is hardly east to many countries in the world. In fact, we might argue that the area should be called the "Middle Center," because it is where Europe, Asia, and Africa come together. It is also a region that contains an incredible amount of human history. And the "Far East?" It is only "far" and "east" to the United States and selected other countries.

People have adopted such terms and perspectives without really questioning the assumptions on which they are based. In fact, what happens when we define the world from another perspective, one that places, say, Africa in the center of the world, as the Peters projection does? In the second map in Graphic 1.4, "north" is Europe, "south" is Antarctica, the "Middle East" is around China, and the "Far East" is the Pacific Ocean and the United States. As you read this book, we challenge you to remember that there are many perspectives in a global society; avoid the temptation to place your view automatically in the center of the universe.

We can learn more from the maps in Graphic 1.4. The Mercator projection badly distorts the size of different regions of the world; in contrast, the Peters projection is one of the most accurate. In the Mercator projection, the equator, which is supposed to divide the world in half, is nearly two-thirds of the way down the map, thereby greatly exaggerating the northern hemisphere. Europe is portrayed as larger than South America, when, in fact, South America is almost twice the size of Europe (see the Peters projection). The Mercator projection portrays North America as larger than Africa, when, in fact, Africa is much larger than North America. And Greenland is a geographic behemoth in the Mercator projection, larger than China; in actuality, China is much bigger than Greenland. Keep in mind that the world's mapmakers typically have been from Europe and North America, leading them to accentuate the size and importance of their own regions.

Finally, we might ask why the two maps in Graphic 1.4 are so different. The Mercator projection is based on calculations made in 1569—more than four centuries ago. Yet this old map has shaped the views of millions of people about the size, shape, and location of different areas of the world. Image basing other facets of our life on 400-year-old technology and views!

The Book's Themes: Global Trends

This book opened with a story about the effects of globalization on the U.S. workforce. But that story only hinted at globalization's effects. Social trends that appear to accompany globalization will affect nearly everyone in the world in the coming years. This section describes seven of those trends, which we refer to again and again throughout this book with an eye toward explaining the causes, nature, and effects of globalization.

The Spread of Technology Is Both Blessing and Curse

In 1998, Microsoft chairman and CEO Bill Gates expressed an opinion about the future of the computer that is hard to dispute several years later.

> The bottom line on all of this is that this Web lifestyle really is going to impact everything. It will change education, it will change buying, and it will change how you find jobs and participate in jobs. We're really just at the beginning of something that can be quite incredible (*Herald-Times,* October 15, 1998, p. A1).

People with a so-called Web lifestyle have substantial advantages: they have access to new information, new ways of thinking, new modes of communication, new worlds of convenience, new research techniques, and new business and employment opportunities. But the Web lifestyle is not equally available to everyone. Only 25% of U.S. families with incomes under $30,000 have home computers, compared to 80% of families with incomes over $100,000. Households with incomes of $75,000 and higher are 20 times more likely to have access to the Internet than those with lower incomes and 9 times more likely to own a personal computer (Sack, 2000). The disparity between the "haves" and the "have nots" is even more pronounced when we compare countries (Graphic 1.5). The United States and other developed countries have, on average, 18.5 times the number of personal computers that middle-income countries do and 85.5 times the number of Internet hosts. Low-income countries have so few personal computers and Internet hosts that they are statistically negligible.

There is no greater form of inequality in the world today than in the area of access to technology, even simple technology that residents in developed countries have long taken for granted. And the gap is increasing. The majority of the two-thirds of the world's population who live in developing countries have never made a telephone call, much less used a computer. The largest democracy in the world, India, has only 5 million telephones for a population of 850 million (as well as only 1.5 personal computers for every 1,000 persons and only 0.05 Internet hosts per 10,000 persons) (World Bank, 1998). The most severe form of inequality in the world today is in the area of access to technology.

Computers, the Internet, electronic publishing, the transfer of images via cellular telephones, interactive teleconferencing, and other forms of digital technology are transforming business, education, medicine, and many other fields in economically developed countries. Without access to those technologies, less developed countries are falling even further behind. A group of South African educators visiting the United States during 1998 toured computer laboratories in elementary schools. Clearly the visitors were impressed with the facilities, but something troubled them. They politely explained that 90% of rural elementary schools in South Africa do not have electricity, eliminating the possibility of computers. By the time South African students are exposed to computers (often in junior high or high school), their American counterparts have used them for many years. The situation

GRAPHIC 1.5 TECHNOLOGICAL INEQUALITY, 1996–1997		
	Personal Computers per 1,000 Persons	Internet Hosts per 10,000 Persons
High-Income Countries		
Finland	182.10	653.60
Germany	233.20	106.70
Japan	128.00	75.80
Switzerland	408.50	208.00
United States	362.40	442.10
Middle-Income Countries		
Algeria	3.40	0.01
Brazil	18.40	4.20
Mexico	29.00	3.70
Russia	23.70	5.50
South Africa	37.70	30.70
Low-Income Countries		
China	3.00	0.21
Ivory Coast	1.40	0.17
India	1.50	0.05
Kenya	1.50	0.16
Uganda	0.50	0.01

Source: World Bank, 1998.

Note: Data on personal computers in low-income countries are estimates; few low-income countries have data on personal computer use.

is even more pronounced in the rest of Africa and parts of Asia. Many students at the university level in those regions have not had any experience with computers.

Despite the desirability of many digital technologies, governments sometimes prefer that those technologies not become widely available. Repressive governments have always been aware that widespread and efficient communication technologies help to expose government repression and brutality. In 1989, for instance, several thousand Chinese college students gathered in Beijing's Tiananmen Square to demonstrate for democracy. The government cracked down and murdered more than 1,000 students. It then tried to censor news reports of the massacre in China and abroad. International television, led by CNN, was one of its targets. But armed with fax machines, Chinese students and their sympathizers transmitted pictures and written accounts of the carnage throughout the world. In turn, sympathizers in other countries (especially Chinese students studying in the United States) were able to fax information back to the demonstrators in China. This almost instant form of communication was partly responsible for the swift denunciation of China by foreign governments and other global institutions. If the events at Tiananmen Square were to occur today, e-mail messages would increase the speed and volume of communication between China and other countries in the global village.

Repressive governments hate the Internet in this era of globalization; it is difficult to stop the flow of information on the Internet or to censor it. For example, in 1999 the fragile government of Serbia responded to antigovernment protests by banning opposition newspapers, preventing television broadcasts of violence (the state owns the television networks), and generally cracking down on government critics. Those actions, ironically, spurred the opposition to create a Web site that immediately broadcast events all over the world. Moreover, some citizens of Serbia and neighboring countries began to send eyewitness accounts of the brutality via e-mail to friends, family, news agencies, and other sympathizers throughout the world. The Serbian government started to receive thousands of e-mails and faxes from around the globe protesting its violation of basic human and civil rights. Foreign governments also used some of the information generated by the Internet to establish economic sanctions and to threaten political (and even military) action.

The Malawian government had a similar experience. Prior to widespread use of fax machines, the paranoid government of Hastings Banda (the self-appointed "president for life") actually opened every single letter arriving in or leaving the country. The letters passed through a special government office in charge of rooting out "agitators." Anyone unfortunate enough to send or receive the "wrong" type of letter would likely experience a knock on the door and a visit to the local police station (or worse). But the number of letters entering and leaving Malawi declined dramatically with the advent of the fax machine in the 1980s. And it declined even more when e-mail arrived in the 1990s. By the time Banda was ousted from power in the mid-1990s, Internet chat groups were regularly criticizing the aging and out-of-touch president for life, and the government was receiving e-mail calling for the election of another president through democratic processes. Repressive governments once exhibited the capacity to control the flow of information in and out of their country, but that era is largely over.

Technology is not always liberating, however. To the contrary, computers can facilitate the restriction of freedom and the invasion of privacy. In the United States, the proposed Cyberspace Electronic Security Act would make it easier for the police and other law enforcement agencies to examine personal computers. The legislation, which is still pending as of the writing of this book, would enable investigators to obtain a sealed (secret) warrant allowing them to enter a home or office, search through private computers for passwords, and install devices to override encryption programs that scramble computer files. After examining the unscrambled files, law enforcement agents could then determine whether they wanted

Although technology is spreading throughout the world, it is not equally available to all people. Starting above and moving clockwise: Students in Calcutta, India, study old books in a dark room; students in Ethiopia also learn in a dark room but without any formal books; children in middle-income Mexico have access to books, some technology, and a better overall learning environment; junior high students in the United States learn in a well-equipped computer lab. American students often give their parents tips on using computer technology.

to download information from the computer, an action requiring another search warrant (O'Harrow, 1999).

The Justice Department claims that it needs such legislation because computers are increasingly used for a variety of crimes. But civil libertarians and many members of Congress are wary of such action. James Dempsey, senior staff counsel at the Center for Democracy and Technology, stated: "They have taken the cyberspace issue and are using it as justification for invading the home" (O'Harrow, 1999). And more than 250 members of Congress have cosponsored legislation that would prohibit the government from allowing "back doors" into computer systems (O'Harrow, 1999).

Private employers already have the authority to enter employees' computers in the workplace and access e-mail accounts. Details about an employee's private life could become known to company officials. A person who works for a state-supported institution (for example, a government office, county hospital, or public university) is afforded more protection, but the courts have not yet defined precisely how much protection. At the very least, it appears that state-supported institutions must honor the Fourth Amendment to the Constitution, which prohibits the unreasonable search and seizure of materials. For example, a program director at Indiana University sued the university in federal court, alleging that it had violated his Fourth Amendment rights and also invaded his privacy during an audit. The university auditors downloaded the director's computer files in his university office without his permission. The case was recently settled out of court; the financial terms were confidential, a sure sign that the institution had to pay the director a substantial sum of money. In a somewhat similar case in the 1980s, a doctor employed by a state hospital won more than $400,000 when two hospital administrators ordered a search of his office without a warrant and violated his "reasonable expectation of privacy." This area of law will explode in the next decade as the courts define the limits of computer privacy. In the process, we will all learn more about the pros and cons of rapidly expanding digital technology.

Economic Ties Strengthen as Political Structures Fracture

A U.S. company produced a popular advertisement for a new cellular telephone service plan featuring the "United State of America." The advertisement claims that when someone from the "state formerly known as Michigan" calls someone in the "state formerly known as California," there are no additional charges because state boundaries no longer exist. As far as technology is concerned, it is one big country without any borders to get in the way.

The explosion in telecommunications technology similarly has created a world economy that is more interconnected and consolidated than ever before, a world economy without national borders. Even though there are thousands of ethnic and cultural divisions throughout the world, many countries share the language of money. Multinational corporations invest in and trade with countries around the world.

National governments and international banks such as Citicorp and American Express loan money to countries and institutions abroad. Travelers, even those visiting developing countries, can often use ATM cards to obtain foreign currency. After the user inserts his or her ATM card, punches in the access code, and specifies the desired amount of foreign currency, technology takes over. The foreign ATM recognizes that the card is from another bank and refers the transaction to the network system. The network sends a message to the home bank account, converts the amount requested abroad into the home currency, verifies that the user has the requested amount in the home account, and sends a message back to the foreign ATM, which adds a service fee and then dispenses the money. All in about 30 seconds.

Economies around the world are also taking advantage of new technologies to establish regional alliances. The most well-known is the European Union (EU), a group of sixteen European countries—Austria, Belgium, Denmark, Finland, France, Germany, Greece, Ireland, Italy, Luxembourg, The Netherlands, Portugal, Spain, Sweden, Turkey and the United Kingdom—that have worked throughout the 1990s to establish a united community with common economic, security, and judicial policies. In 1999, eleven of the sixteen countries successfully converted to a single European currency, called the Euro. Weaker economies (such as Italy) suddenly have a currency that is worth the same as the currency of stronger economies (such as Germany). All member countries using the Euro will benefit because trade and financial transactions will take place without exchange rates and other charges formerly applied throughout Europe. The EU hopes that more European countries will adopt the single currency.

Although not as formal as the EU, other regional economic alliances are emerging.

✦ *Asia.* Japan, Taiwan, South Korea, Singapore, Hong Kong, Thailand, China, Malaysia, and Vietnam trade with each other and maintain strong economic linkages outside of Asia. Despite recent economic problems in the region, this bloc of countries is dynamic, powerful, and expanding.

✦ *North America.* In 1993, after a bitter debate, the U.S. Congress passed the North American Free Trade Agreement (NAFTA). The agreement eased trade barriers and other economic restrictions between the United States and Mexico and between the United States and Canada. Thomson's move to Mexico, for instance, was facilitated by NAFTA policies, which make it easy to move businesses across the border.

✦ *South and Central America.* Most Latin American countries have their own versions of NAFTA and are opening economic talks with the EU and other bodies. Several economic pacts (specifically, MERCOSUR, the Andean pact, and CARICOM) unite the region and increase its economic vitality.

✦ *Southern Africa.* Twelve countries (led by South Africa) have formed the Southern African Development Community (SADC). These countries have pledged to trade more with each other, ease travel restrictions between countries, and create a single currency.

✦ *East Africa.* Kenya, Uganda, and Tanzania have revived the old East African Union in an effort to formulate common economic and political policies.

Around the world, in region after region, nations are finding economic power in numbers. What is more remarkable, however, is that economic unification is occurring during a period of political fragmentation. To put it simply, there are more and more countries in the world today. Countries are dividing up along ethnic, cultural, or religious lines, with different groups calling for self-rule based on one or more characteristics (Naisbitt, 1994). Graphic 1.6 shows how rapidly the number of countries has expanded since the United Nations was founded in 1945. Twenty-five countries were added to the globe between 1991 and 1993 alone, as the former Soviet Union and other parts of Eastern Europe disintegrated. There are literally thousands of ethnic groups, cultures, and languages in the world. Moreover, with few exceptions, most countries have at least two ethnic, cultural, or religious groups within their borders. Because many groups want independence, we could have as many as 1,000 countries in the future (Naisbitt, 1994, pp. 33–37).

A good example of the trend toward fragmentation is the former Yugoslavia, where ethnic and religious conflict killed at least a quarter-million people during the 1990s. The violence erupted when ethnic provinces declared independence from the capital province of Serbia. Slovenia (where ethnic Slovenes live) and Croatia (where ethnic Croats live) declared independence in 1991, and Bosnia and Herzegovina (where Muslims, Serbs, and Croats live) declared independence in 1992. The United Nations now recognizes four independent countries within the state formerly known as Yugoslavia: the Republic of Slovenia, the Republic of Croatia, the Republic of Bosnia and Herzegovina, and the Federal Republic of Yugoslavia (Serbia).

The United States and its North American neighbors are also experiencing political fragmentation. In 1995 Canadian voters in Quebec province narrowly defeated a referendum to separate from Canada and establish their own country. (The separatist side received just under 50% of the vote.) French-speaking Quebec has a culture much different from that of English-speaking Canada. But Quebec is also an economically vibrant province that contains a substantial portion of Canada's industrial and financial base. If Quebec had separated from Canada, both countries would have faced serious economic consequences. In fact, many Canadian companies (and citizens) transferred large sums of money out of Quebec in the final days leading up to the election. Moreover, other countries (especially the United States) campaigned against Quebec's separation because various trade and political agreements with the new country would have to be renegotiated. The U.S. government breathed a sigh of relief after Quebec voted to stay in the union. But Quebec will vote again on its independence in the future and could still leave larger Canada (Farnsworth, 1995).

Other independence movements in North America are also important to mention. In Mexico, the Zapatista National Liberation Army has engaged in an armed struggle with the Mexican government to separate the state of Chiapas from the

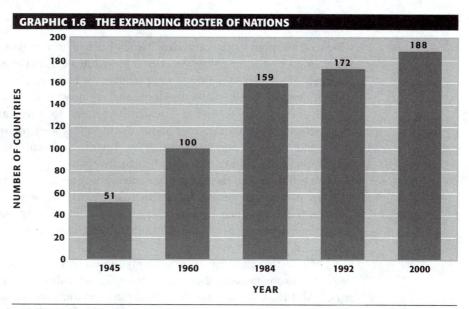

GRAPHIC 1.6   THE EXPANDING ROSTER OF NATIONS

Source: United Nations (various documents).

country (Golden, 1995). And, in the United States, there is a growing movement among the 140,000 native Hawaiians (13% of that state's population) to separate from the U.S. mainland and create their own nation ("Movement for Sovereignty," 1994). Although neither movement will likely prevail in the near future, they are examples of the sorts of movements that are increasing the number of countries in the world.

Political unity is harder to achieve than economic unity. In Europe, for example, economic cooperation and even a single currency may become a reality, but true political union will be more elusive. John Naisbitt, one of the strongest advocates of that position, states emphatically:

> I feel confident that the [EU], which seeks to go beyond trade and bind countries politically—moving toward a common foreign policy and defense, as well as a common currency—is doomed to failure. There are many who disagree with me—vociferously. But that is because they do not understand that although people want to come together to *trade* more freely, they want to be *independent* politically and culturally. There will be no real union of Europe. (1994, p. 10)

Some people argue that European countries themselves are likely to break apart politically. In the United Kingdom, Scotland now has its own parliament and may eventually declare complete independence from England. Several other European countries could experience similar disintegration. Differences in culture, ethnicity, nationality, and religion work against political consolidation.

Culture Is at the Center of Globalization

Conservative presidential candidate Patrick Buchanan rocked the 1992 Republican convention by claiming that "America is locked in a cultural war for the soul of our country." The war, according to the candidate, is between those espousing a traditional view of "family, faith, freedom, and country" and those adhering to "the gospel of New Age 'relativism,'" which he blamed for everything from crime to pornography to economic stagnation. Buchanan decried multiculturalism, tolerance, and inclusion and claimed that "if America is to once again be 'one nation under God,' this cultural war must be won."

The problem with Buchanan's assessment, of course, is that America is culturally diverse; it is a land of immigrants that, in theory, celebrates its differences. Buchanan and a few others have long argued that national unity can never be achieved until there is some type of cultural unity. But true cultural unity, as Buchanan conceives it, is not really possible.

The idea that all members of a society should embrace a common culture often leads to **ethnocentrism,** the belief that one's own culture is superior to other cultures. Multicultural societies must foster appreciation and respect for all cultures; otherwise, such societies will suffer from intolerance, discrimination, and, in the case of some countries, war and killing.

A young Kenyan man who works at a professional job in the city has returned to visit his parents in the village. He is expected to remember the culture and values of his ancestors. Although highly educated and "modernized," this young man will observe local culture while in the village and pay homage to his elders and the village chief.

GRAPHIC 1.7   RACIAL COMPOSITION OF THE UNITED STATES, 1990

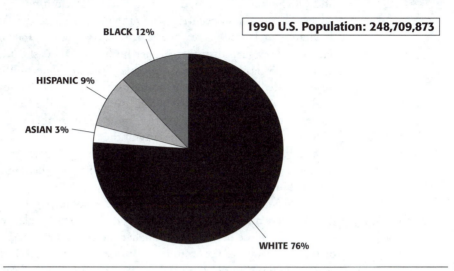

Source: U.S. Bureau of the Census, 1990.

The United States is one of the most multiracial, multiethnic, multicultural societies in the world. In the 1990 census, racial and ethnic minority populations made up approximately 24% of the population (Graphic 1.7). That number is expected to reach 35% by 2005. In some states, such as New Mexico and California, whites soon will no longer be the majority population.

The fastest-growing minority group in the United States is the Hispanic population, especially in California, Texas, and other border states, a demographic shift that could have far-reaching consequences. El Cenizo, Texas, recently passed an ordinance declaring that all city meetings must be held in Spanish (English translations are available, if requested forty-eight hours in advance). Moreover, the town also passed a measure prohibiting city employees from turning in illegal immigrants. Although El Cenizo is believed to be the only U.S. town that has adopted an all-Spanish policy, there may well be similar acts against the traditional, dominant culture in the future. The result could be increasingly strident confrontations between people trying to promote one culture over another.

The world is full of cultural clashes. In 1992, I was living with a young couple in Lusaka, Zambia, while teaching at the University of Zambia. Although the couple, Joseph and Mukolo, had grown up in the traditional rural areas of Zambia, they had long ago moved to the city, obtained higher degrees at the country's main university, and traveled to several other countries. The couple appreciated their background, but they were now very Western in their orientation and lifestyle. They spoke English at home, watched television shows produced in Europe and the United States, and worked and socialized with friends from around the world.

One day Mukolo's mother came to visit, traveling many miles from the countryside. She spoke no English, dressed in traditional clothing, and followed traditional values. The first clash occurred when the mother noted that Mukolo did not kneel down to serve Joseph his tea, the accepted norm in her rural village. How could her daughter show such disrespect to her husband? Didn't she know that her husband would surely leave her because of this dishonor? The mother and the daughter argued heatedly over the issue while Joseph and I left the house. Mukolo tried to tell her mother that things were done differently in the city today, that Joseph did not expect her to serve tea on her knees. The mother countered by telling the daughter that she was losing her way in the city, that she was influenced by corrupt outside values that would undermine the family name. And, the mother noted, Mukolo's children (when they arrived) would forget their ancestors and the values they had imparted.

That scenario is played out all over the developing world, especially in places like Africa, where many first-generation city dwellers try to balance urban values (which carry a heavy dose of Western influence, both good and bad) with the rural values of their upbringing. For example, educated Kenyans speak three languages: their ethnic language (understood only in particular regions), Swahili (the national language, understood by most Kenyans regardless of ethnicity), and English (the language of education, understood by relatively few people). What language should educated parents first teach their children? The parents may agonize over the choice, but grandparents do not. Grandparents in Kenya seldom have an English education and see little reason why their grandchildren should initially learn the language of colonizers. They believe that children should learn the ethnic language first, to encourage them to remember their ancestors and to appreciate traditional values of family and village life. And grandparents let parents know their concerns when the parents visit "home" in the rural areas and the grandchildren cannot speak the local language.

Such cultural clashes reflect a larger issue. Specifically, there is no question that Western culture is continuing to spread rapidly around the world. Television, movies, the Internet, newspapers, magazines, and retail chains expose millions and millions of people around the world to the English language and Western life. And the impact has been significant. People in developing regions, even seemingly remote developing regions, imitate the values and lifestyles they see in the West. Some observers believe the world will become almost culturally homogeneous as local languages and lifestyles are eclipsed by the unrelenting spread of Western culture.

But is the world really becoming culturally homogeneous? On the one hand, it is difficult to argue against the notion that the world is increasingly Western in orientation. On the other hand, some local cultures are fighting back. For example, Islamic conservatives are fighting hard against the spread of Western values by encouraging governments (primarily in the Middle East) to censor television, movies, even the Internet. The fragmentation of the world's political structures is also helping to strengthen local languages (an estimated 3,500 worldwide) and cultures. Apartheid South Africa designated Afrikaans and English as the country's official languages. After the country's democratic political transformation, though, the new government designated eleven official languages; the additional nine languages were ethnic languages spoken throughout the country.

Apparently, culture is simultaneously becoming more homogeneous around the world and more fragmented. One place where the paradox is apparent is Egypt. Tourists can eat at their favorite American fast-food restaurant while looking out at the Great Pyramids, a symbol of Egyptian culture. Egypt has also experienced a rise in Islamic conservatism over the years, no doubt encouraged by what Muslims see as the threat of greater and greater Western influence in the country.

Ethnicity Shapes People's Lives

One of the strongest influences on culture is ethnic identity. Consider the following two stories, one from an intensely multiethnic society and the other from a relatively homogeneous society. Both stories illustrate how important ethnicity is in shaping the way that people live day to day.

In 1986 a very modern, successful, and wealthy trial lawyer, S. M. Otieno, died suddenly of heart failure in Nairobi, Kenya (Harden, 1990, p. 95). Although he lived in a poor country, Otieno's lifestyle resembled that of many upper-middle-class Westerners: he had a high-paying job, a nice home, TVs, a VCR, and other amenities. He sent his children to school in the United States, an enormously expensive undertaking. No outsider would ever have known that Otieno had grown up among the very traditional Luo ethnic group, 200 miles from Nairobi. Rural Luos shun modern lifestyles, embrace traditional marriages (with dowries), believe that improper burials will encourage evil spirits to haunt the group, and think that male circumcision is disgusting.

But Otieno had long since renounced Luo ways. He refused to follow their customs and rituals, rarely spoke their language, and refused to visit "home" for more than short periods of time. He infuriated his relatives by marrying a member of the rival Kikuyu ethnic group; some relatives had not spoken to him for more than twenty years because of that action. Otieno considered himself an individual (a Western concept), not a member of an ethnic group. While living, he had declared that he wanted to be buried on his own land according to his own beliefs. After Otieno's death, his wife, Wambui, intended to honor his request and so scheduled his funeral and burial.

This sad but ordinary event suddenly turned extraordinary, even slightly bizarre. Immediately after Otieno's death, his estranged Luo relatives showed up in Nairobi and declared their intentions to return the body to Luo country for a proper Luo burial. The Luos believed that because "once a Luo always a Luo" Otieno's spirit might haunt Luo villages and communities if he was not buried in a Luo ceremony. Like Otieno's widow, the Luos also scheduled a funeral and dug a grave for him

A clash of cultures within a country. Here a Guatemalan woman from the countryside has entered Guatemala City to shop and market her products. Her way of life is much different from that of city dwellers. Intra-country culture clashes normally revolve around differences based on regional culture, ethnicity, or religion.

back "home." Each side filed for a court injunction against the other side. The court canceled both funerals, and the body was transferred to a Nairobi morgue and held under twenty-four-hour police guard.

Court proceedings over the corpse lasted for three weeks. In the end, the court was more persuaded by Luo arguments; it ruled that Otieno's body should be returned to Luo country because tribal customs are more important than the wishes of an individual. The ruling was upheld months later by a higher court, and the body was turned over to the Luos. Five months after he had died, Otieno's decaying corpse finally was buried. Before burial, the corpse was placed on public display, as stipulated by Luo custom. Witnesses reported that the body "did not look good. His face needed a shave and his lips had shrunken away from his teeth. His tongue was hanging out" (Harden, 1990, p. 127).

Unfortunately, Otieno's corpse is symbolic of Kenyan politics. The country is divided along ethnic lines, and most Kenyans vote for the party that represents their particular ethnic interests. Moreover, the country has experienced substantial violence in recent years, with one ethnic group lined up against another. Citizens of Kenya understand that no one force unifies their society.

But not all countries are divided along ethnic lines. Consider this story from Japan. Baseball, the uniquely American game, is extremely popular there. People follow the Hiroshima Carp, the Yomiuri Giants, the Yakult Swallows, the Taiyo Whales, and the Nippon Ham Fighters (owned by a pork producer). A handful of American players have joined Japanese teams in recent years, expecting to find the familiar rules and rhythms that guide American baseball. Yes, there are nine players on a team, nine innings to a game, and a Japan Series in October to crown a national baseball champion. At the same time, there are also profound differences between American baseball and Japanese *besuboro,* differences that transcend sports and reflect deep cultural differences between the two societies (Whiting, 1990).

First, Japanese baseball is most concerned with group harmony, or *wa,* a characteristic that permeates every aspect of Japanese society. For example, few Japanese players demand exorbitant contracts because doing so would show that a player is placing his own interests above those of the team. Few players throw temper tantrums, fire beanballs at opponents, fight, complain, pout, or do anything else that draws attention to themselves or upsets team *wa.* By contrast, American baseball players are not shy about holding out for more money, even if it creates tremendous salary inequality on the team. Moreover, American baseball fans have seen their share of arguments, fights, whining, and complaining on (and sometimes off) the field. Yes, American players are a team, but they also are individuals who look out for their own interests. One of the biggest authorities on Japanese baseball notes the essential societal differences that are reflected in the two nations' games: "'Let It All Hang Out' and 'Do Your Own Thing' are mottoes of contemporary American society. The Japanese have their own credo in the well-worn proverb, 'The Nail That Sticks Up Shall Be Hammered Down.' It is practically a national slogan." (Whiting, 1990, p. 70).

A second difference between Japanese and American baseball is that the Japanese version allows ties. Several American players in Japan have complained that their teams, on occasion, actually play for a tie. Happy with a tie? Yes, because above all else the Japanese value harmony, conformity, and teamwork. If the teams play hard and the game ends in a tie (or is a close game), both teams can go home without losing face. The key is that each team must put forth its absolute best effort, or *doryoku,* in every game (Whiting, 1990, pp. 60–61). Teams do try to win, but a hard-fought tie is also fine because it combines two of the most important elements of Japanese society: *doryoku* and *wa,* effort and harmony. By contrast, the American emphasis is on winning, with little appreciation for ties. When American baseball players are interviewed, they might well mention the words *win* and *effort* but seldom the word *harmony.*

Japanese society, an ethnically homogeneous society, is also very different from Kenyan society. Japanese society stresses unity, harmony, and teamwork, whereas Kenyan society expects conflict along ethnic lines. Harmony and teamwork across ethnic lines would be nice, but few Kenyans expect it to become a reality any time soon. At the same time, Japanese society and Kenyan society do have one strong similarity: both favor the group over the individual. Japan focuses on the national group, whereas Kenya focuses on the ethnic group. In that respect, both societies differ from American society, which values individualism.

The two examples from Kenya and Japan make a simple but important point: societies around the world vary dramatically. What is appropriate in one culture may be entirely inappropriate in another culture. The maps in Graphic 1.4 may help you appreciate the differing perspectives of ethnic groups around the world.

Modernity and Progress Depend on Perspective

The preceding section noted that "modern" Kenyans consider themselves part of a nation, not an ethnic group. That issue raises the larger question of what constitutes "modern" in today's changing world. Westerners typically consider economic development, multiparty democracy, and advanced technology to be signs of progress. But those characteristics of modernity have some negative by-products. For instance, economic development often is accompanied by high rates of pollution, and advanced technology may lead to high levels of alienation as people rely on communication through machines (for example, e-mail) rather than face to face. The United States, a bastion of modernity, has very high child poverty rates, high rates of broken homes, high teen-suicide rates, and high hand-gun death rates.

Conventional justifications for embracing modernity seldom consider the attractive aspects of more traditional ways of doing things. For example, contemporary African countries considered primitive or backward by some people have a family and social structure that could be a model for other regions around the world. Divorce is rare (although becoming more common in urban areas), retirement homes are virtually nonexistent because old people live with their relatives, and families and villages take care of each other. Many African languages do not even

In a pure display of democracy, a group of villagers in the Gambia discuss issues, debate their merits, and make decisions—often striving for a consensus. The surroundings may not be elaborate, but the democratic process is more complete and "modern" than that followed in many Western countries, where special interests pollute the system.

have a word for *niece* or *nephew* because people regard the children of a brother or sister as practically their own. So, who has made more progress, African societies or North American societies?

African countries also are often considered undemocratic by casual observers, who correctly note the recent history of one-person rule in many African countries. But what people fail to realize is that many African societies (as opposed to governments) have a strong tradition of democracy. In traditional African villages, elders talk about each issue until they reach a consensus. At the same time, communities, churches, and other nongovernment organizations in Africa are putting great pressure on African governments for democracy (Ndegwa, 1996). They are assisted by outside organizations and governments, which put political and economic pressure on African states for democracy. This vibrant system of civic action is what we might call *modern*. And the pressure is working. Democracy at the national level is spreading across Africa. Twenty-five years ago, the continent had few democracies. Today most scholars would agree that 50 to 60% of African countries are democracies. When apartheid came crashing down in 1994, South Africa became probably the most dramatic example of a country that has moved from an extremely authoritarian regime to an open democracy.

As you go through this book, think about what is "modern" and what is "primitive." Some societies are modern in some ways but primitive in others.

Internal and External Forces Interact to Change Societies

Social phenomena in a society are influenced by events that occur inside and outside that society. Consider the social history of guinea worm disease, a parasitic illness that used to be prevalent in nineteen African and Asian countries. It is a painful affliction caused by drinking water contaminated with guinea worm larvae. The worms literally grow under the skin and attack the joints, eventually crippling and debilitating their victims. Fortunately, the disease is now 95% under control (smallpox is the only disease to be completely eradicated).

In 1980 U.S. president Jimmy Carter lost his bid for reelection to Ronald Reagan. One year after leaving office, he started the Atlanta-based Carter Center at Emory University. In 1986 the Carter Center, a nonprofit organization that brings people together to promote peace, resolve conflict, foster democracy, and fight disease around the world, targeted guinea worm disease as its number-one priority, calling for eradication of the disease by the year 2000.

A plan of action was formulated. Former President Carter mobilized many international health organizations to help coordinate the effort and persuaded the Dow Chemical Company to manufacture (free of charge) hundreds of water filters to screen out the guinea worm larvae. And, while these developments were occurring outside the afflicted countries, various efforts were taking place inside the nations to advance the fight against the guinea worm. Most important, the Carter Center and other organizations worked with local governments, institutions, and volunteers to teach people how to filter drinking water.

There is no greater symbol of social change than the fall of the Berlin Wall in 1989. For nearly thirty years, it was brutally effective in enforcing the separation between East and West. An estimated seventy-five East Germans were killed trying to climb over the wall to freedom. But it all ended in November of 1989, when a social revolution swept through Eastern Europe and resulted in the ouster of the East German government and the tearing down of the Wall. In the final protests leading up to the destruction of the wall, there was a sign in the crowd that read: "Sorry chaps, it was just an idea." Above the words was the likeness of Karl Marx.

The guinea worm eradication effort, like the smallpox program before it, has been successful precisely because of the interaction between external and internal forces. The external forces (the mobilizing health organizations and the Dow Chemical Company) would be useless without the strong local efforts in each country. Regardless of the number of filters produced, the guinea worm could not be eradicated without the considerable efforts of people working in villages to train people to filter river water before drinking it. Likewise, local efforts alone would not win the battle, because local initiatives could not produce a proper filter and the international support required to eliminate the disease.

Some of the great social movements in modern history were also a product of interaction between internal and external factors. In 1989 a series of revolutions spread across Eastern Europe and killed communism. It was an amazing year: Poland had its first free elections in forty years, and the communists lost almost every seat in government. Hungary cut its electrified barbed-wire fences along the Austrian border, allowing many East Europeans to emigrate to the West. Encouraged by events in Poland and Hungary, East German citizens began demonstrating, and within weeks the long-time communist leader (Eric Honecker) was ousted as head of the country and the Berlin Wall was torn down. The government of Bulgaria was next to fall, then Czechoslovakia, and finally Romania, where the long-time dictator, Nicolae Ceausesçu, refused to step down voluntarily, as his aging contemporaries had done in other countries. Ceausesçu went the hard way—his own soldiers captured, tried, and executed him on Christmas Day 1989.

Why was 1989 such an eventful year? Stated briefly, there were three reasons for the fall of communism in Europe—the first two were primarily internal reasons and the third was a major external one (Chirot, 1991).

+ Economic problems were increasingly prevalent across Eastern Europe. Bulgaria, Poland, and especially Romania were in terrible shape. They were better off than the Third World but far from the standards of Western Europe. Hungary, Czechoslovakia, and East Germany were much better off economically although not as developed as Western European countries, a fact that was clear to citizens of both Eastern and Western Europe.

+ Eastern European governments had completely lost legitimacy. Citizens no longer had confidence in their governments' ability to deliver services or to act with any degree of moral authority. Repression, secret police forces, and lack of democracy eroded citizens' confidence in the state. Economic problems helped cause—and worsen—this crisis of legitimacy.

+ Meanwhile, Soviet leader Mikhail Gorbachev was calling for economic and political reforms throughout the Soviet Union and Eastern Europe. In a clear break with the past, he also made it clear that no Soviet troops would be used to put down demonstrations in Eastern Europe. Soviet troops had rolled into Hungary in 1956 and into Czechoslovakia in 1968 to put down popular uprisings against communist regimes. Before Gorbachev, the threat of Soviet intervention had always loomed in the background to discourage popular revolts. Previous Soviet leaders had also provided billions of dollars in military and nonmilitary assistance to their Eastern European allies. Gorbachev cut off much of that aid in an attempt to save the ailing Soviet economy and to force economic and political reforms throughout the communist world.

The combination of internal and external forces brought down communism in Europe. If the internal factors had been present but Gorbachev had been willing to commit Soviet troops to Eastern Europe, the revolutions probably would not have occurred, at least not as quickly. And if Eastern Europe had had strong economies and abundant state legitimacy, there would have been no need for Soviet intervention.

Inequality Grows within Societies and across Societies

Much of what has been discussed in this chapter is related to inequality. People have unequal access to technology, economic opportunities, political power, health care, and other factors that help determine life chances. Inequality within a society is usually based on social class, ethnicity or race, and gender. As globalization takes hold, it is also becoming more apparent that societies have unequal clout on the world stage.

Nowhere is inequality more pronounced than when we look at children, a group that is especially vulnerable and disadvantaged in many societies around the world. Throughout the world and in the United States, the number of children falling into poverty is growing, as are cases of child malnutrition, disease, and abuse. Without question, the most exploited group in Third World countries is children, who work for little or no money and often turn to drug running or prostitution to survive (United Nations International Children's Emergency Fund [UNICEF], 1995).

Children in the United States are also in trouble. Almost a quarter of all U.S. children under the age of six live below the poverty line. The numbers for African-American and Latino children (Graphic 1.8) are astounding for a rich country. Part of the reason for high poverty rates is the growing number of single-parent

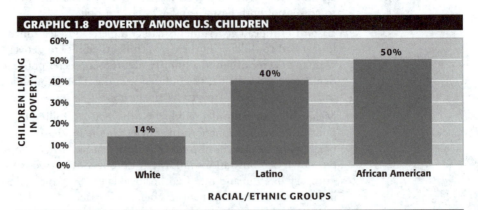

GRAPHIC 1.8 POVERTY AMONG U.S. CHILDREN

(Bar chart — CHILDREN LIVING IN POVERTY by RACIAL/ETHNIC GROUPS: White 14%, Latino 40%, African American 50%)

Source: U.S. Bureau of the Census, 1996.

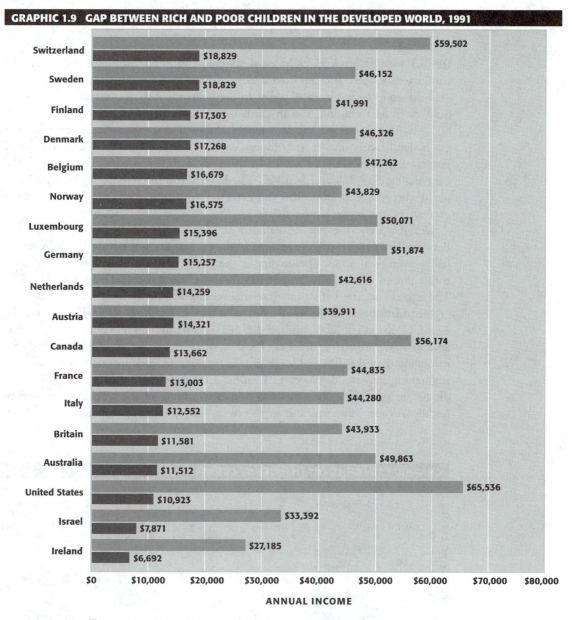

GRAPHIC 1.9 GAP BETWEEN RICH AND POOR CHILDREN IN THE DEVELOPED WORLD, 1991

Country	Affluent	Poor
Switzerland	$59,502	$18,829
Sweden	$46,152	$18,829
Finland	$41,991	$17,303
Denmark	$46,326	$17,268
Belgium	$47,262	$16,679
Norway	$43,829	$16,575
Luxembourg	$50,071	$15,396
Germany	$51,874	$15,257
Netherlands	$42,616	$14,259
Austria	$39,911	$14,321
Canada	$56,174	$13,662
France	$44,835	$13,003
Italy	$44,280	$12,552
Britain	$43,933	$11,581
Australia	$49,863	$11,512
United States	$65,536	$10,923
Israel	$33,392	$7,871
Ireland	$27,185	$6,692

ANNUAL INCOME

■ Households with four children that are more affluent than 90% of households in the country.

■ Households with four children that are poorer than 90% of households in the country.

Source: Bradsher, 1995.

households in the United States. In 1970, 12% of all households were headed by one parent; in 1996, nearly one-third of all households were headed by one parent (U.S. Bureau of the Census, 1996).

The gap between rich and poor children is much worse in the United States than it is in Europe, especially Scandinavia. Graphic 1.9 shows the income gaps among families with children in eighteen developed countries. Although the study was conducted in 1991 and reported widely in 1995 (see Bradsher, 1995), the results are believed to be just as valid today. In the United States, the average "poor household" with four children has an annual income of only $10,923, compared with $65,536 for the average "affluent household" with four children. By contrast, the gap is significantly smaller in European countries, largely because of generous social programs that redistribute wealth in those societies. In Sweden, for instance, the extremes are $18,829 and $46,152. The basic lesson of Graphic 1.9 is clear: compared with people in most other industrialized countries, the rich are richer and the poor are poorer in the United States.

Unfortunately, the poorest families in the United States are getting poorer. Between 1995 and 1997, the income of the poorest 20% of female-headed families fell an average of $580. The income of the poorest 10% of female-headed families with children fell an average of $810 during the same time period (Sawyer, 1999). Those losses occurred at a time of overall economic growth in the United States.

Inequality between rich and poor countries is startling. Each day around the world, more than 35,000 children die, not from natural disasters but from preventable or easily treatable diseases. Perhaps there is no better indicator of global inequality than the different levels of child survival in poor and rich countries. The frightening statistics displayed in Graphic 1.10 show the number of children who die before age five in the forty-two poorest countries of the world, in sixty-seven middle-income countries, and in the twenty-three richest countries. Among rich

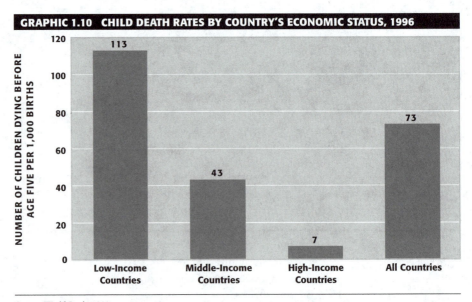

GRAPHIC 1.10   CHILD DEATH RATES BY COUNTRY'S ECONOMIC STATUS, 1996

Source: World Bank, 1998.

countries, the United States is slightly worse than average, at eight deaths per 1,000 births; the lowest death rate is Finland's 5 deaths per 1,000 births.

The incredible gap in life chances between rich and poor countries could be narrowed with a relatively small expenditure of resources. UNICEF estimates that a child can be immunized fully for about $1.50; a child dying from acute diarrhea can be treated with packets of oral rehydration salts that cost ten cents each (the salts are mixed with water). A child suffering from pneumonia can be treated successfully with antibiotics that cost one dollar. A coordinated program to control the major childhood diseases, reduce child malnutrition by half, bring safe water and sanitation to every community, provide basic education for all children, and make family planning universally available would cost only $25 billion each year. That is less than U.S. citizens spend on beer each year and only half of what Europeans spend on cigarettes each year (UNICEF, 1993).

Inequality is an enduring feature in the world and the gap between rich and poor is increasing. This chapter has provided only a few examples; more are presented throughout the book. The study of inequality is one of the most important features of sociology.

A Look Forward

We live in an era of globalization, in which political, economic, social, cultural, and other factors in one country often are affected by events in another country. The United States is an influential country to be sure, but it is only one piece of a giant and complex global puzzle. The remaining chapters underscore that point. They provide substantive information about the United States and other societies around the world, as well as theoretical and conceptual models you can use to understand the sociological implications of that information.

Chapters 2 and 3 introduce the major theoretical and methodological issues in the study of society. Theories are important because they are the framework that enable us to make sense of and explain social phenomena. Methodology is important because it gives us the tools we need to study society.

Chapters 4 through 10 examine the foundations for sociological thought, the important concepts and substantive issues that concern sociologists, including culture, stratification by social class, ethnicity and race, gender, the family, crime and social control, and economic and political institutions.

The last part of the book consists of six articles that apply sociological thinking to global issues. The first five articles focus on several global challenges: global conflict and war, work in the global economy, environmental issues, population challenges, and health care. The sixth article is about creating positive changes in the world. Although this book discusses a myriad of problems, the world is not hopeless. To the contrary, people are creating positive changes each day.

Key Concepts

1. The world is becoming more global in orientation; events that occur in one society affect events in other societies. Thus, many societies are increasingly similar with respect to economics, politics, and culture. Even societies that remain different are influenced by the international economic and political structure.

2. Sociologists are interested not just in the effects of globalization on individual societies but also in the ways that globalization affects the inherent nature of society. They seek to understand this dynamic process by developing expertise in some topic, constructing theories, and conducting research.

3. To understand the effects of globalization and other social processes, we must abandon ethnocentric perspectives and see the world from the perspectives of other societies. Only then can we shake our intellectual and perceptual biases about the things we take for granted, such as technologies, economic and political structures, culture, and modernity and progress.

Active Learning

1. Global Issues in the Press: Document Research. For this exercise, you will use current newspapers from around the globe to examine the relevance of the seven global trends presented in this chapter (the spread of technology, economics versus politics, culture, ethnicity, modernity and progress, internal and external forces, and inequality). For example, you might come across a news story about civil strife or rebellion that illustrates political fragmentation or news of some invention that makes the world even more technological. This project can be done individually or with other students.

a. Make sure you are familiar with the global themes examined in Chapter 1.

b. If you are working alone, search for articles with global themes in the front sections of at least two newspapers for today and the past several days. Choose from your local paper, one of the nationally circulated U.S. papers (for example, the *New York Times,* the *Washington Post,* or the *Los Angeles Times*), or a paper from outside the U.S. (for example, the *London Times*). If you are working in a group, each member should read a different paper, providing a good cross section of local, national, and non-U.S. viewpoints. Your library will have print copies of many newspapers, and electronic versions are available on the Internet (some of the URLs are listed on the Web site for this book, www.pineforge.com/snc).

c. Find relevant news items and, if you are working with a group, compare notes. Write a report explaining the issues and how they relate to the trends outlined in Chapter 1. (A specific news item can relate to more than one trend.) Also note any differences in perspective and coverage between local and national papers and between U.S. and non-U.S. sources.

2. Global Inequality: Internet Research. In this exercise, you will use the Internet to collect information that further illustrates global disparities in access to technology, levels of education, and health care. The nations you choose for this exercise should represent three levels of economic development. Developed nations have industrial economies and are, as a group, the most affluent. Developing nations are in the process of industrialization. Least developed nations rely on agricultural technology—often outmoded and unproductive—to satisfy basic needs. You also will get summary information on low-, middle-, and high-income nations, categories that reflect the level of development. Your sample will be small in size but should still illustrate the extent of inequality among nations.

a. Begin by downloading the scoring form from our Web site (www.pineforge.com/snc) to use in recording scores. Be sure to check the Web site for any changes or updates relevant to this assignment.

b. Go to the home page of the World Bank at www.worldbank.org/. Under "Resources," click "Data & Maps" and then click on "DATA BY TOPIC," which takes you to an index of subjects. Begin by clicking on "HEALTH AND POPULATION" and then on "DEVELOPMENT PROGRESS" (under "HEALTH"). On the form you downloaded from our Web site, record the most recent scores for the net primary enrollment ratio for males and females, the infant mortality rate, and the maternal mortality rate for each of the nine nations in the sample and for low-, middle-, and high-income nations (see the summary of world data at the end of the chart). Note the explanations for the variables in the chart and at the end of the chart. If data are not available for a nation, mark NA ("not available") on the form.

c. Return to the "Data by topic" index and click on "INFRASTRUCTURE." Then under "Power and communications," click on "The information age." Record the number of TV sets and the number of personal computers per 1,000 persons for each nation and for low-, middle-, and high-income nations.

d. Write a report in which you summarize the differences recorded on your form. What do the data suggest about access to technology, education, and health care in the nine nations? Do the data justify the comment in this chapter that "inequality between rich and poor countries is startling"?

3. Ethnocentrism and Cultural Relativity: Group Discussion. (Adapted from an exercise designed by Virginia Teas Gill, Illinois State University.) This chapter argued that sociology requires that we put aside our everyday assumptions and biases about how the world works and overcome ethnocentrism (the belief that one's own culture is superior to all other cultures). The opposite of ethnocentrism is cultural relativity, a perspective that tries to see the customs and practices of other cultures on their own terms. In this exercise, you will view a specific incident from both perspectives, write your own response to some questions about the incident, share your responses with other members of a group, and construct a group response.

a. As an individual, read the following paragraphs and then respond to the questions on the worksheet you have printed out from our Web site (www.pineforge.com/snc). Put your name at the top of the page.

A couple of years ago, Annette Sorensen, 30, an actress from Copenhagen, Denmark, and Exavier Wardlaw, 49, a movie production assistant from Brooklyn, New York, were arrested for leaving their 14-month-old daughter outside a Manhattan restaurant on a chilly day while they ate inside. They left the child in her baby carriage on the sidewalk. Many passersby called 911 to alert the police. New York authorities took the child away from her parents and temporarily placed her in foster care.

In an ensuing article in the *New York Times,* one Danish commentator observed that leaving a baby outside a restaurant is a common practice in Denmark. The commentator wrote, "Often, Danish parents . . . leave their babies outside. For one thing, Danish baby carriages are enormous. Babies ride high above the world on horse-carriage-size wheels. It's hard to get such a carriage into a cafe. . . . Besides, Danish cafes are very smoky places." The commentator continued, "In Denmark, people have an almost religious conviction that fresh air, preferably cold air, is good for children. All Danish babies nap outside, even in freezing weather—tucked warmly under their plump goose-down comforters. . . . In Denmark all children own a sort of polar survival suit that they wear from October to April, and they go out every day, even in winter."

b. Break into groups of three or four. Choose one group member to be the transcriber. Read aloud your answers to the questions on the worksheet, then write one group response to the questions on a separate sheet of paper. Do not merely recopy one of the individual responses. As a result of your collaboration, the group response should be superior to the individual responses. Every group member must approve the group response.

c. Turn in the three or four individual responses with the group response stapled on top. Print the name of each group member at the top of the group response.

My Personal Journey to a Global Perspective

TRACEY JANE DAWSON

I can feel the African sun beating down on my dry, flaking shoulders. My two friends are amusing themselves by throwing stones into the vast savanna that lies at the foot of the road. We have been traveling in Africa for eight months, meeting tribe after tribe and being greeted with nothing but interest and love. My fears have deserted me, leaving me with feelings of joy and confidence. I have learned to communicate without opening my mouth—just with a smile or a laugh. Every day has been as adventuresome as the one before and every sunrise more devastatingly beautiful. Sitting there waiting, hoping for a lone vehicle to come by and transport us to our next adventure, I begin to reflect on my life.

I grew up in a working-class environment in northwest England. My father was a truck driver and my mother a seamstress. I was the youngest of three children, my sister and brother being five and six years my senior. My father was on the road at least three days a week, leaving my mother to raise three children and work all the hours God sent.

The highlights of those early years were centered on the evening meal. It was quality time in the Dawson household, especially when my father was home. We all knew that the topic of conversation would be politics. It created a charged atmosphere in which all of us could express our personal feelings. Being the breadwinner and head of the household, my father would reiterate what was going on in the world. He would tell us stories about Karl Marx, about social injustice and revolution. It was the late seventies, and our political debates focused on apartheid in South Africa, the Arab-Israeli conflict, and England's class system. Under my father's tutelage I became more aware of the social, political, and economic issues that determined the paths of peoples' lives. I realized that those issues would never change. People would always have to suffer. Of that I was certain.

By the time I turned sixteen, I felt I knew all there was to know about political philosophy. I was a revolutionary, my beliefs were set in stone, and nothing would ever change them. My politics soon moved from the kitchen table to the pub, where my friends and I would argue the rights and wrongs of social and political issues. With an air of superiority, I would always bring in Marx and win the argument. The fact that I had never read any of his works had no bearing on the matter; he was a revolutionary and at the time that was all that mattered. I had begun to understand how little control individuals have over their own lives. People's attitudes and values are not their own; they are taught and shaped by their social environment. That realization was the beginning of my sociological understanding of the world. I felt I could step out of my reality and into someone else's. I began to see the evolution of our society, its institutionalized norms and beliefs. I had gone through a secret door in my mind where the world was larger and much more complex than I had ever imagined. My friends had a hard time with that perspective; they had not yet gone through the door and could see the world only through their own reality.

I was seventeen when Margaret Thatcher came to power as prime minister of Great Britain. Little did I know how much worse life could become. Much like her contemporary, U.S. President Ronald Reagan, Thatcher blamed the people for their poverty and inability to find work. She viewed the working class as lazy and ignorant. She took their jobs and cut social assistance programs, condemning them to lives with no hope for change. It was a rude awakening for the working class. I watched helplessly as the changing political dynamics robbed the people not just of work and stability but of human dignity. I watched factories and mines close their doors, leaving working families with no way to survive other than taking meager handouts from a government that despised its citizens.

The society I knew crumbled into depression and despair. I began to hate England. I felt trapped and frustrated and just wanted to get out, but how? I had a poor education, no money, and little chance of making any. Upward mobility for the working class was not an option. We had the ability to look up at the sky, but we were prevented from reaching for it by a glass ceiling, the monstrous, outdated class structure that serves as the foundation of England's political and social system. In essence, it is a state of mind, a conditioning instilled in us from birth. It is made up of four elements—fear, doubt, uncertainty, and anger.

I did not know it at the time, but it was not a lack of money that stopped me from creating a future for myself, it was my conditioned class consciousness. I was not responsible for the social structure in England. I did not choose the limitations imposed on the working class, which meant I was free to make my own limitations.

Then one night I watched a documentary about the Dalai Lama. I had heard about the plight of the Tibetan people, but I knew nothing of Buddhism and its philosophy. As I watched this strange man talk about his life and beliefs, I could not help but smile. His expression was so peaceful and loving and his laugh like that of a child. I saw no stress, fear, or anger, and yet, like me, he struggled for freedom. I could feel my emotions rising to the surface, and tears began to run down my face. It was the strangest feeling because I did not

Tracey meets new friends in South Africa. The fall of apartheid in the early 1990s ushered in a new era of democracy and inclusion for black South Africans, who could not vote under the apartheid system. South Africa is trying to create more opportunities for its black citizens, an effort that will require a lot of time, patience, and resources.

know why I was so emotional. When the documentary was over, I turned off the television and stared at the blank screen. I realized I wanted some of what he had.

The next day I bought a book on Buddhism. That was my first step toward mental and physical freedom. Reading Eastern philosophy was a liberating experience. It pushed me back through the secret door in my mind where the world was not conditioned by one reality but by many. I learned I could create my own world, one where I could take from many different realities to create my own, one with no fear, no doubt, no uncertainty, no anger. It was the best feeling I had ever had.

There was no going back, only forward into the unknown. I wanted to experience the world, meet new people, and learn what they knew. I wanted to climb mountains and have wild adventures. I began buying travel magazines and searching the advertisements for jobs abroad. There were many ads for nannies. I had never thought about being a nanny, but the agency paid your way and the family paid for everything else, which made the prospect of being a nanny in a foreign country exciting. Three months later, I was on my way to Paris to take care of three children. I felt sorry for the family I was going to live with, because my only experience with children was growing up with two dogs. Paris turned out to be a very good experience, and after eight months I was ready to step a little further into the unknown.

Since then, I have traveled to many places and have had many wonderful experiences. After Paris I spent a year in Israel, working as a volunteer on a kibbutz in the Golan Heights.

Tracey makes friends with a group of Hindu women in India. Again, travel helps us learn about new religions, cultures, and lifestyles. It also helps us to expand our individual horizons and see the world (and its people) in new ways. In fact, world travel probably helps us learn more about ourselves than anything else.

There were volunteers from all over the world who were also looking for something more in life than what they had been given. In Israel I learned that my understanding of the Arab-Israeli conflict was rudimentary and that there are always at least two sides to a story. My beliefs and opinions that were set in stone when I was sixteen deserted me, and I was left with a feeling of emptiness. My understanding of what was right and wrong was also gone. It was a strange feeling because I was like a child, learning and seeing everything for the first time.

After Israel I went home to England, got a job in a factory, and saved enough money for a plane ticket to India and South Africa. Apartheid was coming to an end in South Africa, and I wanted to see it. I had always wondered how white South Africans would explain that political system. After my experience in Israel, I should have known what would happen. I found that their reality was much like my own growing up in England, small and narrow, maintained by their families, their education system, their church, and the media. Once again my opinions dissipated—they were the product of a conditioned state of mind, a built-in value system that one rarely questions.

In India, a country full of extremes, I had many moving and emotional experiences during my three-month visit that added to my understanding of the way people are affected by—

and triumph over—their social circumstances. I remember none more vividly than the act of love I witnessed on my final journey, on the train from Varanasse to Bombay.

It was a hot sticky day, and the train was moving at a snail's pace. There was a distinct smell of feces in the still air. The train was crowded with people even before we left the station. Little did I know that hundreds more would join us before the journey's end. The aisle was jammed with women breast feeding their babies, children crying with confinement, and men playing cards on their suitcases. Going to the bathroom was an impossible task. I anxiously waded through stifled bodies, praying I would not step on any fingers or toes.

On one of my adventures to the bathroom, I returned to find that a man and his teenage son had taken my seat, with his large family crouched on the floor between the two bunks. I was hot, sweaty, and impatient. I flew into a rage, pushing and kicking people into the aisle. They moved slowly and passively—there was nowhere else for them to go. I watched the man and the boy out of the corner of my eye. They were both perched on the edge of my seat, the last step before merging into the cramped aisle. They were very quiet. Their expressions told only one story, one of hardship and poverty. Yet there was no sign of self-pity or sorrow.

My anger left me. Feeling guilt well up inside me, I noticed there was something wrong with the boy. His eyes were drawn and his legs were unusually thin. The father noticed me looking; he stared back and put his arm around his son and pulled him close, as if to protect him. Then he bent his head and kissed the boy's cheek with such passion and unconditional love. I felt a sharp pain in my chest but did not know why. Months later, after returning many times to that moment in my mind, I realized I had never seen such an expression of love between a father and his son. The lesson learned was compassion. I was concerned with my space on the train, a space I had paid for and considered mine. The man and his child needed only a small part of that space. Why was my first reaction one of anger and contempt? How conceited was I to think because I had paid for it I deserved it?

My nostalgia broken, my mind returns to the present. The African sun has started its descent, casting majestic shadows across the land. I look up to see my partners in crime still amusing themselves with their stone throwing. I glance down the neverending road, but there is nothing in sight. I smile to myself, enjoying the unknown. As I look out over the vast African savanna, my smile broadens. My God, it's beautiful! England seems a world away—its miserable rainy days, its depressing unemployment lines, and its frustration. I think about all the wonderful places I have visited, the diverse cultures rich with religion and tradition. I wonder at what specific point or place I let go of all that anger and fear that came from knowing only one reality, a reality in which I looked at the world with condemnation and judgment, struggling under its limitations—limitations that were really only illusions.

Thinking about the Essay

In Chapter 1, we pointed out that it's not easy to overcome our ethnocentrism—the beliefs and values into which we are socialized—but that it is valuable to make the attempt. We illustrated that point with a map exercise (see Graphic 1.4). How do the experiences described in this essay reinforce that idea?

2 Sociology and Society

How does sociological theory help us interpret the world?

One evening in 1987, four teenagers—two sisters, ages 16 and 17, and two males, both 19—climbed into an aging Camaro and began cruising their small New Jersey town. Around 3:00 A.M., they stopped at a gas station, bought three dollars worth of gas, and attempted to take the hose from the station's vacuum cleaner. The manager stopped them and the kids didn't push it. Later, the manager said that he didn't really think anything about the incident and that the teenagers seemed to be in good spirits.

Early the next morning, the Camaro was found in an abandoned garage, the four teens dead of carbon monoxide poisoning. Autopsies showed that they died sometime between 4:00 and 5:30 A.M. In a suicide note, the teens criticized their families, said they felt unloved, and asked to be buried together. Their families were stunned, the town mourned, and their friends wondered why. The story made the national news and, for at least a while, Americans everywhere wondered why four teenagers—at the beginning of life, with all its possibilities and surprises—would commit such an act of despair.

Who were those four teenagers? What had their lives been like? How could people so young be so sad and hopeless? Were they depressed? Drunk? High? Crazy? Why end it all? Why as a group? Did they talk each other into it? Did they dare each other to stay in the car as the deadly fumes built up? What was their final conversation like? What were their final thoughts?

Most of those questions will never be answered. It is always a challenge to understand society and human behavior, but some topics are more difficult—and more heartbreaking—than others. Can we really know why someone would take his or her own life? Can we ever understand suicide?

This chapter introduces the discipline of sociology. Sociologists study a broad range of issues and problems: ethnic and religious conflict, inequality, and the control of disease, to name just a few examples. Although sociology does not claim to have all the answers (or even all the questions), it does offer a powerful and useful way to think about social life, the differences between societies, and social problems. We wrote this book, in part, to demonstrate the power of our discipline and the usefulness of the knowledge that sociologists have accumulated. We hope to convince you that sociology can answer important questions about society and that sociologists have something worthwhile to say about a wide array of topics, from threats to the survival of the globe to the suffering of a few families in a small town in New Jersey more than a decade ago.

We also wrote this book to provide you with a set of intellectual tools—concepts, theories, and techniques—that you can use to analyze the social world and come to your own conclusions and answers. We began that process in Chapter 1 by introducing some of the central concepts and main themes of this book; you will become familiar with many more sociological ideas and theories as you move from chapter to chapter.

This chapter continues to unpack the sociological toolkit by considering the origins and the development of the discipline. Sociology is less than two centuries old, but it has a complex intellectual past and supports a variety of viewpoints, some of them contradictory, on society and social issues. We do not attempt a comprehensive review of the history of the discipline but, rather, focus on three scholars who have profoundly influenced the development of sociology. We examine how they thought about society in the context of their times and also see what parts of their thinking survive to the present day in the work of contemporary sociologists.

We begin this exploration by considering the conditions that led to the emergence of sociology. All ideas are shaped by the context in which they originate, and, as you will see, sociology was profoundly influenced by the nature of everyday social life at the time of its origin. Modern sociology arose in Western Europe at a time when industrialization and urbanization were stimulating rapid, even revolutionary change. Early sociologists had an unending string of urgent questions to consider and ponder. They probed and researched virtually every aspect of their societies, from inequality and the relationships between classes to culture and religious values, from bureaucracy to democracy, and from the mechanization of production to the causes of suicide. Their work was wide ranging, and the themes and ideas at the core of this book are rooted in their analyses.

The Origins of Sociology

People have always wondered about human behavior and social problems, but the distinct discipline of sociology emerged only when a certain set of circumstances came together. One major catalyst was the sweeping change the industrial revolution stimulated in Western Europe. Beginning a little more than two centuries ago,

industrialization, the process by which machines and new forms of energy are applied to economic production, transportation, and other tasks, began to transform the economy, politics, culture, language—the very nature of everyday life. The new industrial technologies first appeared in Great Britain and by the turn of the nineteenth century had spread to other Western European nations. Eventually, industrial technology transformed the globe and helped to mold the modern system of societies, with all its complexities, interconnections, possibilities, tensions, and inequalities.

Before the industrial revolution, the huge majority of Europeans were small-scale farmers (peasants) who lived in scattered rural villages. Their way of life was traditional and slow changing, and their farming techniques were centuries old. The level of productivity was low, and virtually all work was done by hand or with animals. People were illiterate, and most never had occasion to venture more than a few miles from their place of birth.

The industrial revolution brought machines and new power sources (steam, coal, and—later—petroleum and nuclear power) to the tasks of economic production. Even though the early machines were primitive by today's standards, they quickly increased the food supply and the volume of goods that could be produced. The productive capacity of the economy exploded in agriculture, manufacturing, construction, transportation, and hundreds of other areas.

Industrialization also brought new forms for the organization of work: factories, mills, and mines, each of which required a large workforce. Cities began to grow, and peasants left their rural villages in huge numbers for work in the city. Industrialization and urbanization became complexly interrelated processes that, as they proceeded, created new problems and challenges. The early factories and mines were dangerous and difficult for the workers, and exploitation (low wages, long hours, unsafe working conditions, and other abuses) was common. City life brought overcrowding, crime, homelessness, and new forms of poverty. The early industrial workforce consisted largely of displaced peasants who, although well equipped to survive in their traditional, "low-tech" rural environment, experienced distress and confusion in the city.

Simultaneously, a host of other challenges to the established conventions of social life appeared. For example, before the industrial revolution, the traditional European political institution was monarchy, which was hereditary, authoritarian, and justified by the doctrine that the king (or queen, or tsar, or emperor) was divinely ordained to rule. The monarchy was supported by an elite class of aristocrats who owned the land and controlled much of the wealth of society. New political ideas—democracy, freedom, liberty, and equality—challenged the status quo, helped to stimulate bloody revolutions in North America and in France, and spread to other peoples. The traditional political order of hereditary monarchs and landed aristocracy came under attack. A new day dawned, the old ways faded, and the political forms of the past fast became irrelevant to the burgeoning industrial, urbanized society.

As economies and politics changed, so did virtually every other aspect of society. New ideas and new problems forced people to think about society in new ways and to seek new answers to the eternal questions of social life. How should society be

The process of industrialization dramatically altered the workplace, family, and social structure. Peasant farmers left their land to work in dangerous and grim factories in the city, where many industrial workers faced new forms of poverty and unhappiness. Today, industrialization has reached an advanced stage, with robots replacing humans in many factories. Corporations increase their profit margins by making products without having to pay so many laborers. And, in the post-industrial information age, fewer and fewer workers will be needed, as people make their own travel reservations, shop on-line, scan their own groceries, and use voice mail instead of operators.

organized? How should resources and wealth be distributed? What is the proper role of religion and the church in everyday life? Who should participate in the governance of society? How should employers treat workers? How should parents treat children? How should rulers treat the ruled?

In the midst of the confusion and dislocation, a French nobleman named August Comte (1798–1857) proposed that those questions could be answered by the development of a new field of study called sociology, which would apply the methods of science to the study of society. Comte felt that a scientific study of society based on research and facts would dispel the myths and misunderstandings perpetuated by superstition, tradition, and "common sense" and uncover the fundamental laws that should govern and regulate human nature and human society. Those laws would provide a blueprint by which society could be organized to minimize conflict and strain and maximize benefits and happiness for all.

Other scholars followed Comte and made further contributions to the new discipline, the new way of thinking about society and social life that grew into modern sociology. This chapter focuses on three of the scholars who made especially important contributions to sociological thought: Karl Marx, Max Weber, and Emile Durkheim.

Karl Marx (1818–1883)

Karl Marx was born in Germany and grew to adulthood during the early days of the industrial revolution. He studied the massive social and economic transformations caused by the shift to machine power and industrial technology, and he documented the enormous productivity of the new economic system as well as its destructive, antihuman features.

Marx was particularly concerned with the enormous class inequalities that lay at the heart of Western European industrial societies. He observed the splendid lifestyles of the wealthy—the huge mansions and armies of servants catering to every indulgence—and the abysmal squalor of the working class and the poor. How could such desperate misery coexist with such affluence? How did such a tiny elite manage to commandeer such a huge share of the wealth? Marx saw class inequalities as unjust, unfair, and—ultimately—doomed. He believed that the economic system that created huge disparities was fundamentally corrupt and would be destroyed in a violent revolution. Following that destruction, a new social order founded on perfect justice and fairness would emerge and carry humanity to a new stage of social development free of exploitation, inequality, and poverty in all its forms.

Marx's conclusions flowed from his analysis of history, philosophy, economics, and social structure. For our purposes, Marx's complex body of thought can be summarized in two key propositions:

◆ The key elements of the structure of any society are the economic system and the class relationships that flow from that system.

◆ Struggle between social classes is the fundamental reality of social life. Class conflict supplies the energy that propels history.

The economic system includes all elements of society involved in producing and distributing goods and services and satisfying the needs (for food, shelter, and so forth) of the population. In Marx's view, sometimes called economic determinism, the economic system is basic, a foundation on which all other components of society are constructed. In other words, the economy shapes the form and content of every aspect of society, including the legal system, religious thought and practice, the family institution, and even a person's consciousness.

Perhaps the most important elements of the economic system are social classes, which Marx defined in terms of their relationship to the means of production, that is, the tools, resources, and organizations by which the society produces and distributes goods and services. In an agricultural society, the means of production include land, draft animals, plows and other farming implements, and the markets through which food and other goods and services are distributed. In an industrial society, the means of production include factories, machinery, energy supplies (petroleum, natural gas, and so on), banking and financial institutions, highways, and shipping firms and railroads.

The means of production are crucial to Marxism. Marx believed that the class that controlled or owned the means of production dominated the rest of the social system and molded the society to suit that class's self-interest. Marx maintained that the ideas, practices, customs, and routines of a society do not "just happen" but are designed to sustain the elite class and the economic system on which its domination rests. For example, societies that base their system of production on slave labor may enshrine such religious beliefs as "the meek shall inherit the earth" to distract the oppressed from their misery in the present by focusing their attention on the next life. Likewise, consumer-oriented economies (like the United States) may enshrine materialistic values to encourage people to purchase goods to the limits of their financial abilities (or even a little beyond). Thus, economic systems, means of production, and the needs of the dominant social class shape all societies.

To say that a society has a dominant class implies that there is an antagonistic or adversarial class that does not own or control the means of production. According to Marx, the disadvantaged class will naturally oppose the dominant class and try to reduce its suffering and increase its share of the wealth. **Class conflict,** the struggle and friction between the two social classes, is therefore inevitable and inescapable, a fundamental part of social life.

Marx wrote that class conflict is crucial because it provides the energy that fuels social change and propels history. Periodically, class conflict will escalate to violent revolution, and the elite class, along with its economic system, will be destroyed and replaced by its enemy class. The newly victorious class will reshape society to suit its own economic interests and, in the process, create a new system of inequality and a new antagonist class, and a new phase of strife and struggle will begin. But the conflicts and episodes of discord are not random, undirected, or neverending: they ultimately will bring human society to a state of perfect peace, harmony, justice, and fairness. Marx believed that the class conflicts of his day were the last stage of a long process that stretched far back into history and that, after a period of bloody revolution, human society would enter a state of utopian perfection.

In the nineteenth-century European industrial societies that Marx studied, class conflict was between the bourgeoisie, or capitalists (the owners of the means of production), and the proletariat, or the workers, who were forced to sell their labor in exchange for wages and who did the actual work of production in factories, mines, and mills. This economic system, called **capitalism,** is based on private ownership of the means of production. In Marx's view, the bourgeoisie (the capitalists) dominated society, and all social arrangements and structures—from the political system to religious beliefs—were designed to sustain and perpetuate their reign. For example, when labor unrest and strikes occurred, the state typically intervened on the side of the factory owners and used its coercive powers (the police and the army) to suppress the labor unions of the proletariat.

Marx believed that the suffering and oppression of the proletariat were inevitable results of capitalism and could not be reduced as long as the system of private ownership of the means of production endured. The self-interest of the capitalists— their need to generate profit, protect and expand their interests, and finance their elaborate lifestyles—dictated that they keep wages and benefits as low as possible. As a result, workers were forced to endure long hours, unsafe working conditions, and misery in all its forms.

He also believed that the working class—the great majority of the population— would soon become so alienated from the capitalist system and so outraged at the inequalities and injustices it generated that they would rise up in revolt, destroy the bourgeoisie, and take control of society. Because the proletariat owned nothing, they would abolish private property when they came to power and construct a society based on socialism, a system in which the means of production and the wealth of society were owned jointly by all.

In anticipation of that revolt, Marx and his collaborator, Friedrich Engels, published *The Communist Manifesto* in 1848. Their slim volume set forth the basic principles of what came to be called Marxism, presented a scathing critique of capitalism, and issued a call to arms to the proletariat ("Workers of all countries unite"). Along with Marx's other works, *The Communist Manifesto* became the intellectual basis for the version of socialism called communism, which seeks to attain a socialist order through violent insurrection. The communist ideology has profoundly influenced the development of the current world system of societies. Revolutions in the name of Marx have taken place in Russia (1917), China (1949), Cuba (1959), and several other countries (none of which, ironically, were fully industrialized at the time of the revolution). An enormous number of people have subscribed to some version of Marxism; for about half of the twentieth century, more than a fifth of the world's population was governed by principles derived from Marx's writing.

The impact of Marxism on the social sciences—political science, economics, and history, as well as sociology—has been great. Modern scholars continue to mine the Marxist body of work for insights on the importance of the economic infrastructure of society, the nature of capitalism, class conflict, and other matters. Today, Marx is regarded as one of the founders of the **conflict school** of social thought, a perspective that stresses the central role of struggle, domination, and competition between groups in social life.

Max Weber (1864–1920)

Max Weber was another monumental figure in the development of the social sciences. His intellectual interests were wide ranging and his work so prolific that he profoundly influenced the development of political science, history, and economics as well as sociology.

Among his numerous intellectual pursuits, Weber took up many of the same questions as Marx, applied his own considerable intellectual and scholarly powers, and came to his own conclusions. Both scholars were concerned with the effects of industrialization on society, inequality, social class, and the future of Western capitalism, but Weber felt that Marx's views on those matters were too narrow. For example, he supplemented Marx's economic approach by developing a more elaborate and subtle analysis of social class that incorporated political power and prestige. (See Chapter 5 for more on social class and stratification.)

Weber also disagreed with the emphasis that Marx placed on the economy in shaping social structures and social change. He argued that cultural factors as well as economic forces shaped the industrial revolution and the rise of capitalism, and he focused especially on a set of values that emerged during the Protestant Reformation and came to be known as the Protestant Ethic. Those values rose to prominence in European culture after the Reformation and provided an essential catalyst for the industrial revolution and the rise of capitalism. (See Chapter 4 for more on culture and values.)

The traditional religion in most of Europe, Roman Catholicism, stressed an other-worldly spiritual orientation, which encouraged people to devote their energies to prayer, meditation, and the greater glorification of God and the Catholic Church. People were urged to devote surplus energy and time to spiritual endeavors, and high status was accorded to persons so committed to their religious duties that they retreated from the world to enter convents and monasteries. Perhaps the most tangible evidence of the medieval world's devotion to the glorification of religion and concern for the next life are the magnificent churches and cathedrals that were constructed in nearly every city and town.

In Weber's view, the traditional trappings of religion were incompatible with the hustle and bustle of industrialization and the hardheaded realism of capitalism. The new Protestant religions provided a more appropriate basis for the economic transformation because they focused on this world instead of the next and extolled the value of hard work for its own sake, not so much for the glorification of the Deity. The religious foundations of capitalism are particularly evident in Calvinism, a branch of Protestantism developed by John Calvin (1509–1564). The central belief of Calvinism is predestination: the idea that God alone determines whether a

Weber believed that cultural values—often emanating from religion—influenced society along with economic factors. The rise of capitalism was prompted by the Protestant Reformation and the Protestant Ethic, which stressed hard work, diligence, and self-discipline. Protestant denominations (right) placed more emphasis on earthly achievement as a sign of worthiness for salvation. "Faith without works" was not sufficient for industrious Protestants. This was in contrast to the Roman Catholic church (above), which placed primary emphasis on prayer, meditation, and other-worldly endeavors. Concern with earthly achievement was misguided, according to medieval Catholicism.

person is saved or damned and that no individual can do anything to change that fate. Indeed, to try to change one's spiritual destiny is to behave as if the will of God is open to negotiation with mere mortals.

The doctrine of predestination created a terrible uncertainty for Calvinists. How could they know if they were saved or damned? According to Weber, they dealt with that anxiety by assuming that they were in fact one of those chosen for salvation. To live life with less than absolute confidence in one's salvation would be evidence of insufficient faith and a sure sign of unworthiness. But how could they maintain that absolute confidence? In addition to following all religious norms carefully and avoiding the temptations of the devil, Calvinism counseled "intense worldly activity" (Weber, 1958, p. 112). Success in this life was seen as evidence that a person was among the few who would be saved in the next life. Also, Calvinism extolled thriftiness, discipline, perseverance, a simple lifestyle, and diligence. In addition to assuaging uncertainty and reducing anxiety, those spiritual values prepared people to succeed in their worldly pursuits.

Whereas the culture of medieval Catholicism directed people's attention away from this world and its mundane activities, Protestantism, particularly Calvinism, did just the opposite. By extolling the value of salvation through hard work and diligence, the newer religious doctrines laid some of the most important cultural foundations for the industrial revolution, the rise of a commercial class, and the success of capitalism. Weber supplemented and extended Marx by demonstrating that the rise of capitalism could not be understood solely in terms of social class or the economy. It also represented a change in how people thought about themselves and their lives.

Marx and Weber also differed in their projections of the future of capitalism. Marx felt that the system of private ownership of the means of production was doomed. Weber, in contrast, thought that capitalism would continue to evolve and that the capitalist class would continue to dominate Western society (and the world) for the indefinite future, a prospect he saw as, at best, a mixed blessing. Although capitalism was enormously productive and had the potential for improving the quality of life throughout society, Weber thought it also had some distinctly negative qualities. He was pessimistic about the implications of the style of thinking that lay at the core of Western capitalism, a form of rational analysis that operates in terms of costs and benefits, profits and loss, simple plusses and minuses. The central search of the true capitalist is for the single most efficient, cost-effective way of accomplishing goals.

Weber termed that mechanical, clockwork approach to business and to life **rationalization** and saw it as powerful and compelling but also destructive of some basic human needs and potentials. How can rationalization be applied meaningfully to the creativity required to compose a symphony or create a work of art? How can a mechanical, clockwork style of thinking speak to the human need for meaning and purpose in life? (Note Weber's emphasis on the cultural forms as opposed to the economic, materialist approach of Marx.)

Furthermore, what is rational for one group may be irrational for another. Consider, for example, the classic assembly line. Work is highly routinized, and the workers have virtually no control over their actions and make no decisions about the production process: they merely follow instructions and obey the procedures established by management. From the point of view of management and the bottom line, highly regulated forms of production may be efficient and perfectly rational. From the perspective of the workers, however, the same procedures may be intensely dispiriting. To the extent that the workers have no autonomy, they have no sense of control or responsibility for their work and no pride or sense of accomplishment in the final product.

Thus, capitalism may be productive and efficient, but it can also be soulless and alienating. The simple, one-dimensional rationality of efficiency is antagonistic to human values and the meaning that people need to derive from life. Furthermore, cold rationality can be harnessed for any purpose, including the most destructive. As demonstrated by the Nazi Party in Germany during World War II, even madness and murder can be rationally organized.

Emile Durkheim (1858–1917)

Marx and Weber affected the development of all the social sciences, but Emile Durkheim's influence is more specific to sociology. In fact, he is probably the single most important figure in the history of the discipline. Durkheim helped clarify the identity of sociology, pioneered many of the methods, approaches, and perspectives used today by sociologists around the world, and addressed some of the most profound and important questions of his (and our) time.

Like Marx and Weber, Durkheim's thinking was shaped by the social conditions that surrounded him. He was centrally concerned with the effects of industrialization and urbanization on social life, especially on the unity and cohesion of modern society (a concern with many echoes in the United States and the world today). Durkheim believed that a society could not function without some minimal sense of togetherness and solidarity among its citizens. The lower the level of cohesion and sense of belonging, the lower the ability of society to meet the needs of its citizens and protect the people from outside enemies (and each other).

In Durkheim's view, the industrial revolution profoundly changed the basis for social unity and cohesion. The mechanisms that had sustained traditional agricultural societies were becoming increasingly irrelevant in modern industrial society. According to Durkheim, traditional agricultural societies are held together by the forces of similarity and familiarity and the weight of tradition. In such societies, most people live in small villages with family, kinfolk, and neighbors, all of whom are well known to each other. Everyone depends on farming for a livelihood, and the division of labor is simple. Each family is virtually self-sufficient, and all adults perform about the same kinds of tasks, following routines and procedures that have been handed down across the generations and that are thoroughly anchored in tradition.

A preindustrial society stresses conformity and sameness: the concerns of today echo those of yesterday and anticipate those of tomorrow. People belong to strong social networks and have numerous, dense ties with others, and their behavior is regulated by a stable, solitary, slow-changing set of cultural beliefs, values, and norms. Durkheim called that form of social cohesion mechanical solidarity.

As industrialization and urbanization begin to change a society, the division of labor becomes more complex, and isolated, rural self-sufficiency declines. In a modern society, people are bound together not by their sameness and the density of their social ties but by their mutual dependency and need to cooperate in order to survive. City life and industrial jobs mean that each person must rely on others (strangers) to produce and distribute food, clothing, housing, heat, water, and other goods and services. People cannot satisfy their needs by themselves: all goods and services, from the trivial to the essential, must be purchased in the marketplace.

Modern societies, then, are held together by cooperation and interdependency rather than by similarity and sameness. Each of us is constrained to carry out our roles and participate in a complex system of exchange with others to perform daily tasks and satisfy needs. Durkheim called that type of cohesion organic solidarity, emphasizing the idea that modern society is like a giant organism that depends on the independent contributions of each component for the smooth functioning of the overall system. That way of looking at society lives on today in American sociology as **structural-functionalism,** an approach that analyzes the role (or function) of each part (or structure) in the system of society.

The shift from mechanical to organic solidarity parallels the shift from agricultural to industrial systems of production and the shift from village life to city life. Like most changes, those shifts have some consequences that might be regarded as negative and others that might be seen as positive. As society modernizes and urbanizes, the weight of tradition declines and the strictures of small-town conformity are lifted. In the city a level of individualism and creativity that would be crushed in a traditional village is tolerated and even encouraged. New lifestyles, ideas, and values have a chance to flourish, and people can live in greater independence, self-expression, and freedom than ever before.

But there is a price to pay for enhanced tolerance and individualism. Social ties and connections become fewer and less dense in the anonymous city, and the moral certainties of previous generations are lost amid the clashing values and cultural relativity of modern society. Under conditions of organic solidarity, people need to cooperate in order to satisfy their needs, but the division of labor separates people into specialized roles and narrow niches. People can become socially disconnected and feel anonymous and alone even in the midst of a densely populated urban landscape.

Parallel with the weakening of social ties and networks, industrial society also tends to lift the weight of cultural tradition and ancient codes of morality. Because the cohesion of modern society is based on cooperation and interdependency, there is no need for a strong, repressive, or monolithic system of morality to reinforce conformity. The resultant decline in moral unity and normative cohesion increases the likelihood that people will feel that they are not bound by any ethical principles, that morality itself is meaningless or irrelevant and does not apply to them or to their lives. Durkheim used the term **anomie** to describe the sense of normlessness or moral drift that affects modern society. Individualism and personal freedom may flourish in industrial society but only at the expense of a loss of moral certainty and unity.

Those ideas are prominent themes in Durkheim's writing, and he pursued their implications in a variety of ways, including, in perhaps his single most important work, a landmark study of suicide. That research project is significant, in part, because it demonstrated that suicide—seemingly the most private and personal of

African village life involves a strong sense of community and solidarity. Social ties are strong, and a well-defined sense of morality and values guides village life. Children are raised not just by parents but also by large extended families. But these social ties are threatened when people move away to urban areas and a more individualistic lifestyle. Most people in this Nairobi traffic jam grew up in villages and return often to visit parents and other relatives. These parents will watch closely to see whether grandchildren growing up in the city are observing the values, traditions, and language taught in the village. If not, they will voice their displeasure.

behaviors—has sociological dimensions and cannot be fully understood as simply an act of individual will. Durkheim demonstrated that suicide is linked to (among other factors) patterns of group membership and the social contexts in which people live. He thereby demonstrated the value of a sociological approach and the need for a scientific study of society.

Instead of asking why specific individuals take their lives (an individualistic approach), Durkheim asked why the rates of suicide varied from group to group. By studying the official records of suicide available from governmental agencies, Durkheim saw that urbanites had higher suicide rates than rural dwellers, single people had higher rates than married people, and Protestants had higher rates than Catholics. What could account for those group differences?

To demonstrate Durkheim's thinking, let's examine one of the group differences he identified: the higher rate of suicide among Protestants than among Catholics. Durkheim rejected explanations based on the content of religious beliefs or creeds because both religions adamantly and clearly condemned suicide. Rather, Durkheim explained the difference in rates in terms of moral cohesion and the strength of social ties. The Catholic Church placed a stronger emphasis on community (social ties with others) and provided an elaborate and detailed theology and a moral code that included detailed answers to all of life's questions. Most Protestant denominations, in contrast, encouraged members to seek the truth for themselves and to strive to be individually responsible for their own spiritual growth and needs. Catholics were thus more likely to be integrated into a moral community of like believers. Although members of both faiths might be equally likely to lose a job, get depressed, suffer the loss of a loved one, and confront other traumas or personal tragedies, Catholics were more likely to find support and solace from others than were Protestants.

> If religion protects . . . against the desire for self-destruction, it is . . . because it is a society [with] beliefs and practices common to all the faithful, traditional and thus obligatory. The more numerous and strong these collective states of mind are, the stronger the integration of the religious community. (Durkheim, 1951, p. 170)

Durkheim's thinking about suicide flowed from his analysis of the impact of industrialization and the shift from mechanical to organic solidarity. An urban, industrial society has greater moral uncertainty, fewer social ties, and lower levels of solidarity than a rural, agricultural society, and one of the prices of modernization is a higher suicide rate.

Of course, Durkheim recognized that modernization is not the sole cause of suicide and that acts of suicide are not all the same. His research convinced him that there are at least four types of suicide and, thus, four different kinds of explanations and patterns of causation for that phenomenon. The first two types of suicide, egoistic suicide and altruistic suicide, are based on the number and density of ties with others, a dimension of social life that can be called social integration. *Egoistic suicide* accounts for the higher suicide rates of Protestants. It results from too few ties with others and is motivated by loneliness. *Altruistic suicide* occurs when a person's ties to the group are too strong. Durkheim recognized that, ironically, group solidarity can be so great that it overwhelms a person's sense of individuality. Altruistic suicide occurs when a person gives his or her life for the group (e.g., Japanese kamikaze pilots in World War II) or when a group commits suicide collectively (as the Heaven's Gate cult did in 1997).

Durkheim's third and fourth types of suicide, anomic suicide and fatalistic suicide, are based on a dimension of social life called moral integration, which parallels the difference between mechanical and organic solidarity. *Anomic suicide* occurs under conditions of normlessness, when rapid change makes moral codes seem irrelevant and people no longer feel committed to or regulated by a normative system. Under those conditions, life itself can lose any sense of purpose and seem empty and devoid of meaning. *Fatalistic suicide* occurs when people are overregulated: they feel trapped and immobilized. This type of suicide is an act of desperation and hopelessness, a final act of futility and despondency.

Students of suicide have argued about the value of this typology for much of the last 100 years. Some find Durkheim's thinking and his classification system to be extremely useful; others argue that his definitions are vague and his explanations, at best, incomplete (see, for example, Lester, 1994, and Thorlindsson and Bjarnason, 1998). Regardless of the outcome of the debate, there is no question about the value of Durkheim's overall contribution. By demonstrating that this seemingly most personal and individual of behaviors has sociological dimensions, he simultaneously increased our understanding of suicide and established the credibility of a young discipline.

The Sociological Perspective

Marx, Weber, and Durkheim are towering figures, but sociology also has roots in numerous other scholarly traditions and world views. Some scholars trace the origins of sociology to ancient Greece, Africa, or Asia; the separate streams of thought that have contributed to the discipline defy enumeration or easy categorization. Still, a fully scientific sociology grounded in research and empirical fact as well as theory and logic is less than two centuries old. Sociology is still a young discipline with much room for growth and many questions left unanswered (indeed, unasked).

The hallmark of the discipline is the **sociological perspective.** Sociologists focus on society, its constituent parts and structures (groups, institutions, political systems, social classes, language and symbol systems), and its processes (interaction in all its forms, cooperation, conflict, dominance and exploitation, group formation and dissolution). While sociology has obvious relevance for understanding the behavior of individuals, sociologists are more concerned with the social contexts in which behavior takes place than with people per se. Sociology is sometimes called a macro discipline because of the focus on social realities that are more general than the individual.

The sociological perspective is interested in the social context that produces behavior. Why do these boys dress and sit in such a similar fashion? Sociologists are interested in the societal factors (for example, peer pressure) that have produced this conformity, which probably extends well beyond dress and posture.

You have already been exposed to the sociological perspective in several different contexts. Chapter 1 discussed globalization, rising levels of inequality, and other key trends, in each case treating society as a unit of analysis in its own right. Marx, Weber, and Durkheim also took a macro approach to social life. For example, all three were concerned with the implications of industrialization—the central engine of social, political, and economic change in their social worlds—for everyday life and ordinary citizens. The process of industrialization happens to a society as a whole and is, therefore, fundamentally sociological.

Perhaps the easiest way to clarify the sociological perspective is to contrast it with what might be called an individualistic perspective, in which behavior is seen as the result of individual decision making and free will. An individualistic perspective is extremely common among Americans and is used to explain everything from poverty ("poor people are just lazy") to crime ("criminals have no morals") and suicide ("people who take their own lives must be crazy"). Explanations of that sort are not so much "wrong" as they are incomplete. As Durkheim demonstrated a century ago, even the most private behaviors have sociological dimensions and cannot be understood apart from the social contexts and processes in which they occur. Ignoring (or deemphasizing) the social context in which choices are made and behavior takes place means ignoring the myriad, complex, and subtle power that society exerts on the individual.

The ability to take social context into account, to see behaviors as jointly produced by individual and societal factors is sometimes called the **sociological imagination** (Mills, 1959). As Chapter 1 argued, if we have any hope of understanding human society and social problems, an approach that takes into account social structures and social processes is essential. Without sociology (and, to be sure, the other social sciences), our understanding will be too narrow, and we will not be able to deal effectively with the urgent problems that confront the world.

Sociology is not, however, a uniform set of views regarding society. Modern American sociology maintains a number of distinct schools of thought and approaches to social reality. Some perspectives flow from Marxism or from the thinking of Weber or Durkheim; others reject those and most other sociological traditions, including the assertion that a scientific analysis of society is even possible.

We do not attempt to cover all the diverse perspectives in any detail in this book. Instead, our version of sociology stresses what we believe are the strengths of the discipline: a reliance on science and empirical research, critical thinking, a comparative, macro focus, and a concern with the urgent problems facing humanity. We make occasional references to other versions of sociology, but this book stresses the themes presented in Chapter 1 and anchors itself in the nineteenth-century origins of the discipline. Those characteristics are evident in the examples of modern sociological research presented in the next section.

The Continuing Relevance of Marx, Weber, and Durkheim

The processes of industrialization and modernization that stimulated the emergence of early sociology have spread far beyond the borders of Europe and continue to shape and reshape social life, but now on a global scale. Just as early sociologists tried to research and understand the maelstrom of changes around them, contemporary sociologists study the effects of globalization, increasing inequality among nations, increasing economic unification, and the other trends identified in Chapter 1. Thus, the mature stages of industrialization, urbanization, and modernization continue to shape contemporary sociology just as their beginning stages stimulated the growth of the discipline in its infancy.

It would not be surprising to find that concepts developed (mostly) in the nineteenth century would have little relevance as we make the transition into the twenty-first century. The social world has become a very different place, and Marx, Weber, and Durkheim could not have anticipated computers, communications satellites, cloning, space travel, cable TV, or the other wondrous technologies that shape our lives. On the other hand, industrialization and its partners, urbanization and modernization, continue to be powerful forces for social change around the globe. The shift from agricultural to industrial technologies has spread far beyond Europe, and some nations, like the United States, are moving into a new stage of postindustrial development. Nonetheless, to the extent that industrialization continues to drive social, economic, and political change around the globe, the ideas of Marx, Weber, and Durkheim—class conflict, rationalization, and anomie—retain their relevance.

Marxism and Modern Capitalism

Marx is the most historically distant of the three sociologists considered in this chapter. He died more than 100 years ago, almost four decades before the deaths of Weber and Durkheim and, indeed, years before they began their major projects. He saw industrialization at its earliest stage, and his predictions of workers' revolts and a utopian future might seem naive today, particularly after the 1989 collapse of the Soviet Union, the first society fashioned in the name of Marx.

It would be a big mistake, however, to ignore the influence of this powerful thinker. Just as Weber, in the view of some, spent his intellectual life in a prolonged debate with the ghost of Marx, modern sociologists (and other social scientists) continue to analyze Marx's writings for insights on the dynamics of western capitalism and its effects on society. Many of his ideas have found their way into everyday life, sometimes appearing in unexpected places. For example, Marx's notion that the economy is the elemental force that drives the rest of society found pithy expression during Bill Clinton's 1992 presidential campaign ("It's the economy, stupid") and remained a theme of the Clinton administration (Cassidy, 1997). Likewise, Marx predicted that capitalism's insatiable need for new markets would transform the globe, destroying traditional markets and cultures in its wake. That prediction seems validated by the worldwide availability of commodities such as Big Macs, rock 'n' roll, and blue jeans. Marx remains a vital presence in a wide variety of analytical viewpoints. This section examines world systems theory, a perspective that has roots in Marxism but that focuses on the globe as a whole and the forces that create and sustain inequality among societies.

World Systems Theory. The central argument of **world systems theory** is that the differences among societies in health, wealth, education, access to technology, and life expectancy are not inevitable, foreordained, or somehow "natural" (see Wallerstein, 1974; Chase-Dunn, 1989). Rather, the inequalities were created by the deliberate actions of the more powerful nations and their dominant capitalist class.

In the modern world, according to world systems theory, societies can be categorized into three groups.

◆ The *core* comprises advanced, affluent nations (the international equivalent of the bourgeoisie or capitalist class). Leading core nations include the United States, the nations of Western Europe, Japan, and Australia.

◆ The *semiperiphery* is a middle group of nations that are moderately developed. Semiperipheral nations include newly industrializing nations such as South Korea, Brazil, and Malaysia.

◆ The *periphery* includes poor, underdeveloped nations (the "proletariat"), located largely in Africa, South America, and Asia.

The magnitude of the differences in quality of life between the core and the periphery are explored in Chapter 5. This section addresses the question of why the core nations are so much more affluent than nations in the periphery and even the semiperiphery. World systems theory argues that the core nations created the disparity by deliberate exploitation and that, just as Western industrial societies are organized to sustain the rule of the capitalist class, so the global system of societies is organized to benefit the core nations. The higher quality of life enjoyed in the core nations comes at the expense of the nations in the periphery.

The current world system started to take shape some five centuries ago, when the nations of Western Europe began to explore the rest of the globe. As they ventured into Africa, the Americas, and Asia, Europeans not only "discovered" new peoples and civilizations, they dominated, conquered, and colonized them. Using their superior military and economic power, European nations established colonies, which they organized for the benefit of the "mother country." England was the most aggressive and successful of the European powers; at the height of its power in the early twentieth century, it had colonies in every corner of the globe. British colonies included Canada in North America, British Guyana in South America, Nigeria and Kenya in Africa, Egypt in the Middle East, and India and Australia in Asia. For centuries, it was literally true that "the sun never sets on the British Empire." Graphic 2.1 shows the extent to which the nations of Western Europe controlled the rest of the world in the early twentieth century.

What motivations fueled the rise of Europe to world domination? For the individuals involved, a variety of motives were at play: thirst for adventure, greed, the desire to bring Christianity to the world, simple racism. At the level of nations, the benefits of colonialism generally were materialistic: the core nations exploited their colonies for natural resources, raw materials, and cheap labor. A stream of goods—minerals, metals, sugar, tobacco, rice, food products of all sorts—flowed to the mother country, where they were transformed into commodities for the marketplace. The wealth that surged into Europe in the fifteenth and sixteenth centuries stimulated the industrial revolution and helped the capitalist class rise to power. As the nations of Europe industrialized and modernized, their dominance in the world increased.

The colonies lost wealth and resources but received little in the way of compensation. In addition, the European imperial powers often used their colonial populations as a source of cheap labor or, even worse, slaves. The plantations in the European colonies in America depended directly on slave labor imported from Africa and harnessed for the profit of the growers, the shippers, and the merchants back in Europe (Curtin, 1990).

Besides exploiting their colonies for raw materials and labor, the core nations imposed their culture, language, and institutional forms. Native cultures and languages were suppressed; educational systems, marriage laws, and political processes were recast to follow forms derived from the mother country; local traditions were ignored or even outlawed. The plundering of wealth and resources and the suppression of native traditions and cultures generated intense anger and resentment among colonial subjects (much of which persists into the present), strong emotions that often were expressed in violent uprisings and revolution.

During the twentieth century, the era of European colonialism began to draw to a close. The nations of Europe were weakened by wars, and the cost of directly

GRAPHIC 2.1   EUROPEAN COLONIZATION IN THE EARLY TWENTIETH CENTURY

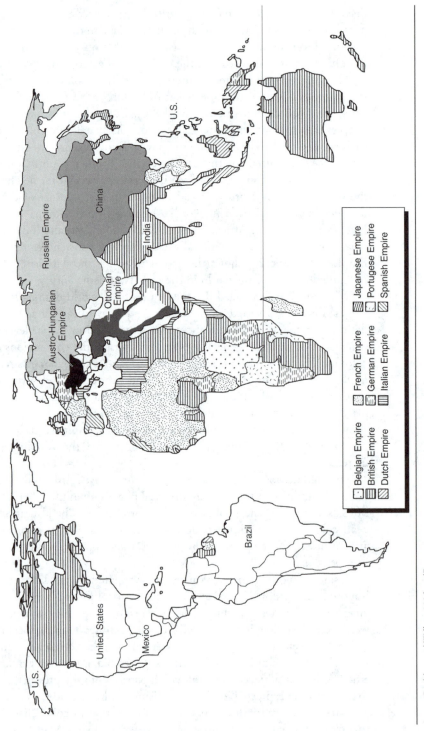

Source: Bradshaw and Wallace, 1996, p. 47.

controlling distant, overseas colonies became prohibitively expensive. The great colonial empires withered and disintegrated, with the end often hastened by violence and warfare. Today, all the European colonial possessions have achieved political independence. The last European colonies were only recently transferred to their original ruling country, Hong Kong in 1997 and Macao in 1999 (both to China).

But, according to world systems theory, the end of direct political control is not the end of colonialism or of the exploitation of poorer nations for the benefit of the core. Direct political rule has been replaced by an economic form of domination operated by powerful transnational corporations (TNCs), economic behemoths controlled by the capitalist class that own companies, factories, mines, and other businesses around the globe. Although TNCs are headquartered in the core nations, they transcend the boundaries of any one nation. TNCs include such well-known companies as GE, Coca-Cola, Exxon, Microsoft, and Wal-Mart, and many of them are richer than most nations. Graphic 2.2 lists the 50 largest economic entities in the world, excluding core nations. Twenty-nine—well over half—of those entities are TNCs (noted in capital letters). Approximately 140 nations in the world have smaller economies than the smallest of those 29 corporations.

Although present-day forms of exploitation are new, the dynamics remain roughly the same as at the height of direct political colonialism. The nations of the periphery are still exploited for cheap food, raw materials, minerals, metals, and cheap labor. The capitalist class dominates not only advanced industrial societies but, through the TNCs, much of the rest of the globe.

The Limits of World Systems Theory. There is no debating the basic historical facts stressed by world systems theory: European nations did control much of the world for the past five centuries, and they used their preeminent position to benefit their own economies at the expense of their colonies. European forms, customs, and languages were imposed on colonial subjects, and native cultures and customs were often denigrated, ridiculed, attacked, and outlawed. The colonial powers were often brutal and racist and commonly practiced slavery and other forms of oppression.

However, as an explanation for present-day global relationships and the levels of inequality among nations, world systems theory is open to question. It is true that core nations and TNCs have been guilty of exploitation, but, as noted in Chapter 1, societies are shaped by internal factors as well as external ones, and the nations of the periphery must share some of the blame for their lack of development and overall poverty. Poor nations have been brutalized by their own elite classes as well as by colonial outsiders, and corrupt and incompetent leadership has sometimes retarded development and squandered resources. The factors that sustain current global inequalities are many and multifaceted and cannot be reduced to a simple equation that blames only capitalism, economic imperialism, or the excesses of the past. (Chapter 10 explores many of those factors.)

Furthermore, the flow of benefits has not been completely one-sided, and the harmful effects of TNCs can be exaggerated (Firebaugh, 1992; Firebaugh and Beck,

GRAPHIC 2.2 FIFTY RICHEST ENTITIES IN THE WORLD (EXCLUDING HIGH-INCOME NATIONS)

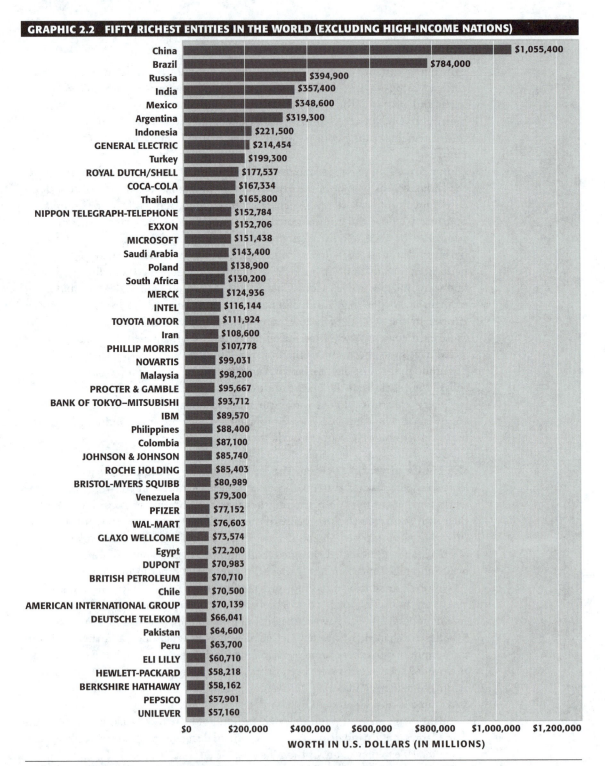

Entity	Worth (US$ millions)
China	$1,055,400
Brazil	$784,000
Russia	$394,900
India	$357,400
Mexico	$348,600
Argentina	$319,300
Indonesia	$221,500
GENERAL ELECTRIC	$214,454
Turkey	$199,300
ROYAL DUTCH/SHELL	$177,537
COCA-COLA	$167,334
Thailand	$165,800
NIPPON TELEGRAPH-TELEPHONE	$152,784
EXXON	$152,706
MICROSOFT	$151,438
Saudi Arabia	$143,400
Poland	$138,900
South Africa	$130,200
MERCK	$124,936
INTEL	$116,144
TOYOTA MOTOR	$111,924
Iran	$108,600
PHILLIP MORRIS	$107,778
NOVARTIS	$99,031
Malaysia	$98,200
PROCTER & GAMBLE	$95,667
BANK OF TOKYO–MITSUBISHI	$93,712
IBM	$89,570
Philippines	$88,400
Colombia	$87,100
JOHNSON & JOHNSON	$85,740
ROCHE HOLDING	$85,403
BRISTOL-MYERS SQUIBB	$80,989
Venezuela	$79,300
PFIZER	$77,152
WAL-MART	$76,603
GLAXO WELLCOME	$73,574
Egypt	$72,200
DUPONT	$70,983
BRITISH PETROLEUM	$70,710
Chile	$70,500
AMERICAN INTERNATIONAL GROUP	$70,139
DEUTSCHE TELEKOM	$66,041
Pakistan	$64,600
Peru	$63,700
ELI LILLY	$60,710
HEWLETT-PACKARD	$58,218
BERKSHIRE HATHAWAY	$58,162
PEPSICO	$57,901
UNILEVER	$57,160

WORTH IN U.S. DOLLARS (IN MILLIONS)

Sources: Hoover Institute, 1998, and World Bank, 2000.

Note: Chart displays 1998 market values for transnational corporations and 1997 gross national products (GNPs) for nations.

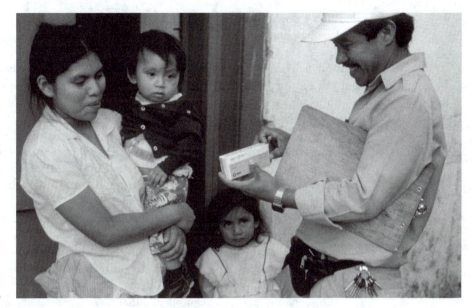

Although transnational corporations have exploited poor countries, they have also manufactured and donated medicines that fight tropical diseases. The Merck Mectizan Donation Program gives Mectizan to people who suffer from river blindness. Here a local health worker delivers the drug to a coffee plantation in the Guatemalan mountains.

1994). Some poor nations have benefited from the infusion of capital that foreign investment brings, and contact with core nations and TNCs has helped to raise the standards of living and increase economic growth in many countries (Rangel, 1989). While international capitalism may not be particularly benign or benevolent, neither is it the unmitigated, callous exploiter that the more zealous adherents of world systems theory sometimes allege.

In short, world systems theory, a modernized and global application of Marxism, provides a powerful account of the origins of the current world system of societies and the inequalities among nations. But no theory can explain everything. To understand the modern global system of societies, we must take into account processes and structures in the poorer nations of the world. Much of the remainder of this book is devoted to the development of that more balanced view.

Rationalization in Modern Society

Weber was very concerned with the implications of the new style of thinking that lay at the heart of industrialization, capitalism, and modern science. He believed that rationalization would drive out all other ways of thinking—traditional morality, sentiment, values, religion, even magic—and imprison people in a sterile system of cold logic. The brave new world of the industrialist might be efficient and predictable, but it would also be profoundly meaningless, purposeless, and dehumanizing.

Bureaucracy. To Weber, the impact of rationalization on human affairs was epitomized by **bureaucracy:** large, hierarchical organizations governed by explicit rules and regulations. The efficiency of a bureaucratic organization is based on its ability to break down complex tasks (for example, manufacturing an automobile) into smaller, separate tasks that can be organized in a coordinated, systematic way (for example, the classic assembly line). Because tasks are narrow and specialized, workers can be trained to high levels of efficiency and skill. The activities of the workers at the bottom of the organization are coordinated and regulated by supervisors, who in turn report to middle managers, who are the subordinates of others still higher in the organizational structure, and so on, to the top layer of management and control. Explicit, written rules and regulations, administered impersonally and objectively, regulate the system. Once the most efficient procedure for accomplishing a specific goal has been identified, it is implemented and committed to writing. A manual of operations is developed that standardizes and regulates employee performance and guarantees maximum productivity.

Highly rationalized bureaucracies can be very productive and predictable: an assembly line can produce exactly the same product built to exactly the same specifications time after time, hour after hour, all day and, if necessary, all night. Bureaucracies can be like machines. They can do their work like a clock ticking away; rigid, routinized, inflexible, precise, unchanging.

Although bureaucracies can operate that way, they usually fall short of the ideals of consistency and maximum efficiency. Ultimately the workings of the organization depend on people, and people, according to Weber, need more from life than rigid rules, a narrow specialization, and a paycheck. In the highly rationalized bureaucracy, individual workers are forbidden to change routines, make decisions, or exercise creativity. Employees have little or no control over the course of their work. In fact, they are controlled by the organizational routine and become servants to the system, appendages of the organization. Because they merely enact the routines and procedures designed by others, they feel little pleasure, satisfaction, or sense of fulfillment from their jobs. The greater the extent to which work is rationalized and specialized, the greater the alienation, boredom, and unhappiness of the workers and the greater the likelihood that the quality of work will suffer. Because it leads to worker dissatisfaction and a lower quality of work, rationality is, ironically, ultimately irrational (Ritzer, 1996, p. 13).

McDonaldization. Writing at the beginning of the twentieth century, Weber saw bureaucracy as the embodiment of both the positive and negative consequences of rationalization. Writing at the end of the century, sociologist George Ritzer finds a modern equivalent: **McDonaldization,** the form of organization pioneered and epitomized by McDonald's fast-food restaurants. Although scarcely a half century old (the first McDonald's opened in the mid-1950s in California), there are today well over 26,000 McDonald's outlets worldwide (McDonald's, 2000). The franchise has been one of the great success stories of American capitalism and has spawned numerous imitators in many other types of businesses as well as in the fast-food industry.

According to Ritzer, McDonald's success is due, in large part, to its adherence to four central principles of a rationalized bureaucratic organization: efficiency, calculability, predictability, and control.

◆ *Efficiency.* The unending search for the optimal method of accomplishing a task is perhaps the heart of rationalization. In the fast-food business, efficiency means moving a customer from a state of hunger to a state of satiation with minimal time and effort. The fast-food industry has devoted an enormous amount of time and effort to find the best (that is, the fastest and least expensive) way to cook cheeseburgers, fry potatoes, and dispense soft drinks.

◆ *Calculability.* Rationalization stresses the quantitative aspects of a process. The food is uniform in weight and size and cooked according to exact time intervals. Portions are as much alike as possible, and quantities (amount of catsup on a patty, number of fries per serving) are carefully measured. Calculability stresses easily measured aspects of performance (for example, number of hamburgers sold each day) as opposed to more subjective and ephemeral dimensions (quality, taste, or the ambience of the dining experience).

◆ *Predictability.* Perhaps McDonald's greatest appeal to consumers is that no matter where or who you are, the experience of dining at McDonald's is as nearly uniform as it can be. Across the country (and, increasingly, around the globe), the customer is greeted in the same way, chooses from the same menu, pays about the same price, and is served in about the same amount of time. Above all, a McDonald's cheeseburger always has the same taste, appearance, smell, and weight.

◆ *Control.* The experience of the McDonald's diner is controlled by the design of the facilities and the process: stand in line, wait your turn for service, choose from the limited menu, finish the meal quickly, discard your trash on the way out. The experience of the workers is even more controlled. Like cogs in bureaucracies everywhere, they are trained to accomplish a narrowly defined set of tasks in a rigid, unchanging fashion. There is little (if any) room for decision making. The food arrives at the restaurant "pre-formed, precut, presliced, and 'pre-prepared'" (Ritzer, 1996, p. 103). Little is left for the workers to do other than follow the prescribed routine to cook (or, in many cases, heat) the food and deliver it to the customer. One long-term trend is to eliminate as much human input as possible and rely instead on machines, timers, and computers. Eliminating people and, thus, the possibility of human error controls the process more completely and enhances the predictability and efficiency that are at the core of the fast-food industry.

So, what's so bad about a mediocre cheeseburger? Certainly, McDonald's model for meal delivery has some powerful advantages. It is convenient, efficient, and (relatively) cheap. People find great comfort in being able to get it "their way" (to borrow the slogan of a McDonald's competitor), even when they actually have virtually no control over the preparation of their meal (try ordering two burgers, one well done and one rare).

In fact, the organizational model pioneered by McDonald's is so powerful and attractive that it has been adopted in many other areas of social life, some of them quite dissimilar from the fast-food industry. McDonaldization has spread to health care ("Doc-in-a-box"), auto maintenance (Jiffy Lube), newspapers (*USA Today* is sometimes called *McNews*), and even education, leisure, and travel. It is now possible to travel around much of the world and never leave the homogenized safety of franchised restaurants and hotels and controlled, prepackaged experiences.

Such hyperrationalized forms of organization do have costs, as Weber would have predicted. First, McDonaldization is dehumanizing to workers. The tasks are broken down into such narrow segments that, in the words of one fast-food worker, "a moron could learn this job" (Ritzer, 1996, p. 130). Workers are allowed to use only a small portion of their skills and abilities. The highly routinized procedures create resentment, dissatisfaction, and alienation. It is difficult if not impossible to derive a sense of fulfillment or meaningfulness from this type of work. McDonaldization also dehumanizes the customers, who are greeted by memorized scripts ("Welcome to McDonald's. May I take your order please?) and then herded through an assembly-line dining experience. The opportunities for actual person-to-person contact are limited (they waste time), even while the impersonality and anonymity is hidden behind what Ritzer calls "false fraternization" (for example, the ubiquitous but meaningless "Have a nice day"). For both customers and workers, the experience is designed to eliminate spontaneity and creativity. Dining becomes an empty experience in which the only need satisfied is hunger.

The dangers of McDonaldization might seem trivial as long as we confine our attention to cheeseburgers and quick, convenient meals. But what happens when

This photo could be from almost any place in America or, increasingly, the world. McDonaldization has spread to pizza, all sorts of fast-food restaurants, and many other types of establishments. Such places hire low-skill workers and pay them little in the way of wages or benefits.

those trends affect other areas of social life? Will more and more jobs become so narrow, specialized, and unchallenging that "a moron" could do them? Will education be reduced to nothing more than a series of multiple-choice tests and standardized curricula, the content of which is selected not for importance but for ease of testing? To what extent can life itself be reduced to choosing narrowly defined options from a carefully controlled menu? What happens to a sense of meaning and purpose when life is prepackaged and experiences are standardized and scripted? What happens to the human spirit, spontaneity, creativity, and the need for meaning when all of life is enclosed in the iron cage of rationalization?

Suicide in the Modern World

A century of research has validated Durkheim's argument that suicide has an important sociological dimension. In particular, his assertion of a connection between suicide and degree of social integration (egoistic and anomic suicide) has been demonstrated time and again by researchers in a variety of nations using a variety of research techniques (Lester, 1994; Thorlindsson and Bjarnason, 1998; Trovato, 1992; Simpson and Conklin, 1989; Pescosolido and Georgianna, 1989). This section briefly reviews some recent trends in suicide and relevant findings from research.

Suicide around the Globe. One of the challenges of doing research on a phenomenon such as suicide is making sure that data are reasonably accurate. This is a problem even in nations like the United States that have sophisticated data-gathering systems. The difficulty is compounded many times over in comparative, cross-national analyses because nations vary in their definitions of and candor about suicide. Nonetheless, Graphic 2.3 compares the suicide rates for twenty-four developed nations. As you can see, the suicide rates are highly variable. Russia's suicide rate, for example, is about six times greater than the rate in England and Wales.

In comparison with other industrialized nations, suicide is not a particular problem in the United States. The U.S. suicide rate falls toward the lower end of the graph in Graphic 2.3 and is only a fraction of the highest rates. The U.S. suicide rate has remained roughly the same since at least World War II. Suicide is currently the seventh leading cause of death in the United States, falling well below heart disease, cancer, and accidents but a little ahead of homicide. Rates of suicide tend to increase with age. In addition, males commit suicide at higher rates than females, and whites have higher suicide rates than blacks (U.S. Bureau of the Census, 1998, pp. 101, 108).

Researchers have reached some conclusions about suicide based on data like these:

◆ Suicide rates are highly variable. Graphic 2.3 shows quite a bit of variation in suicide rates among developed nations, but variability would be even greater if nations at all levels of development had been included.

◆ Just as Durkheim would predict, suicide rates seem to increase with modernization and industrialization (see, for example, Zhang, 1998, p. 538).

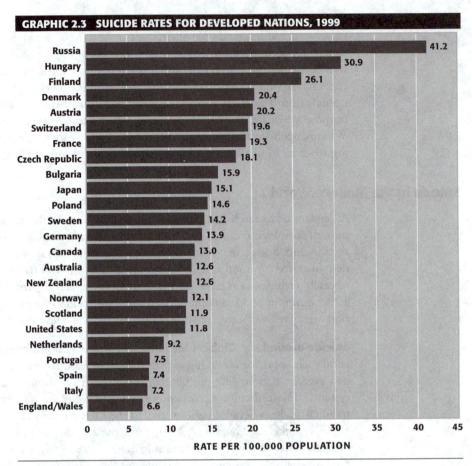

GRAPHIC 2.3   SUICIDE RATES FOR DEVELOPED NATIONS, 1999

Nation	Rate per 100,000 Population
Russia	41.2
Hungary	30.9
Finland	26.1
Denmark	20.4
Austria	20.2
Switzerland	19.6
France	19.3
Czech Republic	18.1
Bulgaria	15.9
Japan	15.1
Poland	14.6
Sweden	14.2
Germany	13.9
Canada	13.0
Australia	12.6
New Zealand	12.6
Norway	12.1
Scotland	11.9
United States	11.8
Netherlands	9.2
Portugal	7.5
Spain	7.4
Italy	7.2
England/Wales	6.6

RATE PER 100,000 POPULATION

Source: U.S. Bureau of the Census, 1999.

Keep in mind that those conclusions are based on data that are incomplete and inconsistent in quality. (See the appendix for more information on dealing with cross-national data.) Conclusions about the sociological dimension of suicide are more trustworthy when they draw on a single set of data, as the study described next did.

Teenage Suicide in the United States. Although overall suicide rates have been fairly stable in the United States, the suicide rates for adolescents and young adults began rising steeply in the 1960s, as shown in Graphic 2.4, and just recently began leveling off. Against that backdrop, the suicides of the four New Jersey teenagers mentioned at the beginning of the chapter caught the attention of sociologist Donna Gaines. She went to the hometown of the victims and tried to develop some understanding of the tragedy. She used a technique called field research (see Chapter 3) to study the social context in which the teenagers lived and, as much as she

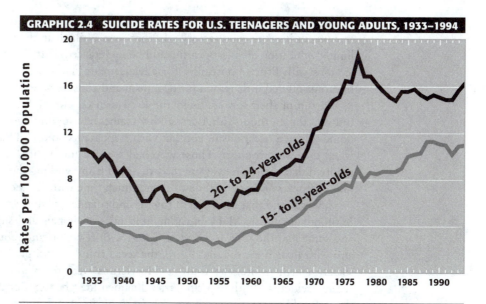

GRAPHIC 2.4 SUICIDE RATES FOR U.S. TEENAGERS AND YOUNG ADULTS, 1933–1994

Source: Holinger et al., 1994.

could, immersed herself in their social world. She spent long hours, days, and weeks in their town, struck up relationships with the same circle of friends, interviewed families, teachers, and acquaintances, and hung out in the same spots. She tried to see their lives from the "inside out," to see the world from their perspective. Gaines was particularly well suited for the task. She is trained in social work and journalism as well as sociology and has extensive experience working with teenagers. In addition, her social-class background and biography were similar to those of the victims.

Arriving on the scene weeks after the incident, Gaines did not attempt to reconstruct the exact dynamics that led to the group suicide. Rather, she tried to place the act in its social context and analyze the biographical and sociological forces that lay behind the incident. Perhaps the single most notable thing about the four victims was that they were members of what Gaines calls the "burnout" subculture: the "losers," or bottom layer of the teenage social world (at least in that particular New Jersey town at that particular time). The members of the subculture were easy to spot. They were marked by their dress (T-shirts honoring heavy-metal rock bands like Metallica and AC/DC), their music (loud and portable), their lifestyle choices (drugs and sex to go with the rock 'n' roll), and their preferred hangouts (the parking lot of a 7-11 store, an abandoned warehouse). Rejected by the "jocks" and the "preps" at the top of the teen status hierarchy, ignored by teachers, labeled as failures and troublemakers by authority figures, burnouts had little status or respect in the present and few options for the future.

Burnouts were generally from blue-collar or working-class families (what Gaines calls the "upper poor"), a group that is suffering more than most from the process of deindustrialization mentioned in Chapter 1. As the economy shifts away from manufacturing, the good factory jobs that were available in the past to workers with limited education are disappearing and being replaced, if at all, by low-paying service jobs with little opportunity for advancement. Thus, the economic future for burnouts offered little reason for optimism and considerable reason for despair.

On top of their low status in the local teen culture and their bleak economic futures, the burnouts interviewed by Gaines commonly reported problems at home: divorce, alcoholism, conflict with stepparents, and child abuse and neglect when they were younger. Those who had avoided those particular problems often reported that their parents were too exhausted from working their second (or third) jobs or from working overtime to spend much time with the kids.

Gaines found that thoughts of suicide and suicide attempts were common in the burnout subculture. Many burnouts told tales of despair and suicidal depression, and some had the scars to prove it. Faced with rejection and failure in the present and with little hope for the future, the teens could see no place for themselves in society. Furthermore, the four suicide victims were upset and depressed by the recent accidental death of a close friend named Joe (the night of the suicide, one of the girls told a friend that she was "going to see Joe"), and most of them were experiencing serious problems with their parents. Somehow, the combination of hopelessness, depression, rejection, and failure combined to impel the fatal decision to end it all. One of the teens' friends voiced a chilling epitaph for these young suicide victims: "They were beaten down as far as they could go" (Gaines, 1998, p. 253).

Significantly, as Gaines begins to develop her conclusions about what caused the multiple suicide, she turns to Durkheim and his typology. She finds that the realities of the teenage deaths (and lives) are too complex to be sorted neatly into only one of Durkheim's four types of suicide. For example, she finds some evidence for egoistic suicide: the kids in the burnout subculture had few meaningful ties with their parents or other adults and felt "less loved and supported than previous generations" (Gaines, 1998). At the same time, though, the kids were deeply involved with their peers, and the social ties within the burnout subculture were intense and numerous (so strong that they might account, in a way, for the group nature of the suicide). The kids in the burnout subculture felt constrained, pushed down, hopeless, adrift, and alienated, as if they did not fit in anywhere and had nowhere to go. Thus, the suicide seems to combine elements of egoism and anomie (disengagement from adults and the community as a whole) with fatalism: the four teenagers had lost the ability to dream and to imagine that the world could get any better for them.

Of course, it is ultimately impossible to know exactly why a person commits suicide. Suicide is a complex phenomenon with multiple causes, including physiological, genetic, and psychological factors. However, intimate knowledge of a suicide victim's thought processes or genetic predispositions is not really necessary to test theories like Durkheim's. The sociological characteristics that are of concern to us—people's involvement in social networks and their connections with others—are more overt and easily measured.

Conclusion

The development of sociology as a way of thinking about social life and the urgent problems that face the world cannot be understood apart from the industrial revolution, which in only two centuries has transformed society. Marx, Weber, and Durkheim wrestled with the implications of the myriad, complex changes wrought by that revolution and tried to understand the consequences for everyday social life and ordinary people. They attempted to apply the principles of scientific analysis to social life and wrestled with the issues raised as society entered the uncharted territory of rapid change and urbanization. The fact that they differed in their conclusions in no way diminishes the importance of the questions they asked or the value of the methods—science, critical thought, careful analysis—they used to study those issues.

Contemporary sociologists continue to study the issues and deal with the questions that Marx, Weber, and Durkheim raised. As we enter the twenty-first century, it is clear that sociology has grown and developed since their time. The boundaries of the discipline are indistinctly drawn, and many questions in addition to those raised by the founders are being addressed. Contemporary sociologists study everything from bulimia to war, terrorism, female genital mutilation, the socialization of jazz musicians, ethnic humor, pornography, population growth, spirituality, UFO cults, baseball, human memory, the process of dying, and aggression in preschool children. Indeed, it is hard to imagine a topic that sociologists, the scientists of all things social, could not study.

The net cast by modern sociology is wide, but the discipline remains centrally concerned with modernization, the impact of technology on society, globalization, inequality, and a range of other topics that also commanded the attention of Marx, Weber, and Durkheim. Like them and other pioneers of the discipline, modern sociologists also search for ways to improve the functioning of human society, reduce the burden of social problems, help people everywhere reach their fullest potential, and seek solutions for the dilemmas that humanity faces. Certainly sociology has not fulfilled Comte's vision of a discipline that would save society, but our failures merely mark the enormity of the task. Now, more than ever, there is a need for a discipline that, in the tradition of Marx, Weber, and Durkheim, responds to the central problems of our time and seeks answers through empirical research, critical thought, and careful analysis.

Key Concepts

1. In the early 1800s, August Comte proposed the creation of a separate discipline called sociology: a "science of society" that would apply the principles and techniques of science to the study of human social life.

2. The sociological perspective focuses on society and its constituent parts and processes. Sociology is a macro discipline, and sociologists are primarily concerned with the social contexts that shape human behavior and interaction.

3. Among the many scholars who contributed to the development of sociology, three stand out: Karl Marx, Max Weber, and Emile Durkheim. All were centrally concerned with the impact of industrialization—the central process of social change of their day—and traced its effects on aspects of social life as diverse as class conflict, bureaucracy, and suicide.

4. Modern sociology has been shaped by many different intellectual heritages and incorporates a variety of viewpoints. Just as the social scientists of the nineteenth century were concerned with the early stages of industrialization, contemporary social scientists (and this book) are concerned with late industrialization and the related process of globalization. The legacy of the early founders remains strong, however, and is evident, for example, in present-day work on the global system of societies, McDonaldization, and teenage suicide.

Active Learning

1. Explorations of McDonaldization: Survey Research. Does McDonaldization really cause workers to become dissatisfied and alienated? In this exercise, you will explore that hypothesis by interviewing people who work or have worked in fast-food franchises or similar McDonaldized environments. Make sure you are familiar with the summary of Ritzer's analysis in this chapter and keep his points in mind during the interviews. This project can be done as a group or individually.

a. Using the questionnaire provided at our Web site (www.pineforge.com/snc) as a guideline, select two people with work experience in a McDonaldized environment. Subjects can be other students, relatives, friends, or acquaintances. If you are working on your own, feel free to modify the wording of the questions, but if you are working with a group, make sure everyone words questions the same way to produce comparable answers. The questions are open ended and general; let the respondents add their own thoughts or go off on tangents. The questions are intended to uncover respondents' feelings about the McDonaldized aspects of work: minimum autonomy, close control by supervisors, and the routinization and standardization of tasks. If the respondent raises issues like those during the interview, you might want to follow up ("Please tell me more") to get a more complete picture of the work environment. Keep in mind that people take these jobs for a variety of reasons and have a variety of experiences, so your subjects may not express dissatisfaction with their work.

b. Limit each interview to ten minutes (or some other maximum agreed on by your group). Take notes during the interviews.

c. Analyze the answers you receive. Did the respondents resent the lack of personal control in the workplace? Did they rebel against the regulations in any way? For example, did they secretly make fun of the supervisor, steal a few moments to gossip or tell jokes, or deliberately break the rules? Did they try to bring some creativity, individual expressiveness, or sense of fun to the workplace? Did they try to somehow humanize the "soulless" environment? Those are the kinds of reactions that Ritzer (and Weber) would predict and that you should be alert for. But be objective—report all reactions, even those that do not match the predictions. Look for explanations for such contradictions.

d. Submit a summary report along with your interview notes. If you are working with a group, discuss your findings, compare conclusions, and write a joint report.

2. Nonroutine Behavior in a Routinized Environment: Observation Research. What are the rules governing behavior in McDonaldized environments? Are they as standardized and as rigid as Ritzer's analysis would have us believe? Most people are not even aware of the rules that guide their behavior in such environments. Typically, however, when someone violates the rules, others will try to restore a sense of order and predictability and reimpose the routines and conventions.

For example, greeting behavior between friends and acquaintances is highly routinized and predictable. You say, "Hi, how are you," and the other person says, "Fine, how are you?" There are "rules" governing both the statement and the response. Try responding with an exact and detailed description of your health (your blood pressure, temperature, pulse rate, and so on) the next time someone greets you by asking how you are. Note how the other person responds to your violation of the rules. He or she will probably try to restore a sense of order and predictability by ignoring your response or dismissing it as a joke.

The purpose of this exercise is to help you see how routinized an environment is through observation research. It should be conducted by a group of two or three students.

a. Select an environment that you consider McDonaldized—organized for efficiency and control. (Check our Web site at www.pineforge.com/snc for suggestions.) Brainstorm about the ways that control is exercised over all the participants. For instance, how is a fast-food dining experience structured to control guests' behavior? Workers' behavior? Managers' behavior? Plan how you will collect information during your observation. Who will take notes about which types of behavior?

b. Visit the environment you have chosen during a busy time and for at least half an hour. As unobtrusively as possible, note the behaviors that seem to indicate McDonaldization. Pay particular attention to any behavior that seems to violate the conventions of the place. What does the violator do? How do others try to restore order? What remarks do you overhear? Do reactions vary by age, gender, race, or other visible social characteristics?

c. As an optional step, visit a similar environment that you would expect to be less routinized and compare it with the McDonaldized workplace. For example, you could visit both a fast-food restaurant and a mom-and-pop café. Watch for the same sorts of behaviors; be objective in evaluating what you see.

d. Write up a group report of your observations. Discuss the rules that seem to govern the environment you chose, exactly how someone may have violated those rules, and how others sought to restore order and routine. To what degree do you think the environment you chose is McDonaldized?

3. Suicide and the Sociological Perspective: Data Analysis. (Adapted from an exercise designed by Virginia Teas Gill, Illinois State University.) For this exercise, you will need to review this chapter's discussion of Durkheim's ideas about suicide, the sociological perspective, and Gaines's study of teen suicide. By combining that information with some additional data on teen suicide, you will be prepared to explore the phenomenon sociologically, individually and with a group.

a. Download the graphic on teen suicide from our Web site (www.pineforge.com.snc). Note that the graph covers the same time period as Graphic 2.4 (suicide rates for U.S. teens and young adults) but presents rates only for teens (ages 15–19) and breaks the overall rates down by race and gender. When (in what time periods) do rates rise and fall? How do they vary by race and gender? Which group has the highest rate? Do all rates for all groups rise over the time period?

b. What are some sociological reasons for the patterns you observe? How could the patterns you observe be explained on a macro level? What kinds of questions would a sociologist (versus a mental health counselor, who might take a micro-approach or an individualistic approach) ask about these rates?

c. On your own, write a brief report describing the patterns you see in the chart, using a sociological perspective. Put your name at the top of the page.

d. In groups of three or four, read your descriptions to one another. Write one group response to the questions on a separate sheet of paper. (Choose one group member to transcribe the response.) Do not merely recopy one of the individual responses. As a result of your collaboration, the group response should be superior to any of the individual responses. Every group member must read and approve the group responses.

e. Turn in the three or four individual responses, with the group response stapled on top. Print the name of each group member at the top of the group response.

The Globalization of Taste

NICKY HART

The hamburger is the quintessential American food. A portable fast finger food designed for consumption on the go, it is also the quintessential capitalist meal. It gets its name from the Hamburg steak, a chopped meat cutlet associated with German immigrants in nineteenth-century America. The constitution of the hamburger is an important feature of its appeal—much of the digestive process is accomplished by industrial production methods prior to human ingestion. The ground meat requires little or no chewing, making it especially suited to the immature jaws and teeth of children. Eating a McDonald's hamburger is a matter of "getting food down your neck" in the fastest possible time. It heralds the return of nomadic hand-to-mouth eating, eliminating the accoutrements of civilization—the dining table, the crockery, and the cutlery; simultaneously it facilitates the end of eating as a specialized and restful experience (Elias, 1979).

By historical standards, the hamburger is an extravagant meal made from the luxury foods of yesteryear—beef and soft white bread (Braudel, 1974). In preindustrial and early industrial Europe, only the most refined people could afford loaves of bread baked from pure white flour. The masses made do with heavy, crunchy whole-wheat, rye, and other dark breads—the type favored today by health-conscious "foodies." Likewise, beef was butcher's meat, an expensive commodity beyond the means of most people even as a celebratory meal. When Western Europe's peasantry dined on meat, they ate home-cured pork in very modest portions.

Today, all that has changed. Industrial farming delivers beef to market in plentiful quantities, and refined white flour is the cheapest variety on supermarket shelves. The meaning of red meat and its corresponding social status have been revolutionized. It is no longer seen as a high-status and protective life-giving substance (Harris, 1986; Fiddes, 1991). Along with sugar and bread baked from processed white flour, red meat has joined the list of modern medical risk factors, foods that rot the teeth, clog the arteries, and constipate the gut. The luxuries of yesterday are now the basic staples of the masses. If hamburger consumption follows the sociodemographic trend of cigarettes, it will increasingly become the food of the lower class, shunned by the health- and status-conscious rich. The anticipation of that changing base of the hamburger's appeal to the American consumer is one reason why McDonald's has shifted its investment strategy to global markets to maintain the momentum of corporate growth.

McDonald's is one of America's most internationally visible and successful corporations. Along with Coca Cola, its logo is virtually equivalent to the stars and stripes as an icon of America and its significance as the epitome of global capitalism. A visit to the company's Web site quickly reveals that McDonald's colonial outreach includes 119 nations and that international investment exceeds home investment. At the end of 1999, McDonald's was operating 26,996 restaurants worldwide, fewer than half of them in the United States.

The disproportionate growth of McDonald's foreign investment is the highlight of Graphic 1. Of the 2,020 new restaurants opened in 1999 (one every 4 hours), only 10% of them were in the United States. The future of McDonald's is global, and, according to the corporate strategy, the scope for invading traditional food cultures in other nations is immense. And, as potential investors were informed at the end of 1999, McDonald's is not yet feeding even 1% of the world's population; further development and increased profit clearly are there for the taking. The corporate plan for the year 2000 was to add 2,000 new restaurants, all but 200 outside the United States.

The McDonald's phenomenon is a rich case study for illustrating and evaluating the predictive power of classical sociological theory. The application of Max Weber's theory of bureaucratic rationality as the core of modern industrial capitalism has received the most attention. Ritzer's (1993) concept of McDonaldization presents formal rationality as the overriding force of change in every sphere of social life, from food and eating through medical care, education, sport, leisure, even birth and death. Though Ritzer acknowledges the salience of profit in this process of institutional colonization (1993, p. 144), he does not assign significance to it as a factor of historical social transformation. Following Weber, Ritzer recognizes the roots of rationalization in capitalism, but his analysis implies that once rationalization has emerged, it acquires a social velocity all its own.

That interpretation downplays the contribution of powerful economic forces propelling the momentum of McDonaldization in the last quarter of the twentieth century, which is how Karl Marx would explain the phenomenon. Marx's theories offer an alternative set of tools for interpreting the spread of formal rationality through the fabric of society. The velocity of McDonaldization reflects the massive concentration of the economic resources in modern capitalist society, whether controlled by multinational corporations or government authorities. Confining the discussion to McDonald's itself, we note how its enormous wealth, exceeding that of many nation states, has been growing exponentially during the last decade. The current international investment strategy represents an 8% annual growth rate and is feasible

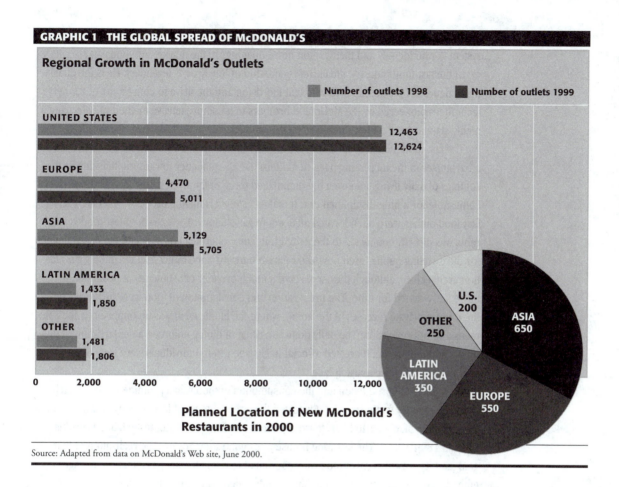

GRAPHIC 1 THE GLOBAL SPREAD OF McDONALD'S

Regional Growth in McDonald's Outlets

Number of outlets 1998   Number of outlets 1999

Region	1998	1999
UNITED STATES	12,463	12,624
EUROPE	4,470	5,011
ASIA	5,129	5,705
LATIN AMERICA	1,433	1,850
OTHER	1,481	1,806

0   2,000   4,000   6,000   8,000   10,000   12,000

Planned Location of New McDonald's Restaurants in 2000

- U.S. 200
- OTHER 250
- ASIA 650
- LATIN AMERICA 350
- EUROPE 550

Source: Adapted from data on McDonald's Web site, June 2000.

only through a massive injection of additional capital. The Marxist explanation for that trend points to the corporation's easy access to capital investment (from a stock market flush with funds) and to its overriding interest in amassing profits by extending its operations abroad.

A Marxist explanation would emphasize the logic of profit rather than the logic of rationalization as the dynamic force of social change. A key concept in the process is the commodity. A commodity is a thing produced for sale, and the production and sale of commodities are the organizing principles of an industrial capitalist civilization. According to Marxist theory, capitalism thrives by converting more and more areas of human existence to salable commodities, including human beings themselves, who sell their labor to earn their livelihood and satisfy the consumption dreams promoted by the capitalist advertising machine. Capitalism is a restless social system, and the health of a modern nation is judged by its annual rate of economic growth. Growth is maintained by entrepreneurs—the heroes of the system—who identify and then exploit novel openings in the market for goods and services.

In the fast-food industry, the entrepreneurship of Ray Kroc is legendary. He is the charismatic figure in McDonald's lore who had the vision and the drive to convert the quick-serve techniques pioneered by the McDonald brothers to a comprehensive method of delivering a highly standardized and profitable fast-food product.

The fast-food industry represents the commodification of daily subsistence. Its progress is a barometer of the increasing pace of modern life, the tendency toward multitasking in the routines of daily living, and even the diminished force of family ties. Fast food is the perfect comestible for a time-disciplined era. It makes eating a refueling process—indeed, early fast-food outlets were often located adjacent to gas stations. The growth of fast-food restaurants was directly connected to the automobile; they offered a convenient form of sustenance for the traveling public. Even now, their garish outward appearance still resembles gas station architecture, although they now serve a much broader constituency of people on the move and pressed for time. The preparation and consumption of food were formerly confined to the private recesses of the home, where the family meal was an opportunity for commensality and relaxation. The daily domestic ritual of dining enforced a demarcation of the public and the private; it created a social backstage where individuals were free of the pressures of a competitive marketplace.

Socializing the production and the consumption of food was a prominent goal of early twentieth-century feminists, who advocated the establishment of large-scale communal cooking and dining facilities to liberate women from the drudgery of domestic labor (Perkins Gillman 1899/1966). The fast-food industry has gone some toward the realization of that goal, and its growth is chronologically equivalent to rising female participation in wage employment and the diminution of kinship dependency in daily subsistence. Fast food is more convenient than family food. It releases people of all ages from the discipline of eating the same food with the same people at the same time. Consequently, the popularity of commodified eating is a primary social indicator of women's liberation. It is also correlated with the widening income inequalities and the growth of flexible work.

"Flexible work" has become a euphemism for exploitation. Such jobs are typically minimum wage, unskilled, part time, and without benefits. The rapid expansion of flexible work over the last decade was pioneered by the fast-food industry. McDonald's does not need a highly or even moderately skilled work force. Its operations have eliminated all but the most minimal requirements of human intelligence. Workers toil ceaselessly filling orders for food prepared on mechanized assembly lines. The division of labor has been taken to an extreme, with the removal of all initiative on the part of the worker. Even cashier work is reduced to punching pictorial buttons on a preset register. The worker is thus denied the opportunity to use, develop, or be paid for any occupational skill. In France, the phrase *McDo generation* highlights growing "flexibility" in the labor market, the consequent deterioration of employment opportunities, and the lack of prospects for young people entering the labor market.

Nevertheless, the global spread of burger culture is a highly progressive development for some contemporary social and political commentators. Thomas Friedman (2000) has even proposed that McDonald's might serve as an international index of global pacification and ideological homogenization. His "Golden Arches Theory of Conflict Prevention" declares that "No two countries that have a McDonald's have ever fought a war against each other." The factor in McDonald's apparent propensity to bring peace on earth is consumer empowerment, which some observers associate with the extension of democracy and human rights. That interpretation is at odds with Durkheim's prediction that a society organized by market forces is a recipe for anomie and social conflict on a grand scale. Durkheim's cultural conservatism challenges the ideas that the global capitalist market is a unifying force and that modern consumerism could forge peace on earth.

McDonald's ambitious program of global culinary colonization depends on a world made safe for capitalist investment. Setting up a McDonald's abroad involves much more than finding a promising location with a flexible workforce. When McDonald's decided to hoist its golden arches in Russia, there were no half measures. Its first restaurant there, built on Pushkin Square in 1990, seats 700, with a 70-foot-long serving counter and 27 cash registers. The globally uniform daily fare—buns, beef patties, french fries, and apple pies—is supplied by the Moscow-McDonald's Food Processing and Distribution Center, a high-security, 10,000-square-meter compound with chain-link fence, armed security patrol, and television surveillance system (the locals refer to it as "McGulag"). Clearly, McDonald's Moscow venture was an expensive undertaking that could be contemplated only by executives convinced that further investment and an increasing stream of profit would be forthcoming. Equally important was the conviction that the Russian population and its political elite could be trusted not to return to their old ideological ways. McDonald's now operates fifty-two restaurants in Russia, with a total work force of 5,000.

In the mid-1990s, before ethnic cleansing in the Balkans prompted a NATO retaliation against Belgrade, which in turn prompted a Serbian trashing of a local McDonald's, Friedman's thesis may have been true. Today the picture is a little less rosy. McDonald's Web site does not give details of the corporate losses connected with politicoeconomic miscalculations. For students of the global economy, a balance sheet of the costs of premises laid to waste by angry nationalist mobs would save a great deal of academic research effort. Interestingly, though, the threat of mob violence against McDonald's has been encountered more frequently in nations higher up the scale of economic maturity than in newcomers eager to prove their reliability to international capitalism.

McDonald's has become hugely popular in countries around the world, including Russia (top) and China (middle). Ironically, during a period of meat shortages in Russia, McDonald's became a reliable source of meat for the middle and upper classes. Recently, McDonald's has also expanded into Africa, opening stores (with drive thrus!) across South Africa. But not everyone is pleased with the spread of McDonald's. In 1999, protesters gathered outside a McDonald's in Toulouse, France (right), claiming that the restaurant chain was polluting French culture. The protesters served bread, wine, and other foods produced and appreciated by the French.

At the end of the twentieth century, the number of McDonald's restaurants trashed and the legal and promotional costs of maintaining corporate credibility probably have been much higher in Western Europe and North America than in the traditionally riskier areas of international capital investment. During 1999, McDonald's restaurants were sites of popular protest, often violent and destructive, in England, France, Belgium, Switzerland, Canada, and the United States. In Seattle, the World Trade Organization (WTO) talks were a venue for a show of solidarity against global capitalism by a diverse collection of international social movements.

Anti-McDonald's sentiment in Europe has complex roots, and demonstrations frequently attract a variety of protesters. To begin with, McDonald's is a convenient target of anti-American feelings in general. Its logo is an icon of American economic, political, and ideological power at the head of the new world order. The American embassy in any foreign country is surrounded by high security, but a McDonald's restaurant is, by necessity, freely accessible and therefore vulnerable to sabotage.

A related source of opposition to McDonald's arises from a more general opposition to modernity as represented in American consumerist culture. That opposition has several dimensions, with anxiety about food a frequent ingredient.

- *Industrial food.* Popular concern about industrial food and industrial farming is much greater in Western Europe than in the United States. The panic brought on by mad cow disease in the 1990s served to focus and heighten anxiety about the dangers of unnatural interventions in the human food chain. For Europeans recently sensitized to the unreliability of politicians and regulatory agencies to protect the public health, U.S.-produced beef with growth hormones and genetically modified food are the leading symbols of "Frankenstein foods."

- *Survival of small farmers.* Safe, wholesome food is associated with small farmers, and protection of their way of life and mode of agriculture is attracting increasing support in both Europe and the United States. In France, farmers have been at the forefront of campaigns against McDonald's. One of the leading personalities of the highly successful protest against the WTO in Seattle in 1999 was Jose Bove, a charismatic French farmer who was briefly imprisoned for methodically taking apart his local McDonald's and delivering it piecemeal to the local police station. In more violent actions on behalf of and by farmers in France, McDonald's premises have been bombed and at least one person has been killed.

- *Ecology and animal rights. Consumer empowerment* is another term for environmental profligacy, disdain for other species, and western selfishness in the face of world hunger. Beef, the heart of a McDonald's meal, is an expensive food to produce. The Beyond Beef Coalition (2000) estimates that while more than a billion people worldwide are starving, 37% of the world's output of grain is fed to livestock. Moreover, the increasing demand for beef directly contributes to global warming; rain forests are being cleared for cattle ranching, and the digestive processes of the world's billion head of cattle give off a formidable volume of methane gas, a major factor in the greenhouse effect. Although McDonald's avoids beef produced in tropical countries, its aggressive promotion of the hamburger habit on a global scale increases the worldwide demand for beef and directly helps fuel the resulting ecological damage. McDonald's is also a prominent target for animal rights activists, who highlight the appalling conditions of livestock that end up in Happy Meals.

- *Cultural homogenization.* The ubiquitous golden arches are a symbol of the increasing loss of local character in commercial enterprises and the tendency for every urban place to become a facsimile of every other. Fast-food chains and coffee houses seeking permits for new outlets increasingly face stiff opposition from community groups keen on preserving territorial individuality or keeping out businesses that would "lower the tone" of the neighborhood. That has happened all over the world, from Martha's Vineyard to London's Hampstead. The reaction against cultural homogenization in mature industrial societies partly reflects a fundamental paradox of modern capitalism—the contradiction between the personal autonomy sponsored by a free and open marketplace and the standardization arising from the massive concentrations of wealth accumulated by multinational corporations. McDonaldization may be the recipe for success in the global market, but it is based on eliminating commercial individuality.

The downside of personal autonomy is individual isolation. Fast food, by making the individual a free agent in matters of daily subsistence, helps to erode the kinship solidarity reinforced by the traditions of family eating. The displacement of home-cooked food has not come about without concerted effort on the part of the fast-food industry. McDonald's allocates 6% of its budget to advertising, the bulk of it directed at children. The strategy is sociologically sophisticated and involves a process of nutritional socialization. By understanding that food preferences are set early in life, McDonald's attracts and secures the loyalty of children, teaching them (in the company of their parents) the lesson of personal sovereignty in the choice of food, and reinforces their unwillingness to stomach communal meals. As a corporate operations manual puts it: "Remember, children exert a phenomenal influence when it comes to restaurant selection. You should do everything you can to appeal to children's love for Ronald and McDonald's." That explains why the corporation invests a large part of its promotional budget on free gifts for small children, who can be counted on to insist that they be brought back again and again for a Happy Meal.

What better place to accomplish the deed than at sites that symbolize the collective consciousness of the nation? McDonald's pays a premium to locate its outlets in the vicinity of national monuments. As Marvin Harris famously observed, "Food must be not only good to eat, it must also be good to think" (1986). The high rent paid for such locations is a small price to pay for a corporation seeking the dual goals of cultural incorporation and nutritional indoctrination.

The tendency of the corporation to seek development sites close to sacred areas of foreign nation states makes it a primary target for critics of economic globalization. Israeli protesters objected to the location of a restaurant opposite the Golani Junction, a monument to the nation's war dead. They feared the site would become known as the McDonald's Junction. Likewise, groups in France, Austria, and the Czech Republic, incensed by cultural desecration and the material pollution connected with McDonald's paper and polystyrene trash, have reacted against plans to erect the familiar fast-food icon in the vicinity of historically significant sites. Italian art restoration experts have sought to evict the largest Italian McDonald's from its site opposite the Column of the Immacolata at the foot of the Spanish Steps—they claim that the greasy cooking fumes blend with dirt and stick to the ancient marble surfaces.

Given those reactions, why is McDonald's not more sensitive in locating its business premises? The answer is not difficult to figure out. Locations adjacent to historically important national sites are highly profitable. In the short term, they produce a quick return by selling familiar fast food to U.S. tourists. But the longer-term economic strategy is to blend insidiously into the cultural landscape.

Karl Marx might have endorsed McDonald's goal of penetrating the collective culinary conscience of international consumers. He admired the dissolvent power of capitalism, seeing its capacity to erode traditional cultures and promote human homogeneity as a potential means of encouraging class solidarity. Whether he would have approved of that process occurring through the channels of commercial advertising is another question, as is the issue of whether the same process stimulates revolutionary fervor in the desired direction. If the global march of burger culture is to be halted, it is not likely to happen through a revolutionary class struggle of the kind that Marx envisaged (Vidal, 1997). The McDonald's phenomenon, including the diverse forms of opposition it engenders, provides an interesting opportunity to explore the membership and potential of revolutionary social movements in the twenty-first century.

From Durkheim's perspective, it is too early to say whether the international spread of the McDonald's franchise should be taken as a stable sign of community harmony and international stability. Contemporary detractors claim that McDonald's exploits the poor both as workers and as consumers. Burger culture is based on a process of economic and environmental exploitation that is not a progressive base for establishing organic solidarity in the mode that Durkheim believed would be needed to ensure cohesion in an advanced national (let alone global) society. On the other hand, the remarkable expansion of McDonald's in the last decade and its significant appeal to other cultures testifies to the importance of capitalism as a motor of acculturation and leaves open the question of the market's effectiveness in the formation and maintenance of social solidarity.

Thinking about the Essay

Is McDonald's a symbol of modernity and economic maturity? Or is it a symbol of capitalist dominance and the spread of western capitalistic consumerism? Do transnational corporations like McDonald's contribute anything positive? How useful are the theories of Marx, Weber, Durkheim, and their followers for answering those questions?

3 Sociology and Science

How do sociologists investigate questions about society?

Imagine a society in which no one talks to anyone else. Most people live alone, dine alone, and drive to work alone. People feel uncomfortable in crowds and are alert for any hint of threat or danger from others. The citizens of this imaginary society are very concerned about crime and violence, and, with few exceptions, they fully trust no one and are wary even in casual conversation. On most jobs, people prefer to communicate by e-mail and memos; face-to-face conversations with coworkers are rare. Computer and communications technology are highly sophisticated, and many citizens are able to work, shop, pay their bills, see the latest movies and the hottest musical groups, and perform hundreds of other tasks from the comfort and safety of their homes. Some people can satisfy all their needs—from the libidinal to the theological—without leaving home or dealing face to face with another person.

In this society, people are active and healthy; virtually everyone exercises regularly and participates in athletics but almost always as individuals rather than in groups or on teams. For example, bowling alleys are crowded and the lanes are always busy but people bowl alone, competing against themselves, trying to break their previous high score—participation in leagues is unknown. Movie theaters, restaurants, and shopping malls are full, but customers generally attend the cinema, dine, and shop alone. In February, restaurants advertise Valentine's Day specials but always include prices for single diners.

Even married couples and families arrange their lives so that everyone has his or her own room, television, sound system, private telephone line (even though they rarely call other people), computer and Internet connection, schedule, and lifestyle.

Everyone is busy and preoccupied with his or her own affairs. Families (let alone friends and neighbors) rarely share a meal, socialize face to face, or otherwise spend any time with each other.

People in this society are not unhappy. They are thoroughly entertained, and there is always something to do: a video or sporting event to watch, the latest computer game to master, the Internet to surf.

Is this society a nightmare or a utopia? Is it imaginary or could it be real? Could it be a preview of life in the United States in the near future? Some social scientists, politicians, ministers, and newspaper editorialists complain that people in the United States are becoming so self-absorbed and self-contained that they are disconnecting from each other, their families, and their communities. Those critics argue that the bonds of friendship and neighborliness are withering away, and they worry that people are dropping out of organized social life and deserting the groups and associations that kept communities functioning in the past.

Those concerns echo some of the questions Emile Durkheim raised (see Chapter 2) about the consequences of industrialization and the decline of social ties and cohesion in modern society. Chapter 4 addresses the way that loss of community may affect a culture. This chapter considers how modern-day sociologists would research those issues, develop explanations for social phenomena, and test explanations to see if they hold water. We illustrate the scientific process with some of the research currently being conducted on participation in civic life in the United States. However, our main focus is the basic philosophy and methods of sociological research and theory testing.

Using Science to Examine a Social Problem: Is American Society Disintegrating?

Sociology is a science, and sociological inquiry involves two intricately related phases. One phase involves the development of a **theory,** an explanation for a social phenomenon. You were introduced to several theories in the first two chapters of this book regarding matters as diverse as suicide, rationalization in the fast-food industry, and inequality. But as a science, sociology cannot rely on theory alone. Theory without evidence is meaningless, which brings us to the second phase of sociological inquiry: **research,** the careful, rigorous testing of theory. Evidence is often gathered in the form of numbers, or data, such as the suicide rate of different societies or the degrees of income inequality. (See the appendix for some ideas on doing research and writing research papers.)

The only way we can know if a theoretical explanation is true is to compare it with the best available evidence. Theories that are consistent with the evidence produced by research are supported. Those that are not are revised or discarded.

Theory motivates research and research shapes theory. The constant interplay between theory and research, between explanation and evidence is the very core of the sociological enterprise. To illustrate the process of scientific inquiry, this section describes a study conducted by Robert Putnam, a leading political scientist, that addressed the issue of social solidarity in contemporary American society. Putnam's study generated strong reactions—some critical, some positive—from politicians, ministers, commentators, and people from all walks of life as well as from social scientists. He raised important questions about the nature of modern American society and stimulated a debate that continues to this day.

Putnam's research on the strength of social networks and community organizations in the United States actually began with a study he conducted of local government in Italy. Putnam found that in certain parts of Italy strong civic traditions and community networks—strong and dense social ties—enabled local government to function efficiently and helped the economy to thrive. In other Italian regions, the absence of such ties and traditions resulted in weak economies and local governments that worked poorly and were corrupt and undemocratic (Putnam, 1993).

Putnam turned his attention to the United States and asked if the civic traditions and local social and political networks were growing weaker and if the social structure in the United States was consequently becoming more like the ineffective local governments of Italy. Though Putnam is not the only social scientist worried about this problem, his book on Italy and a series of articles and a book about the United States have put him in the forefront of those examining the issue.

Putnam has tried to measure the decline of interaction in the United States, explore its implications, and trace its causes. He has presented an impressive collection of evidence demonstrating that, since the 1960s, there have been dramatic declines in the membership of groups of all kinds (PTA, the Girl Scouts, labor unions, the Red Cross, the Lions Club, even bowling leagues) and in many forms of civic engagement (voting, attending political rallies, volunteering for community groups). He believes that the decline in civic involvement has had negative consequences for American culture, attitudes, and behavior patterns. As people in the United States have become more isolated and socially disconnected, they have become less trusting and more suspicious and cynical. As participation in civic and group life declines, society is losing its ability to solve problems, meet common needs, and deal effectively with crises. Do such trends threaten the viability of the social system?

Approaching the Problem: The Scientific Method

What if Putnam asked you to help him develop his theory and figure out why civic engagement and levels of trust are declining? Where would you begin? What possible explanations (theories) for those patterns might you suggest?

Perhaps you would propose that interaction and trust have declined because of the high rates of geographical mobility in the United States. How, you might ask, could transient, rootless Americans be engaged in community life when so many are strangers? How could people trust one another when they do not even know each other?

Or perhaps you might suggest that the root causes of the problems lie in the recent increase in the participation of women in the labor force. In the past, you might argue, wives and mothers did not have jobs outside the home and had the time and energy to volunteer and keep civic associations and community groups functioning. Are working moms today too exhausted to take on the social responsibilities that women held in the past? Has the resultant decline in civic involvement caused people to grow more wary and suspicious of each other?

You might also call Putnam's attention to a third set of suspects: television, the VCR, the home computer, and other recent electronic innovations. Those devices and technologies make it possible for people to be entertained, conduct business, find information, and even hold jobs from the isolation of their own homes. Have we been so seduced by virtual reality that we have lost interest in the real communities and neighbors that surround us?

It probably would not take you long to develop a lengthy list of other possible causes for the decline in civic involvement and trust. In fact, a major challenge of this inquiry is not so much to identify the possibly guilty as it is to eliminate the clearly innocent.

Like detectives everywhere, social scientists use time-tested investigative methods to tell which leads are promising and which evidence is not worth further attention. Sociology was founded on the belief that the **scientific method** can be used to analyze and understand human society and social problems. Pioneered by natural scientists, the scientific method requires that its practitioners be disciplined and careful investigators, that they use the highest standards of logic and self-criticism in their thinking, and that they base their conclusions on the most reliable and trustworthy information available. Scientists strive for objectivity and agree to be guided by what the facts say, not what they wish the facts would say. The ultimate goal of the scientific study of society is to construct explanations of the social world that are theoretically sensible, logically consistent, and thoroughly grounded in research.

This chapter examines the methods that social scientists use to investigate human society. As you will see, Putnam's argument that civic engagement and interpersonal trust have fallen to dangerously low levels is theoretically and logically compelling. But as you will also see, other social scientists disagree with Putnam's reasoning and explanations, and some believe that the data do not actually show a decline. Some think that his solution to the puzzle of declining civic engagement is wrong, while others believe that there is no puzzle worth solving.

Description, Explanation, and Causation

A theory describes and explains relationships between **variables.** A variable is anything in the social world whose value or score can change. Different individuals or groups of people may vary on (or have different scores on) any number of socially significant qualities. Important social variables include gender, marital status, family size, level of interpersonal trust, number of community organizations to which a person belongs, and age. Variables may refer to individuals or larger groups. For

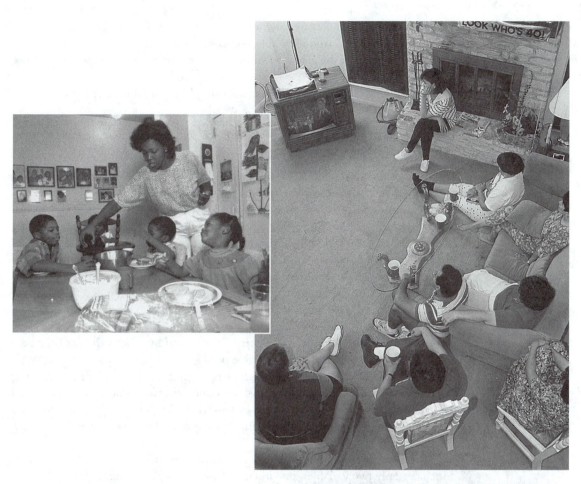

Why has there been a decline in civil involvement and trust? There are many causes, according to Putnam, including working mothers who no longer have time to volunteer to assist various associations and community groups; television, which entertains people and reduces their desire to join and invigorate civic institutions; and long commutes, which place people in their individual cars for many hours each week. By contrast, village life in many developing countries has far more civic involvement and trust, again leading us to ask the question: "Which type of society is really more developed?"

example, an individual may or may not be married; in addition, marriage rates vary among communities, among whole societies, and over time. A theory, then, describes and explains the extent to which variables affect each other and why those relationships exist.

The following two statements illustrate a simplified social science theory:

> Civic involvement decreases as geographical mobility increases. Newcomers to a community have relatively few social contacts and are, therefore, less likely to be drawn into civic organizations.

The first sentence describes a relationship between variables, and the second explains why the relationship exists.

If we wanted to see if a theory holds up, we would have to break it down into specific, testable propositions, or **hypotheses.** Our hypothesis in this case is that people who have recently moved into a community (say, those who have arrived within the past two years) will have lower rates of involvement in civic organizations than more settled residents (those who have lived in the community for two years or more). Complex theories generate a whole set of hypotheses, each of which must be confirmed if we are to accept the theory.

Theories usually explain relationships in terms of cause and effect. We assume that some variables (like civic involvement) are caused by other variables (like geographic mobility). When a causal variable occurs or changes values, the effect variable also occurs or changes values. In the language of science, the effect variable is called the **dependent variable** (because its value depends on other variables), and the causal variable is called an **independent variable** (because, in this particular research, we are not interested in explaining what caused it or what variables, if any, it is dependent on).

Our theory regarding mobility and civic involvement is simple in the sense that it includes only two variables, one independent and one dependent. Actual theories in the social sciences include many variables and complex models of relationships among those variables. The complexity of theories reflects the complexity of the social world we are attempting to understand and explain.

Interaction between Theory and Research

Under what conditions can we regard a theory as true? Scientists accord some degree of credibility to a theory only when two conditions have been met:

◆ The relationships described by the theory do in fact exist.

◆ The explanations proposed by the theory are consistent with the evidence.

Even when a theory meets those two criteria, acceptance is tentative. Theories that seem well supported today may be supplanted by new theories or refuted by new evidence tomorrow.

Because both theories and the realities they try to explain are complex, theories usually need to be tested over a series of research projects. No single project could possibly take into account all the factors and conditions that might affect the relationships among variables. For example, if our theory about mobility and civic involvement were supported by research done in a specific town or community, we (and our colleagues) would still have to wonder if the theory would be supported by research conducted in a different community. If the research were based on an entire society, would the same patterns appear in other societies? Have the same relationships existed at other times or in other historical eras?

Before it can be accepted, a theory needs to be tested in multiple settings with diverse people under a variety of situations. The more often a theory is supported by research, the greater our confidence in it. Still, no theory could be tested under all imaginable conditions, and all the relevant facts could never be collected. Technically, therefore, theories are never regarded as "true" or "proved" in a final sense. They remain open to question, and all theories are tentative to some degree.

In science the term *theory* has much more weight than it does in ordinary speech or in statements like "it's just a theory." A social science theory is much more than an idle speculation or a casual assertion. Some theories, like Durkheim's theory about social integration and suicide rates, are so well grounded in years of research that they cannot be casually dismissed. Even weaker and more tentative theories have to be taken seriously as long as they have generated testable hypotheses that have been partly confirmed by research.

Scientific knowledge accumulates gradually as various research projects build a body of evidence. It is not uncommon for each specific test to result in partial or ambiguous support for the theory. For example, what if a test of the mobility theory found low civic involvement for unmarried newcomers but not for married newcomers? That partial confirmation could lead to a revision of the theory to account for the effect of marital status. The newly revised theory would need additional testing, which might result in additional partial confirmations, more ambiguities, and further revisions of the theory. A theory might be progressively revised and retested over an extended period, with each research episode (we hope) improving the ability of the theory to describe and explain the social relationships we are interested in understanding.

The process of interaction between theory and research is depicted in Graphic 3.1. Theorizing is not an end in itself; theories need to be tested and refined by research. Research is guided by theory, and new data lead to decisions about which explanations have promise and which need to be revised or discarded. Thus, theory drives research and research shapes theory.

The circular shape of Graphic 3.1 is not meant to suggest that science simply spins in one place, going nowhere (although that type of stagnation does occur). Rather, the geometry of the figure illustrates the idea that improvements in our understanding of the social world require interaction between theory and research. Knowledge and understanding accumulate gradually as groups of scientists address similar problems, share theoretical ideas and research results, argue (sometimes bitterly) over meanings and interpretation, and develop increasingly valid and complete answers to important questions. The process of testing a theory can generate

GRAPHIC 3.1   INTERACTION OF THEORY AND RESEARCH

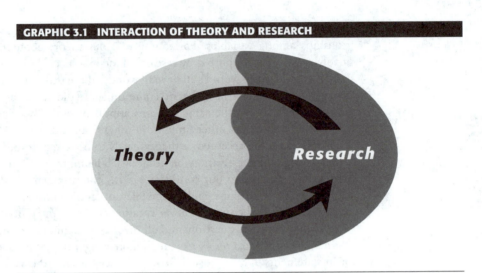

Source: Based on Wallace, 1971.

long-term, sustained traditions of research conducted by large communities of scholars, which is usually how major theoretical advances are made.

Scientific Inquiry

Science is a collective enterprise with its own culture, traditions, institutions, organizations, routines, and procedures. As one of the social sciences, sociology has its own shared set of assumptions about how the world works, namely, that it can be understood through disciplined investigations and careful thinking anchored in empirical research. This section examines several additional characteristics of the scientific enterprise, each of which is illustrated by Putnam's inquiry into declining civic involvement and trust.

Skepticism and Critical Thinking. Let's begin with some of the most important attitudes a good social (or any other kind of) scientist can have: skepticism and the patience and curiosity to look beneath surface appearances and beyond first impressions. Those are not easy attitudes to maintain. The glib, superficial, "commonsense" views of the social world can be powerful, and the social pressure to conform and accept them can be considerable. Try being skeptical all the time—probing and questioning everything everyone says—and see how many friends you still have at the end of a week.

To illustrate the value of skepticism, recall the discussion of suicide in Chapter 2. Suicide may seem to be an intensely personal and private decision, a subject more suited for the field of psychology or psychotherapy than sociology. Some careful thinking and a consideration of the data, however, reveal a more complex picture that has strong sociological dimensions.

In the same way, high rates of mobility, the increasing participation of women in the workforce, or television might seem, at first glance, like important causes of the decline of civic involvement in the United States. Like a suspicious jury in a criminal trial, however, social scientists would not "convict" those suspects unless the weight of the evidence was overwhelming. Before endorsing a theory, scientists would demand proof and lots of it.

In fact, the first thing a scientist would require, before investigating any of the alleged suspects, would be a demonstration that a crime has actually been committed. What evidence is there that civic involvement and trust are in fact declining? Putnam is not short of facts, but neither are his critics.

Putnam supports his argument with empirical evidence drawn from a variety of sources and times. He uses public opinion polls, the work of other researchers, and the membership records of various national organizations to support his conclusions. The diversity of the evidence adds credibility to his case. Just as in a criminal trial, the wider and deeper the pool of facts, the more confidence can be placed in the conclusion.

Here is a sampling of Putnam's evidence.

◆ Membership rosters in organizations as diverse as the Elks, the PTA, and the Red Cross show declines of 25% to 50% since the 1960s.

◆ Time budgets, in which all activities over a single day were recorded by ordinary Americans in 1965, 1975, and 1985, indicate that the time spent on informal socializing and visiting is down by as much as 25%. Furthermore, time devoted to clubs and organizations has declined by as much as 50% over the period.

◆ Participation in collective political events (attending a rally or a speech or working for a political party) is off between 33% to 56% since the 1960s.

◆ National public opinion surveys show a drop of about 25% in membership in all sorts of groups, ranging from sports clubs to labor unions, since 1974. Church attendance is also down, perhaps by as much as 30%, since the 1960s.

◆ National surveys also show that the extent to which people say that other people can be trusted has dropped by roughly 33% since 1972 (Putnam, 1995b, p. 666; Putnam, 2000).

Consistent with the need to be careful, critical, and objective, Putnam also analyzes trends and facts that do not support his argument. He notes, for example, that some forms of engagement have actually increased over the past two or three decades. Organizations such as the American Association of Retired People (AARP), the National Rifle Association (NRA), and the Sierra Club are very active, have large memberships, and can greatly influence local and national affairs.

Putnam points out, however, that those organizations require little of their members other than the payment of dues. The membership does not meet to discuss and act on matters of mutual concern. Such organizations cannot enhance civic engagement because they do not connect people to each other in face-to-face interactions or provide occasions for people to interact with others from their community (Putnam, 2000, p. 51). Like so many other aspects of our daily lives in the United States

Putnam argues that people are less socially engaged than in the past. Suburban neighborhoods, once thriving with children running through yards and playing together, are now often quiet as children play inside or spend time on the computer. In this particular neighborhood (top photo), many homes even have their own basketball hoop, enabling children to play by themselves if they want to. Further evidence in favor of Putnam's theory includes the fact that many churches have declining attendance as people look elsewhere for spiritual and other forms of fulfillment. And shopping malls have become a favored form of entertainment, providing an ability to move quickly and anonymously from store to store.

today, these new organizations are drop in, drive by, or, on the Internet, "surf by"; they cannot duplicate the community-based, local associations of our past.

Scientists are expected to be just as critical of their own arguments as they are of the arguments presented by others. Putnam is careful to acknowledge the limitations and ambiguities in his evidence. He readily admits that his facts are partial and circumstantial and do not, by themselves, provide an airtight case that civic involvement and trust have declined. Taken as a whole, however, he finds the collective evidence convincing. Do you?

Evaluation of Evidence. Since 1993, Putnam has reported the results of a number of tests of possible explanations for the decline of civic engagement in the United States. Although we cannot present his deliberations in detail here, we can use his research to illustrate how social science investigations are anchored in facts and supported by empirical data.

Let us begin with some of the suspects that Putnam has exonerated because of insufficient or ambiguous evidence. First, he finds no evidence that would implicate geographical mobility as a cause of the decline in civic engagement. Data from the U.S. Bureau of the Census show that rates of residential mobility in the United States have not increased over the past fifty years. Rather, rates of mobility actually declined slightly between the 1950s and 1990s. In the 1950s, about 20% of all people in the United States moved each year; the comparable figure for the 1990s is about 17%. If mobility has been steady or falling slightly since the 1950s, it cannot be a cause of a decline in civic involvement, which first became apparent in the 1960s. The timing is off, and Putnam concludes that the mobility explanation is "simply wrong" (Putnam, 2000, p. 205).

Putnam also concludes that the increasing participation of women in the labor force is, at best, a minor cause of the decrease in civic engagement. While overall rates of civic participation for women have declined since the 1960s, the extent of the change varies sharply depending on whether work is full or part time and motivated by economic necessity or by personal satisfaction. The movement of women into the paid labor force is one of the most momentous social changes of the last half-century, but its effect on civic engagement has been "quite modest" (Putnam, 2000, p. 202).

Putnam examines other possible causes of the decline in involvement and trust, including the growth of government, changing family structure and rising divorce rates, and the increasing busyness of people in the United States. As he sifts through the evidence, his attention increasingly focuses on two primary causes: changing generations and the rise of television and other forms of electronic entertainment. The generation that came of age around World War II had unusually high levels of civic engagement, an apparent consequence of the national unity and patriotism that gripped the nation during the midcentury cataclysm (Putnam, 2000, p. 267). As the members of that generation age and pass away, they are being replaced by generations with different formative experiences and lower levels of involvement in community life.

Television, augmented by personal computers, VCRs, DVDs, cable and satellite reception, and digital surround sound, is a major reason we are turning into a nation of asocial, suspicious isolates (Putnam, 2000, p. 283). The effects of television are inextricably bound up with the succession of generations: television became a common fixture in U.S. households as the children of the World War II generation entered adolescence, and its effects have been pervasive for more recent generations. By 1959, 90% of all U.S. households had at least one TV set, and since the 1950s the rate of TV watching has increased in every segment of the population. Television watching now consumes as much as 40% of the leisure time of Americans, an increase of one-third since 1965 (Putnam, 2000, p. 222).

Today, over 98% of U.S. households have at least one television set, more than have telephones (a little less than 94%). In fact, because the average number of television sets per household is 2.4, more and more of us are able to watch TV not only in the privacy of our own homes but in the privacy of our own rooms, reinforcing the tendency toward privatism and isolation (U.S. Bureau of the Census, 1999, p. 581). The growth in the popularity of TV coincides precisely in time with the decline in civic engagement.

Putnam also cites more direct evidence of TV's culpability. Surveys and other sources of evidence indicate that at all levels of education and in all social categories (young and old, black and white, and so on) people who watch a lot of TV are less engaged in civic life than those who watch little or no TV (Putnam, 2000, pp. 228–235). Furthermore, an impressively large literature on the effects of TV watching has found that heavy viewers tend to be less trusting of others and more likely to see the world as dangerous and unfriendly (Putnam, 1996b, pp. 678–679).

Use of media other than TV (newspapers, books, or radio) does not lead to decreased involvement with others. In fact, just the opposite is true. People at all levels of education who spend a lot of time reading newspapers are more likely than heavy TV watchers to be joiners (Putnam, 1996b, pp. 678–679).

In sum, Putnam finds the evidence against television persuasive. The timing is right, the correlations are in the correct direction, and the evidence that TV isolates, privatizes, and disengages us from each other comes from a variety of sources. Should a verdict of guilty be entered? Putnam concludes: "At the very least, television and its electronic cousins are willing accomplices in the [decline of civic engagement] . . . and, more likely than not, they are the ring leaders" (2000, p. 246).

Probabilistic Relationships. You may be annoyed by the tentative and hesitant nature of Putnam's conclusion. If the evidence is on your side, if the facts line up consistently with your theory, why not just go ahead and say that the theory is true? The desire for certainty is understandable, but the nature of science, particularly as applied to the social world, places some important limits on our ability to draw definitive, final conclusions.

First of all, explanations in the social sciences are stated in terms of probabilistic relationships between variables rather than as absolute or invariable relationships.

That is, causal relationships are described using terms such as *tendency, likelihood,* or *trend.* The relationships we investigate are complex and subtle, and any given dependent variable might have many causes. Social scientists rarely make statements of the sort "If variable X occurs, then variable Y will also occur" or "Every person who scores high on variable X will also score high on variable Y" because Y is affected by many factors other than just X. Rather, they explain relationships and discuss causation in phrases like "If X occurs, Y will also tend to occur" or "As X increases, Y will also tend to increase."

For example, Putnam does not claim that the rising popularity of television is the only cause of civic disengagement but rather that it seems to be one of the most important causes. Also, he would not argue that everyone who watches a lot of TV is socially isolated or that all non–TV viewers join civic organizations. His argument is less sweeping and absolute: As TV viewing increases, civic engagement and the willingness to trust other people tend to decrease.

To be sure, partial and probabilistic statements are not as satisfying as robust, unqualified conclusions. Recall, however, that theory and research have an interactive, circular relationship and that our knowledge of the social world accumulates gradually as theories are tested and refined over a series of research projects. If Putnam's case against TV has merit, he and others will find additional ways to gather evidence and test the relationship. If the argument stands up against repeated testing, knowledge about the effects of television will grow and conclusions will become less tentative.

Correlation and Causation. Another reason that scientific explanations are tentative relates to the difference between correlation and causation. There is a **correlation** (or association) between two variables when they tend to occur and change together. When one variable is present, the other variable tends to appear; when one variable changes value (increases or decreases), the other also tends to change (increase or decrease). A **causal relationship** exists if one variable actually produces (or tends to produce) the other variable. Just because two variables appear and vary together (are correlated) does not mean they are causally related. Putnam presents evidence showing that increased television watching and declining civic engagement are correlated, but that finding does not prove that one variable causes the other.

The problem is that variables may be correlated for a variety of reasons, only one of which is a causal relationship between them. For example, it may be that increased television viewing has no actual effect on civic engagement. The variables may only appear to be related because both are caused by a third variable: a rising fear of crime, for example. What if people stopped participating in community affairs because they were afraid they would be assaulted, robbed, carjacked, raped, or murdered if they left the safety of their homes? What if TV viewing increased only because people were staying home more to avoid the dangers of the streets? Increasing rates of TV viewing and declining civic engagement would be correlated but not because one caused the other. Rather, the correlation would result from the fact that both variables were caused by a rising fear of victimization. Once levels of fear were taken into account, the correlation between TV viewing and civic engagement would disappear because it is not causal.

Actually proving that two variables have a causal relationship is a difficult and time-consuming task that requires substantial research and sophisticated statistical techniques. But the logic used to infer causality is not that difficult to understand. A researcher interested in the relationship between TV viewing and civic engagement might identify a number of possible other variables that, like fear of victimization, might be related to the independent and dependent variables. Using statistical techniques, the researcher could control the other variables and see if they affected the relationship between the independent and dependent variables. If, for example, we found that people who watch a lot of TV are less likely to be involved in community organizations regardless of their level of fearfulness, we could be more confident that the relationship is causal and not just a matter of correlation. The more often we controlled for other variables and still found a relationship between TV viewing and involvement in community affairs, the stronger the evidence for a causal relationship.

The point to remember is that even strong correlations between variables do not prove that they are causally related. We must control for the possible effects of many other variables before we can argue that a correlation is genuinely causal. A correlation between variables can be taken as support for the existence of a causal relationship but cannot, by itself, prove that such a relationship exists. Because Putnam relies on correlations to back up his case against television, he is well advised to keep his conclusions tentative.

Traditions of Research

A scientific investigation begins with a question or a problem, but that starting point does not materialize from thin air. Typically, the investigator has been working in a general topic area for some time, and the question or problem represents only the current phase of an ongoing, broader project. Putnam, for example, has been researching political participation and citizen involvement for some time, and his concern with declining civic engagement in the United States flows directly from that line of research.

Putnam's 1993 study of governments in Italy was so well received that he decided to extend his research to the United States. In his book on Italy, he looked at regional Italian governments (which are somewhat parallel to state governments in the United States). The Italian political units were created at the same time and were similar in form but were highly variable in their performance and responsiveness to citizen complaints. What was the cause (independent variable) of the differing levels of government performance (the dependent variable)?

Putnam applied a variety of theories to the problem and investigated many possible independent variables. In the end, he concluded that the varying levels of governmental performance could be explained by the varying levels of social capital in the regions. The concept of social capital encompasses civic engagement and other elements: "Social capital . . . refers to features of social organization, such as trust, norms [of reciprocity] and networks [of civic engagement], that can improve the efficiency of society by facilitating coordinated actions" (Putnam, 1993, p. 167).

That definition identifies three separate components of social capital: trust, norms of reciprocity, and networks of civic engagement. To appreciate the importance of those elements, consider what social life would be like in their absence. What would everyday life be like in a community in which no one trusts anyone else and no one feels obligated to honor debts to others (no norms of reciprocity)? In a community in which no networks of social relationship exist to organize work, meet needs, or solve mutual problems? If they could act at all, individuals in such a society would behave as self-interested, wary, disconnected atoms, each pursuing his or her own selfish goals with no concern for the needs or desires of others. Even the most rudimentary forms of collective action would become extremely difficult because, without trust, people would not subordinate their individual aims to collective goals.

In contrast, a social system with high levels of social capital would function efficiently. People would not need to invest so much time and energy in protecting their own interests; thus, more energy would be available to meet common needs and solve common problems. In short, the greater the store of social capital, the smoother and more efficient the operation of the social system.

From Putnam's conclusion that varying levels of social capital caused the difference in the performance of Italian regional governments, it was an easy step across the Atlantic to see if those same relationships could be applied to everyday life in the United States. Putnam's current project is only one chapter of a continuing, long-term concern with social capital, civic engagement, and interpersonal trust.

It is important to note that Putnam did not invent the concept of *social capital.* His use of the term is based on the work of another social scientist, James Coleman, in the 1980s (1988, 1990, pp. 300–321). In fact, some of the intellectual antecedents of the concept go back to Alexis de Tocqueville (1835/1969), a nineteenth-century French scholar and observer of life in the United States. Thus, Putnam's current thinking is in a tradition of research and theory that stretches back many decades.

Communities of Scholars: The Loyal Opposition

Predictably, Putnam's argument that people in the United States are becoming dangerously disengaged and distrustful has generated a variety of reactions and questions from other social scientists. (Reactions from politicians, philosophers, journalists, and others have also been considerable, but we need not treat them here.) Although we cannot review all aspects of the debate, we do present enough opposing views to show that the tentative nature of Putnam's conclusions is justified.

Issues of Definition and Measurement. First of all, a number of scholars dispute Putnam's assertion that organizational memberships and civic engagement have been declining, an extremely serious criticism. If he were wrong about the direction in which his dependent variables are changing, he would be left with nothing to explain.

Given the variety of evidence presented by Putnam, how could there be any dispute about the decline in involvement? Some of his critics argue with his definition of civic engagement and community groups; others present additional data sources that must be considered. Consider this sampling of those objections.

◆ Some researchers have criticized the way in which community groups are defined in some of the data sources on which Putnam relies. For example, the YMCA is counted as a community group, but commercial, for-profit health clubs and fitness centers are not. If a person decided to exercise at a privately owned health club instead of the Y, that would be counted as a decline in community group involvement instead of simply a change in membership (Schudson, 1996, p. 17). Is what Putnam takes to be civic disengagement simply a shift in the form and locale of involvement?

◆ Several of Putnam's critics argue that the data sources he uses to measure civic engagement in the United States are limited to well-established, more traditional forms and groups like the PTA or the Lions Club. New community groups (like neighborhood Crime Watch programs or Habitat for Humanity) and temporary programs (for example, spontaneous, grassroots efforts to raise funds for victims of natural disasters) fall through the cracks. If the critics are correct on this point, community involvement could be constant or increasing even while Putnam's measures show it is declining (Greeley, 1997; Schudson, 1996; Skocpol, 1996).

◆ Similarly, a research project conducted by Robert Wuthnow (1994) shows that people in the United States are continuing to join groups and seek affiliation and a sense of belonging but are doing so by joining small, informal groups that are, by their nature, difficult to locate and count. Wuthnow reports that about 40% of people in the United States belong to support groups of various kinds. Most of those groups have a religious theme (adult Sunday schools and Bible study classes), but they also include self-help groups (many related to dealing with addictions) and special-interest groups (groups to discuss books or politics, play music, share poetry, or participate in a wide variety of other activities). In direct contradiction to Putnam, Wuthnow argues that people in the United States do join organizations, are still connected to one another, and are still finding emotional support and a sense of community through their interactions with others. As older forms of affiliation (like neighborhoods) weaken, people are finding new ways to connect and belong.

◆ A recent survey conducted on the Internet by sociologists Witte and Howard (1999) shows that people may be finding a form of community in cyberspace. Based on the responses of some 50,000 people, the researchers found, consistent with Putnam, that the longer a respondent has been online the less likely he or she is to report feeling "close to other people in my community" or that "my community is a source of comfort for me." On the other hand, and

Putnam's critics point out that civic involvement is not declining and that people are seeking new ways to connect with each other and influence their communities. Here a citizen voices her opinion at a town meeting in Laguna Nigel, California, dealing with the future of her city.

contrary to Putnam, long-time users are more likely to be politically active, belong to organizations, and feel a sense of community with other Internet users. Those findings suggest that cyberspace is not populated by asocial, alienated isolates but rather by "digital citizens" who are finding new ways of forging community and connecting with others.

◆ A 1999 analysis of community involvement and social capital by Everett Ladd challenges many of Putnam's most basic assertions and interpretations. Ladd examined rates of civic engagement and found that, indeed, some groups, such as the PTA, have lost members over the past several decades. He argues that such losses have been more than balanced by increases in other forms of group membership and community involvement. For example, parents have developed new organizations—variously called "Parent Activity Clubs," "Parent Councils," and so forth—to replace the PTA and keep them involved in their children's schools. Like many forms of belonging, what looked at first glance to be a decline in involvement turns out, on closer inspection, to be a shift in involvement with no overall decrease. Ladd concludes that "not one set of systematic data shows a decline in parental involvement while many show increases" (Ladd, 1999, p. 43).

◆ Finally, at least one data source not cited by Putnam shows that the United States has relatively high rates of group membership and community involvement compared to other advanced industrialized nations (Knack and Keefer, 1997) and that those rates increased between the early 1980s and the 1990s (Greeley, 1997; Ladd, 1999). Graphic 3.2 shows levels of trust and the strength of norms of civic cooperation for twenty-one industrialized nations. Contrary

GRAPHIC 3.2   MEASURES OF SOCIAL CAPITAL IN TWENTY-ONE INDUSTRIAL NATIONS

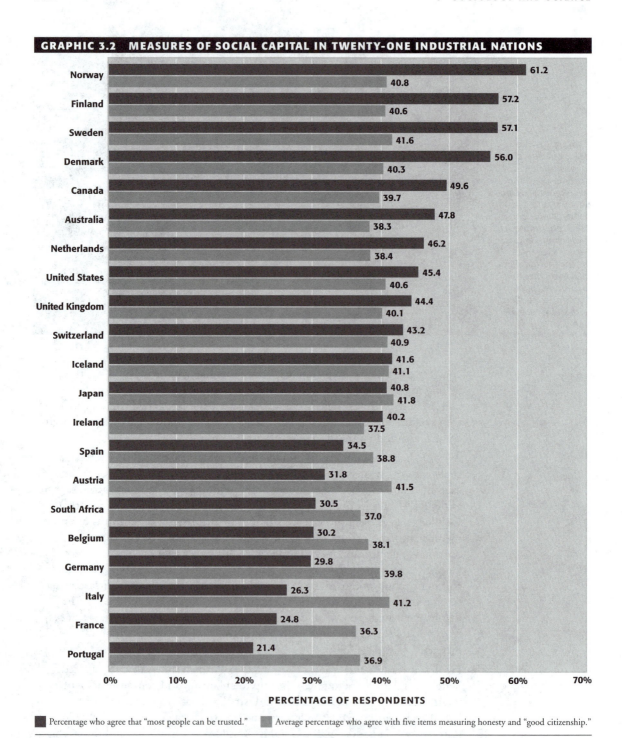

Norway: 61.2 / 40.8
Finland: 57.2 / 40.6
Sweden: 57.1 / 41.6
Denmark: 56.0 / 40.3
Canada: 49.6 / 39.7
Australia: 47.8 / 38.3
Netherlands: 46.2 / 38.4
United States: 45.4 / 40.6
United Kingdom: 44.4 / 40.1
Switzerland: 43.2 / 40.9
Iceland: 41.6 / 41.1
Japan: 40.8 / 41.8
Ireland: 40.2 / 37.5
Spain: 34.5 / 38.8
Austria: 31.8 / 41.5
South Africa: 30.5 / 37.0
Belgium: 30.2 / 38.1
Germany: 29.8 / 39.8
Italy: 26.3 / 41.2
France: 24.8 / 36.3
Portugal: 21.4 / 36.9

PERCENTAGE OF RESPONDENTS

■ Percentage who agree that "most people can be trusted."   ■ Average percentage who agree with five items measuring honesty and "good citizenship."

Source: Knack and Keefer, 1997.

to what one might expect based on Putnam's argument, the United States ranks high on both variables. Of course, a graph can present only a partial picture of the complexities of group life in those societies. A different picture might emerge if we could measure all forms of belonging and all dimensions of social capital.

It is not easy to resolve the debate about the level of civic engagement or the trends in group membership. There is no comprehensive national or cross-national count of all the different types of groups to which people could belong and all the different ways in which they could be involved in their communities. Without a definitive way of measuring those variables, the evidence presented by both Putnam and his critics must be regarded as tentative and circumstantial. That part of the debate might not be resolved for some time.

The Effects of Changing Age Distribution. Some of the trends cited by Putnam may reflect changes in the demographic structure of the population rather than declining patterns of engagement and belonging. For example, decreases in the participation of adult volunteers and leaders in youth groups simply may be the result of the fact that the number of children and adolescents decreased after the 1960s. If the supply of children decreased, so would the demand for adult leaders.

To illustrate further, Putnam specifically cites the PTA as an organization that has lost membership. However, the PTA's membership history seems quite understandable when changes in the numbers of schoolchildren are taken into account. The number of children between the ages of 5 and 14 decreased by over 14% between 1970 and 1980 but then began to increase in size and is now approaching the levels of the 1970s. Although PTA membership is lower now than in the 1960s, it actually reached its lowest point in the early 1980s. Since 1994, it has increased by 28%. ("American Survey," 1995, p. 21; Ladd, 1999). Changing membership levels in groups such as the Boy Scouts and Girl Scouts may similarly reflect the changing age structure of U.S. society.

If the decline in civic engagement is due to changes in the age structure of the U.S. population, Putnam's case against TV would lose credibility. The relationship between civic engagement and television viewing might be more a case of correlation than causation.

The Importance of Comparison Points. To some extent, conclusions about whether rates of involvement and civic participation are rising or falling can be determined by the exact dates that are used for the comparison. For example, Everett Ladd (1996, p. 2) examines voter turnout in U.S. presidential elections and concludes that the patterns do not support Putnam's thesis of declining civic engagement. In Ladd's view, after reaching its modern high in 1960, voter turnout has plateaued at a level typical in the United States in the twentieth century.

As you can see from Graphic 3.3, whether voter turnout is considered to be rising or falling can depend on which dates in the past are being used for comparison. Putnam believes that the decline in civic involvement first became noticeable in the 1960s; in fact, voter turnout has generally trended down since that decade. If the

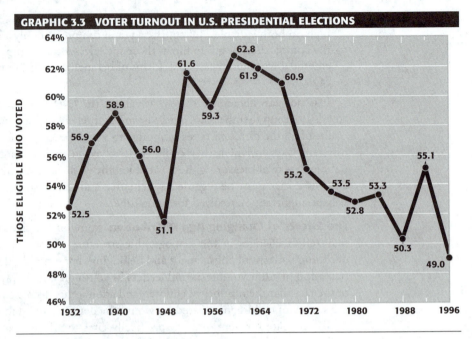

GRAPHIC 3.3   VOTER TURNOUT IN U.S. PRESIDENTIAL ELECTIONS

Source: U.S. Bureau of the Census, 1998, p.297.

comparison takes into account all elections since 1932, however, then perhaps Ladd's conclusion that turnout is hovering rather than declining is more sensible. Note that if the comparison had been made only between the 1948 and 1992 elections, we might have concluded—contrary to both Ladd and Putnam—that turnout generally has risen over the past several decades. Which is the most sensible comparison date for the case at hand?

On the matter of involvement in politics, a 1999 study confirms some of Putnam's conclusions and raises some troubling questions about the future health of the U.S. political system. Based on a survey of U.S. respondents aged 15 to 24, the study found that young people are disengaged from politics and that they distrust and lack knowledge about politics, politicians, and public life in general. In 1972, when the right to vote was first extended to 18-year-olds, some 50% of them voted. Since that time, turnout has steadily declined; in the presidential election of 1996, it fell to about 32%. Although some forms of youth volunteerism are actually increasing (for example, in church-related activities), the survey found that young people generally give a very low priority to being involved in democracy and community (National Association of Secretaries of State, 1999).

Alternative Causes. Some critics argue that even if there has been a decline in engagement, Putnam has identified the wrong cause. For example, research conducted by Pippa Norris (1996) shows that the relationship between television viewing and civic engagement varies by the content of the shows people watch. Although, consistent with Putnam, she found a generally negative relationship between TV viewing and civic engagement, she also found that people who watch news and public affairs programming are more likely to be involved in all forms of political and community activity. Television viewing can have a variety of effects on people, and some forms of viewing do not seem to be damaging to the health of the society. Norris argues that, compared with the people in most other democracies, those in the United States are much more involved in organizations of all types and have constructed a dense network of civic associations. If U.S. citizens lack confidence in government and trust in each other, it is unlikely that such deep-rooted problems could be resolved simply by turning off the television.

Michael Schudson also argues that television is not to blame. Declines in local civic participation may instead be the result of a growing orientation to nationwide (or even global) organizations by "civic spark plugs," people who in the past would have provided leadership at the local level. If people who in the past would have been key volunteers, presidents of organizations, and chairs of committees are today directing their attentions to broader or more distant concerns, then declining civic engagement at the local level may reflect only a shift in focus (Schudson, 1996, p. 19).

Other investigators raise the possibility that declining participation (in politics at least) reflects fundamental changes in the way in which elections in the United States are conducted. Since the 1960s, local efforts to mobilize and involve voters directly have declined, as have opportunities for personal, face-to-face contact

Some civic causes are increasingly global in scope. Movements calling for equality for women, gays, and minorities are no longer confined to the local community. Other global causes center on the environment, fair trade, human rights, fair labor, child labor, and peace. The era of globalization is not restricted to economics.

between political leaders and citizens. Grassroots organizations have given way to pollsters, special-interest groups with deep pockets, focus groups, and television advertising (Skocpol, 1996, p. 24). The trends cited by Putnam may reflect a shift in the way the society conducts business (especially political business) from the local to the national levels. One scholar suggests, "Maybe it's not that the people have lost interest in the polity. . . . Maybe the polity . . . has lost interest in the people. It's not that Americans are tuning out. They're being left out" (Vallely, 1996, p. 26).

The criticisms of Putnam's conclusion show the importance of taking into account the context—the internal and external factors impinging on a society—in which events take place. As various economic, political, and cultural changes occur, social relations also change. But it may be the general context, rather than any specific, identifiable independent variable, that is the cause. Yes, people in the United States watch more television than before, but the whole society has changed so much since the early 1950s that increased TV watching may be less important than other deeper, more powerful changes. It may be true that there is a problem with civic engagement in the United States, but a narrow focus on television may miss the point. Many sociologists would argue that the lack of interest in community simply reflects the shallow materialism and pervasive self-absorption that is fostered by modern American culture. The problem may be too fundamental to be resolved, as Norris suggests, simply by unplugging the television set. (See, for example, Etzioni, 1993; Bellah et al., 1991.)

Attending to social context also raises the issue of television's effects beyond U.S. borders. If Putnam is correct, the social capital of other societies may erode as those societies become more technologically advanced and begin watching more television. That is a difficult point to research, however, partly because the cultural content and the nature of television programming can vary so much from nation to nation; as Norris suggests, content may be more important than the amount of viewing. At any rate, much of the world's population does not have easy access to television, and questions about the effects of TV on community life are largely moot. For example, in the United States in 1999 there were about 85 televisions per 100 population, or more than 8 TVs for every 10 persons (World Bank, 2000). Other advanced industrial societies (like Canada, Japan, and the United Kingdom) also have a high ratio of TVs to people, but across much of Africa, Asia, and South America, especially in low-income nations, the ratios are more like 5 or 10 sets for every 100 persons. Those ratios reflect differences in levels of development and affluence and suggest that the ill effects of TV, if any, may be confined to the industrialized world. Graphic 3.4 illustrates the global variation in access to television as well as to personal computers and the Internet.

The Value of Debate. Both Putnam and his critics build logical arguments and back up their cases with data and research. So who is right? Recall that the debate, at least in its present form, began only in 1993. This early in the research process, it is probably best to withhold judgment and wait for the results of further research or

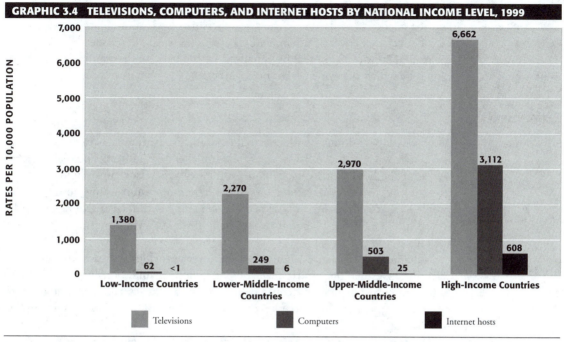

GRAPHIC 3.4 TELEVISIONS, COMPUTERS, AND INTERNET HOSTS BY NATIONAL INCOME LEVEL, 1999

Source: World Bank, 2000.

the appearance of better theories. What would you do to resolve the debate? What specific information about trends, relationships, and variables would you gather to determine who is right and who is wrong?

By way of conclusion, it is important to note what Putnam and his critics are arguing about and how the argument is being conducted. These scholars are attempting to figure out what is true in the United States at the turn of the new century by sorting through each other's logic and facts and critically assessing each other's interpretation of the data. Although messy at times, freewheeling, open discussions about theory and research—attacks and counterattacks—improve our understanding and increase our knowledge base. Although the debate may never be resolved, social science assumes that, if we argue long enough, think carefully, and conduct sufficient research, we will ultimately understand.

Gathering Data

All scientific inquiries follow the same general logic, rules, and procedures, but specific investigations may use a variety of different techniques to gather data and test theories. Social scientists can choose among experiments, surveys, direct observations, analyses of existing data, and a number of other research methods. The choice depends on the nature of the problem, the availability of time and money, and the talents and interests of the researchers involved. Your ability to assess critically the debate between Putnam and his critics (as well as other social science arguments and controversies) will be enhanced with a basic understanding of the techniques by which the evidence has been gathered.

Experiments

Most sociologists do not conduct actual laboratory experiments because the format is too narrow or artificial for most of the problems they address. The major exception is at the border of sociology and psychology, where social psychologists often pay subjects to perform certain tasks in a laboratory while being observed. But problems that require the study of people interacting within large groups cannot be forced into a controlled laboratory, especially if we are trying to understand whole societies.

Nonetheless, the classic laboratory experiment provides the basic model for all scientific investigations, and a review of its logic is helpful. To illustrate, imagine how a simplified experiment could be used to study the effects of violent TV programming (independent variable) on people's levels of trust and suspiciousness (dependent variable).

The researchers in this imaginary experiment would begin by gathering a group of subjects and then dividing them into two subgroups that are as similar as possible. One group would be the experimental group, and its members would be exposed to violent television programming. The other group would be the control group, and its members would be exposed to nonviolent television programming.

It is crucial that the two groups be comparable in size, individual characteristics, and so on. The only important difference between them should be their exposure to the independent variable (violent TV programs). If the groups are not comparable, the researchers would not be able to determine if differences in the dependent variable (level of trust) at the end of the experiment are due to TV violence or merely reflect the differences that existed at the beginning of the experiment. In effect, using a control group is the same thing as controlling for (or holding constant) other possible variables such as age, religion, gender, wealth, type of community in which the subjects live, and so on.

Normally, comparability is ensured by assigning people to groups randomly. If group assignments are based on chance, people with the same characteristics will be equally likely to be assigned to either group. In the end, the two groups should have similar mixtures of types of people.

Once experimental and control groups were established, the experiment would begin with a pretest of the dependent variable (level of trust). Then the members of the experimental group would be exposed to the independent variable (violent TV programming). They might spend each evening for a week viewing three hours of television programming featuring violence, aggressiveness, and various forms of mayhem and brutality (for many viewers in the United States, that would be a normal week). Over the same time period, the control group would watch three hours of nonviolent programs each night.

A posttest of the dependent variable (trust) would be conducted at the end of the experimental time period. If the posttest level of trust is lower for the experimental group but not for the control group, the researchers could conclude that trust had declined because of the violent television programming.

The great power of the laboratory experiment is that it allows the researcher to rule out all factors other than the independent variable that might affect the dependent variable. In the real world outside the laboratory, all sorts of things could affect the results. For example, what if during the week of the experiment something happened—an act of betrayal by a high government official or a scandal involving a respected public figure—that might change people's levels of trust and suspiciousness regardless of their exposure to TV violence? How could we know that the lower posttest levels of trust in the experimental group were caused by violent TV and not by the extraneous event? An experiment is designed to control for just that sort of occurrence. If the experimental and control groups are truly comparable, we can assume that events external to the experiment affect both groups equally. Thus, the posttest trust levels might fall for both groups, but the decrease would be greater for the experimental group. The difference still could be attributed to television violence. In a well-designed, carefully conducted experiment, the researcher can anticipate and guard against all possible influences on the dependent variable other than the independent variable.

All scientific experiments, not just those conducted by social scientists, follow similar procedures. Medical experiments testing the effectiveness of new drugs, for example, use the same steps. The experimental group with a particular disease receives the drug, and the control group with the same disease receives a placebo, (an inert substance that looks like the drug being tested but does not actually contain it). The point is to see if the experimental group shows signs of improvement. Medical experiments usually add one more control: neither the subjects nor those administering the drug are told who is getting the drug and who is getting the placebo. The procedure, called a double-blind experiment, further reduces the chances of bias in reporting as well as any psychological effects that sometimes occur when people think they are getting a useful drug and start to feel better just for that reason.

The power and usefulness of any social science research project can be enhanced by following the principles of the experiment. A main principle is to compare groups (experimental and control) and different times (pretest versus posttest). Comparisons are especially crucial in the social sciences because we rarely deal with absolute values. No level of civic engagement is, on its face, "high" or "low"; we can judge only people's relative participation. Thus, comparisons across time, groups, and societies become extremely important. For example, if Putnam can show that the average level of civic involvement is lower for heavy TV viewers than for light viewers, he can make his point about the harmful effects of TV without having to specify exactly what a "low" level of involvement is. By the same logic, the fact that

Putnam uses extensive comparisons over time and across societies increases the credibility of his case. Of course, his critics make the same kinds of comparisons and are entitled to the same degree of credibility.

Field Experiments. An experiment that tests the effect of TV on trust would be simple compared with an experiment that realistically tests the effect of TV on membership in community groups and civic engagement. Entire communities cannot be reproduced in the lab, and neither can the complex, long-term processes that, at least according to Putnam, link TV to increasing isolation and self-absorption.

Instead of trying to bring the community into the lab, social scientists sometimes attempt to bring the experiment into the community. This variation, called the field experiment (or natural experiment), involves reproducing the basic elements of the classic experiment in a real-life setting.

To apply the field experiment method to Putnam's argument, we would need, at a minimum, comparable experimental and control groups and tests of the dependent variable (civic engagement) before and after (pretest and posttest) the introduction of the independent variable (TV viewing). Those conditions are not easy to create in a society so permeated with TV, but a quasi-experimental study of the impact of TV on community involvement actually has been conducted.

In the early 1970s, a research project began in a Canadian town that was about to receive television reception for the first time. Although not particularly isolated, the town lay in a low valley and broadcast signals could not reach the residents' homes. The researchers selected two other nearby towns of comparable size and makeup to serve as the control group. At the time of the experiment, one control town could receive only one television channel; the other control town had multiple channels and a cable TV system.

The researchers measured participation in a wide variety of community activities in all three towns before TV reception was introduced to the experimental town and again two years later. They found that civic engagement and participation in community activities declined significantly in the experimental town but not in the other two towns. The decline was greatest for sports activities and greater for young people than for adults. The researchers also found declines in attendance at community dances, suppers, parties, and other forms of informal socializing (Williams, 1986). The results are exactly what Putnam would predict.

Surveys

Social scientists commonly use surveys, standardized sets of questions or requests for information administered to a group of respondents. Interviewers can conduct surveys face to face with respondents, over the telephone, or through mailed questionnaires. Combined with computers and other technologies, surveys allow social scientists to collect enormous amounts of information from very large groups of people. For example, the General Social Survey (GSS), a public opinion poll that has been conducted almost every year since 1972, includes hundreds of different items of information for each respondent. The GSS database makes it possible to estimate population characteristics as diverse as household income, religious affiliation, and support for the death penalty.

Surveys are extremely useful techniques for gathering large volumes of information from large numbers of people. For many variables of interest to social scientists, there is no other way to map the characteristics of a sizable population. Like any research technique, however, surveys have their limitations. The main limitation is that they tell us only what people *say* is true, which may be different from what is actually true. Bluntly put, people can lie, shade the truth, or "misremember" information. For example, the percentage of survey respondents who say they voted in an election commonly is far greater than the actual turnout. Although 71% of the respondents to the 1994 GSS claimed that they had cast a ballot in the 1992 presidential election, only 55% of the electorate had actually voted (U.S. Bureau of the Census, 1993, p. 261). As we might expect, the frequency of acts associated with being a good citizen are likely to be inflated in surveys, and deviant or disreputable acts tend to be underreported.

For "big" sociological issues that have implications for the entire society—like the possibility that civic engagement in the United States is declining—surveys ideally should be based on the entire population. But a moment's reflection should convince you that, no matter how desirable, questioning all 270 million Americans about their group memberships, engagement in civic affairs, and television-viewing habits would be virtually impossible.

As a substitute for testing entire **populations** (like all U.S. citizens) social scientists use smaller, carefully chosen subsets (**samples**) of the entire group. The information collected from the sample then becomes the basis for estimating the characteristics of the population.

You probably are most familiar with sampling from public opinion polls and election forecasts. Particularly during presidential-election years, the news media are filled with almost daily polls tracking the latest shifts in public opinion and voter sentiment. Although they are somewhat controversial, election projections generally are quite accurate. In fact, they can estimate, within ±3 percentage points, the likely behavior of the American electorate (which can number 100 million people or more) from samples of about fifteen hundred respondents. The key to such accuracy lies in the process of selecting cases for the sample. To permit inferences, samples must be **representative** of the populations from which they were drawn, that is, a sample must reproduce the general characteristics of the population. For example, if a population is 25% Catholic and 51% female, then a representative sample also will be about 25% Catholic and 51% female. Every important characteristic of the population should be reflected in a representative sample so it can be treated as a miniature version of the population.

The actual mechanics of sample selection are complex and beyond the scope of this book. We can say, however, that if samples are selected randomly (so that every case in the population has an equal chance of being selected) and they are large enough, there is a high probability that they are representative of the population. Once samples are selected, they can be tested to make sure they are representative.

Having some understanding of sampling is important for a couple of reasons.

◆ Large representative samples are becoming increasingly available to social science researchers. Along with other technological advances (mostly related to computers), many sociological theories can now be tested on state-of-the-art samples and databases. Sociologists hope such advances will provide more definitive and authoritative tests of their ideas and, thus, greater confidence in sociology's knowledge base.

◆ More relevant to this chapter, much of Putnam's (and his critics') information about civic engagement and levels of trust in the United States are based on data collected from representative samples, not from the entire population. Specifically Putnam relies heavily on the GSS (as do his critics). Thus many of Putnam's conclusions (and many of his critics' arguments) are based on some of the most trustworthy information available about the U.S. population. Of course, although the source of his data may increase our confidence in his conclusions, it does not guarantee their accuracy.

Observation (Field Research)

Observation, sometimes called field research, requires that the investigator be in direct contact with the subjects of the study, usually for an extended period. Observation is appropriate for the intense study of small groups. This research technique has been used in many different settings to study, among other subjects, peasant villages, doomsday cults, blue-collar neighborhoods, bank robbers, doctors, street-corner men, juvenile gangs, and restaurant workers. Donna Gaines used the technique in her study of teenage "burnouts," which was presented in Chapter 2. Observation is especially useful for studying deviant or criminal groups (such as gangs), groups on the fringes of society (such as new religious cults), and other groups that are difficult to reach by standard sampling techniques (such as the homeless).

Contrary to what you might think at first, observation is a demanding research method and should not be undertaken lightly or casually. It usually requires a massive commitment of time and energy on the part of the researcher, who must be thoroughly prepared to observe accurately and objectively. Maintaining scientific objectivity can be especially challenging because the researcher may come to know the subjects well. To the extent that ties of friendship and intimacy are formed, the investigator's ability to analyze the subjects objectively can be compromised. Also, to the extent that the observer is in direct contact with the subjects, he or she may inadvertently alter their behavior, thus raising questions about the validity of the observations. Would the subjects have behaved in the same way had the observer not been there?

Observation can be a powerful research methodology and has been the basis for some important sociological work. It is limited, however, to what one person or a few people can see in one place. Observation has been used to study things like interaction patterns, rates of group membership, and strength of social networks in local communities. It is much more difficult to directly observe those same variables on a national level or over a long stretch of time. Think about the difficulties of observation for Putnam and his critics, who are concerned with social patterns that have been changing over the better part of three decades.

Analyses of Existing Data

Social science researchers often conduct research by analyzing data collected by someone else. Organizations as diverse as businesses, professional sports leagues, government agencies, and labor unions collect and publish huge amounts of information that can be useful for testing theory and understanding how society works. Such information is easily available, often in libraries and on the Internet, and researchers can gather it quickly and cheaply.

The U.S. Census Bureau is perhaps the single richest source of data for the social sciences in the United States. A census of the entire population, conducted every ten years, gathers an enormous variety of information about U.S. residents. The Census Bureau also gathers more detailed information from smaller samples of citizens. The census is the source of most of the information reported by Putnam and his critics about voter turnout, number of televisions per household, and the age distribution of the population. Other sources of information relevant for this debate include publications of the national offices of the PTA, labor unions, and other associations and organizations.

Perhaps the chief limitation on the use of existing statistics is that the definitions and procedures used to collect information may not exactly match the concepts in which a social scientist is interested. A difference in definitions can create errors of measurement and inaccuracy in conclusions. But when sociologists study large-scale social issues, such as civic behavior, they often have no choice but to adapt their research to data previously collected by large organizations.

Conclusion

This chapter introduced the scientific method as practiced in the social sciences and illustrated the nature of scientific investigations with a current debate about civic engagement in the United States. Research like this is not an academic exercise, relevant only to sociologists and scholars; the results can help us understand the social world more thoroughly and perhaps even help us change it for the better. If Putnam is right about the decrease in civic engagement in the United States and the culpability of television, perhaps measures can be taken to forestall further deterioration of our social capital. Perhaps other technologies can be used to reconnect people to each other and to strengthen social networks. Indeed, as suggested by the research done by Witte and Howard, Internet chat rooms and discussion groups, which seem to be flourishing, may represent one way to reconstruct community.

One of the great strengths of science is that it is a collective enterprise in which communities of scholars examine similar questions over time to arrive at a better understanding of the world. Even if Putnam ultimately is proved wrong about the impact of television, he still has raised issues that make us—ordinary citizens, politicians, journalists, and social scientists alike—critically examine who we are, how we live, and where our society is going. His research has stimulated an important debate about the nature and future of American society and thus already served a valuable purpose.

Key Concepts

1. Science is a method for testing ideas and theories. The scientific method stresses the need for careful, self-critical empirical research and the objective assessment of evidence.

2. When sociologists develop a theoretical explanation for some social phenomenon, they—like all scientists—are obligated to test their ideas by empirical research. Science involves a constant dialog between explanation and verification: theory motivates research and research shapes theory.

3. In general, sociologists seek to analyze and verify causal relationships among variables: relationships in which one or more independent variables cause one or more dependent variables. Causal relationships are expressed in terms of probabilities and tendencies.

4. Theories are tested by communities of scholars over time. As evidence gradually accumulates, conclusions about the validity of a theory typically are tentative and partial.

5. Social scientists use a variety of techniques to gather data and test theories. Among the most widely used research designs are experiments, surveys, observation, and the analysis of existing data.

6. This chapter focused on issues of social capital and social ties for examples and illustrations. The questions and concerns raised by Putnam are still under investigation and await final judgment based on empirical research and logical analysis.

Active Learning

1. TV and Civic Involvement: Debate. In this exercise, you will debate and discuss with your classmates the issues raised by Putnam and his critics regarding the relationship between TV viewing and civic involvement. You will present your own conclusions and evaluate the arguments and opinions of others. You will also come up with some ideas for researching the issues further.

a. Review the arguments and evidence in this chapter both for and against Putnam's conclusion that the spread of television is related to a decline of civic involvement in the United States. On a single sheet of paper, list Putnam's arguments and evidence in a column on the left and the arguments and evidence of his opponents in a column on the right. As much as possible, line up related pro and con positions. At the bottom of the page, write a short paragraph stating your understanding of the issues and your (tentative) conclusion.

b. Use your library or the Internet to update the debate. Search both the popular press and scholarly journals for recent (since 1999) articles that speak to topics such as the health of civic life, involvement in politics, and rates of participation in voluntary associations and community service groups. You might look especially for information about the effect of the Internet or other new technologies on community life. Add the information or ideas you find to your list of arguments for and against Putnam's conclusion.

c. In a group of four to six students, take turns presenting your understandings of the debate and your conclusions. Is Putnam right? Try to resolve any disagreements and come to a common view.

d. How can your group help resolve the issues? Develop three specific questions for further research in this area, one applying to local communities, one to the United States as a society, and one that would require a comparison of many societies.

e. Submit a summary of the group's deliberations, the list of three questions, and the papers brought to class by each member of the group. As an option, the groups may appoint spokespersons to share views and opinions in class.

2. Student Involvement in Campus Civic Life: Survey. This project may be done individually or as a group. You will test on your campus some of the ideas explored in this chapter about the relationship between civic involvement and television viewing habits. If Putnam is correct, students who watch more TV should be less involved in campus life, less likely to attend events (games, concerts), and less likely to belong to organizations such as clubs and sororities. They also should be less likely to socialize with other students informally or attend parties.

a. Make sure you understand Putnam's argument and the responses of his critics. Also familiarize yourself with the material in this chapter on surveys.

b. Develop a short (five to ten questions) survey that you can administer to other students. A suggested list of questions is available at our Web site (www.pineforge.com/snc). You can measure the independent variable by asking your respondents to estimate how much time (in hours during a typical week) they spend watching TV or videos. We also suggest that you ask respondents about time they spend on the Internet, listening to music on personal stereos, or participating in other individual activities. To measure the dependent variable, devise questions that will determine how many campus organizations respondents belong to, how much time they spend in group or club activities, how much time they spend with friends on campus, how often they attend campus events, and the like.

c. Administer your survey to five to ten students. Identify yourself, explain the purpose of the project, and make sure the respondents understand that all information will be kept strictly confidential. A suggested introduction is available at our Web site. Leave a copy of the questionnaire with each respondent and arrange to pick it up at a specific time. Give the respondents at least an hour; try to get all questionnaires back within a day. Make sure you thank the participants for their time.

d. When you get the completed questionnaires, analyze the results. One way to do that is to first organize the questionnaires in rank order by extent of TV viewing. Place the questionnaire with the greatest number of hours on top, followed by the next highest, and so forth (place ties together). Then divide the pile of question-naires into two equal piles: one half for heavier viewers and one for lighter viewers.

e. Look through the two piles one at a time and see if the heavy viewers are less involved in campus life than the lighter viewers. To make that determination, you might count the number of club memberships of the students in each pile and com-pare the totals. Or you might compare average number of friends or campus events attended. Regardless of the exact technique you use, if heavy viewers are less involved, Putnam's idea is supported. If heavy viewers' involvement in campus activities is the same as or more than light viewers' involvement, Putnam's idea is not supported.

f. Repeat the process by dividing the questionnaires into two piles reflecting students' level (heavy or light) of Internet use or other item you have chosen to measure the independent variable. What patterns do you find? Do the data support Putnam's idea?

g. Write a report (jointly if you are working with a group) in which you present your results and come to a conclusion about the relationship among TV viewing, other individual activities, and civic involvement on campus. Also consider these ques-tions: Are there ways of being involved in campus life other than those you meas-ured on the survey? Do you suppose your conclusions would change if you had included those other types of involvement? What would happen to your conclu-sions if you had measured involvement in off-campus activities? Going beyond your survey, what is your impression of the level of civic involvement on your campus in general? Are students involved and engaged or apathetic and uncaring? In your opinion, what role do TV and the Internet play on your campus? If you could design your own research project, what questions would you ask about involvement and apathy on your campus?

4 Culture and Society

*Can local culture coexist
with global culture?*

The Blasket Islands, off the western tip of Ireland, are rugged hogbacks of land that jut from the treacherous waters separating the Atlantic Ocean and Dingle Bay. For centuries, these remote outposts sustained a vibrant and colorful community. The people spoke Irish Gaelic and passed on their traditions from generation to generation in stories, legends, poetry, music, song, and dance. Their love of language ran deep and blossomed into literature when the art of writing reached the islands. By the middle of the twentieth century, this tiny community of several hundred souls had produced several widely acclaimed biographies and memoirs of island life.

Today, the Blasket Islands are deserted. The last members of the community moved to the mainland in the 1950s, drawn by the comforts of the outside world—easier jobs, better healthcare and schools, the pleasures of central heating. Some of the rich verbal and musical heritage of the Blaskets has been written down or recorded, but without an ongoing community to sustain them many of the ancient traditions are lost forever.

Around the globe, hundreds of other local cultures—indeed, entire national traditions—are similarly perched on the brink of extinction. For example, the language of everyday life in Ireland is English, a legacy of centuries of British colonization. But the Irish value the Gaelic language, as they do all their traditions, and they are making a concerted effort to preserve their native tongue. Gaelic is a requirement in all the schools and for certain government jobs; all official documents are published in both English and Gaelic; and Irish TV features an all-Gaelic station. Yet the percentage of people who consider Gaelic their first language or who actually use the language extensively is tiny. Students widely regard Gaelic as irrelevant and say they would prefer to study French, German, or some other language that might help them get a job in modern, unified Europe. One Irish educator has remarked, "It's hard to find a reason to [require Gaelic] at a time when we are trying to strengthen our role in Europe, not fall off the edge of it" (Ardagh, 1995, p. 293).

Will the Gaelic language disappear like Blasket Island culture, preserved only as a curiosity or a museum piece? It seems that western culture is spreading across the world and that people everywhere, like the Irish, are abandoning their traditional languages in favor of English or some other widely used language. How concerned should we be? On one hand, a universal language and a single, global culture certainly would be advantageous for efficiency and ease of communication. Also, people everywhere are attracted by some aspects of modern western culture: movies, computers, clothing, food, advanced medical care, and technology. At the same time, people lament and fear the loss of the traditional cultures that have given meaning to their lives or to the lives of their ancestors. Can the world afford to lose cultural diversity, distinct languages, unique ways of expressing complexity and emotion, manifold visions and viewpoints? Does it really matter when a culture dies?

The main concern of this chapter is the issue of cultural variation and survival, not only of the Blasket Islands or the Gaelic language but of local cultures around the globe. One of the most interesting things about human beings is our ability to produce an endless variety of values, lifestyles, and languages. Such variations are interesting in their own right and may even increase our ability to survive. The more diversity in the global cultural "gene pool," the more likely we will be able to devise solutions when crises arise.

Until the Blasket Islands were abandoned in the mid-1950s, they had maintained a small but vibrant community since at least the 13th century. The community spoke Gaelic. What will happen to the generations of stories, poetry, music, and dance that maintained this community for so long? Ironically, at a time when the Gaelic language is threatened by such developments, the popularity of Celtic music is growing around the world.

Will modernization and globalization destroy cultural diversity? We address that issue by first defining and explaining the concept of culture from a sociological perspective, examining culture's role in society, and introducing a vocabulary for discussing culture. Then we examine the processes by which culture is created, transmitted, and changed. In the final section, we explore the effects of globalization directly.

A Sociological Perspective on Culture

The first thing you need to do in studying culture from a sociological perspective is to understand the different ways of thinking about culture. When people talk about "culture," at least in a western society, they often are talking about fine arts and high-minded discourse. "Getting some culture" means learning to appreciate things like painting, drama, and orchestral music and to be at ease with conversations about things like the deconstruction of violence in Quentin Tarantino's films.

It wouldn't hurt you to "get some culture," if for no other reason than to understand something about the society in which you live. However, we want you to be able to understand **culture** as sociologists use the term: a set of tangible and intangible elements—things like diet, tools, technology, language, and values—that gives shape and meaning to the everyday lives of a particular group of people. Perhaps an analogy will help: if the structure of a society—its groups, organizations, networks of relationships, and patterns of interaction—are the hardware, then culture is the software that provides the operating instructions (Kanagy and Kraybill, 1999).

You know how important it is for a computer to have operating instructions. You can appreciate, then, what culture does for us in our everyday lives: it helps shape our perceptions and thus determines the nature of the reality in which we live. If you were to wake up tomorrow morning in the home of an Asian peasant, you might be dismayed by what you perceive as the poverty and backwardness of the household. They might have a refrigerator and a TV, but where are the microwave and the coffeemaker? Why do they eat just a little chicken or fish, no beef? Why do they spend so much time fussing with a household shrine when they could be out earning money to buy the things that might make their lives easier? Why aren't the kids in school getting a high school diploma instead of staying at home for weeks at a time to help out on the family farm? You might be surprised to learn that, in many parts of the world, that household epitomizes cultural expectations for the good life. Far from envying the lush and fast-paced lifestyle you might be accustomed to, they might just pity you for being so far removed from the things they value: the land, strong kinship systems and communities, and deep connections with ancestors.

In addition to being concerned with the ways that culture affects perception and everyday life, sociologists also are concerned with how culture is related to the structure of society. For example, think of the way women are regarded in two very different societies. In Sweden women generally are considered equal participants in

Culture helps shape the structure and everyday life of a society. The culture guiding this middle-class African-American family (right) is very different from that guiding an extended Cakchiquel family in Guatemala (top). Both cultures are dramatically different from the disappearing culture of the Tsaatan reindeer hunters in Mongolia (above). The long arm of Westernization is widely thought to harm some local cultures by exposing people to new lifestyles and values in movies, videos, and television. In this photo, the Tsaatan are watching a TV/video run off a generator. The video is an Italian documentary about how the Tsaatan are abandoning their culture and way of life.

GRAPHIC 4.1   STATUS OF WOMEN IN INDIA AND SWEDEN

	Sweden	India
School Enrollment		
Primary and secondary schools		
Males	100%	83%
Females	100%	62%
Colleges and universities		
Females per 100 males	120	49
Political Power		
Percentage of government positions occupied by women		
Ministerial level	38%	3%
Subministerial level	27%	6%

Source: United Nations, 2000.

society, whereas in some parts of India they are considered the property of their husband or their father. Those cultural attitudes and perceptions are associated with two very different sets of social institutions, organizations, and laws. Like most western societies, Sweden requires that women have rights in the workplace equal to men. The government also provides generous maternity benefits (for up to one year following the birth) so women can spend adequate time in their equally important role as mothers before returning to work. Many Indian women have jobs as well, but in some segments of the society they are expected to stay at home their whole lives, serving first their father's household and then their husband's or mother-in-law's. Traditionally, a bride's family provides a dowry to the groom at marriage. Abuses of women related to the dowry—the abandonment of wives, even their murder when the dowry is considered insufficient—are against the law in India, but sensational cases still come to light on a regular basis. The role of women in India, the tradition of the dowry, and a legal system that does not sufficiently deter the abuse of women are all quite different from the social arrangements that affect Swedish women. But the more important point is that such social arrangements reflect different cultural beliefs about women's abilities and their value to society. Graphic 4.1 presents some data on the comparative status of women in the two nations.

Much of what sociologists have to say about culture comes from their analysis of anthropological studies. Anthropologists systematically observe the artifacts and behaviors of people who share a way of life, often comparing their observations with patterns from another time or a different place. For instance, an American anthropologist might visit the Philippines for an extended period and note how the Filipino lifestyle differs from what the anthropologist knows to be the American lifestyle. Or the anthropologist might visit the Philippines several times over a decade or more, noting any changes in lifestyle that have taken place.

Sociologists also study culture by conducting surveys (see Chapter 3) about what people believe or what they consider is the right way to act. Data from sources like the U.S. Census, which describe how people live and how much they value things like marriage and parenthood, are also useful tools for studying culture.

Sociologists use information and data to develop theories and models to analyze the diverse dimensions of culture and society and to predict what might happen under various circumstances. This chapter presents several theories and models developed to help us understand what culture is, how it affects society, and what might happen to local cultures as globalization proceeds.

Culture and Community

Chapter 1 stated that "culture is at the center of globalization"; now we will explore the implications of that assertion. On an individual level, learning one's culture makes it possible to communicate and interact with other members of the society. From the perspective of society, culture helps to tie individuals, groups, and institutions into a single unit. Culture provides a basis for **community:** the sense of cohesion that develops among a group of people who are linked by shared interests, understandings, and identity. People who share a common culture share a similar reality and attach similar meanings to the things and the events in the world around them. That cultural unity and sense of solidarity was one of the many topics that fascinated Emile Durkheim, one of the founders of sociology discussed in Chapter 2.

Although the people within a community are linked by a common culture, they also are affected by distinct, shared variations on the overall culture, called subcultures. Thus, they will all have somewhat different understandings of how society is supposed to work. For instance, everyone who grew up in your hometown may associate July 4 with a big public fireworks display, but the younger generation and the older generation or people from diverse backgrounds may have different ideas about the foods, dress, and behavior that are appropriate at the picnic.

Subcultural variation is linked to two different types of community (Griswold, 1994, p. 139):

◆ *Territorial community.* People are often linked as much by geography as by anything else. The Irish—or any other national or regional group—base much of their identity on the fact that they inhabit a common territory. If you have lived in a small town or a tight-knit neighborhood, you know what it means to be part of a territorial community. Although you may have tried to distinguish yourself from other members of your home community from time to time, you probably still identify yourself as being from, say, the Bronx or St. Cloud or Chattanooga, and you expect other people to understand something about you from such an affiliation. You may be more trusting of people "from home" or perhaps seek them out if you find yourself in some remote locale. Such has been the case from the beginning of human society. We believe that we have something important in common with people from our home territory. This is a traditional view of community. When we talk about "local culture," we generally are referring to territorial community.

◆ *Relational community.* A more modern type of community may form among people linked by shared circumstances, ideas, and activities rather than by geographical ties. Think of friends you have made through a shared interest in some sport or avocation. Think of a chat room you are part of or your instant identification with people who share your gender or ethnicity or dedication to a cause. With faster, cheaper communication and transportation, relational communities have become more common. Ironically, the ancient Gaelic language is being preserved, in part, by modern technology. A number of Web sites (for example, http://metalab.unc.edu/gaelic/) offer translation services, dictionaries, and a variety of other resources, and there is a discussion list for people with a shared interest in Gaelic, at gaelic-L@listserv.heanet.ie.

One big question that sociologists are only beginning to address is what happens to community in a globalizing world. When people are more geographically mobile—moving across town, across the country, or even to the other side of the world, perhaps every few years—how do they develop a sense of shared culture? Obviously, the territorial aspects of community become less important, and local culture begins to have less of an effect on a highly mobile population. The lament that a person has forgotten her or his "roots" recognizes that the local culture has lost its pull.

On the other hand, even the most mobile, "rootless" people can still identify with a relational community (human beings are, after all, social animals) formed around a certain profession, industry, or activity. Regardless of physical location, people may maintain ties with others who share an experience, like a spinal cord injury, graduation from a particular college, or an interest in mountain biking, or glass blowing, or Irish culture. With modern transportation and communication, people can maintain a strong sense of community and build a common culture that transcends geography.

Elements of Culture

Imagine you are a sociologist trying to analyze a culture. You could observe the artifacts and behaviors of the people in the culture and, through survey, research, or another methodology, try to determine the ideas they have in common. As you proceeded, you would observe the elements of culture, including the material (tangible) and nonmaterial (intangible) components, the technology they use, and their methods of communication.

Material Culture

The things you can see and touch and hear make up **material culture.** If you were to visit another culture, you would readily notice differences in the way people typically dress, the look of their homes and work spaces, the foods they eat, their music, their behavior on the street, and so on.

You don't have to travel far to see variations in material culture. An ethnic restaurant in your own town—whether it serves sweet and sour pork, pierogi, burritos, or lasagna—brings a little bit of material culture from a faraway place. You can find variations in material culture just by traveling to another region of America: cowboy hats and boots versus wingtips and three-piece suits; skyscrapers versus frame houses versus adobe haciendas; a snowmobile in the front yard versus a swimming pool in the backyard; clam chowder versus gumbo.

In a big city, ethnic enclaves preserve a lot of "foreign" culture in the form of specialty groceries and restaurants, foreign-language video stores, houses of worship, newspapers and magazines, pastimes, and home decor. Smaller towns, too, might have sections that you can tell, just by looking, house people of different cultures. When you drive through a town, can't you tell where the "rich" people and the "poor" people live? Whether an establishment caters to hunters or retired people or young families or athletes?

Although it is easy to identify, material culture is a relatively superficial manifestation of culture. For example, if you wanted to have a Caribbean-themed party, all you would have to do is buy a few palm-and-beach-type decorations, make a few spicy dishes, serve rum and fruit drinks, tell everybody to wear "island" clothes, and play reggae music. For a few hours, you could adopt the outward trappings of a different culture. You can easily re-create (at least superficially) the material aspects of another culture and, thus, sample and experience it without making any major changes in the way you think or live. To truly absorb a new culture, however, you would have to do a lot more than put on different clothes and eat different foods.

This busy shop in Chinatown, New York City, underscores how material culture can be imported. Prices and descriptions are in both Chinese and English, as are the conversations. Large cities across the United States have a number of "towns" that help preserve the local "foreign" culture by offering distinctive food, entertainment, houses of worship, newspapers, and clothing.

Nonmaterial Culture

The intangibles that make one group of people different from another group, their **nonmaterial culture,** are much more difficult to identify, re-create, and adopt than material culture. You would have to infer those intangibles from an individual's or a group's behavior and then change your basic outlook to incorporate them. The elements of nonmaterial culture include beliefs, values, norms, and rituals.

Beliefs. People have long sought to define the nature of the reality they perceive by making statements like "Step on a crack and you'll break your mother's back" or "Virgos are perfectionists" or "The world is flat" or "There is only one God" or "God is a woman" or "Disease is caused by microbes, invisible to the naked eye." Such statements are **beliefs.**

Beliefs incorporate the information accumulated through people's senses and the knowledge that comes from others and from thinking about that information. People interpret information differently, and differing interpretations of the sensed world can (and do) produce differing beliefs. What is not so obvious, perhaps, is that people also sense things differently. Just think about the last time you disagreed with someone about who exactly said what.

In spite of the diversity of perception, people who share a culture come to agree on some interpretations of reality. The resulting cultural system of beliefs gives a group of people a particular world view that differs, to a greater or lesser degree, from the world views of people who live in different places and at different times. For example, an Orthodox Jew "knows" that pork is unclean and must not be eaten, just as an Indian peasant "knows" that beef is forbidden. Consider how the western belief system regarding the meaning of certain physiological conditions has changed over the past several centuries. A seizure that today would be diagnosed as a medical problem might have been seen in the 1700s as evidence of demonic possession or witchcraft.

Beliefs can be expressed in a number of ways. Modern cultures have a tendency to explain the world in terms of science, philosophy, and sometimes religion; traditional cultures rely more on myth, folklore, and religion. The difference is the degree to which beliefs are based on objective perceptions of reality, observing the natural world, testing beliefs against the evidence, and using logic to understand cause and effect. Every belief system and explanation makes assumptions about the nature of reality, but myth, folklore, and religion take a lot more on faith than does science.

Regardless of the basis for a belief, those who do not agree with it are likely to deride it as superstition. We may wonder how anyone could believe that a dead family member would care about being invited to a feast; people in other cultures might wonder how we could believe that simply giving someone a little pill is enough to effect a real cure.

We all have to be careful about our reactions to others' beliefs. Not only does "the truth" depend on the time, the place, and the social setting in which we find ourselves, but in today's complex world each of us is also likely to deal with multiple belief systems. For example, consider a woman we know who grew up in a traditional Pueblo community in New Mexico and then became a software engineer with the military. What must it be like to reconcile a linear, scientific, time-centered way of thinking with a cultural belief system that is more in tune with nature's patterns and rhythms? Many people struggle to reconcile religious or spiritual beliefs with the belief system that governs our capitalistic, technologically oriented, competitive society. Others may find their belief systems challenged as they take major steps in life and enter college, marry, take a new job, or move to a new community.

Values. Beliefs are associated with **values:** attitudes about what is desirable and moral. Someone who "values diversity" believes that society should be made up of all types of people, groups, and subcultures. "Family values" are a particular set of judgments about how people should feel about and operate within families. "Values training" helps people sort out their views on right and wrong.

A cohesive culture has a distinctive set of values. As diverse as the United States is, researchers have been able to define a set of "traditional American values," which are summarized in Graphic 4.2. These values are similar, but not identical, to those of other western, capitalistic societies. For instance, Americans traditionally have been more individualistic than the English or the Germans, who have different cultures and histories. American values today are also somewhat different from the traditional American values. For instance, it appears that modern Americans are giving

---

GRAPHIC 4.2 TRADITIONAL AMERICAN VALUES

Individualism and freedom. Self-reliance; freedom from external constraints and convention; right to think for ourselves, live as we see fit, express ourselves

Equality. Equal opportunity—not equal outcome—and a fair chance to succeed; inequalities in income, education, and prestige based on differences in talent and effort

Achievement. "Getting ahead" and improving one's situation; competing for the limited resources and opportunities available

Efficiency and practicality. Simple, common-sense, practical solutions to problems

Progress and technology. High value on the new and novel ("state of the art"); belief that technology can solve most problems and that the future will have better technology and will, therefore, be better

Material success and consumerism. Success measured by material well-being, possessions, and comfort

Work and leisure. Hard work, effort, staying active, avoiding "laziness"; free time, relaxation, personal development, and expression

Source: Adapted from Williams, 1970.

up a little of their preference for individual achievement in favor of collaborating to achieve common goals, especially at work.

Although the information in Graphic 4.2 is helpful in understanding U.S. culture as a whole, we need to remember that individuals have different values—they have different biographies, different experiences within subcultures, and different responses to those unique experiences. The Amish in the United States, for example, value simplicity and community and shun modern technology. But members of the Amish community who have business dealings with the outside world may find their values affected by the larger culture and decide that it is okay to install a telephone—but for business calls only and at restricted times of the day.

The result is that multiple value systems may be incorporated into a society's culture. Recall the story in Chapter 1 about S. M. Otieno, the westernized African attorney whose death ignited a fight between Kenyans with conflicting values and beliefs. All over the world, conflicting values are behind many arguments, fights, lawsuits, and wars. It is not easy to accept someone else's ideas about right and wrong.

Values play a crucial role in social life: they provide guidelines for people to make choices in their lives, channel people's energies, and help answer fundamental questions like "What's the difference between right and wrong?" and "What's the meaning of life?" An individual may have a uniquely personal value system, but it is deeply shaped by the culture that person shares with other members of society.

Norms. Every culture includes rules of conduct and codes of behavior called **norms.** Norms are related to values and beliefs and regulate behavior and thought, from the mundane (driving on the right side of the road) to the sublime (how to approach gods and spirits).

A college classroom is a good place to see norms in action. Why is it that students generally sit still during the entire class period and let the professor tell them what to do? In western school culture, as we might call it, that is the unwritten rule. But every class is also a subculture that develops its own norms. Some of your classes may begin precisely on time, others a little late; the students in one class might passively absorb what the professor says, while in another they engage in animated discussion.

Several types of norms exist.

◆ *Folkways* include matters of etiquette, convention, and custom, such as when and how to use a salad fork or when and how firmly to shake hands with someone. Folkways have less moral content than other norms, and violations are treated more as embarrassments than as crimes.

◆ *Mores* have strong moral content and are closely related to a culture's values. Violations are considered to be serious matters. The Ten Commandments are good examples of mores—many Americans call on them to judge and condemn the behavior of others. In stricter, more traditional cultures, codes of conduct like the Ten Commandments have the force of taboos, or very strong mores. Anyone caught violating a taboo might be shunned by the rest of the community, run out of town, physically punished, even killed.

◆ *Laws* are formal norms, written down, codified, and organized. Laws may relate either to folkways (traffic laws, for example) or to mores and taboos (laws regarding homicide). Because they're written down, laws are characteristic of literate cultures.

Norms are important to a culture because they regularize and standardize behavior and thereby create order and predictability. Without norms, you would not be able to anticipate the behavior of others and, thus, could not organize your own behavior: social interaction would be impossible. Imagine trying to drive across town if you could not predict with a high degree of certainty that people would stop on red, go on green, drive on the right, and so on.

One of the biggest problems for people visiting other cultures is learning the norms. Except for laws, norms are not written down, and they may be so automatic and ingrained that people aren't even aware of them. Imagine trying to tell your socially inept cousin how to behave at your favorite club. To fit into another culture, you must carefully observe what others are doing (or rely on someone else's systematic observation), ask questions, and be prepared for the occasional embarrassing or difficult incident.

Rituals. Another important nonmaterial element of culture has to do more with behavior than with attitudes and rules. **Rituals** are the customary, often ceremonial, activities that signify a culture's shared beliefs, values, and norms. More than that, rituals give a group of people an opportunity to celebrate community. For instance, reciting the pledge of allegiance or singing the national anthem at the start of a ballgame is an American ritual that demonstrates the crowd's shared patriotism. It also serves to unite them in a common endeavor: expressing their competitive urges in a sporting match (which is itself a ritual). A ritual is a way for a group to reaffirm its values and beliefs.

Rituals that are important to some cultures may be deemed unacceptable—even morally repugnant—in others. For instance, some traditional African and Middle Eastern cultures still advocate female circumcision, removal of the clitoris and perhaps other genital surgery when a girl enters adolescence. The ritual is intended to celebrate passage into young adulthood and ensure an adult woman's "purity," an important cultural value. Many other cultures denounce female circumcision because it permanently disfigures young girls, creates lifelong discomfort and medical problems, and even increases the risk of death in childbirth. Critics of the practice call it female genital mutilation (FGM) and are trying to get laws passed throughout the world to ban it.

We might concur that female circumcision should be banned, but we need to be careful about how we view the practices and beliefs of others. For example, some cultures think that male circumcision is repugnant and would be deeply offended by the bris ceremony of Judaism. Others would be appalled by some common American practices: aging parents living by themselves, drunken bachelor parties for prospective bridegrooms, the hazing rituals of college fraternities and sororities.

Rituals help celebrate a group's sense of community revolving around shared beliefs, values, and norms. Starting at the top of the page: In India, large groups of people participate in the Holi festival, also called the Festival of Color. It celebrates the start of spring. Hindus cover themselves in colorful dyed water and colored powder called gullal. Another interesting ritual is the Marian pilgrimage in Slovakia (above). As many as 250,000 Catholics travel to the church on Marianska hora, the sacred hill that is more than a mile north of the town of Levoca. Families, school groups, and the elderly walk long distances to participate in the pilgrimage. Of course, American college students have their own spring ritual, here along the Texas coast (right).

Many rituals, like circumcision, mark an individual's transition from one position or status in society to another. For example, the "tooth fairy" ritual marks a child's transition from dependence to a more independent and responsible status around the age of 5 or 6 (Corsaro, 1997). When the child loses a baby tooth, the mythical tooth fairy visits while the child sleeps to leave money under the pillow and take the tooth in exchange. This ritual coincides with the child's entry into formal schooling and the start of the shifting allegiance from family to peers. Although many cultures ritually mark the shedding of baby teeth, the tooth fairy and her surreptitious gift of money are peculiar to western cultures.

Some rituals are performed by large groups of people acting simultaneously, but others are carried out in private by individuals acting alone. Consider anthropologist Horace Miner's (1956) classic description, from "Body Ritual Among the Nacirema," of one culture's daily ritual activity meant to avert disease and disability. Miner begins by describing the use of the household shrines that are the center of such activity.

> The focal point of the shrine is a box or chest which is built into the wall. In this chest are kept the many charms and magical potions without which no native believes he could live. . . . Beneath the charm-box is a small font. Each day every member of the family, in succession, enters the shrine room, bows his head before the charm-box, mingles different sorts of holy water in the font, and proceeds with a brief rite of ablution.

Sound familiar? Spell Nacirema backwards, then think about your own morning ritual before the bathroom mirror.

Whether they are carried out en masse or individually, all ritual activities have some meaning beyond pure function. They do not simply aid people in carrying out the necessary tasks of daily life; rather, they demonstrate and support the culture as a whole.

Technology

Some elements of culture cannot be classified neatly as either material or nonmaterial. Consider **technology,** which consists of a culture's tools and methods for producing the things it needs. We can talk about the business process known as change management as a technology (an element of nonmaterial culture) or about piston technology (material culture). Some technologies are so broad and pervasive that they encompass both material and nonmaterial aspects. Computer technology comes to mind, with its hardware (material) and its software, networks, protocols, and graphic user interfaces (nonmaterial).

Technology helps define a culture. A nomadic culture, for example, is characterized by technologies that enable its people to move easily from one place to another to make good use of natural resources. An agricultural culture has technologies that facilitate cultivating plants and nurturing animals. You should be well acquainted with industrial technologies, because we are enmeshed in them. You probably are also well aware of the information technologies that many social thinkers believe are the most obvious signs of an evolving information-based or postindustrial culture. Chapter 5 explains how the eras of technological development are related to one aspect of culture, the system by which a society determines who gets how much of its resources.

Technological innovations are often portable from one culture to another. Like foods and some of the other more superficial aspects of culture, tools that make life better can be an appealing import. Cell phones, for instance, have become instantly popular in places that have limited or expensive wired-phone service, like China, Israel, and parts of Africa. But process technologies may be harder to import. Cultures with massive populations of able-bodied workers, such as India and Bangladesh, have declined to accept some labor-saving construction and manufacturing technologies. They would rather rely on traditional, labor-intensive processes and low-tech tools, which allow them to support an important cultural value: self-reliance and meaningful work for their own people.

Communication

Like technology, communication is an element of culture with both material and nonmaterial aspects. **Communication** is the verbal, nonverbal, and visual language that allows the members of a culture to convey meaning or thoughts from one person to another. Books, correspondence, and street signs are just some of the material manifestations of communication. The vocabulary and grammar of a language are nonmaterial manifestations, ephemeral vessels for meaning.

Communication is a centrally important element of culture. It helps a group of people develop a shared understanding of reality, coordinate activities, and transmit accumulated information and knowledge to new members of the culture. A person who cannot communicate fully with those in the surrounding culture cannot participate fully in social life.

To communicate, people must share a set of symbols: socially defined, learned representations of meaning. The symbols of a society include an alphabet and words; gestures, like a wave of the hand; and graphic designs, like the male and female silhouettes on restroom doors. A great deal of human communication is conducted with symbols, but a lot also takes place through signs: forms of communication that are genetically fixed and universally understood. An example of a sign is a smile; all people, in all cultures, use this sign to mean the same thing.

Each culture develops a set of arbitrary symbols with agreed-upon meanings and then teaches those meanings to new members of the culture. The vocabulary of a language is an obvious example, but even gestures and graphics have a culturally determined meaning. Some cultures do not wave in greeting, or they use a different kind of wave. In some cultures, the graphic representations of male and female silhouettes look quite different from what we've grown used to—if they even use human forms to indicate gender-specific bathrooms.

Symbols can be used to communicate because they have socially determined meanings. That is, the culture comes to associate a particular symbol with some particular aspect of reality. To talk about the tall plants with woody trunks, for example, English-speaking cultures have adopted the word *tree;* to indicate the same thing, German speakers use *baum,* and Spanish speakers say *arbol.* Anyone in an English-speaking culture understands what a person means by the word *tree.* The meaning is somewhat individual: I may think of a shady oak, you may think of a fragrant pine. But we are able to communicate some basic meaning because the symbol we use to signify the thing means roughly the same to both of us.

As cultures evolve, so do the meanings of the symbols they use for communication. However, meanings are grounded in the beliefs, values, and circumstances of a culture. For example, most middle-class Americans understand a wide variety of terms indicating forms of intangible wealth: *stocks, bonds, mutual funds, money-market accounts.* Those terms help a person in that culture more accurately communicate with others who have, want, or trade in those forms of wealth. A person who measures wealth in livestock, however—such as an African or Central Asian nomad—does not need to know or want to know what a mutual fund is but has a rich and subtle vocabulary for discussing livestock. The term *mutual fund,* even if it could be translated somehow into the language, would have little meaning to a nomad. It seems, therefore, that how we communicate has a lot to do with our culture.

The Construction of Culture

Sociologists commonly use an approach called the **social construction of reality** to explain how cultures are created and maintained. The underlying idea is that reality is, for any person, a collection of beliefs about what exists, in both a material and a nonmaterial way, and what it all means. Our beliefs about reality are products of our social experiences and communication with others; they reflect what the people around us believe to be true, moral, and important.

Reality can be different for different groups of people. For instance, in the two world maps presented in Chapter 1, you got a feeling for the impact of different cultural perspectives. If all you've ever seen is the map with North America in the center, then naturally you think of that continent as the starting point for all discussions of place. If the only culture you've ever experienced is middle-class American culture, then naturally that's your standard for judging what is good, bad, true, disgraceful, necessary, useful, wasteful, polite, tasty, disgusting, beautiful, funny, and so on. But imagine seeing the world from the perspective of a Blasket Islander, an Australian, or a citizen of the Aztec Empire. Your perspective and thus your reality would be completely different from those of an American.

Experiences also contribute to a person's perspective. Once people have the opportunity to travel and see other ways of life, they often are more open-minded and appreciative of other ways of doing things. The other side of the coin is that social reality can change as people and groups develop different ideas about what is true, valuable, and right. At a mundane level, think about changes in the American diet in the last half of the twentieth century. In the 1950s, the epitome of fine dining was a big, richly marbled steak, a baked potato with sour cream, thoroughly

Until the 1960s, African Americans in the south had to use separate entrances, as at this theater in Mississippi. Few whites questioned segregation. But times have changed. Although American society has not reached racial equality, it still has come a long way since those days. The children of people who sat on the balcony have become mayors, professors, businesspeople, artists. Black and white people work closely together in many organizations.

cooked vegetables swimming in butter, and iceberg lettuce with Thousand Island dressing. Today's health-conscious eaters would look at such a meal and see mostly cholesterol. But imagine how insubstantial and precious today's gourmet meals—combining a little bit of lean protein artfully arranged with crisp-cooked vegetables and an exotic sauce—would appear if served to diners in the fifties.

On a grander scale, the civil rights movement in North America in the last half of the twentieth century offers another good example of how social realities can change. Through a complex and multidimensional series of changes in the educational system, the justice system, politics, media, sports, entertainment, and daily life, our society has changed its ideas about acceptable attitudes toward and treatment of racial and ethnic minorities. In the 1940s and 1950s, many white Americans wouldn't have considered a black American capable of leading a major enterprise. Even Jews and people of Irish, Italian, and Polish extraction were suspect. But today our society takes for granted that members of those groups can be not just capable but excellent leaders in government, business, the military, the media, and the arts. As a society, our social reality has changed.

This section discusses in more detail how the social construction of reality takes place, particularly in regard to culture. Three questions concern us: how do individuals adopt the reality of their culture? How do cultural elements develop meaning in a society? Why and how do the salient elements of a culture change? The answers offer insights into how globalization is likely to affect local culture.

The Transmission of Culture to Individuals

As soon as a baby is born, it begins to acquire experiences and ideas about reality from the surrounding culture, and those early perceptions will have lasting effects. Most of us become more and more embedded in the culture of our birth as we grow up. How does that happen? And what happens when we change cultures, marry someone from a different subculture, take a new job in a different industry, or move to a different region? Those questions all relate to the process of cultural transmission, in which the content of a culture is passed along from one generation to another or to a new member of the group.

Socialization. The process by which an individual becomes a functioning member of the surrounding society is called **socialization:** learning about and adopting the values, norms, beliefs, and other nonmaterial elements of a culture and becoming familiar with its material elements. Through communication, interaction, and formal instruction, children learn not only about cultural elements but also about the meaning of those elements. In that way, they absorb the culture that surrounds them. Through socialization, individuals learn their culture so thoroughly that they come to take it for granted.

The agents of socialization are many. Young people learn about their culture mainly through interaction with "significant others," such as parents and friends, but all of the following help to transmit culture.

◆ *Family.* It is difficult to totally rid ourselves of the beliefs and values picked up in our earliest years. If your family stressed kindness and responsibility—if that was the behavior you saw in your parents and other relatives and that was the behavior they reinforced—you might value kindness and responsibility the rest of your life. In addition, some of our most cherished rituals throughout life are those we experienced in childhood with our family, such as the special birthday dinner with the unvarying guest list, menu, and games or the summer vacation at the lake involving the same activities every year.

◆ *Schools.* The educational system presents explicit lessons about the larger culture—teaching us to value democracy and freedom, for example—as well as implicit cultural lessons about things like relationships to authority (in the form of teachers), time (in the form of semesters and class periods), and success (good grades, popularity, athletic prowess, and so on).

◆ *Peers.* Typically in childhood and especially in adolescence, a group of friends forms a subculture with its own beliefs, values, norms, rituals, and even its own material culture. (Which particular toys, clothing, and after-school or weekend activities did your group favor?) Groups of adults do the same thing, although usually not as intensely. The elements of culture picked up from peer groups often conflict with family subculture and sometimes (for deviant groups) with the larger culture as well.

◆ *Workplace.* When you walk into a new job, you have a lot to learn: how to do your task in this particular setting, whom to emulate, whose favor to curry, how to dress, how seriously to take deadlines and dictums, and so on. Some workplaces make cultural transmission a bit easier through a formal socialization process called orientation, although it seldom tells you the most important things you need to know about workplace values, norms, and rituals. Bosses, mentors, and peers participate in socializing you too.

◆ *Mass media.* Most Americans absorb a great deal of nonmaterial culture from TV, movies, the Internet, magazines, CDs, and other mass media. Studies have shown, for instance, that Americans' fear of crime is related to the plethora of crime and violence we see in the media (Croteau & Hoynes, 2000, pp. 15–16). The media also give us ideas about material culture: we get much of our sense of style and manners from sitcoms, soap operas, talk shows, action movies, and, of course, ads. American media messages also have a great deal of influence in other parts of the world, which is part of the reason that preserving traditional cultural elements, such as the Gaelic language, can be so hard. It is why some "closed" cultures (such as a few Asian and Islamic nations) try to prohibit access to the Internet and western media. Even a democracy like France takes steps to limit the influence of American films and TV programs. The authorities deem outside influences harmful and destructive, precisely because they threaten local cultures and values.

◆ *Social institutions.* **Institutions** are clusters of social structure (groups, patterns of interaction, statuses, and networks of relationships), culture (both material and nonmaterial), and technologies aimed at satisfying basic human and social needs. The educational system, for example, is an influential institution that combines material culture (school buildings), statuses (student, teacher), organizations (the PTA, labor unions for teachers), values, norms, and a host of other elements to socialize students and disseminate culture and knowledge. For many people, the institution of religion also plays an important role in transmitting beliefs and values. Government, through laws, taxes, and spending policies, also guides us into certain behavior patterns. And anyone who is taken in by a "total institution," such as a prison, the military, a nursing home, or a mental institution, is socialized into a new culture with distinctive norms, both formal and informal.

Agents of socialization interact in complex ways. In effect, children are actually socialized into a set of subcultures rather than a single culture. Family, neighborhood, classroom, and other social groupings to which a child belongs each have a somewhat different set of values, norms, technologies, and so on. Thus the individual acquires a commitment not only to the larger culture but also to various subcultures. If you grew up in North America, you absorbed a general culture. Just as significant, however, are the variations you experienced as a member of various subgroups.

Sometimes the lessons of one subculture are reinforced by another. For example, schools and workplaces both value punctuality, consideration of others, and submission to authority. However, the lessons may also be contradictory, as when a peer group's norms of rebelliousness conflict with a family's norms of obedience. Those variations are what contribute to both inner conflict (Do I follow the teachings of my family and church or the norms of my peer group?) as well as social conflict among subgroups.

In a broad sense, variations in the lessons derived from socialization may be due to your family's makeup and ethnic heritage, your geographic location, and the era(s) in which you have lived. But an equally significant influence is your social class (see Chapter 5). The socialization practices among the upper class, the middle class, the working class, and the underclass vary a great deal: how parents discipline their children, what they expect their children to experience in adulthood, the cultural experiences they provide, how they communicate caring, how (and if) they reinforce the norms of the school and the workplace, and so on (Newman, 1999). People from different social classes are likely to have different sorts of role models and learn different values. Consider the effects on career aspirations and preparation for adult life. A person enmeshed in what has been called the "culture of poverty" is focused on surviving in the here and now and has little immediate hope of a fulfilling career in the business world; she or he is likely to value street smarts and "attitude" more than good grades in school and the acceptance of authority.

Socialization is an interactive process, not a one-way street. While children are absorbing culture, they are also reinventing or creating new meaning for aspects of it (Corsaro, 1997, p. 18). For example, picture a kindergarten class in which one of the teacher's rules is that all the toys have to be cleaned up before the children can hear a story. The children themselves, through their creative efforts to avoid participating in the cleanup, may redefine the norm: the teacher will read the story if all the toys are put away except for one toy that a particular child might put in a special place for later play. Adolescent culture has an even wider influence on the larger culture. For instance, the cool irony and edgy spirit of Generation X has prompted innovations in clothing, automotive, and entertainment styles. Those are just two examples of how the younger members of a society not only are socialized into it but also participate in constructing its culture and thereby changing its content and meaning over time.

Acculturation. What happens when a person who grew up in one culture is transported into a distinctly different culture? A person who, because of immigration (see Chapter 6), marriage, adoption, or job status, is immersed in an unfamiliar culture may at first experience "culture shock," a variety of unsettling emotions, including anxiety, suspicion, and loneliness. Gradually, however, through observation, trial and error, the guidance of others, perhaps even classes in the language, norms, and rituals of the new culture, the person in the new environment becomes more comfortable.

Acquiring the ability to communicate with other members of the culture is a key step. If you don't know how to ask questions and understand the answers, you are at a disadvantage. Immigrants obviously face that task if they don't know the local language. But you may not be aware of how your college studies are acculturating you to a new language (jargon) that will help you communicate with other members of your profession and other members of the middle or upper-middle class. Learning a language also acquaints you with the thought patterns of the new culture. As you learn more words for the things and ideas you encounter in the new environment, you gradually learn more about the new culture's beliefs and values and thus find it increasingly easy to fit in.

The Social Production of Culture

Understanding how individuals acquire cultural knowledge is one thing. Understanding how the elements of culture come to have meaning, to represent reality for the members of the culture, is quite another. At least two broad processes are at work (Griswold, 1994, p. 52):

◆ As people interact and communicate, they develop a common way of life and a shared sense of what is true, valuable, and right.

◆ Certain elements of a society are organized into systems that work to find, promote, distribute, and consume cultural objects and, thereby, give meaning to those objects.

The first process has already been described in this chapter; it is the relationship between individuals and their culture. But that doesn't tell us much about the relationship between a culture and the social structure in which the culture is embedded. For that, we can call on the production-of-culture model (see Peterson, 1976), which originated with industrial and organizational sociologists. The production-of-culture model focuses on the organizations, industries, and other structures of society that create cultural objects.

In modern, industrial societies (and, increasingly, around the globe as a whole) cultural objects—movies, museum exhibits, fashions, and the like—become meaningful through the efforts of a vast culture industry, systems of organizations that produce, distribute, and market the objects (Hirsch, 1972). Graphic 4.3 shows how the four subsystems involved in the culture industry interact (Griswold, 1994, pp. 72–80).

◆ *Technical subsystem.* The creators who provide the input: the stories, the songs, the movies, the TV shows. The technical subsystem for a cultural object may be an individual (a novelist, for instance) or a group of people (such as a band, script-writing team, or sitcom cast).

◆ *Managerial subsystem.* Those who produce the product, such as publishers, music companies, and movie and TV studios. The producers typically are large organizations (increasingly, they are branches of transnational corporations), but they also may be small firms or individuals.

◆ *Institutional subsystem.* The disseminators of information. The media play an important role in producing cultural objects by spreading the word. They also provide feedback through reviews, interviews with artists, and other publicity, giving the managerial subsystem important information about what types of products to produce in the future.

◆ *Cultural market.* The consumers of the cultural object, who might be called the "interpretation-producing subsystem," the ones who ultimately give meaning to the object. They are also important sources of feedback through their purchase of tickets, recordings, books, and the like; their attention to particular TV programs, Internet sites, and so on; their interest in celebrities; and their purchase of spin-off products like toys based on movie and TV characters.

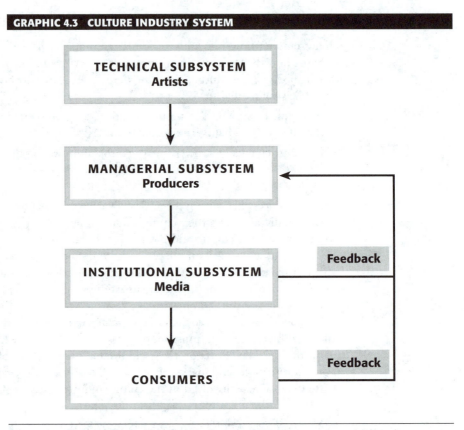

GRAPHIC 4.3   CULTURE INDUSTRY SYSTEM

Sources: Adapted from Griswold, 1994, p. 73, and Hirsch, 1972, pp. 639–659.

Although this model was developed to describe the production of cultural objects presented to the public in general, it can be used to understand the production of any cultural element. For example, say we want to analyze the production of the belief that the U.S. government is a threat to individual freedom, a popular notion among some U.S. citizens. If we looked into the source of this idea, we would find a technical subsystem consisting of certain organizations and activists, politicians, newspaper and magazine columnists, book writers, Web sites, and radio and TV talk-show hosts who have put this idea into words and created other symbols to represent it. We would also find a managerial subsystem consisting of publishers, producers, publicists, and the like who have put the idea into forms suitable for public consumption and who fund production and distribution. The idea is then disseminated to the general public by the institutional subsystem, which consists of various media outlets. In this case, another important part of the institutional subsystem is the network of political, religious, and other organizations that see the government as a threat or that benefit from undermining public faith in it.

Their financial and political support further encourages the technical and managerial subsystems to develop the idea. Likewise, the other subsystems would not work for long to produce this cultural object if they did not find a receptive audience in the cultural market.

The general public can help refine the meaning of any cultural element, including the message of mistrust of the government. For example, the American public tolerates and even endorses (sometimes enthusiastically) complaints about big government and overregulation, but it finds extreme antigovernment actions, such as the bombing of the federal building in Oklahoma City by Timothy McVeigh, unacceptable (a violation of mores). Many Americans regard the government as an annoyance (even a major annoyance), but they do not see it as "the enemy."

The production-of-culture model is useful, then, for focusing our attention on the way the social world participates in the construction of culture. Cultural elements, whether things or ideas, gain meaning for a group of people and become significant to their lives not just because of individual interactions and communication but also because of the workings of a complex, multilayered system of organizations, structures, and networks.

Culture Change

Cultures are in a constant process of change as individuals and societies adapt to new circumstances. You could say that cultures evolve much as living beings do. However, cultural change can be much faster than biological or physiological evolution. You would probably see few physical or genetic differences between, say, ancient and modern Egyptians. But if modern Egyptians were to travel back to the time of the pharaohs and the pyramids, they would undoubtedly find much foreign about both the material and the nonmaterial culture. Even just going back to the 1950s in North America, you would find some significant differences not only in the trappings of culture but also in language, norms, rituals, and so on.

Cultures change in two main ways. First, people invent or discover new cultural elements. That is, they create new ideas and things, like democracy or microwave ovens, or they give familiar things and ideas new meaning — for example, the perception that the wide open spaces are a valuable public resource rather than a wasteland or a wilderness that needs to be tamed. The second avenue for culture change (and the more important to us in this chapter) is **cultural diffusion,** the process of importing both material and nonmaterial cultural elements from one society into another. Culture diffuses through trade, migration, and other types of interaction among people from different cultures, contacts that are greatly facilitated by advances in communication and transportation technology. Diffusion brought the English language to Ireland and helped to change the ways in which Blasket Islanders thought about the larger world beyond their community.

People usually are quick to adopt elements of material culture that are clearly advantageous in terms of efficiency or productivity. The Plains Indians, for instance, quickly saw the utility of the horses introduced to the American continent by the Spanish and, later, rifles and manufactured blankets. The Indians adapted those technologies to their existing lifestyle. However, they were far less willing to adopt the nonmaterial culture of the invading Euro-American cultures, such as farming technology or the belief in private ownership of land. Some Plains Indians acquiesced to the new nonmaterial culture only after their people had fought against European values and been defeated in war; generations later, many Native American tribes still proudly hold to their traditional values and practice the ancient rituals of their tribes.

The Plains Indians are not unique. Generally speaking, material culture diffuses more rapidly from one culture to another than does nonmaterial culture (Ogburn, 1964). People often adopt the superficial elements of a different culture—the tools, foods, music styles, clothing—without thinking twice. But values, beliefs, norms, and rituals rely more on shared meaning for their existence than things do and thus are more deeply embedded within a culture. This point has great significance in our search for an answer to the fate of local cultures in a globalizing world.

Cultures are inherently resistant to rapid change, at least on a nonmaterial level, but societies can reform and modify their cultures when they realize that some elements are dysfunctional. An unmistakable sign that things are not going well for a society is a defeat in war. More subtle hints, however, may come from a loss in global economic or political status or from internal disruptions such as financial disaster, social strife, violence, or increasing hunger and homelessness (Chirot, 1994, pp. 121–122). For example, the Soviet Union dissolved in 1992 because its client states, its people, and its leaders, Mikhail Gorbachev and Boris Yeltsin, saw a need to emulate the more successful industrialized nations of the West. To improve productivity and raise the quality of life in their societies, the leaders of the former USSR and its satellite states set aside their cultural beliefs in totalitarianism and communism and adopted forms of democracy and capitalism.

As an additional example, consider the changes in the United States that resulted from the civil disorders of the 1960s and 1970s. Many of the issues and demands of that era were resolved by such cultural changes as new civil rights laws, the end of the Vietnam War, and the rise of new beliefs about the roles of men and women. It will be interesting to see when and how American culture might change in response to some of today's signs of social strain, such as hate crimes, computer scams, and the widening disparity between rich and poor.

Some types of cultural change create a condition called **cultural lag:** a gap between the material and nonmaterial parts of culture. Disruptive cultural upheavals can occur when changes in material culture outpace changes in nonmaterial culture, just as an earthquake suddenly and dramatically relieves the tension between two tectonic plates. Social institutions don't change easily, so they may "crack" under the strain (Chirot, 1994, p. 120). For instance, in the United States today, people are having trouble reconciling their cultural beliefs about the proper beginning and end of life with medical technology that can control fertility, create life in a laboratory, and keep a body "alive" even when the brain is "dead." The sometimes bitter culture wars between pro-life and pro-choice forces, conservatives and liberals, traditionalists and cosmopolitans attest to the culture's struggle to reconcile its values, beliefs, norms, and rituals with the new possibilities provided by material culture and rapidly changing technology.

Social disruptions are resolved when the strain created by cultural lag is reduced (Griswold, 1994, p. 63). For example, doctors, lawyers, ethicists, and politicians have developed new cultural elements (living wills, protocols for dealing with brain death, federal and state legislation) to help reconcile the conflicts between technological capabilities and folkways and mores. The production of new cultural elements reduces the strain created by cultural lag, at least until the next strain erupts.

The Globalization of Culture

Interestingly, many societies today are facing cultural lags. Rapid advances in technology have introduced new dilemmas for cultures all over the globe. Tradition and old assumptions about community based on geographic location are rubbing up against the realities of a networked, changing world. The strain is accompanied by violent conflict in some places (like Serbia and Indonesia), social repression in other places (like Afghanistan), and denunciations of globalization virtually everywhere. What seem to get the most attention in the media are the difficulties of various local cultures faced with the rapid, widespread, and sometimes overwhelming diffusion of western consumerist culture—the McDonaldization of society, the hegemony of Hollywood, and so forth.

Not everyone is hostile toward global culture, however. In the past decade, city dwellers in China, for instance, have avidly embraced some elements of western culture. Entrepreneurism, individualism, and consumerism are new values in this communist country. Graphic 4.4 shows some of the results of three consumer surveys conducted by the Gallup Organization in the People's Republic of China. Keep in mind that rural Chinese are far less likely to have access to western technologies or to have experienced western culture to the extent that urban Chinese have, which probably affects their values. In addition, the Chinese government continues to erect formidable barriers to the diffusion of culture from the West. Within months after the 1999 Gallup survey was completed, the government enacted new laws that restrict the gathering and reporting of such data and that control access to the Internet.

For many people around the world, global culture is scary, and they strongly prefer their traditional ways. Author Thomas L. Friedman, on a recent book promotion tour to Cairo, observed many middle- and upper-class Egyptians using cell phones and computers and many other less well educated, lower-class Egyptians plowing their fields with water buffalo and praying for a successful trip in an elevator. Friedman notes:

> Many Americans can easily identify with modernization, technology and the Internet because one of the most important things these do is increase individual choices. At their best, they empower and emancipate the individual. But for traditional societies,

GRAPHIC 4.4   CHINA'S CHANGING CULTURE

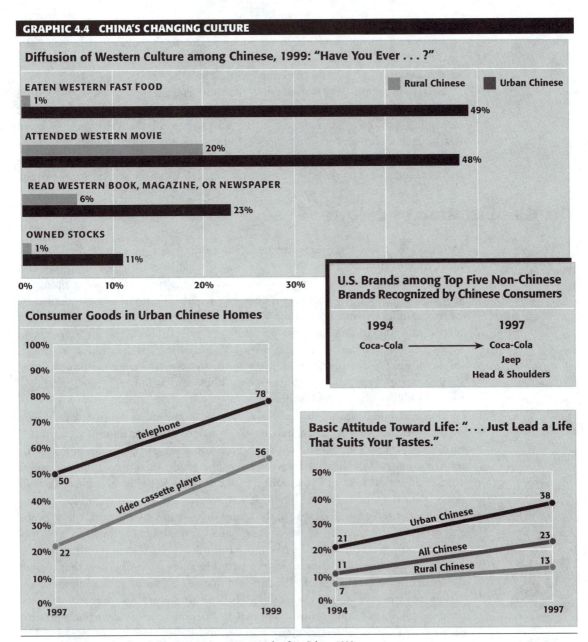

Diffusion of Western Culture among Chinese, 1999: "Have You Ever . . . ?"

■ Rural Chinese   ■ Urban Chinese

EATEN WESTERN FAST FOOD
1%
49%

ATTENDED WESTERN MOVIE
20%
48%

READ WESTERN BOOK, MAGAZINE, OR NEWSPAPER
6%
23%

OWNED STOCKS
1%
11%

0%   10%   20%   30%

U.S. Brands among Top Five Non-Chinese Brands Recognized by Chinese Consumers

1994	1997
Coca-Cola ——————→	Coca-Cola
	Jeep
	Head & Shoulders

Consumer Goods in Urban Chinese Homes

100%
90%
80%   78
70%
Telephone
60%   56
50% 50
Video cassette player
40%
30%
20% 22
10%
0%   1997   1999

Basic Attitude Toward Life: ". . . Just Lead a Life That Suits Your Tastes."

50%
40%   38
Urban Chinese
30%   23
21   All Chinese
20%
11   Rural Chinese   13
10%
7
0%   1994   1997

Sources: 1994 and 1997 data from Gallup Organization, 1997; 1999 data from Palmer, 1999.

such as Egypt's, the collective, the group is much more important than the individual, and empowering the individual is equated with dividing the society. . . . And
that is why, for all of globalization's obvious power to elevate living standards, it is
going to be a tough, tough sell to all those millions who still say a prayer before they
ride the elevator. (2000, p. A-27)

In short, the beliefs, values, norms, and rituals of the emerging global culture,
which are predominantly derived from western industrial culture, are incompatible
with the perceptions and meanings of local nonwestern, often agrarian culture and
threatening to their integrity.

So what makes the difference between cultures like urban China and rural
Egypt? Perhaps one more idea about culture can help us understand: societies
not only construct culture, they construct social problems (Griswold, 1994, pp.
93–100). Unsettling things happen in societies all the time. People lose their jobs or
homes, disagree about religion and politics, are forced to adjust to new ways of
doing things, and watch children move away from home. But those things become
social problems only when the community assigns some problematic meaning to
them that is consistent with its culture and has some way of attributing a cause.

Take the issue of McDonaldization, the worldwide, pervasive spread of the principles used to run fast-food restaurants, which was discussed in Chapter 2 (Ritzer,
2000). As McDonald's established outlets in Moscow, Beijing, and other far-flung
locales, people flocked to them, standing in line for hours to try a Big Mac. In some
places, particularly in Asia, McDonald's is now considered a local phenomenon as
much as an agent of globalization (Watson, 1997); the meaning of McDonald's has
been constructed as something consistent with the local culture rather than bad.

In other places, however, McDonaldization has been interpreted as a social problem. For instance, a grass-roots "Slow Food" movement arose in Europe when an
Italian restaurant critic began inveighing against the opening of a McDonald's
restaurant in Rome (Ritzer, 2000, pp. 217–218). Italy and other European cultures
assign a great deal of meaning to food and eating. The culinary arts are highly
respected, and meals are long and convivial. Many Europeans were highly offended
by the idea that their culture was being invaded by cultural elements that they considered to be in complete opposition to their traditional values and rituals.
Although some Europeans were undoubtedly eating less-than-gourmet meals as
efficiently as possible when the Slow Food movement started (and still are), the
movement took hold in large part because McDonald's offered a convenient target.

Nevertheless, the demise of local culture is not always regarded as a loss, and the
spread of modern, western consumerism is not always seen as a problem. Indeed,
we feel confident in asserting that the world would be a better place if some traditions (war, slavery, infanticide, prejudice) did not survive. On the other hand, the
loss of a tradition or the demise of a culture reduces the richness of expression, perspective, and point of view that make human beings so diverse and so interesting.
When the world loses something like the stories and music of the Blasket Islands or
the poetry of the Gaelic language, social life everywhere is diminished.

Fortunately, even as modern western culture spreads across the globe, people are finding ways to preserve the local traditions that are meaningful to them. For example, many forms of traditional Irish culture, language, and music are being preserved, reproduced, and, in some ways, transformed. The vehicle is a contemporary Irish cultural industry on the Internet, in local clubs and community groups, and in small, specialized, "niche" concert venues, recording companies, and summertime festivals. Even as the elements of a traditional culture slip to the edges of everyday life, they can survive and grow in other forms.

Conclusion

When people visit the Indian Ocean city of Mombasa, Kenya, they often are surprised at the mix of cultures. For instance, it is not uncommon to see street preachers from elsewhere discussing either the Christian Bible or the Islamic Koran while using an interpreter to ensure that the message is understood in Swahili, the local language. The preachers often use microphones or speaker systems, an element that gives the event a decidedly western flavor. Thus, the local culture has adopted and assimilated some aspects of outside culture, which have changed life in Mombasa for some local people. But local customs and lifestyles are still very much alive. Throughout the world, in fact, it seems that local cultures can coexist, albeit uneasily at times, with global culture. There are four reasons why that would be so.

First, what really matters about culture is the sense of community that people—even individualistic Americans—derive from it. Although we are used to the sense of belonging that comes from being part of a territorial community, many of us are finding fulfillment in relational communities as well. Our links to others with similar interests and concerns may or may not diminish our links to others from our same geographic location, but they won't change the human need to join with others in creating shared meaning about the things and ideas around us.

Second, local culture is surprisingly resilient and durable, even in the face of threats from outside forces. Language, religion, beliefs, and values are deeply entrenched so that, instead of global culture replacing local culture, we often find that local culture can accommodate global culture. For example, Christian church services held in Africa incorporate local customs, music, dance, and language. Missionaries learned long ago that a foreign message is much more effective when it is presented in a local language.

Third, human beings have long been products of multiple subcultures. As a species, we are highly experienced in reconciling conflicting cultural demands and expectations. More important, it is extremely unlikely that all the world's peoples will suddenly become hostage to a single, global superculture. Complete homogenization is not possible as long as we are still subject to the influence of diverse families, friends, coworkers, social institutions, and other socializing agents.

Fourth, many people value cultural diversity for its own sake. They like to experience new things and ideas that add spice to life, and they don't want to abandon old customs and ideas that have deep personal meanings. They resist homogenization by learning and using Gaelic, worshipping in the same way as their ancestors, resurrecting some nearly forgotten craft or type of music, and savoring a fine meal with friends.

To be sure, globalization will continue to threaten local cultures. Clearly, modern, western culture is seeping into all corners of the globe, just as English is becoming a universal language. The result will certainly be some loss of cultural diversity. Local cultures will change, and some will disappear, as did the traditions of the Blasket Islands, swallowed up by globalization.

But at least some elements of local culture can survive those pressures. For one thing, human beings are likely to always be waging culture wars—some intense, others more frivolous—to preserve the cultural elements they most value. Such battles will be fought for centuries to come, and the process of cultural evolution will continue as it has since the dawn of time. At the same time, other people will joyously preserve many cultures and customs in some form, sometimes by the latest, most modern technologies. Irish Gaelic survives, and, if you look hard enough, you can find recordings of Blasket Islands songs and stories for sale on the Internet. Thus, cultural extinction is not a linear or inevitable process, and, unlike biological extinction, it does not have to be forever.

Key Concepts

1. Culture is a set of tangible and intangible elements that give shape and meaning to the everyday lives of a particular group of people. Culture includes beliefs, values, norms, material objects, rituals, technologies, and a host of other components. In addition to studying culture itself, sociologists also study the relationships between culture and social structure.

2. Culture provides the basis for communities, including those based on territory and those based on common interests and experiences. The latter, called relational communities, are becoming more important in postindustrial society.

3. Culture is socially constructed and is transmitted by socialization to newborn members of a society and by acculturation to newly arrived immigrants.

4. In modern societies, new cultural forms, ideas, and objects are continually being produced, promoted, distributed, and consumed. Cultural change is caused by the discovery or invention of new elements and by diffusion. Culture lag occurs when some material elements or technology change more rapidly than norms, values, and beliefs.

5. Can local cultures survive the threats of globalization and western culture? The answer appears to be a tentative "yes": local cultures can survive in some form, often with the assistance of modern technology.

Active Learning

1. Changes in Socialization Value: Interview. In this project, you will question an older American about his or her socialization experiences. What values were stressed when that person was a child? What agents of socialization were most important in his or her childhood? How has socialization changed since then?

a. Find a respondent, someone who is at least a generation (roughly 20 years) older than you but preferably at least 60—the older, the better. You can interview anyone, but this project might be an excellent excuse to call an older relative and renew family ties. Conduct the interview face to face or by phone.

b. Introduce yourself and the project. Tell your respondent that you are conducting interviews as an assignment for a college class and that responses will be held in strict confidence. You need to make that guarantee (and mean it) even if you are related to the respondent. A suggested introductory script is available at the Web site for this book, www.pineforge.com/snc.

c. Conduct the interview. A suggested format is available at the Web site, but you do not need to read the questions verbatim or follow a particular order. For this project, you can be informal and chatty—try to get the respondent to relax and talk about his or her childhood. What was expected of children then? What kind of relationship did your respondent have with his or her parents? How did discipline work? Make sure you record the current age of your respondent, the social class of his or her parents (rich, poor, middle class, etc.), and the setting in which the respondent was socialized (e.g., urban or rural). Take notes during the interview or, with the respondent's permission, tape the interview.

d. This step, which is optional, is designed to help you learn about cultural lag. During the interview, ask your respondent to think about the things (items of material culture and technologies) that were available to children then and the things that kids have today. Ask your respondent to identify the single biggest difference between then and now (an answer might be television or the Internet) and to evaluate its impact on family life and child rearing. Ask for opinions: has the change been good or bad for kids? For values? For family life? Whatever your respondent says, don't argue or react—just record the thoughts as completely as possible. If the interview bogs down, seek further information with a gentle prompt ("Can you tell me more about that?").

e. Summarize the interview. Review your notes or recording. Write a brief paper in which you summarize the thoughts of your respondent and relate them to this chapter. Identify the following, as relevant: norms, values, material culture, technology, rituals, and symbols.

2. Faculty Doors as Symbolic Statements: Observation Research. (Adapted from an exercise designed by John W. Eby, Messiah College.) In this group exercise, you will study some naturally occurring symbolic statements, postings on office doors, to help you develop skills of observation, use your sociological imagination, and understand one aspect of campus culture. Postings on faculty doors are symbolic statements of individual beliefs and values and symbolic representations of the subcultures in the area the doors are located.

a. In class, break into groups of four to six. With your group, visit the campus building or the section of a building to which you have been assigned by your instructor. Be prepared to explain what you are doing to anyone who asks. You may also talk with those in the offices in the area you visit to get additional information.

b. Observe what is posted on office doors in order to "read" the subculture of the area. Record your observations on the worksheet available at the Web site for this book, www.pineforge.com/snc.

c. Share observations with other members of your group. Be prepared to summarize your findings for the class as a whole.

3. Cultural Diversity: Data Analysis. This chapter focuses on the tension between globalization and cultural diversity. How much cultural diversity is there in the world? You often hear that "people are pretty much the same wherever you go." Is that really true? This project may be done as a group or individually.

For this exercise, you will use data from the World Values Survey, which was administered to representative samples of the populations of about forty societies in the early 1990s. You will observe responses to two items that measure socialization values: how important it is for children to be obedient and how important it is for children to be independent.

The results for ten of the forty societies are presented at our Web site (www.pineforge.com/snc) in three tables. The first table simply lists the nations in rank order for each variable, the second organizes the nations in terms of geographical regions, and the third groups the societies in terms of affluence and quality of life. Study the tables and answer the following questions. Your instructor may suggest some additional items for analysis.

a. Analyze how much diversity there is. Look at Table 1 (Rankings) on our Web site. How much difference is there between nations? What is the relationship between the two variables, obedience and independence? For example, do societies that stress obedience tend to deemphasize independence?

b. Analyze patterns of differences by geographical region (Table 2) on our Web site. For example, do Asian nations stress different values than European nations? To manage the comparisons, you might calculate average scores for each region. Instructions for doing so are available at the Web site.

c. Analyze differences in socialization values by level of affluence. Do poor nations stress different values than more affluent nations? Are poor nations more "traditional"? Do they stress obedience more? Why might such differences arise? Again, to manage the comparisons, you might calculate average scores for each region; instructions are available at the Web site.

d. Write a brief paper evaluating your three analyses. Remember that you are making the comparisons with very limited samples. If this is a group project, be prepared to discuss your conclusions with other members of your group.

How Culture Shapes Schooling

STEVEN BRINT

Sociologists have long been aware that the world's educational systems are converging on a common form of organization, a common set of subjects to be taught, and a common set of mechanisms for evaluating student performance. A cross-national study undertaken twenty years ago by sociologist Alex Inkeles showed the spread of a standard set of educational practices that defined schooling throughout the world—even in the most remote and isolated villages. Those standard practices included public funding and responsibility for schooling; compulsory attendance for a set number of years; a ladder structure connecting all levels of schooling, from preschool to higher education; formally prepared and certified teachers; an administrative hierarchy of superintendents, principals, and teaching staff; school days and years of similar length; primary school curricula comprising the same subjects—language, literature, math, science, social studies, and arts—with the same emphases on language and math; and regular testing to measure how well students are learning the curricular materials (Inkeles & Sirowy, 1983). International tests of achievement, which had come into existence in the 1960s, were, by the time Inkeles was writing, leading to a new kind of "space race"—countries were competing to reach the stratosphere in their students' average mean scores in math, science, and reading.

Why do we see so much standardization in the midst of so much human diversity? Some point to Western "hegemony," the capacity of North American and European elites to impose their own conceptual schemes on the rest of the world. Others agree that the global system of schooling is based on a vision of modernity originating in the West, but they argue that it is now endorsed freely in countries around the world (Meyer, Nagel, & Snyder, 1993). That vision of modernity links individual development to social progress through the medium of schooling. Undoubtedly, the first generation of postcolonial leaders in the developing world found the idea of mass public schooling to be both a symbol of modernity and a means of economic development. In the words of one of those leaders, Sekou Toure of Guinea: "Man's social behavior and economic activities are directly conditioned by the quality of his . . . education. It is in order to free the youth of this country from all the social evils inherited from the past that [we] are anxious to develop educational facilities and allocate an important share of . . . [the] budget to educational purposes" (Toure, 1965, p. 125).

The active efforts of Western elites to build global institutions should not be discounted. In the years after World War II, educational consultants from the industrial societies actively spread a vision of modern schooling linking individual development and social progress. In recent years, the World Bank, which wields unusual clout throughout the world, has been a particularly important advocate of that vision of modern schooling in the developing world.

The world's educational systems have not become alike in every respect, however. In the remainder of this essay, I discuss some differences in teaching and learning in a number of different countries, especially Japan, the United States, and France. The differences provide a window on the important sociological concept of culture. Understanding differences in cultural understandings remains an important part of social analysis.

Two social psychologists, Harold Stevenson and James Stigler, spent several years comparing primary school teachers in Japan, China, and the United States (Stevenson & Stigler,

1992). Their studies included observations, interviews with teachers, and analyses of videotapes of instruction. The two researchers concluded that American teachers are, by and large, highly caring and sensitive to children's interests and needs and excel in kindness and empathy. In the words of another observer, American teachers "have a knack for discerning latent grace in an awkward gesture" and "applaud those who try no matter how slight their success" (Jackson, Boorstrom, & Hansen, 1993, p. 259). In Asia, by contrast, teachers are expected, above all, to be skilled performers. The teacher's job is to lead students skillfully through coherent and engaging lesson plans that eventually bring them to new knowledge. Teachers are expected to be lively and to engage students' attention, but they do not feel pressured to be sensitive and nurturing. "As with the actor or musician, the substance of the curriculum becomes the script or the score: the goal is to perform the role or piece as effectively and creatively as possible" (Stevenson & Stigler, 1992, pp. 166–167). Not surprisingly, as Graphic 1 shows, teachers in Asia choose clarity and enthusiasm as the most important attributes of good teachers, while teachers in the United States choose sensitivity and patience far more frequently.

Children in a classroom in Muroto, Japan. Japanese schools stress effort, discipline, and order. Graffiti and vandalism are seldom problems because students, not janitors, normally clean the schools. Why make a mess when you are going to have to clean it up?

Japanese teachers also are far more likely to consider school performance to depend primarily on effort rather than ability, the reverse of the American pattern. Stevenson and Stigler describe one scene from a Japanese classroom that would probably never occur in an American classroom. A young Japanese student was having trouble drawing a three-dimensional cube. The teacher called the boy to the board and asked him to draw the cube. The boy failed repeatedly, but the teacher kept the boy at the board, providing help and asking the class whether the boy was improving. The boy showed no visible signs of embarrassment; he remained at the board for nearly a full hour until he finally produced a passable

T O P I C A L   E S S A Y

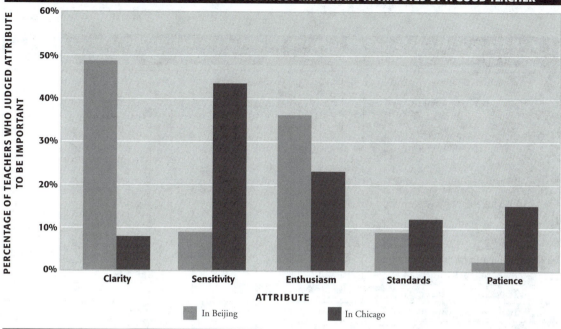

GRAPHIC 1   TEACHERS' JUDGMENTS ABOUT THE MOST IMPORTANT ATTRIBUTES OF A GOOD TEACHER

Source: Stevenson and Stigler, 1992, p. 167.

three-dimensional cube. Errors are not regarded as cause for embarrassment in Japanese classrooms or a threat to students' self-esteem. Instead, they are seen as an index of what students still need to learn and a necessary means to improvement.

At the upper reaches of the French and English secondary school systems, the most admired teachers embody a third distinct cultural style. Teachers in those systems have broad, esoteric knowledge and are at ease with the repartee of refined society. The approved style is marked by witty lectures, provocative questioning, and bantering exchanges with students. The English literary critic Cyril Connolly provides a reminiscence of one such teacher at Eton, the leading British preparatory school:

> Wells taught the classical specialists; he was a fine cricketeer and a judge of claret, a man of taste with a humour of understatement. . . . [He] was theatrical, he liked knotty points and great issues, puns and dramatic gestures. He was . . . fond of paradoxes and we learnt to turn out a bright essay on such a subject as "Nothing succeeds like failure" or "Nothing fails like success." (Connolly, 1938/1973, p. 220)

In line with the values of their teachers, elite English and French secondary students are expected to show signs of brilliance, not mere correctness or competence. Sociologist Pierre Bourdieu (1988, pp. 195–208) conducted a study of some 150 student records from an elite preparatory school for girls in Paris. Bourdieu analyzed the remarks instructors made supporting grades on each of several exercises submitted by the girls (Graphic 2). He found

GRAPHIC 2   SOCIAL CLASS AND EVALUATION OF TWENTY-THREE STUDENTS IN A PRIVATE GIRLS' SCHOOL IN PARIS

Occupation and Residence of Student's Father	Simplistic, silly	Servile, vulgar	Insipid, flat	Clumsy, slow	Poor, partial, narrow	Dull, boring, mediocre	Empty, banal, bland, conventional, superficial	Just about correct	Awkward, gauche, confused, woolly	Flabby, nice, puerile, childish	Strong, vigorous	Sincere	Interesting	Full, vast, rich	Ease, skill	Fine, ingenious, subtle, intelligent	Cultivated	Personal, lively	Mastery, research, philosophical spirit
Tradesman, provinces		■		■			■												
Tradesman, provinces										■			■						
Craftsman, provinces										■									
Chief technician, provinces				■	■				■										
Tax clerk, provinces	■					■													
Chief technician, Paris			■		■			■											
Post office clerk, Paris					■		■												
Health visitor, Paris						■		■											
Tax collector, Paris					■														
Engineer, Paris									■			■				■			
Company secretary, Paris										■									
Managing director, Paris																			
Sales director, Paris			■	■						■						■			
Export director, Paris																			■
Diplomat, Paris							■		■										
Secondary teacher, Paris													■						
Secondary teacher, Paris																■			
Pharmacist, provinces							■									■			
Doctor, Paris		■																	
Doctor, Paris																■		■	■
Surgeon, Paris										■	■								■
Law professor, Paris										■						■			■
Philosophy professor, Paris										■		■							■

Source: Adapted from Bourdieu, 1988.

that the descriptive adjectives "careful," "conscientious," and "thorough" were located closer to the pole indicating poor performance (marks supported by such adjectives as "simplistic" and "insipid") than to the pole indicating excellent performance (supported by such adjectives as "masterful," "cultivated," and "ingenious"). Nor were the adjectives "sensible" or "right" terms of praise in this hierarchy of judgments. They, too, were slightly closer to the pole that indicated poor performance. The scale of evaluating remarks corresponded closely to the socioeconomic background of the girls. Girls whose parents were highly educated were more often labeled with adjectives suggesting brilliance. Those lower down the social scale were more often labeled with adjectives suggesting mere competence.

The U.S. educational system has long stressed the ideal of equal opportunity for all students, even those with learning disabilities. The system is expected to accommodate students of very different aspirations and abilities. The end result is that a higher proportion of Americans enroll in higher education than in any other country in the world.

Culture can be defined as a set of cognitive, expressive, and emotional understandings shared by members of a group and communicated through symbols. To be effective, teaching practices must align with the understandings of the culture in which they exist and thereby fit the expectations of students who have become attuned to that culture. Where those alignments do not exist, students are likely to be confused or hostile and teachers less effective than they otherwise would be. A "caring," American-style teacher might confuse Asian students, just as a "cultivated," European-style teacher might seem insufferable to American students. Divergent national ideals of teaching and learning suggest that no universally valid set of pedagogical principles exist. Instead, the ability of teachers to align with the particular expectations of their culture will always be an important part of their effectiveness.

Sociologists usually are not satisfied simply to describe differences among cultures. They also search for the underlying causes of those differences. In the cases described in this essay, some deeper features of social organization are evident beyond the differences in cultural understandings. For example, behind the "caring" ideal of the American teacher, we can see the imprint of the long effort in the United States to provide equal opportunity to students from heterogeneous backgrounds and the need to move students of mixed abilities through a system that depends on large numbers of students entering higher education.

In contrast, behind the "skilled performer" ideal of the Japanese teacher, we can see the relative homogeneity of Japanese society and the special status in which Japanese teachers are held. Japanese teachers undergo a much longer apprenticeship than American teachers. They are paid as well as other professionals and are addressed by students in deferential terms. The Japanese term for teacher, *sensei,* implies great respect and applies equally to teachers at all levels, including university professors. Japanese teachers also have shorter in-class days, leaving them with longer periods in which to prepare their lessons and discuss them with other teachers.

This French school provides a rigorous education to young students. How well students perform in class and on national examinations will determine whether they will enter the elite higher-education system. The system is widely accepted in France and other countries, but it is seen as elitist and even discriminatory by many Americans.

Finally, behind the "cultivated" ideal of the French elite secondary school teacher, we can see, among other things, the residue of a class struggle between "court society" and the lower classes in French society. That struggle originally pitted the aristocracy against the plebian classes at a time when the aristocracy set the tone for so-called polite society. As the aristocracy receded in importance, other classes, such as urban professionals and intellectuals, took up the old aristocratic ideals as a way of expressing values markedly different from those of the more sober-minded, narrowly practical, and profit-conscious business classes. Those cultural values persist at elite levels of schooling, because they serve an important function in marking off the elite from the "merely competent." They are reinforced by a higher-education system that has a clearly distinguished elite track, the *grandes écoles,* whose graduates monopolize the highest-level jobs in French society. The same relationship obtained between the cultivated classes and the elite English universities of Oxford and Cambridge until those schools became more science-oriented and open to the middle classes in the 1950s and 1960s (Soares, 1999).

By looking at education comparatively, social scientists are able to show that many styles of instruction can work, if the understandings and expectations of teachers and students about what education means and how it is produced are aligned. Social scientists are also able to probe for the roots of the particular teaching and learning styles that different societies develop. This is one example of what social scientists mean when they say they "study culture."

Thinking about the Essay

Chapter 4 discussed globalization and the survival of local cultures. How does this essay fit into that discussion?

Local Gods and Universal Faiths

LESTER R. KURTZ

When our bus arrives in Harran, an ancient city in what is now southeastern Turkey near the Syrian border, children dressed in brightly colored clothing pour out of the mud and straw "beehive" houses to greet us. We descend the hillside to the ruins of the old city. The occasion is an interfaith symposium on Abraham, founder of the three major Western religions—Judaism, Christianity, and Islam—who lived in Harran thirty centuries ago.

We make our way through the crowds, past television cameras and security guards armed with guns and cell phones. We sit under a large open tent amid the ruins. Men's choirs sing ancient Jewish and Muslim prayers, and a girls' choir sings in Aramaic, the language of Jesus.

Our group includes Jewish rabbis and scholars from Israel (including an Israeli family with two young boys), a Muslim journalist from Tanzania, and the papal nuncio from the Vatican. We have Syrian Orthodox nuns from Iraq, Muslims from Turkey, Protestants and Catholics from Europe, and three Americans: a retired clergyman, a priest now teaching in

These "beehive" houses are still found in Harran. People have lived in such structures for at least several hundred years.

Istanbul, and a sociologist. Soon the patriarch of the Eastern Orthodox Church arrives from Istanbul, formerly Constantinople, the capital of the Eastern Empire for more than a thousand years and a battleground for many of the Crusades of the Middle Ages. He is followed by the head of the Russian Council of Muftis, other Muslim religious leaders, a head rabbi, the provincial governor, a member of parliament, and other dignitaries. Each new arrival is greeted by a rush of cameras and reporters.

According to a leader of the sponsoring Interfaith Dialogue Platform, the gathering is the first of its kind in the 5,000-year history of Harran. The conference is front-page news because the leaders of the three ancient traditions are meeting not to insult or shoot one another but to celebrate their common heritage. The goal of the conferences is no less than to think about how Jews, Christians, and Muslims can learn to appreciate each other and live together in peace.

In today's global village, we (especially those of us who are Americans) tend to think that something 100 years old is an antique—radio stations play "oldies" from only 20 years ago. For the people of Harran, however, the last 500 years are recent history. Humans have inhabited the planet for a long time and have changed how they live in many ways. Throughout most of human history, people lived in relative isolation, but all that changed during the twentieth century. People have always been in contact with other civilizations through trade and war, but the scale and scope of such encounters have increased exponentially in the modern world. Our friends and colleagues are not just the people in our tribe or village but include people from around the world and from a variety of cultures—we truly live in a global village.

We also are more likely than ever before to encounter people from other faith traditions. Most human beings interpret the world through a religious lens (unlike many people in modern colleges and universities). Most people worship God with a perspective similar to that of their ancestors and with rituals that go back hundreds, if not thousands, of years. Their faith shapes their daily lives and gets them through life's crises; it helps them to interpret the origin and meaning of the cosmos and to understand their place in it. Religious traditions provide the moral bedrock and ethical training of entire civilizations and guide people through life's changes—birth, puberty, marriage, and death. They also teach people how to wage war and how to make peace.

During the 5,000 years that human beings have lived in Harran, people have gotten very good at war. We are now so good at fighting that we threaten to blow each other up with nuclear weapons or some other form of mass destruction. One major question is whether our religious traditions and institutions will justify the continued use of militaries to solve our large-scale problems or help us find a path to peace. All the world's religions have at one time or another promoted killing and denounced anyone who followed in a different tradition. In these dangerous times, we may need to find some way, as Abraham did, to break with certain aspects of the past while building new institutions of faith on ancient cultural foundations.

The life of Abraham was remarkable in many ways. Although he is considered by Jews, Christians, and Muslims to be the model man of faith, people of his own day considered him a rebel, perhaps even antireligious. He broke with many of the ancient religious practices of his own family and at the age of 75 left his family's homeland and migrated to another region (see Graphic 1).

A sociological perspective sheds an interesting light on the story of Abraham and his first wife, Sarah, and his second wife, Hajar (reputedly an Egyptian woman who had been Sarah's slave). That perspective illuminates 3,000 years of history and the relationship between that

GRAPHIC 1   ABRAHAM'S JOURNEY THROUGH ANCIENT LANDS

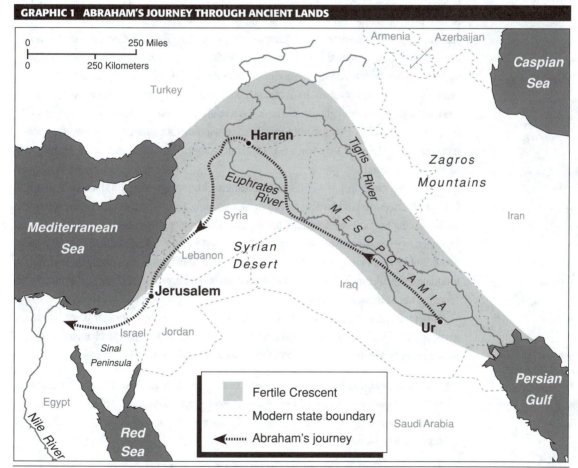

Source: Adapted from World ORT Union, 1996.

time and now. Like us, Abraham, Sarah, and Hajar lived in a time of economic, social, and cultural change. They lived at the beginning of the agricultural era; we are at the dawn of the information age. New developments in the economy were changing everything; wandering tribes were beginning to settle down in villages and even small cities. People were trading across large distances, pushing back the boundaries of the unknown, and witnessing the migration of much of the population around the Fertile Crescent, rich land east of the Mediterranean Sea. Those contradictory trends—settling down and moving—were great historical movements that affected the nature of human life and beliefs about God for millennia to come.

Economic and cultural change go hand in hand, and ideas about God and methods of making a living (modes of production) affect and change one another. As people began to change their ways of living, they also developed different images of God; changing theologies in turn promoted different ways of life. Hunting and gathering societies, for example, envision multiple and sometimes equally important gods and spirits, to reflect their own conditions of equality and mutual interdependence. Agricultural societies are more hierarchical, so the gods are organized into hierarchies of importance and power. The end product is monotheism and universalism. In Abraham's time, most gods were considered local and were associated with a single place. There were many gods, each of them representing a different aspect of reality or a natural force, such as wind or rain. Some were believed to protect cities (like Helen of Troy, just west of Harran); others were clan gods, often represented as statues (or idols).

Like all the great prophets and spiritual leaders of human history, Abraham built on the faith of his ancestors, but he also forged dramatic innovations—and got in trouble for doing so. According to tradition, Abraham, Sarah, and Hajar rejected the common idea that God belonged to one clan or lived in one place. Their God was the Creator of the universe who was full of love and compassion for "all the families of the earth." Thus Abraham laid the foundations for the monotheism and universalism that emerged in the later traditions of Judaism, Christianity, and Islam.

Abraham believed that God told him to migrate with his family to another place. Abraham was convinced that God would go with them and that God had told him to change his name from Abram to Abraham. According to the Hebrew scriptures (Genesis 12:1–3),

> Now the Lord said to Abram, "Go from your country and your kindred and your father's house to the land that I will show you. I will make of you a great nation, and I will bless you, and make your name great, so that you will be a blessing . . . and in you all the families of the earth shall be blessed."

According to the Islamic tradition, Abraham left Harran because of religious persecution. It must have been a scene of intense conflict: according to the tradition, the king tried to

The "Abraham Mosque" in Sanliurfa, Turkey. Legend has it that an ancient king wanted to kill Abraham and had him thrown into a massive fire. But God turned the fire into water at this site, a place revered by Jews, Christians, and especially Muslims.

execute Abraham in Sanliurfa (near Harran) for his rebellion against local religious practices. Abraham miraculously escaped and left the country, becoming an immigrant much like those who today are forced out of their old culture because of social forces beyond their control.

Abraham, Sarah, and Hajar were open minded and generous in their attitude toward others and were convinced that God would bless them as they migrated. Abraham was not bitter and prayed to God to bless his father and the family he had left behind.

Abraham's encounters with cultures other than the one in which he was raised probably stimulated a great deal of thinking. As immigrants in new lands, he and his wives were forced to change their perspective about many things, including ideas about God. Abraham may have changed his opinion about the meaning of life, the nature of the universe, and the religious rituals he had practiced growing up; as his experience broadened, his cultural outlook became less local and more universal. The trend toward universalism that marked Abraham's thinking is, of course, widespread in the modern world—people on the other side of the globe seem much closer to us today than they did even a generation ago. Universalism reflects the growth of ties among societies, the growth of relations among different types of people, and the need to build new nations out of disparate ethnic, racial, and religious groups.

Abraham also believed that, no matter where he lived, God provided all the basic necessities and blessings of life: food, land, even children. That belief did not distinguish Abraham much from his ancestors, except that Abraham believed that the God he worshipped was the

God of all creation and blessed all people. The story of how that belief was tested is a dramatic one, celebrated everywhere in Western art and literature. Despite the promise of many descendants, Abraham was an old man when his first child, a son named Ishmael, was borne by his second wife, Hajar. Then, when Abraham was 100, his 90-year-old first wife, Sarah, gave birth to Isaac. Although traditions disagree as to which son was involved, Abraham believed that God told him to make a human sacrifice. Abraham climbed a mountain with his son prepared to carry out God's command. Just as he was about to kill his son, he heard an angel of the Lord commanding him not to. He saw a ram caught in a thicket and substituted it for his son, renouncing the violence of human sacrifice that was probably widespread at the time.

As we repeat and discuss stories, those of us who are gathered in Harran for the Abraham symposium gain a new sense of our 3,000-year common heritage. Despite the fact that Jews, Christians, and Muslims have been killing each other for centuries, they share common ancestors and a belief in the same God. As I watch the gathering with a sociological eye, it seems to me that the parallels between the social transformations of Abraham's time and of ours are striking: people encountering one another across diverse cultures and creating new ways of thinking about the world and of living together. I wonder what new spiritual movements might emerge from the turmoil of the twenty-first century and whether a new universalism similar to Abraham's vision would help us figure out how to live together in a global village booby-trapped for self-destruction.

Thinking about the Essay

Is the point of this essay that all religions are merging into a single faith? Would such a consolidation be desirable? Given the pressures of globalization, is it inevitable?

5 Inequality

*Are the rich getting richer
and the poor getting poorer?*

The world may be developing into a single global village, but not everyone is living on Main Street. Consider, for instance, Guler Sabanci, who lives, metaphorically speaking, in the mansion on the hill. She is a top executive in her family's company, the largest privately owned enterprise in Turkey. The family is worth an estimated 4.5 billion dollars and is involved in a variety of areas, including banking, tires (Guler's major area of responsibility), cigarettes, and automobiles. Guler began attending family business meetings when she was three and gradually worked her way up to an executive position after college. She is the head of four related family-owned companies, on several other company boards, and involved in other service and educational organizations. She devotes her spare time to reviving the Turkish wine industry (Rossant, 1999).

Closer to Main Street is Lauren Caulder, who comes from a middle-class, suburban American family. Her father worked in the city, and her mother was a housewife. Lauren enjoyed a secure and advantaged childhood and did everything she was supposed to at home, at school, and then on the job. She is now a professional, respected by her colleagues, better educated than her parents, and earning more than her father ever did. Yet Lauren feels cheated. Even when her income is combined with her husband's, she knows that she cannot match the lifestyle of her parents. The big house in the suburbs, the good schools for her kids, the comfort of economic security—it all seems to be slipping further away. She has worked hard and fulfilled all expectations, but, somehow, she "never got to Candyland." For all her efforts, she still cannot provide for herself and her children what her parents provided for her (Newman, 1993, pp. 2–3).

Nevertheless, Lauren is far better off than Sadisah (the only name on her pay stub), who lives in Indonesia. Sadisah considers herself fortunate to have a job in a plant where she assembles tennis shoes for a huge multinational corporation. In parts of her country where civil strife has had its harshest effects, many have no job, no home, and no food or medicine except that donated by relief agencies. Still, Sadisah is hardly prospering. She typically works 60 hours a week and earns about 14 cents an hour. Her salary (without overtime) works out to $8.40 a week, or about $430 a year. At the same time, the shoes she makes, which cost about 12 cents a pair to assemble, are sold in more affluent nations for $80 or more. The top executives of the shoe corporation earn a million dollars or more a year, and the company pays well-known athletes millions of dollars to endorse its products. How many years would Sadisah have to work to buy a pair of the shoes she makes? How many lifetimes would she have to work to have the wealth of the Sabanci family or even the Caulders (Ballinger, 1993)?

These extremes of wealth and poverty probably seem as old as human society itself. Doesn't it always work this way: a small group controls most of the wealth, leaving the rest of the population to divide up whatever is left over. Don't the rich always find a way to get richer? Aren't the poor always with us?

As we enter a new millennium, those questions about wealth and want seem especially appropriate—and on more than one level. If you recall, one of the central trends listed in Chapter 1 was growing inequality within and across societies. On a global level, wealth and resources appear to be increasingly concentrated in the hands of a few nations, corporations, and individuals, and a growing percentage of the world's population, like Sadisah, finds itself locked in unrelenting poverty (United Nations, 1999, p. 3). Graphic 5.1 displays the growing income gap between the richest and poorest fifths of the world's population. In 1965, the richest 20% of the population received almost 70% of the income, while the poorest 20% got only 2.25%, an income ratio of about 31:1. In other words, in 1965, for every dollar of income that went to the poorest 20%, $31 went to the richest 20%. As you can see, the income gap has generally increased; in 1997, it stood at 74:1, more than double the degree of income inequality in 1965.

On the level of individual nations, increasing inequality is also a common trend (United Nations, 1999, p. 3). Even in the United States, the self-proclaimed bastion of equality and opportunity, inequality is greater and increasing faster than in any other advanced industrial nation (Gottschalk & Smeeding, 1997, p. 634). We examine those trends in greater detail later in the chapter.

This chapter discusses some of the reasons for inequality at both levels. But first, let's introduce some sociological concepts that can help to make sense of this complex and multilayered phenomenon.

Sociological Perspectives on Inequality

Inequality has been a central concern of sociology virtually from the beginning of the discipline, and contemporary sociologists have a well-developed toolkit for

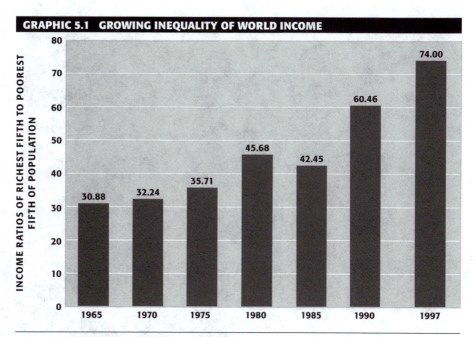

GRAPHIC 5.1 GROWING INEQUALITY OF WORLD INCOME

Sources: 1965–1990 data from Korzeniewicz and Moran, 1997; 1997 data from United Nations, 1999.

describing and analyzing what they call **stratification,** the system by which valued goods and services are distributed in a society. The most obvious aspect of stratification is wealth and income, but virtually anything—health, life expectancy, literacy, happiness—can be distributed unequally. The stratification system is a part of the economic system of a society, but it is also closely connected with politics, culture, the educational system, and other institutions.

One of the features of stratification that interests sociologists is social mobility, individuals' ability to move up or down within the stratification system. In some societies (caste or closed stratification systems), mobility is minimal and people inherit the status of their parents. An example of such a system can be found in traditional India. For thousands of years, the population was divided into four main castes, ranging from the Brahmins (highly respected priests and scholars) at the top to impoverished peasants at the bottom. Generally, each caste and subcaste was linked to an occupation (for example, farmer, artisan, or merchant) and people inherited their occupation from their parents.

Other societies have an open stratification system, in which individuals can compete for the higher, more lucrative and powerful positions, albeit with a relative advantage or disadvantage from their birth families, their race or gender, or other personal characteristics. In the United States and other advanced industrial societies, the stratification system is relatively open, and people can attain positions in the class system that differ radically from those of their parents.

The effects of inequality start early in life. A mother and six-month-old baby share a bed and uncovered mattress in Warren County, North Carolina (top), home to the highest poverty rate in the state. Many families in that area lack indoor plumbing and running water. These conditions produce higher levels of sickness and a poorer quality of life. The situation is especially bleak for homeless families in the developing world, such as this mother and her young daughter, who live on the streets of Jakarta, Indonesia (middle). By contrast, the little girl in the bottom photograph has more material comforts and probably better learning opportunities, such as books around the house, to develop physically and mentally. Material comforts do not always translate into a stable emotional environment, but they can provide basic necessities that healthy children need.

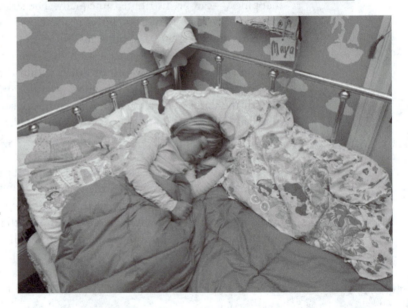

Social inequality and mobility are complex issues and must be approached from several angles. This chapter focuses on social class and, especially, on the distribution of income and wealth, but that is only one aspect of stratification. Chapter 6 approaches the topic from a different angle and focuses on racial and ethnic inequality, and Chapter 7 investigates patterns of inequality based on gender. All three chapters examine the ways in which class, race and ethnicity, and gender interact and intersect to form a matrix of domination that shapes the life chances of individuals, the rhythms of everyday social life, and the structure and operations of the larger society (Hill-Collins, 1991, pp. 225–227).

To understand the need for this multidimensional approach, consider the three women whose biographies opened this chapter. Their access to power and valued resources is determined partly by their social class, but race and gender also shape their lives. Sadisah's position in society, for example, has a lot to do with her family's heritage. In Indonesia, ethnic Chinese often fare better than native peoples like Sadisah and her family. In Guler Sabanci's case, gender is an important issue. Her family is very traditional—she is the only woman who talks business with the men before meals (while her female relatives do the cooking). Furthermore, in spite of her high status in the company, it took her two years to persuade her family to permit her to live alone, an uncommon living arrangement for a Turkish woman (Rossant, 1999, p. 192). Lauren Caulder's experience may not seem to be so dramatically shaped by class, race, and gender, because it is similar to what most middle-class Americans experience. But make no mistake: it is, as you will learn in this chapter and the next two.

The sociological perspective has another important lesson to impart about social inequality. People have long been fascinated by wealth and concerned about (or repelled by) poverty and have developed a variety of explanations, ranging from the theological ("It is God's will") to the genetic ("The strong will prevail") for patterns of stratification. But sociologists believe that inequality is a social phenomenon, the result of complex economic, political, and cultural forces. The social nature of inequality is reflected in the fact that it varies across time and space, sometimes increasing, sometimes falling, and sometimes approaching zero. Inequality is a part of social life and requires a sociological perspective to understand fully.

Sociologists agree that inequality is a social phenomenon but not on why it exists. The rest of this section examines some of the most influential sociological answers to the question of why inequality exists. Many useful and important theories and concepts have been developed, but most, in one way or another, have roots in the ideas of the founders of the discipline, especially Karl Marx, Max Weber, and Emile Durkheim (see Chapter 2).

Class Interests and Inequality

Inequality was a central concern for Marx. He thought that conflict between social classes was the fundamental reality of social life. He defined social class specifically in terms of people's relationship to the means of production, that is, the tools, resources, and organizations by which a society produces and distributes goods and services. In an agricultural society, the means of production would include draft animals and plows, while in an industrial society they would include machinery, energy supplies (petroleum, natural gas), financial institutions, and transportation systems. According to Marx, in an industrial society, the capitalist class, or bourgeoisie, controls the means of production and does whatever is necessary to squeeze wealth out of the workers, or proletariat.

A Marxist scholar might see today's increasing inequality as simply another case of the capitalist class expropriating wealth from other classes. In fact, as discussed in Chapter 2, Marxist-based world systems theory provides a powerful way of viewing modern day inequality both within and between nations. On the other hand, most modern day sociologists would agree that Marx placed too much stress on economic factors, a shortcoming that Max Weber addressed.

Three Dimensions of Stratification

Weber extended Marx's analysis by demonstrating that inequality has (at least) three different, closely related dimensions: property (class), prestige (status), and power. The **property,** or class, dimension is the closest to the Marxist conception of inequality. Weber agreed with Marx that the most important class distinction was between people who own or control income-producing property (that is, the capitalist class that holds investments and owns businesses) and those who do not. Weber also agreed that the owners generally dominate the nonowners. But he then went on to dissect the distinctions within those two broad categories. Property owners can be divided according to the nature of their assets (for example, large businesses, farms, small businesses), and nonowners can be differentiated according to the type and quality of skills they possess (for example, technicians and professionals, skilled laborers, unskilled laborers). Thus, each broad class could be subdivided into a multiplicity of smaller divisions.

The second dimension of stratification, according to Weber, is **prestige,** or the respect and honor accorded a person by others. The distribution of prestige reflects the cultural values of a society, and individuals or groups that exemplify those central values are accorded more prestige and deference. A martial society would regard warriors with great respect, while a religious society would have saints and martyrs as its cultural heroes. (What do the current cultural heroes of American society say about its values? Do they support the traditional values described in Chapter 4?) In many societies, group membership also affects prestige. For example, in the United States, certain groups (whites, males, Protestants) traditionally have commanded higher status regardless of class or wealth.

Prestige and social class position can be closely related, and it is not uncommon for respect and honor to increase with a person's wealth. However, those dimensions can vary independently. For example, a person involved in an illegal enterprise like drug trafficking may be quite wealthy (rank high on property) but be held in low esteem in the community (rank low on prestige). The reverse can also be true:

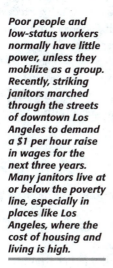

Poor people and low-status workers normally have little power, unless they mobilize as a group. Recently, striking janitors marched through the streets of downtown Los Angeles to demand a $1 per hour raise in wages for the next three years. Many janitors live at or below the poverty line, especially in places like Los Angeles, where the cost of housing and living is high.

a person devoted to serving the community or working with the poor (like Mother Theresa) may command great respect and be universally revered but live in poverty.

Weber's third dimension of inequality is related to the political system: **power** is the ability to affect decision making to favor one's interests. One source of power is, of course, wealth and property: politicians typically pay close attention to the needs and desires of the affluent. Fortunately for the middle class and the poor, however, power has its own dynamics and is not solely a function of money. The civil rights movement against legalized segregation in the American South, for example, was a successful attempt by African Americans, a relatively impoverished and powerless group, to improve their status in society.

Prestige can be linked to power in a variety of ways. For example, prestige is used as a power resource when billionaires, sports stars, or entertainers are allowed to testify about and influence public policy in Congress or at the White House. The person of average or below-average prestige rarely is consulted when it comes to public decision making. Also, many political issues involving beliefs and values (for example, abortion rights or gun control) are battles for prestige. Instead of fighting for position in the class hierarchy to gain power, the combatants are vying for prestige and public approval.

Weber's multidimensional model gives us more flexibility than Marx's model to explain how inequality is structured in a society. The three dimensions of inequality are independent of each other, and a change in one does not necessarily imply changes in the others. For example, income inequality is increasing in the United States today, but that does not mean that power and prestige are undergoing similar changes. In fact, recent declines in sexism and racism suggest that access to fame and political power is open to more Americans today than ever before.

Weber did not deny the power of the capitalist class, but he also saw that people at every level have means they can mobilize to pursue their interests and protect their resources. Factory owners might use their hiring and firing power to resist workers' demands for a pay raise, but the workers have the power to control membership in their unions and thus access to their jobs. Middle-class people with knowledge and skills that are in high demand, such as computer systems engineers in today's high-tech economy, also have power they can exchange for valued goods and services. Modern sociology continues to view inequality in the multidimensional style of analysis established by Weber.

The Functions of Inequality

Structural functionalism is one of the strongest analytical traditions in American sociology and has its roots in the work of Durkheim and many others (see Chapter 2). Structural functionalists believe that each part of human society is designed to perform some specific function, and the overall system functions smoothly only when all parts play out their roles. From that perspective, inequality is a central feature of society because it has a vital role to play.

Writing in the 1940s, two American sociologists, Kingsley Davis and Wilbert Moore (1945), argued that the purpose of inequality is to match qualified people with important positions, and they used a medical analogy to illustrate their reasoning. Some jobs in a modern hospital (for example, neurosurgeon) require higher levels of skill and more training than others (for example, receptionist or janitor). Jobs also vary in terms of their importance: a highly skilled neurosurgeon is a much more valuable resource than is a highly skilled janitor. The health (literally and figuratively) of society is best served if the most competent people are motivated to pursue the most difficult and important tasks (like neurosurgeon). Thus, the more important and demanding positions carry higher rewards (wealth and prestige) as a way of motivating people to attempt to achieve them. Far from being oppressive or exploitative, inequality is a way of matching competent individuals with top positions for the benefit of all.

That hypothesis might seem sensible enough at first glance, but there are a number of problems with it (see Tumin, 1953). First, it is difficult to define exactly how "important" a position is. Is the janitor really less important than the neurosurgeon? Could the hospital continue to function if all the neurosurgeons went to a convention for a month? Could it function if all the janitors went instead? In the United States, athletes and entertainers earn millions, but are they more "important" than elementary school teachers or police officers?

Second, the hypothesis assumes an open stratification system, with opportunities for upward (and downward) mobility, and deemphasizes the social and political processes that sustain privilege and inequality for the benefit of some. The hypothesis does not account for racial or gender discrimination or for the ways in which groups and individuals try to maintain their status and control their access to resources. In contrast, Weber recognized that occupational groups of all kinds (medical associations for neurosurgeons, labor unions for janitors) try to protect their share of the rewards. Physicians might support efforts to raise the standards of admission to medical school, thus artificially keeping the supply of doctors low and creating leverage for higher rewards. Labor unions try to win the exclusive right to represent a group of workers and then control who gets to join. The less open or fair the competition, the less likely it is that the social system can neutrally and objectively match talented individuals and important positions.

The Davis-Moore hypothesis may be fully applicable only to a pure meritocracy, a society in which the importance of each job would be objectively and clearly measured and in which a person's gender, race, or religion would be completely irrelevant. All advanced industrial societies have open stratification systems, but none of them, including the United States, approaches that ideal. Nevertheless, the Davis-Moore hypothesis does point out that inequality can play a positive role in society by motivating capable individuals to strive for important positions.

The Evolution of Inequality

The theories presented in the preceding section give us an array of important concepts for analyzing stratification in industrial societies. But it can be just as useful to understand how stratification systems have evolved over time—some sociologists analyze inequality in the context of the development of human society. Gerhard Lenski (1966; Lenski, Lenski, & Nolan, 1995) is a contemporary American sociologist who, like Marx and Weber, connects inequality primarily to the economic system of a society. He argues that the nature and degree of inequality and mobility reflect the **subsistence technology** of a society, or the manner in which basic needs such as food, shelter, and clothing are satisfied. Over the millennia, human beings have lived in societies supported by several different subsistence technologies, including hunting and gathering, agricultural, industrial, and, most recently, postindustrial. As you learned in Chapter 4, technology has a lot to do with culture. It also has a lot to do with stratification systems.

Although hunting and gathering societies are rare (perhaps nonexistent) today, all human beings lived in them until just 10,000 years ago. The first agricultural societies emerged in 8000 B.C., and most of the world's population still lives in societies in which basic needs are satisfied by some form of farming, whether simple gardening or more ambitious agricultural enterprises. The shift to industrial technology began just two centuries ago, with the application of machines to the tasks of production in agriculture, manufacturing, transportation, and other areas. The industrial societies of the world include Japan, Australia, most of the societies of western Europe, Canada, and the United States. In postindustrial societies, manufacturing and other industrial enterprises are being supplanted by new enterprises based on the control of information, computers and cyberspace, biomedical engineering, communications, and other advanced technologies. The United States is entering the postindustrial age, as are Japan and several nations of Europe.

Societies based on different subsistence technologies differ in hundreds of important ways, including, for example, population size. While hunting and gathering technology supports a limited number of people, agricultural technology can support populations in the hundreds of millions, even billions. Large cities and complex civilizations, including the ancient Chinese, Egyptian, Roman, and Aztec empires, were built on agriculture. However, industrial societies are many times more productive than even the most advanced agricultural societies and can support large populations at high standards of health and affluence. In fact, citizens of industrial societies enjoy the highest standards of living in history. The wealthiest, most powerful societies today are based on industrial technology, and the new, postindustrial era seems to augur even greater wealth and power. Those differences in economic productivity have important implications for the stratification system.

Hunting and Gathering Societies

Contrary to the idea that inequality is inevitable, families in hunting and gathering societies, such as Plains Indian tribes, varied hardly at all in their property, prestige, or power. There was little difference in lifestyle, amount of possessions, dress, or diet. There were no permanent or full time leaders (rulers), and decision making was based on consensus or agreement.

Gender and age were usually the only important sources of differentiation and inequality. The division of labor was based on gender (typically, men hunted while women gathered), but gender inequality was minimal. In decision making, the advice of elders would be given more weight in recognition of their wider experience and greater fund of information. Because hunting and gathering societies were small and homogeneous (indeed, the entire membership of the society might consist of blood relatives), racial and ethnic diversity was not an issue.

What little inequality existed in hunting and gathering societies often reflected differences in personal prestige, awarded to individuals with talent in a needed or valued area, like hunting, storytelling, or communication with spirits. In addition, the individuals in such a society were highly interdependent. People were constantly assisting each other in the struggle to secure food, safety, and health—everyone played a part in ensuring everyone else's welfare. As a result, everyone tended to be more or less equally important to the group.

Inequality was also minimal, in large part, because these societies produced so little wealth. In addition to having limited technology, they were nomadic and moved every few weeks or months as the seasons changed and as game migrated. Their possessions had to be portable or disposable, and clothing, weapons, and tools could not be accumulated. With this most basic of subsistence technologies, resources tended to be equally shared and quickly consumed.

Agricultural Societies

The earliest agricultural societies were not much different from hunting and gathering societies in the way they were organized. The people adopted simple new technologies for gardening a small plot and tending a few animals, but the effect on structures of inequality evolved slowly. Changes became more obvious as more advanced agricultural technology evolved. Social classes and large differences in wealth grew as societies became more productive and larger in population. The largest and most powerful agricultural societies, such as ancient Egypt and the pre-Columbian Aztec empire, were notable for the extreme differences between the small but wealthy elite class and the miserable conditions of the majority of the population.

Advances in agricultural technology, such as irrigation systems and plows, made it possible to increase the amount of land that each worker could cultivate (environmental and other conditions permitting, of course), thus creating a stable surplus of food and other goods and services. The surplus was crucial to the development of human society because it freed some people from laboring in the fields and supported additional occupations, such as weavers, toolmakers, and carpenters. The surplus thus laid the groundwork for dramatic increases in population size, specialization, and further advances in productivity. It also created the possibility of greater inequality.

Elite families, clans, or classes often dominated agricultural societies, becoming wealthy and powerful because of their control of two equally important resources: land and labor. Work in those preindustrial societies was **labor intensive,** that is, done by hand or with the aid of a draft animal. Thus, agricultural production depended on controlling not only the fields but also sufficient laborers to work in the fields.

The elites in agricultural societies expropriated a disproportionate share of the surplus. They used their resources to subsidize luxurious lifestyles and to coerce others, living far less luxuriously, to obey them. They differentiated themselves from ordinary citizens by giving themselves noble titles and passing their high status on to their children.

Often, the workers who produced the surplus resented their exploited position, and the landed aristocracy had to resort to force to reinforce their dominance and preserve internal order (and to conquer neighboring societies and commandeer their neighbors' surplus as well). As exploitation increased, the peasant class tended to grow more discontented, necessitating even greater repression and tighter controls.

Life at the bottom of agricultural societies was harsh, especially so when the elite classes used slavery and other forms of repression to maximize their control over the labor supply. When there were racial or cultural differences between the labor force and the aristocratic classes—as in the antebellum American South—prejudice and racism were often used to reinforce inequality.

Thus, as they evolved, agricultural societies tended to feature high levels of inequality and low rates of social mobility. A small elite class controlled land, labor, and wealth, while the great majority of the population languished in grinding poverty and harsh repression. The elite class of agricultural society—the top 1 or 2% of the population—typically controlled not less than 50% of the wealth and economic assets (Lenski et al., 1995, p. 182). In between the nobles and the peasants was a small class of merchants, artisans, and tradesmen who came to play a much larger role in human affairs as societies switched from agricultural to industrial technology.

Industrial Societies

The industrial revolution began in England in the 1700s. Machines, powered at first by water, then by steam, coal, petroleum products, and nuclear power, began to replace people and draft animals and dramatically increase the productive capacity of society. Tractors replaced horse-drawn plows, steamships replaced sailing ships, buggies gave way to automobiles, and factories came to dominate production. Industrial technology is **capital intensive:** the new machines were expensive and required large investments of capital (for example, lots of money) to develop and purchase.

The shift to industrial technology had profound consequences for society, changes so vast and sudden that they thoroughly justify the term *revolution*. Machines made the labor of the peasants irrelevant, and traditional agricultural systems could not survive in competition with modern forms of production. New employment opportunities sprang up in the cities, and industrial societies urbanized as people shifted from the old order of work (peasant, rural, labor intensive) to the new (industrial, urban, capital intensive). Populations grew, levels of education rose, family size fell, new forms of government appeared, and—of particular interest here—the agricultural nobility and the peasants on whose labor they depended faded in importance.

As the landed aristocracy fell, new classes and forms of inequality arose. The new elite class of capitalists consisted of the owners of factories, mines, and financial institutions. Below them in the social hierarchy, the middle class—shopkeepers, factory managers, small business owners—grew. One step further down, the modern working class—people who ran the machines and the expanding industrial infrastructure (railroads, canals, and factories)—came into being.

The new capitalist class acquired enormous wealth, and the distance from the top of the stratification system to the bottom grew wider. In part, the increasing inequality was a result of greater productivity. Even in the early stages, industrial technology produced much more material wealth than agricultural technology had, and the new capitalist elite had a strong tendency to conserve the bulk of the wealth for themselves, as the agricultural nobility had before them. The new urban working class (Marx called them the proletariat), on the other hand, were working long, hard hours in dangerous conditions with precious little reward. Conditions in the early factories, mines, and mills were dreadful, wages were minimal, and workers

Industrialization helped create a new class structure in the United States, as it has in other countries and is doing today in developing countries. These photographs illustrate class inequality in housing about 1900. At the top of the page, tenement wash lines are stretched across a working-class neighborhood of New York City. Below it is a middle-class neighborhood in Maine. In the late nineteenth century, Americans began moving to new suburbs and the quiet of tree-lined streets, grassy yards, and more spacious homes. The urban homes of the elite, such as this mansion in New York City (bottom), were much more opulent than middle-class homes. Although there have been changes in the American class structure during the last century, the basic system was in place by 1900.

had few means (for example, unions or government regulation) to protect themselves from exploitation and abuse by their bosses.

At the same time, much of the population continued to live in the countryside as peasants, in the labor-intensive agricultural sector. Industrial laborers may have been abused, but they were still participants in the process of industrialization and were eventually able to claim some of the benefits of greater productivity. Peasants, in contrast, were stuck with the same old distribution of resources, and the pie was getting smaller as the agricultural sector became less and less important to society. The increasing inequality of early industrialization thus reflected not only the gap between capitalist and industrial laborer but also the widening gap between the traditional rural economy and the emerging urban-industrial economy.

Around that time, Karl Marx noted the plight of the industrial working class and developed his theories of class conflict. He and many of his contemporaries assumed that things would only get worse without some sort of major overhaul in social relations. But then something interesting happened.

The Kuznets Curve. Contrary to folk wisdom about "the rich getting richer" and the expectations of many social thinkers, the degree of inequality leveled off and then actually declined as industrial economies matured. Wealth and income (and power and prestige) came to be more evenly distributed across the population and less concentrated in the hands of a small, super-wealthy, all-powerful elite. As shown in Graphic 5.2, after 10,000 years of widening gaps between the wealthy and the rest of society, the trend actually reversed. That decline in inequality is referred to as the **Kuznets curve,** after Simon Kuznets (1955), who first documented and explored the phenomenon. The same curve has been found in contemporary societies that are just beginning to industrialize as well as in the history of societies that are currently industrialized (Nielson and Alderson, 1997, pp. 12–13). One important cause of the decline in inequality was the gradual movement of the population from the traditional agricultural sector to higher-paying jobs in the cities. That shift raised the bottom level of the stratification system and portended a variety of other changes that eventually had an even greater impact on inequality. At the heart of those changes were the rising levels of education demanded by an increasingly sophisticated technology and the growing power of the middle and working classes.

In the earliest days of industrialization, simple strength was an important asset for workers because the first machines were often cumbersome and difficult to operate. As the technology matured, however, the demands shifted from brawn and endurance to brains and **human capital:** investments in people's literacy, education, and skill development. Industrial societies responded to escalating technological demands by investing in schooling and opening up opportunities for education to a larger and larger share of the population.

As levels of education rose, the middle class (and the working class as well) became more articulate, more aware, and more demanding. They got involved in politics at all levels and made their demands known to the state, a process made easier by urbanization and modern forms of communication. (Chapter 10 sketches the

GRAPHIC 5.2   KUZNETS CURVE

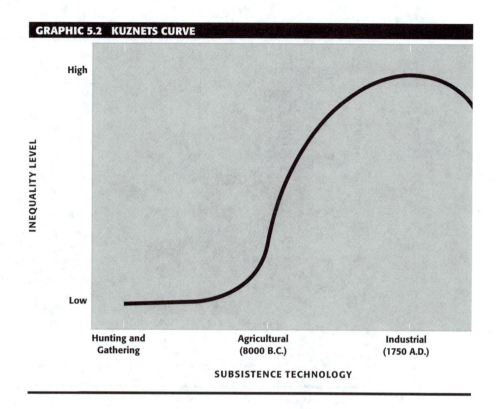

evolution of democratic involvement in policy making.) Thus, industrialization created a more educated, articulate workforce, and urbanization made it easier to organize and mobilize their strength. The decline in inequality described in the Kuznets curve reflects the increasing political power of those nonelite groups and their successful demands for a more equitable distribution (in the form of higher pay, shorter workweeks, better working conditions, pension plans, and so on) of the growing surplus created by industrial technology.

Labor Sectors. A convenient way to track the changes represented in the Kuznets curve is to examine the structure of the workforce over time. Graphic 5.3 shows the changing structure of the job market in the United States from 1840 to 1996. Similar changes occurred in other industrialized nations.

As Graphic 5.3 shows, the job market can be divided into three sectors:

◆ *The extractive sector* extracts raw materials from the environment. Extractive occupations include mining, forestry, and fishing, but at the start of industrialization, farming was by far the most common extractive occupation, comprising almost 70% of the workforce. However, during industrialization, this sector declines rapidly; in industrial societies today, it accounts for a tiny minority of all jobs (about 3%).

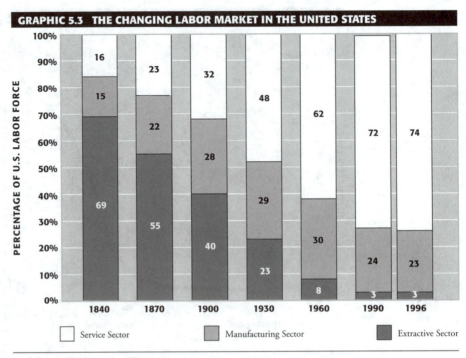

GRAPHIC 5.3 THE CHANGING LABOR MARKET IN THE UNITED STATES

Source: Adapted from Lenski et al., 1995.

◆ *The manufacturing sector* transforms raw or unfinished materials into finished products ready for sale in the marketplace. An example of this type of job would be a factory worker who produces finished goods (shoes, cars, vacuum cleaners) from leather, plastic, or aluminum. This sector increased in the United States well into the twentieth century, but since the mid-1900s, it has declined as the United States moved into the postindustrial era.

◆ *The service sector* provides services instead of producing "things." Examples of service jobs include waitress, cab driver, policeman, physician, and teacher. Today, the great majority of U.S. jobs (about 74%) are in this sector. Service jobs are highly variable in terms of income and prestige, but they tend to fall into two segments. The more desirable jobs—like neurosurgeon—feature higher pay, more prestige, greater job security, and more benefits. The less desirable jobs—like janitor—provide lower (often much lower) pay levels, little security or opportunities for upward mobility, and few (if any) benefits. The difference between the two segments, more than any other single factor, is human capital, with the better jobs requiring higher and higher levels of education.

In part, the growth in the service sector reflects the greater demands for services (grocery stores, clothing stores, and so on) in an urban, industrial society in which people cannot be self-sufficient. It also reflects the coming of the postindustrial era. In the United States, recent economic growth has been concentrated in the finance, computer, communication, and other high-tech industries that produce, control, and disseminate information. Most jobs in those growth industries, from computer programmer to financial analyst, fall into the more desirable segment of the service sector. You might think, then, that inequality would be continuing to decrease. In fact, it has started to rise again in the United States, as the next section explains.

Increasing Inequality in the United States

Even though the industrial revolution began in England, the United States has been the world's most advanced and powerful industrial society for many decades. Like all industrialized nations, the United States experienced a period of declining inequality, but during the transition to a postindustrial stage of development in the latter half of the twentieth century, income inequality began to increase once more.

The notion that income inequality is increasing was hard to accept in the face of abundant evidence that the U.S. economy was booming at the turn of the twenty-first century. Unemployment and inflation were low, satisfaction with the economy was widespread, and discrimination based on race or gender seemed to be at its lowest level in the history of the nation. Now more than ever, some were saying, the sky is the limit, and any American can become anything if only he or she works hard enough.

These two shopping centers underscore the increasing inequality that is present in the United States. Large suburban malls have become more than "shopping" centers. They provide more affluent residents with entertainment and food, as well as a place to walk, take children, and "hang out" with friends.

But prosperity has been selective, and the economic news has not been equally rosy for everyone. Since the 1970s, the income gap between affluent and impoverished Americans has been generally increasing, some people and groups are as far from prosperity as ever, and the share of the nations' paycheck going to middle-income Americans generally has fallen. How can booming prosperity and increasing inequality exist side by side?

The Great U-Turn

Since the end of World War II, the United States has been through two very different periods of economic growth. The first was favorable for the middle class, but the more recent period has seen a decline in real wages (that is, wages corrected for inflation). Today, despite the nation's prosperity, the dream of middle-class prosperity may be of reach for more and more Americans. (See Bluestone & Harrison, 1982; Farley, 1996; Levy, 1998; Newman, 1993.)

From 1945 to the mid-1970s, the golden age of the American middle class, the economy grew steadily, incomes rose, and the American middle class grew and prospered. A high school graduate (or, more accurately, a white male high school graduate) had a reasonable chance at a good, secure blue-collar job or even a white-collar job (Farley, 1996). With hard work, the middle-class dream—the house in the suburbs with the car and all the appliances—could be financed with a single salary.

However, the Kuznets curve bottomed out in the 1970s, and the **"Great U-Turn"** (Bluestone and Harrison, 1982) began. Average wages (corrected for inflation) stopped rising, poverty began to increase, and the middle class stopped growing. Today, a high school graduate (even a white male high school graduate) faces an

The Great U-Turn, which began in the 1970s, led to stagnant wages, increasing poverty, and a shrinking middle class. Many industrial workers lost their jobs to cheaper labor in developing countries. In 1980, a group of unemployed autoworkers queued at an unemployment office in Detroit.

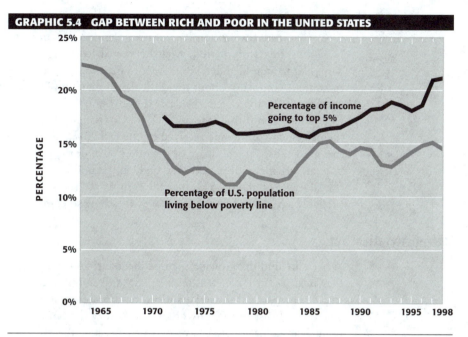

GRAPHIC 5.4 GAP BETWEEN RICH AND POOR IN THE UNITED STATES

Source: U.S. Bureau of the Census, 1999.

economy in which secure jobs that pay well are scarcer than they were forty years ago. To have a chance at the middle-class dream, people almost certainly need, at least, a college education or other training beyond high school and the combined efforts of two wage earners.

The changing distributions of wealth and poverty resulting from the Great U-Turn are clearly visible in Graphic 5.4. The top line represents the percentage of all U.S. income that went to the richest 5% of the population. In 1967, that group earned about 17% of all income, but by 1998, the top 5% of earners were bringing home over 20% of the nation's income, a thirty-year high. (U.S. Bureau of the Census, 1999).

The graph also shows the percentage of the U.S. population living below the poverty level, as defined by the federal government, between 1959 and 1998. A dramatic decrease in poverty is evident through the 1960s, and a low point was reached in the mid-1970s. Then poverty began to increase (with some fluctuations) and reached high points in the mid-1980s and early 1990s. The percentage of poor decreased in the mid-1990s—a reflection of a robust economy and full employment—but it remains several points higher than the low point of the 1970s.

It is also likely that the number of very poor people—people well below the poverty line and with little chance of entering even the lowest ranks of the working class—has been growing in recent decades. There is much concern in the social sciences about the increase in extreme poverty in the United States, and a new term—the *underclass*—has come into use to describe that group, which is so disconnected from the economic mainstream and so distant from affluence.

During this same period, what happened to the great mass of the population who, like Lauren Caulder, are in between the rich and the poor? Is there any truth to Lauren's complaint about the difficulty of matching the standard of living of her childhood? Graphic 5.5 displays the changing shares of the national income received by each fifth of the population. Consistent with Graphic 5.4, it shows that the percentage of income received by the top 20% has increased dramatically since the late 1970s. But the share of the other 80% of the population has declined (the poor are getting poorer, as is everybody in the middle). If you factor in the decrease in real wages of about 15% since the early 1970s (Farley, 1996, p. 341), you would probably agree that Lauren does have something to complain about.

Deindustrialization

What is behind the growing income inequality in the United States? What sparked the Great U-Turn? The reasons are many and complex, but one set of forces, collectively known as **deindustrialization,** has been commonly cited as a major culprit. The basic thrust of this line of analysis is that the economic fortunes of people at middle levels of income have declined because the American economy has lost many "good" jobs (jobs that pay well and that offer security and fringe benefits). Deindustrialization was caused by many interrelated forces, of which three of the most important are cited here.

◆ The transition to a postindustrial society has caused the job structure to shift. Unionized, well-paying, secure factory jobs have declined and been replaced by jobs in the service sector, many of which pay low wages. Job growth in the 1980s, for example, was largely confined to minimum wage occupations (Farley, 1996).

◆ By the 1970s, the physical infrastructure of U.S. industry—the buildings, machines, and transportation networks—reached the end of its useful life and needed to be either refurbished or abandoned. For the capitalist class, it was more profitable to build new structures designed to accommodate the latest technology. Very often, the new plants either were built outside the United States to take advantage of less expensive workforces (hence, Sadisah's job opportunity) or replaced people with machines. In either case, the U.S. workforce lost good jobs.

◆ Because of economic globalization, U.S. businesses are facing growing competition from abroad. This trend is described in detail in Chapter 10. In response, American businesses of all sorts have become "leaner and meaner" by downsizing their workforce (firing people) and reducing their payrolls and overhead. The result, again, is the loss of many good jobs, blue collar and white collar alike.

The result of deindustrialization has been downward mobility for many members of the great American middle class, blue collar as well as white collar. They have experienced downward mobility either in their own lives (as they took lower-wage

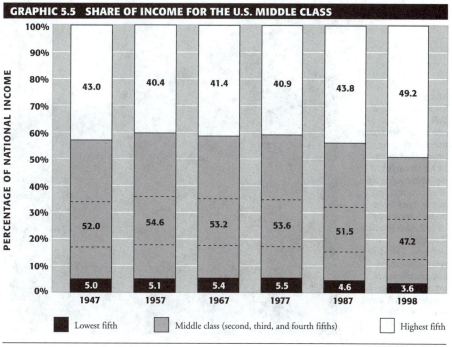

GRAPHIC 5.5 SHARE OF INCOME FOR THE U.S. MIDDLE CLASS

Source: U.S. Bureau of the Census, 2000.

jobs to replace the disappearing good jobs) or in their economic well-being relative to their parents.

These trends have had different impacts on different segments of society. For example, those who have acquired higher levels of human capital—technical skills and advanced training—often prosper in the postindustrial U.S. economy. But it seems likely that the less-well-trained and less-well-educated will continue to lose class position and drop into the lower reaches of the service sector.

Deindustrialization also affects men more than women, because men tended to monopolize the good manufacturing jobs in the industrial economy. Women have been more concentrated in the service sector and, thus, have been less negatively affected. The result is that the income gap between the sexes has actually narrowed in recent years (Farley, 1996, p. 351). However, the U.S. job market still incorporates striking gender differentials in pay. For example, in 1998, median income for women high school graduates was 71% of the median income for men with the same educational level, and the gap for college graduates was 70% (U.S. Bureau of the Census, 2000).

Not all women are benefiting equally, however. Minority-group women have found it somewhat easier than minority-group men, who are among the main victims of deindustrialization, to find work in the service sector. However, the service jobs tend to be the ones with low salaries and are unlikely to generate sufficient

Abandoned factories, such as this one in Detroit, are common across manufacturing areas that have been devastated by deindustrialization. More important, many lives have been harmed by deindustrialization. The typical industrial worker who loses a job eventually finds work in the service sector, which pays less and offers fewer benefits.

resources to provide adequate housing, medical care, and nutrition for themselves and their children. Middle-class, dominant-group women, on the other hand, may command higher wages. But they still face limitations on promotions and raises, "glass ceilings" that do not affect middle-class, dominant-group males.

Regardless of race and gender, deindustrialization has hit the urban poor hard. The older plants and factories that have been closed generally were located in or near center cities. Increasingly, the urban, less educated, working and lower class faces an economy dominated by poorly paid, insecure service sector jobs or, worse still, no jobs at all (Farley, 1996). The so-called urban underclass is not only impoverished but has become increasingly marginal to the evolving, postindustrial economy. That is, the economy of the future will offer few places for this population (especially for people who are both poor and members of minority groups of color), and they will become increasingly disconnected and increasingly irrelevant as a workforce. (See Kasarda, 1989; Massey & Denton, 1993; and Wilson, 1987, 1996.)

Thus, it seems that the future holds very different prospects for different types of Americans. People who can acquire marketable skills and advanced training—those with more human capital—may prosper, but others may fall further behind. Perhaps if the economic boom that began in the 1990s sustains itself, it will, like the proverbial rising tide, eventually lift all boats. Perhaps another Kuznets curve will appear, and income inequality will level off and then decrease once more. In the near future, however, the trends examined here seem to point to increasing frustration for the squeezed middle class and increasing misery for the poor.

Inequality around the Globe

The processes analyzed to this point affect every nation and the globe as a whole, not just the United States. Every country in the world has some degree of social stratification, some more than others. This section looks at inequality in selected countries around the world, investigating the different ways that inequality manifests itself. But first let's take a look at inequality from the other perspective mentioned at the beginning of the chapter: the broad, global level.

Inequality among Nations and the Effects of Globalization

Even the most casual observer notices that some countries are better off than others. If nothing else, you know that the United States is wealthier, more prestigious, and more powerful than, say, Cuba or Thailand. Social scientists formalize such observations in several ways. One is by dividing nations into three categories based on the productivity of their economies, which reflects the subsistence technology that they typically employ.

◆ *Low-income nations,* such as Nigeria, Cambodia, and Haiti, generally are the least developed or industrialized. A very high percentage of the workforce—as much as 80% or more—is in the traditional (labor-intensive) agricultural sector, and farming technology is primitive and relatively unproductive. Most people try to satisfy their basic needs by working small plots of land, perhaps supplemented with herding or occasional part-time jobs. Most low-income, least developed nations are located in Africa (World Bank, 2000).

◆ *Middle-income nations,* such as Brazil, South Africa, and Bulgaria, are a mixture of agricultural and industrial technologies and are in transition from more labor-intensive, agricultural economies to fully industrialized economies. Typically, the population is split between a more traditional, agricultural sector and a more modern, urban sector.

◆ *High-income nations,* such as the United States, Japan, and Switzerland, are often referred to as "developed," or industrialized. This category includes the technologically most advanced societies in the world.

It is clear that there is a gap between rich and poor nations and that the gap has a great impact on the well-being and life chances available to the populations of lower-income nations. But how large is that gap? Is it increasing or decreasing? As you may recall, Graphic 5.1 showed that inequality worldwide has been increasing in recent decades, just as it has been in the United States (see Korzeniewicz and Moran, 1997, pp.1000–1021).

One major cause of the rising inequality in the world is globalization. Some nations have been able to capitalize on the opportunities presented by globalization while others have not. Consider the distribution of computer technology, which has led the more advanced nations into the postindustrial age but has also divided the world into the "connected" and the "unconnected." The 20% of the world's population living in the highest-income nations have 93% of the world's Internet users, while the bottom 20% have only 0.2% (United Nations, 1999, pp. 2–3). Those nations without a large group of people who know how to use computers to gather information are at a distinct disadvantage in the competition for new industries with high-paying jobs.

The dividing line between the computer literate and illiterate reinforces the gap between industrialized, high-income nations and the rest of the world. As long as access to modern technology and information is unevenly distributed, the nations that control the new technology will tend to grow and prosper while other nations will tend to fall further behind.

Globalization is also helping to open up new markets, but once again the nations that are benefiting the most are in some ways the ones that need it least. China, for example, has an enticing market of over a billion consumers, some of whom are jumping right into the middle class. Although "communist" China is still politically repressive, some Chinese citizens watch soap operas (from Taiwan), listen to talk radio, and watch CNN. They avidly purchase all sorts of western goods and services. The Chinese economy is advancing rapidly, but Chairman Mao (the leader of the Communist revolution) would spin in his grave at the thought of a Chinese youth dressed in Calvin Klein jeans heading to a 7-Eleven store to buy a Coca-Cola, a common sight in the major Chinese cities today.

As the leading corporations penetrate the Chinese economy and other emerging markets, they generate profits that flow to the more developed nations, where their headquarters are located. The expanding global marketplace thus tends to favor high-income nations, international corporations, and those who control the economic behemoths. Globalization contributes to inequality between nations by creating a flow of goods and services to the new markets largely located in the low- and middle-income nations and a flow of profit back to the high-income nations.

Of course, the benefits of globalization are not entirely one way; the process has brought, among other things, job opportunities, modern medicines, and access to advanced technology and forms of communication to developing and least developed nations. In some cases, globalization has done more than that, as illustrated by four middle-income Asian nations known as "the little dragons": Taiwan, South Korea, Hong Kong, and Singapore. The dragon is a symbol of power in Asia and reflects the increasing importance of these tiny nations in the regional and global economies. The four little dragons did not begin to industrialize until the 1950s, but they have relatively high average incomes (gross national product, or GNP, per capita), high life expectancies, and low mortality rates (see Graphic 5.6), all signs of a healthy society. The four little dragons, together with high-income Japan (which began to industrialize in the early twentieth century), are leading the industrial development of Asia. Together, they account for less than 1% of the world's land mass, less than 4% of the world's population, but nearly 21% of the world's industrial output.

GRAPHIC 5.6   KEY CHARACTERISTICS OF THE FOUR "LITTLE DRAGONS," JAPAN, AND THE UNITED STATES

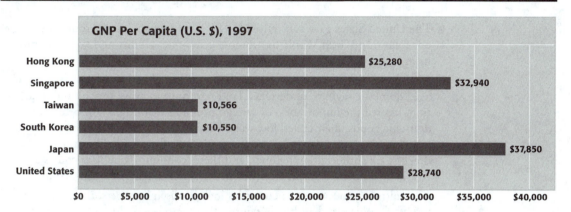

GNP Per Capita (U.S. $), 1997

Hong Kong	$25,280
Singapore	$32,940
Taiwan	$10,566
South Korea	$10,550
Japan	$37,850
United States	$28,740

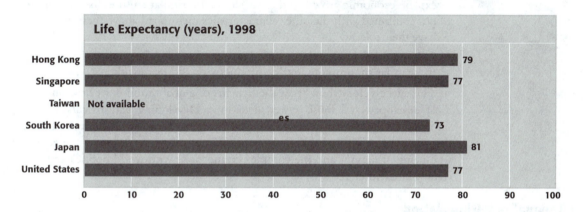

Life Expectancy (years), 1998

Hong Kong	79
Singapore	77
Taiwan	Not available
South Korea	73
Japan	81
United States	77

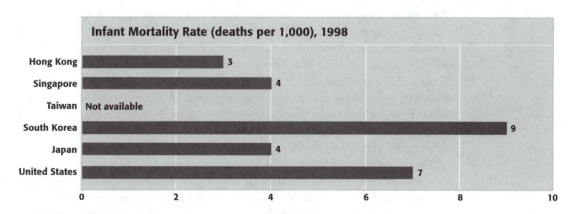

Infant Mortality Rate (deaths per 1,000), 1998

Hong Kong	3
Singapore	4
Taiwan	Not available
South Korea	9
Japan	4
United States	7

Sources: World Bank, 1999; Taiwan GNP from Bradshaw and Wallace, 1996, p. 95.

This success story can be attributed to many factors, four of which are listed here.

◆ The United States gave substantial foreign aid to Japan and the four little drag-ons following World War II to promote economic stability and fight commu-nism.

◆ Their governments have developed strong industrial and trade policies, encour-aged domestic savings, undertaken land reform to increase agricultural produc-tion, limited the importation of foreign products that might compete with domestic goods, maintained low wages, and exercised heavy-handed tactics to keep order at home. Japan has been a democracy for decades, but the four little dragons are authoritarian regimes, and their economic dynamism comes at a cost in civil liberties, harsh criminal justice systems, and press censorship.

◆ The cultural values of Asian countries include discipline, personal control, and respect for elders and authority figures. By themselves, cultural values cannot explain economic growth (other societies with similar cultures have not grown), but combined with the other characteristics mentioned above these traditions have their role.

◆ Although the situation is changing to some extent, Asian companies, especially those in Japan, promote loyalty, productivity, and teamwork.

This success story shows that the benefits of globalization don't flow only to the most developed and most powerful nations. Developing nations can sometimes find ways to dramatically change their positions in the world economy and increase the quality of life for their populations. We return to the topic of the economic well-being of nations and the complex connections with world politics and global-ization in Chapter 10.

Inequality within Nations

Patterns of inequality within nations tend to reflect differences in level of develop-ment. As Graphic 5.7 shows, inequality tends to be higher in low-income agricul-tural societies and lower in high-income, fully industrialized societies, a pattern roughly consistent with the Kuznets curve. A particularly revealing element of Graphic 5.7 is the "ratio of income inequality" (Lenski et al., 1995, p. 329), which is derived by dividing the average percentage of total income received by the richest 20% of the population by the average percentage received by the poorest 40%. The ratio of income inequality for low-income nations is 2.4, which means that the richest 20% earn $2.40 for every dollar of income going to the poorest 40%.

On the average, middle-income nations have even more income inequality (4.2) than low-income nations, but they are also highly variable (have the greatest range of scores) and thus include both the most unequal and most equal societies. The middle-income societies with the highest ratios of income inequality are Brazil (7.8) and Guatemala (8.0). Middle-income nations with the lowest ratios, which tend to be former members of the Soviet bloc that collapsed in the late 1980s, include the Slovak Republic (1.1) and the Czech Republic (1.5).

GRAPHIC 5.7 INCOME DISTRIBUTION FOR NINETY-SEVEN NATIONS				
		Average Percentage of Income Received by		
Income Level	Number of Nations Studied	Poorest 40% of Population	Richest 40% of Population	Ratio of Income Inequality	Range of Income Inequality Ratios
Low-income societies	32	18	44	2.4	1.7–6.8
Middle-income societies	45	13	54	4.2	1.1–8.0
High-income societies	20	23	38	1.7	1.3–3.0

Source: World Bank, 2000.

High-income nations have much lower ratios of income inequality on average than either low- or middle-income nations (1.7) and are also much less variable. However, high productivity and national income are not universally or invariably associated with lower inequality for the citizens of a country. As Graphic 5.8 shows, income inequality in the most advanced and productive nation in the world—the United States—is 3.0, dramatically higher than in any other advanced industrial nation (World Bank, 2000; Gottschalk & Smeeding, 1997). Moreover, the pay differential between the highest and lowest paid workers is much greater in the United States than in a place like Japan (Byrne 1991, p. 93).

These general points about income inequality and level of development can be supplemented by taking a closer look at selected nations and regions. The different histories, cultural values, and political ideologies of nations create a diversity of stratification systems, which in turn influence the size of the gap between rich and poor.

High-Income Nations: The European Welfare States. European countries, especially those in northern Europe and Scandinavia, often are referred to as "welfare states" because they have relatively big governments and high taxes. They also have high levels of equality, an excellent quality of life, and progressive social policies.

One way to examine the size of government is to look at the amount of money a government spends as a percentage of its total economic output. Big governments, quite simply, spend a lot of money. Graphic 5.9 shows that Europe's welfare states spend substantially more money (about double, on average) than the United States, relative to each country's gross domestic product, or GDP. Moreover, these countries tend to spend relatively less money on defense (about one-quarter of U.S. expenditures) and more on health, education, welfare, and social security. Expenditures on welfare-related items tend to equalize incomes, because the poor effectively get more income while the rich give up some income through higher taxes.

The European welfare states, along with Japan, have long been considered some of the most equal in the world. These states also tend to provide a higher quality of life for the children of poor families and to subsidize education, thus making a greater investment in the human capital of future generations. The gap between rich and poor children is much smaller in Europe than it is in the United States,

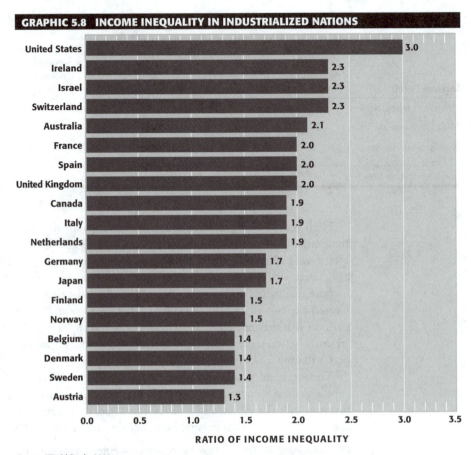

GRAPHIC 5.8   INCOME INEQUALITY IN INDUSTRIALIZED NATIONS

Nation	Ratio
United States	3.0
Ireland	2.3
Israel	2.3
Switzerland	2.3
Australia	2.1
France	2.0
Spain	2.0
United Kingdom	2.0
Canada	1.9
Italy	1.9
Netherlands	1.9
Germany	1.7
Japan	1.7
Finland	1.5
Norway	1.5
Belgium	1.4
Denmark	1.4
Sweden	1.4
Austria	1.3

RATIO OF INCOME INEQUALITY

Source: World Bank, 2000.

Note: Data are from different years, 1982–1994.

largely because of generous social programs that redistribute wealth in those societies (Bradsher, 1995).

We should be careful not to idealize these welfare states: they do have poverty and inequality, and many European states are looking for ways to cut government spending and taxes. But these nations have built an enviable quality of life through substantial government intervention. Europeans tend to believe in government and continue to want strong government programs. In contrast, American culture maintains strong antistatist values and is deeply suspicious of anything labeled "welfare." Americans generally believe in sharp limitations on the role of government, and they would be horrified to pay European-level taxes. On the other hand, Europeans cannot understand why Americans tolerate high levels of inequality and poverty. That difference in perceptions underscores the differing histories and philosophies of the American and European systems.

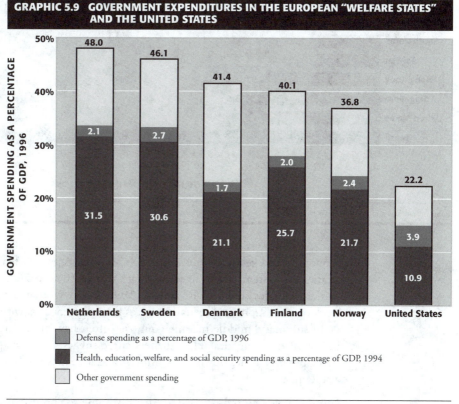

GRAPHIC 5.9 GOVERNMENT EXPENDITURES IN THE EUROPEAN "WELFARE STATES" AND THE UNITED STATES

GOVERNMENT SPENDING AS A PERCENTAGE OF GDP, 1996

	Netherlands	Sweden	Denmark	Finland	Norway	United States
Total	48.0	46.1	41.4	40.1	36.8	22.2
Defense	2.1	2.7	1.7	2.0	2.4	3.9
Health, education, welfare, social security	31.5	30.6	21.1	25.7	21.7	10.9

■ Defense spending as a percentage of GDP, 1996

■ Health, education, welfare, and social security spending as a percentage of GDP, 1994

□ Other government spending

Source: Adapted from World Bank, 2000.

Middle-Income Nations: Newly Industrializing Countries. Some middle-income nations are called newly industrializing countries (NICs). In these societies, economic growth and modernization have so far reached only a small proportion of the population. In Brazil, for example, the ratio of income inequality is very high, and the majority of people still live in the low-income, traditional agricultural sector even as the elite classes benefit from industrialization and greater productivity. If (and it's a big if) NICs follow the trajectories of the nations that are fully industrialized today, income inequality will decline in the future as people move into the industrial sector of the labor force.

Despite rapid industrialization, the four Asian dragons have avoided the extreme inequalities that characterize Brazil and some other NICs. Graphic 5.10 shows that the four little dragons have inequality levels more comparable to that of the United States than of Brazil.

As with the European welfare states, it is important not to idealize the situation in the four dragons. Rapid economic growth has been possible at least partly because of the hard work of young, poorly paid female factory workers. (Recall the earlier story of Sadisah, from Indonesia; Chapter 7 examines the intersection of

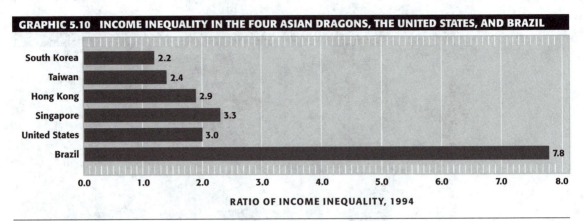

GRAPHIC 5.10   INCOME INEQUALITY IN THE FOUR ASIAN DRAGONS, THE UNITED STATES, AND BRAZIL

South Korea — 2.2
Taiwan — 2.4
Hong Kong — 2.9
Singapore — 3.3
United States — 3.0
Brazil — 7.8

0.0   1.0   2.0   3.0   4.0   5.0   6.0   7.0   8.0

RATIO OF INCOME INEQUALITY, 1994

Source: Bradshaw and Wallace, 1996, p. 105.

economics and gender.) One study in Taiwan indicates that female factory workers' salaries are systematically fixed at a rate that is 10% to 20% below male factory workers' salaries (Bello & Rosenfeld, 1990, 216). Women also must endure poor working conditions and sexual advances from male bosses, with little recourse.

In summary, middle-income countries often have more inequality than highly industrialized countries. The Kuznets curve suggests that inequality will lessen as development trickles down to the middle and lower classes, but of course that is not a certainty.

Low-Income Countries: Africa. Africa is home to about two-thirds of the world's low-income countries. Tellingly, about 75% of Africans work in agriculture. Food is produced for domestic consumption, and coffee, tea, peanuts, and other crops are exported for money. Fewer than one-third of African citizens reside in cities, and only 10% to 20% of urban citizens have "modern" wage-earning jobs as professionals, laborers, or office workers. Many urban jobs (such as shoe shining, auto repair, street sweeping, and prostitution) are in the "informal sector" and do not pay steady wages. Some informal workers earn a very good living, but others make barely enough money to keep from starving. Still other urban citizens are unemployed and resort to begging and crime for survival. An increasing number of beggars in African cities are street children with no homes or means of family support. Graphic 5.11 shows some key characteristics of selected African countries and compares them to the United States.

The tragedy of Africa is that it has grown progressively less economically developed since its countries achieved political independence from European colonizers some 40 years ago. Independence was supposed to usher in a new period of prosperity for Africa. But the continent had few educated citizens, little money, little advanced technology, and an unrealistic vision of what development would entail. When national boundaries were drawn by colonizers, they paid little heed to the existing territorial boundaries of distinctly different cultural groups. A journalist

GRAPHIC 5.11 INDICATORS OF AFRICAN ECONOMIC DEVELOPMENT

	GNP per Capita (U.S. $), 1997	Child Mortality Rate (deaths per 1,000, 0–5 years of age), 1997	Percentage of Population Living in Urban Areas, 1997	Percentage of Workers in Nonagricultural Jobs, 1990
Botswana	$3,260	88	65%	54%
Congo, Democratic Republic of	$110	148	35%	32%
Ghana	$370	102	37%	41%
Kenya	$330	112	30%	20%
Namibia	$2,220	101	38%	51%
Nigeria	$260	122	41%	57%
Rwanda	$210	209	6%	8%
South Africa	$3,400	65	50%	86%
Tanzania	$210	136	26%	16%
Uganda	$330	162	13%	15%
Zambia	$380	189	44%	25%
United States	$28,740	9	77%	97%

Source: World Bank, 2000.

wrote, "The colonialists designed the scenario for disaster and the Africans seem to be trying their best to fulfill it" (Lamb, 1985, p. xv). In many cases, the new African leaders proved to be just as exploitative and rapacious as the white colonial rulers they succeeded.

The class structure of African and other low-income societies tends to resemble a triangle, with a small elite class at the top and a large poor class at the bottom (Graphic 5.12). By contrast, the class structure of a developed country is more diamond-shaped, with a small elite class, a large middle class, and a small poor class. The class structure of NICs is somewhere between those two extremes.

In considering the case of Africa, it is important to recognize that nations awash in poverty and poor "life chances" (for example, poor health) may be relatively "developed" in ways other than economic. For example, African countries are more developed than the United States when it comes to strong family and community structures. In addition, patterns of inequality can shift over time. Consider the case of South Africa, where the apartheid system ended in 1994, after nearly 50 years of state-sanctioned racial segregation. Virtually overnight, the black population had new opportunities in jobs, schools, and political institutions. The national government, which had been primarily white, is now primarily black, and companies are recruiting well-qualified black South Africans in large numbers. Still, white South Africans own 85% to 90% of assets in the country, and it will take a long time to change the economic institution and the stratification system. Nonetheless, political change did occur in the country, and there is no reason to think that economic change will not follow.

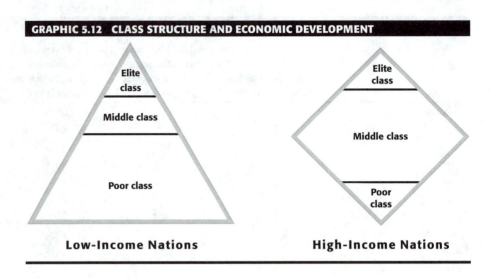

GRAPHIC 5.12   CLASS STRUCTURE AND ECONOMIC DEVELOPMENT

Conclusion

We began this chapter with a question: Is inequality increasing around the globe and in the United States? How much truth is there in the folk wisdom that the rich get richer while the poor get poorer? Clearly, this is a question that has no simple or final answer. We have seen that inequality is a social phenomenon that reflects the level of development, the history, and the value system of a society. Some societies have virtually no inequality, and the amount of income inequality seems to be generally lower for societies at higher levels of development. Some analysts, like Marx, see inequality as a straightforward result of class exploitation and domination, while others, like Davis and Moore, argue that inequality is not only inevitable but desirable.

The time frame we use when addressing the issue is crucial. Inequality seems to have increased in the United States and across the globe as a whole over the past several decades. However, if we take a long-term view and compare industrialized nations today with the most advanced agricultural nation of two centuries ago, we would find lower levels of inequality along with an enormous improvement in quality of life for citizens in all social classes. The industrialized nations of the world provide a level of comfort and health for their citizens that could not have been imagined in the past. Even the homeless in the modern United States often have a higher standard of living than did ordinary citizens of agricultural society 200 years ago (see DeMuth, 1997, for more).

Some degree of inequality may be inevitable in societies above the hunting and gathering level; in advanced industrial societies, the degree of inequality may be increasing as a result of deindustrialization and globalization. Nonetheless, inequality is a social product, and its extent and nature generally reflects the interests of the elite classes. If the rich do tend to get richer, it is because of the deliberate, self-protective actions of the wealthy and powerful, not because of some immutable law of nature.

In the world system of societies, we have seen that some nations (the four dragons—Taiwan, South Korea, Hong Kong, and Singapore) have found ways to prosper, even though the global economy is dominated by a few technologically sophisticated and economically powerful societies. Can other nations and regions find their way out of poverty and marginalization? Can the degree of inequality among the peoples of the world be reduced? If Levis and Pepsi-Cola can be spread around the globe, why can't the knowledge that will help people in more parts of the world participate more fully in the emerging global village and find a way to move to Main Street? The global patterns of inequality, like those in the United States, are the results of sociological forces that can be measured, analyzed, understood, and, ultimately, changed.

Key Concepts

1. Inequality, whether due to discrepancies in class, race, ethnicity, gender, or some other characteristic, is fundamentally a sociological matter. Stratification (the unequal distribution of valued goods and services) is a central feature of social structure and must be understood in terms of the social context (for example, the degree of openness in the system), not in terms of individual characteristics. Stratification is part of the economic system, but it is affected by—and in turn affects—cultural values and individuals' access to political, educational, and other institutions.

2. Sociologists use a variety of perspectives on inequality, but most theories can be traced back to one of the founders of sociology. Marx focused on the competition of social classes for control over the means of production, while Weber emphasized the multiple dimensions of stratification. Modern-day structural functionalism is derived from Durkheim and focuses on the way that stratification serves the purposes of the social organism.

3. A society's stratification system—how open or closed it is, what dimensions matter in determining a person's position within it—reflects its subsistence technology. Inequality is virtually absent in hunting and gathering society and tends to increase as societies adopt agricultural and then begin to adopt industrial modes of production.

4. According to the Kuznets curve, the degree of economic inequality in industrial societies tends to decrease after the early stages of industrialization. Urbanization, democratization, and better education and communication give workers greater power to press their interests with the elites. However, the process appears to reverse as deindustrialization takes hold and societies enter a postindustrial era. Only those who can invest in human capital—education, training, and skill development— seem to prosper in the new service economies.

5. At present, the powerful sociological forces of deindustrialization and globalization are two of the most important trends shaping inequality and determining the life chances of individuals in the United States and around the globe. A nation's overall status in the world economic hierarchy seems to rely on its ability to capitalize on the opportunities brought by globalization.

6. Middle-income nations have greater inequality than either high- or low-income nations. Among high-income nations, the United States may have the highest level of economic inequality. Also, compared with other nations in its category, primarily the western European nations and Japan, the United States offers fewer support services to its less privileged citizens.

Active Learning

1. The Titanic Game: Role Play. (Adapted from an exercise designed by John R. Bowman, University of North Carolina, Pembroke.) This exercise is based on events that actually happened a few minutes before midnight on April 14, 1912. On her maiden voyage to New York, the luxury ocean liner Titanic struck an iceberg in the North Atlantic. Of the more than 2,200 passengers and crew onboard, only about one-third survived. Similarly, in this exercise, you will find yourself on a sinking ship, although one with just twelve passengers. Only four of the twelve individuals on your boat will survive. Although the actual sinking of the Titanic took nearly three hours, this group activity will take about thirty minutes.

a. Your instructor may distribute copies of the Titanic Game worksheet before class. If not, download a copy from the Web site for this book (www.pineforge.com/snc) and bring it to class.

b. Once in class, form groups of twelve, preferably in a circle, so everyone can see everyone else. Each group represents a separate "ship." Each group will imagine itself dealing with the following scenario:

> You are on a luxury liner and the ship's captain announces: "Please do not panic! The ship has just hit an iceberg and we are about to sink. Unfortunately, there is not enough room on the lifeboat to save everyone. Since we won't sink for at least another twenty minutes, we must decide who among us will be saved. Only four of us will survive."

c. Randomly assign each person in the group a number from 1 to 12. The person's number tells which of the following roles he or she will play:

1. Retired person	7. U.S. Senator
2. Ship's captain	8. President of the Titanic ship line
3. Physician	9. Spouse of the president
4. Nurse	10. Baby of the president
5. Migrant worker	11. Army captain
6. Welfare mother (or father)	12. Elementary school teacher

d. Have the group members in turn, identify their roles to the group. Then each person must try to convince the group to allow him or her to get on the lifeboat. Remember that everybody wants to live and you are fighting for your life!

e. After everyone has made a case, decide as a group how you will make the decision who is to survive. After a system is established, discuss who should be permitted to get on the lifeboat. Keep in mind that each person selected for the lifeboat reduces the number of seats left for you.

f. Prepare a list of survivors (by role) for the instructor. Discuss what your list indicates about the relationships among property, power, and prestige.

g. After completing this role play, answer each of the discussion questions on the Titanic Game worksheet as an individual. Be prepared to share your answers with the rest of the class.

2. Low-Income Budgeting: Research and Role Play. (Adapted from an exercise designed by Brenda Beagan, University of British Columbia.) In this exercise, you will individually conduct some informal research on the cost of living in your area. You will then discuss your findings with classmates and attempt to develop a monthly budget for a low-income household. The purpose is to get a better understanding of the effects of economic inequality on daily life.

a. Visit our Web site (www.pineforge.com/snc) and download a copy of the Cost of Living worksheet. Complete a copy on your own before the next class. You will need to do some informal research into basic costs of living: use your own knowledge and experience, ask friends and family about their costs, read newspaper ads for housing costs, skim fliers from grocery stores, look at your utility bills, and so on. Bring the completed worksheet to class.

b. In small groups, work together to develop a budget for a household living as described in the scenario distributed by the instructor. You will also discuss and answer a few questions about living in poverty and the decisions your group made in its budgeting. Be alert—your economic situation may change even during the course of your discussion!

c. When your group is finished, hand in the group worksheet and the individual worksheets for each group member.

3. The Importance of Social Class: Data Analysis. This exercise asks you to analyze some data and then reach conclusions about your analysis in small groups. It draws on Graphic 5.13, which presents some results from a 1998 survey of 3,000 U.S. residents, a representative sample of the total population. Assume that the results in the table can be generalized to all adult Americans in that year.

Across the top of the table, you will find four social classes listed: lower, working, middle, and upper. The respondents were asked to select one of those categories to describe their own class situation.

The table presents results for a number of survey items—from opinions about abortion to leisure time habits—that might be associated with social class. The numbers in the table are the percentages of people in each class that responded "Yes" to the item. For example, 42% of the lower-class respondents were pro-abortion, as were 34% of the working-class respondents. Complete wording for the items and a more detailed key are included at our Web site (www.pineforge.com/snc). Before conducting the analysis outlined below, make sure you understand what the questions are actually asking.

GRAPHIC 5.13   SOCIAL CLASS, VALUES, AND LIFESTYLE

Values and Lifestyles	Percentage Answering Yes			
	Lower Class	Working Class	Middle Class	Upper Class
Pro-abortion for any reason	42%	34%	42%	42%
Have been divorced	28%	23%	23%	19%
Afraid to walk on streets at night	62%	40%	41%	32%
Happy	18%	25%	38%	54%
Health excellent	13%	24%	38%	59%
Primary socialization values:				
Obey	32%	20%	16%	12%
Think for self	29%	45%	55%	66%
Voted for Clinton in 1996	64%	56%	50%	35%
Went to a movie in the past year	43%	66%	71%	67%
Socialize with friends several times a month or more	33%	43%	44%	49%
People can be trusted	18%	31%	46%	52%

Source: National Opinion Research Council (NORC), 1998.

a. Before class, analyze the results shown in Graphic 5.13 item by item. For each item, find the highest and lowest percentages in each row and subtract the lower number from the higher one.

b. Use the following rough guide to assess the importance of class for each item, based on your calculations in the preceding step.

If the difference between high and low percentages is . . .	*. . . the item is*
less than 10	not affected by class
between 10 and 20	somewhat affected by class
between 20 and 30	moderately affected by class
more than 30	strongly affected by class

c. Write a brief paragraph that describes the relationships. Which items were related to class? How strongly? Bring your written assessment to class.

d. In class, form groups of four to six and share your descriptions of the relationships. Make sure everyone agrees on which relationships were strongly affected by class, which were not affected by class, and so on. Once you agree on the description, try to analyze why the variables are related in that way. What is it about life at different class levels that might create those patterns?

e. Write a joint report summarizing the group's analysis and conclusions. Turn in the joint report along with the individual descriptions you each brought to class.

Biopiracy and Gene Theft

PHILIP McMICHAEL

For centuries, dwellers in the South American rain forest have used the poisonous secretions of an Amazonian frog on the tips of their arrows to tranquilize the birds and animals they hunt. Recently, when a scientist from Abbott Laboratories isolated the frog chemical to develop a painkiller, the Ecuadorian government demanded compensation on behalf of Ecuador and the Amazonian indigenous tribes. It did so under the terms of the 1992 Convention on Biological Diversity, which confirmed national sovereignty over genetic resources and affirmed the principle that nations are entitled to "fair and equitable sharing of the benefits." Many modern commercial drugs derive from chemicals found in tropical flora and fauna. Our lifestyle is directly connected to the extraction of genetic resources, such as drugs from the rosy periwinkle of Madagascar to fight childhood leukemia and testicular cancer; Brazzein, a powerful sweetener from a West African berry; biopesticides from the Indian neem tree; and human cell lines to identify genes that cause illnesses like Huntington's disease and cystic fibrosis. It seems obvious and rational that the world's biodiversity, like the frog secretion, should service all of humankind. That is why so much attention is being paid to preserving the tropical rain forests, given their rich biological variety. But the greater the attention, the more controversy that erupts. At issue is the relationship between the lifestyle of developed nations, mostly in the northern hemisphere, and the rights of indigenous peoples in developing nations, which are mostly to the south.

The more southern regions of the world contain 90% of global biological wealth, while scientists and corporations in more northern countries account for 97% of all patents. Patents on biological wealth give patent holders exclusive control over use of the genetic materials. In many cases, a corporation has patented genetic material obtained from a developing country without payment or obligation, turned it into a commodity such as a medicine, and then charged either a fee for use of the genetic resource in local production or high prices for the commodity, even to the country where the material was originally in use, perhaps for centuries. Many people, particularly in developing countries, view appropriation

The author thanks Rajeev Patel for useful suggestions on an earlier draft of this essay and for his help in compiling Graphic 1.

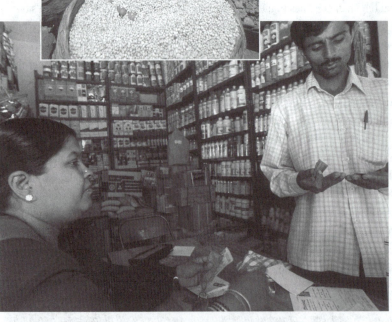

Genetically modified (GM) seeds, patented and marketed by multinational corporations, are supposed to erase world hunger. The "Zapper" is seen fortifying these seeds in an advertisement (above right). But farmers who use GM seeds must sign a contract that bans saving, selling, or exchanging seeds. When a crop fails, these farmers do not have seeds for the next season's crops and have no money to buy new seeds. The Deccan Development Project in Karnataka, India, is fighting back. Seeds are being saved to ensure against crop failure and financial ruin (above left). Nonetheless, the sale of GM seeds continues (below left), increasing farmer dependence on multinational corporations.

of genetic material by foreigners as biopiracy. ActionAid, a London-based antipoverty and community development organization that operates worldwide, defines biopiracy as

> the granting of patents on plant varieties or individual genes, proteins and gene sequences from plants in the South by commercial and industrial interests. This privatisation of living organisms often involves companies taking indigenous plant varieties from developing countries and using these species for the extraction of genes, or genetically modifying . . . existing plants—many of which are also indigenous to the South (ActionAid, 2000).

Biopiracy is not limited to plant varieties. Attempts have been made to acquire human and other animal genetic material, as well as nonplant microbiological material. The entire living world is up for grabs.

As the twentieth century came to a close, spontaneous and organized protests against biopiracy proliferated across the world. For example, in 1993, the 10-million-strong Karnataka Farmers Association in Bangalore, India, demonstrated against Cargill Seeds because of that company's plans to patent local seed germplasm and gain monopoly rights to its use. During the 1990s, tens of thousands of Indian farmers demonstrated in Delhi against "gene theft." By the late 1990s, the Karnataka Farmers Association was targeting the biotechnology corporate giant Monsanto, which claims patent rights over thirty "new" crop varieties that originated in India, including corn, rice, tomatoes, and potatoes, all genetically altered by Monsanto to survive application of one of Monsanto's herbicides.

Another significant protest movement has arisen in Mexico. In December 1999, eleven indigenous peoples' organizations mobilized against a five-year, $2.5 million, U.S. government–funded bioprospecting project in Chiapas, one of the richest biodiversity sites in the world. The purpose of the project is to collect thousands of plants and microorganisms used in traditional Mayan medical practices and to develop them into patented drugs.

Arrayed against those protesting biopiracy are some formidable interests. For instance, the U.S. government has formed an International Cooperative Biodiversity Groups consortium. Its commercial partners are several large global pharmaceutical and agrochemical firms. The consortium has funded eleven bioprospecting projects worth $18.5 million (Rural Advancement Foundation International [RAFI], 1999). The targeted countries are all in the south: Mexico, Peru, Chile, Argentina, Panama, Suriname, Madagascar, Vietnam, Laos, Nigeria, Cameroon, and Costa Rica. Hope Shand, the research director of the Rural Advancement Foundation International (RAFI), an organization fighting biopiracy, remarked: "The use of public money to subsidize biopiracy is a form of corporate welfare for the Gene Giants" (RAFI, 1999). Despite their overwhelming superiority in terms of resources, corporations do not always win. On November 4, 1999, indigenous peoples from nine South American countries successfully overturned a patent issued by the U.S. Patent and Trademark Office to a U.S. citizen for the *ayahuasca* vine. The director of the Coalition for Amazonian

Peoples remarked: "Given that *ayahuasca* is used in sacred indigenous ceremonies through-out the Amazon, this patent should never have been issued in the first place" (Center for International Environmental Law, 1999).

The instances of the growing controversy over genetic heritage and property pose several significant but unresolved questions of our time:

◆ Should genetic properties of living things be bioengineered, patented, or owned?

◆ How can plant varieties be "discovered," when they embody the practical result of centuries of experimentation in plant cultivation by indigenous peoples?

◆ Isn't biodiversity a part of the common heritage of humankind? If so, who should be charged with protecting that common heritage? Who is in the best position to preserve biodiversity: local communities, multinational agencies, or global corporations?

Regarding that last question, the biotechnology industry argues that it alone has the resources to collect the fruits of biodiversity and ensure their global dissemination. The Council of Indigenous Traditional Midwives and Healers of Chiapas retorts that bioprospecting "is a robbery of traditional indigenous knowledge and resources, with the sole purpose of producing pharmaceuticals that will not benefit the communities that have managed and nurtured these resources for thousands of years" (RAFI, 1999).

We hear a lot about the economic and cultural aspects of globalization. But when we examine globalization from the biopiracy angle, we can see that it has a fundamentally political dimension. Like the anticolonial movement, the movement against biopiracy challenges the projection of European and, more recently, North American experience as the universal experience. According to critics of biopiracy, gene patenting presumes that scientific practice and private rights are the norm—at the expense of traditional knowledge and sustainable agricultural and cultural practices.

The battle over access to biodiversity is a contest between corporate and human cultures, played out in local settings as much as negotiated in institutional settings like the World Trade Organization (WTO). When *ayahuasca* is protected as a nonpatentable plant, the consequences go beyond Amazonian ceremony or the U.S. Patent Office—they alter political possibilities for both indigenous peoples and the biotechnology industry in similar struggles across the world.

The ramifications extend to the general issue of intellectual property rights as well. The term *intellectual property rights* refers to ownership of, through a multiyear patent, the rights to a discovery or an invention. In the twenty-first century there is a new form of colonization, a proposed intellectual property rights regime based on a synthesis of European and U.S. patent laws and administered by the WTO. Advocates of the new regime claim that it will simplify operating across national borders and protect and promote innovation for everyone by guaranteeing a way to profit from technological developments.

But once again, Western societies assume that their scientific and legal arrangements are the optimal framework. That stance devalues the existence, integrity, and viability of non-Western knowledge and values and channels the benefits to private investors rather than communities. In the case of biopiracy, the idea of intellectual property rights allows private parties to view diversity in an instrumental way as something that can be used for immediate benefit and discounts the intricate and historical connections between cultural and ecological diversity on which our planet's sustainability may well depend.

Another attempt to deploy the WTO as the regulator of intellectual property rights on a uniform, worldwide scale is the 1995 Trade Related Aspects of Intellectual Property Rights (TRIPS) protocol. Its framework was defined by a coalition of twelve major U.S. corporations, a Japanese federation of business organizations, and the official European business and industrial agency. The TRIPS protocol privileges governments and corporations as legal entities but ignores communities' and farmers' rights over traditional knowledge. The irony is that TRIPS grew out of an attempt to stem pirating of Western products (watches, CDs, etc.) but appears now to sanction a reverse form of piracy by the producers of technological goods.

A notorious instance of the reach and bias of TRIPS is the patenting of Indian basmati rice by the Texas-based company RiceTec Inc., which sells "Kasmati" rice and "Texmati" rice as authentic basmati. Once patented, the next steps are to demand financial compensation from the hundreds of thousands of Indian small farmers who cultivate basmati rice and to monopolize the control and reproduction of seed, using biotechnology. Meanwhile, in Thailand hundreds of farmers staged their own protests against RiceTec, which was targeting the jasmine rice on which five million farm families in Thailand depend.

Thus far, the TRIPS agreement has allowed a choice between protection via patenting and an effective *sui generis* system, a political-legal framework in which local knowledge is respected and protected and local participants can help to make decisions about collective rights. Use of the qualifier *effective* to describe the *sui generis* system assumes that local protection is worked out between governments and user communities, which do not always agree on the mode and goal of protection. Nevertheless, the *sui generis* system is potentially a better guarantor of agricultural and medicinal plant biodiversity than is the patent system. Indian physicist Vandana Shiva has noted that "indigenous knowledge systems are by and large ecological, while the dominant model of scientific knowledge, characterized by reductionism and fragmentation, is not equipped to take the complexity of interrelationships in nature fully into account" (Shiva, 1997, p. 8).

The *sui generis* option in TRIPS has been used successfully, in at least one case, to resist biopiracy. In 1996, the small Indian village of Pattuvam, in the southern state of Kerala, declared its absolute ownership over all genetic resources within its jurisdiction. The move to preempt corporate genetic prospecting is protected by the Indian constitution, which mandates decentralization of powers to village-level institutions. The initiative stemmed from a group of young villagers disaffected with Indian politics and committed to sustainable development. They came up with the idea of having the village youth document native plants and crops growing within the village's boundaries. By registering its biodiversity in local names, the village claims ownership of genetic resources, denying the possibility of corporate patents applying to those resources and indeed making subsequent patenting of life under their jurisdiction impossible. As Shiva observed: "The declaration gives recognition to community rights, to the intellectual and biological commons and provides a new interpretation to the *sui generis* option of TRIPS" (Alvares, 1997, p. 12).

Thus far the protection of genetic resources under TRIPS has been overwhelmingly undertaken not through the *sui generis* option but by the filing of patents by northern, developed countries. Graphic 1 shows that some developed countries, most notably the United States, have already filed patents on a number of important biological materials. The last row of the chart gives the scores assigned to patenting countries by the Rural Advancement Foundation International (RAFI). Compare those scores for the top ten offenders (the higher scores, in this case, are worse than lower scores) to the scores for less developed countries: China, 28; South Korea, 18; South Africa, 15; Brazil, 15; Mexico, 13.

Although the idea that genetic diversity is a human heritage has universal appeal, biodiversity can be defined from two opposing points of view. The instrumental view underlies commercial patenting, while the cultural view encourages respect for local knowledge and protection for the farmers and communities that have so carefully husbanded many of the world's genetic resources. The instrumental view has been dominant, but the cultural view gained valuable support from the 1992 Convention on Biological Diversity, an international commitment to conserve biological diversity. In addition, the convention empowered states to enact national laws to protect biodiversity. How states will interpret that right and that obligation remains to be seen.

Thinking about the Essay

Chapter 5 made the point that inequality among nations is increasing because of globalization: some nations have been able to capitalize on new opportunities while others have not. How do biopiracy and gene theft illustrate that point?

GRAPHIC 1   COUNTRIES THAT HAVE FILED THE MOST BIOLOGICAL PATENTS

Representative Sample of Patents Filed

Biological Resource	Region	Purpose	USA	UK	Germany	France	Italy	Belgium	Netherlands	Switzerland	Luxembourg	Austria
J'oublie	Africa	Sweetener	■	■	■	■	■	■	■	■	■	■
Barbasco	Amazon	Pharmaceutical	■	■	■	■	■	■	■	■	■	■
Greenheart	Latin America	Pharmaceutical	■	■	■	■	■	■	■	■	■	■
Neem	Asia	Agriculture	■	■	■	■	■	■	■	■	■	■
Bitter melon	Asia	HIV/AIDS	■	■	■	■	■	■	■	■	■	■
Snakegourd	China	HIV/AIDS	■	■	■	■	■	■	■	■	■	■
Mamala	Pacific	HIV/AIDS	■	■	■	■	■	■	■	■	■	■
Sangre de drago	Amazon	Pharmaceutical	■	■	■	■	■	■	■	■	■	■
Kava	Pacific	Pharmaceutical	■	■	■	■	■	■	■			
Basmati rice	Asia	Agriculture	■									
Quinoa	Andes	Agriculture	⬦									
Endod	Africa	Molluscicide	■									
Ayahuasca	Amazon	Plant patent	■									
The Terminator	World	Seed control	■	✕	✕	✕	✕	✕	✕	✕	✕	✕
The Verminator	World	Seed control	✕	✕	✕	✕	✕	✕	✕	✕	✕	✕
Animal cloning	World	Cloning	✕	✕	✕	■	■	■	■	■	■	■
Human cell lines	World	Diagnostic test	■	■	■	■	■	■	■	■	■	■
Human growth hormone	World	Gene patent	■	■	■	■	■	■	■	■	■	■
Human umbilical cord cells	World	Disease treatment	■	■	■	■	■	■	■	■	■	■
Transgenic soya	World	Species patent	■	■	■	■	■	■	■	■	■	■
Transgenic cotton	World	Species patent	■	■	■	■	■	■	■	■	■	■
Transgenic *Brassica*	World	Genus patent	■	■	■	■	■	■	■	■	■	■
		PATENT SCORE	**95**	**83**	**83**	**83**	**83**	**78**	**78**	**78**	**78**	**75**

Legend:

■ At least one patent issued

✕ Country designated by patent o in patent cooperation treaty

⬦ Patent abandoned

Scoring: 5 points for patent issued by country, 2.5 points for international patent issued, 2.5 points for voluntary abandonment of patent.

Source: INPADOC, 1998.

6 Assimilation and Pluralism

Will racial and ethnic groups persist?

The killing began in 1994. The president of Rwanda, a member of the Hutu tribe, was killed when his plane was shot down near the capital city. Some said that rebels, members of the Tutsi tribe, fired the fatal rocket. Others suspected extremist Hutus who resented the President's conciliatory overtures to the Tutsis. Either way, the incident sent shock waves through the tiny African country and then through the world. Hutus reacted by attacking their Tutsi neighbors. In the weeks and months that followed, 800,000 people—perhaps many more—died in the killing fields, and millions fled to neighboring nations (Gourevitch, 1998, p. 133).

The victims of the massacre and their attackers knew each other, and the killing was done face to face, with machetes, fists, firearms, and grenades. No one was spared: babies, women, children, and old people fell in the frenzied attacks. People were decapitated, pregnant women were cut open, and children were murdered by having their heads smashed together.

Today, the massacre is fresh in the memory of all Rwandans and tribal hatreds remain strong. Revenge motivates new killings, more innocents are slaughtered, and the burden of grief and outrage continues to grow. The Rwandan economy is decimated, fertile fields lie fallow, and villages, once teeming with life, have been abandoned. In one prefecture, only 8,000 Tutsi remain of the 250,000 who lived there in 1994. And they remember who the killers were (Public Broadcasting System, 1997).

This story, sadly, has many echoes across time and space. Merciless slaughters of "others" and horrific attacks on outsiders have been common throughout history. Sometimes the victims are strangers or newcomers, sometimes they are seen as threatening or inferior, and sometimes they are neighbors. The details vary, the names of the dead change, but the world never seems to outgrow its capacity for bloody atrocity and bitter enmity. Today, deadly assaults on "others" continue in the former Yugoslavia, the Middle East, Russia, Mexico, Germany, Northern Ireland, and scores of other places around the globe.

The United States has also seen its share of racial and ethnic hostility. The repressive brutality of slavery and bloodthirsty wars with Native Americans marked the nation's birth; as the nation grew, other groups—Mexican Americans, Chinese immigrants, newcomers from Europe—were victimized and attacked. Recent victims of this unfortunate American tradition include James Byrd, an African American dragged to death and decapitated in Texas, and Joseph Ileto, a Filipino mailman murdered by white racist Buford Farrow because Ileto was "Asian and held a government job."

Will these atrocities ever end? It may seem that the world will never outgrow prejudice and racism, but not everyone agrees that the situation is hopeless or that racial hatred and ethnic violence are inevitable. For example, Robert Park (Park & Burgess, 1924) and Gunnar Myrdal (1944), social scientists who pioneered the study of U.S. race relations, argued that industrialization and globalization—the very same forces that have transformed the world and that have been featured so prominently in this book—would eventually dissolve the cultural and racial lines that divide us. They argued that industrialized societies have higher levels of education, stronger democratic institutions, greater protections for civil liberties, and more elaborate, bureaucratic rules, regulations, and routines. Those forces tend to increase the extent to which people are judged objectively, by their capabilities and talents, not by their appearance, language, or religion. As the world grows more rational and more complex, tolerance will increase and the ancient enmities and narrow attitudes of the past will fade away.

Ethnic conflicts continue to kill many people around the world. Hundreds of bodies were buried in this mass grave in Rwanda. In 1998 the International Criminal Tribunal for Rwanda convicted Jean Kambanda, former prime minister of Rwanda, of genocide and crimes against humanity. He is the first head of government to be convicted and punished for genocide. He will serve his life term in either Mali, Benin, or Swaziland.

After a century of Nazi death camps, ethnic cleansing, lynching, race riots, and myriad other forms of brutal racism, can there really be a basis for such optimism? This chapter explores that question. We begin with a theory about the evolution of racial and ethnic relations that can be used to interpret events in the world today, then outline some of the ways that societies deal with racial and ethnic difference. The remainder of the chapter examines racial and ethnic relationships resulting from two very different processes and the ways in which ethnicity and race shape people's lives. The end of the chapter presents some conclusions on the future of prejudice, racism, and the kinds of atrocities that gripped Rwanda in 1994. Is it possible that the racial and ethnic violence that has plagued the world for so long can stop? Were Park and Myrdal prescient and insightful or just naive, wishful thinkers?

Global Species Consolidation: Analyzing Race and Ethnicity

Walter Wallace, a distinguished sociologist and scholar, recently revived and updated the predictions of Park and Myrdal. He envisions "the eventual consolidation of all ethnicities into one *global ethnicity,* all races into one *global race,* and all nationalities into one *global nationality*" (Wallace, 1997, p. 3, emphasis in the original). To be sure, the future will have conflicts and disputes, and other dimensions of inequality—social class and gender, for example—will continue to divide people into hostile camps. In Wallace's view, however, the boundaries of culture and color that are so significant today—the group affiliations that people daily fight and die for—will become meaningless as humans complete the process of **global species consolidation.**

Wallace's argument, presented in summary form in Graphic 6.1, is sweeping. It covers virtually all of time and the entire globe, beginning with the first appearance of our species some 100,000 years ago and ending in the distant future. The starting point of the model ("point of origin") refers to East Africa, the area in which the oldest fossil evidence of our species has been found and, thus, the area in which human beings first emerged. The sections that follow examine the remaining stages of the process: dispersion, differentiation, contact, and consolidation.

Dispersion and Differentiation: The Origins of Ethnicity and Race

As noted in Chapter 5, our distant ancestors relied on hunting and gathering for their sustenance, moving as they had to in search of food and security (Wallace, 1997, p. 17). The small groups in which they lived grew and split, grew and split again, gradually dispersing and slowly wandering until, by about 10,000 years ago, they had wandered far from the African homeland and peopled virtually the entire globe.

As they migrated, they accommodated themselves to many different environments: deserts, rain forests, ice and snow, and searing heat, to name but a few. Our

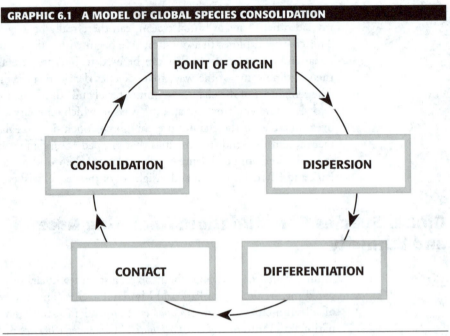

species is clever and resourceful, and our ancestors grew more diverse as they adapted to local conditions. Groups that settled in deserts, for example, naturally developed lifestyles different from those of groups that had adapted to rain forests. Migration thus led to cultural differentiation: an increasing diversity in language, customs, religious beliefs, and technologies (Wallace, 1997, p. 15). By 10,000 years ago, there were thousands of distinct societies, each a unique combination of institutions and culture.

Physical and anatomical differentiation sometimes followed cultural differentiation. When groups were isolated from each other, high levels of inbreeding altered the gene pool and created the differences in appearance that we label "racial" today. Exactly why and how our species developed the various combinations of so-called racial traits—skin color, hair texture, and so forth—is unknown. While some traits may be adaptations to particular environments, many others appear to confer no significant benefit or advantage. Our species relies on culture, intelligence, and problem-solving ability to survive, and our racial features are not very important from the standpoint of adaptation and evolution.

That is not to say that race is unimportant in human affairs. Racial differences, along with the cultural differences that evolved during the 90,000-year-long human diaspora, have become primary markers of group membership, social boundaries that differentiate friend from foe, allies from enemies. But this prominence derives not from biology or genetics; it is the result of specific historical, political, and social circumstances that this chapter explores later.

Contact and Consolidation: Evolution of a Global Species

The period of migration and differentiation began to end with the invention of agriculture, in about 8000 B.C. The invention of agriculture brought new dynamics to human social life. Agricultural societies were more productive than hunting-gathering societies and could become larger in size and more complex in their division of labor and institutional structures. Increasing populations meant a greater demand for land to produce food, a dynamic that often led to contact, conflict, and warfare between neighboring societies.

With the invention of agriculture, the 90,000-year-long process of differentiation stopped, and the globe began to slowly shrink. As farming fueled the growth of societies and increased the value of land, intersocietal contact and conflict increased and produced larger and more complex social forms. Small, local societies were forged into regional states through military conquest, and some of the more powerful states—ancient Egypt, the Roman Empire, China, and the Aztecs—built empires that covered vast territories and incorporated a diversity of cultures and races. When nations and empires united separate peoples and exposed them to a single culture and language, they reversed the differentiation created by the preagricultural migrations. In many ways, the extinction of local languages and cultures that is going on today (see Chapter 4) is a continuation of the process.

Thus, world history since the invention of agriculture can be seen as a series of miniglobalizations, and each multiethnic and multiracial state represented at least a small step on the path to species consolidation (Wallace, 1997, p. 55). Our species spent 90,000 years flying apart and the last 10,000 years gradually, haltingly coming back together (with, of course, some spectacular reversals of the process). By connecting the consolidation phase to the point of origin in Graphic 6.1, Wallace suggests that we will become in the future what we were in the distant past: a single, unified species.

In the years since the industrial revolution, the trends toward global unity have continued in economics, politics, culture, and other areas. Economically, the world increasingly functions as a single global system with a variety of organizations operating on an international scale. Politically, several trends toward global unity are notable. As you will learn in Chapter 10, democracy, in all its various, imperfect forms, has become the most common form of government and the universal model for political institutions around the world (Wallace, 1997, p. 122). Also, a wide variety of international political organizations have been established, the most significant of which is the United Nations.

On the other hand, not all the evidence supports Wallace. As pointed out in Chapter 1, the world is—at least at present—growing more fragmented politically, and a variety of ethnic, racial, and religious groups are demanding their own nations. What would persuade these groups to stop flying apart?

For Wallace, what's at stake is not just a reduction in prejudice and ethnic and racial violence but the very survival of our species. At the dawn of the twenty-first century, the greatest threats facing our species lie in the natural world: global warming and climate change, pollution, acid rain, destruction of rain forests, microbial epidemics. Such dangers—some distant, some immediate—are life threatening not to a single individual, group, or nation but to the globe. They have no respect for group boundaries and don't care who is white or black, Tutsi or Hutu, Catholic or Protestant. In a shrinking, increasingly interconnected globe, they threaten everyone and, thus, require a global approach to deal with them effectively. What will end the current phase of political fragmentation and drive global species consolidation is the recognition that, without it, the possibilities of survival for our species decrease (Wallace, 1997, p. 163).

Social Relations in a Differentiated World

The world today may be entering Wallace's consolidation phase, but racial and ethnic differences continue to shape societies and thus individual lives. Such differences contribute to inequalities in wealth and opportunity, oppression, conflict, and a wide variety of petty, nagging slights. Some groups are more likely than others to blend in with the larger culture. As you will see, however, the experience of difference depends to a great extent on how racial and ethnic groups originally came into contact. Group relations that originated in force and violence, through conquest and colonization, generally result in patterns of subordination and oppression that are more rigid and longer lasting. On the other hand, group relations that originate in immigration tend to evolve more easily into mutual acceptance and harmony.

Minority Groups and Dominant Groups

In a differentiated world, we often find that groups are not equal in their access to resources or the power they have to shape their own lives. The less powerful groups are called **minority groups,** regardless of their numbers relative to the more powerful groups. Minority groups may be quite large and even be a majority of the population, as people of African descent were during the days of apartheid in South Africa.

Regardless of relative size, minority groups are defined by two characteristics (Wirth, 1945). First, they are the targets of differential and unequal treatment and have fewer opportunities and less access to wealth, status, power, and other resources. The severity of the inequality varies and, at the extreme, may include genocide and mass extermination. Second, the members of the minority group have some characteristic that makes them highly visible and easily identifiable. Racial minority groups are defined mainly by physical characteristics (for example, skin color) and ethnic minority groups by cultural traits (for example, language, religion, dress, or accent). In either case, to maintain a system of group inequality, it must be plainly obvious who is in the minority and who is not.

Where a minority group exists, so too must a **dominant group.** By definition, the dominant group enjoys greater access to resources, political power, wealth, opportunity, and status. Indeed, dominant groups create minority groups and, as in the case of American slaveholders, perpetuate the differences in status for their own benefit. Given the history and power dynamics of the world over the past several centuries, it is not surprising that recent dominant groups have often been white Europeans. However, a longer view of time reveals that dominance is hardly a European monopoly, and virtually every identifiable group has, at some time or some place, experienced minority status. For example, in the context of recent world history, the British would normally be thought of as a "dominant group." However, the modern day population of Britain is a blend of Saxons, Normans, Celts, and other ethnic groups (not to mention Protestants and Catholics), each of which was, at one time or another, recent immigrants, a persecuted minority, or an oppressive dominant group.

Prejudice and Discrimination

Any dominant-minority relationship generates—and is partially defined by—prejudice and discrimination. **Prejudice** is the tendency to think about other groups in negative ways, to attach negative emotions to those groups, and to prejudge people based on their group membership. Prejudice includes negative emotions such as contempt, disgust, or hatred and **stereotypes,** or overgeneralizations about entire groups of people (for example, statements such as "Jews are miserly," "Italians are hot-tempered," and "African Americans are irresponsible"). A person is prejudiced to the extent that he or she maintains rigid stereotypes about other groups and associates strong emotions with those perceptions. While prejudice involves thoughts and feelings, **discrimination** is the unequal treatment of others based on their group membership. Examples would include not hiring or promoting persons because they are African American (or Puerto Rican or Filipino). Of course, prejudice, stereotypes, and discrimination don't affect just racial and ethnic minorities; they also affect people in minority positions because of their gender, sexual orientation, body type, and so on.

Both prejudice and discrimination can be characteristic of an individual, a group, or entire societies and cultures. Some stereotypes are embedded in culture and passed on from generation to generation during socialization, which you learned about in Chapter 4. Thus, in a society with a strong heritage of racism, children learn prejudice in the same way they learn language, values, and customs (Brown, 1995, pp. 119–160). Groups and entire societies can also discriminate. During the days of racial segregation in the American South and apartheid in South Africa, institutions and legal systems were organized so as to reinforce and perpetuate black inequality in education, politics, jobs, the criminal justice system, and virtually every other aspect of society.

Assimilation and Pluralism

In sociology, Wallace's concept of consolidation is usually referred to as **assimilation:** the process by which two or more formerly separate and distinct groups merge into a single group. A useful model of this process for minority groups was developed by sociologist Milton Gordon (1964). The model separates assimilation into a number of stages, of which we will focus on the first three:

1. *Acculturation.* Assimilation begins when the minority group learns the culture and language of the host society (Chapter 4 explained the process). A group's level of acculturation can be measured by its changing values, speech, and behavior patterns.

2. *Integration.* During this phase, members of the minority group begin to enter the more public sectors of the larger society, including the job market, the school system, and churches. Assimilation at this level can be assessed by measuring the minority group's economic, educational, and political standing relative to the dominant group. As integration in the public sector proceeds, people from different groups begin to form acquaintanceships and then friendships. Integration at this more intimate level can be measured by counting the number of friends, acquaintances, and neighbors people have with members of other groups.

3. *Intermarriage.* The third stage of assimilation occurs when the intimate relationships yield marriage partners.

In Gordon's view, assimilation proceeds through a series of fixed, interlocking stages: acculturation is followed by integration in the public sector, which leads to more intimate forms of association and, finally, to marital assimilation.

Groups that come into contact do not always consolidate or assimilate; sometimes they retain distinct racial and ethnic identities within the larger society. One alternative to assimilation is **pluralism.** Pluralistic groups, like the Amish (or Pennsylvania Dutch) and many Native American tribes in North America and the Hutus and Tutsis in Rwanda, are structurally separate and maintain distinct identities and sets of traditions. Pluralism in the United States is manifested by multiculturalism, celebrations of ethnic or cultural holidays such as Kwanzaa or St. Patrick's Day, and the preservation of the music, cuisine, or other lifestyle elements of particular groups and traditions.

A more radical alternative to assimilation is **separatism.** A separatist racial or ethnic group wishes to sever ties with the dominant group and become independent and autonomous. Political fragmentation and separatism are widespread in the world today and can be found in Canada, Great Britain, many African nations, the Middle East, Russia, Tibet, and Mexico.

The extent of pluralism in a particular society is sometimes described in terms of Gordon's stages of assimilation. Complete or cultural pluralism exists when the minority group is neither acculturated nor integrated. An example would be the Cuban immigrants to the United States who have established a self-contained social

American society is full of examples of assimilation—in the workplace, in social circles, in institutions, on campus, everywhere. The highest level of assimilation involves intermarriage. In the photo at the top of the page, Sakinabai marries Gregg in a Jewish ceremony. She is Asian but spent the first few years of her life in Uganda, until tyrant Idi Amin expelled all Asians from the country in the 1970s. Her Muslim family moved to the United States, and she met Gregg while both attended Trinity College in Connecticut. Their marriage represents a merging of cultures, religions, and histories.

structure in Little Havana, a part of Miami. There they can find jobs and housing and obtain all the goods and services they desire while speaking only Spanish and maintaining cultural values and beliefs distinct from "American" culture. Churches, schools, political bodies, and other social institutions in Little Havana, although linked to institutions in the larger society, are dominated by people who maintain a strong Cuban identity. Some Asian immigrant groups, such as the Chinese and the Vietnamese, have taken a similar path.

Structural pluralism, in contrast, exists when the group has substantially acculturated but has not integrated. Groups share a common culture and value system with the larger society but maintain separate and distinct institutional structures and communities. Black-white relations in the United States might be described in terms of structural pluralism. The groups share a language and many common cultural elements and may even be "together" (integrated) in the school system and at work. At the same time, blacks and whites are "separate" in their neighborhoods, churches, and voluntary organizations and service clubs, such as Boy and Girl Scout Troops.

Contact Situations

The last element of racial and ethnic differentiation we will discuss in this chapter is the most important one for our analysis of the likelihood of global species consolidation. Wallace argues that the **contact situation**—the conditions under which groups first come together—is a crucial determinant of future relations. He identifies four separate contact situations, of which we will focus on two: minority groups created by colonization and conquest and those created by immigration. Wallace hypothesizes that groups created by immigration (particularly when they are physically similar to the host group) are more likely to consolidate. In contrast, groups created by colonization and conquest (especially when they are racially different from the dominant group) are more likely to experience long-lasting discrimination and prejudice and to face more serious problems of poverty and powerlessness (see also Blauner, 1972).

The key difference between the two types of groups is power. Minority groups created by colonization or conquest are unlikely to be left with the power to defend themselves against unfair treatment or to be able to combat discrimination and inequality. Immigrant groups, even though they may be impoverished and desperate when they first arrive, have more freedom and more control of their fate. For example, an immigrant group can choose to sever ties with the dominant group by going somewhere else or by independently establishing a separate, self-sufficient enclave, choices that are not available to minority groups created by conquest or colonization. Furthermore, immigrant groups are more likely to possess some skills or resources they can use to improve their status within the social structure of the dominant society. The rest of the chapter examines the profound impact that the contact situation can have on group relations.

Contact Situations: Conquest and Colonization

Virtually every intergroup conflict that has made headlines in recent decades—Northern Ireland, the former Yugoslavia, Rwanda, Canada, the Middle East, Russia—has its origins in some form of conquest or colonization. Even a cursory examination of group relations around the globe lends credence to the hypothesis that such situations are longer lasting and more difficult to resolve than those created by immigration. In many cases, the task of merely ending open hostilities, let alone establishing a basis for peaceful coexistence, seems impossible, and one searches in vain for support for Wallace's thesis of global consolidation. On occasion, however, even the most ancient and bitter situations can take some surprising twists.

The European Colonization and Conquest of Africa

The continent of Africa was one of the primary targets of European domination over the past five centuries, and white Europeans invaded and conquered most of the continent, expropriating resources, enslaving and killing millions of Africans, and establishing intense prejudice and systematic discrimination in the process. Consider the maps of Africa in Graphic 6.2. In 1950, there were only three independent African nations (Egypt, Ethiopia, and Liberia); the remainder of the continent was controlled by European powers.

Why were European nations able to conquer and colonize virtually the entire continent? Wallace attributes European dominance to the luck of territorial draw. While the environmental conditions in Europe favored the growth of agricultural technology, those in Africa did not, especially in the bulk of the continent that lies south of the Sahara Desert. In Africa, poor soil combined with a highly seasonal rainfall limited the development of farming and the large, more complex social structures that agriculture supports (Wallace, 1997, pp. 48–52). Thus, when regular contact began, European nations were able to use their greater power to dominate the smaller, more fragmented, and less developed societies of Africa.

As we pointed out in Chapter 2, the age of European empires has ended. By the 1960s, most African nations had achieved independence, and the map of Africa today bears only a faint resemblance to the 1950s map. On the other hand, modern boundaries were established during the European colonial period and do not reflect the everyday cultural realities of the African peoples. In some cases, postcolonial boundaries separate ethnic and tribal groups; in others they combine groups that traditionally have been rivals, thus creating huge problems for national cohesion and internal peace. Consider, for example, the nation of Rwanda.

Rwanda. Hutus and Tutsis have been living together in the area that is now the nation of Rwanda for centuries. Traditionally, the more aristocratic Tutsis ruled the more numerous Hutus (about 85% of the population) in a pluralistic, unequal, but not particularly rancorous or violent relationship. When European nations colonized the area, they allied with the Tutsis and allowed them to accumulate even

GRAPHIC 6.2   EFFECTS OF EUROPEAN COLONIZATION OF AFRICA

European Control of Africa, 1950

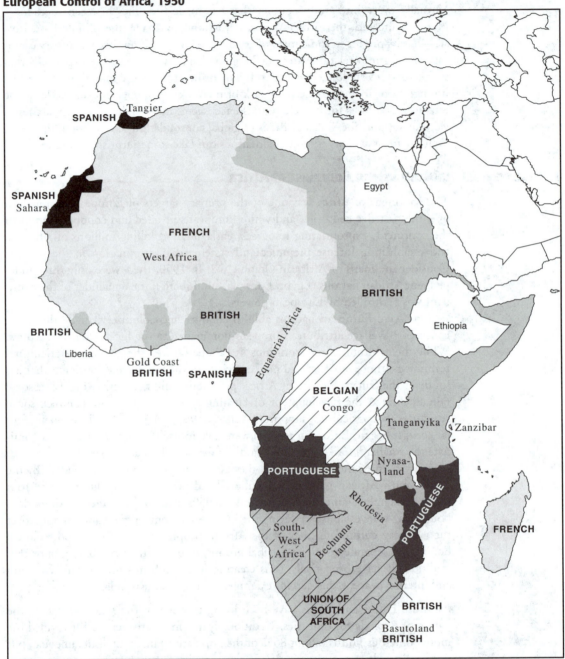

Africa, 2000

more power and resources at the expense of the Hutus. That policy exacerbated tribal rivalries and Hutu resentment, and relations between the groups deteriorated, sporadically erupting into violent attacks. The 1994 killings described earlier were simply the most spectacular chapter in a very long story.

While the European colonial powers did not create the rivalry between the Hutus and the Tutsis, they escalated the mutual hostilities by playing one group off against the other. After independence, the new nation of Rwanda was left with the task of consolidating two extremely antagonistic tribes into a single nation—a challenge that, at least for now, is not being met. The recent history of this tiny nation provides little support for Wallace's consolidation thesis, but one case should not cause us to dismiss the theory entirely.

South Africa. Until very recently, most observers might well have cited South Africa along with Rwanda as evidence against Wallace's prediction. Before the late 1980s, South African race relations were governed by apartheid, one of the most elaborate systems of racial repression ever constructed. The tiny white dominant group (about 15% of the population) controlled and exploited black South Africans in virtually every way possible: politically, economically, and in everyday encounters and interactions.

The Dutch were the first Europeans to arrive in the area that was to become South Africa, in the 1600s. They fought with the native tribes for control of the land; eventually their superior military technology allowed them to prevail. From the time of the Dutch conquest, the main role of black South Africans was to provide a cheap, powerless, easily controlled labor force for the benefit of the dominant group.

In the 1800s, South Africa became a British colony. The British also were committed to maintaining white privilege, and in 1948, the apartheid system of racial repression and exploitation was formally enacted. Apartheid resembled legal segregation in the American South but was even more elaborate and repressive. Black South Africans were accorded virtually no political or legal rights and were the objects of unrelenting prejudice, degradation, and humiliation. They were forced to carry identity papers and live in bleak segregated townships with inferior social services, far from their workplaces in the white areas of South Africa. Until recently, one would have been hard pressed to find any evidence of consolidation between blacks and whites in South African society.

Then, in the late 1980s, apartheid began to crumble. Within a few years, the system was dismantled, the vote was extended to all citizens regardless of race, and in 1994 Nelson Mandela, a black man who had served 27 years in prison for his opposition to racial injustice, was elected president. In the second democratic presidential election in the nation's history, Mandela was succeeded in 1999 by another black man, Thabo M. Mbeke.

What caused apartheid to end? The reasons are complex and generally consistent with Wallace's views of the effects of globalization on group relations. By the late 1980s, South Africa was an outcast nation, subject to boycotts and trade embargoes and excluded from many international organizations (for example, the Olympics). While black South Africans conducted a protest campaign from the inside, a variety of nations, organizations, and groups brought pressure from the outside. (Recall this theme from Chapter 1: "Internal and external forces interact to change societies.") Isolation and economic uncertainty brought the white leadership to the realization that some accommodation had to be made if South Africa was to survive in the global system. Apartheid ended not with a bloody race war but with a series of reforms initiated by the white leadership, the very group that had repeatedly vowed to defend the system of racial privilege to the death.

Today, more than a decade after the end of apartheid, South Africa still faces enormous challenges of racial integration and justice. The black population now has political power, but the wealth of the nation remains concentrated in the white community. The segregated school system did little to prepare blacks for positions of leadership or jobs that require technical expertise or sophisticated skills, and most high-level positions in government and business continue to be held by whites. This experiment in consolidation could still fail, and South Africa might still become the site of devastating race wars. On the other hand, the dramatic transition from racial repression and separation—the legacy of conquest and domination that began centuries ago—could also provide a model of change and consolidation for other equally divided societies. (For more, see Beinart, 1994; Mallaby, 1992; and Van den Berghe, 1967.)

Before the fall of apartheid in South Africa, all citizens carried an identity card that classified them according to race. Blacks could be stopped at any time and asked for their papers. Their movement was restricted, and they were not allowed in "white areas" without a documented reason, such as a job. When in white areas, blacks had to use separate facilities, such as this bus marked Slegs vir nie Blankes, or "Non-Europeans Only."

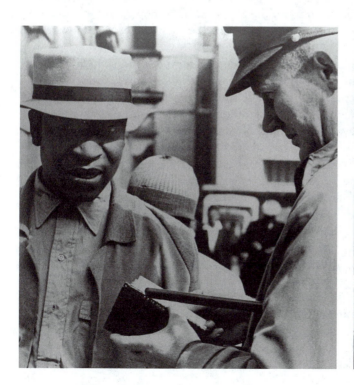

Involuntary Americans: Slavery and Segregation

Relations between blacks and whites in the United States also began with the European domination of Africa. This contact situation began with the transatlantic slave trade, which became a vital leg in the system of commerce that brought labor to the Western Hemisphere and precious metals and agricultural crops to Europe. The slave trade was also an early chapter in the development of the world system of societies and a global economy.

The first permanent English colony in the Americas was founded at Jamestown, Virginia, in 1607, and the first Africans arrived about a decade later. For several decades, African Americans remained few in number, and most were treated as indentured servants (persons required to work for a specific master for a term of years), not as slaves. That situation began to change in the 1660s, as large plantations began to dominate agricultural production and the demand for labor rose. American slavery originated as a solution to a labor shortage, a business decision made consciously and deliberately (Noel, 1968; see also Morgan, 1975; Smedley, 1993).

The institution of slavery was constructed gradually and carefully in the decades following the 1660s. The system institutionalized the low status of African Americans and gave slave owners virtually unlimited power, up to and sometimes including the power of life and death. In the eyes of the law, slaves were considered property, not people, and they had no standing in court and few ways to defend themselves or protect their interests. When the Civil War (1860–1865) ended slavery two centuries after its creation, the Southern black population was impoverished, largely powerless, and uneducated and had few skills other than those related to plantation work.

African Americans under slavery did undergo a form of consolidation or assimilation. The masters and overseers needed to communicate with their workforce and insisted that the slaves learn English and other American ways. The acculturation was coerced and involuntary and did not, of course, lead to integration—such a progression would have been unthinkable during the days of slavery. One of the legacies of this contact situation was a kind of structural pluralism combined with extreme inequality. Blacks and whites were both separate and together: they shared a common culture and language but lived in separate institutional structures, with blacks having virtually no access to power, wealth, or status.

After the Civil War, slavery was replaced by another system of race relations that combined structural pluralism and inequality: de jure segregation (segregation by law). Under this U.S. version of apartheid, black southerners continued to be an unskilled, inexpensive, relatively powerless agricultural labor force. That status was institutionalized by a series of laws passed by the Southern states beginning in the 1880s that separated blacks and whites in virtually every phase of social life, consigned blacks to an inferior status, and sustained the powerlessness and poverty of African Americans.

Segregation ended in the 1960s as the result of the combined impact of the civil rights movement, federal legislation, and Supreme Court decisions. At that time,

Race relations have improved in the United States over the centuries. The country no longer has slaves working at cotton gins. It no longer has theaters for "colored people," as shown in this photo from Leland, Mississippi in 1937. But the country remains largely segregated for a variety of reasons: African Americans earn lower wages and have less education than whites, and they continue to experience other forms of discrimination and prejudice. Greater equality will be reached only with strict enforcement of antidiscrimination laws, continuation of affirmative action programs, and, perhaps most important, a new attitude of tolerance and inclusion that hopefully will emerge with younger generations.

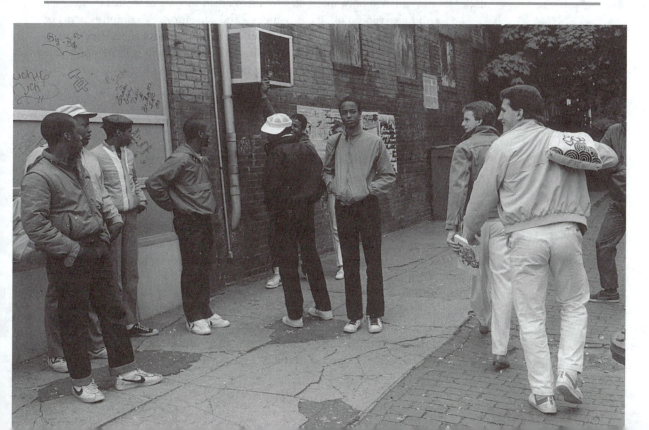

the majority of African Americans still lived in the South and, not surprisingly for a group that had experienced three centuries of extreme inequality, remained relatively powerless and impoverished.

Contemporary Race Relations in the United States

Today, African Americans are free from rigid systems of oppression and control, but they have been in that position for less than half a century, only a few generations. The legacy of three centuries of oppression is predictable: significant racial inequality on most measures of economic well-being and quality of life and a strong tradition of antiblack prejudice.

Are American race relations today tending toward consolidation? In answering that question, we might stress the progress that has been made ("the glass is half full") or the work that remains ("the glass is half empty"). Clearly, however, the experiences of African Americans verify the hypothesis that colonized and conquered minority groups experience more extreme forms of rejection and exclusion and challenge Wallace's ideas about eventual consolidation.

For example, consider the two measures of racial inequality in the United States in Graphic 6.3. One chart displays median family incomes for blacks and whites over the past half-century. While incomes for both groups have risen, the racial income gap remains quite noticeable. In the late 1940s, black families earned about 50% of the income that white families earned; after five decades of changing race relations, black families still earn only about 60% of the median income of white families.

The second chart in Graphic 6.3 compares the educational accomplishments of blacks and whites. Since 1960, racial differences in level of education have diminished but have not disappeared. The narrowing of the racial gap is more noticeable at the high school level, and the continuing racial gap in college graduates is a particularly ominous sign for racial equality in a postindustrial economy, where access to better jobs is increasingly tied to educational credentials.

Why does racial inequality persist in the United States? We consider two forces, employment patterns and residential patterns.

The Impact of Deindustrialization. We briefly considered the effects of deindustrialization (the shift from a manufacturing or industrial economy to a service and information-based economy) in Chapter 5 and will return to that issue in Chapter 10. Here, however, we consider its effects on black Americans and other minority workers of color. The changing structure of the economy and the job market has produced winners and losers. Unfortunately, a large percentage of African Americans and other minority groups of color have social and educational characteristics that make them more likely to be in the latter category.

The postindustrial job market for African Americans is segmented. That is, poorer African Americans with more modest educational achievements are largely restricted to the low-wage service sector and face a job market marked by high rates of unemployment and insecurity. More-educated African Americans, on the other hand, have prospects for upward mobility that are unprecedented in U.S. history.

GRAPHIC 6.3   BLACK-WHITE INEQUALITY IN THE UNITED STATES

Family Income

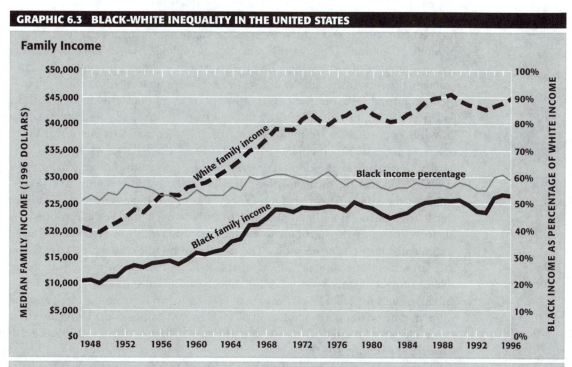

Education Completion Rates

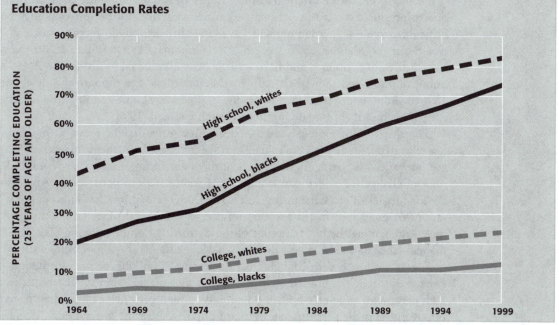

Sources: Family Income graph adapted from U.S. Bureau of the Census, 2000; Education Completion Rates graph adapted from U.S. Bureau of the Census, 1999, p. 169.

Well-qualified black Americans still face discrimination and prejudice, but their prospects for success and achievement in the larger society are greater than for any previous generation. The favorable situation of middle-class African Americans is due to a number of factors, including the growth of white-collar occupations, government pressure (for example, affirmative action programs) to increase employment opportunities for minorities, and the efforts of millions of individual African Americans to improve their lives and those of their families and communities.

While opportunities for middle-class African Americans have increased, many observers argue that their affluence is more tenuous than that of whites with comparable occupational positions. For example, in one study Oliver and Shapiro (1995) found that the median income of white-collar blacks was only 70% that of whites at the same occupational level. They also found huge gaps in the total net worth (real estate, stock holdings, and so on) between middle-class whites and blacks, a difference they attribute to the racial gaps in wealth and income that have accumulated over past generations. The families of middle-class whites have access to a larger pool of economic assets and resources and are much more likely to be able to provide financial assistance for college education, business ventures, home purchases, and so forth. Thus, the present economic gap between the black and the white middle class is partly a function of the current realities in the job market and partly a legacy of racial discrimination in the past (Oliver & Shapiro, 1995; see also Cose, 1993; Landry, 1987).

Furthermore, to the extent that the advance of the black middle class has been due to pressures created by affirmative action programs, further progress may be difficult to achieve. Those programs have tended to atrophy in recent years (Cancio, Evans, & Maume, 1996; Feagin, 1991; Thomas, 1993; Willie, 1989), have very little public support, and have actually been eliminated in California. A 1998 public opinion poll showed that affirmative action had the support of only about 10% of whites and was, in fact, "strongly" opposed by almost a third of the African Americans polled (National Opinion Research Council, 1998).

The situation of more-educated African Americans may be tenuous, but their less educated counterparts are in danger of becoming a permanent underclass: jobless, powerless, surviving on the fringes of the mainstream economy, and with little hope of change. The dilemmas facing the African-American poor stem partly from the long legacy of racial inequality and partly from their current low levels of preparation for good jobs in the growing service sector. African Americans (especially males) are among the major victims of the decreasing number of good blue-collar, manual-labor jobs located near the cities, a decline that is at the root of many of the problems associated with "the ghetto." For example, no jobs for men in the inner cities means that the burden of child support falls on the women. The result is a high percentage of female-headed households, a high percentage of children reared in poverty, and the perpetuation of urban poverty across the generations. To some extent, such marginalization faces all people with lower educational credentials, regardless of race or ethnicity, but African Americans (and other peoples of color) also face barriers of race above and beyond the handicaps of lower social class.

Deindustrialization clearly has adverse effects for people with low levels of educational accomplishments, exactly the characteristic of a minority group that so recently escaped from legalized segregation and inferior school systems. But, you might wonder, if employment opportunities are moving elsewhere, why don't African Americans move too?

Residential Segregation. Sociologists Douglas Massey and Nancy Denton (1993) argue that residential segregation, one aspect of structural pluralism combined with racial inequality, is the single most powerful force sustaining the social class differences between black and white Americans. The races remain sharply segregated in virtually every large metropolitan area in the United States. The pattern almost everywhere (see Graphic 6.4) is for blacks and other peoples of color (many of them recent immigrants) to be concentrated in an inner city surrounded by rings of largely white suburbs. African Americans have been increasingly concentrated in metropolitan areas in recent decades. They are now much more urbanized than whites and much more likely to live in the center city (55% versus only about 22% for whites). Thus, even as good jobs disappear or move away from the urban areas, a large percentage of African Americans remain in the cities (Farley, 1996, p. 266).

These modern patterns of segregation and inequality, unlike those created by slavery and de jure segregation, are the results of complex and subtle forces. For example, although doing so is illegal, real estate agents continue to guide prospective black home buyers away from areas inhabited by the dominant group (a practice called "racial steering") and to utilize other techniques to maintain residential segregation. Banks and other financial institutions reject minority-group loan

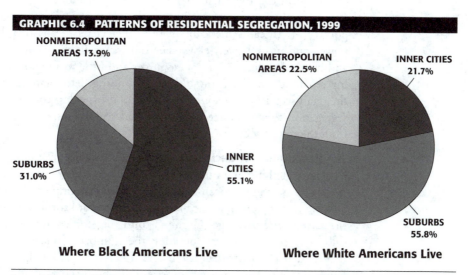

GRAPHIC 6.4   PATTERNS OF RESIDENTIAL SEGREGATION, 1999

NONMETROPOLITAN AREAS 13.9%
SUBURBS 31.0%
INNER CITIES 55.1%

Where Black Americans Live

NONMETROPOLITAN AREAS 22.5%
INNER CITIES 21.7%
SUBURBS 55.8%

Where White Americans Live

Source: Adapted from U.S. Bureau of the Census, 1999.

Well-educated African-Americans have more opportunities than ever before, creating upward mobility for this segment of the population. Overall, however, educational attainment for African-Americans is lower than that for whites. People with little education must settle for low-paying jobs in the service sector. The result is low family incomes and high rates of poverty among African-American children.

applications at higher rates than dominant-group applications. Furthermore, affordable housing and public transportation are often lacking in the suburban areas to which jobs are moving, and impoverished inner-city residents have few options for commuting long distances (Massey and Denton, 1993, p. 182).

The result is that black Americans are more racially segregated than other minority groups and their neighborhoods tend to be more impoverished as well. Massey and Denton call the phenomenon "hypersegregation," or the extreme concentration of poverty combined with racial segregation. The residential isolation and poverty of African Americans in the inner cities means they have little political power, and it is relatively easy, when dollars get tight, to cut their services, schools, and medical clinics. With few resources and little income, maintenance and housing repair suffer. When the quality of housing deteriorates and poverty increases, the retail sector (and the jobs and services it provides) collapses. Poverty and racial segregation thus reinforce each other and seal off inner-city black neighborhoods from the rest of society.

The Persistence of Racial Inequality. Black-white relations in the United States present something of a mixed case for Wallace's theory of global species consolidation. The status of African Americans clearly has improved on many dimensions, and the races are integrating and consolidating, at least in some ways. For example, the rate of intermarriage (Gordon's third stage of assimilation) has risen dramatically over the past several decades: the number of black-white married couples increased fivefold between 1970 and 1995 (the glass is half full). On the other hand, interracial marriages comprise only about 0.6% of all married couples (the glass is half-empty) (U.S. Bureau of the Census, 1998, p. 60).

Massive problems of racial inequality remain, and the racial inequality that has been thoroughly built into our history continues in the present and threatens to remain a feature of the future. Deindustrialization, residential segregation, and urban poverty are some of the key factors limiting further movement toward racial equality and consolidation.

Contact Situations: Immigration

Immigration has shaped the history of many nations, but perhaps none more than the United States. Graphic 6.5 shows the rates of legal immigration to the United States since the 1820s. We focus on two periods of immigration: the first from the 1820s through the 1920s, the second covering more recent decades.

In the earlier period, immigrants were overwhelmingly from Europe. Most, especially toward the end of the period, were peasants forced off the land by industrialization and the mechanization of agriculture. The United States was an attractive destination for them because it had a vast, thinly settled frontier (once Native Americans were eliminated as a threat) and relatively more opportunity, even for poor, uneducated peasants, than was available in Europe.

In the more recent period, immigration is more diverse in national origin but continues to reflect the forces of industrialization and globalization: the crowded conditions in less developed nations and the concentration of opportunity in the

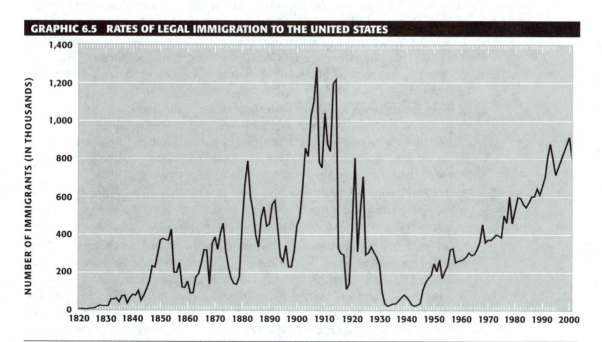

GRAPHIC 6.5   RATES OF LEGAL IMMIGRATION TO THE UNITED STATES

NUMBER OF IMMIGRANTS (IN THOUSANDS)

Source: Adapted from U.S. Immigration and Naturalization Service, 1997.

industrialized world and in the United States, the leading economic power in the world. As in the nineteenth century, immigration today is global in scope and one of the fundamental forces shaping the modern world.

This section examines the two different eras of immigration to the United States in more detail. As you shall see, the outcomes of the earlier era tend to support Wallace's consolidation thesis. The more contemporary period, on the other hand, raises some troubling questions.

Immigration and Assimilation Then

Immigration from the 1820s through the 1920s had an enormous impact on the young, industrializing United States. It provided workers for the factories and mines, helped to settle the frontier, and provided much of the energy that fueled the rise of the United States to the position of a world power in the twentieth century. Many immigrants—from places like Italy, Ireland, Sweden, and Poland—arrived penniless, uneducated, and unskilled, and they were often the victims of severe rejection and harsh discrimination. Today, in sharp contrast, the descendants of even the most destitute and miserable of the European immigrant groups are assimilated and, on the average, equal to national norms in terms of income, education, and virtually all other measures of equality. We can analyze the consolidation of European immigrant groups in terms of Gordon's model. Keep in mind that the movement of these minority groups through the stages of assimilation took decades and was often marked by the passing of the generations.

1. The first generation (the actual immigrants) tended to not assimilate very much. They often lived in ethnically distinct neighborhoods such as "Little Italy," where they could maintain their original culture: speak the old language, find familiar foods, and live in accordance with the old ways.

2. Assimilation began in earnest with the children of the immigrants (the second generation), especially in the public schools. The schools socialized this generation into the broad American culture and prepared them to integrate into the mainstream society. As adults, they often left their ethnic neighborhoods and raised their children—the third generation—in nonethnic settings.

3. The third generation continued the process of integration into the private, more intimate associations of the larger society and laid the groundwork for rising rates of intermarriage for themselves and for the generations that followed.

Today, European immigrant groups are in their fifth or later generation. Intermarriage has been so extensive that many people can no longer sort out their exact ancestry. The sense of ethnic identity for these groups is fading and has become largely symbolic and voluntary, a part of the self-image that may be emphasized on certain family or ceremonial occasions but otherwise ignored. Their identification with their ancestors may manifest itself as an interest in family history, participation in clubs and organizations that have an ethnic theme, or in other ways that are not central to their jobs, their circle of friends, or even the daily lives of their families.

Unlike their ancestors or members of minority groups of color, the descendants of the European immigrant groups can choose the extent to which they want to identify with their group. They can stress their ethnicity, ignore it completely, or vacillate between the two extremes. Overall, however, the white ethnic groups are at the end of the consolidation or assimilation process and are in the "twilight of ethnicity." (See Alba, 1990; Lieberson & Waters, 1988; Steinberg, 1981.)

According to sociologist Douglas Massey (1995), several factors explain the successful assimilation of European ethnic groups:

◆ *Declining rates of immigration.* Graphic 6.5 shows that immigration from Europe declined dramatically after the 1920s. The Great Depression of the 1930s brought skyrocketing unemployment to the United States and much of the rest of the world and decreased the incentive to immigrate. Also, immigration policy in the United States became very restrictive in the 1920s. Legislation was passed to greatly reduce the overall number of immigrants permitted each year and to limit them to the more Protestant and Anglo-Saxon nations of northern and western Europe. The rapid decline in immigration was crucial because it cut off the supply of newcomers to the European ethnic neighborhoods. With no fresh arrivals to maintain their vitality, the old ways faded after the 1920s. As the second and third generations Americanized and the first generation passed away, the ethnic neighborhoods were abandoned (or came to be occupied by other minority groups and more recent immigrants) and the European cultures and languages became echoes and memories.

◆ *Good economic times.* The second major factor accounting for the successful assimilation of European ethnic groups was the economic boom that followed World War II. From the 1940s until the 1970s, real wages rose, poverty fell, and there were abundant opportunities for economic advancement (at least for white males). During this period, the white ethnic groups that had not previously reached parity with national norms finally did so. By the 1970s, the descendants of even the most penniless, least educated, most unskilled European immigrant groups had, on the average, achieved equality in income, occupational prestige, and education.

◆ *Expansion of education.* In large part, the groundwork for this rise to middle-class status was laid by the expansion of public education, an investment in upgrading the skills of the workforce necessitated by the need to keep pace with the demands of continuing industrialization for literate, educated workers (Farley, 1996, p. 229). When the economy expanded after World War II, the descendants of the European immigrants had the educational credentials necessary to rise in the American job structure.

Although their sense of ethnic identity may be fading, many white ethnic families still remember their immigrant ancestors who arrived with nothing and forged a place for themselves and their families in a new and often hostile world. Without trivializing the truths of those legends, Massey reminds us that this success story was made possible by the structural conditions that existed in American society. If emigration from Europe had continued after the 1920s, if the school systems had not expanded, or if the postwar economic boom had not occurred, the assimilation of these groups (particularly those from peasant backgrounds) would have been a very different story. Heroic tales of immigrant resolve aside, the experiences of these groups are a study in sociology, not biography (Massey, 1995, p. 643).

Immigration and Assimilation Now

Will present-day immigrants follow the pathway to full assimilation forged by the European ethnic groups? In Massey's view, the answer is both yes and no. The exact social conditions that made assimilation possible in earlier times will not recur; therefore, the models of the past may not be relevant for the future. Some present-day immigrants (or their descendants) will consolidate and reach equality, but others may find themselves in a permanent urban underclass. Let's examine the conditions that are affecting today's immigrants.

Racial and Cultural Differences. Immigrants to the United States today are much more diverse—racially, culturally, and linguistically—than those that came before the 1920s. The latter were virtually all Europeans, while immigrants today come, literally, from every corner of the globe. At the end of the twentieth century, about half of all immigrants were from Central and South America, with Mexico being the single largest country of origin. Most other immigrants (about 40% of the total) came from Asia, and the remainder were coming from Europe, Africa, and other places.

The contemporary immigrant stream includes people of every racial background, social class, level of education, and religious background and languages from Armenian to Korean to Spanish to Pakistani. Consolidation and assimilation of such diversity are hard enough, but lingering racism and intolerance make the task even more challenging and difficult.

Permanent Immigration. Massey believes immigration to the United States has become permanent and little can be done to alter that reality. Immigrants today are pushed from their homelands by overpopulation, slow economic growth, and lack of opportunity. They are pulled to the United States and other developed nations by relatively high wages, greater opportunities, and the strong demand for cheap labor in certain parts of the economy (for example, garment industry sweatshops, some forms of agriculture, and domestic work).

Furthermore, stable networks of social relations within the United States have been established over the years to channel the movement of immigrants (illegal as well as legal) and match them with employment opportunities. For example, Mexican immigrants and migrant workers have provided seasonal labor for the U.S. agricultural sector for many decades. The system is well established, predictable, and reliable. Growers rely on it and would be hard pressed to harvest their crops without it. With such well-established channels, the pressure to immigrate to the United States is unlikely to diminish in the foreseeable future.

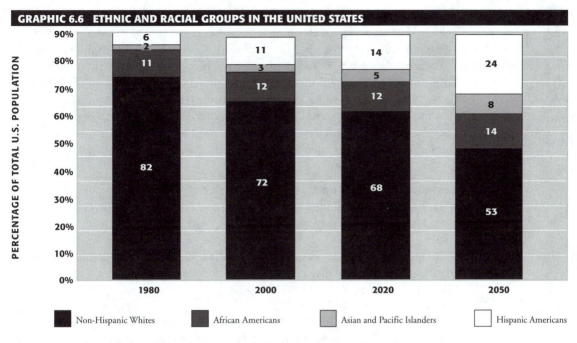

GRAPHIC 6.6 ETHNIC AND RACIAL GROUPS IN THE UNITED STATES

Sources: U.S. Bureau of the Census, 1999, p. 14; Pollard and O'Hare, 1999, p. 10.

Note: Values for the years 2000, 2020, and 2050 are projected. Native Americans, Eskimos, and Aleuts make up less than 1% of the total U.S. population and are projected to continue at that level.

With no interruption in the supply of newcomers, the new immigrants will sustain non-Anglo cultures and non-English languages even as the second and third generations Americanize and integrate. The racial and ethnic diversity of American life will therefore continue to increase. Graphic 6.6 shows the relative sizes of various ethnic and racial groups, one indicator of increasing diversity in the United States. The growing percentages of Asian and Hispanic Americans are due largely to "permanent" immigration. For the next half-century, the United States will become significantly less "white," and Asian and Hispanic groups and cultures will have a much greater impact on every aspect of social life.

Diversity in the United States will be further increased by modern means of communication and transportation. Jet travel, satellite television, computers, and the Internet can link modern-day immigrants to their home societies and cultures in ways that the European immigrants of the past could not imagine. Thus, even as some immigrants follow a generational pattern of Americanization, new arrivals and modern technology will sustain the old ways and assimilation will proceed in the midst of growing pluralism and diversity.

Economic Trends. Massey believes that continuing deindustrialization will ultimately lower occupational mobility, increase inequality, and throw some groups into permanent poverty. The last of the European immigrant groups were lifted to middle-class status by an economic boom that lasted several decades. According to Massey, it is unlikely that such a lengthy period of economic growth will be repeated.

In any case, at a time when education is becoming increasingly important for employment and upward mobility, the public schools that are most likely to serve recent immigrants (and racial minority groups) have fallen into disarray. Many face the daunting task of trying to teach children who speak scores of different languages at a time of limited support and shrinking budgets. Thus, far from riding an economic escalator to equality, many contemporary immigrants face permanent poverty and marginality.

Segmented Assimilation. In an analysis that parallels Massey's argument, some sociologists have concluded that the important question for contemporary immigrants is not whether they will assimilate but rather to what segment of American society (Portes & Rumbaut, 1996; Portes & Zhou, 1993). The European immigrant groups all eventually entered the great middle class. But contemporary immigrants are much more diverse in their social situations. It may be a long time—if ever—before some of them have the same opportunities for integration and equality that the earlier immigrants had.

Some recent immigrants are highly educated professionals who experience little overt discrimination in American society and often take well-paid, high-status jobs in the mainstream occupational structure. Proficient in English and often trained in American universities, these immigrants are most likely to duplicate the success of the European immigrant groups, often in fewer than three generations.

Most inner-city areas in the United States reflect growing levels of immigration. In downtown Los Angeles, for instance, many stores advertise a variety of goods and services in both English and Spanish. Immigrants face special economic, social, and cultural challenges. And their children often experience cultural confusion: Should they follow the cultural values of their parents or adopt the culture of their American peers?

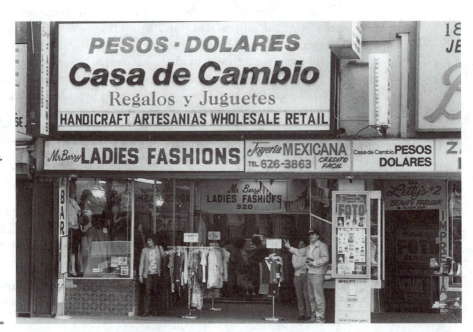

On the other hand, unskilled and uneducated immigrants usually find work in the low-wage sector of the economy. Especially for those who are also nonwhite, assimilation can mean occupying a place in the social structure from which any upward mobility would be unlikely. Many of these immigrants live in deteriorated inner-city neighborhoods, where they come into close contact with urban poverty and the lower-class segments of racial minority groups. In this ghettoized environment, the children of the immigrants are exposed to a culture that, in many ways, rejects middle-class conventions. To the extent that they absorb the oppositional culture, the second generation will move away from, not into, the middle class (Portes & Rumbaut, 1996, pp. 248–249).

For an example of the uncertainty facing some contemporary immigrant groups, consider the Haitian community in Miami, Florida. The first generation is strongly committed to preserving a separate Haitian identity and using their cohesion and solidarity to help each other become successful in America. Their children attend inner-city, largely African-American schools. Haitians are racially similar to African Americans, but their Haitian ways bring ostracism and sometimes ridicule. Should the second generation remain "Haitian" and resist the culture of their peers at school? Or should they assimilate to African-American culture and reject the ethnic solidarity and communal cohesion of their parents? Or should they aspire to assimilate into the larger society (Portes & Rumbaut, 1996, pp. 253–255)?

Prospects for Consolidation. The United States has been, from its birth, a nation of immigrants. The dominant group—white and Anglo-Saxon in heritage—has resisted the absorption of each group of newcomers, but the ultimate outcome for immigrants from Europe was assimilation and integration (consolidation). Will the process repeat itself with the current wave of immigrants, so much more diverse in language, culture, and race? Massey feels that many contemporary immigrant groups will never attain middle-class prosperity and that some will wind up as members of the urban underclass. Of course, countless nineteenth-century observers made similarly dire predictions about immigrants from Ireland, Italy, Poland, Russia, and other places, groups that seemed, at the time, to be outlandishly exotic and permanently unassimilable. At any rate, Massey's analysis offers little support for Wallace's consolidation thesis.

Conclusion

This chapter evaluated Walter Wallace's ideas about global species consolidation by considering a variety of racial and ethnic group relations around the world, both past and present. Wallace argues that the trajectory of world affairs over the past 10,000 years is toward consolidation and that all peoples everywhere will eventually merge into a single entity, undifferentiated by race or ethnicity. Wallace's prediction finds support in the recent events in South Africa and, in the United States, in the assimilation of European immigrant groups and the unprecedented opportunities currently available to the black middle class. Other situations, however—Rwanda, the growth of an underclass of poor African Americans and other minority groups of color, segmented assimilation—are, to say the least, less hopeful.

Furthermore, by concentrating on racial and ethnic differentiation, we have deemphasized other forms of inequality that have implications for global consolidation. For example, Chapter 5 noted that economic inequality within and between the nations of the globe is currently increasing. If global species consolidation should happen under those conditions, the globe would resemble a huge feudal society: a small percentage of the world's population would enjoy great comfort and affluence while most people would be locked in grinding poverty (Wallace, 1997, p. 123). A society with such massive internal inequalities would be inherently unstable. Thus, one key prerequisite to successful global species consolidation is the more equitable distribution of resources and opportunities across the globe. What are the prospects for such redistribution? Both short- and long-term trends in economic inequality suggest that the possibilities are remote.

Wallace is largely silent on one other aspect of inequality: gender, the subject of the next chapter. Clearly, however, the fading of racial and ethnic boundaries does not imply a reduction in gender inequality. A world that is no longer divided by race and ethnicity may still be split by gender. For example, organizations struggling to bring freedom to a racial or ethnic group are often militaristic in tone and male-dominated in structure and often consign women to less visible, subordinate roles. Liberation from racism is no guarantee of liberation from sexism.

Perhaps inevitably, there are other aspects of inequality and domination that we have failed to address. Thus, the evidence we have examined is ambiguous and partial. Is it still possible to come to some conclusions about Wallace's theory? Final judgments must await future developments—and that is the major weakness of Wallace's theory. Wallace does not (and cannot) specify a time frame for the completion of global species consolidation; indeed, he suggests that the process may take hundreds or thousands of years. But without a clear time frame, the theory cannot be falsified. Until the exact moment the process is complete, we won't know if the theory is wrong or we just have not waited long enough.

On the other hand, what is the alternative? If we dismiss Wallace, do we accept the idea that prejudice, racism, massacres, and attempts at genocide are inevitable—and through our acceptance make those horrors more likely? By accepting ethnic and racial atrocities and hate crimes as "natural," do we help to institutionalize them? If the heroes of the past—Martin Luther King, Nelson Mandela, Mahatma Ghandi—had merely accepted the oppressive, unjust systems that limited them, would those systems ever have changed? Wallace may well be wrong; even if he is right, global species consolidation and intergroup peace may be so distant in the future as to be irrelevant for today. In the meantime, however, if we can assume that he is right, what might happen to group relations in places like Rwanda, Northern Ireland, the former Yugoslavia, and the United States?

Key Concepts

1. Although conflict among people of different racial and ethnic groups persists, some social theorists believe that such intolerance can be overcome. For example, the theory of global species consolidation predicts that all racial and ethnic boundaries will gradually disappear as globalization enables people from different parts of the world to interact more regularly and more intimately.

2. Members of a minority group are not necessarily less numerous in a society than members of the dominant group. Rather, a minority group is an easily distinguished group that has less opportunity to achieve wealth, prestige, and power because of prejudice and discrimination from members of the dominant group and within the society's institutions.

3. Relations between dominant and minority groups can be analyzed in terms of prejudice, discrimination, assimilation, and pluralism.

4. The situation faced by a minority group is very much affected by the contact situation in which it encountered the dominant group. A racial or ethnic minority forced into contact against its will—for example, colonized peoples and peoples imported into a society as slaves—experiences greater powerlessness and poverty and is less likely to integrate fully with the dominant group. Virtually all the trouble spots around the globe originated in some type of conquest or colonization. In contrast, immigrant groups are more likely to assimilate and enter the society's economic and cultural mainstream.

5. Global trends in consolidation and assimilation are ambiguous. The United States faces ongoing challenges of achieving racial equality and absorbing a new wave of immigrants, many of whom are not well educated for success in a postindustrial society.

Active Learning

1. Race and Gender Stereotypes: Drawing Pictures. (Adapted from an exercise designed by Jacqueline C. Simpson, McMurry College.) This exercise requires drawing, but you will not be graded on your artistic ability. During the exercise, you will deal with stereotypes, that is, overgeneralizations about entire groups of people. People with strong stereotypes believe that almost all persons who belong to a certain group will have a certain characteristic, whether they do or not. Stereotypes ignore or overlook individual assets.

Because stereotypes have a negative connotation, it is difficult for most of us to admit that we all have them. The stereotyping process can work two ways. The first, and most common, is that an image is seen (for example, a member of another racial or ethnic group) and a label is automatically attached to the image (that person is lazy, or dangerous, or not very smart, and so on). In the second process, a label is heard or seen and an image is generated. The following exercise illustrates this second process and shows how ingrained stereotypes can be.

a. Before class, draw two separate pictures, one of a pretty child and one of a bully. Use a whole sheet of paper for each drawing, and draw the child and the bully full length, that is, include a body, arms, and legs in addition to a head. If possible, use crayons, colored pencils, or markers for your pictures. Give your pretty child and your bully names.

b. Bring your drawings to class and be prepared to discuss stereotypes and prejudice.

2. Group Conflict: Periodical Research. This project can be done individually or with other students. In either case, you will use newspapers and newsmagazines to update or extend the points made in this chapter.

a. Skim recent newspapers or newsmagazines for stories about conflicts between groups. Choose a nationally circulated U.S. newspaper (for example, the *New York Times,* the *Washington Post,* or the *Los Angeles Times*), a U.S. newsmagazine (for example, *Newsweek* or *Time*), or an English-language paper from outside the United States (for example, the *London Times*). If you are working in a group, each member should read a different periodical, providing a good cross section of national and international viewpoints. Print copies of many of these papers and magazines are available in your library; electronic versions are available over the Internet, and some relevant addresses are listed on our Web site (www.pineforge.com/snc).

   Look for a group conflict in the United States or some other nation. The conflict could involve racial, ethnic, or even religious groups but should be a matter that is regional, national, or international in scope. Ignore local issues that are specific to a certain city, area, or state (be aware, however, that local issues can quickly become national or international). As one suggestion, you might endeavor to update the material in this chapter on group relations in Rwanda, South Africa, or one of the other trouble spots mentioned. If you are working with other students, try to find different conflicts for purposes of comparison.

b. Analyze the conflict in terms of the concepts presented in Chapter 6. Identify the dominant and minority group and the issues involved. Did the current situation originate with conquest or colonization? Did the minority group immigrate to its current location? Does the minority group desire assimilation, pluralism, separatism, or some other relationship with the dominant group? What does the dominant group want? What other concepts from the chapter can you apply to this situation? You may not be able to answer all those questions from press reports, and your instructor may suggest some limits on the amount of research you are expected to do.

c. Write a report summarizing your information. Your instructor will specify whether you will present your findings to the rest of your group, the class as a whole, or as a paper.

3. Personal Prejudice: Assessment. This is an individual project that requires access to the Internet. You will visit a Web site that offers a test called the Implicit Association Test, a measure of your personal level of prejudice.

a. Begin by going to the Web site www.yale.edu/implicit/. Be sure to read the introductory material first; on the opening screen, click on the button offering preliminary information. After you have familiarized yourself with the nature of the test, proceed to "Measure Your Implicit Attitudes." The site offers four different tests, and you are free to take them all, but only the Race IAT is relevant for this assignment.

b. Once you have completed the test, write a brief report on your experience. Did the test measure your feelings about other groups, your ideas (stereotypes), or both? Did it seem that the test resulted in a reasonably accurate assessment of your level of prejudice? Why or why not?

4. Assimilation: Data Analysis. According to Milton Gordon, the process of assimilation occurs in stages and often takes place over the course of generations. For this exercise, make sure you are familiar with these sections of this chapter: Gordon's model, the material about assimilation by generation for pre-1920s immigrants from Europe, and the material on assimilation for post-1965 immigrants.

a. Study Graphic 6.7, which includes information from a 1999 survey administered to a representative sample of Latinos. Write a brief analysis of the information from

GRAPHIC 6.7 LATINO ACCULTURATION SURVEY

LANGUAGE

"What language do you usually speak at home?"

	Only/More Spanish	Both Equally	Only/More English
First generation	73%	20%	6%
Second generation	17%	43%	40%
Third generation	1%	21%	78%

"In what language are the TV programs you usually watch?"

	Only/More Spanish	Both Equally	Only/More English
First generation	31%	42%	27%
Second generation	5%	26%	68%
Third generation	1%	11%	88%

FAMILY VALUES

"Is it better for children to live in their parents' home until they get married?"

	Yes
First generation	87%
Second generation	62%
Third generation	46%
Non-Latinos	42%

"In general, the husband should have the final say in family matters."

	Yes
First generation	46%
Second generation	27%
Third generation	24%
Non-Latinos	26%

Source: *Washington Post*, 2000 (January 16).

Note: These results are from a telephone survey of about 2,400 Latino and 2,000 non-Latino adults conducted in the summer of 1999. Projections to the population are accurate within ±2 percentage points.

the perspective of Gordon's generational model of acculturation. Bring your written report to class.

b. In class, divide into small groups and discuss your individual analyses. Is the information in Graphic 6.7 consistent with the generational model? Why or why not? Are Latinos acculturating?

c. With your group, consider Graphics 6.5 and 6.6. Graphic 6.5 shows high rates of immigration in recent decades, and Graphic 6.6 projects rapid growth for both Hispanic and Asian Americans as percentages of the U.S. population. Consider those trends in combination with the information in Graphic 6.7 and discuss the following statements:

◆ Immigration is fast, assimilation is slow.

◆ "Even as some immigrants follow a generational pattern of Americanization, new arrivals and modern technology will sustain the old ways and assimilation will proceed in the midst of growing pluralism and diversity." (This is a quote from the chapter.)

d. As a group, write a report summarizing your deliberations and conclusions. Your instructor may ask you to share your thoughts with the class.

7 Gender

How is globalization affecting inequalities between women and men?

Ladies and gentlemen, allow us to introduce you to Khokha, Filfil, and NimNim—three Muppets who will star in the new Egyptian television show *Alam Simsim* (Arabic for "Sesame's World"). Khokha, the program's star, wants to become a pilot, a doctor, and an engineer—all at the same time. She is joined by her friends in skits, activities, and songs, some of which focus specifically on gender equality. "There's nothing women can't be," sing the colorful Muppets at one point. It is hoped that the new show will help change attitudes in male-dominated Egyptian society: "Khokha is our gateway to break down negative, gender-based stereotypes," said the show's head researcher, who is also a child psychologist. That is a strong statement because women have a long way to go in Egypt. For instance, the country's literacy rate is 24 percent lower for women than for men. Until recently, Egyptian women were not even allowed to initiate divorce proceedings against their husbands, who, by contrast, could divorce their wives at will (Abdel-Hamid, 2000).

Egypt is not the only country experiencing changes with respect to gender. Consider a few other examples from around the world.

◆ The Israeli Supreme Court recently issued a landmark decision allowing women to pray out loud at the Western Wall in Jerusalem. The ruling was the result of an eleven-year court battle to end the ban on women praying at this holy site.

◆ Since the Fourth World Conference on Women in 1995, more than sixty countries have changed laws that discriminated against women. For example, one law allowed rapists to escape punishment if they married their victims.

◆ Many American women are leaving corporate America and starting two-thirds of all new businesses in the country. Groups such as the Women's Technology Cluster in San Francisco assist women who launch new companies.

◆ Girls throughout the world are achieving higher levels of education, although they still lag behind boys. In an effort to further girls' education, Nigeria actually prohibits girls from leaving school early.

◆ Women are making progress even in conservative bastions such as the Islamic world. For instance, more Arab girls are going to school, and more Arab women have the right to work outside the home. Dubai even has the Persian Gulf's first female taxi drivers; they work for a company that caters to women customers who do not feel comfortable with male taxi drivers.

◆ Although they still lag far behind men, more women are being elected to office. Across southern Africa, for instance, more than 35% of local representatives in Parliament are women. Some countries have female heads of state. Reflecting on her own tenure in office, former Norwegian Prime Minister Gro Harlem Brundtland said that people were so used to her tenure in office that young Norwegian girls asked, "Mommy, is it possible for a boy to grow up to be prime minister?"

Egyptian women, like those in many other parts of the world, are becoming more actively involved in the workforce. A policewoman patrols the streets of Cairo, and an ophthalmologist works at her desk in her private practice.

But all those positive developments do not mean that women have reached equality with men. In fact, women still make less money, receive less education, are subjected to more domestic violence, and have fewer overall opportunities. Worldwide, 70% of all women live in poverty. This chapter, like Chapters 5 and 6, touches on the economic mechanisms that divide rich nations from poor ones and the haves from the have-nots. The focus here is on how societal forces on a global scale affect the opportunities of women and men to participate equally in society. We begin with a look at the way sociologists view gender and then examine some theoretical insights that explain why men and women are treated differently in

various societies around the world. Next, we focus on those differences across several historical time periods, with an emphasis on how globalization affects gender inequalities today. Throughout the discussion, there is an emphasis on examining data and linking the data to both theoretical concerns and substantive events.

Sociological Perspectives on Gender Relations

Studies by anthropologists, historians, sociologists, and other social scientists indicate that most societies have been and continue to be organized in a way that perpetuates gender differences and inequality. In almost every society, men dominate and have certain rights and privileges that women do not have. Sociologists have pursued explanations for that inequality from nearly the beginning of the discipline. Why does gender inequality exist? How were differences and inequalities created, and why do they continue?

To begin answering those questions, we first must understand what gender is. **Gender** refers to the social differences assigned to people of different sexes. The different social roles that men (and boys) and women (and girls) participate in, the activities in which they are involved, the clothes they wear, and many other aspects of culture help to define what society characterizes as gender. Sex, on the other hand, is based on biological differences. Most often, although there are clear exceptions, gender and sex are parallel: biological males take on masculine gender roles, and biological females take on feminine gender roles.

Generally the differences and ultimately the inequalities that people perceive between females and males are due to the social construction of gender. To underscore that point, one "diversity consultant" who conducts seminars for large companies often does a fun exercise. He asks male and female volunteers from the audience to complete several tasks: the men are asked to "walk, talk, and interact like women," and the women are asked to "walk, talk, and interact like men." Both genders tend to exaggerate the perceived behaviors of the other (often in very humorous ways), but nearly everyone agrees that, on balance, men and women have different styles. Although biology may be partly responsible, most people would agree that much of the difference is based on how society defines gender roles. As discussed in Chapter 4, over time people tend to create, recreate, and transform their perceptions of a certain reality. Our individual perceptions of gender are based on the larger collective understanding of what gender is.

Of course, we have come to realize that because gender is a social construction, it is susceptible to redefinition. Thus collective understandings of gender are likely to differ through time. For instance, when young people today watch a TV comedy or drama from the 1950s, they often take note of (or laugh at) the gender differences. Why are all the women in dresses? Why is Mom always in the kitchen? Why does Dad do all the talking, especially on weighty issues? Why does Mom always defer to Dad? Such differences also are apparent across societies today. For example, Western societies generally define gender roles differently than do strict Islamic societies, which tend to place more restrictions on what women can do, wear, and say. Those conflicting definitions can lead to confusion, even resentment. We know several American businesswomen who conduct business in Saudi Arabia: they are politely ushered through the back of a restaurant—the "women's entrance"—while their male colleagues go in through the front.

A good way to begin addressing gender differences is by examining relevant theoretical explanations for them. One explanation is the **feminist perspective.** Although the term *feminist perspective* makes it sound as if there is only one theory that would address gender relations, in fact, many different theories have evolved from and encompass the feminist perspective.

◆ *Marxist feminism* asserts that gender inequality is rooted in social class inequality. The same capitalist system that produces social inequality also creates inequality between men and women. Thus, the only way to eliminate gender inequality is to eliminate capitalism and implement an alternative system.

◆ *Radical feminism* argues that the cause of gender inequality is deeper than just capitalism. In fact, gender inequality is due to the fact that men are in power and dominate all aspects of society. According to radical feminism, male oppression of women occurs in the family, the economy, politics, and most other areas (Tuana & Tong, 1995).

◆ *Liberal feminism* argues that the existence of gender differences and inequalities is due to the lack of opportunities for women and that if laws were changed to create opportunities for women, gender equality would increase (Tuana & Tong, 1995).

◆ *Multicultural feminism* argues that a number of contributing factors reinforce gender differences and inequalities (Tuana & Tong, 1995). Some factors would include race, class, ethnicity, age, religion, sexual orientation, and disability.

If we overlook the differing theoretical branches, we find that there are common threads that tie those theories together to form a feminist perspective. All the feminist theories attempt to explain gender differences and inequalities by examining social institutions, although they emphasize different institutions. For example, Marxist feminists focus on economic institutions; liberal feminists focus on legal institutions (and the implementation of legal action); and radical feminists focus on cultural institutions. Unlike the classic sociological theories, which mainly represent the thinking of people who hold a dominant position in society, feminist theories explain gender inequalities from the perspective of people who are in a subordinate position. Instead of accepting those inequalities, feminist theories acknowledge them but then attempt to change them or suggest means by which to change them.

Feminist theorists explain gender differences in employment, education, and politics as due primarily to male privilege. They explain the differences through a number of contributing factors, including economics, culture, class, and race. They also explain how the differences are perpetuated, and they attempt to bring about change that will allow for increased equality between men and women.

Understanding the feminist perspective will help us explore gender differences, as well as explanations for those differences. Note how a different perspective affects our view of male and female roles as we examine gender across different societies and historical time periods. That is a fundamentally sociological way of looking at the world.

Gender Roles and Subsistence Technology

In Chapter 5 we saw that as subsistence technologies changed, so did societal structures. It is not surprising to see that gender roles also changed over time as populations transformed from hunter-gatherer societies to agricultural societies to industrial societies. As gender roles have changed, so has the **sexual division of labor,** the way that work is divided among the female and male members of society.

Hunter-Gatherer Societies. Hunter-gatherer societies generally are extremely small, consisting of about 25 to 100 members. Their technology is basic, and they rely primarily on knives, spears, arrows, bows, digging sticks, containers, and nets to hunt their prey and to gather and transport their resources. The fact that so few people are involved in the organization of the society allows for more equality. Because there is no private property and all members work together, there is no stratification based on wealth or private property (O'Kelly & Carney, 1986). In fact, hunter-gatherer societies discourage aggressiveness and encourage cooperation (Silberbauer, 1982; Wiessner, 1982).

Because of their organization, many hunter-gatherer societies value women and men equally and give both leadership opportunities. Leadership positions are usually determined by personality and accomplishments rather than by traits like gender, race, or parents' social class or circumstances of birth.

If we examine the division of labor in hunting and gathering societies, we find that, for the most part, men hunt and women fish and gather nuts and seeds (Friedl, 1975). The men also help to gather food after they have finished hunting. Because women may not be as productive hunting if they are pregnant or have small children in tow, most women do not hunt. However, there are variations to that general pattern. For example, among the Tiwi on the islands off the coast of Australia, women hunt for land animals and gather vegetable foods, while the men hunt aquatic animals and birds (Goodale, 1971).

What is of most interest in hunter-gatherer societies is that the work men and women do is equally valued. Because they are collecting food for subsistence, all food collected is of importance. Therefore, the act of women gathering nuts, proteins, and vegetables is just as important as men hunting animals.

In hunter-gatherer societies, gender is based primarily on the work that men and women do. Men, for the most part, are the hunters, and women, for the most part, are the gatherers. Gender tends to be divided by type of labor. That division of labor, however, does not indicate gender inequality. In fact, in hunter-gatherer societies, gender inequality is minimal. Both men and women value what each brings to the society, and all are equally respected, regardless of sex.

Agricultural Societies. In the evolution from hunter-gatherer to agricultural societies, the roles for women and men begin to differ, and organizations of societies become more stratified (Lenski & Lenski, 1978). Hoe agriculture allows women to remain at home and farm, while the men hunt game. The group's lifestyle is no longer nomadic. A more sedentary lifestyle leads to a greater separation between the genders. Whereas in the hunter-gatherer societies men and women might hunt and gather together on occasion, in agricultural societies the division of labor leads to increased segregation between men and women and emphasizes the differences between men and women (Murphy & Murphy, 1974; O'Kelly & Carney, 1986).

The number of individuals involved in an agricultural society is greater than that of hunting and gathering societies; therefore, the organization of the society becomes more crucial. Family ties play a larger role, coupled with the development of private property. Because people are able to accumulate household goods and have more wealth to pass along to heirs, tracing family lines becomes more important. Some agricultural societies are organized on the basis of **matrilineal descent,** meaning that family ties are determined by relationships on the mother's side of the family. Children belong to the woman's side of the family, and land and other resources are passed down according to her relatives. More often, however, **patrilineal descent**—family ties determined by relationships on the father's side of the family—is the organizing principle (O'Kelly & Carney, 1986).

Patrilineal descent tends to be associated with **patriarchy,** a system in which decision-making positions are held primarily by men. Agricultural societies often become patriarchal societies, and the stratification of individuals on the basis of gender becomes more apparent. Even in matrilineal societies, decision-making positions usually are held by men, even though women have more power than they do in patrilineal societies. Malawi's two major ethnic groups, the Yao and the Chichewa, are both matrilineal societies. Land is highly valued in both societies and is passed on to the daughters. Yao women are allowed to initiate divorce proceedings against their husbands and, unlike in most African societies, no stigma is attached to such action. However, leadership positions in Yao and Chichewa societies are held mainly by men, and the country as a whole is governed almost exclusively by men.

Gender stratification increases as agricultural technology improves and as access to land shrinks. As people are introduced to more technology and the lands for hunting and gathering decline, many turn to settled agriculture. Use of the plow, which requires greater upper-body strength than previous agricultural technologies, furthered the division of labor between men and women. Men typically spend long hours plowing in the field to produce crops that feed the family and that can be sold in the marketplace, while women stay at home to watch the children and focus on processing and preserving the goods that the men provide. That contribution to the household is not valued as equally as the work that men perform, since women no longer contribute economically. Moreover, women become more economically dependent on men and lose decision-making power within the home due to the

Gender stratification, typical of agricultural societies, is apparent on this farm in southeastern Missouri during the Great Depression. Women (and young children) planted a spring garden to feed the family and to earn a little extra income. Men plowed the fields, raised livestock, and hunted for meat.

unequal balance (Martin & Voorhies, 1975; O'Kelly & Carney, 1986). At the same time, towns and cities are beginning to form, and men are entering decision-making positions within the community.

We can see how, with the change to agricultural societies, the social construction of gender transforms dramatically. Women's work contributions are no longer viewed as equal to those of men. While men are working outside the home, holding decision-making positions, and contributing to the home economically, women are working at home, baking, sewing, preserving goods, and tending to small farm animals. Gender stereotypes and expectations transform with the roles that change. Men begin to be seen as strong, intellectual, and fit for agricultural labor and for public roles, while women begin to be viewed as needing male direction and suited solely for domestic tasks (O'Kelly & Carney, 1986). Hence, women move from being viewed and treated as equals in a hunting and gathering society to being viewed and treated as inferior due to the division of labor found in agricultural societies.

Industrial Societies. Gender remains stratified in an industrial society (O'Kelly & Carney, 1986; Saffioti, 1978), but income-earning work becomes even more separated from the home than in agricultural societies. With industrialization, men and

These photos from about 1960 reflect sharp gender inequality: male managers and female typists. Although there has been progress over the last forty years, there remains great gender inequality with respect to wages, jobs, education, status, and other factors. Upper-level management is still dominated by men, and clerical jobs are still handled overwhelmingly by women.

women find it economically attractive to leave the farm, move to the city, and find work in factories. Yet tradition and law may continue to discourage women from working outside the home. If women do enter occupations, the occupations tend to be stratified by sex, such as seamstress or teacher. In addition, the primary role of child care remains the woman's responsibility, whereas the role of economic provider belongs to the man. As in agricultural societies, women lose decision-making power in both the public sphere and the private sphere because they do not make a significant economic contribution to the household.

As industrial societies progress, we see some additional gender transformations. Traditional gender definitions begin to break down in the looser culture of urban areas, and many families discover they need two incomes to pay for goods and services in the city that families once would have provided for themselves on the farm. Women begin to enter the workforce at higher rates, although employment remains segregated by gender, and the jobs women hold tend to pay less than men's jobs. At the same time, women remain responsible for housework and child care, which further limits their employment opportunities. Although men remain more active than women in the public sphere, women do begin to make their presence felt.

The Social Construction of Gender: The U.S. Women's Movement

Clearly, the social construction of gender is continually transforming. The gender patterns that evolve in industrial societies can be seen more clearly when we examine the evolving social construction of gender through the women's movement in the United States.

The gender roles that we see today in the United States have changed significantly over the last century. Many of those changes are due to various movements that attempted to address women's concerns. However, as we shall see, women's concerns were vastly different in the early 1900s than they are now. One of the themes stated in Chapter 1—"Modernity and progress depend on perspective"— certainly applies in this case. Nevertheless, the way in which women's concerns evolved throughout the past century helped to construct the gender roles we find today.

Early 1900s. During the second half of the nineteenth century, factories and mills rapidly multiplied in the United States. Nearly anyone who needed a job, including women and children, could find one. In the absence of laws protecting workers' rights, however, abuses of workers were rampant, leading individuals to press for government intervention. Purposely or not, the laws created to protect workers helped to define gender roles in the early 1900s.

During that period, the proper roles of men and women were hotly debated. Many viewed the very fact of women working in factories as an abuse, never mind the conditions of their employment. Campaigns to protect women from work-related abuses brought the debate over gender roles to the fore, and educated women were prominent in the battle.

Florence Kelley, for example, became a top leader of the Progressive Movement by fighting for improvements in the treatment of women and children. She developed strategies like consumer boycotts of garments produced in sweatshops and lobbied for legal requirements that employers document workers' ages as a step to ending the exploitation of children (Sklar, 1995). She also pioneered the use of scientific data to sway the U.S. Supreme Court. With her friend Louis Brandeis, she influenced the 1908 case of *Mueller v. Oregon,* which established women's "protected status" as workers. Kelley and Brandeis successfully argued that women's maternal functions were of greater importance to society than their property rights or other rights as citizens. The court subsequently ruled that women's rights in the workplace, specifically the hours they were allowed to work, could be curtailed—for their own good, of course. Women could not be expected to work under the same conditions as men

That sort of protective legislation was a two-edged sword. On the one hand, it was a beneficial response to the savage effects of unrestricted labor markets and the abusive practices of employers. But it also created barriers for women's autonomy and negotiating capacity. Because it gave the right to time off from work for childbearing and child care, the new legislation made women, especially mothers, more costly to hire. In effect, it created new incentives for the employment of men. Social reformers thus aided female segregation into less desirable jobs in the workplace with the underlying presumption that woman's primary role is in the home (Lehrer, 1987).

During the early 1900s, the social construction of gender—women in the domestic sphere, men in the public sphere—was based on the fact that women gave birth to children. That construction was used to implement laws that placed more pressure on men to earn money and support their families. Those changes affected both men and women.

The ever stronger definition of men as providers and women as homemakers was buttressed by the struggle for the **"family wage"**—a wage large enough to support family members—as a masculine entitlement. Samuel Gompers, the first president of the American Federation of Labor (AFL), captured rising feelings on that subject when he stated, "It is wrong to permit any of the female sex of our country to be forced to work, as we believe that men should be provided with a fair wage in order to keep his female relatives from going to work" (Leckie, 1996, p. 12). In addition to male-dominated organizations like the AFL, leaders and participants in women's groups like the American Association for Labor Legislation and the Women's Trade Union League also backed the idea that working men should earn enough to support their families. For that reason, they provided steady pressure for restricting women's involvement in paid work, heightening women's dependence on men (Kessler-Harris, 1988, p. 8). Florence Kelley herself saw the family wage as a means to reinforce an order in which husbands would support "the wives throughout life and the children at least until the fourteenth birthday" (Skocpol, 1992, p. 408).

The family wage had a moral as well as an economic dimension. Reformers saw the family wage as a way to control footloose men by charging them with the support of their families. At the same time, the family wage would safeguard feminine morality by keeping women out of the workplace, where they would come into contact with unrelated men (Smith-Rosenberg, 1985).

For industrialists, the transformation of men into household providers secured a disciplined labor force. And women themselves went along with this definition of gender roles. A retreat into the home and reliance on men's earnings exacerbated their subordination, but it reduced the strain of trying to combine paid and domestic labor.

The campaigns to protect women in the workplace and give men a family wage thus helped to reinforce existing notions of male supremacy, women's subordination, and patriarchal rule. Women were relegated to their motherly positions and had to remain dependent on the work of their husbands. Even unmarried women, confined to low-paying "female" occupations, felt the effects. Meanwhile, men continued to work in the public sphere, taking part in employment and other institutions outside the home. Thus, men were the ones who made decisions in the home, which affected other family members, and in the public sphere, which affected the structure of business and politics, generally reinforcing their privileged role in society.

Mid- to Late 1900s. The gender identities created in the early 1900s prevailed for almost a century, but World War II first showed how fluid those arrangements were. When working men joined the armed forces as soldiers, they left behind vacant positions in industry and services, which were quickly occupied by women. In addition, almost 300,000 women served in the Army and Navy, performing such noncombatant jobs as secretaries, typists, and nurses.

Government campaigns during the war stretched the limits of gender definitions by portraying women's employment as a patriotic duty. Capturing the sense of the age was Rosie the Riveter, a character promoted by the media to encourage the idea of factory work as an extension of feminine skills (Honey, 1985). Shown in posters as a muscular but winsome operative, Rosie became a new model of womanhood. Evans and Loeb sang of her, "All the day long, whether rain or shine, she's a part of the assembly line. She's making history, working for victory. . . . That little girl will do more than a male will do, working overtime on the riveting machine" (Evans & Loeb, 1942). When women were needed in the public sphere, the U.S. government actively worked to reconstruct the notion of gender to encourage women to enter vacated jobs.

Another reconstruction effort took place with the end of the war, when women who had adopted Rosie the Riveter as a role model were pushed back into the home to make way for returning veterans in need of jobs. Hollywood movies of the 1950s and 1960s are filled with the tales of women who, having experienced the passing allure of career and financial independence, discover true happiness in their voluntary surrender to marriage and family. Still, the heightened participation of women

Gender roles are influenced by other events occurring in society. During World War II, women took over many industrial and service jobs that were vacated by men. Women even played in a professional baseball league to fill the void left by the suspension of major league baseball during the war. During the conservative 1950s, many women were traditional housewives and catered to their working husbands. These gender roles were challenged during the 1960s, when the sexual revolution began to expand women's options and redefine what was expected of men and women. Fathers became increasingly involved in playing with and caring for young children, although mothers still normally assume greater responsibility in these areas.

in paid employment during World War II had irreversible effects that became all the more apparent as the structure of society changed in the two decades that followed.

In the 1960s, a series of social changes, including new efforts to improve race relations, began to redefine gender roles. The sexual revolution of the 1960s lifted the stigma from premarital sex and divorce, expanding women's options by giving them more power to control their roles as mothers and wives. Extensions to civil rights legislation made sexual discrimination a matter of legal concern. Innovations in contraceptive methods and the legalization of abortion in 1973 further increased women's capacity to compete on an equal footing with men in the labor market. In the 1970s, the feminist mobilization involved a new generation of women and men who saw women's advances in education, employment, decision making, sports, and many other areas as birthrights, not privileges. By the end of the 1970s, images of female executives in "power suits," clutching briefcases and marching confidently into the workplace, had replaced those of mothers in aprons. The new professional woman burst onto the scene as a culmination of yearnings for emancipation, but, as we will soon see, not without troubles all her own.

The effects of women's liberation were felt in every aspect of culture. During the last two decades of the twentieth century, the popular media, television in particular, obsessively reviewed emerging definitions of gender with alternating glee and horror. Phil Donahue, the man who created the modern-day TV talk show, donned a skirt more than once while discussing the new sensibilities. His influential programs contributed to a new climate of tolerance for sexual minorities, including homosexuals and transsexuals. Just as Donahue was exploding the myths of unchangeable masculinity and femininity, innovative marketing campaigns presented images of men sensitively holding babies and women in army fatigues forcefully clutching rifles. Unisex fashion and haircuts further expressed a yearning for gender equality. The first woman on the Supreme Court, Sandra Day O'Connor, was appointed in 1981, and the first female Vice Presidential candidate, Geraldine Ferraro, came shortly thereafter in 1984. Hard-fought battles to allow women greater opportunities in the military began to demolish the last bastion of male exclusivity.

Large-scale economic change simultaneously eroded the material foundations that had supported the notion of men as family providers and women as subordinate wives and mothers. What changed was not so much the idea that men should be providers as the expectation that domestic and reproductive work should be only women's responsibilities. Americans of both sexes now expect everyone to be at least potentially able to support himself or herself through paid work and make substantial economic contributions to the household. Men are expected to take more active responsibility for home life—caring for children and performing some household labor—instead of just being providers. The new mores reflect, to some extent, value systems that grew in the aftermath of the women's movement of the mid- to late 1900s, but they also are the effect of a deep economic transformation—much of it related to globalization—that has had a significant impact on gender.

Gender Inequality Today: A Global Concern

Globalization was a primary theme in 1995 at the Fourth World Conference on Women in Beijing. The successful conference was marked by 189 countries adopting a statement that outlines areas of concern and enunciates an agenda for improving the lives of women and children around the world.

Five years later, in June 2000, the world met again in New York for a United Nations special session titled "Women 2000: Gender Equality, Development, and Peace for the 21st Century." The purpose was to assess the world's progress on women's issues since 1995 and to formulate a new plan of action for the future. Twelve critical areas drew primary attention: women and poverty, education and training of women, women and health, violence against women, women and armed conflict, women and the economy, women in power and decision making, institutional mechanisms for the advancement of women, human rights of women, women and the media, women and the environment, and the girl-child.

Not surprising for any international conference, some notable disagreements underscored the gender inequality that exists in the world today. For example, the delegates could not agree on language related to the sexual rights of women. A handful of Islamic and Catholic countries, along with the Vatican, opposed any platform language that appeared to endorse abortion, homosexual unions, or equal rights for women within the family (American Broadcasting Company, 2000).

Despite those differences, which emanated largely from certain cultural and religious traditions, there was remarkable agreement on many topics. (The full platform agreement is available on the United Nations' Web site, www.un.org.) For instance, discussion often focused on the harmful effects of globalization on women, particularly in developing countries. We next look at two examples of that trend: the exploitation of female factory workers and the hardships imposed on women by economic development programs.

Low-Wage Factories in Mexico

Our first example is the *maquiladora* **phenomenon,** the establishing of assembly plants in developing countries by corporations based in high-income countries. The appeal is the lower wages and less restrictive labor and environmental laws in countries hungry to join the economically developed world. In Mexico, such plants, known as *maquiladoras,* are encouraged by the governments of the United States and Mexico to operate along the border in Mexico as directly owned subsidiaries of foreign corporations, most of them headquartered in the United States. Many of the jobs eliminated in the United States as a result of deindustrialization (see Chapters 5 and 10) ended up in Mexican *maquiladoras.*

Twenty years ago, when Mexico's *maquiladora* program was still new, researchers and public officials often saw it as a temporary solution for rising levels of unemployment along Mexico's northern border. The abrupt termination of the *bracero* program, which had enabled Mexican men to enter the United States as guest

This electronics factory in Mexico employs primarily women, who are supervised by male managers. The workers often labor in an unsafe environment for long hours at low pay. Ventilation is poor, protective eyewear and gloves are not provided, and medical care is hard to find.

workers, heightened joblessness and the possibility of popular turmoil (Fernández-Kelly, 1983). Mexico's government reacted by creating incentives for foreign investment in export manufacturing. The *maquiladora* program, in full bloom by the 1970s, exported mainly garments and electronics products. *Maquiladoras* multiplied rapidly, but, ironically and against the expectations of many, they did not create jobs for men; instead, they targeted young, single, working-class women as the preferred providers of labor.

For over 30 years, an overwhelming majority of the workers hired by *maquiladoras,* about 85% of their total labor force, have been working-class women. That carries momentous implications because in both the United States and Mexico (and, for that matter, throughout the world) female employment has been associated with declining terms of employment for working people in general. Employers tend to pay women very low wages and expect them to leave their jobs when they get married or are pregnant. The result is a marginal existence, with little hope of improvement. The point is captured in testimony from a young woman working for a large *maquiladora* operated in Tijuana by a foreign corporation.

I make 38 pesos a day—264 pesos a week. [U.S. $1 = 7.50 pesos.] Our wages are so low the company gives us a weekly bonus of food coupons worth 55 pesos. . . . Between my oldest son and myself, we bring in about 410 pesos a week. Water is very expensive. Gas [for cooking] is very expensive. Food is very expensive. Better to say that I have to go to all the sales, where everything is the cheapest and on special, so that my paycheck can cover everything. If we want to eat meat, it can't stretch that far. It's more like we eat bones than we eat meat. I have to buy what I can afford—the cheapest things. At the beginning of the year there's always a general wage increase, but before the increase takes effect, you see the prices going up on everything. Everything. Last January, sugar went up a peso. Milk, which cost 15 pesos, went up to 17.50. I only make 38 pesos a day, so I work half a day for a gallon of milk. I don't want to gain weight, so I don't drink it. But the kids need it. . . .

I talked to an engineer, the assistant manager on our shift. I asked him, why do they pay us so little, why can't they pay a little more? On the other side of the border, people working for the same company earn in an hour what we earn in a day. He told us that we couldn't pressure the owners to pay better. The company came here because we work so cheap. If we pressured them to pay more, he said, they would just take the work somewhere else, and we would be left without jobs. But I think this is really just an excuse, to make us grateful for our jobs (Bacon, 1996).

The *maquiladora* phenomenon tends to exacerbate women's already limited power in labor markets around the world. Because women tend to see themselves mainly as wives and mothers and because they tend to occupy low positions in the labor market, they have had little power to organize and bring about improvements in their general terms of employment.

Structural Adjustment in Ghana

Another example of gender inequality on a global scale relates to international programs that are providing economic aid to developing countries. Organizations like the International Monetary Fund and the World Bank, which are dominated by high-income countries, have attempted to reform the economies of developing countries so that those countries can repay their massive debts. The societal strains that the reforms have created are particularly evident when we examine the devastating effects of **structural adjustment programs (SAPs).**

SAPs require developing countries to devalue their currencies. A national currency might be devalued by 25% compared to the U.S. dollar and other major currencies, meaning the local currency would be worth 25% less than it was prior to the devaluation. The rationale behind devaluation is that it makes it cheaper for rich countries to purchase products from developing countries. After a 25% devaluation, a U.S. company would pay 25% less for products from a developing country than before. Theoretically, SAPs stimulate business between developed and developing countries and enable developing countries to generate additional income and repay their debts. Although that is partly the case, the increased business also comes at a high price. Following a 25% devaluation, local wages also are worth 25% less than before, meaning that people have to cut back on expenditures and often take an additional job. Household budgets, already meager, must be stretched even further to cope with SAPs.

SAPs also require the governments of developing countries to reduce their spending on health, education, social services, and food subsidies to the poor (Bradshaw et al., 1993; Buchmann, 1996; Gladwin, 1991). The rationale is that the governments

Structural adjustment places increasing pressure on women to earn additional income. Women in Ghana carry items intended for sale to a local outdoor market (left). Other women in Ghana learn textile work in a classroom (below). They will make clothing and other items that can be sold to supplement dwindling family incomes.

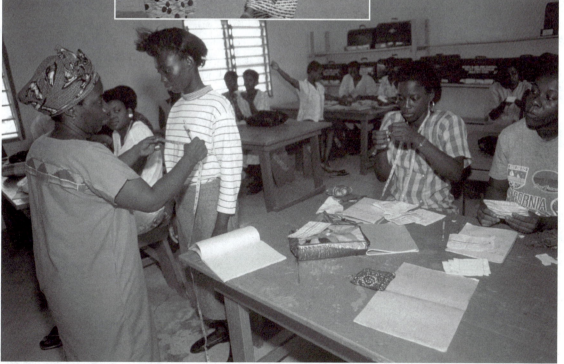

will then have more money to repay their debts. Unfortunately, women are affected greatly by such reductions. Women's access to education has decreased in some countries: literacy programs have been cut and a number of schools have been closed, increasing the traveling distance between home and school (Massiah, 1993; Vickers, 1991). Many girls are held back from attending because the increased distance between home and school limits their contributions to household chores, which are needed. In addition, school fees have increased. Parents prefer to send boys over girls to school, and girls' attendance rates have fallen as parents have less money for school fees (Herz, Subbarao, Habib, and Raney, 1991). Currently, boys already have an advantage over girls at the secondary and tertiary levels of education, increasing their access to employment and providing them with higher wages. In sum, the cut of expenditures in education increases men's socioeconomic status while decreasing women's.

Because most women in developing countries prepare the family's food and are the caretakers of the children, SAPs often lead to increases in the overall amount of work women need to do both at home and on the job. With the falling wages, rising prices, and elimination of food subsidies, women must either work longer hours to stay even under SAPs or participate in supplementary activities to increase their finances (Vickers, 1991). For example, SAPs in Ghana forced market women to increase the prices of the goods they were selling to maintain their income (Gladwin, 1991). But the higher prices led to decreased demand among their customers, who were also suffering under the SAPs. The market women also had to cope with trade restrictions, confiscations, and interrupted trade, as well as increased charges for water, electricity, transport, and health care. The Ghanaian government established a program to reduce the social costs for the rural poor, the unemployed, and the underemployed, but it does not assist market women. Under the SAPs, market women must either work longer hours or find different sources of income.

Some aspects of globalization clearly have harmed women. The masses of desperately poor people in developing countries are an excellent source of exploitable labor for the developed world. Young women are especially vulnerable because they need the work and lack the power to change their conditions and seek other opportunities. Even outside the workplace, women disproportionately suffer from social and economic adjustments because of their disadvantaged status in the labor force and their greater responsibilities for maintaining a household.

Gender in Comparative Perspective

Few things define a society as much as its patterns of work, education, and political decision making. This section discusses those areas for a wide variety of countries, showing again that there are acute gender inequalities across societies and within societies. Although the discussion is global, we focus special attention on the United States (an economically developed country), Mexico (a middle-income country), and Ghana (a poor country).

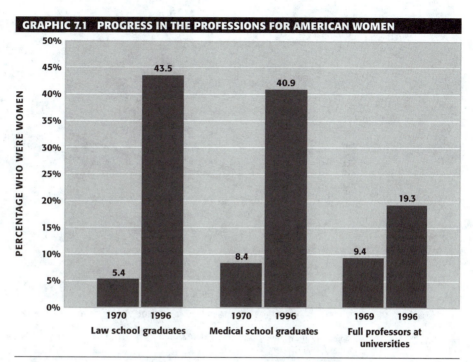

GRAPHIC 7.1 PROGRESS IN THE PROFESSIONS FOR AMERICAN WOMEN

Sources: For law school and medical school graduates, U.S. Bureau of the Census, 1999a; for full professors in 1969, U.S. Department of Health, Education, and Welfare, 1972, p. 90, Table 106; for full professors in 1996, *Annual report*, 2000, Table 8.

Work and Gender

Newspapers tell us that things are going well in the United States: economic expansion continues, unemployment is low, and the stock market has done remarkably well in recent years. For those at the top, it has been (and continues to be) a time of prosperity. The demand for specialized and professional workers has been unprecedented. Throughout the 1980s and 1990s, jobs grew most rapidly in the finance, insurance, and real estate (FIRE) sector: between 1960 and 1994, the percentage of workers almost quadrupled. Lucrative and demanding FIRE positions have provided golden opportunities to many American women.

More and more educated young women are joining the ranks of highly paid professionals. Graphic 7.1 shows their progress since 1970 in law, medicine, and academia, measured by the percentage of women graduates from professional schools and the percentage of full professors at universities who are women. More women are also moving into positions of upper administration at major universities. Prestigious universities such as Duke, Iowa, Michigan, Yale, Dartmouth, and Brown have female presidents or provosts. By contrast, the nation's largest companies are moving much more slowly with respect to naming women to CEO or

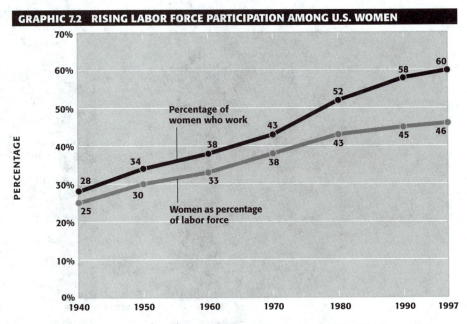

GRAPHIC 7.2   RISING LABOR FORCE PARTICIPATION AMONG U.S. WOMEN

Source: 1940 data from U.S. Bureau of the Census, 1960, Series D13–25; 1950–1997 data from U.S. Bureau of Labor
Statistics, 1998.

Note: Labor force participation includes those who work full- or part-time and those who are currently unemployed. The
1940 data include females 14 years old and over; the 1950–1997 data include females 16 years old and over.

equivalent positions. Only three companies in the Fortune 500 are currently
headed by women: Avon, Hewlett-Packard, and Golden West Financial.

Some people see the growth of high-paying jobs for women as a natural result of
the fact that more women have entered the workforce during the twentieth century.
However, not all working women have found high-paying jobs. Since the 1960s, as
the capacity of men to earn a family wage has declined, working-class women have
entered the labor force primarily to enhance family earnings.

Regardless of their reasons for entering the workforce, women have done so in
increasing numbers over the last century. Female participation in the labor force
increased from 20% in 1900 to 55% in 1988, with much of the growth among
mothers in families with annual earnings below $20,000. By 1988, 67% of mothers
who were single parents, 65% of mothers in dual-parent families, and 53% of
mothers with children under three years of age were in the labor force (Hayghe,
1997). Those proportions continued to increase during the 1990s. Graphic 7.2
shows that, by the end of the century, 60% of adult women were working outside
the home, with that figure representing an unprecedented 46% of the total labor
force.

It is important to note that increased female participation in the labor force does
not mean that all women are doing well. In fact, as demonstrated in Graphic 7.3,

GRAPHIC 7.3   "FEMALE PROFESSIONS" AND THE WAGE GAP IN THE UNITED STATES, 1997

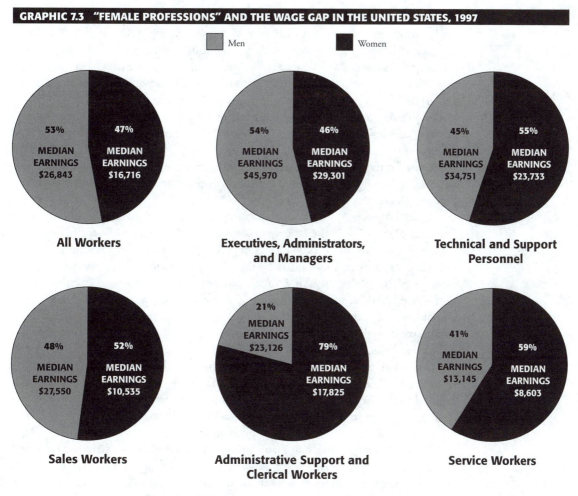

Men   Women

53%
MEDIAN
EARNINGS
$26,843

47%
MEDIAN
EARNINGS
$16,716

All Workers

54%
MEDIAN
EARNINGS
$45,970

46%
MEDIAN
EARNINGS
$29,301

**Executives, Administrators,
and Managers**

45%
MEDIAN
EARNINGS
$34,751

55%
MEDIAN
EARNINGS
$23,733

**Technical and Support
Personnel**

48%
MEDIAN
EARNINGS
$27,550

52%
MEDIAN
EARNINGS
$10,535

Sales Workers

21%
MEDIAN
EARNINGS
$23,126

79%
MEDIAN
EARNINGS
$17,825

**Administrative Support and
Clerical Workers**

41%
MEDIAN
EARNINGS
$13,145

59%
MEDIAN
EARNINGS
$8,603

Service Workers

Source: Adapted from U.S. Bureau of the Census, 1999b, pp. 60–200.

Note: "Female professions" are those in which women outnumber men; dollar amounts are the median annual earnings of women and men in each occupation.

women are still disproportionately represented in so-called "female professions," such as secretaries, nurses, and clerical workers (U.S. Bureau of the Census, 1999b). Not surprisingly, the result is gender inequality in the U.S. labor force with respect to pay—a "wage gap." For every dollar that a man makes, a woman makes 74 cents (U.S. Bureau of Labor Statistics, 2000). Even if women's and men's salaries are compared across the same occupation, similar patterns exist. For example, for advertising, marketing, and public relations managers, weekly earnings are $1,059 for men but only $736 for women, an average annual salary difference of $16,796 (American Federation of Labor–Congress of Industrial Organizations [AFL-CIO], 1997). If we examine the pay wage of elementary school teachers, 83% of whom are women, we still find that men earn approximately $719 per week and women earn $655 per week, an average annual salary difference of approximately $3,328 (AFL-CIO, 1997).

The situation is even bleaker when we examine the interaction between race and gender. For every dollar a white man earns, a white woman earns 74 cents, a black man earns 74 cents, a black woman earns 63 cents, a Hispanic male earns 62 cents, and a Hispanic woman earns only 53 cents (U.S. Bureau of Labor Statistics, 2000). Generally, men and women who are black or Hispanic are limited in their employment opportunities and tend to get tracked into low-wage employment sectors. The combination of the historical treatment of blacks and Hispanics, the current economic limitations of blacks and Hispanics, and the persistence of racism, as discussed in Chapter 6, leads to the radical differences between men and women and between workers of different races.

In fact, African-American males living in impoverished neighborhoods have long faced obstacles in the labor market. Chapter 6 explained how the history of African Americans, marked by residential segregation and racial exclusion, has limited their options in the United States to a larger extent than any other group. Changes in the global economy, such as corporate downsizing and deindustrialization, exacerbated even further the conditions surrounding this nation within a nation. The decline of manufacturing that resulted from the transition to an information-based economy broadened the gulf between those able to benefit from the new opportunities and those left behind. Clustered in inner cities with collapsing infrastructures, negligible investment, and appalling school conditions, new generations of urban black Americans are more likely than their ancestors to be permanently unemployed. They increasingly constitute a nonworking class whose very existence challenges every previous hope for assimilation. Clearly, gender, race, and class all affect employment outcomes in developed countries.

Gender is also an important factor in the way developing countries are stratified. As you can see in Graphic 7.4, throughout the world a large proportion of workers are women. However, most women in developing countries are more restricted than their counterparts in developed, high-income countries in the types of jobs they can find. Many of them enter fields that emphasize sewing, cooking, or other skills transferred from the domestic sphere. Others become secretaries and enter female-dominated professions, similar to the patterns we see in the United States and other developed countries.

Colonization has played a role in the sexual division of labor in many developing countries. During the colonization process, women in Europe were expected to stay close to the home and help with domestic activities, while the men were expected to work outside the home to provide support for the family. Those values were brought with the colonizers when they settled in Africa, Latin America, and Asia. That pattern remained even after the colonizers left, and men are still preferred over women for employment. However, many families in developing countries cannot survive with the income of just the man, especially in urban areas.

Often, the best jobs available to women in developing countries are in the informal sector, employment not formally recognized by the state. For example, few

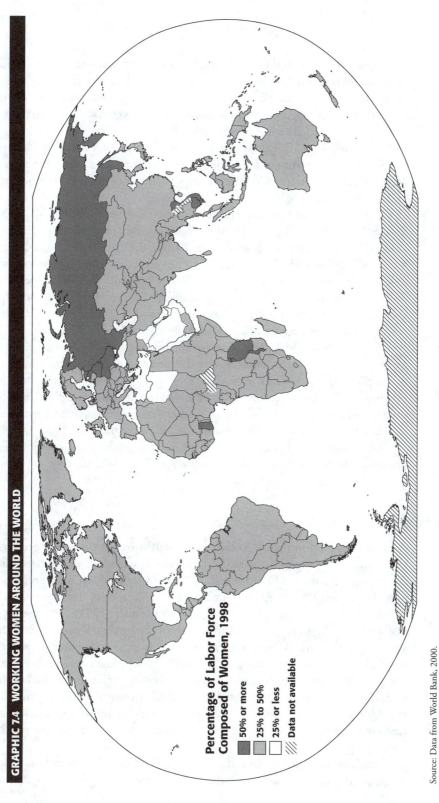

**Percentage of Labor Force
Composed of Women, 1998**

- 50% or more
- 25% to 50%
- 25% or less
- Data not available

Source: Data from World Bank, 2000.

Note: Calculated from ratio of female to male labor force participation.

women in Ghana have the opportunity to work in the formal sector because they must concentrate on farming, child care, housework, and attempting to gain supplemental income through activities like trading. Those activities occupy their entire day. A small segment of professional women, who have access to more money and resources, may hire inexpensive household help to care for their children and perform housework. That affords the small groups of middle- and upper-class women the opportunity to enter the formal workforce and expand their economic opportunities. Differences in class are important in developing countries, as well as in developed countries.

Globalization and rapid industrialization have further disrupted labor markets in developing countries by instigating a massive exodus from outlying areas to the cities. Although many men were ejected from the countryside as a result of the mechanization of agriculture, mining, and forestry, it was mostly women who had to leave their hometowns in search of survival, especially in Mexico and other parts of Latin America. Diminished opportunities in the rural sector and growing demand for domestic workers in large cities partly explain that trend. Alone and often without protection, young women from small towns and villages in Latin America face multiple dangers. For example, young female servants newly arriving in Lima, Peru, are defenseless against the sexual advances of men in the homes where they work or in the streets where they spend some of their free time (Chaney & Bunster, 1988). If the young women become pregnant, they are routinely dismissed and must become peddlers or market vendors, occupations that allow them to eke out a living while simultaneously looking after their children.

The examples from Ghana and Mexico demonstrate the limited employment opportunities for women in developing countries. Unfortunately, the educational system reinforces those patterns.

Schooling and Gender

A popular education theory, known as the **world-institutions perspective,** argues that societies throughout the world have adopted remarkably similar educational institutions based on Western ideals. A Western-style education is seen as modern and developed; therefore, all countries aspire to model their systems after the United States or Europe (see Bradshaw, 1993; Fuller, 1991). The theory is especially relevant as globalization continues to homogenize education throughout the world. More students from developing countries are studying in economically developed countries and then taking ideas back home; textbooks and curricula published in developed countries are adopted by developing countries; and most educational resource centers are located in developed countries and provide materials throughout the world. For those reasons, when we examine gender inequalities in developed countries, we can better understand how inequalities are reinforced in developing countries.

Emphasis on women's education has expanded throughout the world in recent years, which is clearly the case in the United States. With the civil rights era in the

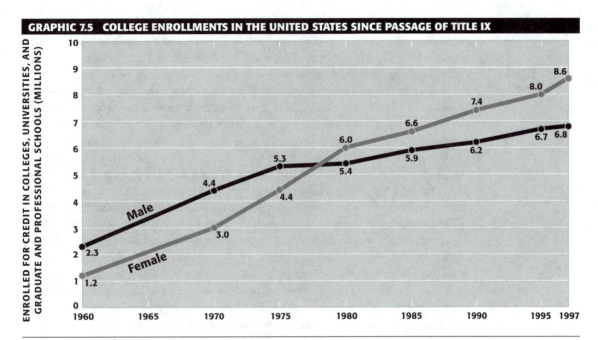

GRAPHIC 7.5 COLLEGE ENROLLMENTS IN THE UNITED STATES SINCE PASSAGE OF TITLE IX

Source: Adapted from U.S. Bureau of the Census, 1999a, pp. 20–516.

1960s and early 1970s, women's access to education increased substantially, particularly with the introduction of the Educational Amendment Act of 1972. That act mandated equal opportunities for men and women in publicly funded educational institutions. Previously, many women were disadvantaged when applying to institutions of higher learning. For example, women's standards for admission into some institutions were higher than men's; in some instances, women were not allowed to live on campus, which limited the number of women that universities would admit (Fox, 1984).

One provision of the Educational Amendment Act was Title IX, which not only enforced equal admissions rates but also provided equal opportunities for both men and women once they were in educational institutions. In other words, women had to have the same opportunities as men to enroll in courses offered, as well as to participate in sports offered. As Title IX has taken hold, women's enrollment in higher education has increased, as can be seen in Graphic 7.5. In fact, more women are now enrolled than men. Clearly, there has been a shift in educational opportunities for women.

However, if we take a closer look at the educational system, we find that while opportunities for girls and women have increased, gender differences remain. School interests for boys and girls begin at the elementary level and are even reinforced by parents and peers before children enter elementary school (Bellew, Raney, & Subbarao, 1992; Sadker & Sadker, 1994). For example, parents are more likely to buy science sets for their sons than for their daughters. At the same time, girls are more likely to be encouraged to play with dolls and other toys that focus on domestic activities. Therefore, when girls and boys enter elementary school, the preferences for certain topics have already formed for most children. Many times girls do not feel comfortable taking science or math since they have not had experience in those areas. On the other hand, boys tend to excel in those subjects because of their previous exposure (Shakeshaft, 1995). The discrepancy is perpetuated even further by the actions of teachers, who tend to call on and encourage boys more than girls (Sadker & Sadker, 1994). Whereas boys are encouraged to continue trying when they fail at problems, girls are encouraged to accept their failure and discontinue their efforts at trying. For those reasons, boys tend to be tracked more toward math and science courses, while girls are tracked away from math and science courses.

The pattern continues throughout high school and into college. The outcomes are particularly evident when we examine university majors by gender. Graphic 7.6 shows the percentage of degrees earned by women in particular fields of study. As expected, the majors dominated by men are computer science, math, engineering, and hard sciences. The majors dominated by women are liberal arts, education, social sciences, and health-related studies. Even if we examine the majors in which women have increased significantly, we also find differences. For example, in medicine women tend to concentrate in pediatrics while men concentrate in surgery. From those patterns, we see that women have gained equal access to educational opportunities; yet, due to influences from parents, peers, and teachers, the gender differences in educational institutions remain. Similar patterns are found throughout the developed countries.

If we look at education today in developing countries, the gender inequalities are more evident than in developed countries. In many developing countries, the gender ratio for primary schooling is fairly equal. However, as students move into secondary schooling, the male-female ratio increases. When the students move into the university level, the ratio is much more apparent (Graphic 7.7). The differences are also evident according to geographic location. The gender divide, for example, is more apparent in Africa and southern Asia than in Latin America.

The reasons for the divide are many. Many have to do with cultural expectations for men and women. First, girls are expected to help more around the house in developing countries. Girls can help on the farms, but, more important, they care for younger siblings. Often, girls are removed from schools to help their mothers care for the home and the family. Many families fear their daughters will become pregnant in school, and they do not want to take that risk. Girls who do become pregnant are removed from the school (Akuffo, 1987) and thus don't make it to the next levels of education. More significant, however, is the fact that boys are seen as bringing more returns to education (Hadden & London, 1996; Herz et al., 1991; Odaga & Heneveld, 1995). The son of a family is expected to leave the home eventually, find a job, and support himself and his family. Because there is an absence of social security in developing countries, sons are expected to support and help their aging parents. Daughters, on the other hand, are expected to marry and leave the

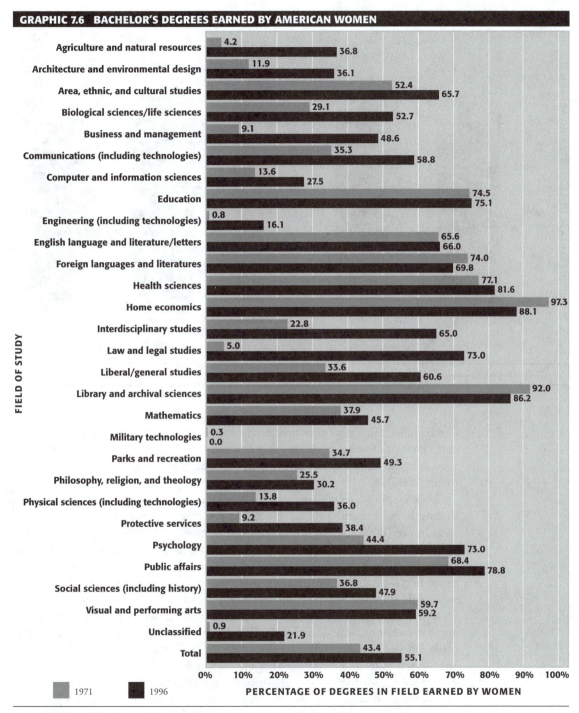

GRAPHIC 7.6 BACHELOR'S DEGREES EARNED BY AMERICAN WOMEN

FIELD OF STUDY

Field of Study	1971	1996
Agriculture and natural resources	4.2	36.8
Architecture and environmental design	11.9	36.1
Area, ethnic, and cultural studies	52.4	65.7
Biological sciences/life sciences	29.1	52.7
Business and management	9.1	48.6
Communications (including technologies)	35.3	58.8
Computer and information sciences	13.6	27.5
Education	74.5	75.1
Engineering (including technologies)	0.8	16.1
English language and literature/letters	65.6	66.0
Foreign languages and literatures	74.0	69.8
Health sciences	77.1	81.6
Home economics	97.3	88.1
Interdisciplinary studies	22.8	65.0
Law and legal studies	5.0	73.0
Liberal/general studies	33.6	60.6
Library and archival sciences	92.0	86.2
Mathematics	37.9	45.7
Military technologies	0.3	0.0
Parks and recreation	34.7	49.3
Philosophy, religion, and theology	25.5	30.2
Physical sciences (including technologies)	13.8	36.0
Protective services	9.2	38.4
Psychology	44.4	73.0
Public affairs	68.4	78.8
Social sciences (including history)	36.8	47.9
Visual and performing arts	59.7	59.2
Unclassified	0.9	21.9
Total	43.4	55.1

■ 1971   ■ 1996

PERCENTAGE OF DEGREES IN FIELD EARNED BY WOMEN

Source: U.S. Bureau of the Census, 1999a.

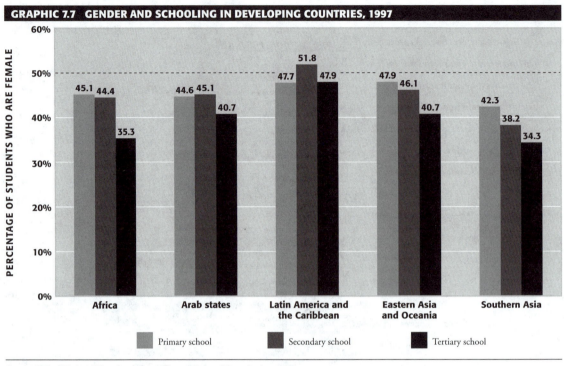

Source: United Nations Educational, Scientific, and Cultural Organization, 1999.

family. Most daughters, once they marry, have no financial obligations to their parents. If a family has to choose between sending their son or their daughter to school, in most cases, it will be the daughter who has to forgo an education (Buchmann, 2000).

In developing countries, the colonial legacy also plays a significant role in determining how boys and girls are educated. When schools were set up in colonized areas in the 1800s, they were built and run primarily for the education of boys and men (Graham, 1971; Pellow, 1977; Robertson, 1984). Initially, girls were not allowed to attend the schools. Because the colonizers needed only certain positions to be filled—mainly lower bureaucratic positions—they worked to educate men who could fill those positions; the education of girls and women would not help to serve their purposes. When girls eventually were allowed to attend school, the emphasis was on domestic activities. Girls and women were taught how to sew and cook and were encouraged to stay at home. At the same time, boys and men were encouraged to leave the home to support the family.

Although girls have fewer educational opportunities than boys in lower- and middle-income countries, the gap between males and females is narrowing. Proponents of the world-institutions perspective argue that developing countries are following the lead of developed countries, which increasingly stress the education of girls. By contrast, opponents of the theory assert that developing countries are fundamentally different from developed nations from a cultural, political, and economic standpoint. The inclusion of women is not necessary to improve economic development.

Again, as we saw in the subsection "Work and Gender," while there has been an increase in the number of girls in educational institutions, they still are lagging behind their male counterparts. Such gender inequality is due to historical development as well as to cultural expectations.

Politics and Gender

If anyone doubts it is a man's world, he or she need only look at who runs governments. Of the 192 countries in the United Nations, only five are headed by women at the time of this writing: Sri Lanka, Ireland, Panama, Bangladesh, and New Zealand. As Graphic 7.8 shows, few countries have parliamentary assemblies that exceed the short-term goal of 30% (on average) established by the recent Women 2000 conference in New York. It is likely that a world with more women leaders would function differently than today's world—there probably would be more emphasis on issues related to women and children and perhaps less on warfare.

The United States, of course, has never had a woman president or even a formidable woman presidential candidate. (In 1984, Walter Mondale ran for President against Ronald Reagan and selected Geraldine Ferraro as his running mate; Mondale and Ferraro were beaten badly.) In fact, although there has been improvement since the mid-1970s, the percentage of women in the U.S. Congress in 2000 was only about 13% in the House and 9% in the Senate—about the world average (see Graphic 7.8). The numbers are better for state legislators, but they still are unimpressive, particularly in a country that considers itself at the forefront of gender issues.

Why aren't there more female government leaders? There are several reasons. First, some countries have cultural traditions that discourage or outright prohibit women from participating in the political structure. The United Arab Emirates and Kuwait do not even permit women to vote. Second, as seen earlier in this chapter, women do not have opportunities comparable to those of men with respect to employment and educational attainment. That limits their potential to gain experience at lower decision-making levels and build the networks and organization necessary to run for office. Third, women do not have as much access to resources (such as money) compared to men. That is especially problematic in the United States, where substantial sums of money usually are required to conduct an effective campaign for national office.

Despite the fact that women's groups and various international organizations are calling for more women to run for office, it is unlikely that dramatic improvements will occur soon. There first must be opportunities for girls and women in the workforce and in schools prior to large-scale political involvement.

Although women have made great strides recently, we still find women are not equal to men as decision makers in the public sphere. Historical and cultural

GRAPHIC 7.8   WOMEN IN NATIONAL LEGISLATURES

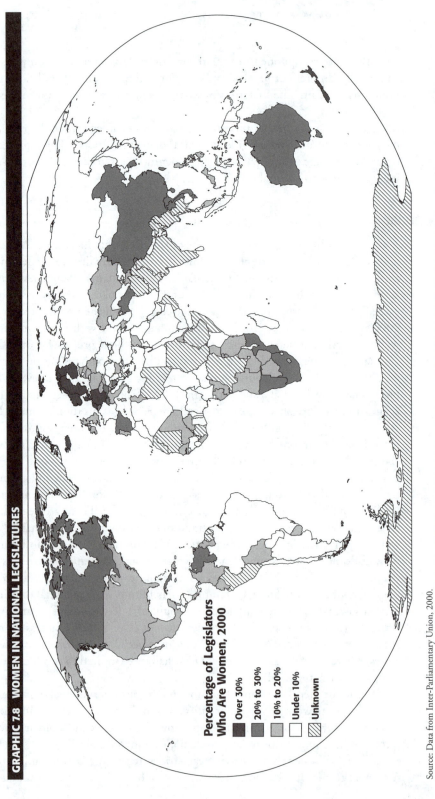

Percentage of Legislators Who Are Women, 2000

- Over 30%
- 20% to 30%
- 10% to 20%
- Under 10%
- Unknown

Source: Data from Inter-Parliamentary Union, 2000.

Note: Percentages include both lower and upper houses of legislature where appropriate.

expectations continue to maintain patterns of gender inequality in both developed and developing countries. Only with a change in those expectations will we find societies with increased gender equality.

Conclusion

Overall, gender inequality has been a feature of society across recorded time and in most cultures. However, in some societal institutions, gender inequality is slowly decreasing, especially in advanced industrial societies. In the past century alone, we have seen significant changes in women's opportunities in developed countries. Changes in the social construction of gender have played a role. And globalization has increased exposure to egalitarian ideas about women's and men's roles.

When examining the effects of globalization on gender, we find opposing outcomes. On the one hand, we could argue that the process of globalization may have a positive affect on gender. In the United States and other developed countries, education and employment opportunities have increased, and women continue to enter the workplace and decision-making positions. In addition, more women in developing countries are attending school and have the opportunity to support themselves and contribute to the household income by working in factories that make goods for international trade, such as the *maquiladoras*. Moreover, with conferences like the Fourth World Conference in Beijing, women can form alliances and begin to institute programs that will increase their presence in education, employment, and decision-making institutions. Connections among women from different nations may help continue to reduce gender inequalities.

On the other hand, we could also argue that globalization has perpetuated gender inequality. The segregation of women and men in educational institutions and in the workplace continues in the United States and other developed countries. In developing countries, girls and women do not have equal opportunities to attend school; women's employment options still are limited and many women still suffer abuses in the factories. Their employment situation is even worse under SAPs. Also, few women are in high decision-making positions, such as governmental posts, in either developed or developing countries. One could argue that globalization is helping to both decrease and increase gender inequality, depending on the specific circumstances.

In the end, all we can say with some degree of certainty is that the most general trend of contemporary gender relations consists of greater stratification of the labor force in terms of sex. The disappearance of the family wage has brought a new expectation that every competent adult, regardless of race, class, gender, or domestic responsibilities, will assume responsibility for the maintenance of at least himself or herself. As more women join the world of employment, they face the promise of added autonomy and economic self-reliance. At the same time, the deteriorating conditions of work in some economic sectors raise concerns about the full meaning of gender stratification for both men and women. The major challenge in the new century will be bringing about a solution to those inequalities.

Key Concepts

1. Gender consists of the social characteristics assigned to people of different sexes. The social roles that males and females participate in, the activities in which they are involved, the clothes they wear, and other characteristics help to define an individual's gender within society. Gender should not be confused with sex, which is based on biological differences.

2. The feminist theoretical perspective became prominent in the 1970s, shortly after the civil rights era. There are many different types of feminist theory, but they all attempt to address the construction and inequality of gender by examining different social institutions from the perspective of women. They also attempt to explain why inequalities are perpetuated and offer solutions to the problems those inequalities present.

3. *Gender* is a fluid concept. What Americans may consider to be typical characteristics of men or of women are not necessarily typical of gender characterizations across time and in different cultures. People's conceptions of gender are specific to their own society and their own time period. Moreover, the social construction of gender is continually changing within societies.

4. The status of males and females in a society varies according to the society's level of technological development. Hunter-gatherer societies maintain a sexual division of labor but generally view the sexes as equal. In agricultural societies, the sexual division of labor increases, the relations between individuals become more complex, and patriarchy becomes more powerful. In industrial societies, the division of labor and the presence of patriarchy remain. However, in advanced industrial societies, both the sexual division of labor and patriarchy are being challenged.

5. Gender inequality has remained a feature of social life throughout time and across cultures. That is evident when we examine the position of women in work, schooling, and political spheres in societies at different levels of development. Although women have made some strides in those spheres in the United States and other developed countries, men and women still tend to be divided according to traditional gender roles. Moreover, women continue to be paid less than men.

Active Learning

1. Gender Socialization: Observation (Adapted from an exercise developed by Professor Betsy Lucal, Indiana University South Bend). In this exercise, you will analyze how gender roles are presented in society and how children learn to "do gender"—that is, how they learn to behave and present themselves in ways that make them easily viewed as boys or girls. You will have a chance to see how gender and socialization work in the real world by analyzing the gender makeup of children's toys and/or clothes.

a. Get the worksheet for this assignment from our Web site (www.pineforge.com/snc) and familiarize yourself with the procedures. Choose a locale for observation: a children's clothing or toy store or a similar area in a department store. Plan to observe for about 20 minutes.

b. As you observe, take notes on the worksheet (a clipboard might come in handy). Be as unobtrusive as possible and try not to disrupt normal daily business. If anyone asks what you are doing, explain the assignment politely and honestly ("This is an assignment for my sociology class") and assure them that you will be gone shortly. Observe how the clothes or toys are organized and presented. How do you know which items are intended for boys and which for girls? Read the worksheet for more information about what to look for.

c. Bring your worksheet to class and be prepared to participate in a group discussion about your observations. In class, break into groups of four to six. Groups should include people who visited different types of stores. Answer the following questions as a group. Each member of the group should take a turn writing a summary of the group's answers.

   i.   Present and compare your findings. What patterns did you see? Did anyone find anything unusual or unexpected?

   ii.   What do you think the clothes and toys you observed teach children about gender? How do they teach them to be boys or girls? Think about the kinds of clothes and how the clothes might affect a child's movements. Similarly, think about the toys intended for each gender and how the toys might affect, for example, a child's school and career interests.

   iii.   Based on your findings with respect to clothing and toys, what does it mean to be a boy or girl? In other words, what do boys and girls look like, act like, enjoy doing, and so on?

   iv.   Are there any ways in which toys or clothing encourage boys and girls to be similar to each other? Explain.

   v.   If we are to be sociologically mindful, we have to take our findings a step further. We can't stop with the patterns. We have to think about what the patterns mean and how they connect to other aspects of the social world. On one hand, these observations show that we use gender as a way to organize the social world. On the other hand, gender in our society is also a basis for inequality, for assigning people different roles, rewards, responsibilities, and so forth. Discuss how children's toys and clothes help to maintain inequality.

   vi.   Submit a summary of the group's discussion to the instructor.

   vii.   Write a reaction paper to this exercise and to the group discussion. What did you learn? How much of an impact do you think children's clothes and toys have on gender socialization and the perpetuation of gender inequality? Can you apply any of these processes to your own socialization? Can you apply them to the socialization of your younger siblings or your own children? Do you think parents realize what kinds of effects the clothes and toys they buy can have on their children?

2. Leadership, Gender, and the Invisible Ceiling: Survey Research (Adapted from an exercise developed by Dr. Keith A. Roberts, Hanover College, Hanover, Indiana). In this exercise, you will gather data from ten students (your instructor may specify a different number) and then use the information to reflect on social conceptions of masculinity and femininity and our society's definitions of leadership. Understanding that our society's definitions of leadership characteristics tend to correspond closely to its definitions of masculinity can help us understand forces that help to limit women's opportunities in employment, education, and politics.

a. Download the "Characteristics of Leaders" survey from our Web site (www.pineforge.com/snc) and make a copy for each respondent and two blank copies for yourself. Also download the summary form for this assignment.

b. Distribute the survey. Relatives, friends, and acquaintances are suitable respondents for this assignment, but try to include people of various backgrounds. Introduce yourself (if necessary) and tell your respondents that the survey is part of a class assignment and that the results will be anonymous (do not ask for names on the sheet). Ask them to follow the instructions on the sheet. Do not tell them that this is a study of gender or of limits on women's opportunities. If they ask, tell them it is a survey on the qualities that Americans look for in leaders (which is true).

c. If all respondents fill out the survey at the same time, shuffle the completed forms so you will not know who might have filled out a particular sheet. If the surveys are filled one by one, place the completed forms in an envelope without looking at them. Later, when all forms have been completed, shuffle them so you will not be able to identify your respondents.

d. Summarize the responses. On one of your blank copies of the survey, add up the number of times each trait was marked with an "X." Write the number of surveys you administered at the top of this form.

e. Download from our Web site the instructions for analyzing the responses. Bring it to class along with your summary form, your summary figures, the other blank copy of the survey, and a calculator.

f. In class, break into groups of three to five. Work together to analyze your group's data, using the instructions you downloaded from the Web site.

g. Analyze the patterns of responses and discuss the implications. How common are positive relationships between "leadership" and "masculinity"? How common are positive relationships between "leadership" and "femininity"? In view of the patterns you identified, discuss the following proposition:

> A woman with "masculine" traits often makes people uncomfortable and may be overlooked for leadership roles. On the other hand, if a woman is not "masculine" (as our society thinks of it), she may not be thought of as a person with leadership qualities.

> Discuss how these patterns might affect women in the workplace. How might they affect men? Can these results help explain why women encounter invisible limits on achievement (an unconscious or unwitting form of sexism)? How might the findings from your survey indicate a pattern that leads to the kinds of gender inequalities discussed in the chapter?

h. Write a brief summary of the group's analysis and discussion and submit it, with the group's data summary, to the instructor.

3. Gender Inequality within and between Nations: Internet Research. In this exercise, you will use the Internet to collect information that further illustrates how gender inequalities play out around the globe and how degree of inequality is affected by national economic level of development and quality of life. You will be gathering information about three nations at each of three income levels (a total of nine). High-income (or developed) nations, like the United States, have industrial or postindustrial economies and very high quality of life. Middle-income (developing) nations are in transition from an agricultural to an industrial society. The chapter uses Mexico as an example of a developing nation. Low-income nations (least developed), like Ghana, have largely agricultural economies and a lower quality of life. Your sample will be small in size but will still illustrate patterns of gender inequality around the globe.

a. Begin by downloading the scoring form from our Web site (www.pineforge.com/snc) to use in recording scores. The scoring form specifies the information you will collect.

b. Choose three nations from each income category below and write their names on the form you downloaded from the Web site.

High income	*Middle income*	*Low income*
Japan	Republic of Korea	Nigeria
United Kingdom	Argentina	Haiti
Canada	Turkey	Kenya
Italy	Algeria	Armenia
Sweden	Philippines	Pakistan

c. Go to the United Nations Web site at www.un.org and find the tables that present worldwide statistics on women (the instructions are on the scoring form you downloaded). Information is organized mostly by region. Click on "Africa" to get data for Nigeria, Kenya, or Algeria; "Asia and Pacific" for Japan, Korea, Armenia, Pakistan, Turkey, or the Philippines; "Latin America and Caribbean" for Argentina or Haiti; and "Developed Regions" for the United Kingdom, Canada, Italy, or Sweden. Record scores on the scoring form.

d. Leave the UN Web site and look at your data. Are the patterns of gender inequality in your small sample consistent with the analysis presented in the chapter? For example, for developing (middle- and low-income) nations, is it true that gender inequality in education tends to be greater at higher levels of schooling? Is female (versus male) participation in the labor force lower for developing nations compared to developed (high-income) nations? Is it true that females have more power (as measured by percentage of government positions) in nations with more gender equity in education and employment? (Remember, you are working with a very small sample, and each nation you chose has a unique history and culture. Thus, it is unlikely that the patterns you find will match exactly the general points made in the chapter.)

e. If you like or if your instructor asks, return to the UN data base and get information on birth rates and family size for each of your nations. What do the statistics tell you about the status of women in the nations you have chosen?

f. Write a report in which you summarize the patterns you have found in terms of the points made in the chapter about the relationships among gender, education, employment, and decision-making power at various levels of national development.

Sex as a Global Commodity

JOANE NAGEL

Soulmates International, an Internet site designed to put "Western" men in touch with "quality Asian ladies" from the Philippines, offers these responses to frequently asked questions:

Why do young Filipino women want an older man 30 to 60? Filipino women are looking for a life partner. . . . They are smart and realise that men 20–30 are not stable, don't have definite goals for their life, and do not treat women with the same respect as an older man.

Are these women loose women or prostitutes? No. These women are not bar girls or prostitutes. Many of these women from 17–25 are virgins.

Do Filipinas make good wives? They are taught that marriage is a life long commitment. . . . When you ask questions of a Filipino woman like how many children would you like to have, or would you like to be a working wife, or a housewife, her answer will always be that it is up to my future husband to decide.

Do they look after their bodies? If you like a petite woman, then you will be pleased with a Filipina. They have very little body hair. They are fanatically clean about their personal hygiene and appearance. . . . Basically a 15 year old Filipino girl has more class that the average 25 year old American girl.

Should you Westernise a Filipino wife? No. You pick this girl because of the fine characteristics they have. If you're foolish enough to want to turn her into an Westernised woman shame on you!

The images and stereotypes imbedded in the questions and answers on this and other similar Web sites reflect ethnosexual images of gender, that is, racialized and sexualized images of masculinity and femininity. The Soulmates International site depicts the traditional, compliant, but sexually available Asian woman desirous of an amorous, but committed relationship with a "Western" (that is, white) man.

Before the Internet, such courtships took place by other, slower means—letters, telephone calls, visits. The Internet is one dimension of the globalization of communication that has made sexual contacts with people in other cultures more accessible to more people in less time than ever before.

More subtle and more profound processes of sexualization are underway in the global village as well. One such sexualization process is embedded in the rise of consumer culture around the world, in particular the desire for Western consumer products and associated lifestyles. Consumer culture is marked by the desire for "stuff"—appliances, clothes, cars, cosmetics, computers, and other gadgets—and by the conspicuous consumption of those products. Participation in global consumer culture and its local variations stands as evidence of economic as well as social success, "modernity," and Western savvy among many diverse populations around the world.

The globalization of consumer culture has had important consequences for understanding sex and globalization. Western marketing around the world not only communicates information about products but conveys implicit messages about the kinds of people who consume the products, messages about their modernity and their desirability. The marketing of Western products puts sexuality in the service of selling goods and peddles a specific vision of Western sexuality, lifestyle, and culture. The spread of Western consumer culture, then, promotes the sexualization of consumption and the consumption of sexuality. It markets a libidinal consciousness, a sexual self-imagining, and an erotic view of ethnic, racial, and national "others."

A Western-style cosmetics counter in Shenzhen, China. Advertisements and marketing campaigns promise women that these Western products will make them more desirable, modern, and exciting. This self-image promotes the globalization of sex.

Examples of the link between globalization and sexualization can be found in some unlikely places. Take, for instance, export processing zones (EPZs), which were established in a number of developing countries during the 1980s as part of a plan to attract foreign investment. EPZs are economic and political borderlands where tariffs, taxes, and production and labor regulations are revised or suspended to encourage companies to build factories and processing plants. EPZs generally are located on the geographic edges of countries and constitute globally connected commercial and cultural spaces. Mexico's *maquiladoras* are examples of EPZs, as are special economic zones in the city of Shenzhen in southern China. Researchers describe these new industrial settings as gendered and sexualized spaces filled with male managers and mainly female workers. In the 1990s, Mexican women comprised 85% of the workers in *maquiladoras* (Vargas, 1998). A similar feminization of the EPZ labor force has taken place in the Philippines:

Light industries such as food processing and the manufacture of textiles, garments, footwear, tobacco, and pharmaceuticals utilize mostly female labor. Women's body parts are idealized, "synergizing" nimble fingers, 20/20 eyesight, and hardy bodies. . . . Women are preferred for all the stereotypical reasons: lower labor costs, traditional feminine skills, manual dexterity, more productivity, greater tolerance of and better performance in repetitive and monotonous tasks, reliability, patience, low expectations, lack of employment alternatives, a willingness to put up with dead-end jobs. . . . young, single, childless women are preferred [because] . . . employers are often reluctant to pay generous maternity benefits. (Tolentino, 1999)

Managers of transnationally owned factories act as marketing agents for Western consumer products and sexual cultural styles for the young single women working in EPZs. For instance, Filipino EPZ factories arrange cosmetic and Western-style clothing bazaars, hold beauty contests, and offer worker incentives and bonuses in the form of gift certificates to department stores. The result is the development of a Western self-conception and consumer culture among workers, the promotion of cosmopolitan standards of beauty, and a sexualization of the industrial workplace. As the young women compete to win beauty contests and department store shopping sprees, and as they spend their EPZ wages on cosmetics and Western-style clothing, they are invited and encouraged to view themselves as potential erotic products, such as mail-order brides and sex workers in a global marketplace (Tolentino, 1999).

Sexuality and romance are areas in which global and local cultures interact to generate new cultural fashions and fantasies. Sometimes the hybrids are surprising—even jarring—mixtures of tastes and designs. Consider this description of the wedding of two educated, local young people that took place in 1993 in the market town of Xijiang, in the rural Miao mountains of Guizhou, China. The bride was an elementary school teacher, the groom the manager of a state-run dry goods outlet.

The guests are arriving bearing shoulder poles of gifts—pork, sticky rice, homebrewed liquor, quilts, fabric. The bride stays in the nuptial chamber . . . and makes up her face with powder, blush, lipstick, eyeliner, then dresses in Miao finery. . . . Just then a group of city friends arrive, classmates from the days when the couple attended high school in the prefecture seat. . . . [They bring] the *pièce de résistance*—a gift borne on shoulder poles. It is an ostentatious yard-long wall hanging behind glass—a photographic decoration slated for the walls of the nuptial chamber. The picture, in a bizarre juxtaposition with or even upstaging of the bride, is of a blonde model in a hot pink g-string bikini lying atop a snazzy racing car. Lovingly, the hanging is given front center placement among the other gifts . . . on display in the nuptial chamber for guests to review. Upon completion of her ethnic adornment, the bride poses with the thing. (Schein, 1997)

How to make sense of this interjection of a crass, cosmopolitan, global image into a quaint, traditional, local scene? Are white women in China in the 1990s signifiers of "self-possessed independence, . . . or fashionable models of bourgeois consumer expertise, or sultry practitioners of erotic extremity?" As capitalist tools and marketing devices, "the white woman sells" (Schein, 1997). What is the meaning of this facsimile of the white woman hanging in Chinese sensual space? Does the presence of the white woman represent some local capitulation to global (Western, that is) standards of beauty and desirability? Or, in contrast, does she represent the appropriation into local culture of what once had been alien and unattainable, the local Chinese consumption of the global white woman? Or does her meaning lie somewhere in between—a kind of hybrid cultural formation, a blending of local and global cosmologies of beauty, gender, and sexuality that bespeaks neither good nor evil, neither submission nor subversion?

Although local/global ethnosexual consumer culture is a blend of East and West, North and South, developing and developed worlds, the power and the location of the originating message should not be underestimated. Despite the rainbow of skin tones in its marketing ads, there is no mistaking the dominance of the color white in the United Colors of Benetton.

No exploration of sex and globalization would be complete without a side trip into the world of sex tourism. A case in point is Thailand and its notorious sex industry, which caters to mainly male Japanese and Western sex tourists. Thailand illustrates the global geopolitical and economic forces at work in the making of a sex tourism destination. Researchers have identified a historical military-libidinal economic connection between sex-for-sale operations catering to soldiers and sex for sale to tourists.

> In 1967, Thailand contracted with the U.S. government to provide "Rest and Recreation" (R&R) services to the troops during the Vietnam War. Today's customers at the go-go bars spawned by those contracts are not only white Americans but also European and Australian— all *farangs* to the Thais. . . . It was in 1971, while the war in Southeast Asia still raged, that World Bank President Robert McNamara, who had been U.S. Secretary of Defense when the R&R contracts with Thailand were signed, went to Bangkok to arrange for the bank's experts to produce a study of Thailand's postwar tourism prospects. (Bishop & Robinson, 1998)

Because of the presence and profitability of the wartime sex industry, the Bank's advice (which Thailand followed) to specialize in tourism led to the convergence of the sex trade and the tourist trade. Thus, the U.S. military and the World Bank became partners in developing what is perhaps the most famous (or infamous, depending on your point of view) sex industry in the world.

Other examples exist of a link between the military's provision of sex for soldiers and sex tourism. For instance, there are historical, political, economic, and cultural parallels between Japan's "comfort women" (mainly Korean and Filipino women forced to sexually service Japanese soldiers in sex labor camps during World War II) and Japan's current role as a consumer market for the Asian sex industry, in particular, for sex tourism.

> Both groups of women have been tricked, imprisoned, raped, and then forced against their will to work as prostitutes. . . . Sex tourism to other Asian countries by Japanese men is a con-

temporary version of the Japanese Imperial Army's sexual exploitation of Asian women. Symbolically, the difference lies only in the way the men dress; instead of military uniforms, they now wear business suits. (Watanabe, 1995)

Researchers also note the intimate connection between sex tourism and the economics of development. In many developing countries that are struggling with international debt, such as Tunisia, Puerto Rico, Haiti, Nepal, and The Gambia, tourism has become a larger industry

than many traditional exports. While all tourist destinations are also sites of sex commerce, in major sex tourist destinations such as Thailand, the Philippines, Belize, Jamaica, and Sri Lanka, the selling of local and imported sexuality is an important component of economic development; in fact, some governments support and advertise sex tourism. For instance, one researcher reports that "Brazil's tourist industry promotes the country as one which offers sexual attractions as part of the nation's natural and cultural resources," for example, *Carnival* in Rio de Janeiro (Larvie, 1999).

Published tour guides have entered the market. Major publishers of tour books like *Fodor's, Frommer's, Rough Guide,* and *Lonely Planet* include sections on straight and gay night life that refer to the sex trade and offer varying levels of advice. For instance, an early 1990s edition of *Insight Guide* to Thailand "explained how to nego-

Japanese tourists in Brazil watch a samba dancer during Carnival *in Rio de Janeiro. Brazil's tourism industry clearly promotes sex-related activities as just another attraction to be enjoyed by foreign visitors.*

tiate the transactions in a massage parlor and how to buy a bar dancer out for the night, advising against taking a prostitute to a first-class hotel" (Bishop and Robinson, 1998). Researchers note that sex tourism and sex workers can be likened to wildlife and other exotic tourist attractions, where the sexuality of local women and men, girls and boys become natural and cultural resources.

It is important to note that the sex industry as a component of local and international tourism is not confined to developing countries. In November 1999, the U.S. Central Intelligence Agency (CIA) completed a two-year study of illegal trafficking and enslavement of mostly women and children primarily in the U.S. sex industry. In the spring of 2000, the *New York Times* summarized the unreleased report *International Trafficking in Women to the United States: A Contemporary Manifestation of Slavery,* which estimated the number of women and children trafficked to the United States for sexual slavery to be as high as 50,000 per year. The report's accounts of forced sexual slavery outside of wartime stand in contrast to the almost festive label "sex tourism."

[The CIA report] describes case after case of foreign women who answered advertisements for au pair, sales clerk, secretarial or waitress jobs in the United States but found, once they arrived, that the jobs did not exist. Instead they were taken prisoner, held under guard and forced into prostitution or peonage. Some of them were, in fact, sold outright to brothel owners. . . . "Latvian women [were] threatened and forced to dance nude in Chicago," the report says. Thai women were brought to the United States "but forced to be virtual sex slaves." Chinese-Korean women were "held as indentured servants." And "Mexican women and girls, some as young as 14," were promised jobs in housekeeping or child care but, upon arrival, "were told they must work as prostitutes in brothels serving migrant workers." ("Once-hidden slave trade," 2000, April 2)

Given that grim reality, it is not surprising that activists have mobilized to counter the sex tourism industry. In Thailand, groups called Empower and Friends of Women work with women in the sex tourism industry to teach them about AIDS prevention. Daughters Education Programme works to provide education for village girls to increase their employability outside of sex tourism and to enhance their local status. Other international anti–sex trade/sex tourism organizations include the Asian Women's Human Rights Council, ECPAT (End Child Prostitution in Asian Tourism), the Global Alliance against Traffic in Women, and the Coalition against Trafficking in Women. More demonstrative methods of protesting sex tourism include airport greeting parties to publicly humiliate Japanese and Taiwanese businessmen arriving home from sex tours and a tactic proposed by a Filipino guerrilla group: "Kill a sex tourist a day" (Davidson, 1998).

Admittedly, sexual commodification with an undercurrent of ethnic exploitation is not new. But the contemporary pace of globalization has intensified and expanded historical ethnosexual processes. Further globalization eventually might result in a blending of cultural values related to sexuality and a weakening of racial, ethnic, and national boundaries and identities. Or globalization might leave racial, ethnic, and national boundaries in place as ethnosexual settlers, sojourners, adventurers, and invaders cross national borders for intimate encounters. Either way, sexuality will remain an important—though often hidden—dimension of globalization.

Thinking about the Essay

What is sexual commodification? How is it related to gender roles and relations as discussed in Chapter 7? How do globalization and the spread of consumerism affect gender?

8 Families

What is happening to families in a changing world?

Have you ever asked your parents or grandparents what life was like in their families? Have you ever asked friends from other societies how family life is for them? You would probably find that family life differs from generation to generation and from society to society. In France, for instance, Parliament recently passed a new law creating arrangements called *Pacte civil de solidarité* (civil solidarity pact), simply known as PACS. PACS are like marriage in some ways: they make each party responsible for financially supporting the other, require the parties to share debts accumulated during the pact, and make each party eligible for the others' work benefits. But PACS differ from traditional marriage in two significant ways: they can be broken in a short period of time, and they can be entered into by gay and lesbian couples. Interestingly, though, nearly 40% of couples opting for PACS are heterosexual couples who feel they are not yet ready for a real marriage (Daley, 2000).

Or consider Wambui, a brilliant Kenyan student studying for her doctorate degree in the United States. She is unmarried and gave birth to a daughter during her graduate studies. The idea of placing the child in a day care center several days a week, even for short periods of time, was foreign to this new mother. It was also foreign to her family. In Kenya, as in most African countries, the concept of the extended family is alive and well. Without being asked, Wambui's aunt, who had held a good job in California for several years after moving there from Kenya, immediately announced that she would move to Wambui's town to provide child care so Wambui could continue her studies. One year later, after completing her studies, Wambui got an excellent job teaching at a university. Again, there would be no day care from nonfamily members. This time, Wambui's grandmother moved from Kenya to take over child care responsibilities. The grandmother spoke virtually no English, but that did not matter. The child needed to begin to learn the extended family's language, Kikuyu, along with the English she was already learning.

This chapter examines changing ideas about the family from an international perspective and addresses several issues. Families differ greatly throughout the world, and we survey some of those differences. Then we ask whether families are in a healthy state. Finally, we look at what might be causing changes in the family, both in the United States and other countries, and what the consequences are for individuals and for society. Sometimes the answers are surprising, especially to people with preconceived ideas about families. By the end of this chapter, the advantage of a sociological approach to studying families should be apparent to you.

A Sociological Approach to the Family

When sociologists study families and try to assess how families are changing, why families are changing, and what the consequences of those changes might be, they make two broad claims. The first is that the **family** is a social institution. The second is that the best way to understand families is to generate hypotheses and then check those hypotheses against the evidence.

Let's begin by examining what it means to regard the family as a social institution:

◆ The family meets fundamental social needs such as child rearing and providing adults and children with companionship, emotional support, food, shelter, and economic resources. To say that the family is a social institution does not imply that those needs could not be met in other ways—only that the family is the main way they actually are met.

◆ The family meets those social needs through the actions of individuals who fulfill the social roles associated with the family: parent, child, husband, wife, and so on.

◆ A set of accepted social rules define the rights and responsibilities of the individuals filling the various roles and specify what behaviors are expected, accepted, and permissible and what behaviors are not. Thus, parents are expected to care for their children; neglect and abuse are a violation of the rules that define the role of parent.

Because the family is a social institution, we refer to *the* family. But that does not mean sociologists think all families are the same. In fact, sociologists have played a leading role in documenting the diverse forms families can take. For instance, **extended families** include grandparents, aunts, uncles, and other relatives. The relatives may not all live together under the same roof, but they normally live close by and make themselves readily available for each other, both physically and emotionally. Many immigrants in the United States continue to express a preference for extended families (like Wambui). The state of being related to others is known as **kinship.** Kin groups include aunts, uncles, cousins, in-laws, and so forth. Some cultures consider all those people part of their extended family, while other cultures distinguish between the "family" (those people with whom they live) and a larger group of "relatives." The term **nuclear family** refers simply to a married couple and their unmarried children living together. The nuclear family used to be the norm in the United States, but it no longer is.

Like any other social institution, the family is dynamic—it is not fixed but is ever changing. The rules that define key family roles vary among societies and over time. Forty years ago in the United States, the roles of husband and wife largely comprised breadwinning and homemaking, respectively. Today's family roles are less gender differentiated: husbands and wives often are expected to share in both breadwinning and homemaking. In the early years of this century, a new family role—grandparent—emerged as people began to live longer. Increasingly, that role has evolved further to include great-grandparent. More recently, the new family role of unmarried partner (heterosexual or homosexual) has developed, and as a society we are still trying to figure out exactly what rights and responsibilities go along with that role. Should an unmarried person be permitted to visit his or her hospitalized partner in the intensive care unit if only family members are allowed? Should an unmarried person be able to inherit from a partner who dies intestate? Should unmarried partners get health insurance from each other's job? France has its PACs, but only one state in the United States—Vermont—has legalized civil arrangements approximating marriage for gay and lesbian partners (called "civil unions"), and that law was not enacted until April 2000.

Because sociologists view the family as a social institution, sociological research tends to focus on the connections between the family and other social institutions, like the economy, religion, and the educational system. For example, some very religious people home-school their children or place them in religious schools, so as to minimize secular influences. Sociologists are studying the way some of those parents are also actively involved in the political process and supporting candidates strictly on the basis of "faith issues," such as prayer in public schools, prohibition of abortion, and tax credits for parents who send their children to religious schools. This is just one example of how the institution of family interacts with other institutions to shape individual values and behaviors.

A sociological approach to the family is in marked contrast to the approach taken by other social science disciplines, most notably psychology, which tends to focus on how individual traits influence and are influenced by family life. For example, both sociologists and psychologists are concerned about the impact of parents' divorce on children. While psychologists stress the psychological impacts (for example, lower self-esteem), sociologists are more interested in the social and economic consequences, such as lower educational achievement. Those two approaches, while distinct, are often complementary: one reason why children of divorce sometimes have problems in school is because they have lower self-esteem. Sociology, however, provides a unique perspective that reminds us that the causes and consequences of family problems are social as well as individual.

In pursuing an understanding of topics like divorce, sociologists use empirical methods. That is, sociologists pose questions like these about families: Which couples are most likely to divorce? How are children affected by their parents' divorce? They then try to answer those questions by gathering and examining relevant data, as described in Chapter 3. The rest of this chapter focuses on some of the data gathered by sociologists to answer the key questions about families today.

Recent Trends in Family Life

Despite their shared reliance on theory and data, sociologists have come up with some widely divergent ideas about what is happening to families. That is not surprising, given the variety of perspectives from which sociologists begin to analyze society and the great volume of data about families. In this chapter, because we cannot do all of those ideas justice, we look at sociological explanations that represent two ends of the spectrum.

Toward one end of the spectrum, sociologist David Popenoe notes that in the United States over the last four decades rates of divorce, cohabitation, nonmarital births, and single-parent households have increased substantially (1993, 1996). He claims that those changes in family life have created more child poverty, adolescent pregnancy, juvenile crime, substance abuse, and other serious social problems. Moreover, men have become less and less involved in the child-rearing process because of the high rate of divorce and nonmarital births. That development is harmful to children, claims Popenoe (1996), because families are better off with both a strong mother and a strong father in the home.

Toward the other end of the spectrum, sociologist Judith Stacey argues that the changes we are witnessing in family life signify that the traditional nuclear family is an outdated and even oppressive institution, favoring men and harming women (1990, 1993, 1996). She asserts that the traditional nuclear family has been replaced in the United States and other developed countries by the "postmodern

Family structure varies greatly these days. From left (on the previous page) to right: a lesbian couple share care of the daughter of one of the women; a "blended family" eats dinner together; a father hugs his daughter; a close-knit Latino family encompasses three generations; and an adoptive family expands. Adoption is increasingly international in scope, as more and more American parents look to Asia, Europe, and Africa for children who need homes.

family," a combination of single mothers, blended families, cohabitating couples, childless couples, lesbian and gay families, communes, and two-worker families. The postmodern family is appropriate for today's rapidly changing society, claims Stacey, and it ensures that a greater number of children will have loving caregivers in the home. A traditional mother and father are not necessarily better caregivers than an unmarried couple, a single parent, or a gay or lesbian couple. Many children have one parent, a stepparent, or parents of the same sex. In fact, only about 25% of all American families fit the traditional model of mother, father, and children. Stacey's position argues that there is no one best model of the family.

Which position is right? The answer remains to be determined. One thing about family life has become clear, however, especially in economically developed, Westernized countries: marriage is indeed becoming much less central to family life. Today many people live together before they marry, and marriage is being put off longer and longer. Some people opt not to marry at all. Women are postponing childbearing, and some are choosing not to have children at all. Most significant, marriage is no longer a prerequisite for childbearing—more children are being born to single women and cohabiting couples. When couples do marry, there is a significant chance that the marriage will not last. Compared to all other societies, U.S. family trends are unique in only one respect: the divorce rate is nearly twice as high as anywhere else.

The data, as you will see, support those conclusions. Let's look first at trends in marriage and cohabitation, then at childbearing, and finally at divorce and remarriage.

Marriage and Cohabitation

In many cultures throughout history, marriage has marked the beginning of family formation. But whether marriage is still a necessary step on the path to family formation is now open to debate. What is clear is that people today are waiting longer than ever before to marry. For example, as the chart in Graphic 8.1 shows, during the 1950s and early 1960s, first-time grooms in the United States were around 23, and their brides were just over 20. But by 1990 the typical first-time bride was 24 and her groom was nearly 26.

As you can tell from the map in Graphic 8.1, the average age of first marriage is generally higher in the economically developed world than in developing countries. Whereas the average age of first marriage for American women is 24 and going higher, the average age for women in much of Africa and South Asia is under 21. Cultural tradition, along with fewer advanced educational opportunities for women, contributes to lower marriage age in the developing world.

As a result of the increase in U.S. marriage age, there has been a dramatic shift in the marital status of young adults. Graphic 8.2 depicts U.S. census data on the percentages of American women aged 20 to 24 who have never been married. For several decades, only about a third of white women in their early twenties were still single. By 1990, however, almost twice as many were single.

GRAPHIC 8.1 AGE AT FIRST MARRIAGE

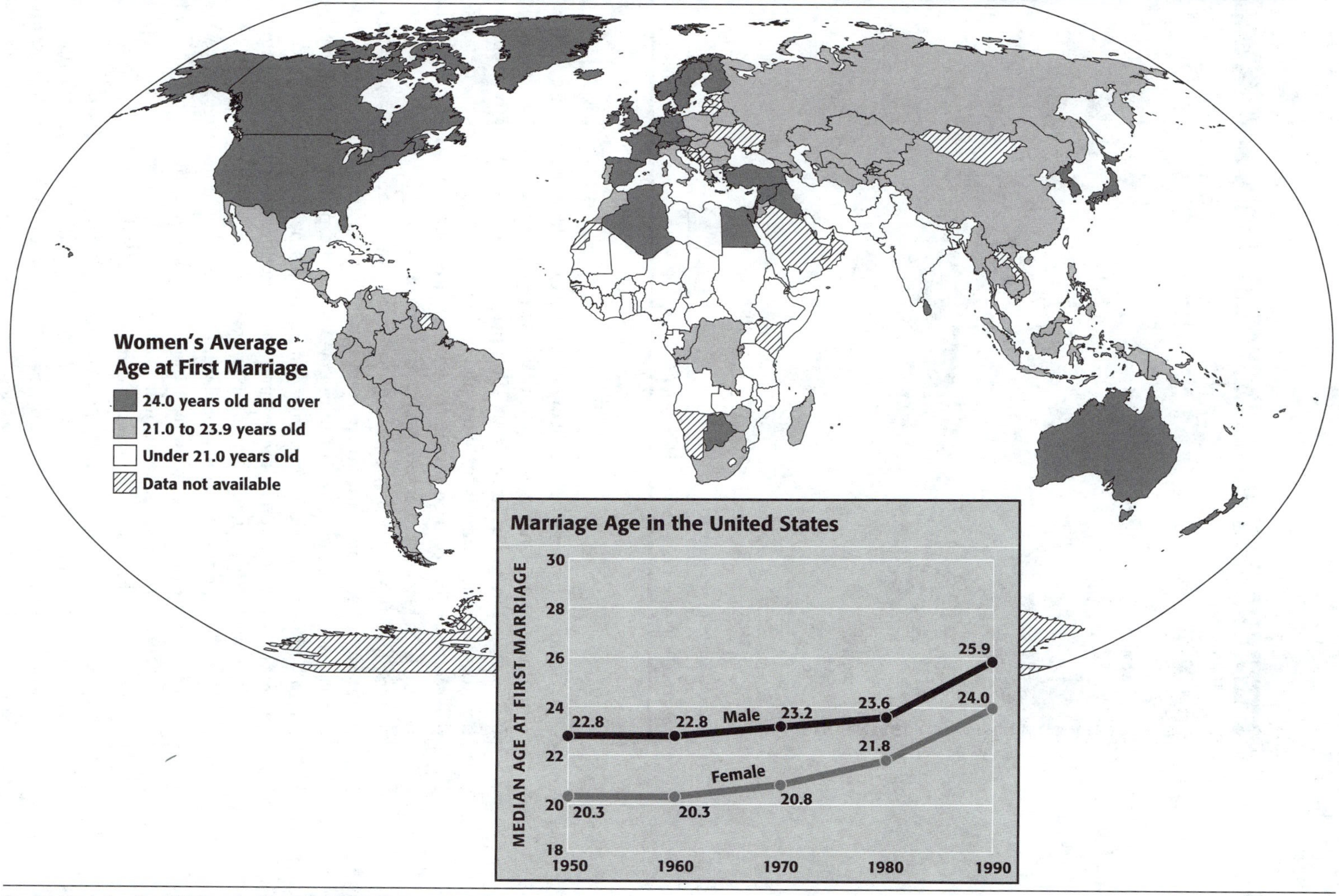

Women's Average Age at First Marriage

- ■ 24.0 years old and over
- ▨ 21.0 to 23.9 years old
- ☐ Under 21.0 years old
- ▨ Data not available

Marriage Age in the United States

MEDIAN AGE AT FIRST MARRIAGE

	1950	1960	1970	1980	1990
Male	22.8	22.8	23.2	23.6	25.9
Female	20.3	20.3	20.8	21.8	24.0

Sources: Graph data from U.S. Bureau of the Census; map data from World Bank, 1994.

287

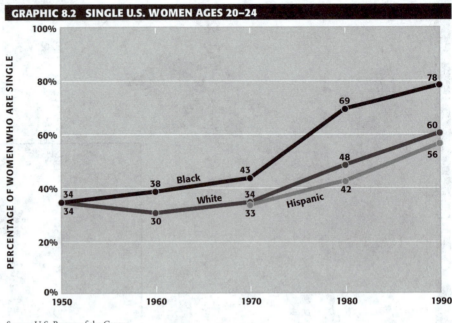

GRAPHIC 8.2   SINGLE U.S. WOMEN AGES 20–24

Source: U.S. Bureau of the Census.

Note: Data for 1950 and 1960 are not available for Hispanic women.

Of course, the experiences of white Americans do not necessarily reflect the experiences of all Americans. Hispanics' marriage patterns have been quite similar to those of whites', but since about 1960 black women in their early twenties have been considerably more likely to be single. Those data suggest that the trend toward delayed marriage (or even nonmarriage) started earlier and has progressed further among U.S. blacks than among whites or Hispanics.

One factor that is clearly related to the trend toward later marriage is the recent popularity of cohabitation. Thirty years ago, living together without being married was considered scandalous and immoral—hence the phrase "living in sin." Only around 11% of Americans marrying for the first time in 1970 had lived together before the wedding. Today, the majority of young people who marry begin living together well before their wedding (Bumpass, Sweet, & Cherlin, 1991). The increase in cohabitation accounts for about half the delay in marriage; the other half reflects an increase in the amount of time young adults spend as singles (Bumpass et al., 1991). In addition, about half the black-white difference in marriage is accounted for by blacks' higher rates of cohabitation (Raley, 1996).

American conservatives often point out the growing rate of cohabitation as a sign of moral degeneration and imply that the United States has the highest rate in the world. In fact, the Nordic countries of Europe actually have the highest international rates of cohabitation. In Sweden, for instance, it is estimated that about 40%

of couples cohabitate, much higher if you consider only young people (McLanahan & Sandefur, 1994).

Although the increase in cohabitation partially offsets the trend away from marriage, cohabitation is different from marriage in several ways.

◆ Compared to similar married couples, cohabitors are less committed to the relationship and are more likely to have other sexual partners (Bumpass et al., 1991; Forste & Tanfer, 1996; Rindfuss & VandenHeuvel, 1990).

◆ Cohabiting relationships are far less stable than marriages. In the United States, about 40% end without the couple marrying, most within 18 months (Bumpass et al., 1991).

◆ Cohabitors tend to be less financially secure than married couples.

◆ Cohabitors are less conventional than married couples in their choice of partners, their attitudes about family life, and the way they manage day-to-day life (Bumpass, 1990; Schoen & Weinick, 1993a; South & Spitze, 1994).

When cohabitation first became common in the late twentieth century, it was usually a step toward marriage, and most relationships ended quickly, either in marriage or a breakup. These days, however, fewer than half of cohabitors in the United States have definite plans to marry. Cohabitors say they do not feel any pressure to marry from either parents or friends or disapproval from friends and family members (Bumpass et al., 1991). The lack of pressure to marry is reflected in an increase in the longevity of cohabiting unions: more than 20% of the cohabiting couples in one large-scale study had been together for five years or more (Bumpass et al., 1991). In addition, childbearing is becoming more common in cohabiting relationships. One-third of never-married cohabiting couples have a child, and half the children were born since the couple began living together (Bumpass et al., 1991). Among blacks and economically disadvantaged whites, rates of childbearing are similar in the first few years of cohabitation and the first few years of marriage, and pregnancy does not prompt a wedding (Loomis & Landale, 1994; Manning, 1993). Taken together, the evidence suggests that, at least for some groups, cohabitation is fast becoming a new route to family formation—an alternative to rather than a step toward marriage.

If cohabitation is becoming an alternative to marriage, we might expect that more people will never marry. But so far that has not happened in the United States: for as long as records have been kept, more than 90% of Americans have eventually married (Cherlin, 1992). Some researchers predict that the pattern will continue as today's unmarried twenty-somethings eventually legalize their relationships. Those researchers point to opinion polls showing that the overwhelming majority of young adults want to marry, expect to marry, and list marriage and a good family among their top life goals (Glenn, 1996). In contrast, other researchers discern the beginning of a trend away from marriage. Demographers predict that if today's marriage rates continue, the eventual percentages of married American women and men born in the late 1950s and 1960s will fall short of the 90% mark; among blacks, it may be as low as 75% (Bennett et al., 1989; Schoen & Weinick, 1993b).

Childbearing

The data reveal three main trends in childbearing: having fewer children, waiting longer to have children, and having children more often outside of marriage. Those trends are especially notable in Western societies, but they are appearing in many other places as well. The major exceptions are very poor countries and countries where religious values are a predominant influence on people's behavior.

Number of Children. Most people know that there is great variation throughout the world with respect to how many children the women in a society are likely to bear. The **total fertility rate (TFR)** is a measure of childbearing that represents the number of children an average woman would bear given prevailing birth rates. Not surprisingly, poor countries in Africa, Asia, and Latin America exhibit much higher fertility rates than rich countries do (Graphic 8.3). In some African countries, for instance, the TFR exceeds six children per woman, whereas in economically developed countries, the TFR is less than two.

The reasons for the variation in fertility have been the subject of countless books and articles, many of which espouse some version of the **demographic transition theory,** which was developed by sociologist Warren S. Thompson (1929). The demographic transition perspective argues that countries go through three stages of development: high fertility and high death rates (underdeveloped country), high fertility and dropping death rates (developing country), and low fertility and low death rates (developed country). The United States and other economically developed countries are in the third stage, whereas much of the developing world is currently stuck in the second stage for several reasons:

◆ Even though death rates have dropped substantially in developing countries because of more vaccinations and other medical advances, fertility rates remain high because the developing world still exhibits relatively high child mortality rates, increasing the perceived need to "overproduce" children.

◆ The developing world has many farmers with little money, increasing the need to have children to work the farms.

◆ The developing world has little or no social security system, increasing the need to have children to provide a safety net for elderly parents.

◆ The developing world has fewer contraceptive options than economically developed countries.

◆ The developing world has some traditions (for example, the desire for male children) that tend to increase fertility.

The result is a rapidly expanding population. One solution is to help poor countries develop as soon as possible, so high levels of fertility will no longer make economic sense.

There are exceptions to the argument that countries must experience development in order to lower their fertility rates. For example, although China is a poor country, the average woman of childbearing age will have only 1.9 children. A major reason for low fertility in China is the country's **one-child policy,** which

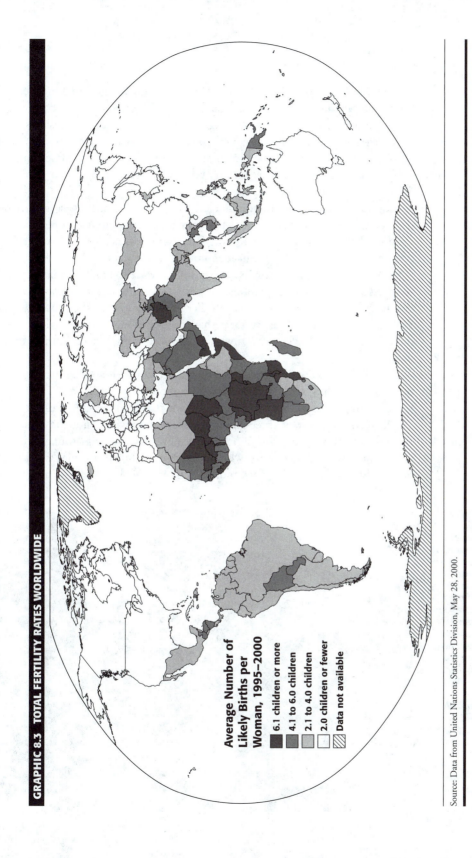

GRAPHIC 8.3 TOTAL FERTILITY RATES WORLDWIDE

Average Number of Likely Births per Woman, 1995–2000

- 6.1 children or more
- 4.1 to 6.0 children
- 2.1 to 4.0 children
- 2.0 children or fewer
- Data not available

Source: Data from United Nations Statistics Division, May 28, 2000.

mandates that people have only one child. Unfortunately, government incentives to limit childbearing are strict, even harsh. The Chinese government provides one-child families with generous housing, health, and education subsidies; strongly encourages abortions for subsequent pregnancies; pays couples to be sterilized; encourages work organizations to monitor workers' menstrual cycles and contraceptive practices; and cuts wages for those who have a third child (Bradshaw & Wallace, 1996, pp. 109–110).

Consider also Kenya, which until recently had one of the highest fertility rates in the world, at nearly eight children per woman. Starting about 10 years ago, social scientists began to notice that Kenya's fertility rate was dropping even though the country was experiencing great economic hardship and a rising child mortality level. Interviews with hundreds of Kenyans revealed that informal networks of Kenyans in women's organizations, factories, agricultural organizations, and other groups are actively encouraging each other to have fewer children (Musalia, 2000). Kenyans are discussing the economic hardships associated with bearing more children during difficult economic times and supporting those who opt for fewer children.

Although the United States is an economically developed country, it has gone through something of a demographic transition of its own since 1950 (Graphic 8.4). Throughout the baby boom years, which lasted roughly from 1948 until 1964, the TFR was over three children per woman, with a notable difference between blacks and whites. But by 1980, the TFR was hovering around two children per woman—slightly lower for whites, and slightly higher for blacks—a level that has barely changed since. Thus, today's families have between one and two fewer

A health worker gives family planning advice and information in The Gambia. African countries historically have experienced high rates of fertility. There is some evidence, however, that these countries are following the lead of Kenya and lowering fertility rates. Severe economic hardship, accompanied by health crises (such as AIDS) and civil instability, may appreciably reduce fertility even more in the foreseeable future.

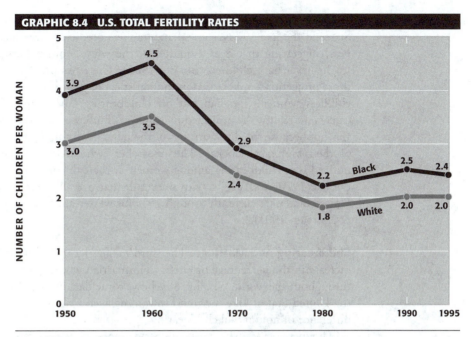

GRAPHIC 8.4   U.S. TOTAL FERTILITY RATES

Sources: U.S. Bureau of the Census; Cherlin, 1999.

children than did those of forty years ago. In addition, blacks' and whites' levels of childbearing are more similar now than they were during the baby boom.

Timing of Childbearing. Not only are women today having fewer children, they also are putting them off until later in life, especially in economically developed countries. In 1960 in the United States, for example, the typical first-time mother was slightly less than 22 years old; in 1992 she was nearly 24 years old (1962, 1996). The trend toward delayed childbearing is even more apparent in the distribution of births by the mother's age; in 1960, 16% of all births were to "older" women, aged 30 to 34, compared to 22% in 1992. Bear in mind that many of the older women giving birth in 1960 were doing so for the third or fourth time, whereas many of the older women giving birth today are first-time mothers.

Most of the trend toward later childbearing is due to a dramatic shift toward later childbearing among more highly educated women, those with at least a college degree. Women with low levels of education continue to have their children at relatively early ages (Rindfuss, Morgan, & Offutt, 1996). The general tendency for more highly educated women to postpone childbearing is similar across all races and in all societies. In the United States, because black women are less likely to attend college than are white women, the trend toward delayed childbearing has been less among blacks than whites. During the 1980s, more than a third of white thirty-year-old women were childless, compared to 15% of black thirty-year-olds (Chen & Morgan, 1991).

When the trend toward delayed childbearing was first noticed in the United States in the late 1970s, some demographers predicted large increases in childlessness, suggesting that over a quarter of the white women born in the late 1950s might never have children (Bloom, 1982). The news media quickly latched on to those projections and colored in the statistical data with real-life stories of regretful, childless women who had put off childbearing "too long" while they pursued careers. In reality, the projected increases in childlessness never materialized—and it was not because the dire warnings of the news media alerted women to the "ticking of their biological clocks." The researchers who made the projections had not noticed that childbearing among women in their thirties actually increased during the late 1970s and 1980s, with the result that overall levels of childlessness in the United States are currently around 15% for whites and below 5% for blacks (Chen & Morgan, 1991).

Childbearing and Marriage. The third major trend in childbearing is a dramatic increase in the percentage of births to unmarried women, a trend that is occurring throughout the world. Graphic 8.5 shows some data on nonmarital childbearing in the United States. Like the trend toward delayed childbearing, there is a large race difference in nonmarital childbearing.

The increase has been most dramatic among younger women. In 1992, 71% of teen mothers were unmarried. Unfortunately it is not possible to calculate the same percentage for 1960 because only 35 states collected information on the ages of unmarried women giving birth. However, in 1960, when nearly half of all women were married by age 20, the total number of unmarried births (to women of all ages) was less than one-third the number of teen births. We can infer that the vast majority of teen mothers were married.

Why has nonmarital childbearing become so much more common over the past thirty years? Among blacks, the reason is clear. Today's black women of childbearing age are far less likely to be married than their counterparts of thirty years ago (refer to Graphic 8.2). In contrast, among whites the retreat from marriage has been less pronounced (Smith, Morgan, & Koropeckyj-Cox, 1996).

Although more children are being born to unmarried women, they are not necessarily being born into single-parent families; a growing proportion of unmarried mothers are cohabiting with their child's father. Data suggest that in the late 1980s about a quarter of nonmarital births were to cohabiting couples (Bumpass et al., 1991). Thus, the rise of cohabitation also has been a factor in the rise of nonmarital childbearing.

Of course, this demographic account of increasing nonmarital childbearing helps us understand only the mechanics of the trend—it has little to say about the underlying social changes that have led black women to abandon marriage and more unmarried white women to become mothers. Next we explore the reasons for those changes, as well as the other changes in childbearing, marriage, and divorce.

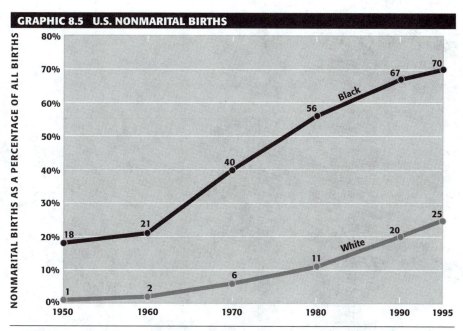

GRAPHIC 8.5   U.S. NONMARITAL BIRTHS

Sources: U.S. Bureau of the Census; Cherlin, 1999.

Divorce and Remarriage

The increase in divorce is undoubtedly the biggest and most far-reaching change in American families over the past forty years. As the small chart in Graphic 8.6 shows, the divorce rate today is twice the level that prevailed for most of the 1950s and 1960s. The high divorce rates imply that between one-half and two-thirds of all American marriages will eventually end in divorce (Martin & Bumpass, 1989; Schoen & Weinick, 1993b).

Divorce rates vary widely across the world. As demonstrated in Graphic 8.6, they tend to be lower in countries influenced by the Catholic Church and Islam. In France and Italy, for example, divorce is discouraged and can take up to five years to complete (by contrast, in some U.S. states divorces can be final in a few months). In reality, however, many couples in those countries break up and live with another person before the divorce is officially granted. That is one reason why PACS are increasingly popular in France—they can be dissolved relatively fast. In much of the Islamic world, it is not possible for women to initiate a divorce at all, thereby reducing the number of divorces. Just recently, Egyptian women won the right to divorce their husbands, but that right is being challenged by conservative Muslims.

In addition to religious intolerance of divorce, other cultural traditions make divorce more difficult in the non-Western world. For example, in some ethnic groups in Africa, it is not just the married couple who form a union; rather, it is the

GRAPHIC 8.6   DIVORCE RATES

Divorce Rates of Selected Countries

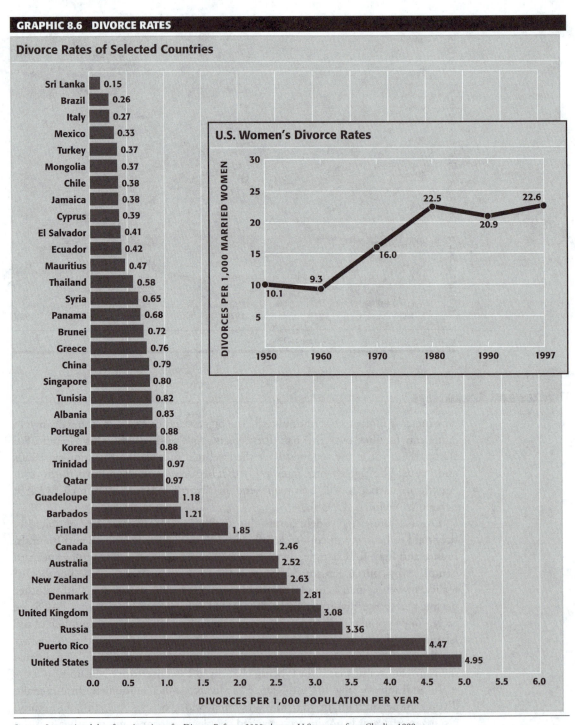

Country	Rate
Sri Lanka	0.15
Brazil	0.26
Italy	0.27
Mexico	0.33
Turkey	0.37
Mongolia	0.37
Chile	0.38
Jamaica	0.38
Cyprus	0.39
El Salvador	0.41
Ecuador	0.42
Mauritius	0.47
Thailand	0.58
Syria	0.65
Panama	0.68
Brunei	0.72
Greece	0.76
China	0.79
Singapore	0.80
Tunisia	0.82
Albania	0.83
Portugal	0.88
Korea	0.88
Trinidad	0.97
Qatar	0.97
Guadeloupe	1.18
Barbados	1.21
Finland	1.85
Canada	2.46
Australia	2.52
New Zealand	2.63
Denmark	2.81
United Kingdom	3.08
Russia	3.36
Puerto Rico	4.47
United States	4.95

DIVORCES PER 1,000 POPULATION PER YEAR

U.S. Women's Divorce Rates

DIVORCES PER 1,000 MARRIED WOMEN

Year	Rate
1950	10.1
1960	9.3
1970	16.0
1980	22.5
1990	20.9
1997	22.6

Sources: International data from Americans for Divorce Reform, 2000; data on U.S. women from Cherlin, 1999.

bride's family and the groom's family. Before the marriage, both families become well acquainted and almost "married" in a sense. If the couple begins having problems, the families will intervene and encourage the two people to work out their differences. As long as the families get along well with each other, it would be difficult (though not impossible) for the couple to part ways permanently. In contrast, in the United States, the two families often do not know each other particularly well prior to the marriage and would be hesitant to intervene if the couple began having marital difficulties.

Some U.S. marriages are at greater risk for divorce than others. The biggest risk factor for divorce is youthful marriage. Women who marry as teenagers are twice as likely to divorce as women who put off marriage till after age 22 (Martin & Bumpass, 1989), most likely because people who marry young lack the emotional maturity needed to sustain a marriage (South, 1995). Low educational attainment also increases the risk of divorce: high school dropouts are twice as likely to divorce as women with college degrees (Furstenberg, 1990). Interfaith marriages are more prone to divorce than same-faith marriages, as are marriages between people with no religious affiliation (Lehrer & Chiswick, 1993).

Women who are sexually active or have a child before they marry and couples who live together before they marry also face increased risks of divorce (Axinn & Thornton, 1992; Billy, Landale, & McLaughlin, 1986; Kahn & London, 1991; Lillard, Brien, & Waite, 1995). However, those relationships probably are not causal; that is, having sex, giving birth, or living together before marriage does not destabilize the marriage. Rather, couples who cohabit, have sex, or give birth before marriage tend to hold less traditional attitudes toward marriage and family in general and may be less committed to marriage and more tolerant of divorce. In recent years, the associations between premarital cohabitation and premarital childbearing and divorce have weakened somewhat. Perhaps cohabitation is no longer such a clear marker for having nontraditional ideas about family life. Also, perhaps, as childbearing within cohabitation becomes more common, more of the women with premarital births marry the child's biological father rather than somebody else.

Researchers used to think that couples with children were less likely to get divorced than childless couples. Recent research, however, suggests that the relationship between having children and the risk of divorce is complex, in part because couples who think their marriage may be unstable are less likely to have children (Lillard & Waite, 1993). In general, children reduce the risk of divorce only while they are very young, roughly through the preschool years. Having older children and having a large family (five or more children) tend to increase the risk of divorce. As a result, parents are only slightly more likely to reach their twentieth wedding anniversary than nonparents are (Waite & Lillard, 1991).

Most divorced people remarry, but levels of remarriage are lower than they were just a few years ago (Schoen & Weinick 1993b). Not only are divorced people less likely to remarry than in the recent past, they also are waiting longer, on average about seven years. Like the trend toward later marriage, the decline in remarriage and the longer waiting time before remarriage are linked to the increase in cohabitation (Bumpass et al., 1991).

Women with children are less likely to remarry than are childless women. In addition, blacks are far less likely to remarry than whites—fewer than half of all divorced black women remarry. Hispanic remarriage rates are intermediate between those of whites and blacks (Bumpass et al., 1991). Thus, although most white children of divorce experience their mother's remarriage, few black children do; because of the lengthening time between divorce and remarriage, most children of divorce spend more than five years in a single-parent family (Bumpass et al., 1991).

Remarriages tend to be less stable than first marriages: about 27% break up within five years, compared to 23% of first marriages. One consequence of that statistic is that about half the children whose mothers remarry (about 15% of all children) experience a second family breakup before their sixteenth birthday (Bumpass, 1984; Furstenberg, 1990).

It used to be thought that remarriages were inherently less stable than first marriages because of the new, complex family relationships they create and because stepparenting was thought to be especially difficult and a source of conflict and strain in remarriages (Cherlin, 1978). Recent research, however, does not support that prediction. Stepfamilies and remarriages are not more conflict prone than first marriages (MacDonald & DeMaris, 1995). In fact, most of the increased risk of disruption faced by remarriages reflects the demographic composition of people who remarry, particularly their tendency to have entered their first marriages as teenagers, (Martin & Bumpass, 1989). The increase in the risk of divorce associated with having been married before is less than the increased risk associated with having married as a teenager.

In summary, although the last thirty years have seen dramatic changes in family life, it is important not to overstate those changes. Most people will marry, and most will have children, waiting until after their wedding to do so. And although marriages are fragile and we cannot say that most will endure, the majority of people who divorce eventually remarry.

The Causes of Family Change

They may not know the specifics, but many people are aware of the general trends in marriage, cohabitation, childbearing, divorce, and remarriage. Like sociologists Popenoe and Stacey, they have differing views on the import of the trends and on their causes. Politicians, media pundits, and armchair philosophers often make the following kinds of statements:

"People just don't seem to care about family life anymore, they're too wrapped up in themselves—that's why they don't get married and why their marriages don't last."

"It stands to reason that easy divorce laws and access to welfare encourage people to get divorced."

"Obviously the increase in women working outside the home is bound to have affected families."

"Young couples these days just can't afford to have families."

On the face of it, all four statements seem sensible and, with regular repetition, have entered into society's collective sense of what has happened to the family and why.

But sociologists are professional skeptics. They do not let those kinds of statements pass without asking hard, explicit questions and then checking their hypotheses about the answers against the available evidence. Sociologists realize that understanding exactly why families are changing—rather than just going along with popular perceptions—helps governments develop better policies in response to cultural change. For example, the widespread perception that easy divorce laws cause an increase in divorce rates is behind efforts in some places to tighten divorce laws or to maintain restrictions on divorce. But if the perception that easy divorce laws cause high divorce rates is wrong, then stricter divorce laws will not reduce the divorce rate. Moreover, they may pose a hardship for some people who are in bad marriages despite their best efforts.

This section presents a sociological view of several of the most commonly proposed explanations for recent changes in the family: weakened family values, increased women's employment, economic adjustments, and social crises. Those explanations have been offered to explain changes in family life all over the world. But as appealing as some of the explanations might be on the surface, they are not all supported by the evidence. The reasons for the changes are, as you will see, elusive and complex.

Weakened Family Values

A lot of people claim that changes in family life are the result of reduced support for traditional family values. There is some debate about precisely which attitudes constitute traditional family values, but they generally include these beliefs: young adults should not have sex or live together until after they are married; most people will be happier if they marry and have children; mothers of young children should not work outside the home; and married couples should stay together forever, except in cases of severe abuse.

Stephen and Megan Scheibner would agree with that explanation. Along with their seven children, ages twenty months to twelve years, they live outside Allentown, Pennsylvania. They are fundamentalist Christians who believe the Bible is the one true guide to life, marriage is sacred, children should be conceived only within marriage, divorce is against God's law, and some "alternative" families (for example, gay and lesbian unions) are sinful. They are appalled by the current statistics about families. The Scheibners "protect" their children from negative outside influences by home-schooling them and strictly regulating their exposure to popular culture (Talbot, 2000). Many American conservatives, particularly religious conservatives, would applaud the Scheibner's attempts to preserve traditional values within their family.

So would many people in other countries. In fact, people in developing countries often blame the same social influences that the Scheibners deplore, which they characterize as "Westernization," for the decline in moral values they witness, especially among young people. Western values that emphasize consumption, designer labels, individualism, easy pleasure, and fast money are transmitted to people in developing countries through motion pictures, television, music videos, and magazines. As a result, young people all over the world are showing a greater tolerance for—indeed they are embracing—Westernization. Their changing culture also extends to new values regarding family as well as new acceptance of nontraditional families.

Although public opinion polls reveal increased tolerance toward nontraditional family behaviors, there is no suggestion of any reduction in the importance people attach to family life. In 1999 Gallup International sponsored a Millennium Survey, the largest survey of public opinion ever conducted: 57,000 adults in 60 countries, spread across six continents. In response to the question, "What matters most in life?" people everywhere placed good health and a happy family life above everything else. People have different ideas about what constitutes a family, but they also demonstrate fairly broad acceptance of other people's definitions of the family.

Why have attitudes toward family life changed so dramatically in recent years? Political conservatives and religious leaders often claim that traditional family values have been undermined by a reduction in support for traditional religious beliefs. Economists suggest that the erosion of traditional family values and the increase in nontraditional family behaviors stem from a rising tide of materialism that encourages people to devote themselves to the acquisition of consumer goods at the expense of other goals like family formation (Crimmins, Easterlin, & Saito, 1991). Sociologists and cultural critics link nontraditional family behavior to growing individualism in society, arguing that individuals are increasingly focused on their personal goals and are reluctant to make the compromises and sacrifices necessary to sustain family relationships (Lesthaeghe & Surkyn, 1988; Swidler, 1980). So far, the evidence provides the strongest support for the claim that waning religiosity is associated with the decline in support for traditional family values, but there is also some evidence that consumerism and individualism may be associated with nontraditional family attitudes (Lye & Waldron, 1997).

The main question here is whether declining support for traditional family values is the reason for changes in family behavior, like the retreat from marriage and the increases in divorce and nonmarital childbearing. The pattern and timing of changes in attitudes toward family are broadly similar to the pattern and timing of changes in family behaviors, which lend support to the "family values" explanation. However, as we have stressed throughout this book, correlation does not equal causation; just because family attitudes and family behaviors changed at the same time, we cannot conclude that a change in one caused a change in the other. It may be

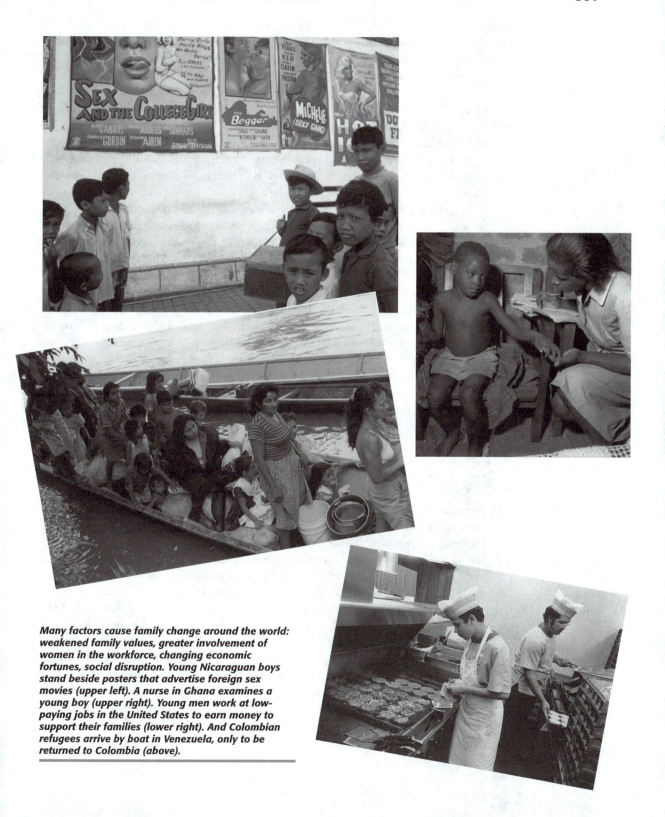

Many factors cause family change around the world: weakened family values, greater involvement of women in the workforce, changing economic fortunes, social disruption. Young Nicaraguan boys stand beside posters that advertise foreign sex movies (upper left). A nurse in Ghana examines a young boy (upper right). Young men work at low-paying jobs in the United States to earn money to support their families (lower right). And Colombian refugees arrive by boat in Venezuela, only to be returned to Colombia (above).

that rather than causing behavioral change, attitudes changed in response to changes in behavior. For example, public approval of mothers' employment increased only after the dramatic increase in mothers' employment (Rindfuss et al., 1996). Greater acceptance of mothers' employment may then, in turn, have prompted more mothers to join or stay in the labor force. In general, it is difficult to assess possible links between changing family attitudes and changing family behaviors because we do not have enough information to tell which changed first—attitudes or behaviors. Few surveys collected information about American family attitudes before the 1970s, but by then the changes in both family attitudes and family behaviors already were well underway.

If changing attitudes toward family life caused the changes in family behaviors, we would expect to find that individuals with nontraditional attitudes would be more likely to behave in nontraditional ways. Testing that proposition is difficult, but sociologist Arland Thornton and his colleagues at the University of Michigan have attempted to untangle the complex relationships using data from a unique study of Detroit women and their children who have been interviewed several times since 1962. Thornton and his colleagues have shown that attitudes do indeed influence behaviors—and that behaviors also influence attitudes. For example, young people with more tolerant attitudes toward cohabitation at age eighteen are more likely to cohabit in the ensuing years—attitudes influence behavior. But the reverse is also true, and young people who cohabit between ages eighteen and twenty-three are more likely to have tolerant attitudes at age twenty-five—behavior influences attitudes (Axinn & Thornton, 1993). Thornton and his colleagues have documented several other similarly complex relationships between family attitudes and behaviors (Thornton, 1985; Thornton, Alwin, & Camburn, 1983). Those findings remind us that we cannot point to one (either attitudes or behaviors) as the cause of the other.

Of course, attitudes are not the only indicators of changes in values; changes in popular culture also reveal value changes. Advocates of the family values explanation argue that by depicting nontraditional family behaviors like divorce and homosexual relationships in a positive or at least neutral way, popular culture includes them in the list of acceptable family choices. However, cultural representations of family life and sexual behavior not only provide individuals with a sense of what behaviors are allowable but also reflect social mores.

Proponents of the family values explanation also emphasize the influence of law and public policy on family behavior. Legal changes since the mid-1960s have indeed reflected nontraditional attitudes toward family life. Family values partisans would argue, however, that traditional family values have been undermined by legal changes like no-fault divorce laws; the repeal or disuse of illegitimacy laws; laws banning discrimination against cohabiting couples and gay couples; the extension of job benefits to domestic partners (heterosexual or homosexual); gay "marriage" (currently valid in only a few places around the world); and welfare benefits for unmarried mothers.

Only some of the claims concerning the impact of public policy on family behavior have been examined in detail. Overall, the research suggests that public policy exerts little direct influence on family behavior. For example, the introduction of no-fault divorce laws generally had only short-term effects on divorce rates; people who live in states with less restrictive divorce laws are not more likely to divorce (Gray, 1996; Peters, 1986, 1992). Similarly, the amount states pay to female welfare recipients is unrelated to rates at which they head households, divorce, and bear children outside marriage (Lichter, McLaughlin, & Ribar, 1997; South & Lloyd, 1992). Contrary to the family values explanation for family change, permissive family law and modest welfare payments do not appear to promote nontraditional family behaviors.

In summary, despite the strong evidence that traditional family values have indeed waned, we simply do not have sufficient evidence to conclude that the changes in values either were or were not the cause of behavioral changes. Studies of individuals reveal complex interrelationships among attitudes and behaviors, which have led many researchers to conclude that changes in attitudes and behaviors are so intertwined they are inseparable and that it is overly simplistic to think of either as causing the other. However, although shifting family values may not be the cause of recent family change, an account of family change that ignores them is seriously incomplete.

Increased Women's Employment

A second explanation for changes in the traditional family concentrates on the impact of increased women's employment, an explanation that has been the focus of much sociological research. Writing over a century ago, social theorist Emile Durkheim (1893/1960) suggested that the sexual division of labor, the tendency for men to work outside the home while women work inside, created a kind of mutual interdependence among women and men that he called organic solidarity (see Chapter 2 for more on the topic). According to Durkheim, any weakening of the sexual division of labor, like an increase in women's employment outside the home, reduces the economic interdependence of married couples, leaving only the sexual and emotional connections, which he regarded as "preeminently ephemeral," meaning unstable and probably short-lived.

In the 1940s and 1950s, structural functionalist social theorists, notably Talcott Parsons, also argued that the sexual division of labor is the foundation of secure marriages and stable families (Parsons & Bales, 1956). According to Parsons, the most important functions of the family are socializing children and meeting family members' emotional needs. Parsons argued that those functions are most effectively fulfilled when women and men occupy the complementary roles of homemakers and breadwinners, because that sexual division of labor eliminates potentially emotionally destructive competition between husbands and wives. Of course, it could be argued that even if complementarity is the basis of a stable marriage, there is no reason why the wife rather than the husband should be the homemaker. However, Parsons emphasized the biological differences between women and men and drew on Freudian psychological theories to argue that women are innately better suited to homemaking and men are better suited to breadwinning. Like Durkheim, Parsons predicted that any attenuation of the sexual division of labor would undermine marriage and render families less able to socialize children and meet adults' emotional needs.

A more recent version of the sexual division of labor argument was devised by Nobel prize–winning economist Gary Becker (1991). Becker argues that marriage is a trading relationship in which men swap wages earned outside the home for domestic services provided by women. Although women could earn money outside the home, because of their biological role in childbearing and child rearing they have a comparative advantage in domestic work, which is more easily combined with child rearing than "market" work. According to Becker, as women's earnings have increased, the advantage to women of getting married and staying married has diminished, particularly as childbearing and child rearing have come to occupy a shorter portion of women's life spans. Based on that analysis, Becker attributes the retreat from marriage, the trends toward less and later childbearing, and the increases in divorce and nonmarital childbearing to the diminution of the sexual division of labor and the increase in women's employment.

The argument that recent changes in families derive from an increase in women's employment seems to make sense. However, research about the impact of women's employment on marriage and cohabitation provides mixed evidence. Some studies support the women's employment hypothesis and show that women who live in areas with good employment opportunities and women with well-paid jobs are less likely to marry. However, the majority of studies show that women who earn more or who are more highly educated and thus presumably have better job prospects are more likely to marry and less likely to cohabit (Oppenheimer, 1988, 1994, 1997; Oppenheimer, Kalmijn, & Lim, 1997).

Research about the relationship between women's employment and childbearing, on the other hand, is more consistent with the women's employment explanation of changing family behavior. Higher-earning women and more highly educated women have fewer children than nonemployed, lower-paid, and less well educated women. Also, the trend toward delayed childbearing is greatest among the most highly educated women, who have the best employment prospects and are most committed to pursuing careers (Rindfuss et al., 1996).

However, many researchers argue that it is a mistake to treat employment behavior as a cause of childbearing behavior, because that implies that women first make decisions about education and employment and then arrange their childbearing to fit in with their employment schedules. Surely, those researchers argue, some women first make decisions about childbearing and then make their education and employment choices in accord with their childbearing goals. In fact, research suggests that few women make one-time decisions about either childbearing or employment; instead, the decisions evolve over time. In the face of those arguments, researchers increasingly have come to view childbearing and employment as jointly determined; that is, one behavior does not cause the other, but the two behaviors are simultaneously balanced (Blau & Robins, 1991; McLaughlin et al., 1988).

Although that view acknowledges the close relationship between women's employment and childbearing, it does not go so far as to say that changes in women's employment caused the trends toward less and later childbearing. Instead, it proposes that women today strike a different balance between employment and childbearing than women did thirty or forty years ago and that the real causes of changes in childbearing and employment are the factors that influence that balance.

In contrast to the rather contradictory evidence concerning the effects of women's employment on marriage and childbearing, there is considerable evidence that rising women's employment has played a role in the increase in divorce. Recent analyses reveal a close association between the long-term increase in divorce and increases in women's employment (Ruggles, 1997; South, 1985). In addition, the more hours a week the wife works and the higher a wife's earnings compared to her husband's, the greater the probability the couple will split up (Greenstein, 1995; Spitze & South, 1985).

Although the evidence points to a link between women's employment and divorce, it is not clear that wives' employment contributes to divorce by increasing women's independence. The impact of wives' employment on marital stability varies according to the husband's attitude toward his wife's work. If the husband is supportive of his wife's employment and takes on some of the housework, then the wife's employment does not increase the risk of divorce. But if the husband disapproves of his wife's employment and leaves her to shoulder the burden of a double day of work and housework, then her employment does increase the risk of divorce (Spitze & South, 1985). These findings suggest that women's employment itself is not necessarily the cause of rising divorce rates. Instead, rising divorce rates may stem from the reluctance or inability of some men to adjust to their wives' employment.

Finally, some of the apparently strong relationship between women's employment and divorce may reflect the impact of divorce on women's employment rather than the other way around (Michael, 1985). Women are well aware of today's high divorce rates and may decide it is safer to be employed throughout their marriages, or they may step up their work hours if they suspect their marriage is in trouble (Johnson & Skinner, 1986).

In summary, although women's employment is clearly associated with both delayed childbearing and increased divorce, the relationships are far more complex than those proposed by the women's employment explanation. The evidence suggests that, rather than being a cause of recent family change, increased women's employment is more properly viewed as a component of recent family change. Forty years ago, American women combined work and family by working outside the home only before their children were born and after their children were teenagers. Today, women take on a different combination that includes more work outside the home, balanced with later marriage and fewer children. One consequence of the new balance is a greater risk of divorce.

Economic Adjustments

The third explanation for recent family change stresses the impact of changing economic conditions in recent decades. According to this standard-of-living argument, the youthful marriages, large families, and relatively low divorce rates of the 1950s and early 1960s were the product of economic prosperity and rapidly rising living standards, particularly in the economically developed world. Conversely, the retreat from marriage, smaller families, high divorce rates, and two-worker families ever since were brought about by a deterioration in economic conditions, especially a decline in young men's ability to support a family (Coontz, 1992, 1997; Levy, 1987; Oppenheimer, 1988, 1994).

Economic trends in the post-1945 period are broadly consistent with the standard-of-living argument. The 1950s and 1960s were years of unprecedented prosperity, and government programs like the G.I. bill and subsidies for home ownership reinforced the impact of the strong economy. In that climate, young men straight out of high school could make enough money to marry, buy and furnish a home, and support a stay-at-home wife and two or three children (Coontz, 1992, 1997). In the early 1970s, however, the economic good times came to an abrupt end. Unemployment rates rose steeply, especially among workers under the age of twenty-five. Those young adults who did find jobs were forced to settle for lower wages and slower wage growth than had been common just a few years earlier (Levy, 1987). As a result, men under 25 who were working full-time in 1994 earned 31% less than their counterparts did in 1973. In 1994, nearly one-third of men earned too little to lift a family of four above the poverty line, compared with only 14% in 1972 (Coontz, 1997).

To make matters worse, young adults seeking to set up new households faced sharply rising prices for everything from food to furniture, including, most important, housing itself (Levy, 1987). In 1952, a typical factory worker could earn enough to cover the closing costs on a new $10,000 family home in the suburban development of Levittown, Pennsylvania, in just one day. By 1991, the same homes were selling for $100,000 and it would take a factory worker 18 weeks to earn enough for just the closing costs (Coontz, 1997).

According to the standard-of-living argument, the reversal of economic fortunes led many young people to postpone marriage and childbearing, which they could no longer afford, and encouraged nontraditional family formation such as cohabitation and nonmarital childbearing. Women's employment is also viewed as a response to worsening economic conditions because many families came to rely on two paychecks. Finally, the increase in divorce is regarded as the result of marital stresses caused by economic hardships and the necessity of having two earners in a family.

Research about the impact of men's earnings on marriage lends support to the standard-of-living explanation for recent family change. Young men who are unemployed, who make less money, who work fewer weeks in a year, or who do not own their own homes are less likely to marry than their more economically secure counterparts (Cooney & Hogan, 1991; Lloyd & South, 1996; Oppenheimer et al., 1997). In addition, men and women who live in areas where male unemployment is high are less likely to marry (Lichter, McLaughlin, Kephart, & Landry, 1992; South & Lloyd, 1992). Finally, cohabiting couples with a high-earning man are more likely to marry than those with a low-earning man, and the man's income is a far more important influence on the decision to marry than the woman's (Smock & Manning, 1997). The studies confirm that men's earnings are an important underpinning for marriage.

Studies of trends in childbearing and divorce are also broadly consistent with the standard-of-living explanation for recent family trends. Women tend to become mothers at a younger age in good economic times but tend to delay childbearing in bad times (Rindfuss et al., 1988). Men who are employed or who make more money are more likely to become fathers than men who are unemployed or in school or who make less money (Blau & Robins, 1991; Rindfuss et al., 1988). Similarly, the divorce rate is generally higher in times of high unemployment and in places with high unemployment, and couples who marry in times of high unemployment are more likely to divorce (Breault & Kposowa, 1987; Preston & McDonald, 1979; South, 1985). Better-off couples, more highly educated couples, and couples in which the husband is employed full-time are less likely to divorce than less economically secure couples (South & Lloyd, 1995). Taken together, those studies provide considerable support for the standard-of-living explanation for recent family change.

In the United States, economic conditions have also been proposed as an explanation for the differences between the marriage patterns of blacks and of whites. Recall that in the United States the retreat from marriage began earlier and is more pronounced among blacks than among whites. Writing in the 1980s, sociologist William Julius Wilson (1987) noted that young black men face far higher rates of unemployment than whites, and that employed blacks tend to earn less than whites. He argued that young women, black and white, evaluate potential husbands by their ability to support a family and rule out jobless and low-earning men. As a result, many black men are unable to marry or must delay marriage because they are not deemed acceptable as husbands, and many black women are unable to marry or must delay marriage because they face an acute shortage of eligible (that is, employed) men.

Wilson's thesis has been subject to intense scrutiny. As predicted, researchers have found that both black women and white women are reluctant to marry men with limited earnings potential (South, 1993). But differences in the economic circumstances of blacks and whites do not explain blacks' lower marriage probabilities (Bennett, Bloom, & Craig, 1989; Lloyd & South, 1996; South & Lloyd, 1992). In one study, researchers asked whether black women would marry if black men had the same characteristics as white men. They found that even under that hypothetical best-case scenario black women would be 50–60% less likely to marry than white women (Lichter et al., 1992). In addition, even though Mexican-Americans are just as economically disadvantaged as blacks, their marriage rates are very close to whites' marriage rates (Oropesa, Lichter, & Anderson, 1994). Findings like those have led researchers to conclude that although economic considerations figure heavily in marriage decisions for all racial and ethnic groups, they provide only a partial explanation for differences between groups in marriage and family behavior.

In summary, the available evidence suggests that economic changes, particularly the decline in young men's earnings, contribute to family change. Many young men do not earn enough to purchase a home or support a wife and children. As true as that is in the United States today, it is even more true in developing countries. You read in Chapter 7 about the way that structural adjustment programs have affected traditional gender relations. The typical result is that both marriage and childbearing are delayed, and more married women are employed, which also tends to delay and reduce childbearing. The economic stresses on families, together with the time pressures faced by two-worker families, contribute to high levels of divorce.

However, economic factors do not explain all aspects of recent family change. The 1930s were also a period of severe economic hardship in the United States and other developed countries, and many young people were obliged to postpone marriage and childbearing—both fell to record lows. But young people did not respond then to the hardships of the depression by cohabiting or having children outside marriage, and few women with children joined the labor force. In the 1930s, those behaviors simply were not an acceptable option. Nor are they an acceptable option in many traditional cultures. The fact that they have become tolerated, if not accepted, family options in developed countries today suggests that in addition to economic change, changes in family values also have played a role.

Social Crises

Weakened family values, more women in the labor force, and decreased earnings for men are important contributors to family change, but they are almost trivial compared to the effect of two profound societal problems with global impact: war and the HIV/AIDS epidemic. Both are discussed at greater length in other chapters, but they bear mentioning here. UNICEF (2000) calls those two problems among the most daunting obstacles to full human development in the world today.

Wars, particularly civil wars, rip families apart in several ways: they result in the deaths of thousands of men, create millions of orphans, lead to unspeakable crimes against women, and produce millions of refugees with no place to go and a bleak future. People in the Western world seldom think about war as a family issue. But to the millions of women and children running across a national border to flee an aggressor or to the hundreds of thousands of families who find themselves in a new country with nothing, war is very much a family issue.

Several years ago, Vice President Dan Quayle created a controversy by criticizing the television series *Murphy Brown* because the lead character was a single mother. The controversy lasted for weeks as the vice president continued to criticize the show (and Hollywood in general) for undermining American values and the family. About the same time, horrifying photographs and videotapes from Bosnia were beginning to appear in the Western news media: Muslim men being packed into rail cars and sent to concentration camps, children on their way to school being bombarded by Serbian forces, and women describing how they had been brutally raped by rival ethnic groups. Thousands of families were torn apart, never to be reunited. The vice president did not comment on those events; instead, he continued his attack on a TV show and other "evils" that harmed the family.

The second global problem with an impact on the family is the HIV crisis, particularly (but not exclusively) in Africa. As much as one-quarter of the population of some African countries (for example, Zambia and Zimbabwe) have HIV and will eventually contract AIDS. The rates are even higher among young adults, the group with children, and the impact on the family is devastating. Millions of AIDS orphans have been created across the continent—in Uganda alone, more than 1.7 million children have lost one or both parents to the disease, the highest number of AIDS orphans of any country in the world (UNICEF, 1999). Although the extended family can take care of some orphans, they cannot care for all of them. The rest of the children end up in orphanages or on the street as beggars or prostitutes. The HIV epidemic will not destroy the African family, but it will alter the structure of the family well into the future. It is a prime example of how large-scale social forces affect individual lives.

The Consequences of Family Change

As you can see, families around the world are in the midst of massive, historically unprecedented change, and the causes are still being investigated. This section examines the social consequences of those changes.

The impact of family change differs depending on region of the world. On average, today's adults in the United States and other industrialized countries spend less time married and more time single (both before and after marriage) or in cohabiting relationships than did adults thirty or forty years ago. Women spend less of their lives involved in child rearing and more time in the labor force. Even in Japan, where women once assumed very traditional roles raising children, younger women are opting for later marriages and entering the labor force in greater numbers.

But, on average, the situation is very different in the developing world. Although there is some evidence that women are marrying at a slightly older age in poor countries, they still are bearing a large number of children and normally do not have a "single life" beyond their early twenties.

As you learned in Chapter 7, both men and women in developing countries face substantial burdens because of structural adjustment programs. Their money is worth less, and the costs associated with raising children are becoming greater. Men living in rural areas often migrate to cities in search of better jobs. Women usually stay behind, and they must simultaneously take care of the children and engage in other activities that will further support the family. Day care centers are not common in poor countries and children are sick more often. Thus, very few women in developing countries have any leisure time, which remains largely a Western concept.

In economically developed countries, family change has affected society quite differently. One-person apartments and condominiums, which were once a rarity, have become commonplace in response to the retreat from marriage and the increase in single living. All kinds of goods and services, like fast food and TV dinners, singles bars and singles travel clubs, have emerged to provide single adults with the things, like meals and companionship, that they previously would have gotten from their families. In addition, the economy has come to depend on the labor and spending power of women, who now make up over 45% of the labor force and who can be found in all types of work in all sectors of the economy (Reskin & Padavic, 1994).

Today's adults in developed countries enjoy far more flexibility and freedom in arranging their family lives than any previous generation. However, other changes, like the increase in divorce, have come at a cost. Women often pay a high price in financial security.

Two consequences of family change include more single mothers raising children alone and more "street children" in many developing countries. This child holds her doll while living on the streets of Sao Paulo, Brazil. Evidence clearly indicates that Brazilian officials have systematically murdered some street children in order to "clean up" the streets. When questioned about this horrific possibility at a conference on children in Norway, a high-ranking Brazilian official (who had been answering questions in English) suddenly held up his hands and claimed he only spoke Portuguese and therefore could field no more questions.

The discrepancies between developed and developing countries are similarly stark when it comes to the effect of changes in family life on children. Around the developing world, a lethal combination of growing poverty, HIV/AIDS, rigid economic policies, war, and overpopulation have harmed children. We could write an entire chapter (or book) on those topics. Instead, we focus on a problem that incorporates many of those issues, namely, the growth of homelessness and **street children** across the developing world. There is no greater sign of total family breakdown than seeing millions of children with no homes, no parents, and no hope. In Kenya, for example, nearly one million children live primarily on the street. Street children are abundant in many other cities in the developing world as well. Their means of survival are fairly well known: begging, pickpocketing, other petty crimes, and prostitution (Bradshaw, Buchmann, & Mbatia, 1994).

Street life takes a considerable toll. Chronic malnutrition stunts physical and mental development, as does the widespread drug use that characterizes street life. In addition, street children seldom attend school for very long, precluding them from developing the basic skills necessary for life. All those problems are compounded by the emotional stress and abuse that go along with trying to survive on the fringes of society.

Although there are some street children in the developed world, they certainly are fewer in relative numbers compared to the developing world. In developed countries, divorce, nonmarital childbearing, and the accompanying financial hardships are a greater threat. In the United States, for example, nearly half of all white children and over three-quarters of all black children spend some portion of their childhood in a single-parent family.

After forty years of research and debate, most family researchers agree that children raised in single-parent families are at increased risk for a range of problems: health problems, low educational attainment, low self-esteem, and behavioral, discipline, and psychological problems (Amato, 1993; Amato & Keith, 1991; McLanahan & Sandefur, 1994). Young adults who grow up in single-parent families are less likely to graduate from high school and attend college and tend to do less well in the labor market than their parents. They also are more likely to leave home early, have sex early, get married or cohabit at a young age, and become premaritally pregnant (Amato, 1996; Furstenberg & Teitler, 1994; McLanahan & Sandefur, 1994). Adults whose parents were divorced are more likely to be unhappy in their marriages and more likely to divorce (Amato, 1996). In general, the longer a child spends in a single-parent family, the greater the likelihood of problems. The risks are especially high for children born to unmarried women. One important reason why children in single-parent families are at increased risk for various problems is that single-parent families generally have only one wage-earner and are more likely to be poor than are two-parent families (Amato, 1993; Furstenberg, 1990; McLanahan & Sandefur, 1994). Overall, about 45% of single-mother families live below the poverty level, compared to only 7% of married-couple families.

We should mention that although the increase in single-parent families has been bad for children, the increased risks associated with being raised in a single-parent family is quite small. The associations between growing up in a single-parent family and the various negative outcomes are not one-to-one. Many children raised in single-parent families do well at school, have no psychological difficulties, and go on to become successful, happy, productive adults. Equally, some children raised in intact families have serious problems. One key factor seems to be conflict between parents (Amato, 1993; Amato & Booth, 1996). In fact, the difference between children from two-parent and single-parent families is less than the variation found within either group of children.

The impact of mothers' employment on children is probably the most extensively researched question in all of social science, even though that research focuses almost exclusively on the economically developed world. It is probably also the most controversial question. But virtually all researchers agree on two points:

◆ There is no evidence that mothers' employment harms school-age children. In fact, for girls there are well-documented benefits of having a working mother—they are more self-confident and do better in school (Barnett & Rivers, 1996). For younger children, too, most of the evidence suggests mothers' employment is not harmful. The exceptions to that occur when mothers work long hours in repetitive, low-skill, low-wage jobs (Parcel & Menaghan, 1994).

◆ Researchers also agree that infants and young children who are cared for by someone other than their mothers usually do just as well as children who are cared for by their mothers. More than one-third of preschoolers with employed mothers are cared for in their own homes—20% of them by their own fathers, as parents juggle their schedules to accommodate the demands of two jobs and child rearing. Roughly another third of preschoolers with employed mothers are cared for in someone else's home, one-third of them by relatives, and the rest are cared for by nonrelatives, as in day care centers (U.S. Bureau of the Census, 1996). Regardless of the exact arrangements chosen by working parents, researchers agree that high-quality child care does not harm children.

In summary, the increase in mothers' employment has not harmed children. In fact, mothers' employment has many benefits for children. For many families, especially single-parent families, it is the mother's paycheck that lifts the family out of poverty. In developing countries, mothers' work is essential for providing basic necessities and caring for children at home. Among nonpoor families, the mother's paycheck provides essentials like college savings accounts and health insurance, as well as occasional luxuries. Once again, then, we cannot conclude that changes in family structure in recent years have been detrimental to individuals or society.

Conclusion

As we were finishing writing this chapter, one of us received a call from a journalist. "What does the next forty years hold for the American family?" the journalist asked. The interviewee began to offer some possible interpretations of the numbers—what it would mean for parents to have fewer biological children and more stepchildren, for example. After a few minutes however, she paused. A disconcerting question had formed in the back of her mind. What would a family sociologist working in 1960 have said to the same question?

Most likely he (nearly all sociologists in 1960 were men) would have based his comments on the assumption that what had been happening would continue. He would not have foreseen the dramatic retreat from marriage that would be underway ten years later. He would not have predicted the surge in the divorce rate. He could not have imagined that the new trend of women going back to work once their children were teenagers would lead to a complete realignment of women's work and childbearing patterns.

We know what family sociologists writing in 1960 had to say about the future because we can still read their writings. Those realizations—that the past forty years have been a time of massive and often unprecedented family change and that the people most in the know did not see the changes coming—left the interviewee reluctant to continue her conversation with the journalist.

We do not know what families will be like in the future. In fact, we are just beginning to understand what has happened to families in the recent past and the implications of those changes. The evidence reviewed in this chapter suggests that a combination of economic forces, globalization, and changing cultural mores led to a wave of family change in developed and developing countries alike. So far the most serious consequence of those changes has been the increase in the number of children who grow up on the streets or in single-parent families and who thus face increased risks for a range of problems.

Although we cannot predict the future of the family, it is clear that as a social institution the family is not in danger. The family continues to meet important social needs, and no other set of arrangements has appeared to take the place of the family. Far from fading, the family is adapting. We are becoming increasingly aware that families don't all look the same. In addition, the rules for some family roles have changed—these days being employed and being a good mother are not incompatible, and it takes more than earning a steady wage to be a good father. Some new family roles—stepfather, partner, ex-wife, former son-in-law—are slowly being institutionalized, and we are coming to understand what the rights and responsibilities of those roles are. Contemporary debates about the family are going to continue. But it is through those debates that we arrive at new understandings of what a family is and does.

Key Concepts

1. The family is a social institution embraced by every known society in the world. However, families vary by society and assume numerous forms, from nuclear families to extended families to "alternative" families. Sociologists focus on the connection between the family and other social institutions, including the economy, religion, the educational system, and so on.

2. Family life around the world has undergone substantial changes over the last three decades. The principal changes include later marriages, more cohabitation, having

fewer children and having them more often out of marriage, and more divorces and eventual remarriages. The changes vary by a society's level of economic development, culture, and other factors. For example, people in developing countries continue to bear more children because there are legitimate economic and cultural reasons for doing so.

3. Explanations about the causes of the changes in the family center on several arguments, including weakened family values, increased women's employment, economic adjustments, and social crises. Although there is some merit to each argument, the two explanations with the strongest support are economic adjustments (lower standard of living) and social crises (war and HIV/AIDS).

4. Family change has important implications for both developed and developing countries. Developed societies are more oriented toward single people and women than in earlier decades, reflecting the fact that people delay marriage and also divorce in larger numbers. Developing societies are forced to deal with many serious problems, such as more street children due to war and HIV/AIDS.

Active Learning

1. The Family in the Media: Group Exercise (Adapted from an exercise developed by Nancy Wisely, Stephen F. Austin State University, Nacogdoches, Texas). In this exercise, you will apply sociological concepts to at least two fictional families as portrayed on video or television. You will develop your sociological imagination by studying the norms, roles, and values that regulate the institution of the family and the behavior of the characters in the videos (not the characters themselves).

For this exercise, you will need to view one of the following: *Pride and Prejudice* (a PBS production of the classic Jane Austen novel), *Parenthood* (a feature-length commercial film), a TV show about a family (either a new series or a rerun), or another video or show specified by your instructor. (*Parenthood* should be available at commercial rental outlets, and *Pride and Prejudice* may be available at university and public libraries.) Leave yourselves a week or so to complete the viewing and remember that other students in this class need access to the videos.

a. In class, divide into groups of four to six. Determine who will view which video or show. As a group, you should view at least two different ones.

b. View the video or show you've chosen, either alone or with other members of your group, and complete the viewing worksheet available from the Web site for this book (www.pineforge.com/snc). Each person in the group should complete his or her own worksheet so you can compare impressions. Bring the completed worksheet to class on the date assigned by your instructor.

c. In class on the assigned date, meet with your group and answer the following questions as a group. Summarize the group's deliberations in writing. Each member should take a turn writing answers.

   i. List the statuses (or positions) in each family (mother, brother-in-law, niece, and so on). What important differences exist between the families in terms of statuses and relationships between statuses?

ii. Why are the families you viewed different? List and briefly explain at least five sociological reasons (for example, level of development of the society, social class, culture, ethnicity).

iii. What values, norms, and beliefs are important in each family? What family rituals are observed?

iv. Describe each family in terms of size and structure (for example, extended versus nuclear). How are the families organized in terms of power dynamics? Who makes decisions? How? What issues threaten the stability of the family? How do they deal with threats?

v. Which of the families viewed by the group represents the strongest family institution? Why?

d. Submit a summary of the group's discussion to the instructor and be prepared to present your conclusions to the class.

2. The Importance of Family Values: Data Analysis. In this exercise, you will analyze relationships between traditional family values and other variables and then discuss your conclusions in small groups. Graphic 8.7 presents some results of a 1998 survey of a representative sample of the total adult U.S. population. Assume that the results in the table can be generalized to all adult Americans in that year.

Respondents were divided into three groups based on their response to the following question: "Do you agree or disagree: It is all right for a couple to live together without intending to get married." Respondents who agreed (about 44%) were labeled "modern" in family values, and respondents who disagreed (about 35%) were labeled "traditional." Respondents who neither agreed nor disagreed (about 21%) were labeled "neutral."

Graphic 8.7 presents the results of the survey in two parts. The first part presents the percentage of respondents in various social categories who selected the traditional response. In the first part, family values are treated as a dependent variable or an effect. The second part of Graphic 8.7 treats family values as an independent variable or a cause and shows relationships with a variety of other behaviors and attitudes. The numbers in the second part are the percentages of traditional, neutral, and modern respondents who answered in a certain way. For example, 48% of the respondents with traditional values attended church weekly or more versus 19% of the "neutrals" and 11% of the "moderns." Complete wording for the items and a more detailed key are available at our Web site (www.pineforge.com/snc).

a. Before class, analyze the results shown in Graphic 8.7 item by item. For each item, find the highest and lowest percentages in each category and subtract the lower from the higher. Use the following rough guide to assess the importance of family values for each item, based on your calculations.

If the difference between highest and lowest percentages is	*The item is*
Less than 10	Not related to family values
Between 10 and 20	Somewhat related to family values
Between 20 and 30	Moderately related to family values
More than 30	Strongly related to family values

Percentage of Respondents Who Espouse Traditional Family Values

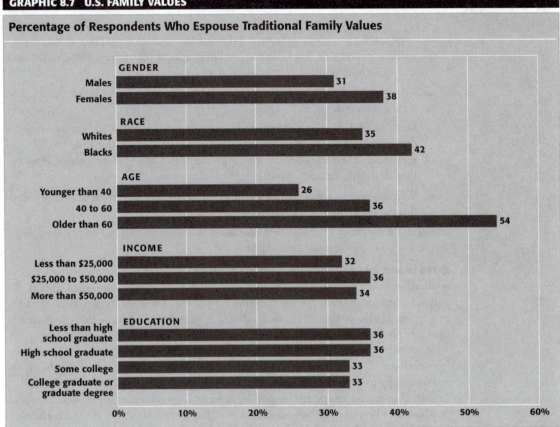

Interaction of Family Values and Other Behaviors and Attitudes

Behaviors and Attitudes	Percentage of Positive Answers among Those Espousing Values		
	Traditional Values	Neutral Values	Modern Values
Attend church weekly or more	48%	19%	11%
Are politically liberal	15%	27%	40%
Have ever divorced	17%	27%	35%
Are very happy	39%	34%	25%
Are very happy with their marriage	68%	58%	59%
Have ever had sex with someone other than spouse while married	10%	13%	17%
Have not had sex at all during past year	31%	24%	15%
Agree that premarital sex is always wrong	58%	10%	7%
Agree that a preschool child is likely to suffer if his or her mother works	56%	36%	30%
Agree that it is sometimes necessary to discipline a child with a good, hard spanking	78%	74%	71%

Source: National Opinion Research Council, 1998.

b. Write a paragraph describing these relationships. Which items are related to family values? How strongly? In your opinion, why are the variables related as they are? Do any of the relationships (or nonrelationships) surprise you? Why?

c. Bring your written assessment to class. Form groups of four to six and share your descriptions of the relationships. Make sure everyone agrees on which relationships are strongly affected by family values, which are not affected, and so forth.

d. Once you agree on the descriptions, try to analyze why the variables are related. Why do the patterns exist? Is there a cluster of values and behaviors in U.S. society associated with attitudes about family? If so, what type of person has those values?

e. Write a joint report summarizing the group's analysis and conclusions. Turn in the joint report along with the individual descriptions you each brought to class.

3. Sociological Family History: Interviews (Adapted from an exercise developed by Mark R. Warren, Fordham University). In this exercise, you will interview members of your family and discover how the larger social world has shaped the history of your family and your own biography. You will write a short paper based on your analysis of the interviews, and your instructor may provide some class time for discussion. Through this exercise and class discussions, you will have the opportunity to consider how the larger social trends we discuss in this book are (or are not) mirrored in the history of your family.

a. Select one branch of your family on your mother's side or your father's side and interview at least one member of each generation (for example, parent, grandparent, great grandparent), going back as far as possible. Fill in information for missing generations from other family members, memorabilia such as photo albums, and so forth as best you can. Get the following information:

  i.   Religion.

  ii.   Educational level.

  iii. Ethnicity or race.

  iv.   Country of birth. Immigrant to the United States?

  v.   Age at first marriage.

  vi.   How did each person meet his or her spouse?

  vii. Number of children. Did any die in childhood or adolescence? Were any born out of wedlock?

  viii. Employment of husband and wife.

  ix.   Were any relationships broken by divorce, separation, or the death of a spouse? If so, was there a remarriage? At what age?

  x.   Did anyone ever cohabitate? Did they know anyone who cohabitated? How do they feel about the practice of cohabitation today? Were they involved in (or aware of) any other unconventional arrangements or marital practices they would care to discuss?

  xi.   Ask the respondents to describe their relationship with their spouse and children. How did they get along? What was a typical day (or week) like? How did routines change over the course of the marriage? What kinds of things did they do together for fun? Were they strict parents? What forms of discipline did they use?

When you conduct the interviews, be as informal as possible and encourage your respondents to chat and tell stories and anecdotes that, for them, summarize how things were. Note significant exceptions (for example, "My family was Baptist except for my great aunt who converted to Catholicism when she married") at your own discretion. Some areas may be sensitive for your family or for a specific respondent. If so, feel free to skip a question or to terminate the interview. Remember to thank respondents for their time.

b. Once you have your family history outlined, think about how prior generations have been affected by changes in the larger society and in the family institution in the United States. Write an essay (length to be specified by your instructor) in which you fit the history of your family into the trends discussed in this chapter (for example, changing divorce rates and childbearing practices, the entry of women into the paid labor force) and previous chapters (for example, changing gender roles, deindustrialization, changing norms and values). To what extent have your family's experiences been the result of social structural forces, of accidental factors, of choices and decisions made by its members? The last part of your essay should address the extent to which you think you are a product of your family's history, the broader social forces operating in the United States, and your own choices.

c. If requested by your instructor, be prepared to share with the class your family's history and your analysis of how your family and your life have been shaped by social forces.

9 Crime and Punishment

Can crime be controlled?

Singapore is a tiny Asian nation of some 3 million people perched on the southern tip of the Malay Peninsula. It is prosperous, modern, and well known for its low crime rate, its intolerance of deviance and disorder, and its harsh treatment of criminals. In 1994, 18-year-old American Michael Fay personally experienced the severity of the Singapore legal system when he was convicted of vandalism after a ten-day spree of spray-painting and damaging cars. His sentence included four months in prison, a fine of $2,200, and—most controversially—six lashes with a cane on his buttocks (Elliot, 1994). In the United States, corporal punishment (short of the death penalty, of course) was abandoned long ago, and the physical brutality of Fay's sentence brought strong responses from his parents, the U.S. government, and concerned people around the world. Singapore responded to the pressure by reducing the number of lashes to four, but Fay received his flogging nevertheless.

Consider, by way of contrast, another encounter of 18-year-old American males with the criminal justice system, this time in the United States. As juveniles, Larry Demery and Daniel Green frequently had been in trouble with the law, and by 1993 they had progressed to serious criminal activities. Green was on parole after serving two years of a six-year sentence for attempted murder. He had smashed his victim in the head with an ax, leaving him in a coma for three months. Demery was awaiting trial for robbing a convenience store and striking the clerk in the head with a cinder block, fracturing her skull.

One night in July 1993, Green and Demery were out searching for an opportunity to rob someone when they spotted a new Lexus parked at a rest area along an interstate highway in North Carolina. They found the driver asleep and shot him in the chest from the partially open passenger side window. When they searched their victim's wallet, they discovered that they had killed James Jordan, the father of superstar athlete Michael Jordan (Thomas, 1993, p. C11). In 1996, almost three years after the murder, Demery and Green were sentenced to life in prison for their crime. But why, many asked, had they been free in the first place? As one North Carolina law enforcement official commented, "Mr. Jordan would be alive now if the [legal] system worked the way it should" (Wooten, 1993, p. 12).

Michael Fay was severely punished for a relatively minor crime while Mr. Jordan's murderers, who were known to be violent, had been left free to rob and kill. The contrast between the two cases almost irresistibly reinforces the widespread popular perception that the criminal justice system in the United States is in a sad state of disrepair, a "revolving door" that releases hardened criminals to commit one outrage after another. Proponents of that view often argue that the United States needs to follow Singapore's lead and tighten up the system, escalate the penalties, and get tough with the vicious predators that stalk our streets. One public opinion poll reported that 38% of a sample of U.S. citizens actually approved of Michael Fay's caning (Elliot, 1994).

Many social scientists agree that the U.S. criminal justice system is soft on crime, but others think that simply getting tough is a narrow, simplistic, and ultimately self-defeating response. They argue that punishment can do little to deter potential criminals and that the true causes of crime in the United States (and, increasingly, around the world) spring from some of the most fundamental characteristics of modern, industrial, capitalist society: materialism, egotism, greed, loss of community, and growing inequality.

This chapter investigates those divergent points of view, considers the nature and causes of crime, and analyzes the relationship between crime and punishment. We begin by considering the scope of the crime problem, matters of definition and measurement, the correlates of crime, and some of the many sociological theories about crime and deviance. Although the focus in this chapter is crime in the United States, we will place the issues in a cross-national, comparative context and apply many of the themes introduced in Chapter 1, including the impact of modernization and globalization, the relevance of culture and subcultures, and the role of inequality in generating crime. We return to the specific issue of crime control after laying a foundation of evidence, ideas, and theories.

Defining and Measuring Crime

When we talk about crime, we aren't just talking about **deviance,** that is, the behaviors and conditions that violate our expectations about "normal people"—things as diverse as drug addiction, physical handicaps, and extreme religiosity. We are talking instead about a subset of deviant behavior, namely **crime,** that consists of acts violating our culture's formal norms, or laws (see Chapter 4).

The public concern over crime and punishment clearly is justified. Crime rates in the United States have risen over the past few decades, and Americans are more likely

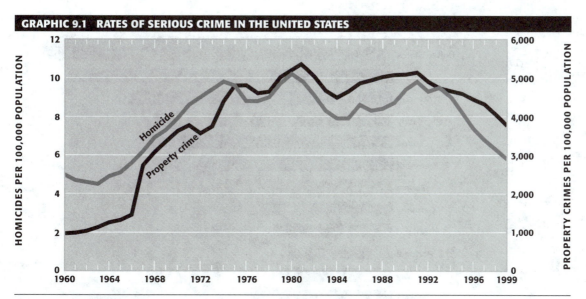

GRAPHIC 9.1 RATES OF SERIOUS CRIME IN THE UNITED STATES

Source: Federal Bureau of Investigation.

to be victimized by crime today than they were a generation ago. Graphic 9.1 shows the trends in the rates of two types of felonies. **Felonies** are serious crimes, such as murder, rape, and robbery—that are punishable by more than a year in prison. (In contrast, **misdemeanors**—less serious crimes, such as petty theft and public drunkenness—are punishable by less than a year in jail.) In Graphic 9.1, you can see a sharp increase in criminal activity beginning in the late 1960s and continuing into the 1970s. By the early 1990s, the homicide rate was more than double the 1960 rate. It then declined, but in 1999 the homicide rate was still higher than it was in the mid-1960s. The rate of property crime (thefts, burglaries, and the like) also declined in the 1990s, but it remains almost four times greater than the 1960 rate. Crime statistics, as we shall see, are subject to various forms of distortion and error, but they document the unmistakable reality of higher levels of crime and victimization for Americans.

Not only are U.S. crime rates higher than in previous decades, they also are higher than in other industrialized nations, often by a considerable margin. For example, Graphic 9.2 shows that the homicide rate for the United States is twice that of France or Denmark, three times greater than that of the United Kingdom, and four times greater than Japan's. In fairness, we should note that the United States does not have the highest homicide rate in the world. In the mid-1990s, at least twenty nations—all nonindustrial and many racked by civil war or struggles between rival criminal gangs—had higher homicide rates than the United States (Kurian, 1997, p. 321).

Although reliable data do not exist for many nations, it seems that crime rates are rising worldwide and that even relatively safe societies like Singapore and China are having to deal with an increase in lawlessness (Stephens, 1994, p. 26). People

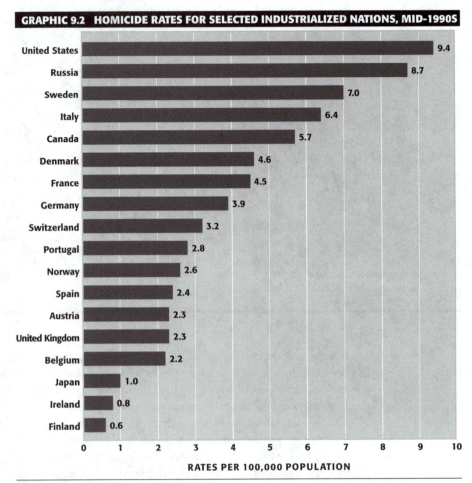

GRAPHIC 9.2   HOMICIDE RATES FOR SELECTED INDUSTRIALIZED NATIONS, MID-1990S

United States	9.4
Russia	8.7
Sweden	7.0
Italy	6.4
Canada	5.7
Denmark	4.6
France	4.5
Germany	3.9
Switzerland	3.2
Portugal	2.8
Norway	2.6
Spain	2.4
Austria	2.3
United Kingdom	2.3
Belgium	2.2
Japan	1.0
Ireland	0.8
Finland	0.6

RATES PER 100,000 POPULATION

Source: Kurian, 1997.

and governments everywhere—not just in the United States—are concerned about controlling crime.

You may have noticed that the data on crime we've provided so far falls into the category of what sociologists call **street crime:** crimes that have personal victims, result in obvious physical injuries or loss of property, and often include a face-to-face confrontation between victim and offender. When people think about or discuss "the crime problem," they usually are thinking of those types of offenses, a tendency that is reinforced by the news media and virtually all aspects of popular culture.

In contrast, **white-collar crime,** or crime committed by "people of high social position in the course of their occupations" (Sutherland, 1940), often lacks a specific victim and a direct, personal confrontation. Examples of white-collar crime include embezzlement (stealing from one's employer), price fixing (collaborations between businesses to keep prices artificially high), insider trading (using privileged information for personal gain in the stock market), consumer fraud (selling products that are known to be dangerous or defective), and even trafficking in human organs (Foster, 1997). Because white-collar crimes lack the clarity and immediacy of being robbed at knifepoint or finding your house burglarized and your most valued possessions gone there is less public recognition that such activities are indeed crimes. Nonetheless, white-collar crimes can have devastating impacts, and dollar losses can be far in excess of the "typical" street crime (Moore & Mills, 1990).

Although we would like to address criminality in all its forms in this chapter, crime is as voluminous as any other human behavior and we cannot hope to cover the subject entirely. Therefore, the remainder of this chapter examines specifically serious street crimes (felonies), in part because the great bulk of sociological research focuses on such crimes and in part because rates for that type of crime are available for cross-national comparison.

How Can the Crime Rate Be Measured?

It is inherently difficult to measure the rate of crime accurately. People obviously are reluctant to reveal their involvement in illegal activity, and victims, for a variety of reasons, may be unable to provide accurate information. Currently, criminologists rely heavily on three methods for measuring crime: "official" crime statistics, surveys of victims, and reports by those who commit crimes. Each method has its strengths as well as some serious limitations.

"Official" Crime Rates. Many governments attempt to measure crime. Those statistics are highly uneven in quality, but they are the sole basis for our (limited) ability to compare crime rates in different societies. This section briefly considers the technique used to gather crime data in the United States. Similar methods are used in other industrialized nations.

The United States Federal Bureau of Investigation (FBI) has been responsible for compiling and reporting statistical information about crime since the 1930s. The data, which constitute what we call the "official" crime rates, are published annually in a report titled *Crime in the United States,* also known as the *Uniform Crime Report* (UCR). Virtually all media reports and everyday discussions of crime are based on those rates. More specifically, media and public understandings of crime reflect the rates of what the UCR calls "Part I" crimes: the eight major felonies (all of them street crimes) that are listed and briefly defined in Graphic 9.3.

It is important to recognize that UCR crime rates (and all government-collected crime data in all nations) are based on crimes known to the police and involve a reporting process that begins at the local level and that is subject to a variety of complications and inaccuracies. In the United States, reports of crimes are tallied locally and then reported to the FBI, a method that suffers from a serious defect: crimes are sometimes (often?) not reported to the police in the first place. Obviously, if an incident is never reported, the police and the FBI cannot count it, and official crime rates will understate actual rates by an unknown but, at least for some crimes, large extent. That flaw creates a considerable challenge for comparisons of

---

GRAPHIC 9.3   MAJOR FELONIES INCLUDED AS PART I OFFENSES IN THE *UNIFORM CRIME REPORTS*

CRIMES OF VIOLENCE

    Aggravated assault: Attack on another person intended to inflict severe bodily injury; includes attempts

    Forcible rape: Carnal knowledge of a female forcibly and against her will; includes attempted rape

    Murder and nonnegligent manslaughter: Willful killing of one human being by another

    Robbery: Taking or attempting to take anything of value from another person by force or by threat of force

CRIMES AGAINST PROPERTY

    Arson: Willful or malicious burning of a building, motor vehicle, or aircraft; includes attempts

    Burglary: Unlawful entry of a structure to commit a felony or theft; includes attempts

    Larceny: Unlawful taking of property from another person without using force, violence, or fraud

    Motor vehicle theft: Theft or attempted theft of a motor vehicle

Source: FBI, 1999.

---

crime rates across jurisdictions, times, and nations. Are lower crime rates the result of sloppy record keeping, or do they indicate greater safety? Do higher crime rates reflect better reporting systems or a greater threat of victimization?

The extent to which crimes are undercounted varies by a number of factors, including the nature of the crime. For example, because almost all homicides are reported to the police (there is a dead body that must be dealt with), we generally can trust official homicide rates, at least for industrialized nations. The crime of rape, in contrast, is known to be seriously underreported, perhaps by as much as a factor of 4, 5, or more. The reasons for not reporting rape are well known (embarrassment, fear that the authorities will not be supportive, fear of reprisal, and so on) and especially likely to affect situations like "date rape," in which the offender is personally known to the victim. The result is a huge reservoir of "hidden" rapes: incidents that are never reported to the police and that are not reflected in official crime rates.

For those reasons, official, government-reported crime rates must be used with caution and, in some cases, not at all. While we can reasonably trust the homicide rate (at least for industrialized nations), we should be circumspect in our use of other official crime statistics.

Victimization Surveys. Since 1972, the U.S. Department of Justice has attempted to address the problem of unreported crime by asking large, representative samples of Americans to list the number of times they have been victimized by crime over the previous six months. Such **victimization surveys** include incidents that were not reported to the police and may provide better estimates of actual crime rates than the UCR reports, at least for some types of crime. For example, in 1998, about 93,000 rapes were reported to the police (Federal Bureau of Investigation [FBI], 1998). Based on victimization surveys, the estimated number of rapes and sexual assaults in the same year was over 330,000 (Rennison, 1998, p. 3). That suggests that in 1998 the actual number of rapes was perhaps 3.5 times greater than the official rate. (See Lynch, 1996, for an analysis of the problems of using victimization surveys to estimate the rate of rape.)

Of course, victimization surveys have their own problems and limitations. People may forget or exaggerate their victimization, and, for crimes like rape, the same dynamics that stop victims from calling the police may prevent them from discussing the incident with an interviewer (which suggests that the actual rate of rape is even higher than that estimated from victimization surveys). Also, victims are often unable to supply detailed or trustworthy information about offenders, especially when the offender is a stranger. Thus, we cannot use victimization surveys for definitive tests of theories about the characteristics of criminals or the dynamics of crime causation.

Self-Reports. A third method of gathering data on criminality is the self-report, in which respondents are asked to describe their criminal behavior. This method can produce the most information about offenders and has been used to good effect in testing and refining criminological theory and ideas about crime causation.

The limitations of this method are fairly obvious: some respondents may not admit their criminal behavior for fear of exposure and arrest, while others may exaggerate their criminality. Nonetheless, self-reports, like victimization surveys, produce estimates of actual crime rates that are many times higher than the official rates.

Who Commits Street Crime?

Based on those three sources of information about crime, we can develop a general profile of typical offenders for serious street crimes. The portrait conforms closely to common perceptions of what a criminal "looks like," and, in broad outline, it seems to characterize street criminals worldwide, at least to the extent that cross-national data permit comparisons (for example, see Gottfredson & Hirschi, 1990).

◆ *Age.* Serious street crime is strongly associated with youth. Graphic 9.4 shows arrest rates by age for all U.S. property and violent crimes and for homicide for 1998. For the first two types of crime, the rates peak in the 15–19 age group and then decline. The homicide rate is more evenly spread across the 15–19 and 20–24 age groups but then drops into the same range as the other types of crime.

◆ *Gender.* Serious street crime is primarily a male activity. In 1998, males constituted about 85% of those arrested for violent crime in the United States and about 71% of the arrests for property crime (FBI, 1998). As displayed in Graphic 9.5, arrests are highest for males aged 15–19 for both property and violent crimes. Arrests of females are also highest in about the same age range but the peak arrest rate for females is much lower than that of males. We should note, however, that the gender differential in arrest rates for serious street crime has been declining in recent years. In the ten-year period from 1989 to 1998, total arrests for females rose 28%, while arrests for males rose only 2%. Over the same period, arrests for violent crimes increased by 2% for males and by 53% for females (FBI, 1998, p. 210).

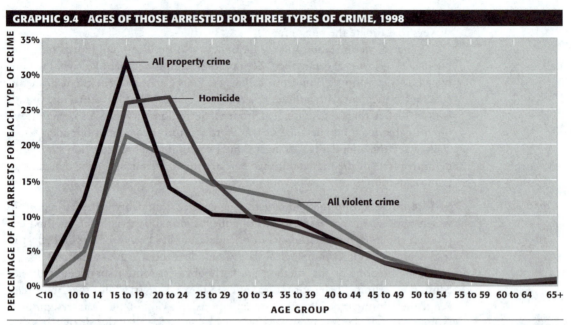

GRAPHIC 9.4   AGES OF THOSE ARRESTED FOR THREE TYPES OF CRIME, 1998

Source: FBI, 1998.

♦ *Race.* In the United States, the majority of people arrested for serious street crimes are white, but African Americans and some other minority groups are overrepresented. Although African Americans are only about 12% of the population, they constituted almost 30% of people arrested for all crimes and over half of those arrested for homicide and rape (FBI, 1998, p. 228). To some extent, that racial differential reflects differences in social class between whites and blacks in the United States (see Chapter 6), but it also reflects racial bias in the criminal justice system (see Tonry, 1995, for a review of recent research).

Keep in mind that this is an incomplete and distorted view of "all criminals." It does not describe people who manage to avoid arrest, a group that may have different racial and social class characteristics than those who are arrested. Arrest rates reflect the behavior of the criminal justice system as well as the criminals. Any class, gender, or racial biases in the police and court system will distort the portrait of offenders created from arrest rates. In other words, if police are more likely to attribute criminality to males, to people of lower socioeconomic standing, or to members of minority groups, those groups will be overrepresented in the statistical profiles. Remember also that this portrait describes only those who commit street crime, not the full array of crime. White-collar criminals, for example, tend to be trusted and "respectable" members of their communities; if they were included in the portraits drawn here, the typical offender would be significantly older, better educated, more middle class, and whiter.

GRAPHIC 9.5   NUMBER OF ARRESTS BY AGE AND SEX, 1998

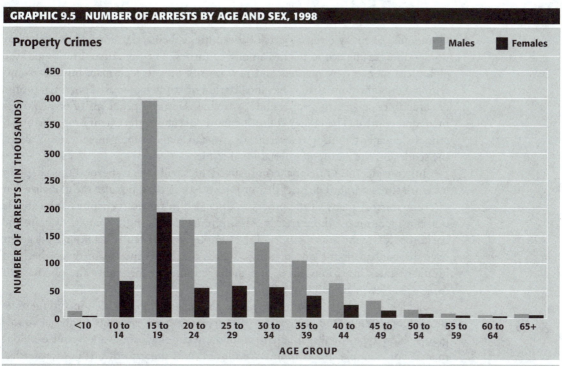

Property Crimes

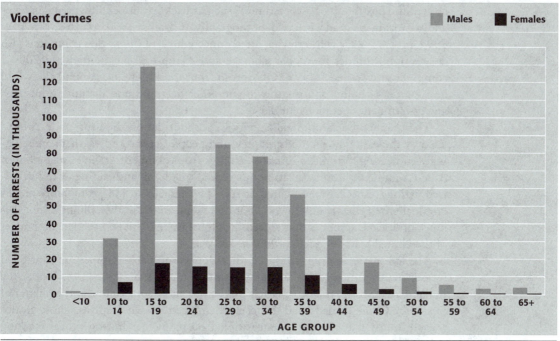

Violent Crimes

Source: FBI, 1998.

How Is Globalization Affecting Crime?

Crime, like so many other aspects of social life, is being transformed by globalization and increasing economic ties among countries. The figurative shrinking of the globe has opened new markets and new possibilities to legitimate businesses and criminal organizations alike. The globalization of crime has created potential profits of sometimes staggering proportions as well as daunting problems of law enforcement and control. The task of collecting hard data about the extent of international crime is equally daunting. Nevertheless, we can make some generalizations about the scope and the nature of international crime.

Our consideration of global criminal activities will take us beyond this chapter's focus on street crime. The brief detour is justified, in part, because the globalization of crime mirrors many of the processes discussed in previous chapters and extends our consideration of those trends. Also, international criminal enterprises are the backdrop for many street crimes, for example, violent feuds between rival gangs over the control of the sale of drugs, which are sometimes blamed for the high homicide rates in various cities, and thefts committed to finance the purchase of drugs (see Newman, 1999, pp. 171–179).

Globally organized crime encompasses a broad array of activities, including prostitution, gambling, and smuggling of everything from weapons to illegal immigrants. New types of illegal activities follow technological advances and developments. For example, the computer revolution and the growth of the Internet has created the possibility of "cybercrimes," such as hacking into confidential databases and a worldwide trade in child pornography (Castells, 1999, p. 167; Newman 1999, pp. 223–227). The growing interconnectedness of the world's computers also creates opportunities for global sabotage and disruption. For example, in 2000 a computer virus called ILOVEYOU spread from the Philippines around the world in a matter of hours, shutting down computer networks and disrupting business and government operations for days.

The premier global criminal activity is, without doubt, the drug trade. Stimulated by the easy flow of goods, money, and people across borders, there are seemingly endless opportunities to transfer drugs from points of origin (usually South America and Southeast Asia) to points of sale (predominantly affluent, industrialized nations, especially the United States). The actual size and profitability of this criminal enterprise are unknown but are surely measured in the billions, if not trillions, of dollars, amounts that exceed the global trade in oil and the federal budget of the United States (Castells, 1999, p. 169).

The international drug trade and other global criminal enterprises are controlled by organized crime groups, including (among many others) the U.S. Mafia, the Italian Cosa Nostra, the drug cartels of Central and South America, the Yakusa of Japan, the Chinese Triads, and the recently emerged Russian Mafiyas. Those groups operate much like any other transnational business: maximizing profits, seeking opportunities for new investment, and limiting risks. Each gang is based in a specific region, where it attempts to minimize interference in its operations by bribing local officials or, if necessary, by ruthless intimidation and violence. Organized crime groups also typically build strong ties with local populations by combining lavish social welfare programs and charities with support of indigenous culture, music, arts, and sports programs (Castells, 1999, p. 199).

Internationally, criminal gangs form a flexible network that stretches across borders and that can respond quickly to changing conditions and opportunities. If local conditions become inhospitable, operations can be moved to safer environments in other locales or other countries. When new opportunities arise, new alliances can be quickly formed. The collapse of the Soviet Union, along with its tight economic and social controls, presented an opportunity for organized crime syndicates both inside and outside of Russia. Alliances between Russian and South American groups were formed to exploit the newly opened market, sell drugs, launder money through now poorly regulated Russian banks, and capitalize on other criminal opportunities (Castells, 1999, p. 187).

The global network of organized crime also mirrors the increasing sophistication of technology and, particularly, the central role of the computer. Consider money laundering. Drug trafficking and other criminal enterprises generate huge profits, which must be "laundered" before they can be used for legitimate purposes. To

Crime is increasingly global in scope. A Colombian anti-narcotics police officer guards packages of cocaine found in the containers behind him at a warehouse in the port city of Cartagena in 1998. Police seized more than 7 tons of cocaine that were to be loaded onto a ship for delivery in Cuba. It was one of the largest cocaine busts in the history of Colombia.

make the ill-gotten funds untrackable, the money is transferred from bank to bank, currency to currency, and nation to nation electronically. In their technical expertise, the criminal cartels mirror the transnational corporations that dominate the formal global economy (Castells, 1999, p. 204).

The criminal cartels have used their profits to penetrate various national governments (most notably, perhaps, Colombia) to protect their operations. The economic stakes are high, and global organized crime threatens the ability of many developing nations to maintain democratic forms of government free of corruption and scandal. The threat is not confined to the Third World, as illustrated by the power of organized crime in Russia, Italy, and other industrialized nations. Sophisticated, flexible, ruthless, and wealthy, the global network of organized crime groups threatens the rule of law and democratic institutions worldwide.

Theorizing about the Causes of Crime

It is one thing to know how much street crime is occurring and who is committing it. More important, that information can help us assess theories about the causes of crime and proposals to reduce crime. Criminologists have been applying the scientific method to the study of crime since the nineteenth century and have developed a rich and varied theoretical base. This section reviews several of those theories, but first it is useful to examine the relationship between modernization and deviance, a concern that has been pervasive in sociology from the beginnings of the discipline. As you saw in Chapter 2, Durkheim argued that industrialization and urbanization cause a decline in mechanical solidarity: a weakening of moral unity, an increase in normlessness, and a decrease in the strength of the social ties that regulate social behavior and bind people to each other. Does that mean that modernization always results in increasing rates of deviance of all types, including crime? Let's review Durkheim's thinking on the matter.

Durkheim noted that traditional agricultural societies are held together by similarity of condition, strict norms of conformity, and strong interpersonal ties (mechanical solidarity). Everyone relies on farming to supply their needs, and people organize their daily lives around routines and procedures that have been followed for centuries. Such close-knit, slow-changing societies have little tolerance for deviance and offer few opportunities for crime.

The conditions of daily life change dramatically under the pressures of industrialization, urbanization, and the shift to organic forms of solidarity. The basis for social solidarity shifts from similarity and conformity to interdependence and cooperation, the weight of tradition is lifted, and there is increased tolerance for diversity in individual expression and lifestyle. Interpersonal ties become fewer and less binding, freeing some for involvement in criminality. Thus, consistent with our theme that modernity is not necessarily synonymous with progress, industrialization may bring higher crime rates along with greater individual freedom.

The idea that modernization and crime are connected has had great appeal to researchers but has been difficult to prove. For one thing, a topic like this requires comparison of societies in different stages of development, and cross-national research on crime is limited by a number of factors: the lack of reliable data for most nations (especially the ones currently undergoing modernization, the very cases most crucial for a test of this hypothesis), problems of comparability, and differences in legal definitions. Nonetheless, researchers have overcome some of those obstacles, and some limited tests of this hypothesis are available. For example, Ortega et al. (1992) found positive relationships between level of development (measured by GNP per capita) and several measures of crime (homicide and theft). On the other hand, a study sponsored by the United Nations found that while rates of theft increased with level of development, homicide rates were higher in less developed nations (Newman, 1999, pp. 50–57).

We need to be careful about drawing any conclusions about the relationship between modernization and crime. It may be, for example, that the rate of property crime increases with development simply because in more affluent societies there is more to steal, not because they lack norms or strong interpersonal ties (see Cohen & Felson, 1979). Also, the higher homicide rates in less industrialized nations may reflect differences in the quality of emergency medical care as much as a difference in rates of violence (Newman, 1999, p. 58). Although crime rates seem to be increasing worldwide and people everywhere lament the decline of traditional morality, not enough research has been done to justify the conclusion that modernity and crime are causally connected, at least in any simple or straightforward way.

Countless other theories about the causes of crime have been proposed and tested. Some ideas led to blind alleys and have been discarded, while others have endured for many decades. No single, unitary theory of criminality has emerged, but a number of ideas are widely accepted by criminologists. To say that they are widely accepted is not, of course, the same thing as saying that they are true. The four theories reviewed here—structural strain and anomie, differential association, deviant subcultures, and social control—are representative of the field, but they continue to be tested and refined, and, as is true in virtually every subfield of sociology, criminologists disagree among themselves about the usefulness of these theories, as they do on virtually every issue related to crime and delinquency.

Structural Strain and Anomie

Writing in the 1930s, Robert K. Merton (1938) developed a theory of deviance based on the relationship between a society's cultural goals and the means it deems legitimate for achieving those goals. All societies encourage their members to pursue a certain set of goals and to judge themselves and each other in terms of their success in those pursuits. Culturally approved goals might include wisdom, physical beauty, self-awareness, military and athletic skills, or inner peace and enlightenment. Industrialized, consumer-oriented societies like the United States stress goals such as acquisitiveness and material success, as measured by possessions—cars, houses, and designer clothes (see Chapter 4 for a more complete list of American values).

A group of young people in Quito, Ecuador, wait to apply for jobs. Failure to find employment or other sources of support may lead to a feeling of anomie. Some people argue that high levels of anomie contribute to criminal behavior.

To regulate competition, each society establishes norms and rules or legitimate means by which to pursue approved goals. In the United States, for example, legitimate means for achieving material success include inheriting wealth, making shrewd stock market investments, and succeeding in school and career.

What happens when the legitimate means are not closely linked to the culturally approved goals? In other words, what happens when playing by the rules and following the approved pathways does not result in success? Even worse, what happens when the legitimate means to success simply are not available? Merton referred to the disjunction between goals and means as structural strain, or anomie, a term you encountered in Chapter 2 in the discussion of Durkheim. For Durkheim, anomie referred to the general sense of normlessness that seems to accompany modernization. Merton applied the term specifically to situations in which the normative or legitimate means are irrelevant or unavailable. He hypothesized that, under that condition, people innovate new means to pursue success and that some of those new pathways are deviant or illegal. Thus, the volume of crime in a society reflects the extent to which culturally approved goals and legitimate means are disconnected, and high rates of deviant innovation and crime are found in societies in which the legitimate means are not available to a large segment of the population. In materialistic America, ambitious people from disadvantaged groups who find legitimate means closed to them may pursue success through street crimes, the drug trade, prostitution, or any number of other illegal or borderline activities.

Merton's thinking seems to lead us to the hypothesis that crime and social class are inversely related: the lower the social class, the scarcer and more inaccessible the legitimate means to success, the higher the crime rate. While that relationship probably has some intuitive appeal, decades of research have failed to establish a simple or straightforward relationship between inequality and crime in general. Some studies have found strong associations, but others have determined that people from all social class backgrounds are about equally likely to be involved in crime, particularly when they are young (Title & Meier, 1996). On the other hand, the specific type of crime that is the focus of this chapter—serious street crime—is disproportionately linked to poverty areas in general, especially to minority neighborhoods in which poverty is compounded by discrimination and segregation (Sampson, 1995). We return to the relationship between inequality and crime in the final section of this chapter.

Differential Association

Another strand of criminological theory also began in the 1930s when Edwin Sutherland (Sutherland & Cressy, 1978) addressed the issue of how criminal behavior is learned. At the time, criminal behavior tended to be explained in terms of mental illness and biological factors. Sutherland challenged these understandings by arguing that criminal behavior was learned much like any other type of behavior: through interaction with others and especially in intimate associations with family and friends, as Chapter 4 describes. People learn about crime from the same people and in the same close relationships that they learn about religion, etiquette, education, and work. Although people learn from agents of socialization like school, television, popular music, and church, the most influential teachers are those who are emotionally closest: parents, siblings, kinfolk, neighbors, and close friends.

In these close associations, people learn the techniques of crime (how to hot-wire a car), the conditions under which a criminal act is appropriate ("insults to honor must be avenged"), and a set of rationalizations ("it's OK to steal something that nobody is using") that can be used to assuage any moral misgivings. Sutherland used the term **differential association** as a way of discussing the frequency and intensity of a person's exposure to deviant influences as opposed to conformist influences. The greater the extent to which a person is exposed to procriminal norms, values, and beliefs in their close, personal relationships, the more likely they are to participate in criminal activity.

Exposure to deviant behavior may well increase the probability that one will engage in such behavior. Peers and their norms have a great influence. Many people are also concerned that violent content in movies, video games, lyrics, and Web sites may provoke "copycat" violence.

To illustrate, consider theft: many otherwise noncriminal people learn that, under certain conditions, stealing is not really theft. For example, is someone who takes company-owned office supplies for personal use a thief? How about someone who exaggerates the amount of their charitable deductions on their federal income tax return? Or, what about a customer who gets too much change back from a cashier and doesn't report the mistake? Our culture provides many ready-made rationalizations to explain or minimize the deviance of such petty acts: "The company is so big, they'll never miss these few things." "It's my money anyway—the government will just waste it." "It's not wrong because this store has ripped me off plenty of times. I'm just getting even." In Sutherland's terms, each of these rationalizations is a "pro-criminal" norm or belief. The greater our exposure to such norms (the greater our differential association with deviant norms and ideas), the more likely we are to engage in crime. The greater the extent to which pro-criminal norms pervade a society, the higher the crime rate.

Perhaps one reason why violence is more common in the United States than other industrialized nations is that we are so frequently exposed to violence (in the media if not in "real life") and to norms and beliefs that justify its use. One study in the Los Angeles area found that teenagers of all racial groups and social classes commonly experienced or witnessed violence in the media, their homes, their schools, and their communities (O'Keefe & Sela-Amit, 1997). Such findings are common in the research literature, as is the argument that exposure to violence leads to desensitization and an enhanced willingness to use it in a wide range of circumstances. In Sutherland's terms, pro-criminal norms favoring the use of violence are pervasive throughout the society.

Deviant Subcultures

Merton's anomie theory and Sutherland's ideas about differential association have been combined in a variety of ways by other sociologists. Some argue that groups that are cut off from legitimate means of pursuing success are especially likely to develop deviant or pro-criminal norms that may grow into **deviant subcultures.** People who live in close contact with deviant subcultures are likely to acquire many procriminal definitions, rationalizations, and points of view.

Cloward and Ohlin (1960), for example, argued that illegitimate pathways to success and status vary just as legitimate pathways do. When the socially approved pathways are not available, groups may have access to illicit activities (drugs, prostitution, gambling, and so forth) controlled by, for example, a criminal gang that operates like a business. Those illegitimate means may provide employment and, perhaps, an opportunity to pursue an illegal career. People socialized into a **criminal**

Rima, 19, is considered part of a deviant subculture by many people. She "spanges"—panhandles for change—during the day so that she can drink beer at night. She was once arrested for "criminal trespass" because she and several friends were found sleeping under an abandoned building. She spent five days in jail before resuming her routine.

subculture have access to stable and well-organized illegitimate means of pursuing success, are likely to acquire many procriminal norms, and are likely to view illegal enterprises in ways that differ sharply from the views of the society at large.

In other situations, a **conflict subculture,** in which success and status are acquired through fighting ability and the use of violence, may develop. Violence is also a part of the criminal subculture, but its use in that context is more instrumental and rational. It is used as a form of social control and a method of doing business, to defend turf, punish enemies, avenge insults, and "demote" employees who fail in their duties. In the conflict subculture, in contrast, violence is valued for its own sake and is a central element in competition for personal status. A related idea is that certain sectors of U.S. society—notably the rural South, urban African-American communities, and "macho" Hispanic communities—maintain subcultures of violence: normative traditions that encourage a quick resort to violence in a broad array of situations. (See Cao, Adams, & Jensen, 1997; Ellison, 1991; Parker, 1989; and Wolfgang & Feracutti, 1967 for more on the subculture of violence.)

When both legitimate and illegitimate opportunities are closed, a **retreatist subculture** may emerge. The norms and values of this lifestyle stress disengagement, getting high on drugs or alcohol, and "dropping out." These activities may be illegal in and of themselves and may also stimulate "junkie" crime, thefts intended to generate funds for the purchase of drugs.

The combination of inequality, lack of access to legitimate pathways to success, and subcultural variations in norms and values have been explored in connection with urban poverty and the contemporary urban underclass. In their work on racial inequality, for example, Massey and Denton (1993) discuss the dynamics in the black urban underclass that lead to the rejection of the larger ("white") culture and to the development of oppositional norms and values, some of which may be criminal or deviant (see Chapter 6). Any group that is isolated from the legitimate opportunity structures of the larger society can develop subcultures with strong pro-criminal norms and value systems that invert those of the larger society.

Social Control Theory

Most criminological theories seek to identify the causes of crime. An alternative approach is to seek the causes of conformity: why do most people obey most norms and laws (at least most of the time)? What is it that limits our behavior, controls us, and keeps us from simply taking what we want, wreaking violent revenge on our enemies, or parking in handicapped spots?

One answer to those questions is provided by social control theory as developed by sociologist Travis Hirschi and others (Hirschi, 1969, 1995; Gottfredson & Hirschi, 1990). Hirschi argues that people are restrained and controlled by the strength of their **social bonds** to others, especially to family and peers. The stronger and more numerous the bonds, the greater the stake in conformity, the greater the risk incurred by committing a crime or deviant act. A lone individual with no bonds to others would risk little by participating in a robbery. It would make much less sense

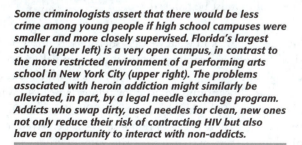

Some criminologists assert that there would be less crime among young people if high school campuses were smaller and more closely supervised. Florida's largest school (upper left) is a very open campus, in contrast to the more restricted environment of a performing arts school in New York City (upper right). The problems associated with heroin addiction might similarly be alleviated, in part, by a legal needle exchange program. Addicts who swap dirty, used needles for clean, new ones not only reduce their risk of contracting HIV but also have an opportunity to interact with non-addicts.

for an individual with strong bonds to many conventional others to commit a similar act.

An example of how social control theory can be applied may illustrate its usefulness. Recall that the rates of serious street crime vary by age, rising during adolescence and young adulthood and then declining. That pattern can be partly explained by the concept of social bonds. In our society, attachment to parents tends to weaken during adolescence, thus "freeing" young people for involvement in deviance. As people move into adulthood, however, new ties form around jobs, spouses, and children, social bonds grow stronger, and the availability for deviance declines. Along the same lines, adolescents who have dropped out of school, have weak ties to family, and have no job are making a lower investment in conformity and have less to lose by involvement in deviance (Hirschi, 1969, 1995).

Controlling Crime

Although they emphasize different points, all the theories described in the preceding section are sociological in that they locate the root causes of crime and deviance not in the nature of the individual but in the nature of society, particularly modern, urban, capitalist society. The theories echo the concerns of Durkheim and other founders of the discipline, but they are also quite contemporary in suggesting that part of the price for the industrialization, urbanization, and modernization of societies around the globe is a rising rate of deviance and crime. That leads to a very important question: What can be done to control the threat of higher crime rates?

Criminologists are not the only ones concerned with issues of crime control. Virtually everyone—politicians, ministers, newspaper editorialists, ordinary citizens—has something to say about how to reduce crime, and everyone seems to have a different opinion. Social scientists, like the general public, are split into various camps and schools of thought. We cannot hope to cover here the full range of ideas and proposals; instead, we examine three key propositions about how to lower crime rates, each of which is currently being debated within criminology, within U.S. society, and around the globe:

Proposition 1: Criminals must be punished more harshly.

Proposition 2: Social control mechanisms must be strengthened.

Proposition 3: Social inequality must be reduced.

In our discussions, we pay particular attention to two schools of thought within the social sciences: the "new penology" and what we call "social disorganization theory." Scholars associated with the new penology focus on the criminal justice system and argue for a get-tough approach to crime. That approach, which is associated with some of America's leading criminologists, including James Q. Wilson (1975, 1983; Wilson & Petersilia, 1995) and John DiIulio (1990; Bennett, DiIulio, & Waters, 1996), arose in the 1970s and 1980s in response to the perceived inability of the American criminal justice system to halt the rising rates of crime. The new penology endorses many popular ideas, including longer prison sentences and the reduced use of parole and probation. The proposition "Criminals must be punished more harshly" is particularly associated with the new penology.

Social disorganization theorists focus more on the causes of crime, specifically on the role of factors such as inequality, discrimination, and deviant subcultures. For the most part, the sociological theories summarized in the preceding section would be included in this approach, and we rely especially on the work of Elliot Currie and Jerome Skolnik, two contemporary American criminologists, in presenting this point of view.

The two approaches differ sharply on many issues, but sometimes the differences are subtle and do not break down into simple, dichotomous pro and con arguments. We should also note that there are other schools of thought in modern criminology and that other criminologists would add other points of view and raise different questions. You can be sure that this section is not the final word on crime and punishment.

Proposition 1: Criminals Must Be Punished More Harshly

We introduced this central proposition of the new penology at the beginning of the chapter when we contrasted the treatment of Michael Fay in Singapore with that of Larry Demery and Daniel Green in the United States. At the heart of this proposition are the related concepts of deterrence (a person's willingness to commit crime can be reduced if the punishment is more severe) and incapacitation (crime can be reduced if criminals are kept in prison).

The idea that the best way to control crime is to control the criminals has a powerful, common-sense logic and is supported by a variety of evidence and research. For example—and contrary to the popular perception that the American criminal justice system is a "revolving door"—the rate of incarceration in the United States has been increasing dramatically for nearly two decades. Graphic 9.6 shows that the rate has more than tripled since 1980; in the opinion of the new penologists, that increase accounts for much of the fall in U.S. rates of crime in the 1990s. For example, DiIulio notes that the cost of crime (for example, the average length of a prison sentence) fell during the 1960s and 1970s and then rose through the 1980s and 1990s, an evolution that matches nicely with the trends depicted in Graphics 9.1 and 9.6 (Bennett, DiIulio, & Walters, 1996, pp. 113–116; see also Reynolds, 1997).

What objections could be raised to the "obvious" connection between a higher rate of incarceration and a lower crime rate? For one thing, critics of the new penology warn that causation and correlation are two different things: just because two variables change together does not mean that one causes the other. It is quite possible that crime rates declined in the 1990s for reasons unrelated to the increase in imprisonment and that longer prison sentences are not the powerful deterrents they seem at first glance. Sociologist Jerome Skolnick (1997, p. 91), for example, suggests a number of factors other than the rising rate of incarceration that might account, at least in part, for the falling U.S. rates of crime in the 1990s.

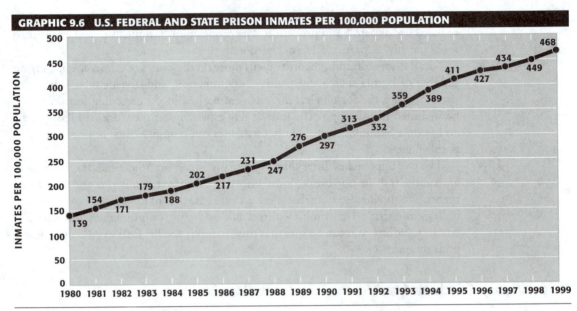

GRAPHIC 9.6 U.S. FEDERAL AND STATE PRISON INMATES PER 100,000 POPULATION

Source: U.S. Bureau of Justice Statistics, 1999.

◆ The age structure of the population has changed. Crime rates rose in the 1960s and 1970s in part because baby boomers (the age cohort created by a high birth rate between 1945 and 1960) were moving through the crime-prone years (ages 15–25). Likewise, crime rates fell in the 1990s in part because boomers had aged beyond the prime years for involvement in crime.

◆ Rates of domestic violence (and killings of spouses) have declined, a reflection of increasing societal disapproval of spouse abuse and more effective intervention by police (see also U.S. Bureau of Justice Statistics, 2000).

◆ Unemployment and rates of poverty are down, resulting in greater social and family stability.

A number of additional issues and questions about the connection between increased punishment and lower crime rates can be raised. First—and again contrary to popular perception—the United States is already one of the most punitive nations on earth. Graphic 9.7 shows incarceration rates for a sample of nations in 1994 (the most recent data available). The U.S. rate of incarceration is exceeded only by Russia's and is roughly five times greater than that of other advanced industrialized societies. Also note that, contrary to the idea that the United States needs to emulate the harsh treatment of Michael Fay in Singapore, the U.S. rate of incarceration is more than double Singapore's rate. Although those patterns certainly reflect the fact that the United States has higher crime rates than other societies,

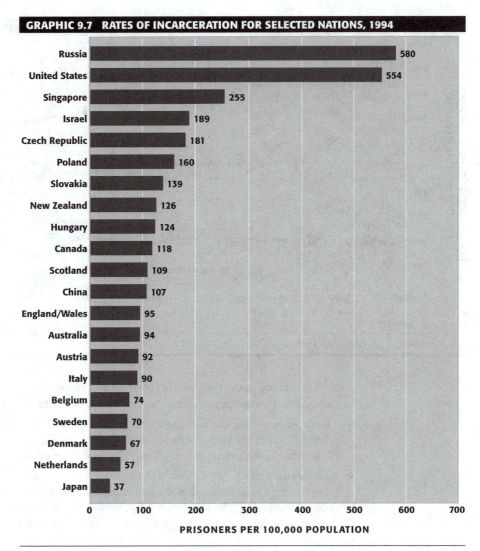

GRAPHIC 9.7   RATES OF INCARCERATION FOR SELECTED NATIONS, 1994

Nation	Prisoners per 100,000 population
Russia	580
United States	554
Singapore	255
Israel	189
Czech Republic	181
Poland	160
Slovakia	139
New Zealand	126
Hungary	124
Canada	118
Scotland	109
China	107
England/Wales	95
Australia	94
Austria	92
Italy	90
Belgium	74
Sweden	70
Denmark	67
Netherlands	57
Japan	37

PRISONERS PER 100,000 POPULATION

Source: Adapted from Newman, 1999, pp. 329–330.

they also raise questions about the characterization of the United States as soft on crime and suggest that the relationship between deterrence and crime is not simple or straightforward.

Most criminologists—both new penologists and their opponents—would agree that longer prison sentences deter crime only if there is some certainty of apprehension. If criminals can reasonably expect to evade the police and the courts, deterrence may well be irrelevant. How successful are the police at apprehending lawbreakers? Some perspective on police efficiency is provided by Graphic 9.8, which

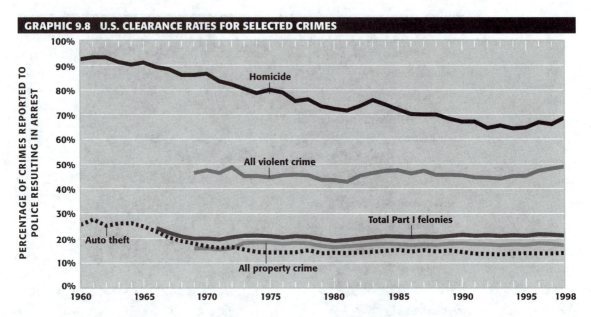

GRAPHIC 9.8   U.S. CLEARANCE RATES FOR SELECTED CRIMES

Source: FBI, 1960–1999.

Note: See Graphic 9.3 for a listing of Part I offenses.

displays clearance rates (the percentage of crimes reported to the police that result in arrest) for various types of crime. Several things about this chart stand out:

◆ The three summary clearance rates (all violent crime, total felonies, and all property crime) are virtually flat over the period, indicating that the efficiency of the police hasn't changed much over the past three decades.

◆ Crime rates (shown in Graphic 9.1) are much more variable than clearance rates (Graphic 9.8), suggesting that the connection between police efficiency and crime rate is weak. The crime rate rose dramatically in the 1960s and has fallen in recent years, yet there is no particular change in clearance rates for either period.

◆ Arrests are much more likely for crimes of violence than for crimes against property. Almost half of all violent crimes and more than two-thirds of all homicides result in an arrest, but fewer than one in five crimes against property have a similar result. Clearance rates apply, of course, only to crimes that are actually reported to the police. When we take account of the large reservoir of hidden crimes, the probability of being arrested for a crime against property falls even lower. If there is less than (or much less than) a one in five chance of being arrested for that type of crime, the deterrent effect of punishment would seem to be weak, and the relative severity or lenience of prison sentences may well be irrelevant.

Deterrence has little effect on some crimes, particularly crimes of violence. Many assaults and homicides occur during emotional conflicts between people who are intimately related (friends, lovers, relatives, spouses) and who are under the influence of drugs or alcohol. The combination of emotion and inebriation clouds the ability to make sound judgments (and partly accounts for the success of the police in solving the crimes). Under those conditions, the deterrent effect of even the harshest penalties—including the death penalty—have little effect: decades of research have shown that there is little connection between capital punishment and reduced homicide rates (Bailey & Peterson, 1999; Sorenson, Wrinkle, & Brewer, 1999).

How can a society in which the rate of incarceration is rising so rapidly still have a high crime rate? Currie suggests an explanation based on what he calls the "replacement effect" (Currie, 1998, p. 30), or the tendency of new criminals to appear even as others are hauled off to jail. The replacement effect is especially evident in crimes like drug trafficking, in which there always seem to be new recruits available to replace those who are imprisoned. Advocates of the new penology agree that replacement tends to nullify the effects of incarceration and that even very large increases in the prison population result in, at best, modest decreases in the crime rate. But, they argue, incapacitation must have some effect. While a street-level drug dealer can be quickly replaced, that may not be true for robbers, burglars, or violent criminals. In the drug trade, there is clear business opportunity, a niche in the marketplace that the leaders of criminal enterprises will want to fill. The

So rapidly is the number of convicts increasing in the United States that a prison-building boom has taken place. The Newton Correctional Facility in Iowa is a new $34 million facility that will house 750 low-risk inmates from overcrowded prisons across the state.

arrest of a thief or a murderer, on the other hand, creates no such "opening" in the job market, and the offender may or may not be replaced.

The effects of incapacitation are also limited because criminal careers have a limited time span. Serious street crime is an occupation of young males, and the aging process affects everyone, criminal and noncriminal alike. If the criminal career of a young male is about ten or fifteen years, then increasing average prison sentences will keep people in prison after they would have stopped committing street crime anyway, and the society will enjoy diminishing returns in safety from an increasingly punitive approach.

Many of the social scientists associated with the new penology would acknowledge the relevance of these arguments. To rely on the criminal justice system alone is to attack the problem at the wrong end; a more comprehensive program of crime control must focus not only on the treatment of criminals but on their production. The next two propositions address the root causes of crime, and once again you will see differences between the new penology, which stresses the breakdown of social control, and social disorganization theory, which stresses factors such as poverty, joblessness, and racism.

Proposition 2: Social Control Mechanisms Must Be Strengthened

James Q. Wilson, a leading proponent of the new penology, believes that the most important cause of crime in the United States and other advanced industrial societies is the breakdown of social control. Part of that argument is reminiscent of other viewpoints previously considered in this book, including Hirschi's social control theory, Durkheim's thoughts about the shift to mechanical solidarity, and Putnam's argument about declining social cohesion in Chapter 3. Wilson argues that the ability of society to control the behavior of its members has grown weaker because of the profound changes that flow from modernization, rapid technological development, urbanization, and higher levels of education and individualism. Modern society encourages personal freedom and self-expression, and the ability of the family, schools, and the state to sanction and limit individual behavior has grown weaker. Self-discipline and the ability (and willingness) to control impulses have declined, and individuals are freer than ever to pursue self-gratification. Although greater individual freedom has manifested itself in artistic creativity, an enhanced spirit of experimentation and entrepreneurship, and more freedom for alternative lifestyles, it also has led to a pervasive and worldwide increase in crime and deviance (Wilson & Petersilia, 1995, p. 491).

In support of Wilson's argument, consider the collapse of the totalitarian, dictatorial Soviet Union and other communist regimes in Eastern Europe in the early 1990s. When those massive, state-operated systems of repression collapsed, crime rates soared. As institutional structures grew weaker, crime and deviance of all sorts—street crime, sophisticated white-collar swindles, political corruption, drug use, and organized criminal syndicates—increased rapidly, exactly as social control theory and the new penology would predict (Frisby, 1998; Gray, 1996).

A weakening of the ability of institutions to constrain behavior and a decline in attachments to others affect all segments of society, according to Wilson, but their power can be greatly magnified by other social forces. For people who generally are law abiding, declining controls may result in modest increases in law breaking: a few more office supplies appropriated for personal use, a few more exaggerations on the tax return, and a lower probability of correcting cashiers' mistakes. However, when weaker controls interact with the alienation of the urban underclass in a setting in which powerful firearms are readily available and pro-criminal norms and role models are highly visible, the possibilities for explosively high rates of violence and criminality are obvious (Wilson & Petersilia, 1995, p. 493).

A variation on that theme was offered recently by another spokesperson for the new penology. John DiIulio argues that the root cause of crime today is not economic poverty but moral poverty: "the poverty of being without loving, capable . . . adults who teach you right from wrong" (Bennett, DiIulio, & Walters, 1996, p. 56). He argues that the probability that a child will grow up to be a career criminal is strongly related to the number and quality of relationships the child has with positive adult influences from parents, teachers, coaches, clergy, and others (p. 60). After presenting a variety of evidence and anecdotes to support that proposition, DiIulio concludes that, to further reduce crime rates in the United States, we must revitalize civic institutions and organizations, strengthen family, religion, and other institutions, reduce the rate of teen pregnancy, and rescue children from abusive situations.

Other social scientists posit a number of objections to that line of argument. Of course, responsible parents, functional families, and cohesive communities are desirable, and their increase almost certainly would reduce the crime rate. The question is what causes breakdowns in social control and how might solutions reasonably be pursued? Social disorganization theorists look for answers not in religion or traditional family values but in the structure of modern industrial, capitalist society, an argument that brings us to our third proposition.

Proposition 3: Social Inequality Must Be Reduced

Social disorganization theory argues that the uneven distribution of opportunities and resources are the root causes of crime. Currie, consistent with Merton and others, argues strongly that the most important and fundamental cause of America's high crime rates is high levels of inequality among different social groups. Currie argues that U.S. crime rates rose in the 1960s because the prosperity and increasing opportunities of that era were unevenly spread across the society. Especially for the urban poor and minority groups, the changing economy meant not greater affluence and mobility but "new forms of disadvantage and blocked opportunities," and the exclusion of those groups was increased after the Great U-Turn (see Chapter 5) that began in the 1970s (Currie & Skolnick, 1997, p. 333). The groups toward the bottom of the American social class system, including the so-called urban underclass, have grown more disadvantaged in recent decades, and they are the groups most disproportionately involved in serious street crime.

Currie points to a variety of research findings in support of this proposition.

◆ Economic inequality and rates of violent crimes are correlated cross-nationally and within the United States. The nations, states, and cities that have wider gaps between rich and poor tend to have higher rates of violent crime (Currie, 1985; Gartner, 1990).

◆ Severe poverty amid affluence is strongly associated with high rates of serious street crime, especially when the poor are highly concentrated in isolated neighborhoods. The relationship between crime and poverty is further strengthened when racial and ethnic discrimination is added to the mix. The recent history of South Africa provides an example of those relationships. The end of apartheid meant the end of rigid controls on the freedom and mobility of the black population. Previously, blacks were allowed in South African cities, where the white population resided and ran their businesses, only during the day and only under conditions of extreme restriction. After the collapse of apartheid, the historically very poor, oppressed, and powerless black population could move freely in the wealthy cities. The combination of the end of rigid controls and a history of extreme inequality led to a rapid increase in crime. Many interpreted the crimes as racial in nature (black versus white), but they also had very strong economic dimensions. (See Louw, 1997, and Ransdell, 1995, for more on crime in South Africa.)

◆ There is an important relationship between joblessness and unemployment and the rate of serious crime. The people who commit serious street crimes and who are filling our prisons are very likely to be not only poor but also persistently unemployed (Grant and Martinez, 1997). They have little "economic viability," or reasonable chances for legitimate jobs that pay well and offer some security, and have rarely, if ever, held a decent or stable job (Currie & Skolnick, 1997, p. 342). One reason that the rate of serious street crime is high in spite of increasing incarceration is because of the decline of the job market for young, relatively unskilled men caused by the shift to a postindustrial economy. The demise of the industrial sector and the increasing importance of education for economic viability have reduced the "already weak opportunities for the kind of solid economic future that can reliably offer an alternative to crime and drug dealing" (Currie & Skolnick, 1997, p. 343).

Although modern societies might suffer from weaker institutions of social control, the key causes of higher criminality are inequality and the limited access of some groups—the disadvantaged in general and racial minority groups in particular—to legitimate means of success.

Implications of the Propositions

Despite their differing perspectives, new penologists and social disorganization theorists broadly agree on many specific ideas for preventing crime and lowering the crime rate. For example, Wilson and Currie agree that the family (not the criminal justice system) must be the focus of effective crime prevention and that interventions in the lives of the children of high-risk families must begin early. They base that conclusion on data about families like those presented in Chapter 8.

Wilson, an advocate for the new penology, believes that the problem is basically one of behavior and that the goal of family assistance programs must be to develop greater self-restraint and impulse control. Because the problems that increase the risk of delinquency and criminality are multiple, programs must address the entire family structure, intervene on many levels, and deal with a variety of risk factors, including nutrition, parenting skills, order and discipline, school, and drug problems in the home (Wilson & Petersilia, 1995, p. 504).

In Wilson's view, households headed by single females are especially at risk. The illegitimate birth rate must be lowered, especially when the mother is young and lives in an impoverished, disorganized neighborhood. Wilson remarks that the illegitimate children of poor, teenage mothers are being given "early admission to the underclass" (Wilson & Petersilia, 1995, p. 505), and he advocates strong programs, such as group homes, for teenagers who are pregnant and poor. But, he adds, the problem is not poverty per se but behavior: irresponsible males sexually exploiting young females and then ignoring their parental duties. The uniquely high rate of violent crime in certain urban areas in the United States is a direct result of the high concentration of illegitimacy, absent fathers, and the lack of legitimate opportunities.

Currie, a social disorganization theorist, agrees that family is crucial but notes that there is considerable disagreement about exactly how the family affects a person's involvement in crime and delinquency. Although Currie agrees with Wilson that the children of broken families face greater risks of delinquency, he argues that the problem is not simply the absence of the second parent but a matter of resources and quality of life. Households headed by single females, especially those of minority group members, are very likely to be poor and to lack the resources to provide a nurturing, supportive environment for their children. More important than the structure of the family is the social context in which the family exists. "What goes on in families cannot be understood apart from what goes on outside them" (Currie, 1998, p. 141).

Wilson and Currie agree that a large part of the problem is the concentration of at-risk families in neighborhoods that are isolated from the rest of society. Currie is concerned that increasing inequality bodes poorly for the future, and Wilson fears for a society that incorporates communities that are growing increasingly permissive and undisciplined. Both social scientists note that programs that provide a wide range of support to low-income families can substantially reduce serious street crime, but they also doubt that the nation has the political will to implement such programs. Instead, Americans will continue to rely on the criminal justice system especially prison, to control crime, however limited that approach proves to be (Wilson & Petersilia, 1995, p. 507).

Given their agreement on several important points, it may seem that the differences between Currie and Wilson are relatively trivial. Consider, however, the implications of their viewpoints. Currie's position—that inequality is the root cause of crime—leads directly and easily to a critique of American society as unfair and unjust. If the problem is too much inequality, then something is fundamentally wrong. That approach can lead to other critical questions: Why is U.S. society so unequal? Who benefits? To what extent is capitalism, with its emphasis on consumption and acquisitiveness, at fault? If the desire for material success motivates crime, what motivates the desire for material success? Why do people in the United States equate their personal worth with their material possessions? Does the ideology of consumerism and individualism generate the criminal impulse? If so, U.S. society itself is in a sense criminal, and any serious attempt to deal with crime must also deal with some fundamental realities of life under capitalism.

Wilson's position—that the problem is the decline in social control and the resultant bad behavior of some individuals—is more conservative in the sense that it tends to lead away from any fundamental criticism of modern U.S. society. From Wilson's viewpoint, the system need not be changed so much as tightened up. If reasonable levels of control and discipline could be restored, crime rates would fall and the problem could be resolved without touching class structure in the United States or the ideology of consumerism and capitalism.

Thus, what might seem like minor differences in emphasis can lead to major differences in views of society. Currie's argument can lead to a highly critical view of modern society and a more drastic agenda for change. Wilson's position can lead to the view that crime is a symptom of a society gone soft and permissive and that what is needed is more effective regulation of individual conduct. As we have seen, strong, fact-based arguments can be made for both viewpoints, and the disputes between those (and other) scholars are unlikely to be resolved in the near future. Sociologists and criminologists have been conducting a complex and subtle investigation of crime for many decades; although the disagreements in the field are numerous and important, they would all agree that there are no simple solutions, no quick-and-easy programs that will make the streets safe once and for all.

Conclusion

Is it possible to control crime and lower crime rates? In spite of their differences, many new penologists and social disorganization theorists seem to agree on three general points:

♦ Reforms of the criminal justice system aimed at increasing punishments and getting tough have limited utility. This chapter began with cases that seem, at first glance, to portray punishment in the United States as soft and weak. The realities are more complex, and all serious scholars would agree that the "lock-'em-up" approach will result in, at best, only modest declines in the crime rate. The criminal justice system is just one of the institutions involved in crime control, and it is not the most important one.

◆ Crime will continue to be a problem in U.S. society, and in other societies, unless some fundamental changes in social policy are made. Social disorganization theorists stress programs that address poverty and jobs; they see recent increases in inequality as especially ominous. The new penologists advocate programs to reduce irresponsible behaviors and see the disintegrating mechanisms of social control in modern society as threatening portents for the future.

◆ Social scientists on both sides of the debate mention that the U.S. population is expected to grow younger and thus produce an increase in the number of people in the crime-prone years. Barring drastic changes in the distribution of legitimate opportunities or the effectiveness of social control, crime rates may well cease their downward trend and begin to rise as the new century dawns. Currie (1997, p. 346) concludes that "It behooves us to think hard about what kinds of families we want [our young people] to grow up in, and what amount of stress and deprivation in the lives of children we are willing to tolerate. . ." (Currie, 1998, p. 161). Wilson is more succinct. His advice is simple: "Get ready" (Wilson & Petersilia, 1995, p. 507).

Key Concepts

1. Crime is a violation of the formal norms, or criminal laws, and includes felonies and misdemeanors, crimes against property and crimes against persons, street crime and white-collar crime.

2. In the United States, serious street crimes rose dramatically in the 1960s and 1970s; although they declined through the 1990s, they remain higher than the 1960s rates. There is evidence that crime rates are increasing worldwide.

3. The "typical" U.S. street criminal is a young, minority-group male, a portrait that seems to generally apply worldwide.

4. For over a century, social theorists have predicted a positive relationship between modernization and crime, but the evidence for such a relationship is, at present, ambiguous.

5. Four current theories of criminality are presented in this chapter. Merton's theory of structural strain and anomie links crime rates to the availability of legitimate means to pursue approved goals. Sutherland's differential association theory stresses the process of learning pro-criminal norms. Cloward and Ohlin combine those two theories and explore criminal, conflict, and retreatist subcultures. Hirschi's social control theory argues that criminal behavior is prevented by strong social bonds with others.

6. Ideas about crime control can be divided into two schools of thought. New penologists stress the propositions that greater punishment will reduce and prevent crime and that stricter social control mechanisms are needed. Social disorganization theorists, on the other hand, argue that the true causes of crime lie in such factors as discrimination, persistent unemployment, and high rates of social inequality.

Active Learning

1. Images of Crime: Individual and Group Interviews (Adapted from an exercise designed by Paul Higgins, University of South Carolina, Columbia). In this exercise, you will conduct interviews to learn about and explore the common images that people hold about crime and criminals. Do people share common assumptions? Do those assumptions distort their view of the reality of crime? Do people equate crime only with street crime, or do they have a broader view of those who commit crime and the harm that comes from crime?

a. Outside of class, ask several people (your instructor may specify an exact number) if they would answer a few questions about crime and criminals. It is fine to interview friends, relatives, and acquaintances, but try to include a variety of people. Introduce yourself (if necessary) and explain that you are asking these questions as part of a class project and that responses will be kept strictly confidential.

b. Ask these questions, one at a time:

- When you think of crime, what specific acts first come to mind?
- When you think of a criminal, what mental picture comes to mind?

c. As your respondents answer, record their responses in writing. List in order the crimes and traits they describe (the ones they mention first might be prominent in their minds). Be sure to thank your respondents for their cooperation.

d. Analyze the ordered lists of responses. Do you see any patterns? Were the same kinds of crimes generally mentioned first? Are the lists similar? Do the lists include white-collar crimes as well as street crimes? Misdemeanors as well as felonies (see Graphic 9.3)?

e. How did the respondents describe criminals? What traits and characteristics did they ascribe to criminals? Write down the specific descriptions or a careful summary of what each person stated. How closely do the descriptions match the profile of people arrested for street crimes presented in this chapter?

f. Bring your analyses of the interview responses to class. Break into small groups of four to six people and compare results.

g. As a group, write a composite view of how the respondents think about crime and criminals. The chapter makes the point that when people think about or discuss crime, they usually are thinking about serious street crime. Do your results support that point? How? As a group, write a brief comparison between this chapter's generalizations about street crime and criminals and the summary your group developed.

h. In your group, discuss the following questions: In what ways might the common view of crime and criminals be useful? For example, how might it help people protect themselves from victimization? How might that same view be potentially harmful? Does it help to lower the visibility of the harm done by white-collar criminals? Write up your conclusions. Be prepared to hand in or discuss your conclusions and summaries, as directed by your instructor.

2. Crime and Punishment in the Press: Document Research. In this project, you will use newspapers from the United States and around the globe to further analyze and evaluate the three propositions regarding crime control presented in this chapter. Review the propositions and make sure you understand the differences between the new penologists and the social disorganization theorists.

a. Choose three newspapers: your local paper, a nationally circulated U.S. paper (for example, the *New York Times,* the *Washington Post,* the *Los Angeles Times*), and a paper from outside the United States (for example, the *London Times*). Your instructor may change the number of newspapers or other details of this assignment. Your library will have print copies of these papers, and electronic versions are available over the Internet. Some of the URLs are listed on our Web site (www.pineforge.com/snc).

b. Scan the editorial pages of recent issues until you find a column expressing an opinion about crime or punishment.

c. For each column, make note of the source, the author(s), and any relevant background information about the author. Then write a brief report summarizing the issue discussed in the column and the position and reasoning of the author.

d. Evaluate the opinion presented in the column. How logical is the argument? What evidence (if any) is used? What is the source of the evidence? How convincing is the argument? What specific facts from the chapter can you use to help you evaluate the column? Is the argument consistent with the new penology or the social disorganization theory? How?

e. Bring your report to class and be prepared to discuss your findings or submit your reports, as directed by your instructor.

3. Propositions about the Causes of Crime: Debate. This chapter presented ideas about crime control from the perspectives of the new penology and social disorganization theory. Which school of thought makes the most sense to you? Why? Make sure you are familiar with the three propositions about the causes of crime presented in the chapter and with both theoretical positions.

a. In class, divide up into groups of four to six. Consider the three propositions one at a time. For each proposition, write a brief summary of the position taken by the new penologists and by the social disorganization theorists.

b. Consider the propositions again. For each proposition, each member of the group should state whether the proposition is true or false and explain the basis for his or her conclusion. What piece of evidence is most persuasive? Which logic or argument makes the most sense to you?

c. After listening to and considering the conclusion of each group member, decide as a group whether each proposition is true or false and cite the evidence or argument that was most persuasive to the group as a whole. Write a summary of your conclusions, the basis for those conclusions, and the votes on each proposition. Be prepared to share your conclusions with the class or submit the summary, as directed by your instructor.

4. Death Penalty: Statistical Analysis. In this exercise, you will gather statistical information from the FBI's *Crime in the United States* to see if the death penalty acts as a deterrent to crime. You will try to determine whether states that do not have a death penalty have higher homicide rates than states that do. This exercise is a greatly over-simplified version of the kinds of research projects that sociologists have been conducting on capital punishment and deterrence for decades.

A key challenge to this type of research is making sure that the comparisons are sensible and reasonable. Simply comparing the homicide rates of all states with the death penalty to all states without would overlook the myriad other factors that could affect homicide rates, such as degree of urbanization or poverty rates. Rather, you should match states as closely as possible on all characteristics other than the existence of capital punishment. (See Chapter 3 on experimental and control groups.)

As of spring 2000, thirteen jurisdictions in the United States did not have the death penalty. They are listed at the Web site for this book (www.pineforge.com/snc) along with a form you can use to complete this assignment. Of those thirteen states we have chosen five, each of which we paired with two neighboring states, on the assumption that neighboring states share many characteristics. You can accept our selection of states and our matching states or do your own selection and matching. You will be using the form at our Web site to do some additional research.

a. Go to your library and get the latest edition of the FBI's *Crime in the United States* and an edition from ten years ago. For each state in the list provided at our Web site, note the homicide rate (make sure you get the rate per 100,000 population, not the total number of homicides) for both years and compute the average homicide rates for all death penalty states and all non–death penalty states.

b. For the latest edition, compare the average homicide rates for the death penalty states and the non–death penalty states (columns A and C on the Web site form). Which group of states has the higher homicide rate? Then compare the average homicide rates for the death penalty states and the non–death penalty states for ten years ago (columns B and D). Which group of states had the higher homicide rate?

c. Are the patterns consistent with the idea that the death penalty has a deterrent effect on the rate of homicide? Explain.

d. Do the patterns "prove" anything about the deterrent effect of the death penalty? Explain. (Remember the difference between correlation and causation, as explained in Chapter 3.)

Septiembre, Car

10 Economics and Politics

Does democracy have a future?

The president of the United States and the mayor of Seattle had been eager to have the World Trade Organization (WTO) hold its last meeting of the twentieth century in that Pacific coast city. The WTO was set up by many of the world's governments in 1995 as an organization for reducing barriers to world trade. It was to have the authority to issue rulings and impose sanctions when it found that a policy of any of its member governments (for example, a tariff on imported goods) violated the WTO's mission. In 1999 President Bill Clinton objected to a number of important WTO policies and hoped that convening its next meeting on American soil would give the U.S. delegation more leverage in getting what it wanted out of the organization. The mayor of Seattle wanted his city to host the event to demonstrate Seattle's friendliness to the ever growing structure of international economic connections. In the end, however, the WTO meetings not only did not accomplish any of the U.S. delegation's goals, they embarrassed the city.

The meetings revealed many of the kinds of conflict that have been swirling around global economic life, some of which you have encountered in previous chapters. To start with, there were bitter disagreements between the delegations of the richer and the poorer countries. Some countries, including the United States, hoped to persuade the conference to take a stronger position on labor standards, arguing that countries with poorly paid labor and no enforcement of workplace safety rules had an unfair competitive advantage in exporting their products to countries whose workers had more rights. But delegates from poorer countries like Brazil, Egypt, and India bitterly and effectively resisted such proposals, arguing that they amounted to an effort by richer countries to block imports from countries that could not afford to pay their workers more or to surround their industrial production with costly regulations.

At the same time, the richer countries had many differences with each other. The United States had hoped to get the WTO to take a position against the policy of the European Union (EU) to provide economic assistance to western European farmers, a policy that the United States sees as an unfair hindrance to the competitiveness of its own farmers in the global marketplace. The Europeans, however, not only resisted, they also showed many signs of being increasingly unhappy about importing American meat from animals fed hormones or American vegetables that had been genetically altered (what the French call "Frankenfood").

The TV news found other disagreements, ones more visually striking to catch their viewers' attention. A variety of disgruntled "nongovernmental organizations," to use the phrase endlessly repeated by reporters, had organized public protests. The protesters appeared as divided as the official delegations. Environmental groups protested the inadequacy of the WTO's environmental rules, labor groups (especially from the United States) protested the failure of the WTO to raise international labor standards, and champions of other countries protested what they saw as U.S. world domination. The leader of a French farmers' movement who had recently made a name for himself by driving a tractor through a French McDonald's (and leading a broad farmers' protest against U.S. imports) turned up to denounce U.S. agricultural practices. And some Americans who called themselves anarchists attacked the WTO as an instrument of a newly emerging global tyranny.

The protestors even disagreed on their tactics. Many made their views known through leafleting, petitioning, holding press conferences, carrying signs, chanting, and wearing T-shirts adorned with slogans. Others blocked the delegates' access to meetings. Still others attacked what they called representatives of the new world economy by smashing windows of places like McDonald's and Starbucks. Some demonstrators who were more peaceably minded ended up stationing themselves in front of McDonald's or Starbucks to shield those establishments from the missiles of their fellow protesters (*New York Times,* November 30–December 6, 1999; Smith, 2000).

In the course of those many clashes, attentive readers of U.S. newspapers, few of whom had even heard of the WTO before, discovered how much power the WTO actually has, despite its not having even existed just a few years earlier. Over 130 countries belonged to the WTO at the time of the Seattle conference, and others were hoping to join in order to have a say in shaping the rules of the global economy. The WTO hears complaints by member governments against each other. The hearings are secret, and the three "trade experts" appointed to resolve the cases do not need to justify their findings in public. No one but delegates of member governments has any right to participate, and there is no mechanism for appealing a WTO decision. Already, the WTO has held that particular tariff policies violate its free-trade mandate, and its critics fear that the WTO has the power to issue rulings that challenge labor rights (for example, safety rules), environmental legislation (for example, mandatory antipollution rules for industrial production), and cultural policies (for example, artist subsidies for work in the national language) on the grounds that such policies constitute restrictions on free trade (Barry, 1999; Wallach & Sforza, 1999).

A sea of people crowd downtown during the Seattle Labor March, where they protested against various policies of the World Trade Organization. The city, normally a relatively tranquil community, was stunned by the intensity of the protests.

The turmoil that swirled around the WTO in Seattle brought many issues to the fore: the relations of rich and poor countries in a globally connected world economy; the capacities of citizens to shape government policy; and, perhaps most basic, the differences between those who want to create a more prosperous world by freeing the global economy from political constraints and those who want to find new mechanisms to control the global economy so it does not produce catastrophe for some (perhaps for many).

For social scientists, the multiple conflicts in Seattle revealed a number of new and puzzling questions. Why had nations apparently given up so much power to this new, mysterious, and secretive international body? If an international organization could wield so much power, what would democracy mean? What could happen if influence over economic life passed out of the hands of democratically organized governments toward organizations like the WTO, which have very little accountability?

Those are the central issues addressed in this chapter. You will find that politics and economics often go hand in hand (as discussed in Chapter 2). Remember that culture matters (Chapter 4) and that today's societies have considerable inequalities (Chapter 5). In this chapter, you will see how the governments of national states arose and accumulated economic power, how state power is being altered by rapid globalization, and how governments and citizens are responding to the breakdown of national economic borders. Let's begin with a bit of history.

The Rise of the Modern State

One way of trying to get a handle on how politics and economics are changing in the global age is by casting a look backward. Although many of the Seattle protesters were concerned about the survival of national policies and identities, we must realize that national states have not always been the focus of political and economic life. The national state is a form of government that evolved over time. When we understand some of the key features of the history of political and economic institutions in society, we will be in a better position to understand the changes of the present and to speculate intelligently about the possibilities of the future.

First, let's look at the political systems of the world five centuries or so ago, during the preindustrial, agricultural era discussed in Chapter 5. In the world of 1500, the nature of the governing authorities under which people lived varied enormously (te Brake, 1998). A great deal of power over the daily lives of most people was lodged in locally based authorities of one sort or another—lords, town councils, religious figures, or village assemblies. There might have been a higher authority in the form of a king or an emperor, but that authority was far away. For many people, especially the vast majority who lived in the countryside, a substantial local landowner was usually a more important figure of authority in everyday life than were the agents of a distant monarch, who (apart from the tax collectors) were rarely seen.

In the years after 1500, power came to be organized differently—and ultimately more uniformly—on the basis of national states. The **national states** came to be identified with clearly demarcated territorial boundaries; within its boundaries, each national state came to be regarded as the **sovereign authority,** not subject to some authority higher still. The states assumed a wide variety of tasks, including making war and building armies, maintaining order and recruiting police forces, constructing roads, providing education, assisting the poor, and supervising commerce. They collected the funds to carry out those and other tasks through taxation, taxation in much greater amounts than any governments had collected before 1500. The states deployed symbols of national identity through flags, anthems, commemorative holidays, passports, athletic competitions, the teaching of nationally oriented histories, and support for national cultures.

By the beginning of the twentieth century, all the richer countries of the world were organized as national states, and many other, poorer countries were organized that way as well. But millions of people in Asia and Africa lived in colonies ruled by European powers. After the Second World War, however, most colonial rule came to an end, and a large number of new states came into existence. If you go back to Graphic 6.2, you can see how many countries in Africa alone have become independent since 1950. As a result, by the 1970s, most people on the planet lived in a national state. Each state had more or less precise territorial boundaries that distinguished it from other states, and each state was held to be sovereign over its own territory. That arrangement has had implications for both political life and economic life within societies.

Politics in the National States

The development of national states went hand in hand with many major changes in political life. Effective power over an increasing array of matters passed from the local arena to the central government. The national states all developed powerful bureaucracies that carried out an increasing number of tasks and collected increasing tax revenues to pay for the activities of the bureaucracies.

At the same time in many of the states, conceptions of **citizenship** developed. People were held to have certain rights not because they were members of a particular family, lived in a particular town, or had some distinctive status (like "noble") but because they were members of a community of people under the authority of a particular national state. Citizens sometimes joined together and developed ways to make demands on the increasingly important national governments. Industrialization and urbanization made it easier to bring people together for concerted action to pressure governments. Modern social movements were born out of campaigns to get the states' bureaucrats to take desired actions and the states' legislators to enact desired laws.

If we look at that process over a long stretch of time, we might summarize the results as a sort of bargain: the state got more power and more tax revenues, and in turn the citizens acquired more benefits and rights. In many of the wealthier countries during the nineteenth and twentieth centuries, for example, extensive welfare systems developed. The states were providing services in return for taxation.

In some countries, citizens were also acquiring the especially important right to participate in choosing who would be the holders of power. The growth of the power of the states, then, was eventually followed, in some of them, by greater **democracy.** States were having a far greater impact on daily life, but citizens had some say in who held power. Citizens' representatives, sitting in parliaments and congresses, wrote the laws.

Many of the richer countries have long histories of democratization, and in the last quarter of the twentieth century, many more countries democratized. Graphic 10.1 shows the long list of countries in the latest democratic wave. At the end of the twentieth century, more people in more countries than ever before were living in national states whose leaders were, at least to some extent, accountable to the people they ruled.

The organizational forms, strategies, and tactics of social movements spread even more widely than democratic institutions. By "social movement" is meant an open, collective, sustained challenge to prevailing ways of doing things. Not only did all the world's more democratic states frequently experience organized movements calling for various sorts of changes, even the less democratic states of the world experienced many such challenges to their authority (Markoff, 1996; Tarrow, 1998a; Tilly, 1997, pp. 193–244). By the last quarter of the twentieth century, citizens in many countries were challenging governments on behalf of a wide variety of causes. Petitions, pamphlets, meetings, and demonstrations on behalf of the environment, women's rights, and many, many more issues had become a routine part of political life.

In summary, at the beginning of the twenty-first century, almost all people are living in some territorial state that claims authority over that territory and whose policies are effective to the national frontier. To a considerable degree, power over everyday life is less and less affected by developments in local arenas and more and more by developments in national ones. In many of those states, people had considerable experience organizing social movements to make demands on their governments, and many of those states had adopted democratic political

GRAPHIC 10.1 COUNTRIES THAT HAVE BECOME MORE DEMOCRATIC IN THE LATE TWENTIETH CENTURY

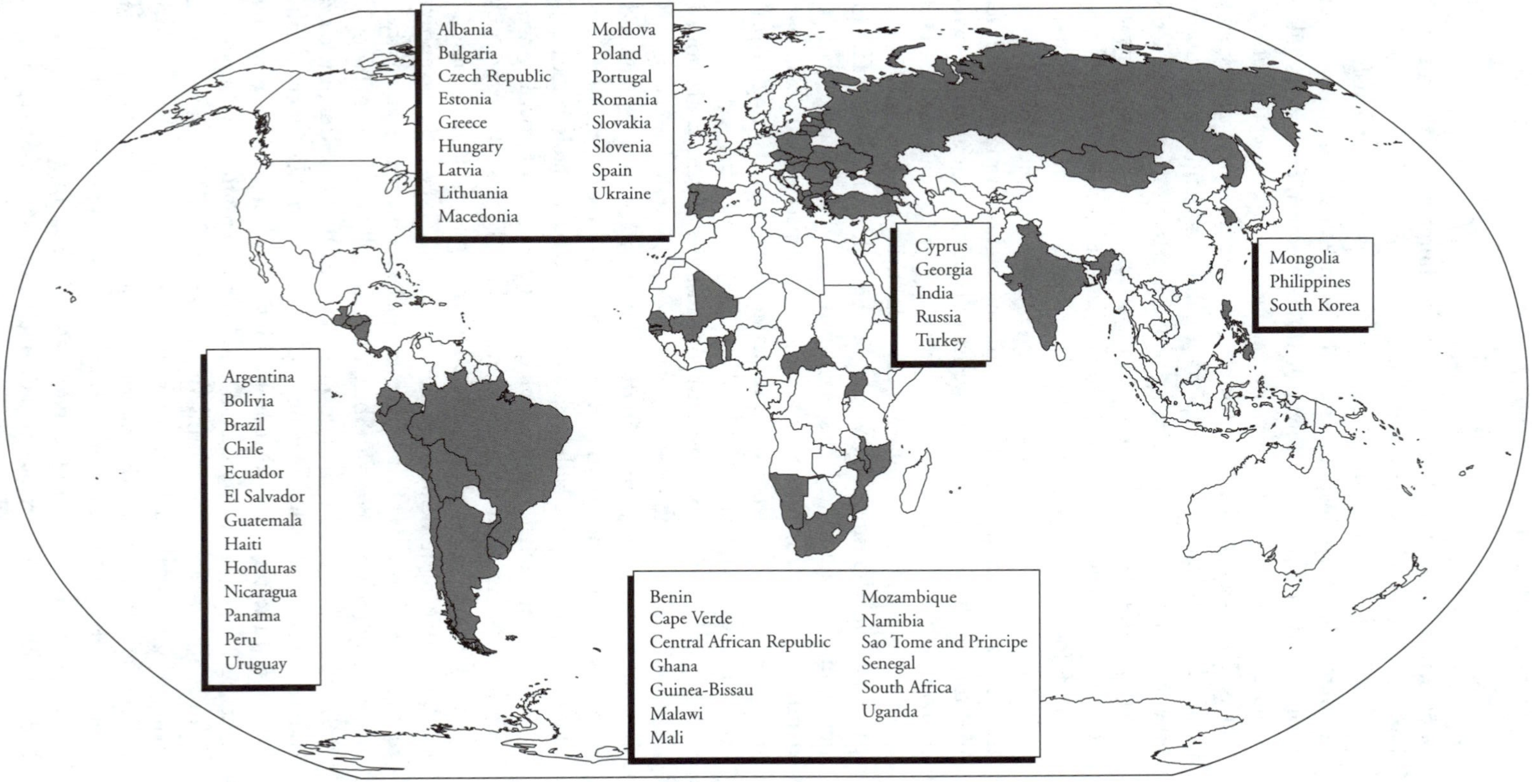

| Mongolia |
| Philippines |
| South Korea |

| Cyprus |
| Georgia |
| India |
| Russia |
| Turkey |

Albania	Moldova
Bulgaria	Poland
Czech Republic	Portugal
Estonia	Romania
Greece	Slovakia
Hungary	Slovenia
Latvia	Spain
Lithuania	Ukraine
Macedonia	

Benin	Mozambique
Cape Verde	Namibia
Central African Republic	Sao Tome and Principe
Ghana	Senegal
Guinea-Bissau	South Africa
Malawi	Uganda
Mali	

| Argentina |
| Bolivia |
| Brazil |
| Chile |
| Ecuador |
| El Salvador |
| Guatemala |
| Haiti |
| Honduras |
| Nicaragua |
| Panama |
| Peru |
| Uruguay |

Sources: Huntington, 1991, pp. 14–15; Gastil, 1989, pp. 50–61; Karatnycky, 1998.

Note: All the countries highlighted here either democratized between 1974 and 1990, according to Huntington, and have not undergone a coup since then or have had a decrease of 5 or greater in the Freedom House index of political rights and civil liberties between 1974 and 1997.

institutions. In a typical high-income state, political life includes a rich variety of arenas for people to press their views:

◆ electoral systems in which organized parties compete for votes

◆ debates between as well as within the many bureaucratic agencies of the powerful state

◆ judicial systems in which individuals, private organizations (including business enterprises), and government agencies carry on disputes with each other

◆ organized attempts, known to political scientists as lobbies, to influence legislators and bureaucrats (often well out of public view)

◆ social movements of people pressing their concerns, as at Seattle, sometimes very much in public view, in the form of demonstrations, blockades, or strikes

Even the less democratic countries have many of those elements. For example, in the People's Republic of China, despite intense official hostility, millions of people are adherents of Falun Gong, a movement for spiritual health, and many participate in public gatherings despite police repression.

Economics in the National States

As the national states dominated or even supplanted local forms of government, they came to have a considerable role in economic life. States impinge on economic life in six broad ways.

◆ *State as enterprise.* All national states employ large numbers of people, purchase substantial quantities of goods and services, and finance themselves through taxation and the borrowing of enormous sums. Those activities profoundly affect what sorts of things are produced, what sorts of job opportunities exist, and how much wealth is available after taxes for other forms of investment.

◆ *State as provider of infrastructure.* The national states build and maintain roads and bridges, operate postal systems and other communications networks, and generally provide the infrastructure for much economic activity. Many essential elements of such infrastructures could not be readily provided in any other way because they rarely are profitable for private entrepreneurs.

◆ *State as shaper of human resources.* States often organize educational systems that produce the next generation of workers, entrepreneurs, administrators, and innovators.

◆ *State as organizer of the legal context.* States provide the police and judicial apparatus without which contracts could not be enforced. Without that background of law, defrauding prospective purchasers would seem more attractive than actually selling them what they want. The state's role in defining the legality or illegality of economically significant activities has an enormous effect on how those activities are carried out or even if they are carried out at all (think about how the manufacture, advertising, distribution, sales, and consumption of tobacco and alcohol are all organized very differently from the manufacture, advertising, distribution, sales, and consumption of other addictive substances that have been made illegal). The state sets regulations that considerably affect the costs of doing business. (Consider, for example, rules about pollution, about wages and working conditions, or about the boundary between enthusiasm and lying in advertising—all of which have enormous consequences for businesses.) One especially important area of state regulation is whether a state enforces, ignores, or prohibits slavery.

◆ *State as warmaker.* States may go to war to obtain or protect access to important resources. Wars can destroy a rival's resources or a state's own. Wars increase state control of the national economy. Taxation, once raised for wartime needs, sometimes long outlives a particular conflict.

◆ *State as maker of economic policy.* In addition to all the other ways that states exert enormous influence on economic life, states may deliberately set out to do so in a wide variety of ways. Those ways include controlling the amount of the national currency in circulation and enacting laws and regulations designed to secure particular economic goals, such as high employment, low inflation, industrial development, economic diversification, investment from abroad, or technological innovation. In pursuit of such goals, states also engage in negotiation with other countries to influence the flow of trade, investment, and workers across national frontiers. At some moments in history and in some countries, states also have owned and managed significant activities, ranging from farms to factories.

The precise character of state involvement in economic life varies from society to society. Economic policies are deeply influenced by the tug of war between power-holders and those trying to influence them, including social movement protesters. In many states, moreover, officials who make those policies either were themselves elected by their fellow citizens or were named by those who were so elected. Either way, in many states there is some significant democratic input into many economically consequential decisions.

Globalization raises important questions about the coming relationship between politics and economics. Those questions were debated in the hotel rooms and over the cell phones of the delegates in Seattle whom the demonstrators had prevented from meeting face to face. But the demonstrators themselves were also using the political influence granted them by the modern state to open up a much wider discussion.

Globalization and the State, Yesterday and Today

People, including social scientists, sometimes speak as though the world has undergone a very recent and very radical transformation known as globalization and is now in many important ways utterly unlike the world of the past. In fact, globalization has a long history. When Europeans began the colonial conquest of non-European peoples toward the end of the fifteenth century, they were quick to set up trading companies that operated on a multicontinental scale. The Atlantic slave trade, which played such an important role in the history of the western hemisphere, brought together peoples from Europe, Africa, and the Americas and created new transnational economic relationships and cultures. Economic and cultural connections that transcend national state boundaries often have been as important as the connections contained within them. Financiers, at many points in history, invested where the profits were, as if their own local identities were an insignificant matter; bankers from Genoa, for example, were extremely important in providing financial resources for the Spanish Empire (rather than financing the economic development of Genoa). So there is nothing especially new about social relationships crossing national frontiers.

What may be most distinctive about recent globalization is the speed and density of cross-border interactions. Tens of millions of people are now hooked into the Internet and are able to send and receive information on a global scale. A great decrease in transportation costs has enabled many more people to move back and forth across great distances, sometimes at supersonic speed, and has enabled vast and complex flows of raw materials and commodities via container ships.

The result has been a proliferation of activity across national frontiers. This globalization has taken place on three levels: the movement of physical objects (from raw materials to manufactured products), the movement of symbols (including entries in bank accounts, documents conferring ownership, and ideas), and the movement of people. The emerging patterns of global mobility seem likely to present a great challenge to the ability of national governments to continue to exercise the kinds of influence over economic life that we have been sketching. The mobility of people and, even more so, of ideas may also be a challenge to state control of political life as well.

The Great Global Mobility of Trade and Investment

In the 1970s, social scientists became extremely interested in what they were calling multinational corporations. Such **transnational organizations** might carry out the extraction of raw materials in one country and manufacturing in a second, transport the manufactured goods to their eventual markets using ships based in a third country, and have distribution outlets elsewhere yet again. It was a difficult challenge for the countries on whose territory the various components of those enterprises were located to monitor the activities carefully enough to collect taxes properly. Moreover, a company based in a country with, say, strict antipollution laws or high minimum wage rates could relocate significant parts of its operation to other countries with a more favorable legal environment while retaining the benefits of keeping other activities, like sales, located near its traditional markets. For example, following the fall of European Communist regimes, foreign firms extended their production into eastern Europe by purchasing or constructing local factories. Postcommunist governments were selling off state-owned resources, often to foreign firms that got bargains, including access to workers who combined high levels of education with low wage demands. For example, to take advantage of those favorable conditions, the Korean auto manufacturer Daewoo bought an existing plant in Poland and the U.S. company General Motors built a manufacturing facility there.

Since the 1970s, however, forms of economic organization have proliferated that are even more difficult for governments to keep track of. Rather than have some single multinational corporation coordinate the various components of transna-

Globalization involves the movement of currency and products across borders. This international banking complex in Frankfurt, Germany (right) houses some of the largest financial institutions in the world. And two fully loaded container ships wait to unload their cargoes at the Hanjin terminal at the Port of Long Beach, California. Combined with the port of Los Angeles, this is the nation's busiest harbor complex.

tional economic activity, the components are connected through a variety of networks without any umbrella organization at all. A great deal of transpacific trade is carried out through networks that link extractors of raw materials, industrial processors, investors, owners of transportation equipment, and dealers who ultimately sell the finished products—and all might be based in different countries. Or an automobile company may have its headquarters in Detroit but farm out the manufacture of brakes to independent contractors in Brazil. One of those contractors might not have all the work done in its own plant by workers on its payroll but hire still another firm—a subcontractor—to do part of the job. Cargo ships, perhaps owned by a Greek company, might carry the brakes to the United States for the final assembly of the car. The U.S. auto company, the Brazilian brake contractor, the subcontractors, and the Greek shipping company might all have significant shares of stock owned by people in other parts of the world, and they might borrow from banks in still other places. All those firms are separate—and we haven't even gotten to the distribution of the finished car.

The new communications and data processing technologies have made it technically feasible for the separate organizations involved in such transnational networks to keep close track of their suppliers and markets. Some of the individual links might exist on paper as a formal contract between a supplier and a buyer, but other links might be based on kinship or friendship or be forged in a face-to-face meeting or over the telephone but not ever written down.

The capacity of governments to keep track of the global flow of investment is especially challenged. Because financial operations largely involve the movement of symbols (words and numbers) rather than goods, their global mobility has been especially enhanced by the new electronic technology. Many observers point out that it is now possible to sit in an office in New York and with just a few keystrokes on your desktop computer move your investments from Thailand to Mexico in response to the news you've just gotten from Tokyo. In fact, if you have a portable laptop, you don't even have to be in your office.

The Considerable but Lesser Global Mobility of People

Workers also flow across borders. The hope of economic opportunity draws many people from poorer to richer countries. In addition, many poorer countries have been the scene of horrific violence—between rebels and governments, as in Algeria and Colombia; between ethnic groups, as in Rwanda; between local forces allied to the great powers during the cold war, as in Vietnam (Chapter 11 expounds on these sorts of conflicts). Millions of refugees from war sit in camps, but millions more have made their way elsewhere, seeking asylum. As one example, roughly one-third of the people who lived in Afghanistan in 1978, at the start of the war between Islamic rebels and the Russian-supported government, were living outside the country in 1988 (Zulfacar, 1998, p. 59). The killing—and the Afghan exodus—was still going on a decade later. (Graphic 10.2 shows just how many refugees sought asylum in Europe in 1999.)

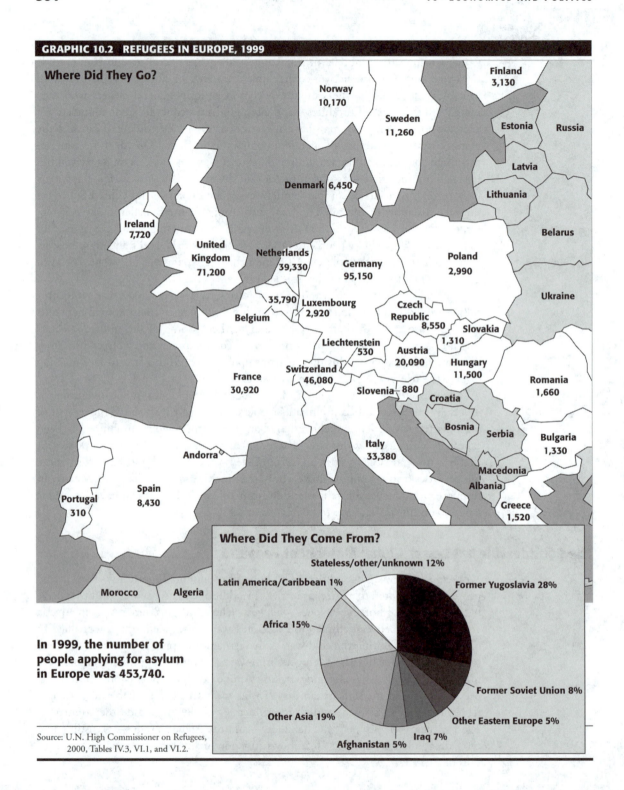

GRAPHIC 10.2   REFUGEES IN EUROPE, 1999

Where Did They Go?

Finland 3,130

Norway 10,170

Sweden 11,260

Estonia

Russia

Latvia

Denmark 6,450

Lithuania

Belarus

Ireland 7,720

United Kingdom 71,200

Netherlands 39,330

Germany 95,150

Poland 2,990

Ukraine

35,790

Belgium

Luxembourg 2,920

Czech Republic 8,550

Slovakia 1,310

Liechtenstein 530

Austria 20,090

Hungary 11,500

Romania 1,660

France 30,920

Switzerland 46,080

Slovenia 880

Croatia

Bosnia

Serbia

Bulgaria 1,330

Italy 33,380

Andorra

Macedonia

Albania

Greece 1,520

Portugal 310

Spain 8,430

Morocco

Algeria

Where Did They Come From?

Stateless/other/unknown 12%

Latin America/Caribbean 1%

Former Yugoslavia 28%

Africa 15%

Former Soviet Union 8%

Other Asia 19%

Other Eastern Europe 5%

Iraq 7%

Afghanistan 5%

In 1999, the number of people applying for asylum in Europe was 453,740.

Source: U.N. High Commissioner on Refugees, 2000, Tables IV.3, VI.1, and VI.2.

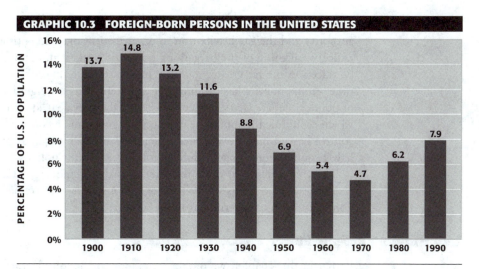

GRAPHIC 10.3   FOREIGN-BORN PERSONS IN THE UNITED STATES

Source: U.S. Immigration and Naturalization Service, 2000.

Americans are well aware of the "new immigration," the recent influx of large numbers of people from places other than western Europe. The French are similarly aware of more than three million Muslims in their country and the Swiss of large numbers of "guest workers." Some of the issues of assimilation and pluralism sketched in Chapter 6 have made the new immigrants more visible than earlier waves of immigrants. Nonetheless, as mobile as people now are, they are not quite as mobile as often suggested. The proportion of foreign-born persons living in the United States at the end of the twentieth century was lower than it was at the beginning of the century. Although their presence rose impressively from 4.7% of the population in 1970 to 7.9% in 1990, it still did not approach the much higher numbers of the first third of the century, as shown in Graphic 10.3. In fact, immigration controls, while not nearly as effective as opponents of immigration would wish, are a great deal stronger than in the nineteenth century, when crossing borders was easier.

Governments can control the flow of people more easily than they can control the flow of money. But both forms of mobility may be a problem for a state and the people living within its boundaries.

Challenges to the Economic and Political Status Quo

In the current era of rapid globalization, societies are facing the challenge of dealing with new global political and economic realities while tied to the old social structures. Four developments in societies all over the world are signaling to social scientists that major change is afoot and creating uncertainty among citizens and political powerholders alike. One development is the erosion of state power and authority and their redistribution to other institutions and entities. A second is the radical weakening of the bargaining power of workers in national politics that can be traced to the far greater mobility of investments than of workers. At the same time, ethnic politics has taken on a new intensity as immigration becomes a focus of political debate (see Chapter 6). Finally, the prevalent ideas about the degree to which economic life should be managed by governments or freed from government control have shifted toward greater market autonomy even as professional experts have acquired much greater clout in forging economic policy.

The consequence of those four trends is that democracy is facing a number of challenges that make its survival less certain just as it seems to have become the predominant form of government in the world.

Reconstitution of State Power

Earlier in this chapter, we took a short look at the long history of national states taking on increasing responsibilities that affected both the daily lives of their citizens and their place among the world's other states. It is a striking feature of the turn of the twenty-first century that power has in some important ways been moving away from the state. Some observers categorize the reorganization of state power as upward, downward, and outward. Graphic 10.4 summarizes those developments, which are described in more detail next.

Upward Reorganization. Political arenas above the level of the national states have been rapidly emerging. States have been entering into agreements setting up a variety of decision-making organizations, like the WTO. Some of those organizations make decisions—as does the WTO—that affect many national states. Others are more narrowly defined, like the North American Free Trade Agreement (NAFTA), set up to reduce national barriers to economic activity among Canada, the United States, and Mexico. One organization, the European Union, has evolved into a true **supranational authority,** making authoritative rulings to which the member states must comply, from issues of how products are to be labeled to decisions about human rights. Such transnational decision-making mechanisms raise considerable doubt about whether national states, each ruling as a sovereign entity over its own territory, are still the basic structure of politics, even national politics.

The decision making of transnational organizations was becoming an increasingly significant matter on the national political scene in many places. For example, a Polish businessman got a judgment from the European Court of Human Rights to the effect that his country's police and judicial authorities had acted improperly in holding him five months without charges (Che ko, 2000). At the same time, a powerful Polish farmers' movement expressed opposition to that country's efforts to join the European Union through widespread road blockades.

Downward Reorganization. As doubts about the quality of national-level decision making grew, many states transferred what had been national-level decision making

GRAPHIC 10.4   RECONFIGURATION OF STATE POWER AT THE TURN OF THE TWENTY-FIRST CENTURY

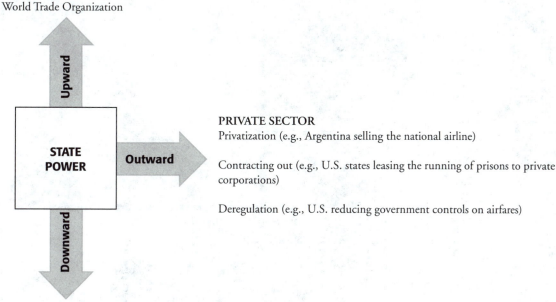

AUTHORITIES ABOVE THE STATES
European Union
United Nations
European Court of Human Rights
World Bank
International Monetary Fund
World Trade Organization

STATE POWER

Upward

Outward

Downward

PRIVATE SECTOR
Privatization (e.g., Argentina selling the national airline)

Contracting out (e.g., U.S. states leasing the running of prisons to private corporations)

Deregulation (e.g., U.S. reducing government controls on airfares)

REGIONAL AND LOCAL GOVERNMENTS
Britain's regional parliaments
France's regional councils
Belgium's powerful regions

to subregions. Some national states, in fact, literally fragmented. In the wake of the overthrow of Communist rule in Eastern Europe, the Soviet Union, Yugoslavia, and Czechoslovakia each divided into separate republics. Out of those three countries, twenty-two new states emerged during the 1990s (Graphic 10.5), and it seemed very likely that there would be further fissioning. In the wake of those events, some observers noticed that complete division was imaginable in a number of other places, including Canada, Belgium, Indonesia, and Great Britain.

Less dramatically, in many high-income countries especially, newly decentralized structures were coming to the fore. Belgium reorganized, transferring a good deal of power to its small number of regions. Great Britain gave new authority to regional governments in Wales and Scotland. France created new organs of regional government, and Italy transferred more powers to its regions. And in the United

GRAPHIC 10.5 NEW NATIONAL STATES SINCE 1989

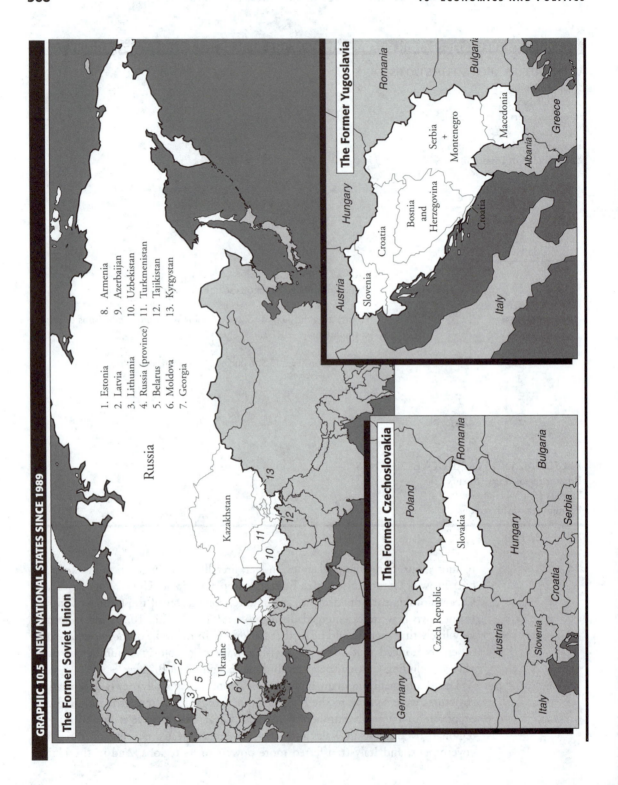

The Former Soviet Union

1. Estonia	8. Armenia
2. Latvia	9. Azerbaijan
3. Lithuania	10. Uzbekistan
4. Russia (province)	11. Turkmenistan
5. Belarus	12. Tajikistan
6. Moldova	13. Kyrgystan
7. Georgia	

Russia

Kazakhstan

Ukraine

The Former Yugoslavia

Austria · Hungary · Romania · Bulgaria · Greece · Italy · Albania

Slovenia · Croatia · Bosnia and Herzegovina · Serbia + Montenegro · Macedonia · Croatia

The Former Czechoslovakia

Germany · Poland · Romania · Italy · Austria · Hungary · Bulgaria · Slovenia · Croatia · Serbia

Czech Republic · Slovakia

States, a majority of the U.S. Supreme Court restricted legislation enacted by Congress on the grounds that it violated the sovereign immunity of the fifty states (Greenhouse, 2000). The court ruled that the national government lacked the authority to enforce rules prohibiting discrimination by an individual state against older workers. The ruling cast into doubt the ability of Congress to issue legislation requiring measures on behalf of women and the disabled as well. Whatever the outcome of those particular questions, the Supreme Court's ruling seemed to indicate that a significant erosion of the authority of the national government over state governments was taking place.

Outward Reorganization. In line with the prevailing view that all sorts of things work better if they are subject to the discipline of the marketplace rather than the supervision of the state, governments are withdrawing from direct control of many activities of great significance for the daily lives of their citizens.

◆ *Privatization.* Embracing the virtues of **privatization,** governments around the world are selling off enterprises they had formerly managed, from factories, shipyards, and mines to airlines. Particularly spectacular in that regard are the countries of eastern Europe, where investors (often including foreigners) and sometimes workers had an opportunity to purchase many previously state-run firms. Because Communist officials were often in a position to know what the good deals were, many took the opportunity to turn themselves into successful capitalists. Latin American governments, as well as others, also have turned all sorts of activities over to the private market.

◆ *Contracting out.* Sometimes governments retain ultimate authority but shift to contracting out some activity. Thus, a city might lease trash collection to a private firm rather than continue to organize it as an activity of the municipal bureaucracy to be carried out by workers on the public payroll. In the United States, a thriving new industry has developed in privately operated prisons. And there is an ongoing great debate about the extent to which the private sector should take over from what are widely seen as failing public school systems.

◆ *Deregulation.* There is also considerable support in the United States and elsewhere for the general notion of deregulation, under which governments give up their claims to issue rules controlling one or another activity that they themselves did not directly administer. But some observers noted an important countercurrent of government action to keep markets competitive by breaking up a few spectacularly large businesses into component parts. In the year 2000, for example, the U.S. government was in court attempting to break up incredibly successful Microsoft, the software giant.

At the beginning of the twenty-first century, the combination of enthusiasm for the private sector, the global scope of communication and economic activity, and diminished regulatory capacity are raising many difficult questions of what governments should do and what they could do.

School districts short on money have turned increasingly to private companies for funding. In exchange for advertising, companies have provided money for computer labs, school transportation, athletic programs, buildings, and other resources. Soft-drink manufacturers as well as apparel and shoe companies are among the leading "donors" to schools.

Weakened Labor Movement

The second major development affecting political life is the general health of the labor movement. The labor movement that emerged in the industrializing countries in the nineteenth century was an important part of democratization (Collier, 1999). By organizing strikes, supporting favorable candidates in election campaigns (and in many places sponsoring political parties), and joining in public protests, the labor movement contributed to the expansion of democratic practice. In the nineteenth century, workers' organizations tended to strongly support the expansion of the right to vote, because they were among those excluded because of insufficient wealth; they often supported voting rights for women as part of a broad movement of the excluded (including women workers); they tended to support expanding the powers of elected parliaments and restricting the powers of hereditary aristocracies and monarchies, which are not accountable to electorates. In trying to satisfy workers, nineteenth- and twentieth-century states enlarged the rights of citizens generally. The labor movement was also a key player in the expansion of welfare rights. Tax-funded pensions, disability payments, unemployment benefits, and public education systems were significant issues for workers (Tilly, 1995).

Today, however, the changing global geography of industrial production, which transfers many factory jobs to places far from the early industrial settings, has shifted the composition of the workforce of the richer countries toward the service sector. Service workers have always been less likely to belong to unions than workers in manufacturing industries, which certainly is a large part of why the proportion of U.S. workers who belong to unions has declined precipitously. (Graphic 10.6 tracks

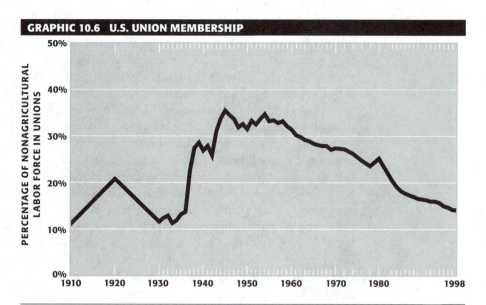

GRAPHIC 10.6   U.S. UNION MEMBERSHIP

Sources: 1910 and 1920 data from Wolman, 1975; 1930–1970 data from U.S. Department of Commerce, 1975; 1971–1998 data from U.S. Department of Commerce, 1974–1999.

Note: Data not available for 1911–1919, 1921–1929, 1971, 1973, 1975, 1977, 1979, 1981–1982, 1990.

the rise and decline of U.S. unionism.) As plants closed in the United States, Germany, France, Great Britain, and other advanced industrial states, formerly industrial towns entered a new and difficult phase. For example, in the early 1970s the steel mills of Pittsburgh provided a nightly fireworks show. Now the mills have largely closed, and a multitheater entertainment complex has been built where a great mill once stood.

But the simple decline in union membership is only part of the story. The greater global mobility of investment has weakened the bargaining power of labor, both directly and indirectly. Workers' capacity to bargain at the workplace, backed by the threat of work stoppages, is significantly reduced in an era in which it is relatively easy for investors simply to take their investments somewhere else, perhaps on the other side of the planet. So, in that direct sense, the global mobility of investment gives investors a new edge in dealing with workers. Workers will not find new jobs nearly as readily as investors will find something else to do with their money. (One wonders whether the kinds of labor conflict we used to think typical of industrial Europe and North America will come to be re-created in newly industrializing places like South Korea [Silver, 1998]).

Indirectly, as well, the gains the richer countries' labor movements won in the nineteenth and twentieth centuries are being threatened, perhaps already being reversed. Remember that national states may be losing control over economic activities that cross their borders and that many activities that had come over the past few centuries to be in the hands of national states were moving upward, downward, and outward. So national states are simply doing less of what workers' movements traditionally have wanted them to be doing. Workers in countries with minimum wage laws, occupational safety rules, and antipollution legislation deal with investors able to move funds to countries without minimum wage laws, occupational safety rules, and antipollution legislation. Moreover, workers in the second country are less likely to be in unions, and their unions are likely to have less clout. The declining position of labor unions is, therefore, more than a loss of members.

A 1990 survey of nineteen high-income democracies documented a remarkable loss of public confidence in labor unions (Graphic 10.7). In western Europe, in fact, only one person in twenty expressed great confidence in unions (Dogan, 1997, p. 29). The political fallout from that loss of confidence was apparent in many countries. Political parties with a long history of appeal to workers were still winning elections and heading democratic governments, but not if they advocated their familiar programs—their leaders talked of the need to change their parties' traditional positions. U.S. President Bill Clinton, for example, as a "new Democrat" championed ending "welfare as we know it." Similar rethinking can be found in Great Britain, France, Spain, and Germany.

One of the great political questions to be faced in the twenty-first century is whether workers can manage to secure the same rights in the new structures of power as they had in some of the national states during the nineteenth and early twentieth centuries. But broad as that question is, it raises one broader still. Because the labor movement, along with other forms of social activism, played such a major role in the democratization of many of the national states, does its current weakness suggest a general weakening of democracy?

New Politics of Ethnic Identity

Chapter 1 noted that ethnicity shapes people's lives. The reorganization of national states goes hand in hand with a renewed emphasis on issues of identity.

As state power passes downward, the shift to greater regional autonomy, as in Belgium, or to outright state breakup, as in the former Yugoslavia, calls into question the rights of those living in the national territory. Group identities are strongly emphasized in the ensuing conflicts. When, for example, Slovene and Croat leaders proclaimed the independence of Slovenia and Croatia from a Yugoslavia dominated by Serbs, they set in motion a decade of murderous violence among Serbs, Croats, Bosnian Muslims, and Kosovo Albanians over who had what kind of rights where (including who had the right just to live somewhere).

As power passes upward, those who identify with existing national states may feel threatened by the claims of new authorities. Many people in Turkey and Poland in the early twenty-first century, for example, fear that the possible entry of their countries into the European Union would mean a significant loss of national autonomy in economic policy, culture, or politics. That fear helps to focus conflict on identity issues.

Such identity issues gain further force from the movements of people across borders. People who move to a country that offers greater safety or prosperity than

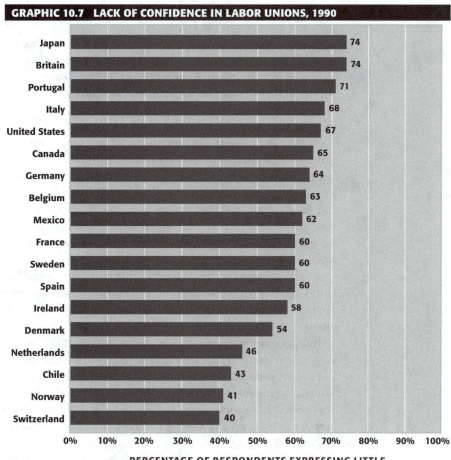

GRAPHIC 10.7 LACK OF CONFIDENCE IN LABOR UNIONS, 1990

Country	Value
Japan	74
Britain	74
Portugal	71
Italy	68
United States	67
Canada	65
Germany	64
Belgium	63
Mexico	62
France	60
Sweden	60
Spain	60
Ireland	58
Denmark	54
Netherlands	46
Chile	43
Norway	41
Switzerland	40

PERCENTAGE OF RESPONDENTS EXPRESSING LITTLE
OR NO CONFIDENCE IN LABOR UNIONS

Source: Dogan, 1997, p. 29.

their native country often bring their culture with them. Some resist giving up their ethnic identity and agitate instead for changes in the host culture. The visible presence of immigrants stimulates debate and conflict among a country's citizens. Some fear that their jobs or their culture is threatened by the new arrivals, while others argue that the newcomers are essential for a prosperous future.

Immigrants often cluster in cities or industries, drawn by friends and relatives who arrived earlier and by a concentration of material and nonmaterial elements that ease their entry into a new culture (Portes & Rumbaut, 1996). That concentration bolsters their ethnic identity and may spill over into their political participation. The political implications are even stronger for immigrants from former colonies of their new home, because they are now living among people who may have the habit of thinking of them as subordinates. Large numbers of Africans from former colonies now live in France, as do Indians in England, Indonesians in Holland, and Filipinos in the United States.

Immigrants sometimes press for their rights in their new home. Muslim immigrants in Britain, for example, have organized to gain recognition for their own culture. And immigrants sometimes press their new country to take positions on the politics of their former home. Immigrants from Cuba, for example, have effectively campaigned for the United States to adopt a wide variety of policies directed against the government of Fidel Castro.

At least as important as movements *of* immigrants are movements *about* immigrants. For example, in Germany fears of cultural invasion by and job competition from Turkish "guest workers" sparked anti-immigrant movements, including violent skinhead organizations to keep zones of certain cities "foreigner free." In France and Switzerland, political parties gain significant adherents around programs of making sure that foreign workers are "kept in their place" or even expelled. In 2000, Austria's Freedom Party waged a successful political campaign in large part around what it called "overforeignization" and entered that country's government, to the great consternation of the fourteen other members of the European Union. In the United States, with extensive numbers of illegal immigrant workers, questions of rights to health care and education for illegal workers' children have generated intense passion on all sides.

Immigration issues are likely to be important in the high-income countries for a long time to come. These countries have very low birth rates and aging populations. In Italy, for example, by the early 1990s the birth rate had fallen to 1.3 children per woman, far too low to sustain the Italian labor force without immigration. Without new arrivals from somewhere, it will not be possible to support the increasing numbers of elderly people in the high-income countries, and it is generally from poorer countries that those new arrivals will come.

The renewed salience of ethnic identities in the richer countries has added to the debates over welfare systems and other social benefits. The provision of services by national governments is, as we have seen, being rethought. The new ethnic consciousness gives considerable impetus to the process. If we think we are all citizens, all fellow nationals, we might willingly contribute to collective needs and consider government agencies appropriate organizers of such collective provision. We will all pay taxes, and we will all use the roads, send our children to the schools, be protected by the police, have access to the medical services, in old age avail ourselves of public support, and have access to unemployment and disability benefits.

But now imagine that we begin to think that in our country there are people who really belong, who are of our kind, but that others do not belong. Although it is "our" country, "they" have access to services paid for by "our" taxes. We would be even less likely to be keen on state provision of services. We don't want to pay for their children's schooling, support them when they are out of work, or pay for their old age. For example, as the Dutch find darker-skinned people from their former colonies of Surinam and Indonesia on their welfare roles, they have begun to rethink their extremely generous (comparatively speaking) welfare policies. In the

Immigration has altered the ethnic identity of countries and communities around the world. The top photo shows a small workshop inside the housing project where Malian immigrants now live and work in a Paris suburb. At left, two Somali girls, ages 5 and 6, laugh during Saturday religion class at a mosque in Fargo, North Dakota. Six hundred Somali families now live in Fargo. Of course, some issues related to ethnic identity have been visible for years and are not the product of recent immigration. In Rhode Island, a group of Narragansett Indians protest their treatment by government officials.

United States, the Welfare Reform Act of 1996 restricted the right of immigrants to income benefits and food stamps. Thus, thinking about ourselves as members of separate—and possibly mutually antagonistic—groups strengthens the tendency to let the private arena "do the job" (we'll pay for ourselves, thank you). In turn, the tendency to let the private arena do the job decreases the sense that we are all in the same boat as far as subjection to state authority and benefiting from state programs are concerned. The new politics of ethnonational identifications in the richer countries and the new politics of individual initiatives (as opposed to collective policy through state action) turn out to be mutually reinforcing.

There is reason for hope, however. Notions of mutual respect among differing cultural traditions, of acceptance of the diversity of the world's peoples inevitably brought together by the world economy in the global age have suggested new ways of thinking and have raised the possibility of altering our very notions of citizenship. In Germany, for example, anti-immigrant violence stimulated demonstrations in support of immigrant rights and cultural difference. That grass-roots political activity was followed by new legislation making it easier for immigrant workers' children who grow up in Germany to acquire citizenship. Moreover—and more broadly—notions that people have rights as human beings rather than just as citizens of particular states are increasingly under discussion for many reasons, including reaction to ethnic conflict in places like Serbia.

State Management of Economic Life

If we were to sum up the relationship of national politics and global economics, we would not want to stop at saying that the national states are unable to manage the changing world economy; we would have to add that in certain important ways those in power have stopped wanting to manage it. At the beginning of the twenty-first century, many prestigious and powerful economists, including economists in government service, favor a retreat from state action in several important arenas.

Economic theorists have for a very long time been concerned about the best relationship between states and markets. In one extreme version, the less we can imagine the state doing, the better. In that view, the wish of individual human beings to improve their own situations is the wellspring of human progress in general and of economic growth in particular. To the extent that people are free to innovate, build, manufacture, and sell as they see fit, they will make things that others want to buy, invent new things, and ultimately create new kinds of wealth that will allow everyone to become more prosperous. We can label this first position **market autonomy:** the state is to leave the market be.

A radically opposed perspective argues that the unguided marketplace merely enriches some people while it impoverishes others. Moreover, all sorts of useful things will not get done because no one can make a profit doing them. In this second view, what is needed is intelligent supervision of the economy by democratically chosen government officials, so that the economy works for purposes decided by human beings in some political process. Let us summarize the second position as **state intervention.**

Proponents of the market autonomy view maintain that states are inevitably inefficient. According to that position, states seize things for themselves, and political elites are as self-interested as the rest of us and inevitably use state power for self-aggrandizement rather than for the common good. Market autonomists go on to say that those with the power to supervise economic life will never have the wisdom to supply what people want nearly as effectively as the marketplace does. Those who favor state action counter that the unhindered marketplace provides not so much what "the people" want as what wealthy people and wealthy organizations want. The argument has gone on for a very long time. (In Chapter 2 you read about how one piece of this enduring debate—Karl Marx's critique of nineteenth-century capitalism—contributed important ideas to sociological thought.)

In the period immediately after World War II, the dominant currents of economic thinking in the higher-income countries—like the United States, Great Britain, and France—lay somewhere between the two poles. There was a place for the market, but there was also a strong place for social and economic policies to guide the market in desired directions. Many economists held that government taxation and spending patterns could guide national economies, a position often associated with the British economist John Maynard Keynes. Others favored significant investment in development projects for the purpose of rebuilding a war-torn Europe; still others favored development projects for the purpose of achieving economic growth in Asia, Africa, and Latin America.

We can summarize those actions, both within a single country and across that country's borders, as **redistributive policies:** resources collected through taxation were to be redistributed to the aged in the form of a government pension plan, to the poor in the form of welfare, and to poorer countries in the form of development assistance. It was believed that such spending would actually trigger more economic growth as a whole. If poorer people could buy more, then manufacturers could sell more and in turn employ more people (who in their turn could buy still more); if poorer countries could produce more, then they would have the funds to buy more of the goods manufactured in richer countries.

During the same period, other governments had their own ideas about state involvement in economic life. The eastern half of Europe, dominated by the Soviet army, put into place systems of economic management—known as socialism—that were dominated by the government and that allowed very little scope to the market. Similar systems came to triumph after civil wars and revolutions in China, Southeast Asia, and Cuba. Some governments in other poorer countries were also attracted to socialist notions, which they hoped would provide some way to achieve economic progress. But even where socialist models were rejected, many governments in Asia, Africa, and Latin America were attracted to the idea that careful government planning of investment, currency values, and tariffs would more likely lead to superior results than would reliance on the market alone.

By the last decade of the twentieth century, such socialist and interventionist ideas were in general disrepute virtually worldwide. Communist regimes with their socialist economies had collapsed in Europe, and new governments proclaimed their attachment to the market. The Communist regimes in Asia began to promote many market elements while successfully maintaining political control. China, to take one important example, allowed far more scope than previously to private initiatives in agriculture, encouraged foreign investment, and began producing goods that people (including people in western countries) actually wanted to buy.

In the richer countries, the economics profession repudiated the theories that justified state management and argued for turning over economic decision making to the private sector. The benefits of free trade across borders was increasingly attractive. In many countries in Asia, Africa, and Latin America, the policy of economic development led by wise state managers was facing failure.

That was a radical shift in ideas about economic policy making. In rich and poor countries alike, political leaders were proclaiming that what was needed was less state, more market. Government was to limit itself to its proper sphere, and economies were to run themselves. The proper sphere of government suddenly seemed circumscribed. One could imagine, for example, private companies competing for tax dollars to run prisons or schools or the replacement of Social Security with privately managed pension funds that would compete with each other to attract investors.

In that climate, many championed freer trade and freer investing across borders, including many in governments. The global economy did not simply erode the ability of states to manage an economy crossing their frontiers: people in power in the states encouraged the building of a global economy. But if economies were to be free from state control, who better to orchestrate economic policy than professional economists? As you will see in the next section, the increasing power of experts in the making of economic policy, particularly in conjunction with the other trends we have been examining, challenges notions of democratic input into political life.

Threatened Democracy

The extent of democratization that has taken place over the past few centuries is impressive. Where there used to be hereditary monarchs and aristocracies, limited public debate, little influence over government policy, and narrowly defined notions of citizens' rights, there are now elected representatives, considerable public debate, electoral accountability of government leaders to citizens, and extensive personal rights. In a more recent perspective, we should be impressed by how many countries have adopted democratic institutions since the mid-1970s. Nonetheless, the processes discussed in this chapter have generated a number of important challenges to effective democratic rule, and some of those challenges are quite novel. This section points to just five of those issues. You will recognize the first four from the preceding discussion of the changing nature of national politics in a global age; the fifth is to some degree a consequence of the other four.

◆ The declining political weight of organized labor has weakened one of the important democratic forces that political elites have long had to reckon with. The advantage of investors over wage earners seems an inherent aspect of the world economy in the global age—inherent, that is, in the absence of concerted political actions to gain control over investment flows. Those who hold power in the national states might wish to regain some of their leverage over the economic activity that flows across their borders. But powerholders seem to be thinking in exactly the opposite direction: how might they push decision making upward, downward, and outward? Thus, trends in state policies seem likely to weaken labor's position further.

◆ Continuing conflict over questions of national identity, in the form of debates about the place of immigration and of minorities in national life, provides fertile ground for openly antidemocratic movements aimed at removing "alien" influences. Another potential danger is that minority groups will stop hoping for gains from the current political process and instigate separatist movements, a form of political conflict often difficult to handle in a democratic framework. Members of ethnic minorities may regard the state's claim to democracy as a fraud or even reject the existing state—whether democratic or not—as a framework for expanding their rights. Members of majorities may aim to shut down the democratic practices that have given the minorities some rights.

◆ Many states have been giving increasing responsibility over economic policy to professional economists. In the 1980s and 1990s, holders of degrees in economics held the highest political office in a variety of national states, including Chile, Greece, Turkey, Ireland, Holland, Taiwan, India, Mexico, Colombia, Guyana, Italy, and Rwanda (Markoff & Montecinos, 1993). Professionally socialized to hunt for optimal solutions to abstractly formulated definitions of economic issues, these leaders have a common outlook forged in graduate seminars, reinforced by international conferences and professional journals, and are to a considerable degree devoted to economic doctrines that support the openness of national economies to the global marketplace. Early-twentieth-century sociologists and political scientists saw the continuing growth of the great central administrations of national states to be a significant challenge to meaningful democracy. How, they asked, could such vast, inert, secretive, and solitary bodies as state bureaucracies be made accountable to voters? The recent professionalization of economic policy poses in a new form the challenge of how to hold expert decision makers accountable to citizens, a problem all the more difficult when those experts are achieving considerable consensus among themselves and all the more important when what is at stake is something as significant as economic policy.

◆ A more subtle and even more novel possibility is that effective power over basic aspects of the global economy will be lodged in supranational structures that lack democratic accountability. In this scenario, more countries may adopt democratic practices, yet the meaningfulness of democracy will be sorely tried. In the late 1990s, for example, the WTO and similar bodies—whose decision-making processes are largely shielded from public view, whose delegates do not

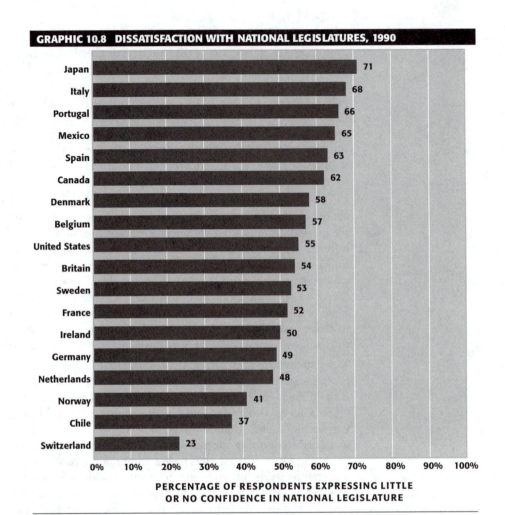

GRAPHIC 10.8   DISSATISFACTION WITH NATIONAL LEGISLATURES, 1990

Country	
Japan	71
Italy	68
Portugal	66
Mexico	65
Spain	63
Canada	62
Denmark	58
Belgium	57
United States	55
Britain	54
Sweden	53
France	52
Ireland	50
Germany	49
Netherlands	48
Norway	41
Chile	37
Switzerland	23

**PERCENTAGE OF RESPONDENTS EXPRESSING LITTLE
OR NO CONFIDENCE IN NATIONAL LEGISLATURE**

Source: Dogan, 1997, p. 28.

have to justify themselves to voters, and whose decisions people have very little capacity to challenge—were gaining authority over the policies of national states. In the global era, it seems, power is passing from the national states and being lodged in transnational structures that are accountable to no one and have no citizens.

◆ Public disappointment with the reality of democracy is spreading, very likely in part as a consequence of the previous four trends. In 1995, at least 40% of those questioned in a European survey on how satisfied they were with democracy in their own country answered "not satisfied" or "not at all" in Italy, Portugal, Greece, Spain, France, Britain, Belgium, Finland, and Sweden. In another survey in 1990 (see Graphic 10.8), in 13 of the 18 nations surveyed, 50% or more had little or no confidence in their nation's legislature (Dogan, 1997,

p. 26–27). The United States is no exception. When asked in the 1960s if they thought that "most elected officials don't care what people like me think," two-thirds of Americans disagreed; when asked the same question in 1998, almost two-thirds were in agreement (Pharr & Putnam, 2000, p. 9).

Despite those threats, democracy has not been discredited in principle. On the contrary, in many countries, including the same countries where dissatisfaction with democracy in practice has run strong, democracy is accepted as superior to any alternative. In Spain in the mid-1990s, for example, a scant 5% declared themselves "very satisfied" with how democracy was working, but four in five agreed that "democracy is the best system for a country like ours" (Dogan, 1997, p. 28; Montero, Gunther, & Torcal, 1997, p. 127).

Attempts by States (and Their Citizens) to Control Globalization

Modern governmental bureaucracies grew within the framework of the national states. But so did mechanisms by which people outside government could influence government action. In our time, globalization is creating transnational political and economic structures that challenge the power of states and citizens to control their destinies. We are witnessing efforts to regain control, efforts that themselves have a transnational character.

Government Organizations

States have sometimes cooperated for joint enrichment. For example, in 1494 Spain and Portugal agreed on how to divide up the world. In 1884, many states agreed to British notions of how to classify the world into twenty-four standard time zones. In the twentieth century, states have set up a large number of permanent organizations for mutual benefit, such as the World Trade Organization.

The sense that individual governments could not manage the issues that confront them has been a powerful spur to such cooperation in the twentieth century. After the catastrophes of the First and Second World Wars, the hope of avoiding war spurred the creation of the League of Nations and then the United Nations. Concern for post–World War II economic reconstruction, which to some meant not only rebuilding a devastated Europe but also encouraging economic development in poorer countries, nurtured two powerful international financial institutions, the World Bank and the International Monetary Fund (IMF). Toward the end of the twentieth century, there was much talk of implementing a powerful international human rights tribunal, but thus far institutions of that sort have remained limited.

One of the most interesting international creations is the European Union. Coming out of the ruins of World War II, some European leaders held that future war might be less likely if neighboring countries had a stake in each other's prosperity. Thus was born the six-member European Coal and Steel Community in 1952. Today the much enlarged European Union has a vast bureaucracy of its own ("the Eurocrats"), writing thousands of rules that govern the details of economic life. Most member states have abandoned control over their own currencies (for centuries an important element of national sovereignty) and are using the Union's common currency, the Euro. European courts are now striking down national laws on matters of human rights as well as on labeling of products like cheese or wine. A court that is separate from the European Union, the European Court of Human Rights, also has considerable influence. After the court ruled that barring gays from the armed forces violates human rights, the British had to bring their laws into line. The German military found that, for the same reason, it would have to afford women in its armed forces the possibility of filling roles previously restricted to men (Cohen, 2000; Lyall, 2000).

A float comparing IMF loans to the Trojan Horse. According to legend, the Greeks tricked the Trojans into taking a huge, hollow wooden horse into the city of Troy. The Greeks persuaded the Trojans that the horse would make the city of Troy invulnerable to enemy attack. Little did the Trojans know that the horse was full of armed Greek troops, who helped to capture and burn Troy. The float reminds people that IMF loans, while promising development, actually carry conditions that can cause harm.

To date, no other transnational structure of governance is so serious a challenge to traditional notions of the sovereignty of individual states as is the European Union. Nonetheless, the remarkable proliferation of transnational governing structures is beginning to erode the very idea of state sovereignty. The World Bank and the International Monetary Fund have long had considerable leverage with countries experiencing economic difficulty and have pressured them into adopting a wide range of policies that the transnational financial community sees as desirable. The WTO, as we have seen, attracts considerable attention from social movements that want to bend it this way and that. And claiming defense of basic human rights, the United Nations has sponsored a range of military interventions in weaker states.

Governments are wrestling with what kinds of powers these new bodies should have and what kinds of problems they should address. Consider the question of human rights, for example. The vast killings of the great world wars, the continuing recourse to brutality by many states, and the violence visited against women and children have been brought to the consciousness of many by the ever denser communications networks that circle the globe. A variety of human rights organizations, like Amnesty International and Human Rights Watch, publicize how widespread and how varied the forms of state brutality are. But now governments and transnational political organizations are getting involved as well, spurred to action by genocidal massacre, as in Rwanda, and mass population expulsion, as in the states of the former Yugoslavia. The post–World War II trials of top Nazis for "crimes against humanity" at Nuremberg suggested a model to follow. However, the Nuremberg court was set up in the wake of a specific horror. Today, governments are debating the establishment of a permanent tribunal to review human rights violations wherever and whenever they occur. The United States, concerned about the threat to its own sovereignty, is especially active in trying to limit the scope and power of any such institution.

When we consider the range of significant issues confronting humanity in the twenty-first century, it seems almost certain that there will be further discussion among governments and outside of governments about the creation of still other structures capable of concerted action across state boundaries. There are many significant dangers that seem extremely unlikely to be managed by any state separately or even any group of separate states without the creation of some sort of organization to take effective action. Those dangers include the following.

◆ *Nuclear proliferation.* During the cold war, the United States and the Soviet Union effectively cooperated in avoiding nuclear conflict. By the end of the cold war, however, the number of nuclear powers had risen considerably and shows signs of rising further. The possibility that weapons of mass destruction might be acquired by parties other than governments (including criminals and terrorists) has increased just as considerably. Nuclear proliferation in combination with the numerous sources of conflict in the world seems virtually certain to lead eventually to the use of nuclear weapons. (You can read more about the threat of war in Chapter 11.)

◆ *Environmental disasters.* The accelerating pace of technological change continues to put new chemicals and new combinations of chemicals into our air and water. Air and water tend to be common resources of humanity, not terribly well separable by socially created national frontiers. Waste and refuse dumped into the Danube upstream pollute downriver countries. If auto exhausts in richer countries and forest burnings in poorer ones combine to put enough heat-trapping chemicals into the atmosphere to raise temperatures globally, melting polar ice will flood coastal areas of richer and poorer countries alike. If coal-burning factories in the Czech Republic do not have adequate emission controls, the smoke comes down in neighboring Poland. If a nuclear power plant in Ukraine malfunctions, any radioactivity released into the atmosphere is inhaled and ingested far beyond national borders. (You can read more about environmental issues in Chapter 13.)

◆ *Global economic instabilities.* The disruptive consequences of volatile transnational movements of investment can wreak havoc as booms turn rapidly to busts. The technological capacity for such volatility seems more likely than not to increase, with the expansion of computer networks, individual investors making spot decisions at their PCs, and the probability that stock exchanges will shift into permanent session and no longer break at traditional quitting time.

◆ *Public health issues.* While global economic growth generates new medicines and medical treatments, new threats to health are also appearing. One threat is the lack of access to new health care measures by the world's poor, which you can read about in Chapter 15. Another threat is the likelihood of increased contact with infectious microorganisms that were once safely isolated in remote areas far from human populations. Still another serious health threat is the overuse and incorrect use of antibiotics, which have been a major weapon in the post–World War II struggle against epidemic diseases. The risk is that disease organisms will evolve drug-resistant forms. Tuberculosis, for example, which once was believed to be on its way out, is again becoming a major threat. The ease and frequency of travel across borders virtually guarantees the spread of new diseases and drug-resistant forms of old ones.

◆ *Transnationally organized crime.* Like other lucrative economic activities, important criminal enterprises are increasingly well organized on a transnational scale, as described in Chapter 9. Vast criminal networks have proliferated to produce, ship, and sell goods and services that are illegal in richer countries but easily obtained in poorer ones. Cocaine and child prostitutes are but two such commodities. The great revenue that flows through criminal networks can cross borders from bank to bank, like other investments in our global age, and to a considerable degree escape the scrutiny of governments.

An important, very general point is that such problems are not only beyond the capacity of any single country to control but are potentially hazardous to people in many countries and in many social classes. People in poorer and richer countries alike worry about the threat to their children posed by the potential for nuclear warfare or new diseases. If the seas rise because airborne pollution leads to climate change, both rich and poor in the increasingly populated coastal areas of the world, from Bangladesh to North Carolina, will find their homes flooded. Violent criminals beyond the control of police scare everyone, too. And although economic volatility on a global scale may make some rich, other wealthy investors worry about their long-term security, and their employees worry about suddenly being out of work. Every one of those issues is likely to generate calls for some mechanism for transnational coordination.

Citizen Organizations

It is not only in the halls of government that people are concerned about transnational issues. Alongside the organizations set up by governments, a variety of citizens' groups have been seeking to make their own views felt and, in so doing, to try to shape the future of the global age. The dramatic Seattle events show that a considerable variety of global concerns are prompting people to organize.

Exploring the emergence of new forms of citizen action is a broad question, but we will also be glancing at an even broader one: what is the potential for democratizing the developing structures of transnational governance?

Let us start by considering some of the elements that prompt political action against transnational organizations by people outside government circles.

◆ *Visible and accessible target.* Organizations that significantly impinge on people's lives and have a well-developed and visible central headquarters are especially suitable targets. The United Nations, despite being a relatively weak body, attracts many demonstrations, probably because of the great visibility of its permanent location in New York City. Probably even more important, various components of the United Nations are open to participation by nongovernmental organizations, which significantly encourages them to use that body as an arena to press their positions (Smith, 1995).

◆ *Resources provided by transnational organizations.* Transnational organizations may provide resources—in the form of activists, ideas, coordination, and funds—that domestic political actors can use in challenging domestic targets. For example, during the later phases of the struggle over South Africa's apartheid system, U.S. campus protesters successfully persuaded American universities to limit or terminate their investments in South Africa. Those activities were part of a broader campaign to get investors to divest their shares of stock in South African corporations, which in turn helped persuade both foreign and South African corporations that the continuation of apartheid promised a future of economic trouble.

◆ *Common cause.* Sympathy for others around the world with whom one can identify is sometimes the basis for citizen action. For example, one of the most common themes of transnational organizing is women's rights. Another is human rights (Smith, 1997, p. 47). Many organizations, such as Amnesty International and Human Rights Watch, have been able to get members based in many countries to engage in actions like letter writing to bring pressure to bear on those abusing fellow human beings far away.

♦ *Incapacity of the states and the state system.* Many transnational issues—war and peace, environment, renewed epidemic threats—clearly are beyond the capacity of single states. At the same time, social activists may find the efforts of governments to manage an issue inadequate or even wholly lacking. The threat posed by the lack of an effective state counterweight to the forces of globalization may prompt vigorous citizen action, as in the case of the environmentalists' activities in Seattle.

♦ *National government as transnational actor.* Because national states remain significant players in the emerging transnational order, because social movements are experienced at making demands on national states, because many of the institutions of transnational decision making do not have the fixed location or visibility of the United Nations, a good deal of social action that aims to affect the transnational scene involves demands that national governments take particular positions in some transnational arena. Even in the case of a powerful and visible organization like the European Union, social movements usually act within—and on—particular member states rather than engage in concerted action across national frontiers or address the Union's governing bodies directly (Tarrow, 1998[b]).

♦ *Lack of input into decision making.* Most political action by citizens has been directed at specific policies of transnational organizations, not at the ways in which global decisions get made. But in Seattle we saw demands for opening up the decision-making processes of the WTO to participants other than governments, and we saw demands to develop some mechanism for more accountable decision making.

The political life of separate national states is still the usual arena in which social movements act. But are events such as the Seattle protests harbingers of a significant shift in the structures of global politics? Many of the organizers of the Seattle protests were hoping for a repeat a few months later in Washington, D.C., where the World Bank and the International Monetary Fund were to meet. However, the obstacles to transnational social movements remain formidable. For one thing, since the rise of the modern state, the centers of national power have been highly visible, providing ready targets for social movements. For example, the beautiful, open design of Washington, D.C., and the placement of the White House and Congress virtually invite citizens to bring their demands to the halls of power. In contrast, many of today's organizations for transnational decision making aim at invisibility. The challenge of democratizing such structures is profound.

Making that challenge more profound still is the difficulty of even thinking about such things. We generally have thought of democracy as something that may or may not characterize the national states but largely have not even considered it an applicable concept in other arenas. During the last quarter of the twentieth century, a period widely considered to have witnessed the triumph of democratic political institutions within national states, only a miniscule proportion of the world's people had any reason to think they had much influence on the organization of the global economy. Beyond that, the gap between the rich and poor of the world grew considerably (Korzeniewicz & Moran, 1997). If democracy is to have a meaningful future in a world of power beyond the states, it will have to be reinvented once again.

Citizens march in front of the White House, calling for an end to economic sanctions against Iraq. The accessibility of government decision makers in democratic countries is in sharp contrast to the inaccessibility of the decision makers in transnational organizations. The Organization of Petroleum Exporting Countries, for example, meets in private and provides only glimpses of its processes, as at this carefully staged public event. Yet OPEC, by controlling the market for petroleum, can greatly influence the price of gas and oil—and thus national economies and people's everyday lives around the world.

Conclusion

The transnational dimension of political and economic life will become increasingly important to all of us, as suggested by the following four reasons.

◆ The web of transnational political and economic activity has reshaped domestic politics, decreasing the role that labor movements have held in the wealthier democracies, renewing the salience of issues of immigration and ethnicity, opening debate on welfare systems, and even mounting a challenge to democracy itself. Transnational decision-making structures increasingly have become the place where major decisions are made. Moreover, economic policy making by national states is increasingly professionalized, further decreasing the sense that citizen input matters.

◆ The transnational decision-making structures will have an increasing impact on many states, not just the weaker players. Already the institutions of transnationally organized finance loom very, very large in the life of many countries; negotiations with the International Monetary Fund or the World Bank may amount to the most important single item on a government's agenda. The WTO may come to be equally weighty, and no doubt other structures of economic governance are still to be created. And we seem to be seeing the beginning of transnational structures that establish human rights rules.

◆ Governments are impelled to seek new forms of coordination to cope with problems none of them can solve alone, but those new transnational structures of governance, in weakening the claims of national sovereignty, themselves encourage further globalization.

◆ Networks of social activists are beginning to address transnational issues in a variety of ways. However, transnational political action by citizens remains far less common than action within the boundaries of states. The question is whether transnational social processes will ultimately nurture effective action from citizens that could have an impact on global political life.

The emerging structures of transnational power are a challenge to democracy. Some in Europe are already calling this the "postdemocratic era," and we may find, if we look, many signs that that might be an accurate assessment. Recall the widespread sense of citizen disillusion with the state of democracy today. But we also may be entering an era in which citizens refuse to give up their power to influence politics. Those in the higher-income democratic countries may decide that they do not want to abandon their two centuries of democratic achievement. Those in poorer countries who have never had much say in the local and global forces that shape their lives may find ways to adapt older modes of social action and to create newer ones in order to democratize the world beyond the states. And here we can point to the transnational networks of social activists, the wide variety of their actions, and the streets of Seattle.

Key Concepts

1. Over the past five centuries, politics came to be organized around national states. Those states came to have the power to make rules about many aspects of social life in the national territory, including many aspects of economic life. By the 1970s, most people on the planet lived in such states.

2. In some of those states, citizens acquired many rights, including the right to participate in choosing those who hold power. Many of the richer countries today have a long history of democratization. Social movements played an important role in the process. Toward the end of the twentieth century, many low- and middle-income countries democratized.

3. In the late twentieth century, social scientists became increasingly aware of what they called globalization. Many important economic, cultural, and political connections were crossing the boundaries of national states. Trade and investment became extremely mobile, and many people moved across borders as well.

4. Globalization went hand in hand with important changes in national politics and national economics. More decisions being made by new transnational bodies, by regional or local governments, and by the private sector. Labor movements, for a long time important in the political life of the industrialized countries, became considerably weakened. Ethnic differences were increasingly important sources of political conflict.

5. Those changes have raised serious questions about the future of democracy. If power passes from the national states into new kinds of decision-making bodies, will it be possible for citizens of the states to find ways of making the new structures accountable to them?

Active Learning

1. Update of Chapter 10: Document Research. This chapter focuses on processes, trends, and organizations that are sure to have a continuing impact on politics and economics in the United States and around the world. In this exercise, you will select an organization or an idea from the chapter and update the information by consulting recent newspapers or other literature.

a. Choose a topic to address from one of the three lists below: an international organization discussed in this chapter; a development that, according to the chapter, is signaling that "major change is afoot"; or an issue requiring transnational cooperation.

Organizations	Issues
Amnesty International	Proliferation of nuclear weapons
European Union	Environmental disasters
Human Rights Watch	Global economic instabilities
International Monetary Fund	Public health issues
United Nations	Transnational criminal organizations
World Bank	
World Trade Organization	

Developments

Reconstitution of state power

Weakened labor movement

New politics of ethnic identity

State management of the economy

b. Review the chapter as necessary to ensure that you understand the importance of the organization, development, or issue you have chosen.

c. Search the press for recent news articles related to your chosen topic. Select a nationally circulated U.S. paper (for example, the *New York Times,* the *Los Angeles Times,* or the *Washington Post*) or a non–U.S. paper (many have English-language editions if you are not fluent in the native language). Your library will have copies of many of the newspapers appropriate for this assignment, and you can also search the home pages of newspapers on the Internet (see our Web site, www.pineforge.com/snc, for some addresses). Using the Internet may be especially useful because most newspapers allow you to search their archives by keywords (for example, "World Trade Organization," "labor unions," or "tuberculosis"). You also can use electronic programs, such as First Search or Proquest, to search popular and scholarly literature in addition to newspapers. Select a news item that is recent, important, and relevant to your specific topic and to the general points made in the chapter.

d. Write a report summarizing the news article and relate it to Chapter 10. What are the implications of your news item for the future of democracy and/or for the economic institutions of the United States and the globe?

2. Evaluation of Globalization and Industrialization: Debate. Chapter 1 pointed out that technology can be a curse as well as a blessing and that what is modern and progressive may depend on one's perspective. Now it is time to critically consider those ideas in light of the points made in Chapter 10 regarding recent economic and political trends. In this exercise, you will review materials from Chapters 1 through 10, develop a position on the benefits and costs of globalization or industrialization, and debate the relative merits of fundamental, world-changing processes with classmates.

a. In class, form groups of four to six and decide on a division of labor for the review phase of this assignment. Members of the group must choose to be for or against either of two propositions:

◆ By and large, globalization is a positive force.

◆ By and large, industrialization and modernization have been beneficial.

Be sure that at least one group member is assigned to each of the four possible positions.

b. Working independently, each group member should review Chapters 1 through 10 for material in support of his or her position. A partial list of the ideas or issues that might be considered in this review include world systems theory, the shift to mechanical solidarity, social capital, local cultures, deindustrialization, rising inequality, gender roles and sexism, racism and global species consolidation, divorce rates, the role of transnational organizations (criminal as well as legal), democratization, and the role of the state. Pick no more than three issues, ideas, or themes to examine in detail and remember that many ideas or issues are addressed in more than one chapter.

c. Write a one- or two-page report that begins with a succinct definition of your central concept (either globalization or industrialization) and that states three important points in support of your position. Note the chapters and page numbers on which your points are based. On the date assigned by your instructor, bring to class enough copies of your report for each group member.

d. In class, discuss in your groups the various definitions of globalization and industrialization. Decide (if possible) on a common definition for each concept.

e. Within your group, debate the two propositions, first one and then the other. The group members assigned to each proposition should present their arguments, followed by discussion by the group as a whole. Consider the evidence and the arguments and weigh their relative merits. The discussion may bring in material not considered by the presenters. If possible, develop a consensus on the issue.

f. Summarize in writing the position of the group on each proposition and state the one or two most important arguments in support of the group's position. If consensus is not achieved, break into subgroups and write separate statements for each position.

g. Submit the summary deliberations of the group along with the individual reports to your instructor. Be prepared, at the discretion of the instructor, to share the conclusions of the group with the class as a whole.

Activists Crusade against Sweatshops

GAY W. SEIDMAN

The news provoked an immediate uproar: in the spring of 2000, the Nike Corporation announced it would withhold millions of promised dollars from three universities, apparently because of the efforts of those universities to improve the conditions in which Third World workers produced sports clothes. Nike's president, Phil Knight, withheld a promised $30-million donation from his alma mater, the University of Oregon, when that school decided to hire independent monitors to examine the factories where Nike manufactured goods with the university's name on them. Simultaneously, Nike backed out of multi-million-dollar contracts with the University of Michigan and Brown University, because student activists had persuaded them to hire independent monitors, too.

To Nike, efforts to develop independent monitoring—monitoring conducted by independent nonprofit groups that would make surprise visits to the factories where Nike goods are made—constituted unacceptable interference in Nike's global operations. Nike's director of global issues, Varda Manager, insisted, "We're not going to give a blank check to dictate our business, our financial terms without us having a seat at the table" (Asher & Barr, 2000). To those who believed that universities are morally obliged to ensure that products carrying their school logos were not made under sweatshop conditions, Nike's actions "struck out at universities committed to finding appropriate ways to safeguard and respect human rights" (Greenhouse, 2000).

What could have pushed Nike to withdraw its donations and contracts knowing, as the company did, that the adverse publicity could harm Nike's sales, already hurt by revelations that some Nike subcontractors paid low wages or polluted local environments? And what could have pushed university administrators to risk millions of dollars of income knowing, as all three schools did, that in an era when governments are trying to balance their budgets, private donations are crucial to university survival? The changing international character of industrial production, or globalization, intersected with an emergent student movement focused on socially responsible investments and consumption. On one hand, globalization allowed corporations like Nike to pursue global production possibilities; on the other, a social movement organized around the social responsibilities of investors and consumers prompted a series of campus demonstrations and sit-ins, as students insisted that their universities improve the conditions under which goods with university labels were made.

Many multinational corporations contract with locally owned factories in developing countries to produce goods according to the multinationals' specifications; the goods are then sold under corporate labels, mainly to consumers in the wealthy markets of North America and Europe. Nike is not unique in that regard, but as a labor-intensive industry it has pursued the strategy further than many other multinational corporations. From its inception, Nike Corporation has run almost no factories of its own, instead contracting a network of local producers across the globe, from Thailand and southern China to Central America, to make shoes marked with Nike's famous "swoosh." The Nike Corporation designs the shoes, oversees the production, controls quality, and then sells the product (Korzeniewiscz, 1994).

Burmese refugees sewing in a sweatshop in Mae Sot, Thailand. Thousands of miles away, in Seattle, protesters demonstrate against the World Trade Organization and the Gap clothing store. The protesters claim that Gap workers in some developed countries must endure sweatshop conditions while earning very low wages.

T O P I C A L   E S S A Y

But Nike is hardly alone: to many multinational corporations across a broad range of industrial sectors, the strategy of outsourcing to subcontracted plants offers corporate executives a way to raise profits without taking on new risks, allowing them to profit from lower production costs in far-flung locations without having to build new plants, hire new workers, or deal directly with foreign governments (Bonacich & Appelbaum, 2000; Gereffi, 1994). International competition almost certainly brings cheaper goods to shopping malls in wealthier nations, but what does it do for the people in poorer countries who don't earn enough to buy anything in those air-conditioned malls? From the perspective of corporate managers and international banks, globalization brings new jobs, and those new jobs often pay better than any of the alternatives, giving incomes to peasant families in impoverished rural areas. Thus, a Nike defender argued that even if the $564 earned *annually* by the average Nike worker in Vietnam "may not seem like much," that figure represents "more than twice the country's average annual income"—thus, it is a good job (Sneider, 2000).

To antisweatshop activists, however, those claims ring hollow: the conditions under which Third World workers produce high-cost running shoes mirror the low pay, long hours, and dangerous exposure to toxic chemicals that marked American sweatshops at the turn of the century. The danger in allowing such sweatshops to exist anywhere, activists argue, is that countries everywhere will be forced to compete in a "race to the bottom." The fear that multinational corporations will move keeps local governments from trying to protect their citizens from exploitative wages, dangerous working conditions, and industrial pollution.

All too frequently, international news accounts provide graphic illustrations that give substance to those fears. In Honduras, a 15-year-old girl tells a camera crew that she earns 38 cents an hour in a factory producing sportswear and that supervisors hit workers and force teenagers to take contraceptive pills. In 1993, more than 188 workers died and 469 were injured when a toy factory near Bangkok burned. Among the bodies were charred toys with names like Toys R Us and Fisher-Price. (That tragedy was a chilling parallel to the famous 1911 Triangle Shirtwaist Company fire, in which 146 immigrant women workers died because the doors had been locked in violation of local fire regulations. The incident prompted New York to pass new labor laws.) In Indonesia, a 23-year-old who tried to organize her fellow workers at a watch factory was abducted, raped, and murdered. The case gained international attention because the military government was implicated in the effort to prevent workers from organizing (Ross, 1997).

In the early 1990s, activists put globalization and international inequality on the American political agenda. But confronted with a process as multifaceted as globalization, where should activists begin to focus their energies? One logical place to begin was close to home. In 1993, while supporters of the North American Free Trade Agreement (NAFTA) argued that increased trade among the United States, Mexico, and Canada would improve all three economies, NAFTA opponents insisted that corporations would move to Mexico so they could pay workers less and avoid the stricter environmental and labor regulations in Canada and the United States. NAFTA was subsequently modified to include tighter environmental regulation across borders and to increase unions' ability to demand enforcement of labor laws.

In the mid-1990s, labor activists also had some success with targeted consumer campaigns. In 1995, for example, The Gap clothing company agreed to pay for independent monitors to keep an eye on working conditions in their Central American factories rather than face persistent picketers outside its stores. Soon, other apparel corporations began to discuss the possibility of monitoring the subcontracted factories where their goods are produced, including publicly naming the factories (rather than insisting that a subcontractor's location remain a trade secret) or creating an independent monitoring system and using "social labels" to indicate that the goods were made under acceptable conditions.

Those discussions followed a rocky path, however. While corporations expressed concern that improved conditions would raise costs and cut profits, activists tried to publicize the effects of unregulated globalization. At the national level, antisweatshop activists developed campaigns around specific corporations, including Disney and the Kathie Lee Gifford line of clothing. Activists also began demonstrating at meetings of the large international institutions that have enforced an open international trade regime, including the 1999 World Trade Organization meeting in Seattle and the 2000 International Monetary Fund meeting in Washington, D.C.

Meanwhile, American university students began to hone in on a target that was closer to home: university administrations. Theories about social movements' success often stress the importance of creating a collective identity, mobilizing potential supporters on the basis that they share interests or grievances. In that respect, antisweatshop activists have found that university campuses offer a unique opportunity. Whereas consumer campaigns often struggle to create a sense of collective identity and must appeal to a diffuse audience of potential shoppers, university-based campaigns have a ready-made constituency and can build on a long tradition of student efforts to hold university administrations to a higher moral standard. During the decades when South Africa was run by an authoritarian white-minority government, student activists demanded that universities divest their shares of companies doing business there. And in the 1980s, many universities came under pressure to divest their holdings in tobacco companies.

In the late 1990s, antisweatshop activists added a new wrinkle: viewing universities as collective consumers, they demanded that the universities withhold school logos from clothing produced under exploitative conditions. Often backing up their demands with sit-ins, protests, and campus referenda and petitions, activists asked universities to intervene in globalization. Markets for university-labeled goods are relatively well-defined, activists argued, so an extra few cents for each garment would not make an appreciable dent in sales or profits. By attempting to ensure that university-labeled goods were produced under

reasonable conditions, major universities could take a moral stance, demonstrating a strategy of constructive intervention to prevent globalization from undermining the conditions of workers and their families everywhere.

In the 1990s, many universities began licensing different apparel corporations (smaller companies as well as big names like Reebok and Nike) to produce goods under the university logos; antisweatshop campaigners suggested that the universities could make independent monitoring a part of the licensing arrangement. By 2000, so many student activists had successfully raised those issues on their campuses that in many universities the terms of debate had changed from whether licensees should be monitored to how best to do it–student activists could well feel that they had begun to make a real difference.

While that strategy suggests new directions for activists, it also raises new questions for sociological theory regarding social movements. Most social movement theorists emphasize the national character of social movements, because activists generally focus on getting local governments to change their policies. But increasingly, sociologists recognize that globalization can change the way social movements mobilize activists and audiences, creating a transnational public sphere in which moral discussions take new forms (Guidry, Kennedy, & Zald, in press). Transnational networks of activists have long provided new information about global developments, but at the turn of the twenty-first century, new technologies of communication almost certainly make such networks increasingly important (Keck &

Many large universities have lucrative, multimillion-dollar contracts with clothing and shoe companies. These companies manufacture apparel with the university logo on it or provide brand-name shoes and clothing to university athletes free of charge. However, under intense pressure from students, some universities have severed ties with companies that use sweatshop labor, particularly in foreign countries.

Sikkink, 1997). Transnational activists also frame issues in global terms, presenting events in ways that persuade others to support a far-off cause or to send donations to an activist group in a poor region. Transnational activists often manage to persuade their listeners that everyone is directly affected by processes taking place in far-flung corners of the world.

At the turn of the century, transnational activism around sweatshops and workers' rights underscore the new possibilities implicit in globalization. It has already helped to promote changes in international policies on issues ranging from human rights to environmental degradation to gender equity. Thus, the same technological and institutional changes that made a "race to the bottom" a dangerous threat might also offer new possibilities. Transnational communication, organization, and advocacy promise to open up exciting new directions for social movement activism as well as for sociological theory.

Thinking about the Essay

Should corporations be free to contract for labor anywhere in the world without restriction? If not, how could restrictions be enforced? Who would decide what those restrictions would be? Who should enforce them? What are the responsibilities of merchants, universities and colleges, and students like yourself?

College students often ask: What does this course have to do with me? How is this material relevant today? How does it apply to the real world? Chapters 11 through 16 answer those questions by applying sociological thinking to critical global problems that affect all of us: war, careers, the environment, population growth, healthcare, and the prospects for making the world a better place. These chapters use the theories and approaches presented in Chapters 1 through 10 to help examine those issues and to place them in broader perspective.

Chapters 11 through 16 differ from the first ten chapters in two ways. First, they contain more personal stories, more descriptive material, and more popular press sources, because they deal with contemporary issues that are affected by breaking news. Second, these chapters have an "activist" or "reformist" slant to them. Their authors use the ideas and evidence of social science to suggest how societies might be improved for more of the world's citizens. The idea that sociology has a moral dimension, in addition to a scientific dimension, is a long and distinguished tradition. As you read in Chapter 2, sociology emerged in response to the social disruptions that attended industrialization in the nineteenth century. In that tradition, the authors of Chapters 11 through 16 take a stand on their particular issues and present their own opinions—informed by sociological thought—on how to solve social problems. You may find yourself arguing with those opinions or perhaps wondering how you can take action on one of the critical issues. That is what we want: your active engagement.

As you read this section, keep in mind all the things you learned about sociology and the world in Chapters 1 through 10. Then flex your intellectual muscles to formulate and defend your own opinions in response to the questions posed by the contributors and the critical-thinking questions posed at the end of each chapter. Take a good hard look at the data in the graphics throughout the book and in the maps in the appendix, and determine for yourself what they all mean.

Good sociologists are interested in substantive events in the world around them and are able to interpret those events within the context of sociological theories, concepts, and methodologies. We hope you enjoy your opportunity to think like a sociologist and continue to apply the same analytical skills you learn in this course long after you complete it..

At Issue

SOCIOLOGY EXAMINES A NEW CENTURY

- ◆ *The Changing Face of War*
- ◆ *The Future of Work*
- ◆ *Can the World Develop and Sustain Its Environment?*
- ◆ *How Many People Is Too Many People?*
- ◆ *The Global Healthcare Challenge*
- ◆ *Creating Positive Social Change*

Under the watchful eye of a United Nations peacekeeper, children in Sierra Leone desperately flee the rebel Revolutionary United Front, which killed thousands of innocent people and chopped off the arms and legs of countless others.

11 The Changing Face of War

YORK W. BRADSHAW

Following Adolph Hitler's annihilation of six million Jews during World War II, the new Jewish state of Israel, the United States, and other countries (including Germany) proclaimed, "Never again": Never again would sadistic madmen like Hitler be allowed to commit genocide against innocent people. In the United States, the states of Illinois, Florida, and New Jersey even passed laws that required schools to teach students about "The Holocaust." But to which holocaust do those laws refer? Any number of conflicts since World War II could be called holocausts: a million killed in Rwanda (1990s), a million slaughtered in the "killing fields" of Cambodia (1970s), hundreds of thousands killed in both Uganda (1970s) and the former Yugoslavia (1990s)—and the list goes on and on. "Never again" has turned into "again and again" despite the world's commitment to stop the mass slaughter of people. In fact, it is difficult to keep up with the latest episode of genocide.

Genocide was not the only form of mass killing in the twentieth century. The last century witnessed two great world wars, many other significant intercountry conflicts, and the threat of nuclear war between the United States and the former Soviet Union. It is estimated that more than 100 million people were killed in wars during the twentieth century (Sivard, 1999). However, the character of war has changed since World War II, especially over the last thirty years. Although intercountry conflicts still occur, the vast majority of conflicts around the world are now intracountry wars, that is, civil wars between two sides in a single country (for example, different ethnic groups) or between the state and a group vying for power (Graphic 11.1).

Civil wars are bloody and often involve the government, which either cannot or will not stop the killing. Moreover, unless their security is directly threatened, outside actors are loath to intervene in civil wars, which are unpredictable and difficult to broker. The difficulties of stopping war were readily apparent in May 2000, when a United Nations Security Council delegation attempted to mediate three African conflicts that had reached the boiling point at nearly the same time: civil wars in Sierra Leone and the Congo and an impending war between Ethiopia and Eritrea. The leader of the delegation, American ambassador to the United Nations Richard C. Holbrooke, noted: "When the trip was planned [one week ago], Congo was the No. 1 crisis in Africa. By the time we got here, it had dropped to No. 3" (Crossette, 2000). Of course, he wasn't counting the continuing civil wars in the Sudan, Angola, Somalia, and Algeria or a new and increasingly violent conflict in Zimbabwe between black

supporters of President Robert Mugabe and white farmers who supported opposition candidates.

There are many possible reasons for the increasing number of civil wars around the world: more weapons, more liberation struggles, more fights over valuable raw materials (for example, diamonds), more religious and ideological conflicts, and more outside actors arming and supporting internal conflicts in other countries. At the heart of it all, however, the cause of civil war is related to a topic central to sociology: inequality. Sociologists are interested in factors that cause and perpetuate wars and other violent activities. Inequality in income, power, and ethnic representation account for a large number of conflicts around the world.

Consider the factor of ethnicity. Chapter 6 provided moving testimony of how ethnicity influenced the horrendous civil war in Rwanda during 1994. Between 500,000 and one million people were killed in the war that pitted Hutus against Tutsis. Six years after the killing, Rwanda remains unstable. Some people have been put on trial for genocide, some have even been hanged for their involvement, but the country has not changed dramatically. It remains ethnically divided and continues to exhibit a tenseness that could erupt into war. Although the primary problem in Rwanda is ethnic conflict, the conflict has historical roots dating back to colonial days, when a colonizer favored one ethnic group over another and therefore exacerbated inequalities of power. Today the outside world has little interest in Rwanda, but the legacy of internal conflict and outside intervention casts a long shadow on this tiny and troubled country.

Too many people assume that Africa is the only continent that suffers from war-based ethnic differences. In fact, however, one of the most intractable ethnic conflicts is in Europe, where, during the 1990s, more than a quarter-million people (many civilians) were killed in the former Yugoslavia. The war also created more than three million refugees, the worst refugee situation in Europe since the end of World War II. Let's take a closer look at that war to see how sociologists seek to understand complex historical situations that influence social conflict and change.

Type of Conflict

Civil war

Intercountry war

Source: Adapted from www.didyouknow.com/conflicts.htm (July 20, 2000).

Yugoslavia, 1990s: Lessons Unlearned

Yugoslavia has experienced wars dating back several centuries (Kaplan, 1993), but the most recent conflict started in 1991. That conflict was caused—and is sustained—by a combination of factors related to history, ethnic hatreds, and inequalities rooted in economics and power. It is a conflict that demonstrates the dark side of Europe, particularly the continent's inability to learn the lessons supposedly taught by Hitler over fifty years ago.

To understand the conflict, we need to examine the ethnic diversity in the "old" Yugoslavia. Take a look at Graphic 11.2, which shows the republics that made up the country in 1990. The Yugoslavian population was 8% Slovene (living mainly in Slovenia), 20% Croat (living mainly in Croatia), 36% Serb (living mainly in Serbia), and 9% Bosnian Muslim

GRAPHIC 11.2 YUGOSLAVIA, 1990

Source: Bradshaw and Wallace, 1996, p. 145.

(living mainly in Bosnia-Herzegovina). The rest of the population comprised several minority groups (Goldman, 1988). The national capital of the former Yugoslavia was Belgrade, located in Serbia, which meant that Serbia retained the primary political and military power in the country, even over so-called autonomous regions like Vojvodina and Kosovo.

Some of Yugoslavia's republics were also ethnically diverse. For instance, 12% of Croatia's population and 31% of Bosnia-Herzegovina's population were made up of Serbs (Goldman, 1988). Despite ethnic diversity, Yugoslavia had maintained relative calm since the end of World War II, primarily because of the skillful leadership of its charismatic long-time leader, Josip Broz, usually referred to as Marshal Tito. But ethnic tensions remained just beneath the surface. Tito's death in 1980, combined with economic stagnation across Eastern Europe and the breakup of the Soviet Union, brought out all of Yugoslavia's simmering ethnic and economic problems.

One important problem was the disparity in wealth throughout the country. Basically, the wealth ran from north to south, with the wealthiest area being Slovenia, followed by Croatia. Both regions resented having to share their resources with southern republics. Of course, the national government in Belgrade (Serbia) realized that the economic vitality of the northern republics was essential to the Yugoslavian economy. However, as Eastern Europe celebrated its independence from the Soviet Union in the early 1990s, Slovenia and Croatia decided to join the action and become independent European countries. Their rationale was understandable: Why be part of a troubled country (with serious economic difficulties) when you can improve your situation by joining the rest of Europe?

Thus, in 1991, Slovenia and Croatia declared independence from Yugoslavia. They would be their own countries. Belgrade saw its economic power base breaking away and eventually sent troops to Slovenia and Croatia to stop the independence movements. The Serbs left Slovenia rather quickly, deciding to concentrate their efforts in Croatia, where 12% of the population was Serbian (Burg, 1994; Goldman, 1994).

In 1992, the majority of people in Bosnia-Herzegovina also voted for independence, more on political grounds than economic. (Bosnian Muslims were sick and tired of being pushed around by Christian Serbs.) As expected, Serbs living in Bosnia-Herzegovina (Bosnian Serbs) rejected the vote and received strong support for their defiance from the national capital in Belgrade. Belgrade could not afford another breakaway republic and therefore sent substantial military aid to its Serbian comrades in Bosnia-Herzegovina. The well-armed Bosnian Serbs initiated a brutal military campaign to force Muslims out of Serbian areas of Bosnia-Herzegovina and to isolate the region's capital, Sarajevo. Sarajevo, once an ethnically diverse and beautiful city that hosted the 1984 Winter Olympics, became a killing field.

Ethnic Cleansing and the "Little Hitlers"

Bosnian Serb troops began to engage in "ethnic cleansing" throughout Bosnia-Herzegovina, a practice of removing other ethnic groups at all costs. Nazi-like tactics were utilized throughout the region, in a display of brutality not seen since the holocaust of World War II. Villages and towns were attacked and Muslims driven out. People (including small children) were burned alive in barns and houses. Muslim men were captured and sent on trains to concentration camps, where they were beaten, starved, and sometimes killed. Many governments (including that of the U.S. administration of President George H. Bush) denied the existence of concentration camps until international photographers took pictures and showed them to the world. Serbs also resorted to another disgusting weapon of war: women, especially Muslim women, were systematically raped. The practice was calculated and unbelievably cruel, considering the sanctity that Islam places on virginity before marriage and fidelity during marriage.

Concentration camps and rape were only part of the Serbian arsenal. Serbian forces also launched missiles, grenades, and bullets at innocent civilians, many of whom were children. This was especially prevalent in Sarajevo, the capital of Bosnia-Herzegovina. The city, surrounded by hills from which the weapons were launched, was an easy target. Thousands of civilians were killed and maimed while walking (and running) down the street, going to markets, lying in hospitals, and attending schools. The indiscriminant killing violated all international treaties on war.

Another particularly brazen attack on civilians occurred in 1995. The United Nations had designated six "safe areas" throughout the country, regions that would function as safe havens for Muslim civilians who had become refugees in the war. A small number of UN troops were placed in each location to guard civilians against attack by the Serbs. It did not matter. On July 11, the Serbs attacked the safe area of Srebrenica, home to nearly 40,000 Muslims, many of whom were women, children, and elderly people. After the attack, the Serbs allowed about half the Muslims to board crowded buses for the difficult trip to another "safe area," called Tuzla. Imagine the scene: hungry and terrified civilians, including many very young children, making the trip north under the watchful eye of the Serbs. Serbian military leaders occasionally boarded the buses to facetiously assure the civilians that nothing would happen to them, never saying anything about those left behind in Srebrenica.

Those left behind were killed, captured, raped, or on the run. (No one knows exactly how many fell into each category.) Young Muslim men (of fighting age) were especially sought after by the Serbs. Photographs taken from a U.S. spy plane on July 13 and 14, 1995, showed people crowded into a soccer stadium near Srebrenica. Spy photographs taken a few days later showed an empty stadium and freshly dug earth next to it. It is estimated that at least 2,000 bodies rest under the soil. Eyewitnesses who managed to escape from the Serbs report that men were taken in groups of twenty to twenty-five from the stadium and machine-gunned. In the end, more than 7,000 men and boys were killed in fields, schools, and warehouses around Srebrenica—the worst case of genocide in Europe since World War II. The PBS documentary *Srebrenica: Voices from the Grave* is a moving reminder that genocide did not end with the Second World War.

Adolph Hitler was not needed to direct the geno-

cide in the former Yugoslavia. He was replaced nicely by Bosnian Serb leader Radovan Karadzic, Bosnian Serb General Ratko Mladic, and Serbian President (in Serbia) Slobodan Milosevic. All three have been indicted on the charges of "genocide and crimes against humanity" by the United Nations International Tribunal for the Former Yugoslavia, a world court based in The Hague, Netherlands. Formed in 1993, it was the first such tribunal since the famous Nuremberg and Tokyo trials following World War II. International warrants have been issued for the arrest of Karadzic, Mladic, and Milosevic, meaning they are wanted by the entire world for their crimes. Karadzic and Mladic are in hiding in Bosnia, protected by large security forces. Milosevic, despised by many Serbs for bringing economic ruin and international isolation, was forced from power by citizens in the autumn of 2000.

Although the "big three" have thus far eluded the law, others have not, including Karadzic's top aid, Moncilo Krajisnik, who was involved in many horrendous crimes. He was captured in April 2000 while visiting his parents' home in Bosnia. Specially trained United Nations forces swooped into their home in the early morning hours, hog-tied Krajisnik's two sons, locked his parents in a closet, and quickly "escorted" a pajama-clad Krajisnik to a waiting airplane. He was arraigned the next day in The Hague for genocide and crimes against humanity. All together, thirty-nine people are now in detention in The Hague. They have been accused of various crimes, including murder, genocide, crimes against humanity, and rape. Some have been convicted and given long prison sentences (there is no death penalty associated with this world court), some are awaiting trial, and some are in detention while their cases are appealed. Another thirty people have been indicted by the International Tribunal but are not yet in custody. It is thought that international troops are actively pursuing Karadzic and Mladic, a difficult and dangerous task. (To follow the International Tribunal, consult *www.un.org/law/*).

We might ask: How could all of this happen? The purpose of sociology is to help us explain such events. We should remember several points. First, civil wars are deeply embedded in historical differences. The former Yugoslavia had experienced ethnic and religious conflict for centuries before the events of the 1990s. Second, various types of societal inequality often are prevalent in violent conflicts. In Rwanda, it was inequalities of land and power. In the former Yugoslavia, it was inequalities of income, power, and military strength. Third, ethnicity remains perhaps the strongest form of identity in the world today. People tend to identify and act with their ethnic groups (although there are clear exceptions), especially over issues of inequality.

Turning Point: Intervention in Kosovo

Ethnic cleansing continued in Bosnia for months, despite threats from the international community that it would not stand by and watch genocide. But the world did stand by and watch. It watched killing, torture, rape, and waves of refugees. It watched the violation of international laws and conventions again and again.

Public opinion in the United States, though normally slow to advocate involvement in war, began to shift in 1995. About half of all Americans felt that the United States and its allies should become involved militarily in the former Yugoslavia. Some publications criticized U.S. officials for standing by so long. The *New Republic,* a left-of-center publication that would like to support a Democratic President, ran a series of blistering editorials against President Clinton's reluctance to use force in the region.

> Since the United States is the only power in the world that can stop the ethnic cleansing, the United States is responsible if the ethnic cleansing continues. Well, not exactly the United States. The American President is an accomplice to genocide. Not so the American people. The President of the United States does not have the right to make the people of the United States seems as indecent as he is . . . more and more Americans want to know why we are standing around and doing nothing ("Accomplices," 1995, p. 7).

The world stopped "standing around" after an event that occurred on August 28, 1995. Yet another Serbian-launched mortal shell fell into the heart of a

Albanian refugees in Kosovo flee Serb shelling of their villages (top). Many refugees were forced to walk for up to seven days before finding relative safety. A French soldier with the NATO peacekeeping force is welcomed by ethnic Albanians in Kosovo (bottom). These refugees might well be dead had there been no outside intervention.

Sarajevo market, killing thirty-eight people. Many of the casualties were children and older people. Blood, limbs, and death were everywhere. Some bodies literally fell apart as they were picked up by family members and rescue officials. International reporters helped civilians and rescue workers load injured people into cars for the drive to the hospital. One driver, a reporter for the Reuters news agency, told about two of his "passengers." A little girl, obviously in shock, quietly said to her mother, "Mommy, I lost my hand. Where is my hand?" The girl's mother could be forgiven for not seeing the problem. Her face was covered with blood and one eye was hanging out of it socket. Their nightmare was not over: The Serbs later delivered a mortar shell blast to the hospital, hitting some victims of the market disaster a second time.

This time, however, the international community handled the attack on Sarajevo differently. Three and a half years after the genocide began and at least two years after the international community threatened to discipline the Serbs, the United States and other Western allies, through the North Atlantic Treaty Organization (NATO), launched punishing bombing raids against Bosnian Serb positions around Sarajevo and other areas of Bosnia-Herzegovina. Wave after wave of bombers destroyed Serbian military headquarters, ammunition depots, antiaircraft equipment, bridges, and communication facilities. Muslim civilians in Sarajevo were literally cheering in the streets as they watched the jets scream overhead on their way to strike Serbian targets. Two weeks and nearly 1,000 bombs later, U.S. warships launched thirteen sophisticated cruise missiles toward Serbian antiaircraft targets in the center of the country.

Western allies mandated that one condition be met before the bombing would stop. All of the Serbs' heavy weaponry (for example, tanks and large mortar launchers) must be moved outside of a 12.5-mile radius around Sarajevo, thereby keeping the city safe from shells directed at civilians. Several days later, the Serbs finally complied with that order and removed their heavy weapons from around Sarajevo.

In September, all sides agreed to a cease-fire and to peace talks. Then, on November 21, the presidents of Bosnia-Herzegovina, Croatia, and Serbia, meeting at Wright-Patterson Air Force Base near Dayton, Ohio, signed an agreement calling for Bosnia-Herzegovina to be divided into a Bosnia-Croat federation and a Serb republic. Since shortly after the agreement was signed, the peace has been enforced by 60,000 NATO troops, including 20,000 from the United States. The troops have done a remarkable job maintaining relative peace in the area; unfortunately, there is little doubt that war would break out all over again if the troops were removed.

Peacekeeping is not the same as nation building. The former Yugoslavia is in the very early stages of nation building, a process whereby institutions and people make possible a relatively smooth system of government. People tend to give their governments legitimacy when those governments demonstrate they have the best interests of the people at heart.

Nation building is a fragile business, especially in regions with a history of conflict. A new round of fighting began in 1998 in Kosovo, an area of the former Yugoslavia that did not have NATO peacekeepers. Kosovo, where 90% of the 2.2 million people are ethnic Albanians, has long sought independence from Serbia. In January 1998, the Kosovo Liberation Army (KLA) announced its intention to unify Kosovo with Albania.

Serbia, which still had grand designs of a "Greater Serbia," was not about to stand by and watch more of its land disappear. Within two months, Serbian forces began a new campaign of ethnic cleansing, burning villages in Kosovo and preventing relief workers from assisting Albanian refugees. There were many documented reports of massacres, rapes, and violence committed by Serbian troops. By September, an estimated 300,000 residents of Kosovo had been driven from their homes. Another 40,000 people had fled to Montenegro, which finally closed its borders. Albania, which had already accepted between 10,000 and 20,000 refugees, accepted another 3,000 people. The United Nations labeled the situation a humanitarian disaster.

Yugoslav President Milosevic largely ignored the warnings of the international community throughout 1998. His troops advanced south into Kosovo, hedging their bets and again testing the resolve of the Western world. They again bet the wrong way. In March 1999, NATO forces launched a campaign of air strikes against Serbian military targets in the former Yugoslavia. Then, for the first time, NATO ground troops entered the scene and helped drive Serbian forces back to Serbia. But the stability of the region remains uncertain today. Again, it is not as difficult to keep peace as it is to address the inequalities and other issues that have contributed to the overall problem.

Voices of War

It is important to remember that wars have victims who experience terrible traumas. Too often, we rely on academic theories and arguments to discuss wars and other conflicts. This section underscores the voices of the victims themselves.

One of the greatest misunderstandings about contemporary warfare is the belief that soldiers kill only soldiers. In fact, soldiers kill civilians. Around the world, 90% of war casualties are now civilians, and at least half of that number are children. During the 1990s, an estimated two million children were killed by armed conflicts, and another six million were severely maimed or disabled (UNICEF, 2000). Beyond the direct killing by knives, bullets, bombs, and land mines, millions of additional children die from the indirect consequences of warfare such as the disruption of food supplies and the destruction of health services. Armed conflict can increase child death rates by up to twenty-four times, a result of both direct and indirect causes (UNICEF, 1996).

One of the most serious consequences of war is the creation of refugees. The number of refugees from armed conflict around the world is growing rapidly, increasing from 2.4 million in 1974 to 27.4 million in 1996. Another 30 million people have been displaced in their own countries. Eighty percent of all displaced people are women and children (UNICEF, 1996). It is those people displaced internally who are most at risk, because they typically are trapped inside their country's borders with an aggressor who knows a lot about where they might hide.

In Kosovo, for instance, there were tens of thousands of refugees during 1998 and 1999. Once the killing started, many ethnic Albanians headed to the mountains and forests to try to evade Serb forces. Not all were successful. In 1999, just days before NATO troops arrived in the area, Imer Delijaj returned to his family's hideout in the mountains of Kosovo and found his family slaughtered. He told Human Rights Watch (1999):

> I continued up the gully, and saw my nine-year-old son Jeton. He had a wound from his left ear to his mouth. I hope it was from a bullet and not a knife [so he would not have suffered]. It is the only body which I am not sure how he was killed. One shoe was on and one shoe was off. . . .
>
> Nearby was the body of Luljeta, the pregnant wife of my brother, about to give birth any day. We had even decided on a name for the baby, Malsore, which means "mountain girl" and related to our suffering in the mountains. . . . [Luljeta's] legs were together. She was lying on her right side and she had wounds on the left side of her face. She was hit a little more on the back of the head, and there was a small wound on her nose . . . .
>
> The other body was that of Valmir, the eighteen-month-old son of [my brother] Adem. He had a wound on the right side of his face near his jaw, and on his right hand he had a hole but not from a bullet, and other small wounds on his body. His pacifier was hanging on his chest.

War destroys childhoods. In the Rwandan conflict of 1994, it is estimated that 80% of children lost immediate family members and that more than one-third actually witnessed the murders (UNICEF, 1996, p. 6). The loss of childhood is particularly obvious among the more than 300,000 children serving as soldiers in thirty different countries. Human Rights Watch, UNICEF, and other organizations have called for an international law that prohibits the use of child soldiers, whose lives are especially bleak. Here is the voice of a child soldier in Sierra Leone, where as many as 10,000 child soldiers have been used recently. She is a fourteen-year-old girl abducted in 1999 by the Revolutionary United Front, a rebel group.

> I've seen people get their hands cut off, a ten-year-old girl raped and then die, and so many men and women burned alive. . . . So many times I just cried inside my heart because I didn't dare cry out loud (UNICEF, 1996).

Susan, age 16, who was abducted in Uganda by a rebel group and forced to fight, had this testimony:

> One boy tried to escape [from the rebels], but he was caught. . . . His hands were tied, and then they made us, the other new captives, kill him with a

stick. I knew this boy from before. We were from the same village. I refused to kill him and they told me they would shoot me. They pointed a gun at me, so I had to do it. The boy was asking me, "Why are you doing this?" I said I had no choice. After we killed him, they made us smear his blood on our arms. . . . They said we had to do this so we would not fear death and so we would not try to escape. . . . I still dream about the boy from my village who I killed. I see him in my dreams, and he is talking to me and saying I killed him for nothing, and I am crying (UNICEF, 1996).

Rape is increasingly used as a weapon of war. In the former Yugoslavia alone, it is estimated that 20,000 women and girls have been raped. There are credible reports of rape camps, where rapes were committed in a systematic and brutal manner. Some war criminals in The Hague have been convicted of such crimes. Many other women and girls were raped and murdered in their own homes by invading soldiers. In Pec, Kosovo, for example, six armed

At left, heavily armed child soldiers in Liberia. At right, a man kneels at the Vietnam Veterans Memorial Wall to rub the engraved name of someone killed in the war onto a piece of paper.

and uniformed Serb men entered a house in June 1999 just two days before NATO entered the city. The Serb soldiers murdered and raped, as described by a witness who survived a chest wound:

> They were wearing military clothes and had black scarves on their heads. They took my sister-in-law into the front room, and they were hitting her and telling her to shut up. The children were screaming, and they also screamed at the children. She was with the paramilitary for one half hour. She was resisting, and they beat her, and the children could hear her screaming. I could only hear what was going on. I heard them slapping her. The children did not understand that they were raping her. After they raped my sister-in-law, they put her in line with us and shot her (Human Rights Watch, 2000).

Not surprisingly, the survivors' physical and psychological scars last a lifetime. If you visit the Vietnam Veterans Memorial Wall in Washington, DC, you will quickly see that the Vietnam war is not over for all Americans, even though North Vietnam defeated South Vietnam (which the United States supported) in 1974. The wall carries the engraved name of every American killed in the war or still missing. Some of the scenes at the wall are heart wrenching. Many veterans, some wearing worn-out

battle fatigues, kneel beside the names of fallen comrades. Families and friends touch the names of loved ones and weep. Some trace a name from the wall onto a piece of paper. Others leave flowers, poems, love letters, and other remembrances. Many young adults come to the wall in search of the fathers they never knew—for some, it is the only gravestone they will ever see.

Some people visit the wall to exorcise the inevitable demons that possess the human soul following war. One day the tattered picture of a North Vietnamese soldier and a young girl (probably his daughter) was left at the wall. This letter, written by an American, lay next to the photograph.

> Dear Sir, For twenty-two years I have carried your picture in my wallet. I was only eighteen years old that day that we faced one another on that trail in Chu Lai, Vietnam. Why you didn't take my life I'll never know. You stared at me for so long, armed with your AK-47, and yet you did not fire. Forgive me for taking your life, I was reacting just the way I was trained, to kill. . . . So many times over the years I have stared at your picture and your daughter, I suspect. Each time my heart and guts would burn with the pain of guilt. I have two daughters myself now. . . . I perceive you as a brave soldier defending his homeland. Above all else, I can now respect the importance that life held for you. I suppose that is why I am able to be here today. . . .
> It is time for me to continue the life process and release my pain and guilt. Forgive me, Sir (Allen, 1995, pp. 52–53).

The Responsibility to Stop Someone Else's War

Discussions about what can be done to stop war are really discussions about what the outside world is willing and able to do in terms of intervention. Civil wars don't end on their own, until there is a victor. In the 1990s alone, civil war has directly contributed to the deaths of nearly two million people, always prompting the same question: Should the United States and its allies intervene militarily to stop the bloodshed? It is a question that will be asked with increasing frequency as the world faces more tragedies born out of poverty, inequality, population growth, government instability, and ethnic hatred.

Before addressing the issue of outside military intervention in civil war, it is critical to underscore the importance of political peace initiatives. Although the 1990s were a period of intense warfare in different regions, they also were a time of historic peace efforts. Northern Ireland, the Middle East, southern Africa, and the former Yugoslavia have all benefited from peace initiatives involving mediation by and assistance from outside sources. As mentioned earlier, for instance, shortly after the United States and its allies bombed the former Yugoslavia in 1995, all relevant parties gathered in Dayton, Ohio, to write the Dayton Accords. The peace agreement, enforced by 60,000 NATO troops, ended the genocide immediately. But a peacekeeping force cannot bring government stability to a region. If the troops left the Yugoslavia region today, there is little doubt that some of the bloodshed would quickly resume. Only intensive political and economic effort will bring stability to a region.

So when should outside forces become involved in other nations' problems? Some people argue that outsiders should be hesitant to get involved in other nations' conflicts, whereas others assert that involvement clearly is warranted under certain conditions.

Let's consider the case against involvement. It has two main points.

- Civil wars generally do not threaten the national interests of most outside countries. Moreover, the wars include intense ethnic hatreds that have been around for centuries. So why should the United States, the United Nations, or any other body become involved, taking on the responsibility for policing the world? Yes, people are dying; yes, the wars are tragic; yes, people are suffering; but no, it is not the responsibility of other nations to intervene in the conflict. Let the local people (and people in surrounding areas) settle their own disputes. Soldiers from far-off lands should not have to die to settle disputes that do not directly concern them.

- Military intervention might stop the killing, but it does not lead to long-term solutions. Outsiders ultimately find themselves in a true dilemma: they can make a commitment to remain in a country for years and years (at a very high cost), or they can leave after a specified period of time and watch the armed conflict start again. At the very least, peacekeeping should be combined with mediation, coaxing each party to the negotiating table to rebuild a national government and nation.

There also are at least two good arguments in favor of military intervention.

- The moral argument is how can the more powerful nations in the world stand back and allow genocide or other major conflicts to continue? Acting to prevent mass killing sends a strong message to other despots around the world. Those against intervention argue that it interferes with the sovereignty of individual nation-states. But Kofi Annan, the Secretary-General of the United Nations, addresses that issue in his Millennium Report (Annan, 2000, p. 24).

I would pose this question: if humanitarian intervention is, indeed, an unacceptable assault on sovereignty, how should we respond to a Rwanda, to a Srebrenica—to gross and systematic violations of human rights that offend every precept of our common ancestry? . . . But surely no legal principle—not even sovereignty—can ever shield crimes against humanity. Where such crimes occur and peaceful attempts to halt them have been exhausted, the Security Council has a moral duty to act on behalf of the international community. The fact that we cannot protect people everywhere is no reason for doing nothing when we can. Armed intervention must always remain the option of last resort, but in the face of mass murder it is an option that cannot be relinquished.

- If the moral argument is not persuasive, then a political argument for involvement may be more compelling. In the former Yugoslavia, for instance, the United States and its European allies would have become more quickly interested in intervention if the war had spread north toward Europe or south toward Greece. When a country's national interests are threatened, it often becomes involved in war. When Iraq threatened Western oil supplies in the Persian Gulf, the United States and its allies launched operation Desert Storm to stop it. Absent a clear threat to national interests, however, this perspective argues that war is not justified.

As shown in Graphic 11.3, UN and NATO troops were involved in eighteen peacekeeping missions around the world as the new century began—more than ever before. And the United Nations likely will be asked to send peacekeeping troops to other troubled regions in the coming years. Clearly the world will be faced on a regular basis with the question of whether to intervene militarily to stop human suffering. As the only remaining superpower, the United States will be asked to shoulder much of the burden militarily and diplomatically, especially for larger missions. Although the United States often has the power to go it alone in military conflicts around the world, it lacks the moral authority that a coalition brings. The nations of the world will need to stand up together to genocide and other conflicts.

The Limitations of Peacekeeping

The west African country of Sierra Leone has suffered greatly over the last eight years, interrupted only briefly with glimmers of (false) hope. Foday Sankoh and his rebel group, the Revolutionary United Front (RUF), waged an eight-year war against the government, during which time the rebels' tactics were brutal. They killed tens of thousands of people and mutilated and dismembered thousands of others, children as well as adults. Their trademark was to chop off the hands of their victims, a

GRAPHIC 11.3   MAJOR PEACEKEEPING MISSIONS IN 2000

Region	Mission	Year Started	Countries Involved
Africa	Democratic Republic of the Congo (UN)	1999	25
	Sierra Leone (UN)	1999	31
	Western Sahara (UN)	1991	28
Americas	Haiti (UN)	1997	11
Asia	East Timor (UN)	1999	44
	Georgia (UN)	1993	22
	India and Pakistan (UN)	1949	8
	Tajikistan (UN)	1994	10
Europe	Bosnia-Herzegovina (UN)	1995	44
	Bosnia-Herzegovina (NATO)	1999	28
	Croatia (UN)	1996	25
	Cyprus (UN)	1964	10
	Kosovo (NATO)	1999	28
	Kosovo (UN)	1999	50
Middle East	Golan Heights (UN)	1974	5
	Iraq-Kuwait (UN)	1991	33
	Israel (UN)	1948	22
	Lebanon (UN)	1978	9

Source: Adapted from *World Press Review*, May 2000, p. 23. Data from NATO and United Nations.

tactic that emerged during the democratic elections of 1996. Worse, the rebels appointed children to be the ones who used the ax.

Indeed, there may be as many as 10,000 child soldiers in Sierra Leone. One group was rescued by the Catholic Church and is being treated at a facility that used to be a Club Med resort. The battle stories are horrific: children hooked on hard drugs and ordered to chop off limbs, kill, rape, and drink the blood of victims. Many of the young soldiers fought for Sankoh's RUF forces.

After years of bloodshed, the RUF signed a peace accord in 1999 that gave Sankoh a prominent leadership position in the new coalition government. In exchange, Sankoh and his rebels promised to put down their arms and cease their reign of ter-

ror. But they repeatedly violated the accord and continued to attempt to take control of the government. One of the main issues is diamonds: Sankoh is widely believed to have amassed a fortune by controlling the lucrative diamond mines in Sierra Leone's interior.

As the RUF continued its march toward Freetown to take over the government, the world began to take notice. The United Nations sent peacekeeping troops, but, amazingly enough, in May 2000, the RUF captured and held hostage 500 UN peacekeepers (about 400 of the hostages were poorly trained and equipped troops from Zambia). Sankoh's grip on the country seemed assured.

Then in mid-May a bizarre series of events occurred in the country. A large crowd of anti-Sankoh demonstrators surrounded his house near Free-town. Sankoh's soldiers and guards opened fire on the protesters, killing nineteen people. Sankoh fled his residence and was not seen again for a week amid rumors that he may have died, had been captured, or was simply hiding in the jungle. Suddenly, however, civilians spotted him back near his residence, reportedly with a sorcerer. Progovernment forces were alerted, and Sankoh was captured, disrobed, and paraded through the streets in an act designed to humiliate him. He was then turned over to British forces to be held at an undisclosed location.

The situation in Sierra Leone has underscored the problems with UN peacekeeping missions. Whether at Srebrenica or in Sierra Leone, UN forces, as currently constituted, are not strong enough to function as effective peacemakers. A primary problem is that individual countries send soldiers to participate in UN missions, but such troops often are poorly trained and equipped. The Serbs knew that at Srebrenica: they pushed the UN troops aside and slaughtered 7,000 people. In Sierra Leone, UN forces again were humiliated, this time by being taken hostage.

Future peacekeeping missions should proceed only under one of two conditions.

- There should be a standing, multinational, professionalized UN peacekeeping force. It must be well trained, well armed, and ready for battle. It also must be large enough and mobile enough to respond quickly to emergencies around the world. This idea was proposed in the early 1990s and killed by conservative American politicians who oppose U.S. involvement in the United Nations; they were supported by voters who oppose U.S. intervention unless vital strategic interests are at stake.

- Absent a professionalized UN peacekeeping force, there should be more NATO-style peacekeeping missions like those in the former Yugoslavia. Although there is a command structure for the multilateral force, each country has its own professional leadership and the soldiers wear the uniforms of their own country.

Whether a professionalized UN force or a NATO-style mission, foreign troops need to be more than mere peacekeepers. They should possess the power to use force to protect citizens and arrest war criminals.

The idea of a multilateral force going into a foreign country and engaging local troops in battle makes many people uneasy. But what is worse: interference with the sovereignty of a country or allowing people like Karadzic and Sankoh to kill and maim civilians at will? At some point, the international community needs to draw a line in the sand, say "No more," and truly mean it. And the other side needs to understand that the "peacekeeping" force has the capacity to do much more than simply keep the peace. That will be a growing challenge because more and more countries exist in the world today, some of them having emerged as a result of conflict.

Five Recommendations for Ending War

Wars kill and maim people, destroy economic infra-structure, and ruin the future of individuals and countries. Ending military conflict is a noble and necessary endeavor. Here are five recommendations that might reduce the number of wars around the world.

- Individual countries and the international community must devote more attention to reducing economic, social, and political inequality within countries and between countries. Inequality is the root cause of many wars. Chapter 16 provides an explicit discussion of how inequality can be reduced.
- The world needs to pay more attention to enacting and enforcing international laws that govern conflict. For instance, many laws and treaties supposedly protect civilians from torture and wanton killing. International war tribunals dealing with Rwanda and the former Yugoslavia are prosecuting and imprisoning those found guilty of violating such statutes. But we need standing war tribunals that are ready to prosecute any war criminal in any country. Once someone is indicted (and there must be strong evidence to indict), a warrant should be issued for the person's arrest. At that point, local forces or an international force could arrest the individual in question and send him or her to The Hague for trial. That would send a strong message to international outlaws: We can always find you, arrest you, and end your freedom.
- Aggressive and skilled diplomacy must be pursued in every conflict, with the recognition that diplomacy and force often go hand in hand. Countries seldom give up land or resources unless they are (or might be) forced to do so. The Serbs joined the negotiating table in Dayton because they had no real alternative; the country was under assault by a stronger outside military power (NATO) that, after many idle threats, finally refused to allow genocide to continue. In addition, diplomats need to be from the countries involved in the conflict as well as from neutral sources. In Northern Ireland, former U.S. Senator George Mitchell is receiving credit from all sides for tirelessly negotiating peace between Catholics and Protestants. He has made more than 100 trips to Northern Ireland in recent

International war tribunals and skilled diplomacy are two avenues for ending war. At top, hundreds of thousands of protesters gather near the home of Sierra Leone rebel leader Foday Sankoh. At bottom, President Bill Clinton attempts to broker peace between Palestinian President Yasser Arafat and Israeli Prime Minister Ehud Barak.

years to meet with all sides. His quiet tenacity has helped bring Northern Ireland to the brink of peace for the first time in decades. Senator Mitchell has talked in moving terms about the difficulties of brokering peace in the region, primarily because the two sides are entrenched and often unwilling to even hear the other side, much less compromise. At one point, Senator Mitchell told both sides at a dinner that he really enjoys opera. He went on to tell them that he

The role of the United Nations will be examined and reexamined as wars, particularly civil wars, continue around the world. Here, Sierra Leoneans bathe while helicopters hover over the beach in front of the United Nations heliport in the capital city of Freetown. The United Nations was backing government forces against the rebel RUF.

loved a particular piece because it sounds the same every time he hears it, not unlike holding peace negotiations in Northern Ireland, where, no matter how many times he meets with both sides, they continue to say the same things over and over again. It was a lighthearted moment and elicited laughter, but the point was clear.

- The world must react when genocide is occurring or could occur. It is arguable that the United States and its allies could have prevented much of the killing in the former Yugoslavia had they acted more quickly in 1991, when the conflict began. As the saying goes, you need only three things for a holocaust: an aggressor, a victim, and a group that stands by and watches. The world will have more and more decisions to make in the coming years about how much watching it wants to do. Although the world cannot have a 911 emergency response line for every crisis, there needs to be a multilateral military force strong enough to prevent gross human rights abuses. That force should possess the power to fight when necessary and not be squeamish about tracking down war criminals and arresting them, even in the face of military conflict. Of course, military efforts should be conducted in consort with diplomacy and should stress peace over war.

- Nation-building efforts must accompany peace-keeping efforts. However, although outsiders can temporarily stop killing and provide assistance in reducing inequality, they cannot build nations. The contending parties are the ones who have to decide how they will structure their society so everyone can live in peace. Many countries around the world are undergoing historical political changes that may lead to stronger, less contentious nations, particularly when those changes are combined with outside economic and diplomatic assistance. The good news is that there are twice as many democracies today as there were only twenty years ago. But democracy is only one step toward political equality and nation building.

At left, a United Nations peacekeeper accompanies local children in East Timor. How many of these boys would be alive without outside intervention? It is a question seldom pondered by those who call for an end to peacekeeping missions around the world. At right, Sierra Leonean refugees return home to Freetown by ferry boat with the assistance of UN troops.

Those are the measures that would help to keep war from devastating societies and lives. All of us are responsible for seeking a solution to war. A special report to the United Nations General Assembly stated:

> More and more of the world is being sucked into a desolate moral vacuum. This is a space devoid of the most basic human values; a space in which children are slaughtered, raped, and maimed; a space in which children are exploited as soldiers; a space in which children are starved and exposed to extreme brutality (UNICEF, 1996).

To do nothing is to let ourselves be sucked into the vacuum. Sociology helps us to understand the history of societies, to point out inequalities, and to work toward solutions. Without an understanding of why wars start and how they are perpetuated, the world will continue to have more—and deadlier—conflicts.

Thinking about the Topic of War

1. What does the term *nation building* mean? Processes similar to nation building were discussed in several chapters, especially Chapters 6 and 10. Taking into account the points made here and in previous chapters, how do you think nation building could reduce the danger of civil war?

2. What responsibility should the United States—the last remaining superpower—assume for peace in the world? Many of the nations suffering from civil wars today were colonized by European nations. Do those nations have any responsibility for the contemporary conflicts in their former colonies? How should the world community of nations—the United Nations—respond to domestic turmoil, civil war, and the threat of genocide? What evidence can you find to support your opinion? Under what conditions does intervention by outside powers seem to work best or to be counterproductive?

Fiber optic cables have transformed technology and communication around the world—and thus today's workplace.

12 The Future of Work

KEVIN T. LEICHT

What type of career do you want when you're finished with college? Some college students aspire to nothing less than a high-paying, prestigious, soul-satisfying job with a well-run company that will reward their efforts over the years with an endless procession of promotions, pay raises, and perks. At the very least, students expect that they will slip into a decent job in their chosen career, with opportunities for growth and a regular paycheck, and eventually work their way up to a position that permits a comfortable lifestyle.

Well, good luck. The world of work you will be entering after college has been affected by a variety of changes that are making traditional work careers—even the "just average" kind—a thing of the past. In their place are patchwork careers in downsized, outsourced, debureaucratized, postunionized, and cyberconnected workplaces where people are hired on a temporary basis and move from job to job at an ever increasing pace. Most people in industrialized societies will never experience hunger, plague, or war. But we stand some chance of becoming "economically redundant," of facing a workplace and a labor market that constantly challenge us to prove we are worthy of having jobs.

The net result of these long-term changes is that Americans are working more hours and making less money than in the past, increasing our sense of living mostly to work. This chapter concentrates on the American work experience because the United States is unique among industrialized societies: our government does less to regulate labor markets and investment decisions than others do. Our society's focus on market-based solutions to problems means that American employees are not sheltered from technological change or global competition.

Those characteristics are responsible for the growth and dynamism of the American economy, but they also are responsible for the decline of the traditional work career. Those workplace changes—and our inability to plan and save for the future—have put many of us on a work-and-spend cycle of growing indebtedness as we try to keep up with the Joneses and buy all the things that will help us maintain what we think are minimal standards of living. At the same time, the demands of the workplace are fraying our understanding of community and further eroding our sense of well-being. Thus career, consumerism, and community are interrelated. Let's take a closer look at how.

Workplace Change and Your Labor Market Prospects

As late as fifteen years ago, most relationships between employers and employees were driven by an implied social contract (Graphic 12.1). Employees started at the bottom of a firm's hierarchy and slowly and steadily worked their way upward during the course of their careers. From an employee's standpoint, the implied contract sounded something like this: "If I work hard and sacrifice for this company, it will take care of me as I get older." From the company's standpoint, it sounded something like this: "We produce long-term commitment to the company by rewarding people less than they're worth when they're young and more than they're worth when they're old." Even if your career stalled out and you were no longer promoted, you could count on remaining with the same company for your entire working life, enjoying coffee breaks and office parties with essentially the same group of people throughout your career. If nothing else, a company always needed thousands of mid-level employees to produce and keep track of a tremendous amount of paper.

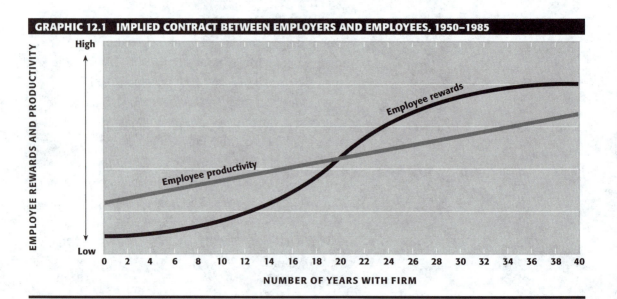

GRAPHIC 12.1   IMPLIED CONTRACT BETWEEN EMPLOYERS AND EMPLOYEES, 1950–1985

EMPLOYEE REWARDS AND PRODUCTIVITY

High

Employee rewards

Employee productivity

Low

0 2 4 6 8 10 12 14 16 18 20 22 24 26 28 30 32 34 36 38 40

NUMBER OF YEARS WITH FIRM

Those who prosper in today's workplace are typically those who can tolerate more independence and more ambiguity than workers faced in the past. They are mobile and flexible about where they work (top left); work well in teams, sometimes assembled for only the duration of a specific project (top right); build their own networks among professional peers and potential employers within their industry (above); and constantly pursue updated skills and knowledge (at right).

Working in that sheltered and protected world was hardly a Shangri-la of bliss and happiness. There was plenty of backstabbing, office politics, racism and sexual harassment (neither of which could be legally remedied at the time), and pressures to conform. There were tyrannical bosses and "golf outings" where you made sure that the boss always won. White-collar, nonunionized employees could be fired at will with little or no recourse. The fact that most people weren't fired was a testimony to the economic boom that followed World War II and reconstruction programs in Europe and Japan and the plentiful job opportunities they produced. But in the 1970s, the implied social contract began to disintegrate.

The Rise of the Disorderly Work Career

The 1970s were a decade of stagnant economic growth, inflation combined with high unemployment (a phenomenon referred to as *stagflation*), and declining profits. Worse still, economic productivity was stagnant or falling. The Arab oil embargoes of the early 1970s (instigated by a relatively new trading block, the Organization of Petroleum Exporting Countries, or OPEC) showed us how vulnerable we were to changes in the political and economic orientations of world traders. (For the first time other than wartime, the price of a U.S. gallon of gasoline rose to over $1. That produced one of the more interesting slogans of the 1970s, "Cheaper crude or no more food!," referring to the dependence of OPEC countries on food exports from the United States.)

As employment rose and fell, profits and investment declined, and prices seemed to be rising without end (inflation in 1979 was 13% and interest rates on consumer loans were around 17%), a subtle but pervasive trend could be seen on store shelves and parking lots. Products manufactured and designed by the Japanese and (increasingly) the Taiwanese and the Koreans began to flood the United States. Those products seemed to be everything their U.S. counterparts were not: cheap, well made, and backed by considerable customer service after the sale. Japanese cars, in particular, were unimaginatively engineered but well built, and they got excel-

lent gas mileage. Japanese electronics seemed far in advance of their beleaguered U.S. counterparts. In scores of industries, it looked like the durable-goods market was going to be taken over by Asian imports, robbing the United States of its identity as a world-class durable-goods manufacturer.

Changes in the market for durable goods had immediate consequences in many other areas of the economy. New financial instruments for financing corporate debt were created and used in a flurry of corporate takeover attempts. Large companies that were deemed inefficient were purchased by corporate raiders and sold off in pieces at a profit. Pay raises became nonexistent; people were glad just to keep their jobs. At about the same time that pay and benefit increases became less common, consumers suddenly discovered they could buy goods with easily available credit cards. Large durable goods (cars and appliances) could be purchased with "no money down."

Beginning in the middle of the 1980s, journalists, social scientists, and policy analysts began to sense that those economic events were having permanent consequences for the world of work. Today, many workers find themselves in a workplace with five new characteristics:

- massive downsizing of the permanent workforce resulting from flatter organizational hierarchies and the replacement of skilled workers by machine tenders
- growing use of temporary workers employed on an as-needed basis to perform specific jobs for the duration of single projects
- extensive use of subcontracting and outsourcing to small firms to produce parts and provide services that used to be provided in house by permanent employees
- flatter organizational hierarchies, as new information technologies eliminated the need for most layers of middle management
- postunionized bargaining environment in which unions have no place and no ability to gain a foothold to bargain with employers

The overall result is a far less stable and secure arena in which to pursue a career. Careers in the

Several economic developments in the 1970s contributed to changes in the typical American work career (clockwise from top): Japanese imports began to flood the U.S. market, thereby lowering prices for many goods and challenging American manufacturers; money and credit became more accessible for consumers, increasing household debt; and oil embargoes led to gas shortages and skyrocketing prices, which further reduced the confidence of American manufacturers.

twenty-first century workplace will be substantially different from the traditional careers of the mid-twentieth century.

Downsizing: Drastic Reductions in the Labor Force

Labor markets in the United States always have rewarded people who can collect and interpret information. In the days before computers, collecting and interpreting large amounts of information required many people to keep track of employee activities, inventories, equipment and maintenance, payrolls, insurance claims, taxes, purchase orders, and legal documents (among other things). Still more people were required to supervise the information gatherers. The companies that hired information gatherers had to rely on those workers' judgment, because mistakes could go undetected for months and cost thousands of dollars. Most of the workers needed to be relatively skilled, and training was critical. With such a large investment in developing information workers, the companies that employed them went to great lengths to increase employee commitment to the firm.

Then computers became cheap, widely available, and easy to use and began to carry out many of the tasks formerly performed by human information gatherers and interpreters. Computers give managers immediate access to the information they need to respond to changing market conditions. Instead of communicating through a chain of command of employees who each interpret what their boss tells them and forward the message to the next level, a small group of managers can communicate directly with those who are responsible for producing the change they want. Some production processes now require almost no human intervention at all.

With computers taking over many of the tasks formerly done by human beings, companies no longer have a need for so many white-collar workers and middle managers. The solution for many companies has been to "downsize," or lay off large numbers of employees, becoming smaller and "leaner, meaner" operations with substantially fewer regular employees. Downsizing was common in the 1980s and 1990s, as Graphic 12.2 shows.

Computers aren't the only reason there has been so much corporate downsizing in the past twenty years. Globalization makes it easier for companies

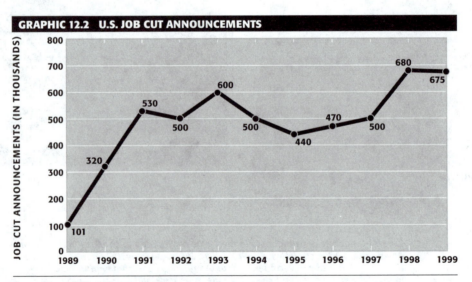

GRAPHIC 12.2   U.S. JOB CUT ANNOUNCEMENTS

Source: "Future of Work," January 29, 2000.

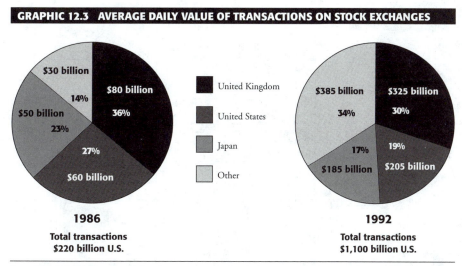

GRAPHIC 12.3   AVERAGE DAILY VALUE OF TRANSACTIONS ON STOCK EXCHANGES

United Kingdom

United States

Japan

Other

$30 billion
14%
$80 billion
36%
$50 billion
23%
27%
$60 billion

1986
Total transactions
$220 billion U.S.

$385 billion
34%
$325 billion
30%
17%
19%
$185 billion
$205 billion

1992
Total transactions
$1,100 billion U.S.

Source: Adapted from Castells, 1996, p. 435.

to move operations to places where labor and materials costs are cheaper, laws are laxer, and markets are closer. When they do relocate, companies typically discover that many employees in their original locations are superfluous.

Furthermore, the transportation system and communications network that increasingly unite economies all over the world have increased the competition that the average U.S. corporation faces. Graphic 12.3 shows that, as Internet access has spread around the globe, this new ability to communicate has drastically increased investment transactions outside the traditional financial centers in the United Kingdom, the United States, and Japan. Now instead of wondering about only local competitors, the well-managed corporation must pay attention to what competitors around the world are doing. The ability to communicate across long distances easily and cheaply makes the accounting firm in Belgium a plausible competitor with the accounting firm in Chicago. Companies around the world increasingly compete in a single market for business and must be ever vigilant to remain competitive.

The era of massive layoffs due to computerization and globalization seems to be over. But down-

sizing will affect your job prospects anyway. It has eliminated the career ladders that reliably employed large numbers of people throughout their entire working lives, which means you may need to jump from company to company to advance your career. In addition, the skilled jobs available in the private sector of the economy will increasingly involve sophisticated customer service work (for example, financial consulting, hotel and restaurant managing) or the service and maintenance of the massive communications network that has replaced thousands of middle managers. Those who are flexible and capable of doing a wide variety of tasks in work teams may actually benefit from the new arrangements. But they probably will have to give up the idea of regular promotions at a single company or regular and steady increases in pay and benefits.

Temporary Workers: Here Today, Gone Tomorrow

Business firms have always experienced fluctuations in demand for their products and services. The fluctuations might be seasonal or predictable in some other way (for example, vacation season is a

busy time for hotels, tax time generates business for lawyers and accounting firms, and auto dealerships and manufacturers experience increased activity at the beginning of the model year). Before computers, firms hired enough employees to meet peak demands and hoped to keep them busy with something moderately useful year-round. But computers and information technologies can monitor fluctuations in product demand (and chart the demand over time), so business firms can plan more efficiently and smooth out the fluctuations. Companies no longer need to keep employees on staff permanently just so they have competent help during peak periods or institute distressing layoffs when demand drops. Instead, they can hire workers from temporary help agencies and subcontractors to work with their permanent employees during peak demand periods.

Another reason for the increase in temporary work has to do with the cost pressures that employers face because of increased competition. Hiring temporary workers on an as-needed basis keeps the total wage bill down while paying workers the prevailing market wage for the time they do work. Graphic 12.4 shows that nearly three-quarters of the firms in the most recent systematic survey of em-

ployment practices report using some form of "contingent workforce" to perform specific tasks: part-time employees (by far the most popular type of contingent worker), temporary employees, and subcontractors. About 6% of the organizations in the survey use all three types of contingent worker (Kalleberg, Knoke, Marsden, & Spaeth, 1996).

Temporary help agencies provide other practical benefits to employers. In exchange for receiving a fee for their services (usually calculated as an hourly rate, only part of which the temporary employee receives), they free the employer from having to hire and screen potential employees, keep track of their payrolls, collect payroll taxes, and provide fringe benefits. The employer also can forgo paying for human resource professionals to motivate a permanent workforce. Temporary employees don't expect to be "taken care of," which, in combination with the cost advantages, makes temporary help agencies some of the fastest-growing employers in the United States.

The implications of the growing use of temporary workers for your career prospects are numerous. You probably will change jobs more frequently than your parents ever did, and your own job performance will have little to do with your tenure on the job. Employers will hire you because you have a specific set of skills and will keep you as long as those skills can be fully utilized. When they no longer need your skills (even for a short period of time), they probably will let you go. You will need to maintain networks of friends, coworkers, and employers to find new jobs and keep yourself employed. On the plus side, your jobs more than likely will be interesting—most dull and boring jobs are now done by machines. Employers will especially value you if you are a flexible, fast learner. Whether this scenario is better or worse than your parents' careers depends on what you want from a job and how adaptable you can be.

Outsourcing and Subcontracting: Why Make It If We Can Buy It?

Many of the same technological and competitive pressures that affect employment relationships also affect where people work. Subcontracting and outsourcing occur when a firm decides to hire an inde-

pendent company to produce products and services that were once produced "in house" by the firm itself. Firms may find existing firms to provide ready-made products, or they can spin off the division or department that once produced products for the firm and organize it as an independent company. Both options allow a firm to transfer control over employees and activities that it used to monitor itself.

Why are subcontracting and outsourcing possible now when they weren't as late as twenty years ago? The ability to communicate instantly with subcontractors through computers and the Internet has helped tremendously. Modular manufacturing, in which robots and computers make mass-produced items to customized specifications, is critical as well, as are innovations in shipping, trucking, and postal services that allow for the rapid movement of products and services over long distances (for example, Federal Express and UPS).

Most production processes are now organized as "just-in-time" delivery systems. Such systems allow

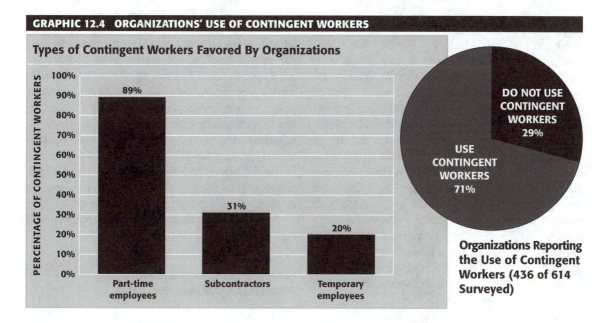

GRAPHIC 12.4   ORGANIZATIONS' USE OF CONTINGENT WORKERS

Types of Contingent Workers Favored By Organizations

Part-time employees: 89%
Subcontractors: 31%
Temporary employees: 20%

(Y-axis: PERCENTAGE OF CONTINGENT WORKERS, 0% to 100%)

USE CONTINGENT WORKERS 71%
DO NOT USE CONTINGENT WORKERS 29%

Organizations Reporting the Use of Contingent Workers (436 of 614 Surveyed)

Source: Kalleberg, Knoke, Marsden, and Spaeth, 1996, p. 264.

Note: Percentages do not total 100% because some organizations use two or three types of contingent workers.

products to be made as they are ordered, delivered to customers right when they are needed, to be used right away. The order is sent over a computer to the manufacturing location, where computers calculate needed resources and modify the robotic manufacturing system to produce the order.

An example of a just-in-time delivery system is the Johnson Controls factory in Toledo, Ohio. Johnson Controls is one of the largest producers of seats for cars, trucks, SUVs, and vans in the country. Instead of producing large numbers of vehicle seats in all sizes, colors, and fabrics, the Johnson Controls factory makes seats to order for specific vehicles. The factory is connected, via computers and the Internet, to automotive assembly plants in southern Michigan. When a plant receives an order for a specific vehicle, the order is scanned into a computer and electronically mailed to the Johnson Controls plant. The exact type of seat is then produced for the specific vehicle, loaded onto a truck, and delivered to the assembly plant a few minutes before it is actually installed. This system eliminates the need to save, store, and keep track of inventory at either end of the assembly process.

Increasingly, communications and manufacturing technologies are so sophisticated that just-in-time delivery systems can work across states, across nations, even around the world. Firms can ask for

bids on the production of the items they want, and the subcontracting firm then bids on delivering the products at the specific times they are needed. They pay one price and get the product exactly when they want it. What could be better?

Subcontracting and outsourcing also have implications for your future work career. Many new jobs are being created not in large, Fortune 500 companies that have been in existence for decades but in relatively small firms that supply large companies with a specific product or service on a contract basis. A company's fortunes depend on maintaining good relationships with suppliers and developing a reputation for quality performance, where *quality* means the right product, at the right price, delivered at the right time, and the right time is measured in minutes. Those changes put additional pressures on employees in subcontracting firms even as they allow firms to branch out and provide products and services to a variety of customers.

Flatter Organizational Hierarchies: Who Needs the Pyramid?

It follows that organizations that don't need middle managers don't need an organizational hierarchy. Instead of messages being passed up and down the organization, a small group of managers in a central office can, via computers and communication technology, monitor and communicate directly with representatives in the field.

Eliminating the organizational hierarchy does raise the question of how to motivate people who are at the bottom of an organization with no realistic prospects for reliable promotions. There are a variety of solutions to that problem. Some firms sell or buy shares of stock for their employees that accumulate as they continue to work for the company. Such ownership stake in the company takes the place of regular promotions and raises. Graphic 12.5 is a hypothetical example of one of those compensation schemes.

Some firms try to keep employees motivated by hiring broadly trained people and moving them from task to task, which keeps them from becoming too bored and offers them a bigger picture of what the company does (Southwest Airlines uses that strategy). Still other firms simply accept high levels of employee turnover and treat their employees as interchangeable parts.

While all those strategies work, depending on the circumstances, they make for a much different workplace than the reliable career of your grandfather's generation. For greater peace of mind, you definitely want to be in a firm that manages people by moving them around rather than expecting you to quit. Instead of a traditional boss, you will be expected to work in teams on collaborative projects that emphasize cooperation and getting along with others. People who like to be told what to do and left alone will be uncomfortable in the new workplace; people who like working with others in situations where they are rarely told what to do by a supervisor should prosper. You won't get to boss people around as your career advances, but you should suffer fewer personal indignities at the hands of tyrannical managers.

The Postunionized Workplace: Can Unions Shoot at Moving Targets?

American society has never fully accepted organized labor as part of the work landscape. But the evolution toward the new workplace has decreased the role of unions considerably (refer back to Graphic 10.6), and declines in private sector unionization

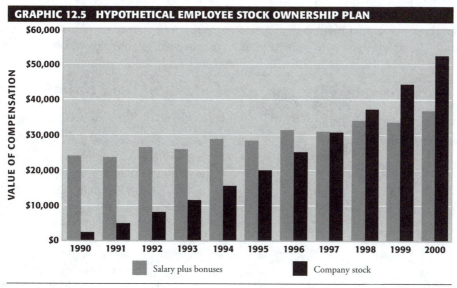

GRAPHIC 12.5 HYPOTHETICAL EMPLOYEE STOCK OWNERSHIP PLAN

VALUE OF COMPENSATION

Legend: Salary plus bonuses / Company stock

Source: Boyett and Conn, 1992, p. 14.

show no signs of stopping. The decline of unionization in the United States is unprecedented among industrialized countries.

The prevailing rules for collective bargaining were established under a different set of assumptions than those we find in the new workplace. For one thing, there was an actual workplace, a fixed location where people congregated to carry out their tasks under the oversight of managers and supervisors. The group of people who worked there were assumed to be relatively permanent employees who weren't replaced very often. The company had considerable fixed costs tied up in specific locations that it could not easily abandon. The employees had to care enough about their jobs with the company to want to improve their lot.

In the new workplace described in this chapter, none of those assumptions hold true. Employers no longer are tied to fixed locations for long periods of time. They routinely hire temporary workers and subcontract and outsource work to other companies. Many employees never come into contact with a physical location called "the workplace," where they can gather with peers to "talk shop." How do you define a bargaining unit in a firm whose employees are never fixed, don't reside in one place, and don't communicate except through e-mail?

None of that is to say that the union movement will completely disappear from the American landscape. Instead, the union movement will have to evolve and change with the new workplace, and representatives of organized labor will have to lobby Congress and state legislators for new and more flexible laws governing union representation.

As technological change and globalization continue to place your work career in the hands of people outside your local community, we can expect organized labor to express more concern for the basic rights of employees in less developed and rapidly industrializing countries. That concern was dramatically illustrated in the demonstrations in Seattle, Washington, at the World Trade Organization Conference in early 2000. Attempts by unions and other concerned American citizens to influence the terms and conditions of work in far-flung corners of the world reflect more than just humanitarian concern for exploited people. They also reflect a growing fear that employers can find cheap replacements for virtually anyone, including college-educated accountants, lawyers, computer software engineers, financial planners, and most other skilled white-collar jobs.

In the twenty-first century, downsizing, temporary work, subcontracting and outsourcing, flatter organizational hierarchies, and the continued decline of organized labor will produce careers with unprecedented numbers of job changes, earnings instability, and anxiety. But those same careers also will be dynamic, ever changing, and never dull. The changes have larger social consequences for our collective life, as you will soon see.

The Social Consequences of the Changing Workplace

The rise of the disorderly work career has had two important effects on working Americans. First, there is no longer an automatic relationship between working harder and earning more, especially in the United States as compared with other industrialized nations. Graphic 12.6 shows that the annual hours that people work in the United States has been rising while the earnings from their jobs have not. Second, those changes not only are dispiriting to the individuals who experience them, they also have social consequences. The disjunction between work

GRAPHIC 12.6   WORKING MORE BUT NOT EARNING MORE

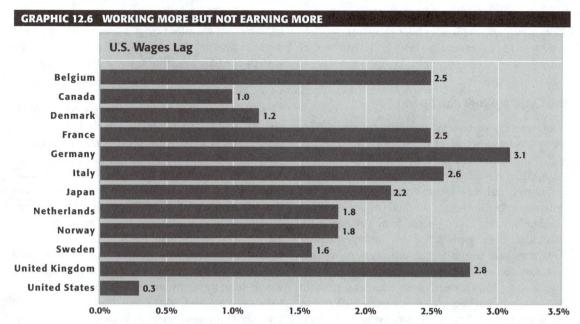

U.S. Wages Lag

Country	Value
Belgium	2.5
Canada	1.0
Denmark	1.2
France	2.5
Germany	3.1
Italy	2.6
Japan	2.2
Netherlands	1.8
Norway	1.8
Sweden	1.6
United Kingdom	2.8
United States	0.3

PERCENTAGE CHANGE IN REAL COMPENSATION, ALL MANUFACTURING EMPLOYEES, 1973–1993

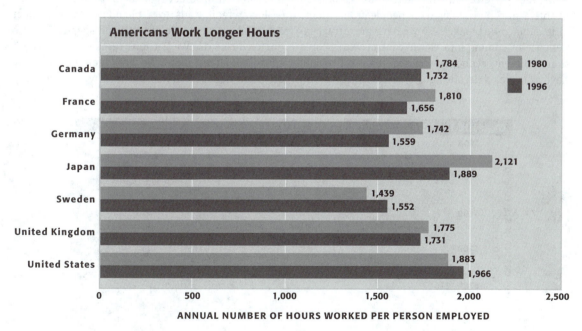

Americans Work Longer Hours

Legend: 1980, 1996

Country	1980	1996
Canada	1,784	1,732
France	1,810	1,656
Germany	1,742	1,559
Japan	2,121	1,889
Sweden	1,439	1,552
United Kingdom	1,775	1,731
United States	1,883	1,966

ANNUAL NUMBER OF HOURS WORKED PER PERSON EMPLOYED

Sources: Top chart from Gordon, 1996, p. 27; bottom chart from Organization for Economic Cooperation and Development, 2000.

and pay leads people to consume at a level beyond their means, and the lack of time away from work is detrimental to communities. Let's explore the social consequences.

The Cycle of Work and Spend

In the process of creating a globalized workplace, we've created a world of globalized consumers as well. Interactions via the Internet, television, and other media have changed our comparison groups, according to Juliet Schor, an economist who studies work and spending habits. Because of our ability to compare ourselves with people from a wide variety of circumstances, income brackets, and lifestyles almost anywhere in the world, our ideas of what is necessary for sustaining an adequate and comfortable lifestyle have moved from comparisons with our next-door neighbors to comparisons with real or imagined others we never personally meet. Furthermore, the new electronic media give us the illusion of interacting personally with people from widely different income brackets, so we have the virtual experience of coming into closer contact with people from different economic classes than we would have as late as a decade ago.

But wait a minute. If our incomes aren't growing, how can we afford what we see on TV and hear about in Internet chat rooms? The answer lies in the growth of easily available credit. Consumer borrowing has risen to unprecedented levels, as Graphic 12.7 makes clear.

According to the Consumer Federation of America, 55 million to 60 million households in the United States have revolving credit card balances (balances not paid in full each month). The average household carries $7,000 in revolving credit card balances and pays $1,000 in interest and fees on those balances each year. The credit card balances of families with incomes closer to the poverty line are actually higher than those of families with incomes that are twice the poverty line or higher. And credit card solicitations are more aggressive than ever before; the Consumer Federation estimates that between 1998 and 2000 credit card issuers offered new credit to consumers at a rate of $24,000 per household (Consumer Federation of America, 1998).

Easy credit leads to a phenomenon that Juliet Schor labels the "cycle of work and spend." We use our credit cards. We get jobs to pay off our credit cards. We charge more. We work more hours to pay off more debt. We try to get jobs with better pay,

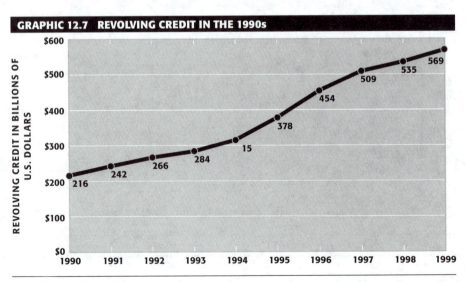

GRAPHIC 12.7   REVOLVING CREDIT IN THE 1990s

Source: Consumers Union, 2000.

whether we like those jobs or not. We work more hours on those jobs to pay off still more debt—all in an attempt to live lifestyles our incomes wouldn't allow us to have without credit cards.

That is one unique feature of the larger social world created by the new workplace. The possession of consumer items like houses, cars, boats, designer clothes, and other prestige consumer items is increasingly divorced from the actual jobs that people do and the earnings those jobs generate. The easy availability of credit and the irrational multiplication of earnings power it produces means we can't look at the consumer items people own and tell how "well off" they really are. That is a relatively new dimension of the social stratification system that has changed well within the last thirty or forty years.

The different means available for obtaining cars is but one example of the bewildering array of consumer choices people have. You can buy or lease a new car with no money down. If you have a bad credit history, there are car dealers who will loan you money at higher rates of interest so you can "reestablish" your credit. Your loan value as a customer is based on whether you can make the minimum payments on the car you want; to keep those payments low, the lender may spread them over longer periods of time. With the additional interest or lease payments, the total cost of the car rises. Some car dealerships even include sales taxes and license fees in a loan so the out-of-pocket expenses really are zero!

Unfortunately, college students are not immune to the cycle of work and spend. A 1999 study of credit cards on campus found that about 70% of four-year college students possess at least one credit card (Manning, 1999). The vast majority of those students are "revolvers," borrowers who carry outstanding balances on their cards. The average student revolver carries $2,000 in debt, and one-fifth of all student revolvers carry more than $10,000 in credit card debt. Credit card debt is being refinanced with student loans and private debt consolidation loans (loans that promise to reduce your credit card debt to "one easy payment"). Many colleges and universities permit credit card marketing on campus

and benefit financially from that marketing through sponsorship for school programs and student activities and exclusive marketing agreements.

But the most striking finding of the study is the costs that credit card debts impose on students. Heavily indebted students from affluent families are bailed out by their (none too happy) parents. But students from families with more modest incomes are forced to cut back on coursework and increase their work time at paid jobs to pay off their debts. Some students are forced out of college entirely to work full time. In 1998, an Indiana University administrator said, "We lose more students to credit card debt than to academic failure" (Manning, 1999, p. 2).

Indeed, the marketing of credit card debt to college students is relentless. In the spring of 1999, I had nineteen students in a political sociology seminar keep track of all the credit card solicitations they received through the mail for the entire semester (around five months). The students were a representative cross-section of students at The University of Iowa; all were in their early twenties, and most had part-time jobs and were taking at least twelve semester hours of course credit. None of them had what they would term "serious" full-time jobs that involved a vocation that they were pursuing as a career. The results of the exercise were amazing. In five months, each student received an average of six credit card solicitations, and the entire group received 115 solicitations, combined. The average amount of credit offered to each student was $36,000. The entire group was offered over $2 million dollars worth of revolving credit at annual interest rates ranging from an "attractive" introductory rate of 3.9% to a rate of 21%. That represents an unbelievable boost in spending power that is not accompanied by visible signs of earnings power.

The problems that undisciplined credit card spending can create extend beyond bankruptcy and bad credit ratings. Increasingly, students with high credit card debts are having trouble getting good jobs because employers are reviewing credit reports. One interviewee was asked by a major Wall Street banking firm, "How can we feel comfortable about

With the easy availability of credit, many college students get trapped in the "work and spend" cycle. They buy so much on credit that they need to go to work to pay off their debts, sometimes jeopardizing their college careers as a result.

you managing large sums of money when you have had such difficulty handling your own credit card debts?" (Manning, 1999, p. 2).

Worse still, the psychological problems resulting from severe credit card debt include severe emotional crisis and suicide. Two testimonials from parents of students who took their own lives provide graphic evidence that the cycle of work and spend involves far more than the inability to balance a checkbook. Here's the story told by the mother of Sean Moyer (Manning, 1999, pp. 4–7).

My son, Sean Moyer, committed suicide on February 7, 1998. He was 22 years old, a junior at the University of Oklahoma and $10,000 in debt to credit card companies. . . . He was a national merit finalist and earned a full-ride scholarship to the University of Texas at Dallas. He was so bright about many things but so stupid when it came to managing money—he just couldn't do it. I remember the day his father and I took him off to college. We were so full of excitement about his future. The excitement about living on campus, being in the big

city, his classes, and the opportunities he would have. I also remember the credit card companies having booths at the union trying to get Sean and other freshmen to sign up. They offered T-shirts and other things just for opening an account. . . . Sean got his first card soon after he started college. While attending UT he worked as a gift wrapper and sales person at Marshall Fields. He was making minimum wage. His meager salary didn't bother the credit card companies. By the time he died he had 12 credit cards including 1 MasterCard, 2 Visas, Neiman-Marcus, Saks 5th Avenue, Macy's, Marshall Fields, Conoco, and Discover. How those companies can justify giving a credit card to a person making $5.15 an hour is beyond me. . . . Sean tried to pay off his debts. He went through credit counseling while in Dallas but he fell further and further behind. When he was 21 he realized he couldn't afford Dallas and moved back home to attend the University of Oklahoma. He worked two jobs while at OU. Still he couldn't make ends meet.

A week before he killed himself Sean and I had a long talk about his debts and his future. He told me he had no idea how to get out of his financial mess and didn't see much of a future for himself. He had wanted to go to law school but didn't think he could get a loan to pay tuition because he owed so much on his cards. His father and I were appalled that he had gotten into so much debt but we also didn't have an extra $10,000 to pay his bills. He thought he was a failure at 22. I will never know the exact reason Sean killed himself . . . but I have no doubt that his credit card debt played a significant part in his decision.

Mitzi Pool's mother tells a similar heartbreaking story (Manning, 1999, pp. 7–8).

My daughter, Mitzi Pool, was a first-year student at the University of Oklahoma in the fall of 1997. She had a small scholarship and student loans to get herself through college. She had grown up most of her life in a single-parent environment and missed out on a lot of the finer things in life. . . . She took a 12–14 hour per week part-time job to pay her car insurance and any spending money. She had applied, received, and maxed out 3 credit cards within the short three and one-half months of her college life. . . . On December 1, 1997 at 7:30 pm, she called me crying and upset. She had lost her part-time job and did not know what she was going to do until school was out at the semester break. I tried to assure her that when she came home for the weekend we would sit down and go over her bills and work some plan out. I was not aware of the credit cards she had gained. This was my last conversation with my daughter. With her checkbook and bills spread out on her bed, my lovely daughter committed suicide that night. No letter, no explanation. The $2,500 credit card debt does not sound like that much to you and me, but for an 18 year old trying to be an adult too fast, $2,500 is devastating."

Are Nikes, new cars, drop-waist jeans, and fully equipped apartments really worth that sort of agony?

Fraying Community Ties

The cycle of work and spend takes a toll on the larger society, not just on the individuals who get

caught up in it. When we're trying to pay off debts by working at unstable jobs whose earnings don't go up regularly, we may stop participating in community activities that once held neighborhoods and communities together.

As discussed in Chapter 3, there are numerous signs that the communities we live in are experiencing difficulties. Americans complain incessantly about the taxes they pay, taxes that are among the lowest in the industrialized world (see Phillips, 1991). Some commentators suspect (as I do) that increased complaining about taxes reflects declining feelings of obligations to the greater community (see, for example, Gans, 1988; Bellah et al., 1985; Carter 1998). There is no firm sociological evidence to back up that suspicion, but it seems that people are less likely to know their neighbors than in times past. We live in bedroom communities that we leave in the morning (when it's dark), commute to an office complex to work all day long, get into our cars and return exhausted (in the dark) to our bedroom community to collapse on the couch in front of the television set. While we're doing that, the trash along the streets isn't collected, Little League baseball teams need coaches, children come home to empty houses after school, we complain about needy people instead of helping them, and our sense of connection to the place where we live might go down the tubes.

Graphic 12.8 presents some results from a 1996 *New York Times* survey covering a wide variety of issues about the relationship between the workplace and community life. The results of the poll are interesting on a number of fronts. Of the 1,265 adults surveyed across the United States, 10% reported experiencing a crisis layoff, a job loss that produced a major crisis in their life. Almost two-thirds reported some other close experience with layoffs, and 14% said they were "very worried" that they or someone in their household would lose their job in the next twelve months. Nineteen percent reported that they took an extra job in the past three years to make ends meet. Overall, the results illustrate exactly what I've been talking about with regard to the growth of disorganized careers.

Graphic 12.8 shows how those changes have affected the commitments that people make to their

GRAPHIC 12.8 COMMUNITY ACTIVITIES AMONG THREATENED EMPLOYEES IN THE 1990s

CHARITABLE
GIVING

"In recent years, has the amount of money you give to charity incr decreased, or stayed about the same?"

	Increased	Decreased	Stayed the Same
Experienced crisis layoff	17%	20%	63%
Worries about losing job	19%	22%	58%
Working extra job	23%	20%	57%
Total	26%	16%	57%

VOLUNTEER
WORK

"In recent years, has the amount of time you devote to doing volunteer work increased, decreased, or stayed about the same?"

	Increased	Decreased	Stayed the Same
Experienced crisis layoff	31%	26%	44%
Worries about losing job	16%	26%	57%
Working extra job	29%	24%	46%
Total	24%	21%	53%

eased,

COMMUNITY
PARTICIPATION

"In recent years, has your involvement in civil community groups increased, decreased, or stayed about the same?"

	Increased	Decreased	Stayed the Same
Experienced crisis layoff	24%	20%	55%
Worries about losing job	15%	23%	60%
Working extra job	23%	22%	55%
Total	21%	20%	57%

RELIGIOUS
PARTICIPATION

"In recent years, have you attended religious services more often, less often, or has there been no change?"

	More Often	Less Often	No Change
Experienced crisis layoff	21%	22%	57%
Worries about losing job	18%	28%	53%
Working extra job	17%	28%	55%
Total	20%	21%	58%

Source: Adapted from *Downsizing*, 1996, pp. 284–292.

communities. Overall, about one-quarter of those surveyed say they are increasing their contributions to charities, volunteering more hours, committing more time to civic and community groups, and attending religious services. But almost equal num- bers of people claim that their commitments to those community activities have decreased in recent years.

However, the overall results don't tell the whole story. If you study Graphic 12.8 carefully, you will see that declining participation is the greatest among those who are worried about future layoffs. How can people reasonably commit themselves to a future in a specific community if they don't know if they will be gainfully employed there, they can't afford the lifestyle they are living, and they have to work longer hours just to make ends meet?

The Hopes and Fears of the New Workplace

It is tempting to look with despair at what we've just seen about growing work instability, indebtedness, and declining traditional communities. Indeed, the workplace is a more uncertain place than it was for your parents and your grandparents. Creating a career for yourself will be harder, and I would be concerned about wages that don't grow, growing gaps between the haves and have-nots, longer hours of work, and the ever increasing trap that consumer credit produces. My aim is not to throw you into a panic, however. I merely want to inform you of the realities that are out there beyond college. Sociologists aren't doing their jobs if they don't tell the truth, even if nobody likes the way the truth sounds.

Things are not as bleak for individuals as they may appear. There are some things to be hopeful about, as there almost always are. Traditional corporate employment—with its grinding conformity, formal business attire, nine-to-five jobs, backbiting office culture, and massive bureaucracy—was spiritually and mentally impoverishing for many people. New workplace arrangements promise greater flexibility; for many people, the price of greater flexibility is more than worth it in comparison to the disadvantages of a standard, nine-to-five desk job. The computers and robotics that eliminated thousands of jobs have also made an unprecedented number of goods and services available to us and opened new economic opportunities in areas that no one had even dreamed of twenty years ago.

If I have one piece of advice to give to you, it is this: learn as much as you can and find work you enjoy, regardless of how much money that work pays. Life is too short (and financial success too fleeting) to base all your decisions on what you can buy. Those who can stay flexible, learn new things, and live within their means have a very good chance of prospering in the new workplace. In addition, avoid the cycle of work and spend and give something back to the community you live in. Doing so not only looks good, it will make you feel good. When you look back in your old age at what you've accomplished, your success in carving out a balanced lifestyle with a sense of belonging will probably matter more to you than the fact that you always had the latest cars or fashions.

Thinking about the Topic of Work

1. Chapter 1 stated that "technology is both a blessing and a curse." How has technology affected your career prospects? Taking both positive and negative effects into account, would you say that technology is more blessing or more curse? What are the implications of the other workplace and lifestyle trends discussed here for your choice of major and desired career? How do you feel about the advice to "find work you enjoy, regardless of how much money that work pays"?

2. Have the trends discussed here (for example, downsizing, the growing use of temporary workers, the declining influence of unions) affected your community? How? Explain your opinion, incorporating material from other parts of the book (see Chapters 3 and 5 in particular). Support your opinion with data published by local newspapers or other sources of information on local economic trends, supplemented by your personal experience and the experiences of friends and family.

Boston, like many other cities, has embraced the automobile, high-rise buildings, and other technologies associated with "progress." However, the small inset photo shows nearby Cambridge, which seeks to maintain a more sustainable environment by encouraging pedestrian traffic and the conversion of old buildings to new uses.

13 Can the World Develop and Sustain Its Environment?

MICHAEL MAYERFELD BELL

A few years ago, I got a chance to visit an old friend—let's call him Carlos Manuel Delgado. By U.S. standards, Carlos is a small farmer. He has about two hectares of coffee trees, another four hectares in sugar cane, and about two hectares of pasture on his farm in the central highlands of Costa Rica. That's equivalent to about twenty acres, a good size for his own country but puny in comparison to the U.S. average of some 450 acres per farm. I first got to know Carlos in 1976 when I was doing some geologic mapping near Platanillo, Costa Rica, a village of about 500 people and where Carlos has always lived.

In 1994, I had a chance to return to Costa Rica (this time as a sociologist, not a geologist, having switched fields in the interim), and I decided, on a lark, to look up Carlos. We hadn't communicated in all those years, and I didn't know for sure that he still lived in Platanillo or that he was even still alive. There are no phones in Platanillo, so the only thing to do was to take a decrepit bus up the switch-back highway to the small mountain city of Turrialba, and from there to take an even more decrepit bus up an even more switch-backed road to Platanillo.

So I did. Eventually, the road turned to dirt, and the bus crested a rise overlooking the upland valley that cradled Platanillo. The sugar cane and coffee fields traced neat lines up the valley sides, and here and there the pastel houses of farmers and farm workers studded the scene like soft-colored precious stones sewn into the folds of a lush green cloak. I could see the church steeples, the small string of village shops, and the village school down by the creek. It was even more beautiful than I remembered.

Why am I telling this story? Because it has much to suggest about the question that I try to answer here: can we simultaneously develop and sustain the environment? In the face of widespread desires for both better human livelihoods and for protection of the environment on which our livelihoods depend, societies around the world are trying to take the new path of what is often called "sustainable development"—development that does not compromise our environmental future. Is that possible, or is sustainable development a contradiction in terms, a global version of the old conundrum that you can't eat your cake and have it too?

But let's cut to the chase. I did find Carlos. He was walking back from his sugar cane fields with a load of cane on his head and the machete he had used to cut it in his hand. He did remember me. The bond between us was immediately remade, and we spent the rest of the afternoon excitedly remembering stories from when we had first gotten to know each other and telling new ones of our lives in the intervening eighteen years. That evening we got together with some of the other local folks that I had met years ago. There was much showing of photographs and drinking of beer as we sat in the single room that served as the sleeping quarters, dining area, and living room for Carlos's family.

Then the conversation turned more serious. The men talked about the difficulty of farming in the region. How there is not enough land anymore. How everyone works so hard and makes so little. How the work is dangerous, accidents are common, and the hospital is far away. How the politicians seem even further away. And this was in Costa Rica, the

"Switzerland of Central America"—a country world renowned for its stable democratic government, its high literacy rates, its high life-expectancy figures (equal to those of the United States, in fact), and its sustainable development policies and extensive system of national parks, aimed at protecting the country's ecological foundations while providing for the needs of its people. If sustainable development is working anywhere, it should be working in Costa Rica. But you wouldn't know it from our conversation.

"So why don't you take us home with you?" asked Carlos, with a laugh that just barely covered the deeper seriousness of his question.

"But why would you want to leave Platanillo?" I asked in return. "The close community here, the safety at night, your friends and family, your closeness to the land. You'd lose all that. It's so beautiful and peaceful here. And Costa Rica is a wonderful country." I meant it. I was in love with the place all over again.

Three of them immediately responded, as if rehearsed, in one voice, with the same laugh that Carlos had used: "For the money!"

For the money—*por la plata,* in Spanish—and all the good things, material things, they imagined would come with it. *Por la plata.*

Yes, Platanillo is beautiful and peaceful. But its residents want more. And who can blame them? Looking around the world, virtually everyone seems to agree. Indeed, there can be little that so much of the world apparently agrees on: more is better. Graphic 13.1 shows the distinctly upward trend in gross world product per person over the past fifty years (keep in mind that production has risen because of increased consumption).

Providing everyone with more is not so simple, however. We must face up to a difficult paradox: wanting more seems to lead to more want. I mean that in several ways:

- *The more you want, the more you want.* Consumption has long been a kind of addiction for us, a hunger that grows the more we try to satisfy it, as sociologists from Thorstein Veblen in the 1890s to Juliet Schor in the 1990s have argued.

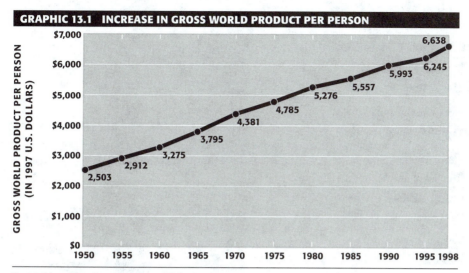

GRAPHIC 13.1   INCREASE IN GROSS WORLD PRODUCT PER PERSON

Source: Adapted from Brown, Renner, and Halweil, 1999, p. 65.

Note: 1998 data are preliminary.

- *The more you want, the more your friends want.* An increasing desire for goods on the part of some people leads to others' increasing desire for goods, as the Changs try to keep up with the Joneses, the Guptas try to keep up with the Changs, and the Carlos Manuel Delgados try to keep up with the Michael Mayerfeld Bells.

- *The more you want, the more people wind up in want.* Increasing desire for goods also tends to promote unequal distribution of goods, as the world divides into winners and losers in the scramble for more. Quite a bit of social scientific research backs up that distressing point, as was shown in Chapter 5.

- *The more you want, the more other creatures wind up in want.* The evidence is now incontrovertible that want also increasingly extends out of the human community and into the biggest community of all: the environment. Nonhuman animals are in want of habitat—and not because the tigers are trying to keep up with the lions and the panthers are trying to keep up with the tigers. Habitat loss for nonhuman animals, soil erosion, global warming, acid rain,

deforestation, the thinning of the ozone layer, hazardous chemicals, and most current forms of agriculture are all dimensions of environmental want. Graphic 13.2 shows some of the effects on ecosystems associated with rising consumption. Several maps in the appendix expand the picture.

So can we simultaneously develop and sustain the environment? As an environmental sociologist I firmly believe that the answer is a definite maybe. And in consideration of the gloomy prospects sketched above, that maybe is cause for optimism, at least for me. I'll try to lay out the sociological case for optimism in the hope that it might extend to you, if you don't already share it. Because, as I'll argue, if we don't come to share what I'll call *sociological optimism* with regard to the environment, there soon will be little reason for it.

We Consuming Humans

Let's start with the pessimistic side of the answer and the sociological theory and evidence that can help us understand it. In 1899, Thorstein Veblen—philosopher,

Carbon Dioxide Emissions of Selected Countries

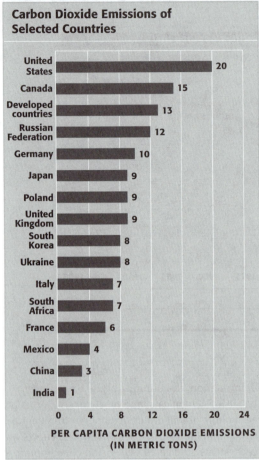

PER CAPITA CARBON DIOXIDE EMISSIONS (IN METRIC TONS)

Source: Adapted from World Resources Institute, 2000; data from Carbon Dioxide Information Analysis Center, November 1997, and United Nations Population Division, 1996.

Consumption of Printing and Writing Paper

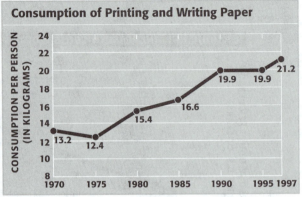

Source: Adapted from United Nations Educational, Scientific, and Cultural Organization, 1999, Table IV.S.2.

Human Encroachment on Natural Forests

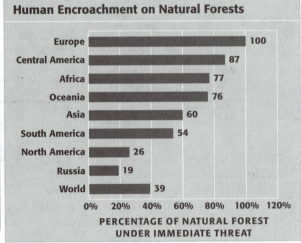

PERCENTAGE OF NATURAL FOREST UNDER IMMEDIATE THREAT

Source: Adapted from World Resources Institute, 2000; data from Bryant, Nielsen, and Tangley, 1997, p. 12.

Link Between Carbon Dioxide and Temperature

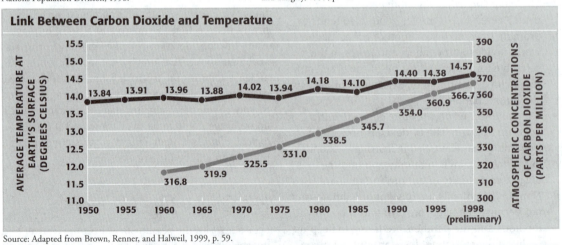

Source: Adapted from Brown, Renner, and Halweil, 1999, p. 59.

economist, sociologist, social critic, Midwesterner—published a devastating critique of the pretensions of upper-class American society, *The Theory of the Leisure Class*. The 1890s were a time of unprecedented social inequality in the United States. It was the decade that produced extravagances like the palatial summer homes in Newport, Rhode Island, for the country's burgeoning ranks of the superrich, homes like The Breakers, the dazzling seventy-room stone mansion completed in 1895 for railroad magnate Cornelius Vanderbilt. It was also the decade that saw the rise of the tenement slums in New York City; the second-worst depression in U.S. history, as a result of the panic of 1893; rampant unemployment; and widespread strikes by steel workers, miners, and railroad workers, as the poor of the country fought for decent wages and living conditions. Meanwhile, the wealthy competed with each other to see who could lay on more marble, gold leaf, and rare woods in their homes and more satin, silk, and embroidery in their clothing.

Veblen, appalled, ripped into the pretensions of what he called the leisure class with his now famous concept of conspicuous consumption, the social processes of competitive display of status through materialist ostentation. There were three elements of such ostentation, said Veblen: conspicuous consumption, conspicuous leisure, and conspicuous waste. Wearing only the most expensive clothing is an example of conspicuous consumption. Taking long vacations in faraway places so you can tell your friends all about it is an example of conspicuous leisure. Holding lavish dinner parties with far more food than the guests can eat and then throwing most of it away is an example of conspicuous waste. All three forms of display can combine, noted Veblen. Take Cornelius Vanderbilt's mansion. The impressive architecture of The Breakers—an imitation Italian palace that was meant to imply that Vanderbilt was an aristocrat—was conspicuous consumption. The fact that it was only his summer home was conspicuous leisure. The colossal size of the place, far more than any one family could possibly need, was conspicuous waste. In fact, said Veblen, all three processes reduce to conspicuous waste, for who truly needs any of it?

Few of us are as wealthy as the Vanderbilts were in the 1890s, but we are nonetheless familiar with those processes among our friends and associates, and we may even recognize them within ourselves at times. It may be that none of us is completely above such tendencies. Even Gandhi struggled with them, as his writings describe. But there is something new in how we engage in status display through goods, argues Juliet Schor in her 1998 book, *The Overspent American*. We increasingly exhibit what she calls the "new consumerism," in which we no longer try to keep up with the Joneses next door but rather with the people we know at work, including the boss, and with the rich people we see in ads and on TV shows. The reference group for consumption used to be people of a similar class background. But today's more informal society brings us into greater social contact with people who make far more money than we do, particularly in the workplace. It is now much more common to mix socially—on the company softball team or at the company coffee pot—with those higher up the echelon. The breakdown of neighborhoods and community feeling combined with the rise of the media age has also led to new emulative patterns, as people think more about Ally McBeal, Dharma and Greg, Madonna, Prince William, and the beautiful people with big houses and nice cars in the ads than they do about the folks next door.

Consequently, Schor argues, we have intensified our competitive consumption in recent decades. For example, the average American home has doubled in size in the last fifty years, new homes are being built with two- and three-car garages instead of the one-car garage that was standard in the 1950s, and the number of bathrooms in new homes often exceeds the number of bedrooms. Not to mention all the spending it takes to fill those rooms and to keep up with constantly rising standards of middle-class comfort. In 1973, 3% of Americans described a second television as a necessity, not a luxury—by 1996, 10% did. In 1973, 20% similarly thought a second car a necessity, and 26% felt that way about home air conditioning. By 1996, the second car had moved up to the necessity category for 37% of Americans and home air conditioning for 51% (Schor, 1998, pp.

11–17). And then there are all the new gadgets—the microwave oven, the portable phone, the cell phone, the VCR, the answering machine, and, of course, the computer—that wouldn't have been found in any homes in 1973. Large percentages of the American public now regard all those gadgets as necessities too. The new "necessities" have been made possible by a 30% to 70% increase (depending on how the measurement is done) in personal spending between 1979 and 1995 (Schor, 1998, pp. 11–17).

Are we any happier because of that increase in consumption? Surveys suggest otherwise. The percentage of Americans reporting themselves as "very happy" peaked in 1957, when our spending levels were about half what they are today, and has never recovered, despite economic growth (Schor, 1992, p. 111). Instead, we are working more than we ever did—the equivalent of an extra month a year—and finding ourselves stressed for time, time, time like never before (Schor, 1992). Leisure time, the great gift modernity was supposed to bring, has actually declined, as Graphic 13.3 shows.

We have become stuck on what might be called the "treadmill of consumption" (Bell, 1998). The satisfying feeling of doing well appears to be, in large measure, a comparative one. If I work more so I can spend more, I feel good about the new house or car or high-definition television set that I just acquired or the Pentium III computer with a DVD drive that now sits in my family room. But if you go out and buy a house or car or gadget that is the same as

mine or better, my feeling of doing well will be undermined, inducing me to buy an even newer and bigger house or car or gadget. It's a race in which we gain psychological ground only momentarily.

Meanwhile, social inequality increases both in the United States and around the world, as you learned in Chapter 5. The reality is that while some of us are racing to stay even on the treadmill of consumption, others of us are being knocked right off that treadmill. In 1976, 1% of Americans held 20% of the nation's wealth; by 1997, they held 40%. Meanwhile, most of those lower down lost ground. The net worth of the bottom two-fifths of the income ladder dropped 80% between 1983 and 1995 (Meadows, 1999). Trends have tempered a bit in the last few years. But even during the roaring economy of the late 1990s, gains have been concentrated at the top. Between 1995 and 1998, income gains for all groups, aside from the rich and the very rich, were flat or slightly down (Stevenson, 2000). Internationally, the situation is even more dramatic. If we compare richest and poorest people instead of richest and poorest countries, the richest fifth of humanity in 1990 (the year for which the calculation was last done) commanded an astronomical 150 times the income of the poorest fifth (Korten, 1995). Given what we know of other trends, that figure is almost certainly quite a bit higher today.

Still, the world economy races along, growing and growing and growing. The world's gross economic product has risen from $6.4 trillion in 1950 to

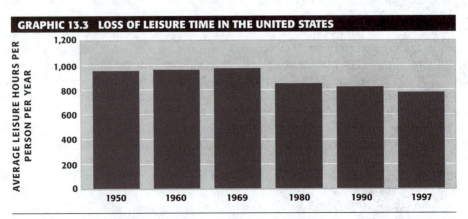

GRAPHIC 13.3   LOSS OF LEISURE TIME IN THE UNITED STATES

(AVERAGE LEISURE HOURS PER PERSON PER YEAR, by year: 1950, 1960, 1969, 1980, 1990, 1997)

Source: Adapted from *Redefining Progress*, p. 19.

roughly $40 trillion today, a sixfold increase (Brown, Renner, & Halweil, 1999, p. 65). Most of those gains have flowed to those on the top, who, caught on the consumption treadmill, nevertheless are no more satisfied now than they were. They may even be less satisfied, given the decline in their leisure time, the decline in their community life, and the increase in their personal stress.

Meanwhile, the environment—remember the environment?—has taken it on the chin as never before. Global warming is up. Species loss is up. Toxins in the environment are up. Deforestation is up. Fish stocks are down. Clean fresh water stocks are down. World grain production per person is down. Our sense of security about the environment is down. But so preoccupied are we with maintaining our place on the treadmill of consumption, sometimes it seems we hardly notice. And when we do notice, sometimes it seems we hardly do anything about it.

Owning Up to What We Own

I'm part of the problem. I live in the United States, the richest country in the world. Between my wife and me, my family makes about $60,000 a year, which is roughly 60% more than the average household income in this richest of all countries. We have two children, a car, a cat, a 1,450-square-foot private home with three bedrooms on a 7,000 square-foot lot, and a share in a vacation home on the St. Lawrence River in Canada. Inside our year-round home, we have a TV, a stereo, a computer, a stove, a refrigerator, a washing machine, central heating, a full complement of furniture, three closets of clothes, kitchen cabinets full of dishes and cookware, a collection of hand and power tools, a camera, three phones, two vacuum cleaners (including the shop vac in the basement), and bookshelf after bookshelf of books (we're all big readers in my family). I'm a semiprofessional musician, and I've got a guitar, a mandolin, a banjo, and several other instruments, as well some sound equipment. We also recently bought a violin for our son, who is learning how to play. In the garage and the tool shed, there is a fair collection of the American usuals: lawn mower, shovels, rakes, a small fleet of bicycles, and several piles of just plain clutter. At the vacation home, there is another house full of furniture, another kitchen, another tool collection—plus a dock, a boathouse, and four boats. We like to travel, and we always take a couple of family trips each year to the east coast of the United States from our Midwestern home, plus a family trip overseas every so often. I also do a fair bit of professional travel, much of it international. All this stuff in my life takes resources, energy, and displaced and despoiled habitat to produce and for me to use and later dispose of it all—some of it a *lot* of resources, energy, and displaced and despoiled habitat.

There are some qualifications I could make. I could tell you that the statistic "average household income" overstates our relative financial position because our household is significantly larger than the standard U.S. size of 2.6 persons. According to the U.S. Census Bureau, per capita income in the United States is $19,241; thus, the per capita income for our family of four is about 30% less than the national median. I could tell you that we hardly ever watch our television, a fifteen-year-old model that we picked up used for $35. We keep it in a closet and haven't watched it in at least the past six months. In fact, the first time my two-year-old daughter watched TV, she thought it was some kind of strange electric lamp and kept dancing around and pointing at it, saying, "Light! Light!" As far as I know, she has watched TV only half a dozen times since, all at

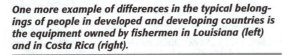

One more example of differences in the typical belongings of people in developed and developing countries is the equipment owned by fishermen in Louisiana (left) and in Costa Rica (right).

other people's houses. I could tell you that we have installed energy-efficient lighting throughout our home, that we have no air conditioning, and that we are very good about turning things off. I could tell you that during the winter we keep the thermostat on our furnace at 63°F during the day and 56°F at night. That is well below the norm in our community—and we sometimes joke that our central heating system is sweaters and our central air conditioning system is skin. I could tell you that the four boats at our vacation house are all small, unmotorized craft and that our lawn mower also is unmotorized. I could tell you that we drive our car only about 8,200 miles a year, just 4,100 miles per driver, well below the U.S. average of about 15,000 miles a year per driver. We do most of our daily travel around town and back and forth to work by bicycle and by foot. I could tell you that we have no microwave oven, no food processor, no portable phone, no cellular phone, no camcorder, no VCR, no dishwasher, and no clothes dryer other than the line outside in the garden. Our electric consumption averages about 300 kilowatt hours a month, which is certainly high by international standards but less than half the usage of a typical U.S. household. I could also tell you that we are seriously looking into windpower to provide electricity for our year-round home (we would be in a group of about fifty households sharing a 50-kilowatt windmill).

I could tell you all those things. Indeed I just did, and they are all true. But the fact remains that my family still consumes a lot, an awful lot.

By comparison, let's take the family of my old friend Carlos Manuel Delgado, the Costa Rican farmer from the village of Platanillo. Carlos is comfortably well off by the standards of Platanillo, indeed by the standards of all of Costa Rica. He and his wife, Esmarelda, along with their two high school–aged daughters, share a duplex with the family of Esmarelda's brother, up the hill from the main part of the village and a couple of hundred meters from the local Catholic church. The house is relatively new, one story with neatly painted stucco sides, glass windows, and a corrugated iron roof. It is perhaps 500 square feet in all. In their 250 square feet of the house, Carlos's family has a living room, a combination kitchen and dining area, two bedrooms, a couple of closets, and a recently installed indoor toilet. (This section of Platanillo got running water a few years ago, thanks to the efforts of Carlos and his neighbors, who, with the support from a small grant from an international development agency, installed a dam up the mountain and a system of water mains.) Their house also now has electricity, which they use to run their new 19-inch color TV, the family boom box, and a few electric lights. There is a sink and a small gas range in the kitchen, but no oven, no refrigerator, no dishwasher or washing machine, and very few dishes and pots and pans. This being the tropics, they have no central heating. Nor do they have air conditioning, although they do have a small electric fan. They own only a few changes of clothing each and only a few pieces of furniture, most of them second hand. They have almost no books, aside from the children's few school books. They do keep up a family photo album with their inexpensive automatic camera, and they delight in showing the album to guests. They have no car and no truck or tractor for the farm, although they sometimes borrow Carlos's father's old truck for farm work and for local trips. They have no vacation home and rarely travel far. In fact, none of the family has ever been outside Costa Rica, a country smaller than most U.S. states. They go regularly by bus to Turrialba, the nearby city of 50,000, and on a few special occasions have gone to San Jose, Costa Rica's capital, about a three-hour journey away. Nevertheless, theirs is a comfortable and full life, even if they are suddenly gripped with want for more upon meeting an old friend from a rich country like the United States.

In terms of consumption levels, it is clear which family are the real environmentalists. Although it would be a challenging task to make a precise calculation, I would guess that my family of four consumes on the order of ten or even twenty times what Carlos's family of four consumes. Yet I do consider myself an environmentalist—an environmental sociologist, no less. But if even a self-described environmentalist can consume at such a level, where is there cause for sociological optimism with regard to the environment?

The Sociology of Environmental Inaction

Let's review what I do that creates the worst environmental damage. According to a 1999 study by the Union of Concerned Scientists, a U.S. group that works on peace and environmental issues, there is a "dirty seven" of consumer activities in the United States, roughly in this order of severity (Brower and Leon, 1999):

1. driving
2. eating meat
3. eating vegetables and grain
4. using household appliances and lighting
5. heating and cooling homes
6. building homes
7. providing households with water and removing the sewage

The authors of the Union of Concerned Scientists study came up with that ordering by performing what are called "life-cycle analyses" of the typical products used in U.S. homes. Usually the consumer focuses only on the useful portion of a product's life. But products have to come from somewhere to get into the store, and they have to go somewhere when we are done with them. Both those somewheres are the environment, and tracing what happens at every stage of a product's "life" quickly leads us to interconnections and implications that we rarely consider in making purchases.

This is not the place to get into the details of the calculations behind the Union of Concerned Scientists study. But if you think through the list, it makes sense. Let's start with the first activity, driving. The United States has an absolutely appalling record when it comes to the automobile. We are far more auto dependent than any other nation, with the highest rates of car ownership and miles driven per driver and per capita, along with the least-fuel-efficient auto fleet of any rich nation, not to mention one of the worst public transportation systems. That is much of the reason that we have the dubious distinction of leading the world in per capita emissions of all greenhouse gases (although China is coming on strong, as it stokes the coal fires of its factories and its enormous population embraces the automobile).

Meat eating, number two on the list, may be a bit of a surprise. But when you calculate the inefficiencies of converting grain to animal muscle, the water pollution caused by livestock and chemically based grain farming, the water drunk by livestock, and the habitat displaced by agricultural land, the toll of environmental damage adds up quickly.

The biggest surprise, I think, is number three: eating vegetables and grain. Here again water use and water pollution figure high, as well as displaced habitat. Virtually all agriculture, as currently practiced, is hard on the land.

Numbers four and five on the list—home appliances and lighting and home heating and cooling—take their environmental bite from energy use and associated greenhouse emissions and air pollution. Home construction, number six, is something hardly ever discussed as an environmental problem in the United States, but when you consider the land, wood, and mined materials needed to put up new houses, you will quickly realize that a house affects not only local habitat but also habitat often thousands of miles away. In addition, manufacturing building materials creates substantial water pollution, and disposing of old building materials takes a lot of landfill space.

Finally, securing and treating the water used in households, number seven on the list, remains a major source of environmental impact, despite many decades of investment in better water supplies and sewage facilities.

The list no doubt would vary by country. For example, people in South America don't drive much in comparison to people in the wealthy nations (see Graphic 13.4). Their homes are a lot smaller and they don't have as many appliances in them. Nobody heats their homes, and few have air conditioning. Water treatment facilities are much worse, though, so water pollution is likely higher. Agriculture is likely the leading cause of environmental problems in Costa Rica, given its high population density, steep slopes, and increasing use of industrial farming techniques.

More significant is the reaction of most environmentally concerned people to the list. (And the overwhelming proportion of people in the United States and elsewhere claim to be environmentally concerned, over 90% in some polls; see Inglehart, 1995.) What can we do about our driving, they ask? We have to get to work, and we have to get our children to school, and we have to get to the stores. What can we do about our eating? We already knew that eating meat is bad, but now we learn that eating anything is bad. What can we do about the inefficiency of our energy use? More efficient brands simply aren't in the stores, at least not at prices we can afford. True, we could turn down the thermostat a bit in winter and up in summer, but to be honest we really don't want to; it makes daily life so uncomfortable to be too cold or too hot. As for home construction, what can we do there? The builders build the homes and we buy them or rent them, and often we're forced to decide in a matter of hours which home to buy or rent, lest someone else snap it up. How can we be expected to first research the comparative environmental damage of different builders' choices of construction materials and site location? It's hard enough to find an affordable place to live. And what can we do about water use and sewage treatment? If we don't water the lawn, the grass will

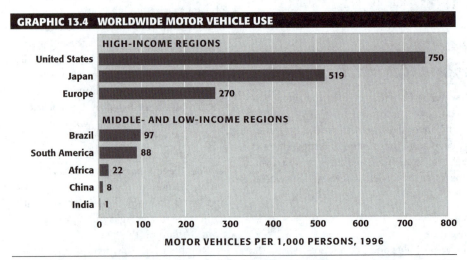

GRAPHIC 13.4 WORLDWIDE MOTOR VEHICLE USE

HIGH-INCOME REGIONS
United States — 750
Japan — 519
Europe — 270

MIDDLE- AND LOW-INCOME REGIONS
Brazil — 97
South America — 88
Africa — 22
China — 8
India — 1

MOTOR VEHICLES PER 1,000 PERSONS, 1996

Source: Adapted from World Resources Institute, 2000; data from American Automobile Manufacturers Association, 1996.

turn brown. It's too expensive to replace all our plumbing fixtures with ones that use less water. And sewage is treated by the government, not us.

In other words, we'd love to do more to help the environment, but if that's your dirty seven list of bad practices, we're very sorry but there's not much we can do. We have to eat the world (our cake).

But we have to have it too. The standard rebuttal to such environmental complacency is suggestions of the Fifty-Simple-Things-You-Can-Do-to-Save-the-World variety. Recycling. Reusing materials like the backs of paper printed on one side, or just using your old things a little longer. Reducing waste through incrementally replacing plumbing and electrical fixtures with more efficient ones when the older inefficient ones break. More recently in the United States, we have seen the growing popularity of another kind of advice: the simplicity movement. The simplicity movement encourages middle-class Americans to give up their high-paying, high-pressure jobs and come home to their families, their communities, and their own sanity. Work less and live more. Give up the second car and the big house. Cut expenses and personal stress. Downshift. Use less stuff and get more out of it. Join a "simplicity circle" and talk with others who are trying the same kinds of things.

All those suggestions have their place, and they would make a significant difference if enough people followed them. Indeed, we can argue for most of them on grounds of personal finances or mental health or something else that has little to do directly with the environment. But there is a persistently individualistic tone to those suggestions, and I worry that, at least by themselves, they feed the very tendencies on which consumerism is based.

In some versions of the simplicity movement, it sometimes seems that the advice is to consume nonconsumption. Nonconsumption itself can become a kind of product. Indeed, there is a vast array of catalogs full of nonconsuming products to buy: thousand-dollar mattresses made from organic cot-

ton; Zen chime alarm clocks; miniature waterfalls for your living room, complete with circulating water pumps to fill your life with the naturally soothing sounds of tumbling water. As a member of a number of U.S. environmental groups, my name and address have been sold to several of the companies that put out nonconsuming catalogs. Copies of the catalogs *Harmony* and *Seventh Generation* regularly come in our mail, despite our best efforts to discourage them. And their main message is the same as that of every other mail-order catalog: Buy more stuff. Buy green, but buy nonetheless.

What we might term *consumptive nonconsumption* may have a subtle cultural consequence in addition to the material consequences of buying more stuff, albeit organic stuff, Zen stuff, naturally soothing stuff. My worry here is that consumptive nonconsumption reinforces the notion that consumption is our best means of taking action in the world. It also reduces the citizen to an individual consumer. But consumption is not citizenship. Buying is not voting, despite the calls from some quarters that "voting with your pocketbook" is a form of democracy. If buying is the measure and the means of democracy, then the richer you are the more you get to vote, which hardly seems in keeping with democratic values. Nor is citizenship a matter of considering only what is best for you: the Zen chime alarm clock or the personal waterfall? I recognize that one may indeed make purchasing decisions that do take into consideration the needs of the wider society, and that form of consumption may indeed be a political statement. I do so myself all the time. And if enough people do it, the impact can be considerable. But such actions are private ones by private individuals in a marketplace of other private individuals, some with more money—more "votes"—than others.

I am not trying to argue against people working less and spending less, or against spending more time at home and recycling more, or against buying products that work more efficiently and using recycled materials. I am doing all those things myself. And they do make some difference in the world, particularly if lots of people do them. They also make me feel that I am actually doing something about my overconsumption, and that feeling is important for motivating me to continue to work on and to identify with environmentalism.

But in addition to the problem of consumptive nonconsumption, there is also the problem of what we might call the *ambivalence of individualized action*. When I set my recycling bucket out on the front step so it can be picked up by our local bicycle-powered collector of recycled materials, I am doing something I can readily see, and that is empowering. Because it is empowering, it helps maintain my commitment to the environmental movement. But as I look up and down the street, I see few of my neighbors doing the same and no evidence that any more of them are likely to in the future. All this effort (it takes us only about an hour every two weeks, I would judge, to deal with our recyclables, although in a family with two young children that hour is sometimes hard to find) and so little tangible change in the wider environmental predicament, I sometimes note with discouragement.

Therein lies the ambivalence of individualized action: it is empowering on one level and disempowering on another, wider level. I can see what I am doing, and yet I can also see what little overall difference it makes. So why bother? The ambivalence of individualized action thus becomes environmental ambivalence, and environmental ambivalence becomes environmental inaction.

The Social Organization of Consumption

The solution to the dilemma must start, I think, with recognizing the *social organization of consumption*—the social structures that pattern our habits of consumption. Let's consider the list of the dirty seven consumer activities. In the United States, recall, driving is number one. That is largely because in the United States if you want to get to work, to school, or to shops, you had best drive.

Take my town of Ames, Iowa, population some 50,000. We have, in most people's estimation, an excellent bus system. But our city government has allowed recent commercial development to be in so-called strip malls, huge collections of stores with huge parking lots lining both sides of a huge road—what planners call "car-oriented development." As a result, our downtown area, where there is little room for parking, has virtually shut down. Most of the major retailers have closed their doors or have moved out to the strip malls. Our bus system is good, as I said, and it does go to the strips. But the fact is that bus systems work best as ways to transport people to and from a centralized area, not as ways to move people from one dispersed region to another. Besides, once you get to the strip, it is quite challenging to move around by foot. Because of their huge parking lots, the stores are far apart. Often there is no sidewalk connecting them, and crossing four lanes of heavy traffic with a toddler clutching your hand to reach a store on the other side is downright dangerous. The bus can't help here: it comes only every twenty minutes and stops at only a few places on the strip anyway. Even if it did go everywhere on the strip, service would be slowed down to the point of near uselessness. Driving your own car is far more convenient, so that's what just about everyone does, except those who can't afford it.

The citizens are told that the city is merely responding to market trends in allowing this kind of development. (Buying is supposedly voting, remember?) But this is no free market, no free "election" by consumers "voting with their feet." These trends are heavily subsidized. The developers of huge

possible only with policies that promote automobile use, has come reliance on huge food producers, huge food processors, and huge food distributors. The producers, processors, and distributors have to compete with other producers, processors, and distributors to get their products on the store shelves. Not surprisingly, the biggest operations typically win out in this competition. The result is something of an American paradox: The huge supermarket is an internationally recognized symbol of freedom and choice, but in fact it closes out choice. If producers, processors, or distributors can't get their products on the shelves of such a store, then scarcely anyone will ever find out that they are out there.

Consequently, it is a constant source of irritation (and a kind of amazement) that I can walk through aisle after aisle of the four supermarkets in my town and see so many things that I have no interest in buying and scarcely any of the products that I would want to buy. (There's a telling measure of American life: just four places for 50,000 people to buy groceries.) Even if I want to purchase environmentally appropriate products, I can't if I don't see them for sale. And if I don't see them for sale, I am less likely to know they exist and to seek them out through other means, such as the two small natural food stores in Ames, one of which is so small that even I—a regular buyer of natural foods—have yet to figure out exactly where it is.

My family is lucky in one regard, living in an agricultural state like Iowa. We eat meat, although only a couple of times a week. But mindful of the environmental issues associated with the conventional ways that meat is raised, as well as the animal welfare issues, we don't purchase our meat in stores. We buy in bulk direct from local farmers whose environmental and animal welfare practices we know and trust and store the meat in our basement freezer (a high-efficiency model). Farms are close at hand everywhere in Iowa, and we have come to know

stores with huge parking lots would not be able to build them without zoning categories like "car-oriented development," and they likely wouldn't try without the expensive roads the town builds for them and without the tax breaks that many of them get for moving out to "the strip." (One big store that recently relocated from our downtown to the strip got an $800,000 tax break for doing so.) If our city instructed developers to build their stores downtown without the big parking lots, they would. Ours is an affluent community, a university town with the most expensive housing market in our state, too good a retail market to pass up.

Yet we, like virtually all other towns large and small in the United States, have guided our development to the fringes, even though it is considerably more expensive for taxpayers to build and maintain the extra roads, not mention to hand out those tax breaks. Several studies document the high costs of the automobile and of sprawl in communities across the United States (for example, MacKensie, Dower, & Chen, 1992; Katz, 1994), and Graphic 13.5 indicates how much farmland and habitat we have lost as a result. But now we are trapped. We drive not because the car gives us freedom. We drive not because the free market allows us to choose to drive. We drive because we must. It is how we have organized our lives.

Similar stories could be told of other activities on the U.S. dirty seven list. Take food production. With our reliance on huge stores, which in turn are

GRAPHIC 13.5   DISAPPEARING FARMLAND AND WILDLIFE HABITAT IN THE UNITED STATES

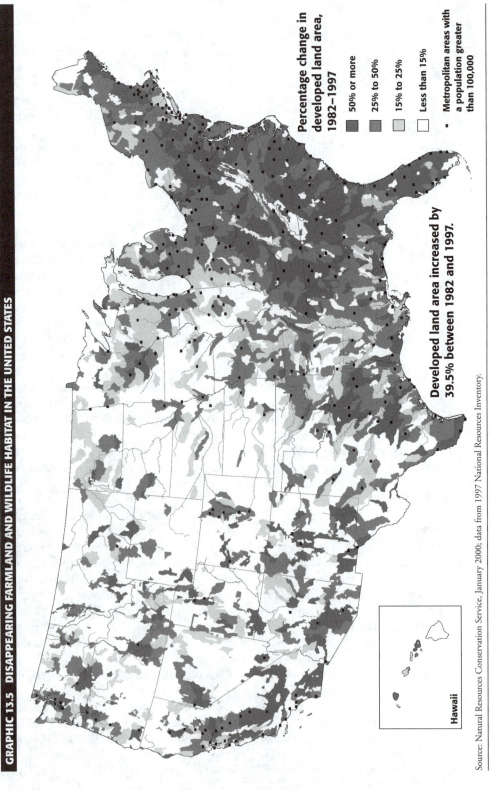

Percentage change in developed land area, 1982–1997

- 50% or more
- 25% to 50%
- 15% to 25%
- Less than 15%
- ■ Metropolitan areas with a population greater than 100,000

Developed land area increased by 39.5% between 1982 and 1997.

Hawaii

Source: Natural Resources Conservation Service, January 2000; data from 1997 National Resources Inventory.

Note: No data available for Alaska.

many farmers through various local events. Most families in the United States, however, no longer have that advantage and are trapped in the dominant patterns of the social organization of food.

I could go on, but I think the point is clear. The problem of consumption is not merely one of individuals making bad decisions in their daily lives and spending habits. It is as well a problem of the structures we have created within which people must make those decisions about their daily lives and spending habits.

Social Power and the Social Organization of Consumption

The problem of the social organization of consumption is not only one of the architecture of daily life—of where the shops are, how we get to them, and what we find in them to buy when we get there. Those are difficult enough problems on their own. Nevertheless, we also must note how the location of every building and every road inscribes on the land property boundaries and the social interests those boundaries represent. Consequently, change in the social organization of consumption is likely to be very difficult. Someone is bound to object to every suggested change, and if those someones are socially powerful, their objections are likely to be socially powerful as well.

In other words, we need to reckon with the distribution of social power within a society and the interests that those with power may have in the current social organization of consumption. That is an issue of enormous importance for consumption. Oil companies seldom have been known to promote laws that advance the use of bicycles and electric vehicles, and pesticide companies seldom have been known to promote chemical-free forms of agricultural production.

And why don't companies promote environmental laws more? A large part of the reason is that business interests are caught on their own treadmill, what Alan Schnaiberg (1980), Walter Cochrane (1958), and others have called the "treadmill of production." To stay in business, companies have to sell

stuff, of course. More than that, to please investors, companies have to sell as much stuff as possible. Even if they don't want to sell more stuff, they probably wind up trying to anyway because other companies making similar stuff likely are trying to sell more. Consequently, prices drop as supplies go up, meaning a company has to try to sell more to keep its income at least even. That inexorably causes prices to drop still further, leading to another round of production increases as companies seek to maximize their profits and to continue to please their investors. Companies commonly try to beat the problem of overproduction by adopting new technologies that allow them to produce more cheaply. But that makes it easier to produce even more, leading to even lower prices, and lower profits, unless a company increases its production yet again. It's another treadmill, and it's a struggle to stay on this one too.

There are a number of important consequences of the treadmill of production. First, companies seek to solve the problem of overproduction by forcing other companies off the treadmill and out of business. That either reduces supply and thus raises prices or allows the companies that remain to pick up the production slack, increasing profits for those still on the treadmill. But soon the race is on again to increase production still further to please investors, and the treadmill speeds up still faster, forcing other companies out of business. The result is that over time the companies on the treadmill are fewer and fewer and bigger and bigger.

Second, as the companies get fewer and fewer and bigger and bigger, they gain enormous political clout. A company as big as Boeing or General Motors or Microsoft can easily set aside funds for lobbying and campaign contributions. They've got plenty of money, and there isn't as much competition anymore—for example, Boeing is now the only manufacturer of large passenger jets in the United States and one of only two in the entire world. Also, for a monopoly, not only is there less competition in production, there also is less competition for the ears and favor of politicians.

Third, companies have little tolerance for anything they perceive as standing in the way of profit, like environmental laws. Even when a company

Treadmill of production in the coal-mining industry (clockwise from top left): To compete, coal-mining concerns abandoned old technology in favor of more efficient blasting and strip mining. They then sought new markets overseas to maintain profits. In the end, however, some concerns couldn't expand markets enough to compete, leaving the landscape littered with abandoned coal mines.

achieves monopoly or near-monopoly status on a production treadmill, investors still want to maximize profit. Because of its political clout, a big company is in a good position to keep environmental laws from interfering with its plans.

Fourth, the public often finds it hard to argue with big corporations. So many of our jobs, as well as the security of our investments, depend on the continued ability of corporations to stay on the treadmill. We're all hooked into it somehow. And without a strong voice of opposition from voters, politicians find it much easier to let corporations have their way.

We all get hooked in another way too. I've discussed several strategies that companies use to stay on the treadmill. Increasing production. Increasing the efficiency of production through new technolo-

gies. Forcing other companies off the treadmill. Using monopoly power to influence the political process (and sometimes to increase prices). Counting on our own interest in the success of a big company, through our jobs and our investments. The other big way is through ads—and more ads and still more ads—opening new markets and expanding existing ones across the world. Buy, buy, buy what we make, make, make, the corporations tell us. Solve our problem of overproduction with your overconsumption. Besides, it will make you happy, happy, happy. To the extent we believe that message, not only do we soak up excess production, we also encourage more of it.

In other words, the treadmills of production and consumption are closely interconnected. Both perpetuate the other and the core value they share: more is better. Eventually, the value of *more* comes to be an independent force in our lives. It has been said many times before, and it likely will be said many times in the future, I fear, that we consume not just to consume but to consume *more*. It is often not the goods themselves that we desire but the very experience of *more* itself—more than my parents had, more than I had last year, more than my neighbor or my coworker has.

And the more *more* we have, the faster the treadmills spin.

My point is not that humans are inherently ruled by an unquenchable appetite for *more*. The widespread desire for *more* is patterned by the social organization of our lives, by the interlocking treadmills of production and consumption. Although it is found beyond the West, the desire for *more* is not culturally universal. Although it has been with us a long time, it is not immutable. Nor is it universal and immutable within the societies in which it is widespread. Indeed, most of us find that our desire for *more* varies across the course of our own lives.

But it is certainly strong within us across most of our lives today, and across much of the world—*por la plata*. We see the desire for *more* in many guises too. There is the common elevation of the idea of profit into a moral good, so that the economy of nations can thrive. As the old expression says, what's good for General Motors is good for the nation, right? There is the similar elevation of consumption into a moral good for the health of the economy: Buy American! There is the equally common moral elevation of the idea of economic growth—which is only an aggregate version of *more*—into the status of a good in itself, in part because increasing the size of the pie is politically more palatable than dividing the pie more equally to begin with. Besides, economic growth means more profits and more consumption. Then there is the equation of moral goodness with economic gain, the secular form of the idea that God rewards those who are the most deserving. Closely connected is the equation of economic status with social status, such that money and goods are desired not for themselves but for what they say about who the person is. In that way, most subtly affecting of all, *more* becomes equated with self.

Meanwhile, we once again have nearly forgotten all about the environment and little consider its needs as we struggle to stay afoot on the treadmills of contemporary life.

Virtual Environmentalism and the Social Reorganization of Consumption

The picture I have been sketching is a grim one, I know. But now it is time, finally, for some sociological optimism about how we might learn to "eat the world" in such a way that we still have it, too. I base my own sociological optimism in the following thought: If we have socially organized our lives so that we tend to make bad decisions about the environment (or anything else), then the solution must be to socially *reorganize* our lives so that we make better decisions.

That may not seem a strong foundation for optimism. Reorganization won't be easy, for all the reasons I have been discussing. Still, knowing that our problems are largely of our own social making suggests that it is at least possible to engage in some social remaking. So let's begin and see where it takes us.

We need to keep firmly in mind a basic reality of life today, one that I have stressed several times in this essay: People are busy, terribly busy, caught as we are on the treadmills of production and consumption. Although we are surrounded by modernity's supposed inducements of choice and leisure,

modernity equally induces us into a treadmill-driven rush from home to work to the point that work becomes home. And when we come home—late, probably—we're still in such a rush that what we do at home becomes work, as the sociologist Arlie Hochschild (1997) observes. The clothes have to be washed, the supper cooked, the dishes done, the children put to bed, the toys picked up, the floor swept, and the bills paid.

When work becomes home and home becomes work, daily decisions have to be made fast. That isn't going to change soon. And if being an environmentalist means a lot of extra thought about the consequences of each act of consumption, if it means delaying buying decisions for days or weeks or months while you track down suppliers of environmentally friendly products, then daily decisions are unlikely to be made with the environment in mind. Environmentalism on those terms is unlikely to become a significant part of everyday life in a modern world. Our daily lives are too full already.

What we need, then, is what might be termed *virtual environmentalism*—environmentalism you don't have to think about because you find yourself doing it anyway. Virtual environmentalism is environmentalism that lies behind and beneath our daily lives. Like environmentalism in the usual sense, virtual environmentalism is taking your bicycle to work, buying food produced with sustainable production methods, replacing old appliances with energy-efficient ones, and using less heating, cooling, construction materials, and water. But virtual environmentalism means doing those things not because you've made a conscious decision to be environmentally good today, but because they are the cheapest and most convenient things to do. Virtual environmentalism is being environmentally good without having to be environmentally good.

I think it is safe to say that virtual environmentalism is likely to be a lot more popular with the general public than environmentalism by cajoling, shaming, issuing court summons, imposing fines, and locking offenders in jail. But it will become popular only if we change the structures of the cheap and the convenient by reorganizing the social organization of consumption. Environmental problems are problems of society, and problems of society require social solutions.

Social reorganization usually requires a terrific effort. But it can be done. One of the most impressive examples is the 1987 Montreal Protocol, an international agreement to steadily cut worldwide production of CFCs, the group of chemicals largely responsible for the thinning of the upper atmosphere ozone layer. Before this agreement, CFCs were everywhere in the products of our daily lives and in the production processes that made them. Today, they are rapidly vanishing, as Graphic 13.6 shows, thanks to an unprecedented international effort to socially reorganize production and thus consumption. The

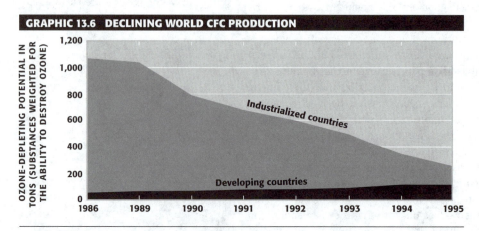

GRAPHIC 13.6   DECLINING WORLD CFC PRODUCTION

Source: World Resources Institute, 2000; data from Oberthur, 1997, p. 30.

ozone layer is still thinning and is expected to for some years to come. But improvement is on the way as chemical reactions in the atmosphere from CFCs already released and from the reduced amount of CFCs currently being released run their course.

That is not to say that individuals do not have a role in change or that ideas and moral values do not either. No reorganization is likely to happen without a broad base of ideologically committed individuals who want change. There is a "top" and a "bottom" to social change (Bell, 1998). The top is the social structures—and the social authority behind them—that guide our lives. The bottom is the popular will. Either may resist the other. Change from the bottom—of the fifty-simple-things variety, like sorting your trash for recycling or bicycling whenever possible—will never achieve dramatic change without structural reorganization from the top. And structural reorganization from the top precipitates political backlash or political repression—or both—if it tries to circumvent the popular will. For lasting and democratic change, we need both the top and the bottom interacting and listening to each other, through what might be called the *dialog of social change.*

The need for virtual environmentalism does not mean there is no need for environmentalism in the traditional sense of the term. Bicycling to work and sorting our garbage for recycling are important ways to keep the dialog going. Environmentalism remains our best route to virtual environmentalism, but we should also try to do more. Maybe one day we won't have to try anymore, as environmentalism becomes virtual environmentalism and as "bottom" becomes "top" and "top" becomes "bottom." We can become environmental without trying—but only if we try.

The contradiction between the ideology and the actual behaviors of even committed environmentalists (and environmental sociologists like me) should not be cynically derided as mere hypocrisy. The implication of such cynicism is that I would be morally better off if I changed my ideology to fit my behaviors. It would certainly be easier for me if I didn't feel that constant discomfort that I feel about what I do. But no, we should see the gap between what we do and what we say we want to do as an essential foundation for social change—it gives us the desire to change our social conditions and thus our behav-

iors to fit our ideologies.

Is there any real chance of achieving the social reorganization of consumption and production through the dialog of social change? Have I really, as I reach the end of this essay, made good on my promise of a message of sociological optimism? Can we really get there, when we think of the deep structures of power and interest arrayed against such a reorganization?

To be honest, I don't know. But I am committed to hoping so and to acting on that hope as best I can given the current structures of social organization in which we live. I hope you, too, will feel some of that commitment and sense the social and environmental actions it suggests to us all.

And I hope you will find some way to tell us about your commitment and about your actions. That way we can keep each other going as we work on the social reorganization of consumption and production, so vital if sustainable development is not to be a contradiction in terms. Therein lies our most basic source of sociological optimism: sharing hope.

Thinking about the Topic of Sustainable Development

1. In your own words, what does the "social organization of consumption" mean? How does it relate to the "social construction of reality" (see Chapter 4)? How do supermarkets actually reduce freedom and choice? List and explain at least five ways in which your community or city is organized so as to sustain and encourage high levels of consumption. For example, how is your town organized to make cars essential for work, shopping, and other elements of everyday life?

2. What is distinctive about a sociological approach to the environment? Think back to the points made about the sociological perspective, especially in Chapters 1 and 2, and explain at least five different ways in which the approach in this chapter is sociological. Which points and which ideas and concepts reflect the fact that the author is a sociologist? What do we gain from viewing environmental issues from a sociological perspective?

14 How Many People Is Too Many People?

DIANE LYE

In October 1999, the world's population reached 6 billion; by the time you sit down to read this book, there will be nearly 6.2 billion people living on earth. World population is growing at a rate of 1.33% a year. That may not sound like a very fast rate of growth, until you consider that 1.33% of 6 billion is 80 million, and that 80 million more people a year is the same as 219,000 extra people each day, or an extra billion people every 12.5 years. That is the staggering arithmetic of human population growth.

To many people, the sheer size of human population and the rapidity with which it is growing seem like major threats to continued life on earth. In the United States, prominent environmental organizations, like the Audubon Society and the Sierra Club, argue that overpopulation and rapid population growth are the principal causes of environmental degradation, world hunger, and poverty. They are joined in those views by writers such as Lester Brown, head of the environmental think tank at the Worldwatch Institute, and Stanford biology professor Paul Ehrlich, another long-time campaigner against the dangers of population growth (see Brown, 2000; Ehrlich & Ehrlich, 1990, for representative views). Many leading scientists share Brown's,

Ehrlich's, and the environmentalists' concerns. In 1993, an assembly of distinguished scientists from fifty-eight countries concluded a conference in New Delhi by issuing a statement referring to population growth as "a great risk to humanity." The scientists pointed to apparent declines in food production and increases in environmental problems as evidence of an impending population crisis (Science Summit, 1994). Since then, reports by the conference organizers suggest that human population may already have reached a level that cannot be sustainably supported by the earth's ecosystems (Royal Society and National Academy of Sciences, 1997).

Fears about the consequences of population growth have led many environmental activists to advocate government-sponsored programs to reduce population growth. Ehrlich, for instance, believes that tough measures are justified because the earth is "a dying planet," and only rigorous government efforts to curtail population growth can minimize the scale of inevitable disaster. Most mainstream environmental and population advocacy organizations reject coercive population policies. Instead, organizations like the Worldwatch Institute and Population Action call for improved education for girls and women and expanded family planning programs in developing countries in the hope that such measures will slow birth rates and prevent a further doubling of world population.

The twin ideas that the most serious problem facing humanity is overpopulation and that the only way to avoid an environmental catastrophe that could wipe out humanity is to slow or halt population growth have entered into mainstream culture in the United States and many other places. Whenever the media covers a human tragedy in a developing country—be it an outbreak of Ebola virus, a famine, or a devastating flood—journalists are quick to point to population growth as the root cause of the problem. People are encroaching into the forests and coming too close to forest animals with strange diseases, we are told. Or the land simply cannot provide enough food for so many people. Or the area is so densely populated that people have to live on flood-prone river islands. Other problems like the loss of tiger habitat, the apparent expansion of the Sahara desert, and the destruction of the Amazon rain forest are all traced to population growth. The population problem is made real by media images of seemingly innumerable children in the developing world's crowded, polluted slums or hard-pressed families scraping a meager living off barren, denuded landscapes.

Looking at population growth through the lens of sociology provides a somewhat different view, however. The reasons for population growth—and its effects—are not nearly so straightforward as is sometimes suggested but are the product of complex interactions among social, economic, cultural, and political forces.

How Does Population Grow?

For most of human history, population grew very slowly (Graphic 14.1). In 8000 B.C., when settled agriculture first developed, the best estimates suggest there were about 8 million people; 8,000 years later, there were an estimated 300 million people—a growth rate of less than 0.05% a year. By 1750, the eve of the industrial revolution, there were around 800 million people, indicating that the growth rate had increased to slightly over 0.05% a year (Coale, 1974). After 1750, as the industrial revolution began, population growth sped up. As a result, in the 200 years between 1750 and 1950, world population more than tripled, to 2.5 billion. But that was nothing compared to the surge in population growth that took place after 1950. The growth rate soared to over 2.0% a year, implying a doubling time of less than 30 years.

Since 1985, population growth rates have fallen. By 1990–1995, population growth rates had eased to just below 1.5% a year and are now close to 1.3% a year. By historical standards, growth rates are still very high, and world population looks set to continue growing for at least another century. However, demographers expect that growth rate to be down to 0.34% a year by 2045 to 2050. Thus, although 1999's growth rate suggested that it would

GRAPHIC 14.1   HUMAN POPULATION GROWTH THROUGHOUT HISTORY

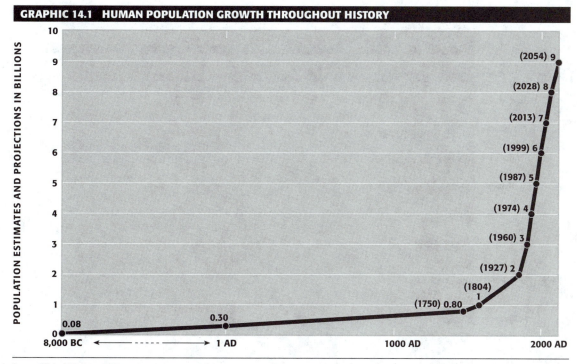

Source: United Nations, 1999a.

take only 12.5 years to reach 7 billion people, demographers project it actually will take 14 years. Fifteen years after that, in 2028, world population is projected to reach 8 billion; however, with the continued slowing down of population growth, it is projected to take a further 26 years to reach 9 billion, in 2054 (United Nations, 1999).

Looking at the world as a whole hides some important regional variations in the timing and speed of population growth. In Japan and the developed countries of Europe, North America, and Oceania (which consists of Australia, New Zealand, and other island nations in the Pacific Ocean), population growth rarely exceeded 1% per year over the 200-year period from roughly 1750 to 1950. By 1970, populations in developed countries were barely growing. Those countries will begin to experience population declines after 2020, so that by 2050 the population of the developed countries will be 2% smaller than they were in 1998. (The U.S. population

most likely will continue to grow through 2000–2050, but its growth will be more than offset by declines in the populations of Europe and Japan.).

In contrast, the developing countries of Asia, Africa, and Central and South America experienced very little population growth before about 1920. However, their late start has been more than offset by the great rapidity of their population growth since 1950; their growth rates have been above 2% for most of the period since then. According to the United Nations, 97% of world population growth between now and 2050 will take place in developing countries. Every year the population of Asia grows by 50 million, of Africa by 17 million, and of Latin America and the Caribbean by 8 million. Population growth rates are still over 2.5% in much of Africa. As a result, although global population growth is now slowing, the world's population will be 50% larger in 2050 than it is today. Nearly all the additional people will live in the

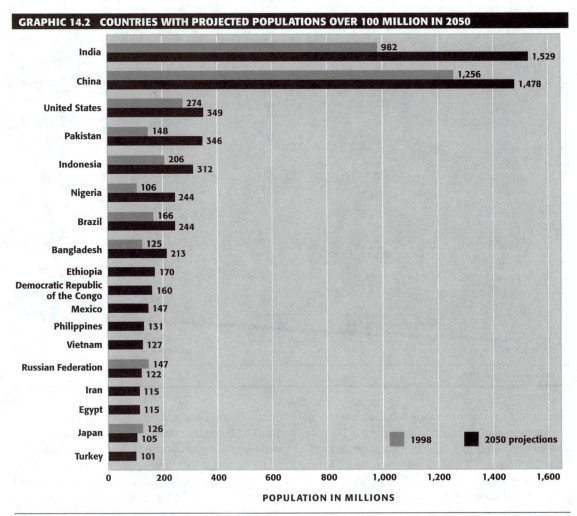

GRAPHIC 14.2   COUNTRIES WITH PROJECTED POPULATIONS OVER 100 MILLION IN 2050

Country	1998	2050 projections
India	982	1,529
China	1,256	1,478
United States	274	349
Pakistan	148	346
Indonesia	206	312
Nigeria	106	244
Brazil	166	244
Bangladesh	125	213
Ethiopia		170
Democratic Republic of the Congo		160
Mexico		147
Philippines		131
Vietnam		127
Russian Federation	147	122
Iran		115
Egypt		115
Japan	126	105
Turkey		101

POPULATION IN MILLIONS

Source: United Nations, 1999b.

poor countries of the developing world. Graphic 14.2 shows the projected members of the "100-million club" (countries with populations over 100 million) in 2050. Very few of them are developed countries.

Causes of Population Growth

Population growth depends on the balance between births and deaths. When more babies are born in a year than people die, population grows; when deaths outnumber births, population shrinks; and when births and deaths are roughly the same, population stays the same.

When Japan and the developed countries of Europe, North America, and Oceania experienced a wave of population growth between 1750 and 1950, it was because there were more births than deaths each year. But, as Graphic 14.3 shows, in 1995 birth and death rates began to approach the same level.

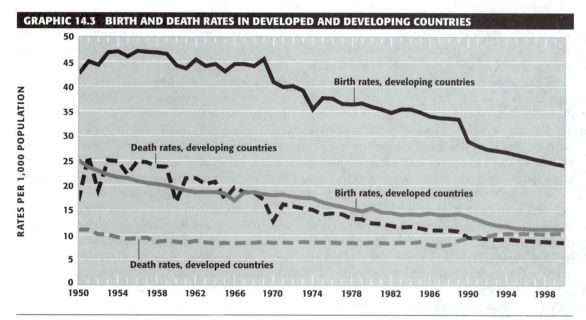

GRAPHIC 14.3 BIRTH AND DEATH RATES IN DEVELOPED AND DEVELOPING COUNTRIES

Source: U.S. Census Bureau, 2000.

Note: Data for 2000 are projections.

These countries are projected to experience population declines over the next fifty years because with today's small families and rapidly aging populations deaths likely will outnumber births.

In the developing countries of Asia, Africa, Central America, and South America, in contrast, population size was stable until the 1940s, because births and deaths were roughly equal. In the 1950s, however, death rates began to fall, so there were far fewer deaths each year than births, with the result that the populations of developing countries began to grow rapidly. In the 1970s, many developing countries began to experience a shift from traditional large families to smaller families, with the result that the number of births began to fall, and population growth began to taper off (see Graphic 14.3). Gradually, a new balance between births and deaths is being established in developing countries.

The short answer, then, to the question "What causes population growth?" is that the number of deaths in a population falls below the number of births. But that mechanistic explanation of population growth raises more questions: Why do death rates fall? Why do birth rates fall, and why do they sometimes stay high? In other words, what are the underlying sources of population growth? To answer those questions, we need a broader perspective.

Population Growth in Developed Countries

Up until about 1750, population growth in today's developed countries—roughly, North America and Europe—was very slow. Most people had large families, often between six and eight children per woman. The idea that people could influence their family size was unknown—children were gifts from God. But those high birth rates were offset by high death rates. Life expectancy was generally in the low 30s, sometimes even lower. When life expectancy at birth is 30, a newborn has only a 75% chance of living to age 1, a 60% chance of living to age 5, and a 17% chance of living to age 65.

Numerous factors contributed to the high death rates. Water supplies were impure; there was no effective sewage removal (waste was simply emptied into the streets, where it eventually flowed into the rivers that people downstream used for water supply); homes were poorly constructed, crowded, and ill ventilated. Given those conditions, it is little wonder that diarrheal disease and other infections were rampant; childbirth and minor injuries could easily become life-threatening events. On top of the hazards of everyday life, epidemics of diseases like plague, measles, influenza, smallpox, yellow fever, and so on periodically decimated communities. Food supplies were often uncertain, and both the quantity and the quality of food depended on the vagaries of the weather. Medical knowledge was too limited to have any significant impact on health or death rates.

Beginning around 1750, a gradual but steady improvement in death rates got underway in what are now the developed countries of Europe and North America. The initial improvement in death rates was fairly modest—for example, in England life expectancies rose from the low 30s to the high 30s—but it was enough to generate a steady surplus of births over deaths and population growth rates of about half a percent a year. The reasons for the early improvement in death rates are uncertain but probably include improvements in both the quality and the quantity of food supplies as agricultural technology and transportation improved, with the result that periodic famines gradually disappeared. Epidemics of plague, which had once killed millions, also disappeared from Europe, partly because housing improved and became less rat infested (rats carry the fleas that carry the plague bacillus) and partly because governments began to take steps, like quarantining suspected carriers, to prevent the spread of plague. Smallpox deaths may have declined as knowledge of an immunization method spread, and there may have been improvements in the care of women giving birth (Schofield, Rehrer, & Bideau, 1991).

It was not until the second half of the nineteenth century that more dramatic improvements in life expectancy took place. The industrial revolution had spawned large, rapidly growing cities. Conditions for ordinary, working people in the cities were ap-

palling: they lived in squalid, overcrowded, unsanitary slums, where death rates were far higher than in the countryside. In some industrial cities, life expectancy was less than 30 years, and one in every five newborns died before its first birthday. But from the 1860s onward, public health activists in Europe and the United States began to argue for and implement public health improvements. The programs included establishing building codes, providing for the removal of sewage, and regulating food supplies to ensure that foodstuffs, especially milk, were not tainted or adulterated. Most important of all was the introduction of water filtration to provide city dwellers with clean, safe drinking water. Those measures had immediate and dramatic effects. For example, the city of Philadelphia introduced water filtration between 1902 and 1909, and typhoid epidemics, which until then had killed several hundred people every summer, disappeared. Public health measures were supplemented by improvements in personal hygiene. The industrial revolution made cheap cotton clothing that could be regularly laundered widely available, as well as the soap to do the laundry. As indoor plumbing spread, people kept themselves cleaner. By 1940, U.S. life expectancy was 65, up from 45 in 1880 (Preston & Haines, 1991; Schofield, Rehrer, & Bideau, 1991).

For the most part, improvements in death rates in Europe and North America were not due to advances in medical science. Until the early years of the twentieth century, disease processes were not well understood; as late as 1900, there were still reputable physicians who rejected the then new theory that germs cause disease. In the absence of any real understanding of the causes of disease, physicians could do little to help their patients (Preston & Haines, 1991). Even when they did learn more, early in the twentieth century, there were few medical treatments for most illnesses until sulfa drugs and penicillin became widely available in the late 1940s. Those innovations, together with other medical advances, have kept life expectancy on a steady but slow upward path since the 1940s. Life expectancy in the United States is now 77 years.

Despite the spectacular gains in life expectancy over the past century, population growth did not accelerate because at about the same time that death rates began to fall birth rates also took a downward turn. Until about 1800, American women were averaging close to eight births each, while European women had between four and five births each. European women tended to have fewer children than American women because they tended to postpone marriage until their mid- to late twenties, whereas American women married young. (Remember, nobody used birth control, so once a woman married she would bear children steadily until she reached menopause.) Between 1800 and 1860, American birth rates fell slightly, to five or six children per woman, probably as marriage age rose and as some couples began to use birth control. In most of Europe and in the United States, birth rates began to fall sharply between 1870 and 1880. By 1900, birth rates were down to three or four children per woman; and by 1930, two children per woman was typical. The largest declines in death rates were in the period 1880 to 1930, precisely the time when birth rates were falling. The result of that pattern was that even when American and European death rates were falling there was no great surplus of births over deaths, so population growth was moderate.

What prompted the shift to smaller families in Europe and North America? Three factors were important:

- As part of a broad cultural change, people rejected the traditional view that children were sent by God and came to view family size as something about which individuals could and should make choices.
- The costs and the benefits of having children changed. When most people lived on farms, children could work and contribute to the family economy. But as people moved into cities and as legislation banning child labor in factories and mandating school attendance was passed, children became less of an economic plus and more costly.
- Changing attitudes about children encouraged parents to spend more on their children for healthcare and education, to produce one or two "quality" children rather than a brood of less healthy, poorly educated children.

Interestingly, the availability of effective contraception played little part in the fall in birth rates. Condoms and diaphragms were not widely available until the 1930s, by which time family size was already down to two children. Letters, diaries, advice books, and first-person accounts reveal that most couples relied on withdrawal as their method of birth control. That such an unaesthetic and demanding method should have been so successful suggests that couples were very highly motivated to have small families.

In the 1950s, after about a hundred years of declining birth rates in the United States and, to a lesser extent, in Europe, birth rates rebounded to between three and four children per woman—the so-called baby boom. But the baby boom had only a short-lived impact on population growth. Most developed countries either already have or will soon have shrinking rather than growing populations.

Population Growth in Developing Countries

In developing countries, birth and death rates remained high and population growth slow until the middle of the twentieth century. In the late 1930s, life expectancy in Africa and Asia was probably no more than 30 years; in Latin America it was closer to 40. Since 1945, there have been spectacular declines in the death rates in developing countries; life expectancy for developing countries as a whole is now 60, a gain of 20 years since 1945. China and most of Central America and South America now have life expectancies close to 70; in India and much of Africa, life expectancy is close to 60. Only the poorest countries still have life expectancies below 50.

Most of the improvement in the death rates in developing countries took place in the twenty years between 1950 and 1970. The speed with which death rates have fallen in developing countries far surpasses anything experienced in developed countries. In the United States, it took sixty years (1880–1940) for life expectancy to improve from 45 to 65; Mexico experienced the same improvement in less than 20 years (1950–1970).

Countries that have large agricultural populations normally have high birth rates, as the United States did during the 1930s (top). Other factors that lead to population growth are improved health care; the middle photo is from a vaccination program in Angola. Population growth is also encouraged by good food production, like the bountiful harvest from this rice paddy in India (bottom).

The dramatic improvements in mortality in developing countries were achieved largely as the result of widespread public health programs. (Chapter 15 examines healthcare programs in the developing world.) However, unlike the public health programs that were so effective in late-nineteenth-century America and Europe, public health programs in developing countries in the 1950s and 1960s did not focus on infrastructure development like the provision of clean water and sewage removal. Instead they were narrowly targeted measures that made use of western medical technology to attack and control specific diseases.

- Nearly 25% of the improvement in death rates is due to dramatic declines in malaria. That was accomplished by widespread insecticide spraying to control mosquitoes, which spread the disease, as well as improved treatments for affected individuals.
- Successful immunization campaigns against tuberculosis, smallpox, whooping cough, cholera, tetanus, and measles, again combined with better treatment for those already infected, explain a further 25% of the decline in death rates.
- Reductions in deaths due to various respiratory illnesses, which ordinarily cannot be vaccinated against, account for 35% of the death rate decline, due in part to the widespread use of effective treatments like antibiotics.

Those imported medical technologies delivered increases in life expectancy that were unprecedented in their speed and that were largely independent of improvements in living standards in developing countries.

The great rapidity of the declines in death rates in developing countries combined with traditionally high birth rates—above six children per woman in most developing countries in the 1960s and early 1970s—sparked a demographic transition, a period of very rapid population growth (Graphic 14.4). The yawning gap between birth and death rates was ex-

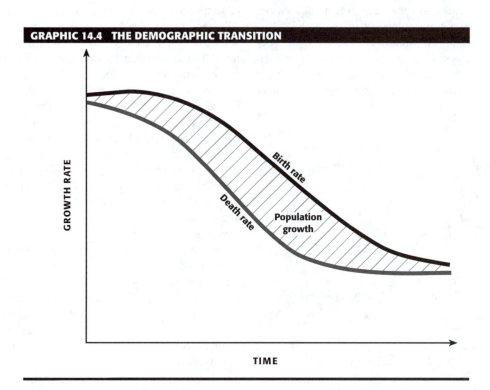

GRAPHIC 14.4   THE DEMOGRAPHIC TRANSITION

acerbated in some countries by increases in birth rates as mothers abandoned breastfeeding (which tends to slow a new mother's resumption of ovulation) in favor of bottle-feeding, which was marketed by international companies as "more modern." That is an example of one of the more negative effects of globalization. From the 1950s onward, population growth rates of 2% a year have been common in developing countries. In parts of sub-Saharan Africa, population growth rates were over 3% a year throughout the 1980s and 1990s (United Nations, 1999).

For developing countries as a whole, population growth rates peaked in the early 1970s. Since then, population growth has slowed as birth rates across the developing world have begun to fall. The most dramatic declines in birth rates were in East Asia, where a number of countries, including South Korea and Taiwan, now have lower birth rates than the United States, despite having birth rates close to six children per woman in the early 1960s. Some Southeast Asian countries, like Thailand and Vietnam, also have birth rates very close to two children per woman, down from above six in the early 1970s. Most important, in China, which accounts for one-fifth of the world's population, births per woman fell from six in the late 1960s to just over two in the late 1980s. Undoubtedly, China's rigorous family

planning campaign, which limits most couples to one child, played a major role in that development.

In other parts of the developing world, declines in birth rates are proceeding more slowly. In Mexico, birth rates fell from close to seven children per woman in 1970 to just over three in the mid-1990s. In India, the second most populous country in the world, children per woman declined from nearly six in the early 1960s, to 3.5 in the mid-1990s. Although those declines are not enough to halt population growth, they certainly have played a role in slowing population growth, and they appear likely to continue. Even in the countries of sub-Saharan Africa, which until recently showed no signs of any reduction in birth rates, there is now indisputable evidence of falling birth rates and slowing population growth. For example, between the early 1980s and the early 1990s, children per woman fell from over six to five in Zimbabwe, and from 7.5 to just over six in Kenya (United Nations, 1999).

The United Nations's projections that population growth rates will continue to slow are based on the assumption that developing countries' birth rates will continue to decline and that those countries will achieve a new balance between birth and death rates. The assumption may or may not be justified. So far, in nearly all the countries for which we have data, once birth rates have fallen by 10%, they do not go back up but continue to fall until they reach two children per woman. However, the countries that have completed the transition to low birth rates are nearly all in North America, Europe, and East Asia. It is possible that the countries of Africa, Latin America, and South Asia will follow a different path, if, for example, unique features of those regions' cultures favor large families. In Iran, for example, birth rates increased after the 1979 Islamic revolution, when family planning clinics were closed and women were encouraged to devote themselves to family life. (Subsequently, birth rates have fallen in Iran.) On the other hand, the globalization of culture tends to promote small families, and middle- and upper-class city dwellers in all developing countries have adopted many of the ways of developed countries.

In summary, most developing countries are now in the midst of the demographic transition. In a few countries, most notably China, a new balance between birth and death rates has been established. In others, mainly in sub-Saharan Africa, birth rate declines are just beginning, so yearly births still far outnumber yearly deaths. The next few decades will be a critical time for population growth. If the downward trends in developing countries' birth rates continue, which seems likely, population growth rates will slow and eventually taper off.

How Many People Can Earth Support?

Although population growth looks set to taper off, world population is projected to double at least once more before the end of the twenty-first century. So far, the world has avoided widespread cataclysms of the type predicted by Brown, Ehrlich, and some environmentalists. But will the earth be able to support the continuing population growth of the new century? Or even of the next few decades?

Population analysts like Brown and Ehrlich argue that there is a fixed upper limit on the number of people that the earth can support over the long run. Ehrlich and Ehrlich (1990) warn that we already may have exceeded that maximum population; Brown (1997) thinks we are fast approaching it. This hypothetical maximum population is known as *carrying capacity*, a biological concept, which is defined as the largest number of any given species that a habitat can support indefinitely.

The first attempt to calculate carrying capacity and answer the question "How many people can earth support?" was made just over a century ago by a geographer named Ernest Ravenstein. He used information on the amount of land currently under cultivation, the average crop yields of the land, and farming techniques being used to conclude that Earth could support about 6 billion people (Smil, 1994).

Since Ravenstein, numerous other attempts have been made to estimate Earth's carrying capacity, using increasingly complex assumptions, ever larger amounts of data, and sophisticated computer simulations. These efforts have resulted in a range of estimates for Earth's human carrying capacity, from Ehrlich's low of 2 billion to a high of over 40 billion (Ehrlich, 1968; Smil, 1994).

Even while efforts to estimate Earth's carrying capacity continue, some researchers have become skeptical about the usefulness of the concept. The fact that the range of estimates varies so widely suggests that the estimates are sensitive to different assumptions about the level of technology. The introduction of new agricultural technologies, such as drought-resistant plant varieties, could, for example, greatly increase both crop yields and the amount of land that could be cultivated. Similarly, shortages of inputs for certain currently used technologies could reduce yields and cultivated land. In other words, Earth's carrying capacity critically depends on the level of technology at our disposal. Carrying capacity is undoubtedly far greater today than in Ravenstein's time, because of advances in agricultural technology, particularly the introduction of high-yield varieties of wheat and rice during the "green revolution" of the 1950s and 1960s.

Economist Julian Simon has carried the argument that carrying capacity depends on technology to its logical conclusion. In his book *The Ultimate Resource*, Simon maintains that the only limits to carrying capacity are those set by human ingenuity. According to Simon, resources such as food are not fixed but can be expanded indefinitely by technological advances. Moreover, Simon argues that, by creating shortages, population growth actually stimulates the research and development that lead to technological advances. According to Simon, without population growth there would have been no green revolution and no improvement in Earth's ability to feed its population. Simon has applied his argument to other resources, such as fossil fuels, and argues that we should not be concerned about the depletion of those resources: when they become scarce, they will become more expensive, which will stimulate research to find cheaper, better alternatives.

Simon's views are not widely shared. Most food researchers, for example, do not believe that Earth's ability to produce food or support human life can be increased indefinitely. However, the recognition that carrying capacity is determined largely by the level of technology has led many researchers to refocus their efforts away from estimating carrying capacity and toward assessing likely future developments in food production. That is, instead of asking, "How many people can Earth support?" researchers are asking, "Will we be able to feed our growing population for the foreseeable future?"

Recent analyses of agricultural production suggest that enough food can be produced to meet the extra demand. The late 1980s and early 1990s saw continued increases in food output in North Africa and Asia, the regions that will account for 60% of the increase in food demand up to 2020 (Dyson, 1994).

Between 1962 and 1989, world food supply increased by about 3.1% per year. A continued gain of only 1.8% a year would be sufficient to meet the projected increase in food demand between 1989 and 2050 (Bongaarts, 1996a). That goal could be achieved by improvements in current resource usage, reduction of waste, and use of more efficient production techniques; it does not depend on major new breakthroughs in farming technology (Smil, 1994). If the people in developed countries could be persuaded to eat less meat, that would increase world food supply by redirecting resources toward cereal and vegetable production. Even global warming would not necessarily pose a threat to world food production, because new plant varieties can be developed far faster than Earth would warm under even the most pessimistic projections of climate change (Smil, 1994). The projected increase in food demand of 1.8% per year includes not only food for extra population but also increases in food per person. That is an especially important goal, because at present approximately 800 million people are chronically underfed.

The finding that not only will we be able to feed the world's population into the twenty-first century but that we will be able to feed them better points to a second flaw in the concept of carrying capacity,

namely that it ignores variations in how people live. The way Americans currently live relies on very high levels of resource use. Clearly, at our present level of technology, Earth could not support 6 billion people living an American lifestyle, a point made in Chapter 13. On the other hand, if we were all prepared to live a much simpler lifestyle—say, along the lines of Chinese peasants, who make up about one-sixth of the world's population—Earth probably could support many more people than it does now.

Thus, the biologist's concept of carrying capacity is of limited relevance to human populations. The size of the human population that Earth can support not only depends on humans' biological needs for food and other resources but also is affected by the level of technology developed by humans and the standard of living achieved by humans. Conservative predictions of food supply and population growth suggest that we will be able to feed our growing population well into the middle of the twenty-first century while at the same time reducing the number of people who are chronically malnourished.

The consequences of rapid population growth, which are less well understood than the causes, remain the subject of heated debates among researchers and academics. As discussed at the beginning of this chapter, some analysts believe that rapid population growth has brought human beings to the brink of disaster and that unless population growth is curtailed we could, as a species, face extinction. But others point out that detailed analyses of the causes of such social problems as famine, environmental degradation, and economic underdevelopment often show that population growth is only one of a cluster of interrelated social, economic, and political factors. Population is rarely the biggest source of the problems.

Famine

In the spring of 2000, the United Nations World Food Program issued an urgent plea for famine relief for Ethiopia. After three years of drought, worsening food shortages in southeastern Ethiopia developed into a full-scale famine. Relief workers projected that emergency food reserves would be completely used up by June 1, 2000, leaving thousands of undernourished people facing imminent death from starvation. As early as February 2000, the death toll in the worst-affected area had reached twelve children every day (*Seattle Times,* April 16, 2000).

The tragedy of famine is familiar. The news in 1997 was that thousands of North Korean children were dying of starvation. In the 1980s, a series of famines in Africa attracted worldwide attention, culminating in a series of pop concerts to raise money for famine relief. In the 1970s, famine struck Bangladesh and parts of India. In the 1960s, famines raged throughout West Africa. The continuing specter of famine seems to be at odds with the claim that there is enough food to feed the world's growing population. If the food supply is adequate, why is there still famine?

One reason is that the food often is not in the same place as the hungry people. North America and Europe are the most productive agricultural regions in the world and produce more food than their populations consume. Government subsidies to farmers in the United States and Europe help keep food prices low for American and European consumers but also lead to huge gluts of some foods. Most of the rich countries' excess food is sold on world markets or, if the prices are too low, is warehoused. If the costs of storage are too high, surplus food is destroyed, although some if it may be donated to famine-stricken countries.

Although it would seem a simple matter for rich countries to eliminate famine by donating their food surpluses to poor countries, there are problems with that approach. To begin with, not all the food that is overproduced is suitable for donation; Europe's food surpluses in the 1970s and 1980s famously included a "wine lake" and a "butter mountain." More important, since the 1960s, development economists have warned that when a country can get large amounts of cheap food from elsewhere there is little incentive for local farmers to improve their own productivity. To avoid that problem, aid agencies provide only short-term famine relief and try to supplement the relief with rural development programs to increase local food production and encourage farmers to grow crops that can be traded on world markets.

But there is another, more surprising reason why famine persists in the face of worldwide increases in food production: famines can occur even when there is plenty of food. During the great Irish potato famine of 1845–1851, for example, huge quantities of food were exported from Ireland, even as one-fifth of the population died from starvation and related diseases. The great Bengal famine of 1943, which may have killed as many as 3 million people, occurred even though the 1943 rice crop was the largest Bengal had ever produced and even though food shops in Calcutta were well stocked. In 1974, famine killed 26,000 people in Bangladesh, even though food production, both total and per head, was at an all-time high, and food exports continued throughout the famine. In 1973, famine killed

Hundreds of thousands of people in southeastern Ethiopia are once again starving. Persistent drought is one cause of famine, but so are war, unequal distribution of food, and other complicated factors—all of which plague Ethiopia. Despite truckloads of food being delivered by groups such as Action Against Hunger, famine will not end anytime soon in this troubled African country.

between 50,000 and 200,000 people in Ethiopia, although food production was up from previous years. As was the case in other famines, during the Ethiopian famine of 1973, food was actually exported from the hardest-hit region, despite the government's claim that bad roads prevented the delivery of food aid.

All those examples are drawn from Nobel prize–winning economist Amartya Sen's book *Poverty and Famines* (1981), in which he presents detailed information about several of the twentieth century's major famines. Sen shows that although famine is usually blamed on food shortages caused by flooding, drought, or some other "natural disaster," the real culprits are the social, economic, and political conditions in the famine areas. In all the examples given in the preceding paragraph, only certain groups of the population were afflicted by famine, so that some starved while others had plenty. Food was available, but those who starved could not get any because the resources they usually traded for food, such as their labor or livestock, were not wanted. In Bangladesh in 1974, farm laborers were hardest hit by the famines, because they were thrown out of work when flooding prevented the planting of second rice crops. In Ethiopia in 1973, nomadic herdsmen were hardest hit, because drought caused the death of many of the animals they traded for grain, and the amount of grain they could get for each animal fell sharply. The same process seems to have occurred in the 2000 Ethiopian famine.

Sen's argument about the importance of entitlements to food was powerfully underscored by events in Somalia in the early 1990s, when widespread starvation prompted a United Nations peacekeeping mission that included U.S. military personnel. The food crisis in Somalia was not caused by population growth or natural disasters but by civil war. Opposing warlords commandeered food supplies and used the threat of starvation to subjugate their enemies and the promise of food to attract supporters. In the eyes of the warlords, their enemies simply were not entitled to food.

Somalia is not a unique example of a famine caused by human malfeasance. One of the worst famines of the century took place in China between 1957 and 1961, when as many as 30 million people perished. That famine was caused by government policies—ironically heralded as the "Great Leap Forward"—that forced farmers into large collective farms and ordered them to prioritize industrial projects over food production. Similarly, the 1997 famines in North Korea were due in large part to forty years of communist policies, which gave farmers little incentive to improve and husband the land. The North Korean government was also extremely reluctant to lose face by accepting food aid (although, to be fair, donor governments demanded political concessions before delivering food aid).

Sometimes food supplies do fail in the wake of natural disasters. Usually, such failures are localized, and famine can be avoided by drawing on food reserves and bringing in food from elsewhere. At other times, famine occurs in the midst of plenty. In either case, when famine occurs, we have to ask why food does not reach the people who need it. The answer usually lies in human action or inaction: leaders who are misguided, inept, or downright evil and institutions that are flawed—like the grain markets that encourage food exports from famine areas or government policies that discourage farmers from making the most of their land. Solving those problems and the tragedy of famine will not be easy, but—so far—humans have had greater success dealing with inept and evil leaders and replacing flawed institutions than they have had controlling the weather.

Environmental Degradation

Another purported result of the rapid growth in human population is irreversible damage to the natural environment. Environmentalists often link increasing air and water pollution and global warming to escalating human activities such as the harvesting of timber and overuse of the land for raising food crops and livestock. But again, blaming it all on population growth is unwise. The human impact on the environment is complex.

For example, a recent study of deforestation in Ghana, in west Africa, found that population growth actually encouraged forest protection and expansion, because people in more populous areas tended to take better care of the forest. In the areas where deforestation was greatest, the problems appear to have been caused by strong economic incentives to tear up the forests in order to plant export crops, like cocoa (Leach & Fairhead, 2000). The authors of that study are careful to point out that the patterns they observed depended, in large part, on the unique social and cultural arrangements of the area—who owns the land and how land is passed from the family members of one generation to those of the next. Different patterns of relationships among population growth, raising crops for export, and deforestation would likely be observed in other parts of the world, such as the Amazon and Southeast Asia.

Even global environmental problems like the buildup of greenhouse gases in Earth's atmosphere are not as closely tied to population growth as is often supposed. The most important greenhouse gas is carbon dioxide, and yearly emissions of carbon dioxide are projected to quadruple during the twenty-first century. But only one-third of the projected increase in carbon dioxide emissions will be due to population growth. Most of the increase will be due to increased industrial production (Bongaarts, 1992). Even if world population growth were halted tomorrow, two-thirds of the projected increase in carbon dioxide emissions still would occur. Slower population growth certainly would help reduce emissions growth, but it would not solve the whole problem.

Economic Underdevelopment

Economists also have become increasingly skeptical that all—or even most—of the economic problems facing developing countries can be traced to population growth. Population growth undoubtedly hinders economic growth, because scarce resources must be directed toward meeting people's basic needs and thus are diverted away from investments in infrastructure, education, and healthcare that can promote economic growth. But slower population growth by itself does not necessarily translate into

faster economic growth, because governments do not always make wise economic policy choices. Often, resources that could have been invested are squandered on grandiose but unsound economic schemes, military adventures, or the personal enrichment of corrupt politicians. Probably the greatest challenge facing developing countries is how to make economic markets operate properly, so that resources, goods, and services are traded at prices that reflect the real costs of using or producing them. Numerous studies have shown that the wasteful use of economic investments, as well as economic resources and food supplies, are due to markets that do not work properly. For example, one reason why many African farmers cannot afford to conserve or improve their land is because governments keep grain prices artificially low to ensure that food is cheap for city dwellers. But the low grain prices leave farmers with too little profit to invest in fertilizing and conserving their soil (Scherr & Yadav, 1996).

It is also apparent that the economic impacts of population growth vary from country to country. Some developing countries, such as Thailand, were able to adjust to the demands of rapid population growth. Those countries benefited from strong economic institutions and enjoyed a surge of economic growth as falling birth rates in the 1970s and 1980s created a large labor force with relatively few children to support. Other countries have not coped well with rapid population growth. Bangladesh, for example, is plagued by corruption, misguided economic policies, nonfunctioning economic institutions, and extreme social inequality. Slower population growth will not solve those problems, and Bangladeshi society might have been better able to meet the challenge of rapid population growth without those additional problems. At the same time, the effects of weak institutions and misguided policies in Bangladesh would have been less severe if the population had been growing more slowly (Barlow, 1994).

The conclusions about the effects of population growth on economic development and on environment problems are parallel. Population growth has adverse consequences for economic development in some countries. But population growth is not the whole or the biggest problem facing developing countries. Instead, population growth is one part of a complex set of conditions that also includes poverty, weak institutions, and bad policy.

Can We Slow Population Growth?

Although population growth generally is not the only or the largest source of global problems such as famine, environmental degradation, and economic underdevelopment, there could be huge advantages to slowing population growth more quickly. Perhaps more people could be better fed and lead healthier, more productive lives. Perhaps we could slow the buildup of atmospheric carbon dioxide and reduce pressure on fragile ecosystems. And perhaps developing countries could direct more resources toward prosperity-promoting investments like education, healthcare, and infrastructure. Given the potential benefits, it is reasonable to ask whether we can slow population growth even more.

Family planning programs have been widely promoted as one way to slow population growth. At present, nearly all developing countries, including more than 90% of the developing world's population, have family planning programs. The programs often are supported in part by aid from developed countries and the United Nations. But do they work?

The record is mixed. Some programs, for example, China's, appear to have been spectacularly successful. The Chinese government began to promote family planning in the late 1960s. The early campaign focused on providing couples with contraceptives, informing them about the advantages of smaller families, and persuading them to have smaller families with more widely spaced births. In the mid-1970s, the campaign intensified, culminating in 1979 with the adoption of the one-child policy. Under that policy, strong persuasion is supplemented with rewards (such as larger food rations and better access to education and health programs) for one-child families and punishments (such as heavier taxes) for larger families. As a re-

sult, China's birth rate is now below two children per woman.

In contrast, family planning programs have been rather unsuccessful in India. During the 1950s and 1960s, the national family planning program was poorly organized and ineffectual—birth rates hardly fell at all before the mid-1970s. In the mid-1970s, the program concentrated on male sterilization, but it aroused widespread hostility as family planning workers crossed the boundary between persuasion and compulsion—men were threatened with the loss of their jobs if they did not submit to sterilization. In the face of public anger, politicians backed away from the family planning program, and it was not until the mid-1980s that family planning efforts were relaunched. By then, the birth rate had finally begun to drop, apparently without the help of the family planning program. Today, India's birth rate is still 3.5 children per woman, India's population is growing at nearly 2% a year, and by 2050 India will have replaced China as the most populous nation on earth.

The differences between the family planning program in China and that in India illustrate one of the most important facts about birth rate declines: for birth rates to decline, couples must have both the means to have smaller families and the motivation. Access to contraceptive devices by itself will not necessarily lead to a reduction in birth rates; couples must also want smaller families. For the first thirty years of its existence, the Indian family planning program, like many other early family planning programs, provided couples with the means to have smaller families but had little impact on birth rates because most couples were not motivated. In contrast, the Chinese family planning program provided both the means for couples to have smaller families and the motivation, in the shape of rewards for small families and punishments for large ones.

So far, most public policy attempts to slow population growth have concentrated on making the means to have smaller families more widely available. Such efforts are important and likely will have some impact on reducing birth rates. At present, an estimated 100 million women worldwide—about one-sixth of all the married women in the developing world—would like either to stop having children or to space their children more widely, but they are not using contraception (Bongaarts, 1994). Improving family planning services and making contraception available to those women could hasten reductions in the birth rates in developing countries. But we should not overstate the impact of extending family planning services to unserved women. When couples are strongly motivated to limit childbearing, lack of access to contraception is not an obstacle to a decline in the birth rate; in the United States and Europe, birth rates declined before the widespread availability of effective contraceptives.

In many parts of the developing world, however, birth rates are high because couples want large families. In the late 1980s, researchers surveyed women in twenty-seven developing countries in Africa, Asia, and Latin America and did not find a single country where the average desired family size was close to two; in sub-Saharan Africa, the average desired family size was six (Bongaarts, 1994). That is something of an improvement, however: some twenty years earlier, most African women were unwilling to say how many children they would like, saying instead that it was "up to God." A similar shift in attitudes was an important prerequisite for developed countries' shift to smaller families.

There are many reasons why couples in developing countries want large families. Some of the reasons are cultural: having many children may be a source of prestige; in societies where a preference for sons is strong, some couples end up with large families because they continue having children until they have one or two sons. Other reasons are practical: children provide old-age support for their parents, in rural areas they work on the farms, and in urban areas they often work in factories and bring in extra wages for the family. In some societies, the women who bear and raise the children have little say over how many children they have; instead, husbands and older family members make those decisions. The Chinese family planning program was successful because it eliminated traditional reasons to have large families and replaced them with incentives to have small families. The government guaranteed old-age support, promising better pen-

sions to couples with smaller families; compulsory education meant that children could no longer work and earn wages, and large families became costly when parents with two or three children had to pay for their children's schooling.

Most governments cannot exercise the degree of control over their citizens' family lives that the Chinese government has been able to exert. Attempts to add incentives and disincentives to the Indian family planning program failed, partly because they were too costly but also because Indian politicians and community leaders saw the program as inconsistent with India's democratic system of government.

Fortunately, government programs such as the ones in China are not the only sources of motivation for couples to have smaller families. When governments invest in education and increase school enrollment, birth rates drop. That was true at the turn of the century in the United States and Europe, as well as in the 1950s in East Asian countries like Taiwan, Japan, and Korea. Today countries that have invested heavily in education, such as Thailand and Vietnam, are experiencing the most rapid declines in birth rates. Increasing school enrollment increases parents' motivation to have smaller families because they must pay for each child who attends school or at least outfit their children for school. It also exposes children and their parents to ideas from the industrialized, developed world, which include a preference for smaller families (Bongaarts, 1994).

Changes in women's roles are another important factor that can increase a couple's motivation to have smaller families. In many high-birth-rate societies, women have few rights and little freedom; children may be their only source of status, and their days are filled with child rearing and domestic or farm work that is easily combined with child rearing. But when women have more education and more employment opportunities, having a large family conflicts with work; an extra child may pose a considerable expense if it means the woman cannot work and stops earning a wage. Last but not least, educated women tend to have a different outlook than their less educated counterparts and are

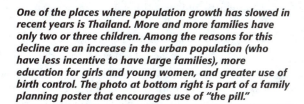

One of the places where population growth has slowed in recent years is Thailand. More and more families have only two or three children. Among the reasons for this decline are an increase in the urban population (who have less incentive to have large families), more education for girls and young women, and greater use of birth control. The photo at bottom right is part of a family planning poster that encourages use of "the pill."

less likely to defer to their husbands and older family members when it comes to reproductive decisions, such as whether to use birth control. Educated women tend to wait longer before getting married and having children, and their children are healthier and more likely to survive, both of which slow the birth rate (Bongaarts, 1994).

A number of steps could be taken to hasten the slowdown in population growth. But if they are to be effective, those steps must go well beyond traditional family planning programs, with their narrow emphasis on supplying the means to have smaller families. In many developing countries, couples want large families. Changing those couples' minds and motivating them to have smaller families is the key to slower population growth. It is especially important that educational programs in high-birth-rate countries include girls as well as boys. Increasing women's education and employment further shifts the balance of costs and benefits away from large families and toward small families and empowers women to make their own reproductive choices.

A Reality Check

There are important potential benefits to slowing population growth. So why not just do it? Unfortunately, there are serious problems, both practical and cultural, with that beguiling vision.

As a practical matter, bringing about slower population growth by increasing education and improving the status of women is a difficult and slow process. Many developing countries simply do not have resources to invest in education. Shortages of educated people who could be teachers are especially problematic, because diverting the most educated people into teaching removes them from other sectors of the economy that also face critical shortages of educated workers.

There are also formidable cultural obstacles to slowing population growth, including these:

- *Values regarding children and education.* In the United States, transportation planners have been spectacularly unsuccessful in their efforts to persuade Americans to ride mass transit. Why should it be any easier to persuade farmers in developing countries to have smaller families and to send their daughters to school, especially when they are so dependent on the labor provided by their children?

- *Traditional expectations for women's roles.* Traditions are often shaped by religious beliefs, and beliefs such as Islam and Roman Catholicism are resistant to change. Religion aside, changing mores regarding women's roles historically has been difficult. In the United States at one time, there was widespread opposition to women's entry into higher education and women's employment, and similar debates are now taking place in many developing countries. Efforts to reduce the birth rate necessarily involve debates over reproduction, an especially sensitive issue. Today in the United States, a passionate debate over abortion rages; a century ago, a similar, equally passionate debate was played out over the morality of birth control. Many developing countries today are embroiled in similar debates about the morality of family planning.

- *Cultural pride.* Debates in developing countries about family planning, women's status, and education often are further complicated by concerns about "cultural imperialism" by developed nations. Many fear that rich countries are imposing their cultural values, including a preference for small families, while destroying poor countries' traditional cultures.

Because of the formidable practical and cultural barriers to implementing policies that might lower birth rates, such policies will not have quick results. Of course, that does not mean we should not try to lower birth rates, especially if the threat of rapid population growth is judged to be the most serious challenge to human survival. It does mean, however, that we should not count on the success of population policies being easy or quick.

Nor will a successful attempt to reduce birth rates automatically make people's lives better. The leaders of developing countries do not have to use the resources freed up by slower population growth to improve living conditions. Recent history is full of examples of leaders who have chosen military spending and self-aggrandizing schemes (like new capital cities, presidential palaces, and heart-transplant centers) over investments in infrastructure, basic healthcare, education, and environmental protection. The citizens of those countries also may opt to continue practices that lead to resource depletion and environmental degradation. For example, people living in the Amazon simply may prefer the immediate gain from selling timber to the hypothetical gain they might reap from protecting the rain forest. Thus, societal development and good policymaking are at least as important as slower population growth to solving problems in developing countries.

We also must recognize that the same values that promote small families also encourage high levels of consumption. We may be able to persuade farmers in developing countries to have smaller families, but the farmer may be willing to have fewer children only if it means he can drive to the market instead of riding a bus and watch television in the evenings. Such increased consumption will not be environmentally friendly. For example, motor vehicles are scarce in China outside the big cities. But in the big cities, congestion and pollution already are problems that will worsen as more of China's billion-plus people buy cars. Our accounting of the environmental damage should include the resources used to build the cars and the pollution generated by the production process. Although slower population growth will mean fewer people to consume limited resources and generate environmental problems, the extent of the environmental harm wreaked by a population depends not on the number of people but on how they live.

In summary, although there are great potential benefits of slower population growth, realizing those benefits will not be easy and will depend on more than just convincing people to have fewer babies. We should not be surprised that population growth is often described as the single greatest challenge facing humanity. It is also humanity's greatest achievement, because it reflects our success at conquering disease and increasing the productivity of the land.

Population growth will taper off over the next half century, although by 2100 there may well be as many as 12 billion people on earth. Will we be able to feed the extra people? In all probability, yes. But how well we will feed the population, how well they will live, and how long they will live are uncertain. Slower population growth may increase the chances that more people will live long, healthy, productive lives, but there are no guarantees that slower population growth will translate into greater well-being. Population is only one of many factors that influence human well-being, and creating strong yet flexible economic, political, and social institutions is an essential prerequisite to meeting the challenge of a world populated by 12 billion people.

Thinking about the Topic of Population Growth

1. Chapter 1 argued that society is changed by the interaction of internal and external forces. List at least three important internal and three important external forces that have shaped the current patterns of population growth and discuss how those forces have interacted. What part have culture and technology played? What are the roles of national governments and international organizations such as the United Nations?

2. Is the world truly facing a population crisis? Is the Earth becoming overpopulated? Is it true that rapid population growth is leading to irreparable environmental damage, disastrous famines, and devastating epidemics? Find evidence to support your point of view. Web sites for organizations like the United Nations, the World Health Organization, and the World Resources Institute are possible sources of data.

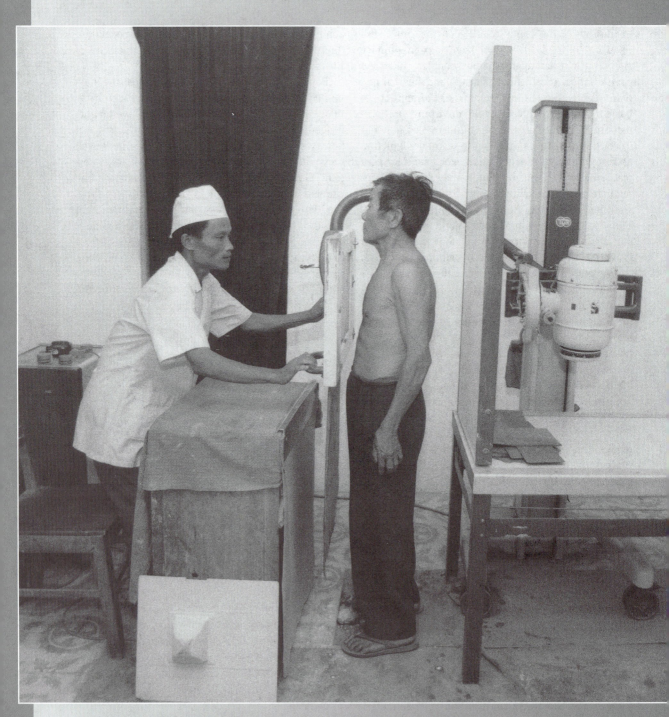

The X-ray room at Ky Anh General Hospital in Vietnam—and, in Idaho, a magnetic resonance imaging machine for brain scans. What constitutes quality healthcare, particularly in developing countries that have so many "basic" needs?

15 The Global Healthcare Challenge

NJERI MBUGUA

In 1984, Kenya's president, Daniel Moi, hastily insti-
tuted a mandatory training program for all Kenyan
students admitted to the nation's public universities.
The students were required to participate in endless
marching drills, cross-country running at 5:00 A.M.,
and lessons taught by inexperienced government
tutors. The training site was located in the foothills
of the rural town known as Naivasha, which is
extremely hot during the day and terribly cold during the night and early mornings. The training site
lacked most basic facilities. Children of the rich
quickly abandoned the program and traveled overseas for their university studies. The rest, like me,
had no choice but to endure the program, which
was a prerequisite for university admittance.

One cold, rainy morning, I feebly walked out of
my barrack, threw up the little food I had eaten for
breakfast, and then fainted. I recall falling on a muddy
pavement, being rushed to the hospital in an uncomfortable military lorry, being carried to a tiny bed, and
then being woken by the woman lying beside me in the
bed, who asked me to straighten my legs so they
wouldn't hurt her stomach. Apparently, I had malaria
and was admitted to Naivasha Hospital. Because of the

483

shortage of hospital beds, I had to share a small twin bed with a woman who was recovering from a stomach operation. Though I shivered with cold and wanted to roll my body into a tight ball for warmth, I had to keep my legs straight and still lest I touch my sick bedmate's stomach.

Neither the hospital nor government officials informed my parents of my illness and subsequent admission to Naivasha Hospital. I was too weak to call them myself. For about a week, I lay motionless on the small bed, dressed in the muddy track suit in which I had fainted. In the hospital's defense, a nurse had brought me a hospital gown. The gown had been washed but it still had spots that resembled blood stains. For that reason, I refused to wear it and for the two weeks that I was admitted at Naivasha Hospital, I never changed my track suit.

The female ward at Naivasha Hospital was a narrow room with twenty-two beds. Eleven beds were squeezed on one side of the room, facing another eleven across the other side. No curtains separated the beds. Across from the bed I shared and to the right was a mentally disturbed, epileptic adolescent girl who had severe burns all over her body. She constantly drooled, muttered to herself, and attempted to lick her wounds. She was a terrible sight to behold. For some reason, she kept staring at me. If I looked at her, she would get agitated and demand to know why I was staring at her, didn't I have something better to do? Did I want her to come to my bed to show me her wounds? To ensure that she did not come to my bedside, I learned to keep my head facing the left side of the ward.

Unfortunately, our immediate bedside neighbor on the left had a bloated stomach and loudly emitted an extremely foul-smelling gas about five times a day and more frequently through the night. At the sound of her gas emissions, all the patients who were physically able to left the ward and waited outside until the smell receded. Those of us who were too weak to escape—the epileptic girl, my bedmate, two old women, a middle-aged woman, and I—remained in the ward, feeling angry and resentful toward her. My bedmate informed me that the middle-aged woman had become partially paralyzed during the delivery of her ninth child, who

was stillborn. Due to the paralysis, the woman no longer could talk or walk. She did seem incapable of controlling her bladder and bowel movements. One of her older children attended her daily, constantly changing her bed pan. When doctors requested permission to perform a tubal ligation on the woman, her husband declined, stating that birth control permitted women to be promiscuous and interfered with God's will.

Other foul smells accosted us. One was from the disinfectant used to clean the hospital floors every day at 6:00 A.M. Patients had to decide whether to brave the cold outside or endure the pungent fumes of the cleaning substance. The smell was so awful that most patients opted to shiver outside in the cold for about a half hour until the odor receded (it never really disappeared).

The third source of foul smell was from the filthy toilets. Fortunately, because I was too weak to eat or drink, I rarely used the toilets. The few times I did, I used the male toilets, which were less filthy. I got away with it because Naivasha was a small rural town where few females wore trousers, and the males did not realize that the skinny short-haired patient in a muddy tracksuit was a female. Or perhaps they did notice but were too sick to bother.

Attending both the female and male wards were two clinical officers (not fully trained doctors), two nurses, and several terribly unprofessional nursing trainees. One of the trainees asked me in a scared voice while administering me an injection, "Do you think this thing has a hole through which the medicine will come out?" Another informed me, "This medicine has expired, but it's still better than nothing. Pray that God uses it to heal you." A third encouraged me to eat the monotonous meal of overcooked cabbage. She kindly let me know that the cabbages had a few caterpillars in the leaves, but since the only thing these caterpillars had ever eaten was cabbage, they really were more like cabbages than caterpillars. I understood her logic. However, I determined never to eat that cabbage whether it was in vegetable or caterpillar form. The little food I ate at Naivasha Hospital was supplied by the kind patients who shared the meager food their families brought them.

It took me two weeks to muster the strength to telephone my parents, who immediately drove from Nairobi (Kenya's capital city) and took me home. They were shocked at my debilitated body. I learned that my brother also had gotten malaria and had been admitted to Nairobi Hospital for a short period. He told me of his hospital experience, which was completely different from mine: constant changes of hospital clothing, a menu that included some gourmet foods, a TV/VCR that entertained him day and night, and a telephone by his bedside. His hospital experience was similar to that found in developed countries.

For the provision of his healthcare, my brother was charged an enormous hospital bill, but fortunately the family's health insurance fully covered it. Because I received treatment accorded Kenya's poor, my hospitalization was free—but it nearly cost me my life.

The Grim Reality of Healthcare in Lower-Income Countries

My brush with the sort of healthcare available to most of the people in the world occurred in 1984. It would be nice if I could report progress and improvement since then, but I cannot. By contemporary standards, 1984 was "the good old days." Since then, the adequate treatment of sick people, especially those in low- and middle-income nations, has been further compromised by a number of changes that accompany the process of globalization: economic development programs that make social spending a luxury for poor nations; rampant political turbulence that has displaced millions of people; burgeoning cross-border trade and travel; the emergence of drug-resistant microbes; the rapid spread of disease around the world; and the HIV/AIDS epidemic. Those developments have raised concerns everywhere about human health but have overwhelmed healthcare systems in developing countries. They demonstrate the pervasive effects of economic and political inequality, which extend to the fundamental issue of the length and quality of a human being's biological life.

Healthcare in the Era of Economic Development Programs

During my hospitalization at Naivasha Hospital, the Kenyan government was still making healthcare in public hospitals available to every Kenyan regardless of socioeconomic status. Soon thereafter, in the early 1990s, the International Monetary Fund (IMF) and the World Bank imposed some drastic conditions on Kenya and other developing countries under structural adjustment programs (SAPs), which were described in Chapters 7 and 8. The main objectives of SAPs are to promote economic growth in developing countries and to ensure the repayment of foreign debts. SAPs stipulate that governments in the debtor countries must impose austerity measures and cut public expenditures on healthcare, education, sanitation, water, transportation, garbage collection, and other vital services. Such cuts ensure extreme poverty and miserable living conditions for many people.

According to the World Bank, the total number of people worldwide living on less than U.S.$1 a day increased from 1.2 billion people in 1987 to 1.5 billion in 2000. If current economic trends persist, that figure will reach 1.9 billion people by 2015. The large majority of the world's poorest people live in low-income countries (in south Asia and sub-Saharan Africa), whose governments spend about U.S.$16 annually per capita on health. The lowest-income countries spend less than U.S.$7 per capita on health. In contrast, the average health expenditure in high-income countries is more than U.S.$1,800 per capita (World Health Organization [WHO], 1999a). People who live on less than U.S.$1 a day cannot afford healthcare and therefore suffer greatly when governments cut back on healthcare spending.

The decline in the quality and the provision of vital public services has also increased susceptibility to disease for the vast majority of people living in developing countries. According to the World Health Organization (WHO), diseases that once were thought to be retreating—among them plague, diphtheria, yellow fever, dengue, meningitis, influenza, and cholera—have made deadly comebacks. Moreover, new killer diseases have emerged. Over the past two decades, over thirty emerging diseases, many of them neither preventable nor treatable, have been identified in humans for the first time (WHO, 1999a). Nevertheless, governments in most developing nations continue to decrease the amount of spending on healthcare. Compared to the U.S.$1,800 spent per person in industrialized countries, the Kenyan government's health spending in 1999 was a mere U.S.$3 per person. With the projected decline in economic growth in most developing countries as SAPs continue, public healthcare spending is set to decline below the levels of twenty years ago.

Even when the governments of developing countries are given foreign aid to improve healthcare systems, corruption, poor planning, and poor program implementation often keep the aid from reaching the targeted populations. Consequently, instead of giving governments the resources to improve people's healthcare, most donor agencies prefer to work with nongovernmental organizations (NGOs), which are better managed and therefore more likely to accomplish the desired objectives. For example, in 1996, the United States channeled more than 30% of its development aid in Africa through NGOs rather than through governments. In 1999, the U.S. ambassador to Kenya, Prudence Bushnell, announced that the U.S. government would start channeling most of its development aid in Africa through NGOs. Less than two months after that announcement, the Dutch cultural attaché to Kenya told journalists that the Netherlands also would decrease direct aid to governments and give more to NGOs. Other major donors, including Britain, France, and Germany, also have told African governments to eradicate corruption or face cuts in aid (Chege, 1999). In 2000, the Dutch government stated that it would freeze all bilateral development assistance to Kenya by 2002 because Kenya's bad governance has made progress in programs funded by the Dutch government impossible to achieve.

Unfortunately, several delivery problems hinder NGOs' efforts to provide healthcare. In particular, NGOs face four key healthcare delivery problems:

- *Transportation difficulties.* Most interior parts of developing nations have poor roads, and most roads are not well maintained. During heavy rains, which usually wash away roads and bridges, many areas become inaccessible. As a result of such delays, some medicines expire and go to ruin without helping the thousands who need them.

- *Physical risks and dangers to healthcare personnel.* NGOs that offer their services in violence-ridden areas often do so at great personal danger to their personnel. For example, Doctors Without Borders provides mobile clinics and relief assistance to those wounded and displaced by civil or international conflict.

- *Ineffective and corrupt government bureaucracies.* It is unfortunate that most public servants in developing countries have to be bribed to perform the services for which they are employed. Corruption by high-ranking government officials has caused some donor agencies to withdraw funds from needy and otherwise deserving nations.

- *Suspicion of the motives of high-income industrialized countries.* Suspicion and distrust have resulted in the loss of opportunities offered freely or at a minimal fee to the needy in developing countries. For example, when Glaxo Wellcome (an international pharmaceutical company) found out in 1999 that the cost for a full treatment of malaria (U.S.$39 per person) was prohibitive for the majority of people in developing countries, it decided to donate up to a million free doses of a highly effective malaria drug called malarone. To the company's surprise and dismay, some African governments did not trust Glaxo Wellcome's intentions and initially resisted the offer.

Developing countries have learned to distrust industrialized countries largely because of three historical events. First, the notoriety of secret experiments such as the Tuskegee Study of Untreated Syphilis in the Negro Male made many people of color around the world wary of charitable services from the United States and other developed countries. In the Tuskegee study, which took place from 1932 to 1972, more than 400 African-American males were promised free medical treatment for their "bad blood" (which researchers had identified as syphilis) yet were refused treatment for syphilis even when a cure was found. The men were never informed that they were part of a study, nor were they ever told that they had syphilis.

Second, and closely related to the first factor, is the export to developing countries of harmful products banned in the developed world. For example, DDT, a highly toxic insecticide that was banned in the United States in 1973, is still being exported to developing countries. Such harmful products are often sold under new, less recognizable trade names.

The fear of counterfeit pharmaceuticals is the third source of distrust of healthcare aid. Many counterfeit drugs are not only ineffective but also toxic, resulting in fatalities. According to WHO, between 1982 and 1997, counterfeit pharmaceuticals were found in at least twenty-eight countries. In about 25% of the cases uncovered, the drugs originated in developed countries, while 10% were from unspecified sources ("Health Agency," 1997).

For a variety of reasons, then, most of the economic development programs advocated by international organizations have resulted in declining healthcare. Governments under financial pressure cut back on public spending. As public healthcare systems deteriorate, the impact is most severe on the poor. A set of complex human circumstances that accompany poverty—reluctance to seek medical assistance, late diagnoses, and self-medication—exacerbate their health problems. In addition, the poor who do develop serious health problems are driven deeper into poverty by their lack of financial protection in the form of health insurance.

Healthcare in the Era of Political Turmoil

My experience at Naivasha Hospital took place during a time when Kenya, unlike its neighbors, enjoyed political tranquility and was referred to as "an island of peace." Gun deaths were almost unheard of, and the police were armed only with batons. Those were the days before ethnic clashes over land, fueled by politics, ravaged the lives of many Kenyans, rendering thousands homeless.

The continuing land wrangles, coupled with increased corruption on the part of the government, a declining economy, and high unemployment rates, have caused Kenyans not only to distrust their government but to turn against each other with firearms. In 2000, Kenyan members of parliament (MPs) voted to have the state provide them with guns and bodyguards for protection, at a cost of 25 million shillings a year. That demand was motivated by the shooting of several MPs, two of whom were still in the hospital at the time of the vote. One MP protested the motion, stating that a popularly elected MP should not need a firearm to tour his constituency. His view was loudly rejected.

Once an island of peace, Kenya has joined the numerous developing countries characterized by "complex emergencies"—armed conflicts that arise from civil wars or insurgencies, as one or several factions fight against a sitting government. Often, countries with complex emergencies divert their limited national resources from healthcare to military spending.

When countries divert national expenditures from healthcare to the military, vulnerable members of the society—the elderly, women, and infants—suffer the most. Indeed, poor countries involved in wars or political unrest are also the countries with the highest rates of infant mortality. (Refer back to Graphic 1.10 for data on child mortality rates and national economic status.) In 1999, Ethiopia, Guinea, Guinea-Bissau, Malawi, Mozambique, Niger, Sierra Leone, Somalia, and Western Sahara—all poor and involved in political unrest—had more than 125 babies die per 1,000 live births. In contrast, the average infant mortality rate in developed countries such as the United States is 7 babies per 1,000 live births. Afghanistan and Western Sahara, despite being rich in mineral resources, have the world's highest infant mortality rate—an astounding 150 deaths per 1,000 births. It is not surprising to find that both countries are involved in political turmoil.

Political unrest causes rapid migrations of large numbers of refugees to new geographic areas. The refugees usually crowd into temporary shelters that are devoid of basic facilities such as clean water, adequate sanitation, and nourishment. They usually have little protection against diseases and receive limited medical care. These environments become fertile breeding grounds for infectious diseases, as was the case in Rwanda during the 1994 ethnic clashes. When about 800,000 Rwandan refugees fled into Zaire, 50,000 of them died from cholera and other infectious diseases in the first month. Among the most affected were infants and pregnant women. In developed countries such as the United States, the maternal death rate from pregnancy complications is as low as 1 in 4,000, but in developing countries more than one woman dies every minute from complications associated with pregnancy. The rate is many times higher in refugee camps.

Political turmoil and war affect healthcare not only in poor nations but also in those that are wealthy. For one thing, they require government expenditures that otherwise could be used to fight disease. As Graphic 15.1 shows, military expenditures are out of proportion to the number of deaths in-

volved, compared to deaths from infectious disease. Warring nations also spend millions of dollars in psychological and physical treatment of soldiers injured during combat. (It is noteworthy to mention that surgeons treating soldiers in the late 1800s and early 1900s developed the basic techniques of reconstructive surgery, which benefit civilians as plastic surgery.) War also interferes with the delivery of healthcare programs such as infant immunization programs.

In conditions of political turmoil, even polio, once nearly eradicated, is reemerging. Three years of fighting in the Russian republic of Chechnya interrupted immunization programs, which resulted in 152 new cases of polio. In 1996, only 53% of two-year-olds in Kosovo received the full vaccination course against diseases such as polio and measles. One of the largest polio outbreaks ever recorded in Africa occurred in early 1999 in Angola, affecting over 1,000 children and resulting in 58 deaths (WHO, 1999b). Those were the reported cases, which implies that the actual numbers may have been much higher. On a positive note, the director general of WHO reported that for the

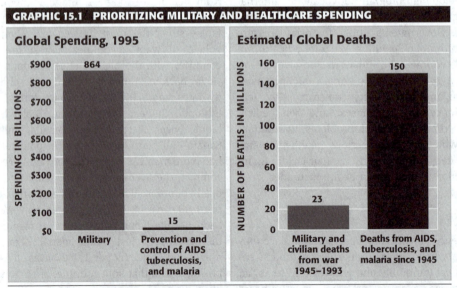

GRAPHIC 15.1   PRIORITIZING MILITARY AND HEALTHCARE SPENDING

Global Spending, 1995

SPENDING IN BILLIONS

Military: 864
Prevention and control of AIDS tuberculosis, and malaria: 15

Estimated Global Deaths

NUMBER OF DEATHS IN MILLIONS

Military and civilian deaths from war 1945–1993: 23
Deaths from AIDS, tuberculosis, and malaria since 1945: 150

Source: World Health Organization, 1999. Available on-line: *www.who.int/infectious-disease-report/pages/graph22.html.*

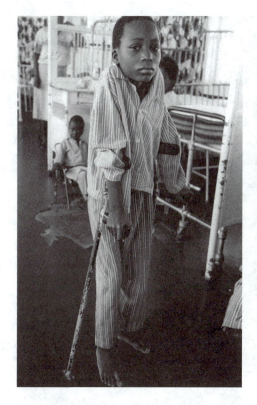

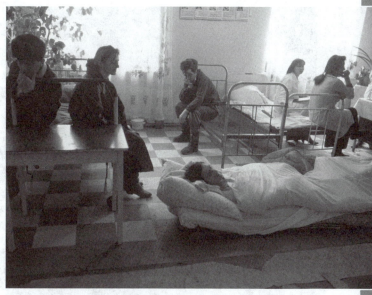

War takes a tremendous human toll across the world. The twenty-five-year war in Angola (with only brief periods of peace) has killed and maimed countless people. It has also disrupted vaccination programs and thereby contributed to a recent outbreak of polio (left). Likewise, the war in Chechnya has severely degraded the quality of healthcare (right).

sake of the health of their children, warring factions in polio-infected countries have set aside their differences and laid down their arms to administer polio vaccine to all children, irrespective of their origins and affiliations (WHO, 2000).

Finally, even when developed nations are not at war or not experiencing internal political turbulence, they still spend a great amount of resources conducting research on methods for dealing with biochemical terrorism. Those expenditures take away from the resources available for conducting crucial research on vaccines to combat existing diseases, and the people who suffer are the poor, in developing and developed countries alike.

Healthcare in the Era of Drug Resistance

Another reason I term my experience at Naivasha Hospital as the "good old days" is that back then malaria was under control. Malaria was (and still is)

preventable by such simple steps as draining stagnant waters, using mosquito-repellent ointments, and sleeping under mosquito nets. According to WHO (1999a), bednets and other prevention and treatment strategies can prevent 50% of all malaria deaths. The cost for an insecticide-treated bednet is about U.S.$10. If bednets were provided to children in developing countries, one in four malaria deaths would be prevented.

Back in the 1980s, malaria was easily cured with first-line-of-treatment medicines such as chloroquine. Although powerful, chloroquine is cheap and easily accessible without prescription. The easy access to this potent nonprescription drug proved to be counterproductive, however, in a continent where most people self-medicate. Most people living in malaria-infected regions use antimalaria drugs to treat all fevers; when the fever subsides, they immediately stop using the medication. In so doing, they expose themselves to suboptimal

A growing number of Americans, particularly those on fixed incomes, cross the border into Canada or Mexico (shown here) to fill their prescriptions. They can purchase many drugs at as little as half the price they would pay in the United States.

drug levels, which allows drug-resistant strains of malaria to proliferate.

The acquired resistance of a disease to treatment is the result of ineffective treatment of the disease—use of a single drug that is not strong enough to knock out the infection, inappropriate prescription, or failure to take medication on schedule or at the right dosage. Ineffective treatment suppresses the growth of strains susceptible to that drug but permits the multiplication of drug-resistant strains. Primary resistance, in contrast, occurs when resistant strains are transmitted from one infectious person to another, which leads to disease that is drug-resistant from the outset. To avoid both acquired and primary resistance, the practice is to offer pa-

tients multiple drugs (referred to as drug "cocktail" treatments) rather than a single drug.

The WHO report (1999a) on anti-infective drug resistance (1990–1999) indicates that over the past decades there was increased use and misuse of antibiotics, which raised resistance in all kinds of microorganisms. The result has been a reemergence of diseases once thought cured, such as tuberculosis (TB). In some parts of Africa, the incidence of TB has increased by as much as 500%. In recent years, there have been outbreaks of TB resistant to even multiple-drug treatment in HIV-infected patients in the United States and in Europe.

The reemergence of such infectious diseases poses new challenges for both healthcare in doctor's offices as well as programs seeking to control the disease. For example, in Kenya, over 95% of the most virulent strain of the malaria parasite *(Plasmodium falciparum)* is now resistant to chloroquine. As a result, by early 2000, malaria accounted for 30% of all outpatient cases in Kenya and 19% of all hospital admissions; 5.1% of the hospital admissions died. Most of those deaths could have been prevented if the patients had been treated with the free malarone drugs donated by Glaxo Wellcome or the new (but costly) first-line drug cocktails (pyrimethamine and sulphadoxine). The optimal solution, however, would have been to prevent malaria through the simple, manageable steps used in an earlier era and to educate the population on proper medicine use.

Reacting to the new malaria epidemic, the Kenyan government in 1999 banned over-the-counter sales of chloroquine-based drugs. That was a good move, albeit too late for four reasons: (1) drug-resistant malaria strains already exist; (2) most Kenyans are poor and cannot afford to pay for a doctor's prescription; (3) the culture of self-medication will be difficult to break; and (4) government bans are ineffective when no viable alternatives are offered.

When governments ban over-the-counter medications, those who need the drugs but cannot afford them develop ingenious ways to acquire medication, either illegally within their own countries or legally from other countries where the drugs cost less. That happens not only in developing countries but also in industrialized ones. For example, in the United States, where the government has made it impossible to acquire most drugs without a prescription, some people travel to Mexican or Canadian border towns to purchase their medications at up to half the price they would pay in the United States. The allergy reliever Claritin is a good example. In Canada, where Claritin is sold without a prescription, a month's supply costs U.S.$17. In the United States, where Claritin is a prescription-only medicine, a month's supply costs U.S.$60 plus the doctor's fee for the visit to obtain the prescription.

The practice of international travel to obtain medication is a growing concern among international health agencies. This sort of travel is another means of spreading drug resistance, involving even more microorganisms and more of the world's population.

Healthcare in the Era of International Trade and Travel

International travel has increased tremendously in the past decade, as shown in Graphic 15.2. For example, the number of international airline passengers soared from 2 million a year in 1950 to over 1.4 billion in 1999 (WHO, 1999c). Increased international travel not only enables people to purchase medications abroad but also facilitates the mobility of a variety of materials capable of carrying infectious agents.

With increased international travel, infectious diseases have come to be perceived as a threat to global health in developed and developing countries alike. As Graphic 15.3 shows, infectious disease is by far the most frequent cause of premature death. Among the six most lethal culprits, the majority are spread by casual contact with infected persons or by contaminated food.

Most infectious microbes can travel to any major city in the developed world via commercial airlines within two days, faster than the incubation period for many diseases (Lederberg, 1996). Before people know they are sick, they may have exposed hundreds of others to a disease. As a result of the increase in the volume of commercial air travelers, deadly airborne diseases such as influenza, pneumonic plague, and tuberculosis can be spread rapidly. For example, WHO reports that in 1977 a passenger with influenza infected more than 70% of the passengers aboard a U.S. airliner that was grounded for several hours. In 1994, a passenger with active TB infected six fellow passengers on a flight from Chicago to Honolulu. Some domestic travelers have contracted malaria after being bitten by a tropical mosquito at an airport. Such cases, termed "airport malaria," have been reported in Brussels, Geneva, and Oslo (WHO, 1999a). Thus, both crafts and ports have become health hazards.

Apart from hitching rides with human cargo, infectious diseases spread internationally through trade in goods. For example, in 1985 the aggressive tiger mosquito *(Aedes albopictus)* was brought to the United States inside waterlogged used tires shipped from Asia. The tiger mosquito is capable of

GRAPHIC 15.2   INCREASES IN AIR TRAVEL

Most Popular Air Routes Between Continents, 1997

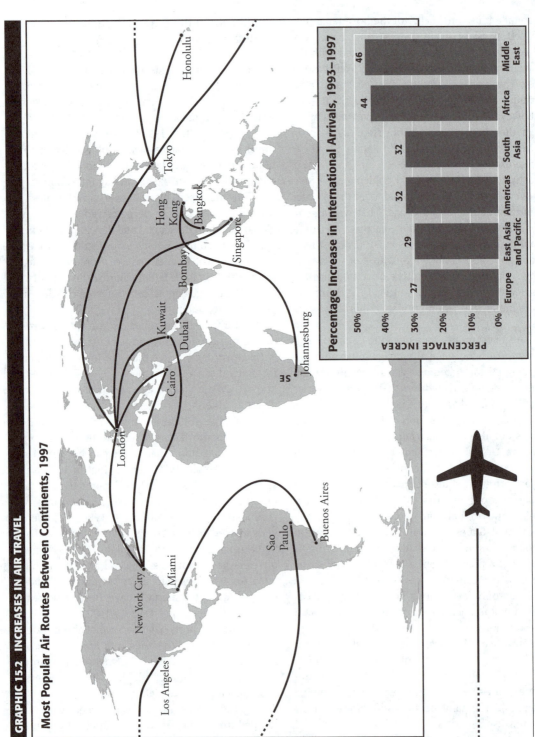

Percentage Increase in International Arrivals, 1993–1997

Sources: Adapted from World Health Organization, 1999. Available on-line: *www.who.int/infectious-disease-report/pages/graph35.html.* Data from World Tourism Organization and International Civil Aviation Organization.

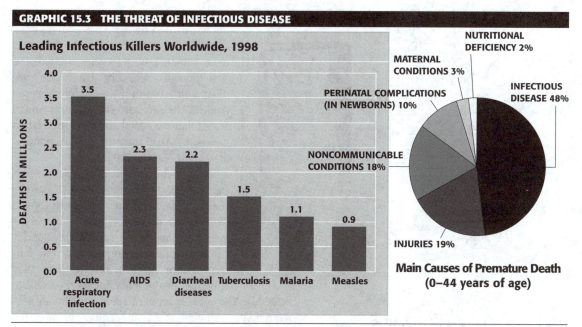

GRAPHIC 15.3   THE THREAT OF INFECTIOUS DISEASE

Leading Infectious Killers Worldwide, 1998

Bar chart — DEATHS IN MILLIONS:
- Acute respiratory infection: 3.5
- AIDS: 2.3
- Diarrheal diseases: 2.2
- Tuberculosis: 1.5
- Malaria: 1.1
- Measles: 0.9

Pie chart — **Main Causes of Premature Death (0–44 years of age)**:
- INFECTIOUS DISEASE 48%
- NUTRITIONAL DEFICIENCY 2%
- MATERNAL CONDITIONS 3%
- PERINATAL COMPLICATIONS (IN NEWBORNS) 10%
- NONCOMMUNICABLE CONDITIONS 18%
- INJURIES 19%

Source: Adapted from World Health Organization, 1999. Available on-line: *www.who.int/infectious-disease-report/pages/graph4.html* and *www.who.int/infectious-disease-report/pages/graph5.html*.

Note: Acute respiratory infection includes pneumonia and influenza; AIDS includes HIV-positive people who died with tuberculosis.

transmitting yellow fever, dengue fever, and other viruses. It became established in Hawaii and within two years got established in at least twenty other U.S. states. In 1997, Mexican-grown strawberries tainted with hepatitis A virus exposed thousands of students in Michigan, Arizona, California, Georgia, Iowa, and Tennessee to the disease when they ate the strawberries in school lunches.

Although some diseases, such as venereal diseases, are spread from developed to developing countries, the bulk of media reports focus on diseases that spread from less developed countries to developed countries. The wording of some media health reports—for example, "Africa breeds nature's assassins" in the *Toronto Star* (May 20, 1995)—demonizes the less developed countries and affects their health both directly and indirectly. First, limiting international travel and shunning goods produced in low-income countries for fear of importing infectious diseases decrease poor countries' foreign income, slow their economic development, and fur-

ther reduce their ability to subsidize healthcare. Second, stigmatizing places and people believed to be the source of infectious diseases transfers international focus from helping the suffering in those countries to ensuring that people in developed countries do not contract the diseases. Thus, international focus is shifted from disease eradication to travel and trade reduction.

It is much more desirable to look at the attempt to eradicate diseases in all parts of the world as an opportunity to forge global unity. Without a concerted effort, some countries may be able to fight off disease, only to have international trade and migrations bring in new cases of disease. Without global consensus on the availability of medications, a country that effectively enforces prescription policies may have its efforts thwarted by its citizens traveling across the border to purchase drugs over the counter and for less. Most important, assisting those afflicted by disease not only protects "us" from contracting "their" disease, it is the humane thing to do.

Healthcare in the Era of HIV/AIDS

Finally, HIV, which leads to AIDS, is a grim reality for anyone who contracts the virus, but it is especially devastating in low-income countries. My experience at Naivasha Hospital took place when malaria, not AIDS, was the most deadly disease in Africa. Fortunately for me, AIDS was not rampant in the early 1980s, and, despite being injected with the same needle that had been used on almost everyone else in the ward, I did not contract HIV.

By the late 1990s, AIDS had spread rapidly throughout eastern and southern Africa, surpassing war, hunger, and malaria to become Africa's number one killer. In the hardest hit countries, HIV-positive patients occupy 40% to 70% of all beds in big city hospitals. With 24.5 million people infected with HIV, Africa accounts for two-thirds of the world's HIV/AIDS cases (UNAIDS, 2000e). In Botswana, the country with the highest HIV prevalence rate, about one in three adults is HIV infected. Life expectancy in Botswana has been reduced from 70 years to about 40 years. Throughout the world, a total of 13.2 million children under 15 have lost their mother or both parents to AIDS since the epidemic began; 95% of them are in Africa (UNAIDS, 2000e).

The devastation of families and economies caused by the AIDS epidemic led the UN Security Council to discuss AIDS as a human security issue in 2000, the first time in its history that it has ever dealt with a health matter. Addressing the council, UN Secretary-General Kofi Annan stated that the social and economic crises caused by AIDS threaten Africa's political stability (UNAIDS, 2000a).

Despite having so many people living with HIV/AIDS, most African governments, because of their immense foreign debt burden, spend very little (about $6 per year per citizen) on healthcare. Specifically, African governments pay out four times more in debt service than they spend on health and education (UNAIDS, 2000d). The meager amount spent by African governments on healthcare is inadequate to meet the cost of AIDS treatment. For example, antibiotics like trimethoprim-sulfamethoxazole (cotrimoxazole), which ward off secondary infections, cost between U.S.$8 and U.S.$17 per person per year. The cost of AZT, which prevents HIV transmission from mother to infant, is U.S.$800 per year. And the cost of the multidrug-therapy cocktails, which have been shown to control the replication of HIV and thus prevent the virus from progressing to full-blown AIDS, costs about U.S.$15,000 a year (UNAIDS, 2000b; "Cost Effective," 1999).

Because most African citizens are too poor to pay for treatments out of their own pockets, the majority of the 24.5 million people infected with HIV lack adequate treatment. The only hope for economically deprived patients is that pharmaceutical companies will provide them with the AIDS drug cocktails free or at an extremely low cost—but it is a very slim ray of hope. For the most part, the large pharmaceutical companies that produce the drugs are driven by profit motives. They do not conduct research on diseases that afflict the poor, nor do they make drugs for people who cannot afford them. Few pharmaceutical firms are likely to develop any new drug for which they foresee less than $350 million in annual sales (Strouse, 2000, p.63).

Realizing the healthcare plight of the millions of poor around the world and that large pharmaceutical companies need economic incentives to conduct research on diseases that affect the poor, the UN Secretary General invited the private sector to participate in expanding the global response to HIV/AIDS and to support the international partnership against HIV/AIDS in Africa. Echoing that call, U.S. President Clinton inaugurated his Millennium Vaccine Initiative, which gives a $1-billion tax credit to pharmaceutical companies to speed up the development of new vaccines. He also gave U.S.$50 million to the Global Alliance for Vaccines and Immunization (GAVI) purchase fund. Similarly, the Bill and Melinda Gates Foundation pledged U.S.$750 million to the GAVI fund. The Gates's foundation focuses on global health with the central goal of preventing disease among poor children by expanding access to vaccines and developing vaccines against malaria, HIV/AIDS, and tuberculosis.

The vast majority of the world's population cannot afford drugs for the treatment of HIV and AIDS. This fact has prompted protests around the world. Here, schoolchildren and AIDS educators march through a Nairobi, Kenya slum calling for a reduction in the price of drugs for HIV-infected patients.

Those initiatives will provide some of the much needed economic incentive for drug companies to facilitate the development of vaccines for diseases that currently afflict millions of the world's poor. As I am writing this piece, five pharmaceutical companies have indicated their willingness to work with other concerned bodies in finding means to improve access to and availability of medicines at affordable rates. Those five companies are Boehringer Ingelheim, Bristol-Myers Squibb, Glaxo Wellcome, Merck & Co., and F. Hoffmann-La Roche (UNAIDS, 2000b).

While the rate of AIDS cases continues to rise in Africa, reports indicate that since 1998, the United States and other developed countries have experienced a substantial decline in AIDS incidence and deaths. That is both good news and bad news. The decline has been brought about by improvements in the treatment and care of adults and children infected with HIV. However, the decreasing rates of AIDS in the United States and other developed countries, juxtaposed against increasing AIDS rates in less developed countries, may make AIDS a disease of the poor. And once AIDS is perceived as a disease of the poor, the resources currently being put into finding an AIDS vaccine may be diverted toward research on diseases suffered by the rich.

The Great Divide: Haves versus Have-nots

The difference in healthcare accorded my brother and me when we suffered the same illness vividly demonstrates inequalities in the life chances of society's privileged and disadvantaged. The rich receive the best healthcare and the poor the worst (or none at all). Whether they live in a developing or a developed country, the poor have a similar fate—they suffer the most and the longest yet receive the worst (if any) healthcare. Poverty, not geography, is what limits the quality of healthcare one receives.

This hospital in Nigeria (top) is well equipped and cares for wealthier citizens. But many hospitals in Africa, including this one in Rwanda (bottom), suffer from an acute shortage of equipment and medications—even basic antibiotics.

What Constitutes Quality?

Before we examine why poverty limits a person's healthcare, let's define what constitutes good healthcare. My experience at Naivasha Hospital was an eye-opener. I had always taken for granted my access to effective healthcare treatment, to clean and well-equipped medical facilities, and to well-trained medical personnel. But after that experience and with my studies of healthcare since then, I have become all too aware that, even when the poor can obtain healthcare, it is of a significantly different quality from what the rich can obtain. It is almost of a different nature altogether. Quality healthcare is differentiated from mediocre healthcare by three

key elements: treatment, facilities, and physician-patient interaction.

Treatment may involve medication or surgery. The two most basic conditions necessary for quality surgical treatment are appropriate sterilized equipment and well-trained surgeons. When one or both conditions are lacking, patients who undergo surgical treatment are not guaranteed safe outcomes. In regard to medication, a basic standard for quality healthcare is receiving the most effective drugs, receiving them before their expiration date, and being instructed in their correct use.

One critical element for maintaining the health of a population is good prenatal and postnatal care, which are vital to a healthy start in life. Any nation in which a large portion of the population lacks quality maternal and natal treatment is bound to suffer poor health. Sadly, that is the case in many developing countries. According to WHO, at least 1,600 women die every day around the world from complications during pregnancy or childbirth, a total of 584,000 women per year. Almost 90% of those deaths occur in Asia and sub-Saharan Africa and less than 1% in the developed world (WHO, 1998). The difference is the prenatal and postnatal care that the women receive and the availability of expert assistance during childbirth. As for the children, thousands in less developed countries die every minute from preventable diseases (WHO, 1999a). In contrast, neonatal and postnatal technological breakthroughs in developed countries save millions of children. So reliable are treatments for mothers and their babies that the focus in developed countries has shifted to technologies that enable sterile women to bear children.

In regard to the quality of healthcare facilities, the basic standard is that clinics, hospitals, and nursing homes (including their kitchens and bathrooms) be hygienically maintained at all times to prevent hospital infections. In 1850, a young Hungarian physician named Ignaz Semmelweis made an important medical discovery: he observed that the failure of doctors to wash their hands spread fatal infections from one patient to another. Before the institution of basic sterilization procedures, hospitals were places of death more often than they should have been. Once medical personnel began routinely washing their hands and sterilizing bedding and other equipment, the association between death rates and hospitalization became spurious; hospitals did not cause patients to die. Unfortunately, in many parts of the developing countries, the association is a legitimate one. The common failure of health workers (doctors, nurses, food providers) to use sterile procedures, as well as the overcrowding of patients in poorly ventilated wards, often results in deaths from infectious diseases. (The situation is not unique to developing countries. Thousands of patients in the developed world also die each year from infections contracted in hospitals.)

In regard to physician-patient interaction, the most basic standard for good healthcare is a high ratio of doctors to patients. A high ratio gives the doctor time to listen to and examine patients

thoroughly. Unfortunately, in poor regions (such as developing countries or minority communities in developed countries), people cannot afford private doctors and end up being served in public hospitals, where the ratio of doctors to patients is extremely low. Patients have to wait hours to see a doctor, and when they eventually do, the doctor rushes through the examination.

Apart from contending with low doctor-patient ratios, most minorities also feel dissatisfied about their interactions with doctors. Some of their complaints include the fact that doctors do not ask sufficiently about pain, do not state how long it will take for medication to work, do not explain the seriousness of an illness, do not discuss test or examination findings, and do not discuss prevention measures. They claim that the doctors do not provide them with the same service they give affluent, mainstream

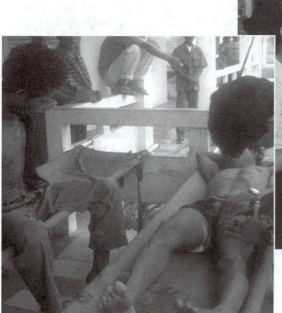

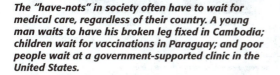

The "have-nots" in society often have to wait for medical care, regardless of their country. A young man waits to have his broken leg fixed in Cambodia; children wait for vaccinations in Paraguay; and poor people wait at a government-supported clinic in the United States.

members of society. In the United States and most other developed countries, those accorded preferential treatment are the more affluent whites (especially white males). Elsewhere, patients accorded preferential treatment usually are the affluent members of the dominant ethnic or religious group.

To protect the well-being of the haves and the have-nots alike, it is crucial that we understand how the elements of quality healthcare—treatment, facilities, and physician-patient interaction—work together. Otherwise, resources devoted to developing a particular health dimension (for example, purchasing appropriate equipment or providing excellent training for doctors) may be negated by failure in another dimension, such as overcrowding, poor doctor-patient relationships, and unhygienic facilities.

Why Are the Poor Denied the Healthcare They Need?

On the surface, it is easy to explain why the poor do not always receive quality healthcare. In most capitalistic societies, such as the United States, the wealthy are accorded more privileges than the poor. But in some societies, such as Cuba, everyone has access to quality healthcare. What sociology helps us do is to discern the deeper reasons for this state of affairs. The way most capitalistic societies structure their healthcare prevents the poor from enjoying the basic healthcare that would lengthen their lives and enhance their well-being. That division is especially evident in regard to health insurance and medical research.

One major reason why the poor are denied the healthcare they so desperately need is because they cannot afford health insurance. To the desperately poor who daily face the dilemma of whether to pay for heat or buy food, health insurance becomes a luxury they cannot afford. Unfortunately, because they lack health insurance, the majority of the poor delay seeking medical help, which further worsens their ill health. In the United States, those who are least likely to have health insurance are racial and ethnic minorities, who are disproportionately poor. The U.S. Census Bureau shows that between 1986 and 1998 the percentage of Americans who went without insurance for at least one month increased from 13% to 16% and that the majority of the newly uninsured were ethnic and racial minorities. In addition, males were less likely to be insured than females in all categories. Graphic 15.4 depicts current patterns of inequality.

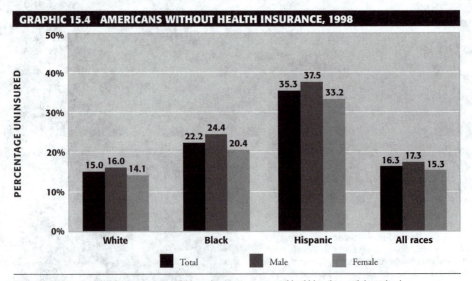

GRAPHIC 15.4   AMERICANS WITHOUT HEALTH INSURANCE, 1998

Source: U.S. Bureau of the Census, 1999. Available on-line: *www.census.gov/hhes/hlthins/historic/hihistt1.html.*

A second major reason for inequities in health-care is the lack of medical research into health problems that affect mostly the poor. According to WHO, the health problems that afflict 90% of the world's population receive less than 10% of the world's medical research financing (WHO, 1999a). As a result, more than 8 million children in less developed countries die each year from measles, diarrhea, malaria, pneumonia, and malnutrition, conditions that are both preventable and treatable. Indeed, preventive efforts have virtually eradicated deaths from these five diseases among children in those developed countries.

Because the wealthy are powerful both economically and politically, they are able to lobby for their health demands to receive top priority in research. Their power, and not necessarily the spread or severity of a disease, determines the type of diseases that receive priority in funding and research. In addition, their power shapes the definition of genuine health "needs." An example from the medical field of cosmetic surgery illustrates the point well. Cosmetic surgery is the most lucrative specialization in the medical realm, generating more than $333 million per year for practitioners in the United States alone. Seeing how lucrative cosmetic surgery is, it is not surprising that medical professionals are starting to define aesthetic surgeries such as breast enlargements as necessary treatments for "deformities" in the same way they define reconstructive plastic surgery, which treats deformities caused by congenital disease or injuries. In a 1982 petition to the FDA, the American Society of Plastic and Reconstructive Surgeons in essence argued that small breasts are really a disease that needs treatment to improve the quality of life for a patient.

The profit motive is behind the discrepancies in funding for medical research and the distortions of medical priorities. It is so strong that some advertisements for brand-name products made by the large pharmaceutical companies give the impression that something is amiss with products made by their competitors, especially generic drugs, which are cheaper than brand-name drugs. Such advertising generates most of the controversies as to whether generic drugs are as effective as brand names. The FDA, however, reports that there are no documented examples of a generic product manufactured to its specifications that cannot be used interchangeably with its corresponding brand-name drug. FDA-approved generic drugs not only are as effective as brand drugs but are cheaper by as much as 50%.

There is need to provide the poor with basic healthcare to relieve their suffering because it is the humane course of action. But it is also the expedient course to take, seeing that diseases do not respect geographic borders. Unless cured, communicable diseases that afflict mostly the poor, especially airborne diseases, eventually will afflict the wealthy. Finally, it is unethical to withhold quality healthcare from the poor, especially when there is health insurance for pets and other animals owned by the wealthy. Innocent children born to poverty should not die for lack of basic drugs.

The Healthcare Challenge of the Twenty-First Century

Worldwide, newly emerging infectious diseases, coupled with the reemergence of drug-resistant strains of formerly curable infectious diseases, are threatening to undermine medical advances achieved during the past decades. WHO (1999a) estimates that, in 1998 alone, the world's people lost a combined 365 million years of healthy life due to infectious disease (see Graphic 15.5)—the equivalent of each of the world's 6 billion or so people being sick and

unable to pursue normal activities for twenty-two days. Imagine what hardship families, communities, nations, and even the world might have avoided and what productivity they might have achieved if even a quarter of that time could have been restored through better healthcare.

The increase in international travel and trade that has accompanied globalization facilitates the rapid spread of diseases around the world. That new threat occurs during a time when most of the less developed countries are becoming progressively poorer (due to internal and external factors) and therefore are unable to provide the social and economic infrastructure necessary for the delivery of quality healthcare. Many of those nations also are involved in political turbulence and are diverting their limited resources from healthcare expenditure to the military. At the same time, capitalism has spread through most parts of the world, making the profit motive supercede humanitarianism.

The problem is global in scope; therefore, the solution must be global as well. The healthcare challenge for the twenty-first century is for the world to unite in combating new and reemerging diseases in all parts of the globe and to combat them as quickly as possible. Delay means wider spread of existing

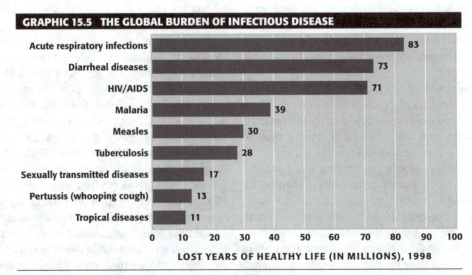

GRAPHIC 15.5   THE GLOBAL BURDEN OF INFECTIOUS DISEASE

LOST YEARS OF HEALTHY LIFE (IN MILLIONS), 1998

Source: World Health Organization, 1999. Available on-line: *www.who.int/infectious-disease-report/pages/graph7.html.*

diseases, mutation of new ones, and reemergence of others.

The big question is, "Can the world meet this challenge?" It is difficult to imagine that a collection of nations with varying interests, many of them too poor to mount effective efforts on their own, can do the job. However, the answer can be yes—*if* a concerted effort is made at three levels.

- At the macro level, the world must unite and national leaders must take responsibility to promote peace in their own countries and across national borders. Some progress has been made on this front. Specifically, some warring countries have laid down their weapons for the sake of the vaccination of their children. More nations and feuding parties must be encouraged to do the same. In addition, to the degree that all nations pay their dues to the United Nations (including the United States, which is seriously in arrears), the organization will be better able to perform its peacekeeping mission.

- At the mezzo level, corporations and healthcare institutions must be driven more by humanitarianism rather than selfish economic gains. Already, several pharmaceutical companies have expressed their goal to conduct research toward finding vaccines for diseases from which they would not profit financially and to form partnerships with concerned bodies to ensure that the poor have access to affordable drugs. If more governments, NGOS, philanthropic foundations, pharmaceutical companies, and health insurance companies work together, not only is a vaccine for most infectious diseases bound to be discovered, other medical advances are likely to be discovered and made accessible to all people.

- At the micro level, individuals must take personal responsibility for their own health and mind their neighbors' health, too. When they are educated regarding hygiene, medicine use, exercise, rest, and nutrition and are given the economic ability to put that knowledge into effect, most people are likely to take good care of their own health. It is possible to reverse the trend of HIV/AIDS if individuals act responsibly by remaining sexually abstinent until marriage or, if they are sexually active, by being monogamous and using latex condoms consistently. Having taken care of their own health, they can then mind the health of their fellow citizens: mowing the lawn of an ailing neighbor, babysitting and feeding children whose parents are incapacitated, sponsoring children through philanthropic organizations, fostering or adopting children, volunteering to mentor the young, feeding the homeless, visiting old people and shut-ins. Such actions are the basis of caring communities. A caring community promotes both mental and physical well-being.

That challenge and the solutions sound simplistic, but they are the basis for more complex solutions promoted by a number of transnational organizations concerned with healthcare. If the world's haves and have-nots opt to form bonds of unity rather than conflict and to use the available resources for the common good instead of selfish gain, we may make major headway in the twenty-first century toward achieving the quality healthcare we all need for a long and productive life.

Thinking about the Topic of Healthcare

1. Discuss how the quality of healthcare for HIV/AIDS patients around the world is associated with the two types of inequalities discussed throughout the book: inequalities within nations based on poverty, race, and gender and inequalities among nations created by the deliberate actions of the more powerful nations and their dominant capitalist class (as world systems theory describes it).

2. Have the developed nations and transnational corporations been positive or negative forces for the improvement of healthcare for everyone? Explain your opinion and support it with data on worldwide trends in sickness, health, financial aid to developing nations, and corporate contributions to or investment in healthcare measures that benefit developing nations.

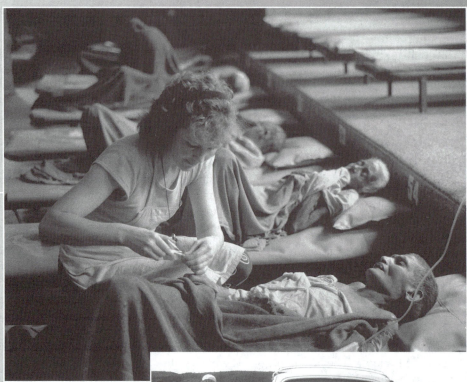

There are many ways to creative positive social changes in the world. A foreign volunteer works at Mother Teresa's Home for the Destitute Dying in Calcutta, India (top); a man visits Kenya to learn more about another culture (and gets help from local citizens); Jewish and Muslim students engage in collaborative activities; young boys volunteer to clean up a roadway (opposite page, top); volunteers unload earthquake supplies; and local citizens clean up after the Los Angeles riots of 1992. Individuals are making a difference all over the world.

16 Creating Positive Social Change

YORK W. BRADSHAW

This book has covered many topics and explored a number of global challenges. But a common theme running through the book is inequality, an important cause of many problems, including poverty, crime, war, disease, overpopulation, environmental destruction, and discrimination. Inequality is not the only factor that explains those conditions, of course, but it often is the most important one.

Just how much inequality exists in the world? Well, let's say the world is a village of 1,000 people distributed in exactly the same proportions as the world's population. Here is what it would look like (derived from Annan, 2000):

- One hundred fifty people live in affluent neighborhoods and control more than 80% of village wealth.
- Seven hundred eighty people live in poorer neighborhoods.
- Nearly half the villagers live on less than $2 a day.
- Two hundred twenty villagers—two-thirds of them women—are illiterate.
- Of the 390 villagers under the age of 20, three-fourths live in the poorer districts and many are looking for jobs that do not exist.

- Less than 10% of health expenditures is aimed at problems affecting people in the poor neighborhoods, such as pneumonia, diarrhea, malaria, and tuberculosis.
- Most wars, preventable diseases, and AIDS cases are in the poorer neighborhoods.
- Fewer than sixty people own a computer and only twenty-four have access to the Internet.

Many world religions have spoken out against inequality, as have well-known atheists such as Karl Marx. Sociology as a discipline has long studied inequality and then recommended societal changes to reduce inequality and create a better quality of life for people.

But the vast majority of positive social changes in the world are created by people who are not widely known. They volunteer to teach people to read; they visit senior citizens who are alone; they counsel distressed people; they coach youth sports; they serve food in shelters; they join the Peace Corps; they fight intolerance and build bridges between ethnic groups; they host foreign exchange students; they build homes, schools, and community centers; they plant trees; they read books to children; they educate people about environmental issues; they give money to charity; they are "big brothers" and "big sisters"; they visit the terminally ill in hospitals; they teach people how to grow food; they stand up to institutions and governments that are unjust; they join community development projects; they perform music and make art; they empower others.

To illustrate, consider the case of Paul Mbatia. He was a devoted young faculty member at the University of Nairobi for several years, where he taught and inspired many students. He volunteered countless hours, helping young people in his home village so they would have an opportunity for a better life. Somewhat unexpectedly, Paul found himself with an opportunity to pursue a doctorate degree in sociology in the United States, where he completed the challenging program in a near-record four years. While in the United States, he was a frequent speaker at seminars and classes designed to promote ethnic diversity. He has a unique gift for helping people of different races and backgrounds to see the other's perspective. Although he could have accepted any of a number of good jobs in the United States after finishing his degree, Paul returned to Kenya to help build and develop his country. He continued to teach at the university, volunteer time for many causes, advise local and international organizations, and donate money to charity. He also started an organization that is devoted to starting and sustaining development programs for the country. Paul has touched many people on two continents and has created positive social changes. The world is a better place because of him.

This chapter has three purposes. Perhaps most important, we want to discuss what you as an individual, like Paul Mbatia, can do to make the world a better place. But first we want to demonstrate that sociology has a place not only in analyzing social problems but in reducing them. We also want to offer specific suggestions for what governments, nations, regions, and communities can do to create positive changes in the world. This book has presented many social problems, because the world is a problematic place. But we don't want you to become cynical or to think that nothing can be done to improve the world. In fact, positive changes occur on a daily basis in many societies and communities across the globe.

What Solutions Does Sociology Suggest?

Sociologists have long proposed solutions to a variety of social problems. Some proposals are fairly modest in scope, while others call for dramatic changes on a global scale. Chapter 2, for instance, discussed world systems theory. World systems theorists often propose fairly radical solutions to global inequality and underdevelopment. According to that theory, the major cause of global inequality and many other problems is exploitation of poor countries by rich countries or by the capitalist class that controls transnational corporations (see Bradshaw & Wallace, 1996, pp. 39–57). According to world

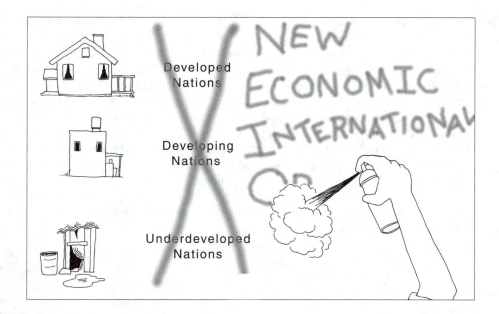

systems theorists, the primary solution to global inequalities involves a fundamental and complete transformation of the world economic and political structure. Some call it a transformation to a new international economic order. Strong advocates of that position even see the necessity of a new world government to promote greater equality:

> We propose a new world political system in which economic and human rights of citizens are guaranteed by a limited federal world state. Such a state would be constitutionally limited from imposing cultural conformity upon citizens or nation-states. It would, however, have certain powers to prevent international war by exercising judicial and military control over conflicting parties, and it would have the power to levy [taxes] to guarantee a basic income for individuals. (Bornschier & Chase-Dunn, 1985)

Although their proposals are vague, world systems theorists basically call for a redistribution of income from rich countries (and people) to poor countries (and people), a redistribution enforced by some type of world government. However, considering the global trend toward political fragmentation and people's enduring tendency to maintain ethnic, racial, and cultural distinctions (contrary to the theory of global species consolidation presented in Chapter 6), a move toward any single entity that governs both rich and poor countries and creates a more equitable distribution probably is unlikely any time soon. (Yes, the European Union is one step toward a limited single state, but it does not include countries at very different levels of development and in different regions of the world.)

The world systems perspective is only one view of change. Sociologists and social scientists have proposed many other solutions. Some focus on what can happen at the global level, others at the regional, national, and community levels. We turn now to an examination of some of the proposals for positive social changes.

Solutions at the Global Level

Three global actions stand out as a feasible way to create positive change: reducing the debt burden of poor countries, providing more foreign aid to poor countries for basic human needs, and forging more public-private partnerships for economic development in poor countries. If enacted, those three actions would make a great difference in the world.

Reducing Poor Countries' Debt Burdens. The first global solution is for wealthy countries and financial institutions to forgive or substantially renegotiate the more than $2 trillion in debt owed to them. The debts started in the 1970s and 1980s, when banks had extra money to lend around the world. The banks anticipated that the economies of developing countries would expand and that the countries would be able to repay the money. Unfortunately, their economies faltered, and developing countries were unable to pay back the debts.

The debt burden is enormous in some countries. Several owe more than 200% of their entire national economy. In the poor regions of Africa, for instance, the average country's debt is slightly more than 100% of its national economy. That would be the equivalent of an individual earning $2,000 a year (a good salary in some African countries) but owing debts that exceeded that amount. Such a person would be overwhelmed and would have to spend all of her or his earnings to pay off interest charges on the debts, much less the principal. The person would not have any money left over for other purposes. It is the same issue for indebted countries, which are struggling to repay their debts and therefore cannot allocate money for health, education, and other basic needs (Bradshaw, Noonan, Gash, & Buchmann, 1993). Many countries spend more money paying their debts than providing resources for basic human needs, a fact that prompted UNICEF (1999) to claim that "debt has a child's face." Graphic 16.1 depicts the magnitude and effects of foreign debt in less developed regions of the world.

The United Nations has called on wealthy countries and the international financial community to cancel all debts owed by heavily indebted countries. Kofi Anan, the Secretary General of the United Nations, states: "Without a convincing program of debt relief to start the new millennium, our objective of halving world poverty by 2015 will be only a pipe dream" (Anan, 2000, p. 38). Debt reduction is beneficial to all parties: it helps poor people, and it also stimulates developing country economies, thereby providing new markets for the economically developed world.

In exchange for debt relief, heavily indebted poor countries must make demonstrable commitments to reducing poverty and to ensuring that they will not accumulate massive new debts (Anan, 2000, pp. 36–38). The world's wealthiest countries and their financial institutions have already endorsed a program that would reduce (but not cancel) debts in exchange for indebted countries meeting certain conditions. Although the plan has not yet been fully implemented, several countries have benefited from it and others are close to qualifying. Countries that qualify have additional money for social programs that improve quality of life.

More Foreign Aid. The second global action that could be taken to create positive change would be for wealthy countries to give more foreign aid to developing nations, especially for basic needs such as nutrition, healthcare, clean water, family planning, and education. In 1990, rich nations collectively gave only $40 billion to developing countries (less than Europeans spent on cigarettes and only slightly more than Americans spent on beer). Six years later, in 1996, that number actually declined, to slightly more than $25 billion (Annan, 2000, p. 38). Equally problematic is the fact that very little foreign aid money—less than 10%—is allocated to basic needs, such as new health clinics.

Some observers point to increasing private foreign investment, that is, overseas investment by private companies, as a means of developing the economies of poor countries and a possible remedy for declining public aid. Private foreign investment around the world nearly tripled between 1990 and 1996 and is currently over $200 billion. However, the money is invested primarily in economic enterprises. Although it stimulates economic growth, it does not directly benefit the poorest citizens of the world. Moreover, private investment is concentrated much more heavily in Asia and Latin America than in Africa, where basic needs are greatest (Annan, 2000, p. 38).

UNICEF and other groups would like to see two developments with respect to foreign aid:

- Rich countries should give 1% of their GNP in foreign aid. On average, during the 1990s the

GRAPHIC 16.1 THE BURDEN OF EXTERNAL DEBT IN DEVELOPING NATIONS

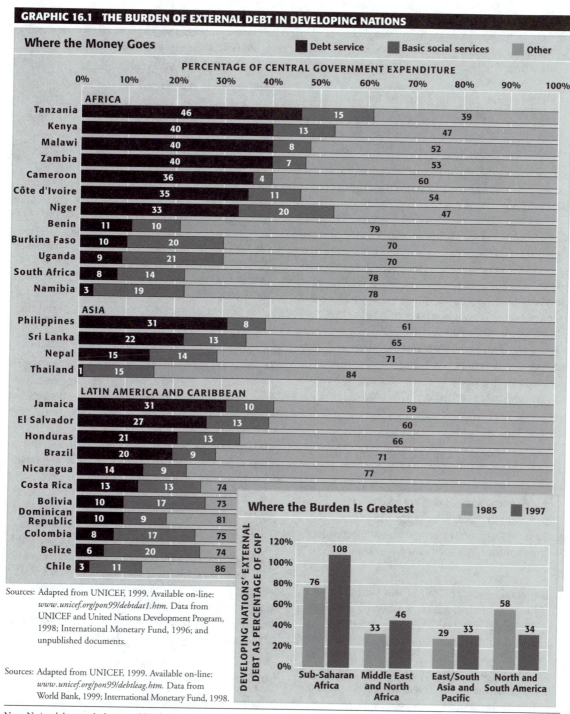

Where the Money Goes

Legend: ■ Debt service ■ Basic social services □ Other

PERCENTAGE OF CENTRAL GOVERNMENT EXPENDITURE

Scale: 0% 10% 20% 30% 40% 50% 60% 70% 80% 90% 100%

AFRICA

Country	Debt service	Basic social services	Other
Tanzania	46	15	39
Kenya	40	13	47
Malawi	40	8	52
Zambia	40	7	53
Cameroon	36	4	60
Côte d'Ivoire	35	11	54
Niger	33	20	47
Benin	11	10	79
Burkina Faso	10	20	70
Uganda	9	21	70
South Africa	8	14	78
Namibia	3	19	78

ASIA

Country	Debt service	Basic social services	Other
Philippines	31	8	61
Sri Lanka	22	13	65
Nepal	15	14	71
Thailand	1	15	84

LATIN AMERICA AND CARIBBEAN

Country	Debt service	Basic social services	Other
Jamaica	31	10	59
El Salvador	27	13	60
Honduras	21	13	66
Brazil	20	9	71
Nicaragua	14	9	77
Costa Rica	13	13	74
Bolivia	10	17	73
Dominican Republic	10	9	81
Colombia	8	17	75
Belize	6	20	74
Chile	3	11	86

Where the Burden Is Greatest

Legend: ■ 1985 ■ 1997

DEVELOPING NATIONS' EXTERNAL DEBT AS PERCENTAGE OF GNP

Region	1985	1997
Sub-Saharan Africa	76	108
Middle East and North Africa	33	46
East/South Asia and Pacific	29	33
North and South America	58	34

Sources: Adapted from UNICEF, 1999. Available on-line: *www.unicef.org/pon99/debtdat1.htm*. Data from UNICEF and United Nations Development Program, 1998; International Monetary Fund, 1996; and unpublished documents.

Sources: Adapted from UNICEF, 1999. Available on-line: *www.unicef.org/pon99/debtleag.htm*. Data from World Bank, 1999; International Monetary Fund, 1998.

Note: National data are the latest available for various years, 1992–1997. Tanzania data exclude Zanzibar.

only countries even approaching that objective were Denmark, Norway, Sweden, and the Netherlands. Most countries are far below that standard. The United States has given, on average, less than 0.3%.

- Of the foreign aid contributed by the economically developed world, a minimum of 20% should be allocated to basic needs. That percentage would be double the current average.

If those two objectives were met, the world's poor would receive at least three times the amount of aid they currently receive.

Cooperation between Public and Private Sectors. The third global solution to inequality is more large-scale development efforts that stress cooperation between public and private sectors. An excellent example is the new Global Alliance for Vaccines and Immunization (GAVI), formed in 1999. GAVI (see also Chapter 15) is a creative alliance comprising national governments, business leaders and their companies, development banks, philanthropic organizations, the World Health Organization (WHO), the World Bank, and UNICEF. GAVI has three goals:

- To improve access to immunizations, especially for the one-quarter of the world's children who remain unprotected against the major child-killer diseases
- To accelerate research and development for new vaccines that would prevent and treat diseases prevalent in the developing world
- To make vaccines more affordable for developing countries and their citizens (Annan, 2000, p. 28)

A key component of GAVI is the Global Fund for Children's Vaccines, which was launched in 2000 and initiated with a $750 million grant from the Bill and Melinda Gates Foundation (Annan, 2000, p. 28).

Another example of potential public-private partnership is in the crucial area of technological and digital development. There continues to exist an enormous digital divide between developed countries and the developing world. For instance, there are more telephones in Tokyo than in all of Africa. The United Nations has announced two new initiatives to try to reduce that divide (see Annan, 2000).

- Establishment of Health InterNetwork, which will create 10,000 on-line sites in hospitals, clinics, and public health facilities in developing countries to provide access to current medical information. The equipment and Internet access will be provided by the WebMD Foundation in conjunction with its consortium partners, among them WHO and the United Nations Foundation.
- A volunteer corps known as the United Nations Information Technology Services (UNITeS), which will train people in developing countries on the uses and opportunities of the Internet and information technology. The volunteers will be a consortium of high-tech professionals from Net Corps Canada, Net Corps America, and the United Nations.

Universities and businesses also are actively involved in programs that train citizens of the developing world to use computers and the Internet. Along with increased knowledge, the developing world also needs computer hardware, software, and maintenance assistance.

Many people benefit from the increased use of computers and the Internet. Economically developed countries acquire new clients, markets, and opportunities to contribute to positive social changes. And developing countries acquire new information and knowledge that can be used in a number of ways: for distance learning, for new businesses, for telemedicine, for utilizing libraries and databases around the world, for checking weather forecasts before planting crops, for evaluating crop prices, for student exchange opportunities, and so on. Many developing countries are taking advantage of those new digital opportunities.

Solutions at the Regional Level

Regional efforts to create positive social changes sound like a great idea and have been attempted all over the world. Chapters 1 and 10 discussed regional initiatives such as the European Union, NAFTA, Mercosur in Latin America, and the Southern African Development Community (SADC). Regional cooperative initiatives are nothing new. One of the most successful regional efforts, OPEC, teaches us a lot about the potential and the limitations of such initiatives.

During the 1970s, the Organization of Petroleum Exporting Countries (OPEC) dominated the world economy for six or seven years. The alliance of mainly Middle Eastern countries set limits on the amount of oil that each member could produce and set the price that each could charge. OPEC's goal was to raise the world price of oil so that its member countries would make a lot of money. The alliance worked incredibly well, and world oil prices went from $3 for a barrel of oil (42 gallons) in 1973 to $39 per barrel in 1979. OPEC countries were rich, making a collective $8.7 billion a day at the peak of profits (Lamb, 1988, p. 30). Of course, oil and gas prices skyrocketed in many countries around the world, including the United States, which had to ration gasoline in some areas. But the OPEC alliance lost power in the early 1980s, when several members became embroiled in pricing disagreements and two members, Iran and Iraq, went to war with each other. The economically developed countries of the world had also begun to produce more efficient automobiles and had implemented other energy-saving measures to lessen their dependence on foreign oil and gas.

OPEC, despite its successes, has taught us that it is difficult to maintain a regional alliance for long. Africa found that out before the formation of OPEC. In 1957, Ghana became an independent country, and its first president, Kwame Nkrumah, called for pan-Africanism, a proposal to create a "United States of Africa." Nkrumah wanted all African countries to unite to make the continent more self-reliant and less dependent on the West. One set of proposals called for the continent's producers of raw materials to come together to demand higher prices for their products. All coffee producers were supposed to agree on a price and a set of rules for trading with developed countries; all tea, sugar, and mineral producers were supposed to do the same.

But the plans failed miserably. The producers could not agree on prices and rules, and a number of them faced political and military instability, making regional cooperation next to impossible. Although Africa has experienced some limited cooperative success stories (for example, SADC), the efforts have never been sustained long enough to muster much clout in the international economic and political systems.

Unlike OPEC and the African cooperative initiatives, the European Union and several Asian alliances have enjoyed a relatively high level of success, at least thus far.

To succeed, regional efforts normally require at least two ingredients:

- Sufficient money and other resources to exert some influence in the world. Asia and Europe have money, technology, skilled personnel, and relative political stability. Africa, notably, does not.
- Skilled diplomacy to formulate creative solutions to the many obstacles that can derail alliances. That may seem an obvious point, but it is one that many world leaders have ignored. Without skilled diplomats and creative initiatives, regional efforts don't last long.

The bottom line with respect to regional success stories is this: rich countries will continue to dominate the world economy, so unless a region brings substantial resources and clout to the table, it probably will not be effective in creating positive social changes on its own. Relatively strong regions, on the other hand, will continue to build regional alliances and become even more powerful.

Solutions at the National Level

National governments are becoming weaker these days, for reasons detailed in Chapter 10. Despite that fact, national governments can undertake a number of useful initiatives to help their citizens. One is to work with outside groups, such as GAVI, to facilitate positive social changes like increased immunization for children. Because of their limited resources, it is essential that the governments of developing countries work closely with nongovernment organizations (NGOs) and civil society to promote development. Governments can provide vehicles, personnel, expertise, and information to various development organizations. Unfortunately, many governments interfere with NGO efforts because they feel threatened by the goodwill generated through nongovernment efforts (Ndegwa, 1996). In Kenya, for instance, Parliament passed a law requiring all NGOs to register with the government so the government can track their activities. Other governments have passed similar laws. Some governments are worried that citizens will follow community leaders more than government leaders. However, without a vibrant civil society—in which churches, community organizations, and other grass-roots institutions flourish—many poor countries will not achieve any level of development in the near future.

Governments also need to work with foreign and domestic companies and organizations to expand development opportunities. A good example comes from India. No developing country has enjoyed greater benefits from the digital revolution than India, whose software industry is expected to increase eightfold, to $85 billion, by 2008. The industry has generated substantial employment and wealth in the country, and one Indian company, Infosys Technologies, has experienced a tenfold increase in its value since being listed on the U.S. NASDAQ stock market in 1999. The Indian government has assisted the revolution through deregulation of the telecommunications and information technology sectors and through creation of government-supported technology parks. Other countries also have stressed digital efforts. The tiny island of Mauritius, for example, uses the Internet to advertise its textile industry throughout the world (Annan, 2000, pp. 33–34).

Today more than ever, the effective national state is a facilitator, a broker, and a coordinator of activities and services. Developing countries are strapped for money, so they must work with others to create positive social changes. NGOs, foundations, and global institutions (for example, the United Nations) are endeavoring to form collaborative relationships with national states in health, education, and other areas.

Solutions at the Community Level

Community efforts are some of the best ways to reduce inequality and create positive social changes. While professors and policymakers debate the merits of various theories and large-scale initiatives, many selfless individuals and groups are working in towns, villages, and other communities around the world. Some projects are based locally, meaning that people from the communities direct them. Local religious organizations work with the poor; local women's organizations help empower women and teach them marketable skills; local charitable organizations work with street children to provide them with food, shelter, and basic education; the list goes on and on.

Other organizations operate in local communities but are headquartered outside the area, usually in wealthy countries. Most are international charities or relief agencies like CARE, Save the Children Foundation, the Red Cross, the Salvation Army, AmeriCares, Doctors Without Borders, and OXFAM. These groups perform outstanding work providing immunizations, helping refugees, fighting poverty, planting crops, and assisting disaster victims. They also work with government agencies and corporations.

Although NGOs have saved and improved countless lives, they often lack money, technology, and other essential resources. To overcome those problems, it is helpful if local groups form an alliance with an international organization or if foreign aid is given directly to poor communities in the developing world, not to national governments that might divert the money elsewhere. For example, one particularly effective NGO is the Green Belt Movement, a grassroots environmental group in Kenya that fights deforestation by planting trees (Ndegwa, 1996). Since its start in 1977, the Green Belt Movement has accumulated 50,000 members in 2,000 communities across the country. Most members are rural women who have planted 10 million trees throughout Kenya. The Green Belt Movement and its dynamic leader, Wangari Maathi, have attracted international attention and substantial funding from abroad. In fact, the movement is almost totally dependent on outside funds for financial support. The Kenyan government does not support the movement because Maathi is a vocal critic of its policies. In particular, she has organized protests against government plans to build on large public parks. She has also advocated greater democracy in Kenya and started the Movement for Free and Fair Elections, which provides educational seminars on the value of democracy. Maathi and her organizations have made a real difference in the struggles for a better environment and more democracy in Kenya, struggles that have occurred at the grassroots level.

Closer to home, University of Illinois clinical psychologist Brenda Krause Eheart was tired of seeing a thousand children a month come into the foster care system in the state of Illinois. The system was overburdened and unable to provide sufficient care for all those children, especially hard-to-adopt children—those with AIDS, other serious illnesses, drug dependencies, psychological traumas, and similar problems. Working with friends and colleagues, she created the Hope for the Children Foundation. They raised a million dollars, purchased sixty-three duplex houses on an old Air Force base in Illinois, and opened Hope Meadows, a vibrant community of children, foster parents, and an incredible network of fifty-three senior citizens who rent their homes in the Meadows for $325 a month in exchange for contributing at least six hours per week as volunteer grandparents. The adoptive families are further supported by a team of resident child psychologists and therapists, who provide crucial assistance to parents dealing with children in stressful circumstances (Covey, 1999, pp. 129–133). Hope Meadows has not absorbed all children in need in the community, but it has provided a new home and additional hope to many children who otherwise would be ignored by an overburdened system.

Few people can influence the global system, regional politics, or national events, but they can improve their communities. Communities greatly affect people's quality of life, as do individual people.

What Can Individuals Do?

Throughout this book we have seen examples of individuals who make a difference, some on a large scale, others on a small scale. Some people have a lifestyle that is designed to create positive changes in the world. For instance, in Chapter 13, Michael Bell discussed how he and his family live their lives in an environmentally responsible manner. He does not have to live that way. He chooses to do so to create a better world for the future.

Each year in my Social Change course, I ask students to form groups and to think of all the ways that they, as students, can create positive changes in the world. The answers normally fall into the following four categories, with a few specifics listed under each one.

1. Learn more about social problems.
   - Take courses on global issues.
   - Read books and magazines on such issues.
   - Teach people about international topics.
   - Talk to people from other cultures, both in the United States and abroad; form friendships at every opportunity.
   - Travel to other cultures and societies.
   - Complete internships related to societal problems in the United States and abroad.

2. Donate time.
   - Teach people to read.
   - Tutor children who need assistance.
   - Join the Peace Corps.
   - Visit people in the hospital.
   - Assist at crisis centers.
   - Assist at day care centers.
   - Build houses with Habitat for Humanity, both in the United States and abroad.
   - House a foreign exchange student.
   - Plant trees and clean up the environment.
   - Give time to a church, synagogue, or mosque.

3. Build bridges.
   - Make friends with people of different ethnic and religious backgrounds.

- Form a cooperative activity with a "rival" group; for example, college Democrats might cosponsor an activity with college Republicans.
- Become a diplomat and "broker": bring together several groups in a cooperative effort to help poor people.
- Encourage groups you are involved with to become more inclusive, more tolerant, and more active in creating positive social changes.
- Spend a day or more helping at a homeless shelter to see another perspective on life.
- Spend a day arguing exactly the opposite point of view you normally assume; for example, political liberals must be political conservatives and vice versa.

4. Donate money.
   - Give to charities.
   - Give to schools.
   - Give to churches.
   - Give to international relief causes.
   - Give to programs that create positive social changes, for example, to programs that immunize children in the United States and abroad.

That is only a partial list of how students—and others—can create positive social changes in our world. We encourage you to add to the list and decide how to make these changes become a reality.

Recently, a group of educators from South Africa spent several weeks at a summer institute in the United States. The twenty-eight participants were carefully selected to represent different races and ethnic groups. They also represented different occupations and positions—teachers, professors, administrators, government representatives. The sole purpose of the institute was to formulate plans for a new educational system in post-apartheid South Africa. It was—and is—a daunting challenge: an educational system that previously had allocated most resources for the minority white population suddenly had to transform itself into a fair and equal system. Near the end of the institute, the participants wanted to make certain that they would stay in touch with each other and maintain their commitment to the lasting social and educational changes discussed during the institute. To that end, they created a ritual of change and commitment. All the participants entered a room and were given a large piece of white poster paper and a box of markers. For the next two hours, without any spoken words, each participant went to every other participant and wrote something on that person's paper about what he or she had learned from that person over the course of the institute and what he or she would do to create the positive changes discussed during the institute. At the end of the time, the group formed a circle and held hands. Without speaking, they listened to several songs that stressed the importance of change and commitment. It was a moving scene—black, white, Indian; Christian, Muslim, Hindu; male, female; younger, older; conservative, radical; beneficiaries of apartheid, victims of apartheid—standing together with loud music playing. The poster paper in front of them represented their pledges to each other and to the many people they would encounter in the future. It was their pledge to change the world.

Thinking about the Topic of Positive Social Change

1. Evaluate the point made in this chapter that inequality is an important cause (perhaps the most important cause) of the major problems facing the world. Think back to the different forms of inequality discussed in other chapters (especially Chapters 5, 6, and 7). What important problems or dilemmas result from those forms of inequality? Given those connections, is it reasonable to argue for the primacy of inequality as a basic cause of global dilemmas? How much weight should be accorded to the arguments of world systems theory (presented in Chapter 2 and summarized in this chap-

ter) regarding inequality? What other important forces are causally related to the problems you have identified (see especially the themes listed in Chapter 1)? What kinds of programs and policies at the global, regional, national, community, and individual levels would address the specific problems you have identified?

2. Pick three of the major problems facing the world that are mentioned in this chapter and assess the ways in which the sociological perspective has increased your understanding of the issues. How have the sociological theories, research, concepts, ideas, and empirical data you have encountered in this course been helpful? Conversely, what sociological theories have not been helpful? Why? From a sociological perspective, what actions could be taken for each of the problems you identified to create positive change?

Authors and Contributors

Michael Mayerfeld Bell ("Can the World Develop and Sustain Its Environment?") teaches environmental sociology and social theory at Iowa State University. He holds degrees in Earth Science, Forest Science, and Sociology and is the author of three books on environmental topics, two of which won national awards. His greatest loves are gardening, fretted instruments, bicycles, human-powered boats, community activism, his family, and his planet. His e-mail address is *mikebell@iastate.edu.*

York W. Bradshaw is Professor and Chair of Sociology at the University of Memphis. Prior to this position, he was director of African Studies and Professor of Sociology at Indiana University, Bloomington. He has also taught and lectured at a number of African universities in Kenya, Zambia, and South Africa. Professor Bradshaw has written and taught on a number of topics, including education and health in developing countries, debt and economic adjustment in poor regions, and African and Asian development. His most recent book is *The Uncertain Promise of Southern Africa* (2000, edited with Stephen Ndegwa). In his spare time, he likes to roller blade, "fire walk," and travel.

Steven Brint ("How Culture Shapes Schooling") is Professor of Sociology at the University of California, Riverside. He is the author of *The Diverted Dream* (1995, with Jerome Karabel), *In an Age of Experts* (1996), and *Schools and Societies* (1998). He is also the author of numerous articles on schooling, the professions, and middle-class politics. He is currently working on a new book about continuity and change in American colleges and universities. Professor Brint lives in Claremont, California, with his wife and two children. His e-mail address is *steven.brint@ucr.edu.*

Tracey Jane Dawson ("My Personal Journey to a Global Perspective"), after the travels described in this book, decided to go back to school at the College of Charleston, South Carolina. She graduated with a degree in political science in May 2000. Before going on to graduate school, she sought volunteer work in Cuba. In the future, Tracey hopes to merge her passion for travel with her formal education and work in the humanitarian field.

Kathleen M. Fallon ("Gender" and "A Sociologist's Atlas") is currently a Ph.D. candidate in the Department of Sociology at Indiana University. She has taught the Sociology of Gender Roles over the past four years and is researching women's nongovernmental organizations in Ghana.

Patricia Fernandez-Kelly ("Gender") holds appointments at the Princeton University Department of Sociology and the university's Office of Population Research. She studies international development. As part of her research on Mexico's maquiladora program, Ms. Fernandez-Kelly worked as a seamstress in a garment factory in Ciudad Juarez. With Lorraine Gray, she coproduced the Emmy Award–winning documentary *The Global Assembly Line.* Her e-mail address is *mpfk@princeton.edu.*

Nicky Hart ("The Globalization of Taste") is a British sociologist and Professor of Sociology at UCLA. She specializes in the sociology of health, family, and stratification and the sociological history of food and eating. Professor Hart believes that the study of "burger culture" should be an important topic for public health in the twenty-first century.

Joseph F. Healey is Professor of Sociology at Christopher Newport University. His research interests include American minority group relations, immigration, and the sociology of sport. Professor Healey has written several textbooks, including *Statistics: A Tool for Social Research* (1999, 5th edition, Wadsworth) and *Race, Ethnicity, Gender, and Class* (1998, 2nd edition, Pine Forge Press). His spare time is devoted to his family and to hammer dulcimers, banjos, and concertinas.

Lester Kurtz ("Local Gods and Universal Faiths") is Professor of Sociology and Asian Studies at the University of Texas at Austin. He has written a number of books and articles on the comparative sociology of religion and on peace and conflict studies, including *Gods in the Global Village* (1995) and the three-volume *Encyclopedia of Violence, Peace, and Conflict* (1999). Professor Kurtz has traveled widely, has lived in India and Taiwan, and has lectured in North America, Europe, Asia, and Africa. His e-mail address is *lkurtz@soc.utexas.edu.*

Kevin T. Leicht ("The Future of Work") is Professor of Sociology at the University of Iowa. He is currently editor of the *Sociological Quarterly* and *Research in Social Stratification and Mobility.* Professor Leicht has been writing about issues related to the workplace for about fifteen years. He became interested in studying changing workplaces and careers while growing up in Omaha, Nebraska, during the farm crisis of the 1970s. His e-mail address is *Kevin-leicht@uiowa.edu.*

Diane Lye ("Families" and "How Many People Is Too Many People?") has a Ph.D. in Demography from the University of Pennsylvania and taught population and family studies at the University of Washington for a number of years. She has been a policy consultant for business and government on important family issues, such as fatherhood, child support, child custody, and welfare.

John Markoff ("Economics and Politics") is Professor of Sociology, History, and Political Science at the University of Pittsburgh. He believes that whether democracy has a meaningful future will be one of the great issues of the twenty-first century and that if academic research is to make a useful contribution it will be by drawing on all the social sciences. His *Abolition of Feudalism* (1996) won prizes from the American Sociological Association, the Society for French Historical Studies, and the Social Science History Association. Professor Markoff's e-mail address is *jm2@pitt.edu.*

Njeri Mbugua ("The Global Healthcare Challenge") grew up in Kenya and is now an assistant professor at Illinois Wesleyan University. Her fields of interest include international health, gender, and race. Dr. Mbugua has conducted field research on HIV/AIDS and adolescent sexuality in Africa and has given numerous public addresses and participated in forums discussing gender, sexuality, and HIV/AIDS. Her practical approach toward international health stems from personal experience and the conviction that academic knowledge can make a difference to those who are suffering. Her e-mail address is *nmbugua@titan.iwu.edu.*

Philip McMichael ("Biopiracy and Gene Theft") is Professor and Chair of Rural and Development Sociology at Cornell University. His research focuses on global political-economic institutions and food systems. Professor McMichael is the author of *Development and Social Change: A Global Perspective* (2nd edition, Pine Forge Press, 2000).

Joane Nagel ("Sex as a Global Commodity") is University Distinguished Professor and Chair of Sociology at the University of Kansas; she has worked and taught in West and Southern Africa. Professor Nagel's recent work includes "Masculinity and Nationalism: Gender and Sexuality in the Making of Nations," in the journal *Ethnic and Racial Studies* (1998); "States of Arousal/Fantasy Islands: Race, Sex, and Romance in the Global Economy of Desire," in the journal *American Studies* (2001); and *Race, Ethnicity, and Sexuality: Intimate Intersections and Forbidden Frontiers* (Oxford University Press, 2001).

Nick Rutter (editorial cartoons) is studying history at Brown University. Apart from his studies, he is active in the student antisweatshop movement and is now at work on a full-length comic book detailing the conditions of New York City's garment sweatshop industry.

Gay W. Seidman ("Activists Crusade against Sweatshops") teaches sociology at the University of Wisconsin-Madison. She is the author of *Manufacturing Militance: Workers' Movements in Brazil and South Africa* (University of California Press, 1994) and has written articles on the South African women's movement, the anti-apartheid movement, and movements for racial equality. Ms. Seidman's interest in South Africa and transnationalism is linked to her involvement in the transnational anti-apartheid movement; she is currently involved in research and activism around transnational labor rights.

Rebecca Smith is a freelance writer and editor who has worked on many Pine Forge Press publications, as well as textbooks and journals on psychology, business, and communication. She has a master of science degree in communication and teaches written, oral, and interpersonal communication skills to working adults through the University of California, San Diego. Her leisure pursuits include gardening and traveling.

References

CHAPTER 1

Bluestone, B., & Harrison, B. (1979). *The deindustrialization of America: Plant closings, community abandonment, and the dismantling of basic industry.* New York: Basic Books.

Bradsher, K. (1995, August 14). Low ranking for poor American children. *New York Times,* p. A7.

Chirot, D. (1991). What happened in Eastern Europe in 1989? In D. Chirot (Ed.), *The crisis of Leninism and the decline of the left: The revolution of 1989* (pp. 3–32). Seattle: University of Washington Press.

Cole, J. (1995, June 12). Jet makers, once keen for a giant aircraft, are drawn to a fast one. *Wall Street Journal,* pp. A1, A9.

Farnsworth, C. (1995, April 18). Quebec separatists split on timing and term of referendum. *New York Times,* p. A7.

Gladwell, M. (1995, July 17). The plague year. *The New Republic, 24,* 38–46.

Golden, T. (1995, February 24). In Mexico, both army and rebels say they're in control. *New York Times,* p. A3.

Harden, B. (1990). *Africa: Dispatches from a fragile continent.* Boston: Houghton Mifflin.

Herald-Times newspaper, Bloomington, Indiana. (1997–1999). Various issues.

Movement for sovereignty is growing in Hawaii. (1994, June 5). *New York Times,* p. A36.

Naisbitt, J. (1994). *Global paradox.* New York: Morrow.

Ndegwa, S. (1996). *The two faces of civil society: NGOs and politics in Africa.* West Hartford, CT: Kumarian Press.

O'Harrow, R., Jr. (1999, August 20). Justice Department pushes for power to unlock PC security systems. *New York Times,* p. A1.

Preston, R. (1994). *The hot zone.* New York: Random House.

Sack, K. (2000, April 4). Core denounces disparities in minority access to computers. *New York Times,* p. A12.

Sawyer, K. (1999, August 22). Poorest families are losing ground. *Washington Post,* p. A7.

United Nations International Children's Emergency Fund. (1993). *The state of the world's children 1993.* New York: Oxford University Press.

United Nations International Children's Emergency Fund. (1995). *The state of the world's children 1995.* New York: Oxford University Press.

U.S. Bureau of the Census. (1990). *Statistical abstract of the United States: 1990* (110th ed.). Washington, DC: Government Printing Office.

U.S. Bureau of the Census. (1996). *Statistical abstract of the United States: 1996* (116th ed.). Washington, DC: Government Printing Office.

Wallace, M. (1998). Downsizing the American dream: Work and family at century's end. In D. Vannoy & P. J. Dubeck (Eds.), *Challenges for work and family in the twenty-first century* (pp. 23–38).

Whiting, R. (1990). *You gotta have wa.* New York: Macmillan.

World Bank. (1998). *World development report 1998.* Oxford: Oxford University Press.

CHAPTER 2

Bradshaw, Y., & Wallace, M. (1996). *Global inequalities.* Thousand Oaks, CA: Pine Forge Press.

Cassidy, J. (1997, October 20 and 27). The return of Karl Marx. *The New Yorker, 73,* 248–259.

Chase-Dunn, C. (1989). *Global formation: Structures of world economy.* Cambridge: Blackwell.

Curtin, P. (1990). *The rise and fall of the plantation complex.* New York: Cambridge University Press.

Durkheim, E. (1951). *Suicide, a study in sociology.* New York: Free Press.

Firebaugh, G. (1992). Growth effects of foreign and domestic investment. *American Journal of Sociology, 98,* 105–130.

Firebaugh, G., & Beck, F. (1994). Does economic growth benefit the masses? Growth, dependence, and welfare in the third world. *American Sociological Review, 59,* 631–653.

Gaines, D. (1998). *Teenage wasteland.* Chicago: University of Chicago Press.

Holinger, P., et al. (1994). *Suicide and homicide among adolescents.* New York. Guilford Press.

Hoover Institute. (1998). *Hoover's handbook of world business.* Austin, TX: Hoover's Business Press.

Lester, D. (Ed.) (1994). *Emile Durkheim: Le suicide one hundred years later.* Philadelphia: Charles Press.

McDonald's. (2000). Corporate Web site. Available: www.mcdonalds.com/corporate/index.html.

Mills, C. W. (1959). *The sociological imagination.* New York: Oxford University Press.

Pescosolido, B., & Georgianna, S. (1989). Durkheim, suicide, and religion: Toward a network theory of suicide. *American Sociological Review, 54,* 33–48.

Rangel, C. (1989). Imperialism does not cause third world poverty. In J. Rohr (Ed.), *The Third World—opposing viewpoints* (pp. 25–31). San Diego, CA: Greenhaven Press.

Ritzer, G. (1996). *The McDonaldization of society.* Thousand Oaks, CA: Pine Forge Press.

Simpson, M., & Conklin, G. (1989). Socioeconomic development, suicide and religion: A test of Durkheim's theory of religion and suicide. *Social Forces, 67,* 945–964.

Thorlindsson, T., & Bjarnason, T. (1998). Modeling Durkheim on the micro level: A study of youth suicidality. *American Sociological Review, 63,* 94–110.

Trovato, F. (1992). A Durkheimian analysis of youth suicide: Canada, 1971 and 1981. *Suicide and Life-Threatening Behavior, 22,* 413–427.

U.S. Bureau of the Census. (1998). *Statistical abstracts.* Washington, DC: Government Printing Office.

Wallerstein, I. (1974). *The modern world system I.* New York: Academic Press.

Weber, M. (1958). *The Protestant Reformation and the spirit of capitalism.* New York: Scribner.

Wright, E. O. (1997). *Class counts: Comparative studies in class analysis.* New York: Cambridge University Press.

World Bank. (2000). [On-line]. Available: www.worldbank.com.

Zhang, J. (1998). Suicide in the world: Toward a population increase theory of suicide. *Death Studies, 22,* 525–539.

CHAPTER 3

American survey: The solitary bowler. (1995, February 18). *The Economist, 334,* 21–22.

Bellah, R., et al. (1991). *The good society.* New York: Vintage Books.

Coleman, J. S. (1988). Social capital in the creation of human capital. *American Journal of Sociology, 94* (Suppl.), s95–s120.

Coleman, J. S. (1990). *The foundations of social theory.* Cambridge: Harvard University Press.

Etzioni, A. (1993). *The spirit of community: Rights, responsibilities, and the communitarian agenda.* New York: Crown.

Greeley, A. (1997). The other civic America: Religion and social capital. *American Prospect, 32,* 68–73.

Knack, S., & Keefer, P. (1997, November). Does social capital have an economic payoff? A cross-country investigation. *The Quarterly Journal of Economics, 35,* 1252–1288.

Ladd, E. C. (1996). The data just don't show erosion of America's social capital. *The Public Perspective, 7,* 1–5.

Ladd, E. C. (1999). *The Ladd report.* New York: Free Press.

National Association of Secretaries of State. (1999). *New Millennium Project, Part 1: American youth attitudes on politics, citizenship, government and voting.* Lexington, KY: National Association of Secretaries of State.

Norris, P. (1996, September). Does television erode social capital? A reply to Putnam. *PS: Political Science and Politics, 29,* 474–480.

Putnam, R. D. (1993). *Making democracy work.* Princeton, NJ: Princeton University Press.

Putnam, R. D. (1995a). Bowling alone: America's declining social capital. *Journal of Democracy, 6,* 65–78.

Putnam, R. D. (1995b). Tuning in, tuning out: The strange disappearance of social capital in America. *PS: Political Science and Politics, 28,* 664–683.

Putnam, R. D. (1996a). The strange disappearance of civic America. *The American Prospect, 24,* 34–48.

Putnam, R. D. (1996b). Robert Putnam responds. *The American Prospect, 25,* 26–28.

Putnam, R. D. (2000). *Bowling alone: The collapse and revival of American community.* New York: Simon & Schuster.

Schudson, M. (1996). What if civic life didn't die? *The American Prospect, 25,* 17–20.

Skocpol, T. (1996). Unraveling from above. *The American Prospect, 25,* 20–25.

Tocqueville, A., de. (1969). *Democracy in America.* Garden City, NJ: Anchor Books.

U.S. Bureau of the Census. (1993). *Statistical abstract of the United States: 1993* (113th ed.). Washington, DC: Government Printing Office.

U.S. Bureau of the Census. (1995). *Statistical abstract of the United States: 1995* (115th ed.). Washington, DC: Government Printing Office.

U.S. Bureau of the Census. (1998). *Statistical abstract of the United States: 1998* (118th ed.). Washington, DC: Government Printing Office.

U.S. Bureau of the Census. (1999). *Statistical abstract of the United States: 1999* (119th ed.). Washington, DC: Government Printing Office.

Vallely, R. M. (1996). Couch-potato democracy. *The American Prospect, 2,* 25–26.

Wallace, W. (1971). *The logic of science in sociology.* Chicago: Aldine-Atherton.

Williams, T. M. (Ed.) (1986). *The impact of television: A natural experiment in three communities.* Orlando, FL: Academic Press.

World Bank. (2000). [On-line]. Available: www.worldbank.org.

Witte, J. C., & Howard, P. E. N. (1999). *Digital citizens and digital consumers: Demographic transition on the Internet* [on-line]. Available: www.survey2000. nationalgeographic.com/links.html.

Wuthnow, R. (1994). *Sharing the journey: Support groups and America's new quest for community.* New York: Free Press.

CHAPTER 4

Ardagh, J. (1995). *Ireland and the Irish.* New York: Penguin Books.

Chirot, D. (1994). *How societies change.* Thousand Oaks, CA: Pine Forge Press.

Corsaro, W. (1997). *The sociology of childhood.* Thousand Oaks, CA: Pine Forge Press.

Croteau, D., & Hoynes, W. (2000). *Media/society: Industries, images, and audiences* (2nd ed.). Thousand Oaks, CA: Pine Forge Press.

Friedman, T. L. (2000, January 28). One country, two worlds. *New York Times,* p. A27.

Griswold, W. (1994). *Cultures and societies in a changing world.* Thousand Oaks, CA: Pine Forge Press.

Hirsch, P. (1972). Processing fads and fashions: An organization set analysis of culture industry systems. *American Journal of Sociology, 77,* 639–659.

Kanagy, C. L., & Kraybill, D. B. (1999). *The riddles of human society.* Thousand Oaks, CA: Pine Forge Press.

Miner, H. (1956, June). Body ritual among the Nacirema. *American Anthropologist, 58*(3), 503–507.

Newman, D. (1999). *Sociology of families.* Thousand Oaks, CA: Pine Forge Press.

Ogburn, W. E. (1964). *On culture and social change.* Chicago: University of Chicago Press.

Peterson, R. A. (Ed.). (1976). *The production of culture.* Beverly Hills, CA: Sage Publications.

Ritzer, G. (2000). *The McDonaldization of society* (New Century edition). Thousand Oaks, CA: Pine Forge Press.

United Nations. (2000). [On-line]. Available: www.un.org.

Watson, J. L. (1997). Transnationalism, localization, and fast foods in east Asia. In J. L. Watson (Ed.), *Golden arches east: McDonald's in east Asia.* Stanford, CA: Stanford University Press.

Williams, R. (1970). *American society: A sociological interpretation.* New York: Knopf.

Word ORT Union. (1996). Abraham and the Patriarchs: Regional and cultural background. *Navigating the Bible* [on-line]. Available: bible.org.org/bible/htm/atlas/History/abr_pats.htm.

CHAPTER 5

Ballinger, J. (1993). The new free trade heel: Nike's profits jump on the back of Asian workers. In R. Jackson (Ed.), *Global Issues, 93/94,* pp. 46–47. Sluice Dock, Guilford, CT: Dushkin.

Bello, W., & Rosenfeld, S. (1990). *Dragons in distress: Asia's miracle economies in crisis.* San Francisco Institute for Food and Development Policy.

Bluestone, B., & Harrison, B. (1982). *The deindustrialization of America.* New York: Basic Books.

Bradshaw, Y., & Wallace, M. (1996). *Global inequalities.* Thousand Oaks, CA: Pine Forge Press.

Bradsher, K. (1995, August 14). Low ranking for poor American children. *New York Times,* p. A7.

Byrne, J. (1991, May 6). The flap over executive pay: Investors, employees, and academics are asking how much is enough? *Business Week,* pp. 99–110.

Davis, K., & Moore, W. (1945). Some principles of stratification. *American Sociological Review, 7,* 242–249.

DeMuth, C. (1997, October). The new wealth of nations. *Commentary,* 23–28.

Farley, R. (1996). *The new American reality.* New York: Russell Sage Foundation.

Gottschalk, P., & Smeeding, T. (1997). Cross-national comparisons of earnings and income inequality. *Journal of Economic Literature, 35,* 633–687.

Hill-Collins, P. (1991). *Black feminist thought.* New York: Routledge.

Kasarda, J. (1989). Urban industrial transition and the underclass. *Annals of the American Academy, 501,* 26–47.

Korzeniewicz, R., & Moran, T. (1997). World-economic trends in the distribution of income, 1965–1992. *American Journal of Sociology, 102,* 1000–1039.

Kuznets, S. (1955). Economic growth and income inequality. *American Economic Review, 56,* 46–59.

Lamb, D. (1985). *The Africans* (rev. ed.). New York: Random House.

Lenski, G. (1966). *Power and privilege.* New York: McGraw-Hill.

Lenski, G., Lenski, J., & Nolan, P. (1995). *Human societies: An introduction to macrosociology* (7th ed.). New York: McGraw-Hill.

Levy, F. (1998). *The new dollars and dreams: American incomes and economic change.* New York: Russell Sage Foundation.

Massey, D., & Denton, N. (1993). *American apartheid: Segregation and the making of the underclass.* Cambridge: Harvard University Press.

National Opinion Research Council. (1998). *General social survey.* Chicago: NORC.

Neilsen, F., & Alderson, A. (1997). The Kuznets curve and the Great U-Turn: Income inequality in U.S. counties, 1970–1990. *American Sociological Review, 62,* 12–33.

Newman, K. (1993). *Declining fortunes: The withering of the American dream.* New York: HarperCollins.

Rossant, J. (1999, July 5). Turkey's tire queen. *Forbes,* 190–192.

Tumin, M. (1953). Some principles of stratification: A critical analysis. *American Sociological Review, 18,* 387–394.

United Nations. (1999). *Human development report: Globalization with a human face.* New York: Oxford University Press.

United Nations. (1999). *Human development report, 1999* [on-line]. Available: www. undp.org/hdro/overview.pdf.

U.S. Bureau of the Census (1999). [On-line]. Available: www.census.gov/prod/ 99pubs/p60-206.pdf.

U.S. Bureau of the Census (2000). [On-line]. Available: www.census.gov.

Wilson, W. (1987). *The truly disadvantaged.* Chicago: The University of Chicago Press.

Wilson, W. (1996). *When work disappears.* New York: Knopf.

World Bank (1999). [On-line]. Available: www.worldbank.org.

World Bank (2000). [On-line]. Available: www.worldbank.org.

CHAPTER 6

Alba, R. (1990). *Ethnic identity: The transformation of white America.* New Haven, CT: Yale University Press.

Beinart, W. (1994). *Twentieth century South Africa.* New York: Oxford University Press.

Blauner, R. (1972). *Racial oppression in America.* New York: Harper & Row.

Bradshaw, Y., & Wallace, M. (1996). *Global inequalities.* Thousand Oaks, CA: Pine Forge Press.

Brown, R. (1995). *Prejudice: Its social psychology.* Cambridge: Blackwell.

Cancio, S., Evans, T., & Maume, D. (1996). Reconsidering the declining significance of race: Racial differences in early career wages. *American Sociological Review, 61,* 541–556.

Cose, E. (1993). *The rage of a privileged class.* New York: HarperCollins.

Feagin, J. (1991). The continuing significance of race: Antiblack discrimination in public places. *American Sociological Review, 56,* 101–116.

Gordon, M. (1964). *Assimilation in American life.* New York: Oxford University Press.

Gourevitch, P. (1998). *We wish to inform you that tomorrow we will be killed with our families.* New York: Picador, USA.

Landry, B. (1987). *The new black middle class.* Berkeley: University of California Press.

Lieberson, S., & Waters, M. (1988). *From many strands.* New York: Russell Sage Foundation.

Mallaby, S. (1992). *After apartheid: The future of South Africa.* New York: New York Times Books.

Massey, D. (1995). The new immigration and ethnicity in the United States. *Population and Development Review, 21,* 631–652.

Massey, D., & Denton, N. (1993). *American apartheid.* Cambridge: Harvard University Press.

Morgan, E. (1975). *American slavery, American freedom.* New York: Norton.

Myrdal, G. (1944). *An American dilemma: The Negro problem and modern democracy.* New York: Harper & Row.

National Opinion Research Council. (1998). *General social survey.* Chicago: NORC.

Oliver, M., & Shapiro, T. (1995). *Black wealth, white wealth.* New York: Routledge.

Park, R., & Burgess, E. (1924). *Introduction to the science of society.* Chicago: University of Chicago Press.

Portes, A., & Rumbaut, R. (1996). *Immigrant America: A portrait* (2nd ed.). Berkeley: University of California Press.

Portes, A., & Zhou, M. (1993, November). The new second generation: Segmented assimilation and its variants. *Annals of the American Academy of Political and Social Sciences, 530,* 74–96.

Public Broadcasting System (1997). [On-line]. Available: www.pbs.org/wgbh/pages/frontline/shows/rwanda/reports/refuse.html.

Smedley, A. (1993). *Race in North America: Origin and evolution of a world view.* Boulder, CO: Westview Press.

Steinberg, S. (1981). *The ethnic myth: Race, ethnicity, and class in America.* New York: Atheneum.

Thomas, M. (1993). Race, class, and personal income: An empirical test of the declining significance of race thesis, 1968–1988. *Social Problems, 40,* 328–342.

U.S. Bureau of the Census. (1998). *Statistical abstract of the United States.* Washington, DC: Government Printing Office.

U.S. Immigration and Naturalization Service. (1997). *Statistical yearbook of the Immigration and Naturalization Service.* Washington, DC: Government Printing Office.

Van Den Berghe, P. (1967). *South Africa: A study in conflict.* Berkeley: University of California Press.

Wallace, W. (1997). *The future of ethnicity, race, and nationality.* Westport, CT: Praeger.

Willie, C. (Ed.). (1989). *Round two of the Willie/Wilson debate* (2nd ed.). Dix Hills, NY: General Hall.

Wirth, L. (1945). The problem of minority groups. In R. Linton (Ed.), *The science of man in the world* (pp. 347–372). New York: Columbia University Press.

CHAPTER 7

Abdel-Hamid, H. (2000). *Big Bird, meet Khokha: Egyptian Sesame Street makes pitch for gender equality* [on-line]. Retrieved June 6 from www.abcnews.go.com.

Akuffo, F. O. (1987). Teenage pregnancies and school drop-outs. In C. Oppong (Ed.), *Sex roles, population, and development in West Africa.* London: Curry.

American Broadcasting Company. (2000). Special section on Women 2000. [On-line]. Available: www.abcnews.go.com.

American Federation of Labor-Congress of Industrial Organizations. (1997). The pay gap by occupations. [On-line]. Retrieved March 3, 2000, from www.aflcio.org/women/a_z.htm#a.

Annual report on the economic status of the profession 1999–2000. (2000). American Association of University Professors survey database. [On-line]. Available: www.aaup.org/2tab800.htm.

Bacon, D. (1996). *The life of a maquiladora worker* [on-line]. Available: www.igc.org/dbacon/Mexico/07MaLife.htm.

Bellew, R., Raney, I., & Subbarao, K. (1992). Educating girls. *Finance and Development, 29,* 54–56.

Bradshaw, Y. W. (1993). State limitations, self-help secondary schooling, and development in Kenya. *Social Forces, 72,* 347–378.

Bradshaw, Y. W., Noonan, R., Gash, L., & Buchmann, C. (1993). Borrowing against the future: Children and Third World indebtedness. *Social Forces, 71,* 629-656.

Buchmann, C. (1996). The debt crisis, structural adjustment and women's education: Implications for status and social development. *International Journal of Comparative Sociology, 37,* 5–30.

Buchmann, C. (June 2000). Family structure, parental perceptions and child labor: What factors determine who is enrolled. *Social Forces, 78,* 1349–1378.

Chaney, E., & Bunster, X. (1988). *Sellers and servants.* New York: Bergin & Garvey.

Evans, R., & Loeb, J. J. (1942). *Rosie the riveter.* New York: Paramount Music Corporation.

Fernández-Kelly, M. P. (1983). *For we are sold, I and my people: Women and industry in Mexico's frontier.* Albany: State University of New York Press.

Fox, M. F. (1984). Women and higher education: Sex differentials in the status of students and scholars. In J. Freeman (Ed.), *Women: A feminist perspective.* Palo Alto, CA: Mayfield.

Friedl, E. (1975). *Women and men: An anthropologist's view.* New York: Holt, Rinehart, & Winston.

Fuller, B. (1991). *Growing-up modern: The western state builds Third-World schools.* New York: Routledge.

Gladwin, C. (Ed.). (1991). *Structural adjustment and African women farmers.* Gainesville: University of Florida Press.

Goodale, J. (1971). *Tiwi wives.* Seattle: University of Washington Press.

Graham, C. K. (1971). *The history of education in Ghana.* London: Frank Cass.

Hadden, K., & London, B. (1996). Educating girls in the Third World: The demographic, basic needs, and economic benefits. *International Journal of Comparative Sociology, 37,* 31–46.

Hayghe, H. V. (1997). Developments in women's labor force participation. *Monthly Labor Review Online, 120,*(9).

Herz, B., Subbarao, K., Habib, M., & Raney, L. (1991). *Letting girls learn: Promising approaches in primary and secondary education.* Washington, DC: World Bank.

Honey, M. (1985). *Creating Rosie the Riveter: Class, gender, and propaganda during World War II.* Boston: University of Massachusetts Press.

Inter-Parliamentary Union. (2000). Web site accessed June 2000. Available: www.ipu.org./wmn-e/world.htm.

Kessler-Harris, A. (1988). *A woman's wage: Historical meanings and social consequences.* Lexington: The University Press of Kentucky.

Lehrer, S. (1987). *Origins of protective labor legislation for women, 1905–1925.* Albany: State University of New York Press.

Lenski, G., & Lenski, J. (1987). *Human societies.* New York: McGraw-Hill.

Martin, M. K., & Voorhies, B. (1975). *Female of the species.* New York: Columbia University Press.

Massiah, J. (1993). Indicators for planning for women in Carribean development. In J. Massiah (Ed.), *Women in developing countries: Making the visible invisible.* Ann Arbor, MI: Edward Brothers.

Murphy, Y., & Murphy, R. (1974). *Women of the forest.* New York: Columbia University Press.

Odaga, A., & Heneveld, W. (1995). *Girls and schools in sub-Saharan Africa: From analysis to action.* Washington, DC: World Bank.

O'Kelly, C. G., & Carney, L. S. (1986). *Women and men in society* (2nd ed.). Belmont, CA: Wadsworth.

Pellow, D. (1977). *Women in Accra: Options for autonomy.* Ann Arbor, MI: Reference Publications.

Robertson, C. (1984). *Sharing the same bowl.* Bloomington: Indiana University Press.

Sadker, M., & Sadker, D. (1994). *Failing at fairness: How America's schools cheat girls.* New York: Charles Scribner's.

Saffioti, H. (1978). *Women in class society.* New York: Monthly Review Press.

Shakeshaft, C. (1995). Reforming science education to include girls. *Theory into Practice, 34,* 74–79.

Silberbauer, G. (1982). Political process in G/Wi bands. In E. B. Leacock & R. Lee (Eds.), *Politics and history in band societies.* New York: Cambridge University Press.

Sklar, H. (1995). *Chaos or community: Seeking solutions, not scapegoats for bad economics.* Boston: South End Press.

Smith-Rosenberg, C. (1985). *Disorderly conduct: Visions of gender in Victorian America.* New York: Knopf.

Tuana, N., & Tong, R. (Eds.). (1995). *Feminism and philosophy: Essential readings in theory, reinterpretation, and application.* Boulder, CO: Westview Press.

United Nations Educational, Scientific and Cultural Organization. (1999). *Statistical yearbook.* Geneva: United Nations.

U.S. Bureau of the Census. (1960). Series D13–25. Washington, DC: Government Printing Office.

U.S. Bureau of the Census. (1999a). Education. Section 4 in *Statistical abstract of the United States: 1999* (119th ed.). Washington, DC: Government Printing Office.

U.S. Bureau of the Census. (1999b). Labor force, employment and earnings. Section 13 in *Statistical abstract of the United States: 1999* (119th ed.). Washington, DC: Government Printing Office.

U.S. Bureau of Labor Statistics. (1998). *Labor force statistics from the current population survey.* Washington, DC: U.S. Bureau of Labor Statistics. [On-line]. Available: stats.bls.gov/top20.html.

U.S. Bureau of Labor Statistics. (2000). Usual weekly earnings summary: First quarter 2000. *Labor force statistics from the current population survey.* Washington, DC: Government Printing Office.

U.S. Department of Health, Education, and Welfare. (1972). *Digest of educational statistics.* Washington, DC: Government Printing Office.

U.S. National Center for Education Statistics. (1972). *Digest of educational statistics.* Washington, DC: Government Printing Office.

U.S. National Center for Education Statistics. (1997). *Digest of educational statistics.* Washington, DC: Government Printing Office.

Vickers, J. (1991). *Women and the world economic crisis.* Atlantic Highlands, NJ: Zed Books.

Wiessner, P. (1982). Risk, reciprocity and social influences on !Kung San economics. In E. B. Leacock & R. Lee (Eds.), *Politics and history in band societies.* New York: Cambridge University Press.

World Bank. (2000). [On-line]. World development indicators. Accessed June 2000: www.worldbank.org/data/wdi2000/pdfs/tabl_3.pdf.

CHAPTER 8

Amato, P. R. (1993). Children's adjustment to divorce: Theories, hypotheses, and empirical support. *Journal of Marriage and the Family, 55,* 23–38.

Amato, P. R. (1996). Explaining the intergenerational transmission of divorce. *Journal of Marriage and the Family, 58,* 628–640.

Amato, P. R., & Booth, A. (1996). A prospective study of divorce and parent-child relationships. *Journal of Marriage and the Family, 58,* 356–365.

Amato, P. R., & Keith, B. (1991). Parental divorce and the well-being of children: A meta-analysis. *Psychological Bulletin, 110,* 26–46.

Americans for Divorce Reform. (2000). *Divorce reform page.* Arlington, VA: Americans for Divorce Reform. [On-line]. Available: www.divorcereform.org/nonus.html.

Axinn, W. G., & Thornton, A. (1992). The relationship between cohabitation and divorce: Selectivity or causal influence? *Demography, 29,* 357–374.

Axinn, W. G., & Thornton, A. (1993). Mothers, children, and cohabitation: The intergenerational effects of attitudes and behavior. *American Sociological Review, 58,* 233–246.

Barnett, R. C., & Rivers, C. (1996). *She works/he works: How two income families are happier, healthier, and better off.* San Francisco: Harper.

Becker, G. S. (1991). *A treatise on the family* (enlarged ed.). Cambridge: Harvard University Press.

Bennett, N., Bloom, D., & Craig, P. (1989). The divergence of black and white marriage patterns. *American Journal of Sociology, 95,* 692–722.

Billy, J. O. G., Landale, N. S., & McLaughlin, S. D. (1986). The effect of marital status at first birth on marital dissolution among adolescent mothers. *Demography, 23,* 329–349.

Blau, D. M., & Robins, P. K. (1991). Child care demand and labor supply of young mothers over time. *Demography, 28,* 333–351.

Bloom, D. E. (1982). What's happening to age at first birth in the United States? A study of recent cohorts. *Demography, 19,* 351–370.

Bradshaw, Y., Buchmann, C., & Mbatia, P. (1994). A threatened generation: Impediments to children's quality of life in Kenya. In J. Best (Ed.), *Troubling children: Studies of children and social problems* (pp. 23–45). Hawthorne, NY: Aldine de Gruyter.

Bradshaw, Y., & Wallace, W. (1996). *Global inequalities.* Thousand Oaks, CA: Pine Forge Press.

Breault, K. D., & Kposowa, A. J. (1987). Explaining divorce in the United States: A study of 3,111 counties, 1980. *Journal of Marriage and the Family, 49,* 549–558.

Bumpass, L. L. (1984). Children and marital disruption: A replication and update. *Demography, 21,* 71–82.

Bumpass, L. L. (1990). What's happening to the family? Interactions between demographic and institutional change. *Demography, 27,* 483–498.

Bumpass, L. L., Sweet, J. A., & Cherlin, A. J. (1991). The role of cohabitation in declining marriage rates. *Journal of Marriage and the Family, 53,* 913–927.

Chen, R., & Morgan, S. P. (1991). Recent trends in the timing of first births in the United States. *Demography, 28,* 513–533.

Cherlin, A. J. (1978). Remarriage as an incomplete institution. *American Journal of Sociology, 84,* 634–650.

Cherlin, A. J. (1992). *Marriage, divorce, remarriage* (rev. ed.). Cambridge: Harvard University Press.

Cherlin, A. J. (1999). *Public and private families: An introduction* (2nd ed.). New York: McGraw-Hill.

Cooney, T. M., & Hogan, D. P. (1991). Marriage in an institutionalized life course: First marriage among American men in the twentieth century. *Journal of Marriage and the Family, 53,* 178–190.

Coontz, S. (1992). *The way we never were.* New York: Basic Books.

Coontz, S. (1997). *The way we really are: Coming to terms with America's changing families.* New York: Basic Books.

Crimmins, E., Easterlin, R. A. & Saito, Y. (1991). Preference change among American youth: Family, work and goods aspirations, 1978–86. *Population and Development Review, 17,* 115–133.

Daley, S. (2000, April 18). French couples take plunge that falls short of marriage. *New York Times,* pp. A1, A4.

Durkheim, E. (1893/1960). *The division of labor in society.* Glencoe, IL: Free Press.

Forste, R., & Tanfer, K. (1996). Sexual exclusivity among dating, cohabiting, and married women. *Journal of Marriage and the Family, 58,* 33–48.

Furstenberg, F. F., Jr. (1990). Divorce and the American family. *Annual Review of Sociology, 16,* 379–403.

Furstenberg, F. F., Jr., & Teitler, J. O. (1994). Reconsidering the effects of marital disruption: What happens to children of divorce in early adulthood? *Journal of Family Issues, 15,* 173–190.

Glenn, N. D. (1996). Values, attitudes, and the state of American marriage. In D. Popenoe, J. B. Elshtain, & D. Blankenhorn (Eds.), *Promises to keep: The decline and renewal of marriage in America* (pp. 15–33). Lanham, MD: Rowman & Littlefield.

Goode, W. J. (1993). *World changes in divorce patterns.* New Haven, CT: Yale University Press.

Gray, J. S. (1996). The economic impact of divorce law reform. *Population Research and Policy Review, 15,* 275–296.

Greenstein, T. N. (1995). Gender ideology, marital disruption, and the employment of married women. *Journal of Marriage and the Family, 57,* 31–42.

Johnson, W., & Skinner, J. (1986). Labor supply and marital separation. *American Economic Review, 76,* 455–469.

Kahn, J. R., & London, K. A. (1991). Premarital sex and the risk of divorce. *Journal of Marriage and the Family, 53,* 845–855.

Lehrer, E. L., & Chiswick, C. U. (1993). Religion as a determinant of marital stability. *Demography 30,* 385–404.

Lesthaeghe, R., & Surkyn, J. (1988). Cultural dynamics and economic theories of fertility change. *Population and Development Review, 14,* 1–45.

Levy, F. (1987). *Dollars and dreams: The changing American income distribution.* New York: Russell Sage Foundation.

Lichter, D. T., McLaughlin, D. K., & Ribar, D. C. (1997). Welfare and the rise in female-headed families. *American Journal of Sociology, 103,* 112–143.

Lichter, D. T., McLaughlin, D. K., Kephart, G., & Landry, D. J. (1992). Race and the retreat from marriage: A shortage of marriageable men? *American Sociological Review, 57,* 781–799.

Lillard, L. A., Brien, M. J., & Waite, L. J. (1995). Premarital cohabitation and subsequent marital stability: A matter of self-selection? *Demography, 32,* 437–457.

Lillard, L. A., & Waite, L. J. (1993). A joint model of marital childbearing and marital disruption. *Demography, 30,* 653–681.

Lloyd, K. M., & South, S. J. (1996). Contextual influences on young men's transition to first marriage. *Social Forces, 74,* 1097–1119.

Loomis, L. S., & Landale, N. S. (1994). Nonmarital cohabitation and childbearing among black and white American women. *Journal of Marriage and the Family, 56,* 949–962.

Lye, D. N., & Waldron, I. (1997). Attitudes toward cohabitation, family, and gender roles: Relationships to values and political ideology. *Sociological Perspectives, 40,* 199–225.

MacDonald, W. L., & DeMaris, A. (1995). Remarriage, stepchildren and marital conflict: Challenges to the incomplete institutionalization hypothesis. *Journal of Marriage and the Family, 57,* 387–398.

Manning, W. (1993). Marriage and cohabitation following premarital conception. *Journal of Marriage and the Family, 55,* 839–850.

Martin, T. C., & Bumpass, L. L. (1989). Recent trends in marital disruption. *Demography, 26,* 37–51.

McLanahan, S. S., & Sandefur, G. (1994). *Growing up with a single-parent: What hurts, what helps.* Cambridge: Harvard University Press.

McLaughlin, S. D., Melba, B. D., Billy, J. O. G., Zimmerle, D. M., Winges, L. D., & Johnson, T. R. (1988). *The changing lives of American women.* Chapel Hill: University of North Carolina Press.

Michael, R. (1985). Consequences of the rise in female labor force participation rates: Questions and probes. *Journal of Labor Economics, 3,* S117–S146.

Musalia, J. M. (2000). *Social networks and fertility decline in Kenya.* Unpublished Ph.D. dissertation, Indiana University.

National Center for Health Statistics. (1962). *Vital statistics of the United States.* Washington, DC: Government Printing Office.

National Center for Health Statistics. (1966). *Vital statistics of the United States.* Washington, DC: Government Printing Office.

National Opinion Research Council. (1998). General social survey. Chicago: National Opinion Research Council.

Oppenheimer, V. K. (1988). A theory of marriage timing. *American Journal of Sociology, 94,* 563–591.

Oppenheimer, V. K. (1994). Women's rising employment and the future of the family in industrial societies. *Population and Development Review, 20,* 293–342.

Oppenheimer, V. K. (1997). Women's employment and the gain to marriage: The specialization and trading model. *Annual Review of Sociology, 23,* 431–453.

Oppenheimer, V. K., Kalmijn, M., & Lim, N. (1997). Men's career development and marriage timing during a period of rising inequality. *Demography, 34,* 311–330.

Oropesa, R. S., Lichter, D. T., & Anderson, R. N. (1994). Marriage markets and the paradox of Mexican American nuptiality. *Journal of Marriage and the Family, 56,* 889–907.

Parcel, T. L., & Menaghan, E. G. (1994). *Parents' jobs and children's lives.* New York: Aldine de Gruyter.

Parsons, T., & Bales, R. F. (1956). *Family socialization and interaction process.* London: Routledge and Kegan Paul.

Peters, H. E. (1986). Marriage and divorce: Informational constraints and private contracting. *American Economic Review, 76,* 437–454.

Peters, H. E. (1992). Marriage and divorce: Reply. *American Economic Review, 82,* 686–693.

Popenoe, D. (1993). American family decline, 1960–1990: A review and appraisal. *Journal of Marriage and the Family, 55,* 527–555.

Popenoe, D. (1996). *Life without father: Compelling new evidence that fatherhood and marriage are indispensable for the good of children and society.* New York: Martin Kessler.

Preston, S. H., & McDonald, J. (1979). The incidence of divorce within cohorts of American marriages contracted since the Civil War. *Demography, 16,* 1–25.

Raley, R. K. (1996). A shortage of marriageable men? A note on the role of cohabitation in black-white differences in marriage rates. *American Sociological Review, 61,* 973–983.

Reskin, B., & Padavic, I. (1994). *Women and men at work.* Thousand Oaks, CA: Pine Forge Press.

Rindfuss, R. R., & VandenHeuvel, A. (1990). Cohabitation: Precursor to marriage or an alternative to being single? *Population and Development Review, 16,* 703–726.

Rindfuss, R. R., Morgan, S. P., & Swicegood, G. (1988). *First births in America.* Berkeley: University of California Press.

Rindfuss, R. R., Morgan, S. P., & Offutt, K. (1996). Education and the changing age pattern of American fertility: 1963–1989. *Demography, 33,* 277–290.

Ruggles, S. (1997). The rise of divorce and separation in the United States. *Demography, 34,* 455–466.

Schoen, R., & Weinick, R. M. (1993a). Partner choice in marriages and cohabitations. *Journal of Marriage and the Family, 55,* 408–414.

Schoen, R., & Weinick, R. M. (1993b). The slowing metabolism of marriage: Figures from 1988 U.S. marital status life tables. *Demography, 30,* 737–748.

Smith, H. L., Morgan, S. P., & Koropeckyj-Cox, T. (1996). A decomposition of trends in the nonmarital fertility ratios of blacks and whites in the United States, 1960–1992. *Demography, 33,* 141–151.

Smock, P. J., & Manning, W. D. (1997). Cohabiting partners' economic circumstances and marriage. *Demography, 34,* 331–341.

South, S. J. (1985). Economic conditions and the divorce rate: A time series analysis of the postwar United States. *Journal of Marriage and the Family, 47,* 31–40.

South, S. J. (1993). Racial and ethnic differences in the desire to marry. *Journal of Marriage and the Family, 55,* 357–370.

South, S. J. (1995). Do you need to shop around? Age at marriage, spousal alternatives and marital dissolution. *Journal of Family Issues, 16,* 432–449.

South, S. J., & Lloyd, K. M. (1992). Marriage opportunities and family formation: Further implications of imbalanced sex ratios. *Journal of Marriage and the Family, 54,* 440–451.

South, S. J., & Lloyd, K. M. (1995). Spousal alternatives and marital dissolution. *American Sociological Review, 60,* 21–35.

South, S. J., & Spitze, G. (1986). Determinants of divorce over the marital life course. *American Sociological Review, 51,* 583–590.

South, S. J., & Spitze, G. (1994). Housework in marital and nonmarital households. *American Sociological Review, 59,* 327–347.

Spitze, G., & South, S. J. (1985). Women's employment, time expenditure, and divorce. *Journal of Family Issues, 6,* 307–329.

Stacey, J. (1990). *Brave new families: Stories of domestic upheaval in late twentieth century America.* New York: Basic Books.

Stacey, J. (1993). Good riddance to "the family": A response to David Popenoe. *Journal of Marriage and the Family, 55,* 237–251.

Stacey, J. (1996). *In the name of the family: Rethinking family values in a postmodern age.* Boston: Beacon Press.

Swidler, A. (1980). Love and adulthood in American culture. In N. J. Smelser & E. H. Erickson (Eds.), *Themes of work and love in adulthood* (pp. 120–150). Cambridge: Harvard University Press.

Talbot, M. (2000, February 27). A mighty fortress. *New York Times Magazine,* 34–41.

Thompson, W. S. (1929). Population. *American Journal of Sociology, 34.*

Thornton, A. (1985). Changing attitudes towards separation and divorce: Causes and consequences. *American Journal of Sociology, 90,* 856–872.

Thornton, A., Alwin, D. F., & Camburn, D. (1983). Causes and consequences of sex-role attitudes and attitude change. *American Sociological Review, 48,* 211–227.

U.S. Bureau of the Census. (Various years). *Statistical abstract of the United States.* Washington, DC: Government Printing Office.

United Nations International Children's Emergency Fund. (1999). *Progress of nations.* New York: UNICEF.

United Nations International Children's Emergency Fund. (2000). *State of the world's children, 2000.* New York: UNICEF.

United Nations Statistics Division. (2000, May 28). [On-line]. Available: www.un.org/Depts/unsd/social/childbr.htm.

Veroff, J., Douvan, E., & Kulka, R. A. (1981). *The inner American.* New York: Basic Books.

Waite, L. J., & Lillard, L. A. (1991). Children and marital disruption. *American Journal of Sociology, 96,* 930–953.

Wilson, W. J. (1987). *The truly disadvantaged.* Chicago: University of Chicago Press.

World Bank. (1994). *Human development report.* Washington, DC: World Bank.

CHAPTER 9

Bailey, W., & Peterson, R. (1999). Capital punishment, homicide, and deterrence: An assessment of the evidence. In M. D. Smith & M. Zahn (Eds.), *Studying and preventing homicide: Issues and challenges.* Thousand Oaks, CA: Sage Publications.

Bennett, W., DiIulio, J., & Walters, J. (1996). *Body count: Moral poverty and how to win America's war on crime and drugs.* New York: Simon & Schuster.

Castells, M. (1999). *End of millennium.* Malden, MA: Blackwell Publishers.

Cao, L., Adams, A., & Jensen, V. (1997). A test of the black subculture of violence thesis: A research note. *Criminology, 35,* 367–376.

Cloward, R. A., & Ohlin, L. E. (1960). *Delinquency and opportunity: A theory of delinquency gangs.* Glencoe, IL: Free Press.

Cohen, L., & Felson, M. (1979). Social change and crime rate trends: A routine activities approach. *American Sociological Review, 44,* 558–607.

Currie, E. (1985). *Confronting crime: An American challenge.* New York: Pantheon Books.

Currie, E. (1998). *Crime and punishment in America.* New York: Holt.

Currie, E., & Skolnick, J. (1997). *America's problems: Social issues and social policies.* New York: Longman.

Elliot, M. (1994, April 18). Crime and punishment. *Newsweek,* pp. 18–22.

Ellison, C. (1991). An eye for an eye? A note on the southern subculture of violence thesis. *Social Forces, 69,* 1223–1239.

Federal Bureau of Investigation. (1998). *Crime in the United States, 1998* [on-line]. Available: www.fbi.gov/ucr.htm.

Foster, T. (1997). Trafficking in human organs: An emerging form of white-collar crime? *International Journal of Offender Therapy and Comparative Criminology, 41,*(2), 139–150.

Frisby, T. (1998). The rise of organized crime in Russia: Its roots and social significance. *Europe-Asia Studies, 50,* 27–49.

Gartner, R. (1990). The victims of homicide: A temporal and cross-national comparison. *American Sociological Review, 55,* 307–335.

Gottfredson, M., & Hirschi, T. (1990). *A general theory of crime.* Stanford, CA: Stanford University Press.

Gottfredson, M., & Hirschi, T. (1995). National crime control policies. *Society, 32,* 30–36.

Grant, D. S., & Martinez, R. (1997). Crime and the restructuring of the U.S. economy: A reconsideration of the class linkages. *Social Forces, 75,* 769–798.

Gray, M. (1996). Nation in fear. *Maclean's, 109,* 29.

Hirschi, T. (1969). *Causes of delinquency.* Berkeley: University of California Press.

Hirschi, T. (1995). The family. In J. Q. Wilson, & J. Petersilia (Eds.), *Crime* (pp. 121–140). San Francisco: ICS Press.

Kurian, G. T. (1997). *The illustrated book of world rankings.* Armonk, NY: Sharpe Reference.

Louw, A. (1997). Surviving the transition: Trends and perceptions of crime in South Africa. *Social Indicators Research, 41,* 137–168.

Lynch, J. (1995). Crime in international perspective. In J. Q. Wilson & J. Petersilia (Eds.), *Crime* (pp. 11–38). San Francisco: ICS Press.

Lynch, J. (1996). Clarifying divergent estimates of rape from two national surveys. *Public Opinion Quarterly, 60,* 410–430.

Massey, D., & Denton, N. (1993). *American apartheid.* Cambridge: Harvard University Press.

Merton, R. (1938). Social structure and anomie. *American Sociological Review, 6,* 672–682.

Moore, E., & Mills, M. (1990). The neglected victims and unexamined costs of white-collar crime. *Crime and Delinquency, 36,* 408–418.

Newman, G. (Ed.). (1999). *Global report in crime and justice.* New York: Oxford University Press.

O'Keefe, M., & Sela-Amit, M. (1997). An examination of the effects of race/ethnicity and social class in adolescents' exposure to violence. *Journal of Social Service Research, 22,* 53–71.

Ortega, S., et al. (1992). Modernization, age structure, and regional context: A cross-national study of crime. *Sociological Spectrum, 12,* 257–277.

Parker, R. (1989). Poverty, subculture of violence, and type of homicide. *Social Forces, 67,* 983–1007.

Ransdell, E. (1995, August 21). The world's most murderous country. *U.S. News and World Report,* p. 44.

Rennison, C. M. (1998). *Criminal victimization 1998, changes 1997–1998 with trends 1993–98.* U.S. Department of Justice Web site. Available: www.ojp. usdoj.gov/bjs/cvict.htm.

Reynolds, M. O. (1997). *Crime in Texas: 1993 update.* NCPA Policy Background Paper. Dallas.

Sampson, R. (1995). The community. In J. Q. Wilson & J. Petersilia (Eds.), *Crime* (p. 194). San Francisco: ICS Press.

Skolnick, J. (1997). Tough guys. *The American Prospect, 30,* 86–91.

Sorenson, J., Wrinkle, R., & Brewer, V. (October 1999). Capital punishment and deterrence: Examining the effect of execution on murder in Texas. *Crime and Delinquency,* 481–493.

Stephens, G. (1994). The global crime wave. *The Futurist, 28,* 22–28.

Sutherland, E. H. (1940). White-collar criminality. *American Sociological Review, 5,* 1–12.

Sutherland, E. H., & Cressy, D. R. (1978). *Criminology* (10th ed.). Philadelphia: Lippincott.

Thomas, R. (1993, August 16). Suspects have spent lives in trouble. *New York Times,* p. C11.

Title, C., & Meier, R. (1996). Specifying the SES/delinquency relationship. In R. Crutchfield, G. Bridges, & J. Weis (Eds.), *Crime.* Thousand Oaks, CA: Pine Forge Press (originally published in 1990).

Tonry, M. (1995). *Malign neglect—race, crime, and punishment in America.* New York: Oxford Press.

U.S. Bureau of Justice Statistics. (1999). [On-line]. www.ojp.usdoj.gov/bjs.

U.S. Bureau of Justice Statistics. (2000). *Intimate partner violence* [on-line]. Available: www.ojp.usdoj.gov/bjs/abstract/ipv.htm.

Wilson, J. Q. (1975). *Thinking about crime.* New York: Basic Books.

Wilson, J. Q. (1983). *Thinking about crime* (rev. ed.). New York: Random House.

Wilson, J. Q., & Petersilia, J. (Eds.). (1995). *Crime.* San Francisco: ICS Press.

Wolfgang, M. & Ferracuti, F. (1967). *The subculture of violence: Towards an integrated theory of criminology.* London: Travistock.

Wooten, J. (1993, September 13). Lessons of Pop Jordan's death. *Newsweek,* p. 12.

CHAPTER 10

Barry, T. (1999). What's this organization? (WTO): An annotated glossary of terms and concepts about the World Trade Organization [on-line]. Available: www.foreignpolicy-infocus.org/wto.contents.html.

Che ko, A. (2000, April 8). Oskar ony ubezpieczony. *Polityka,* p. 32.

Cohen, R. (2000, January 14). A European identity: Nation-state losing ground. *New York Times,* p. A3.

Collier, R. B. (1999). *Paths toward democracy. The working class and elites in western Europe and South America.* Cambridge: Cambridge University Press.

Dogan, M. (1997). Erosion of confidence in advanced democracies. *Studies in Comparative International Development, 32*(3), 3–29.

Gastil, R. (1989). *Freedom in the world. Political rights and civil liberties, 1988–1989.* New York: Freedom House.

Greenhouse, L. (2000, January 12). Supreme Court shields states from lawsuits on age bias. *New York Times,* p. A1.

Huntington, S. (1991). *The third wave. Democratization in the late twentieth century.* Norman: University of Oklahoma Press.

Karatnycky, A. (1998). *The annual survey of political rights and civil liberties, 1997–1998.* New Brunswick, NJ: Transaction Publishers.

Korzeniewicz, R., & Moran, T. (1997). World-economic trends in the distribution of income, 1965–1992. *American Journal of Sociology, 102,* 1000–1039.

Lyall, S. (2000, January 13). British, under European rights ruling, end ban on openly gay soldiers. *New York Times,* p. A1.

Markoff, J. (1996). *Waves of democracy: Social movements and political change.* Thousand Oaks, CA: Pine Forge Press.

Markoff, J., & Montecinos, V. (1993). The ubiquitous rise of economists. *Journal of Public Policy, 13,* 37–68.

Montero, J. R., Gunther, R., & Torcal, M. (1997). Democracy in Spain: Legitimacy, discontent, disaffection. *Studies in Comparative International Development, 32*(3), 124–160.

New York Times (1999, November 30–December 6). Various articles.

Pharr, S., & Putnam, R. D. (2000). *Disaffected democracies. What's troubling the trilateral countries?* Princeton, NJ: Princeton University Press.

Portes, A., & Rumbaut, R. (1996). *Immigrant America: A portrait.* Berkeley: University of California Press.

Silver, B. (1998). Turning points in workers' militancy in the world automobile industry, 1930s–1960s. In R. Hodson, (Ed.), *Research in the sociology of work, Vol. 6* (pp. 41–69). Greenwich, CT: JAI Press.

Smith, J. (1995). Transnational political processes and the human rights movement. *Research in Social Movements, Conflicts, and Change, 18,* 185–219.

Smith, J. (1997). Characteristics of the modern transnational social movement sector. In J. Smith, C. Chatfield, & R. Pagnucco, (Eds.), *Transnational social movements and global politics: Solidarity beyond the state* (pp. 42–58). Syracuse, NY: Syracuse University Press.

Smith, J. (2000). Globalizing resistance: The battle of Seattle and the future of social movements. Paper presented to the Workshop on Contentious Politics, Columbia University. [On-line]. Available: www.sociology.columbia.edu/conpol/feb28.htm.

Tarrow, S. (1998a). *Power in movement: Social movements, collective action, and politics.* New York: Cambridge University Press.

Tarrow, S. (1998b). Building a composite polity: Popular contention in the European Union. Cornell University Institute for European Studies working paper 98.3.

te Brake, W. (1998). *Shaping history: Ordinary people in European politics, 1500–1700.* Berkeley: University of California Press.

Tilly, C. (1995). Globalization threatens labor's rights. *International Labor and Working-Class History, 47,* 1–23.

Tilly, C. (1997). *Roads from past to future.* Lanham, MD: Rowman & Littlefield.

United Nations High Commissioner on Refugees. (2000). Available: www.unhcr. ch/statist/99oview/toc.htm.

U.S. Department of Commerce. (1975). S*tatistical abstract of the United States.* Washington, DC: Government Printing Office.

U.S. Department of Commerce. (1974–1999). *Statistical abstract of the United States.* Washington, DC: Government Printing Office.

U.S. Immigration and Naturalization Service. (2000). *Immigration fact sheet* [online]. Available: www.iminfo.com/library/articles/immfacts/html.

Wallach, L., & Sforza, M. (1999). *Whose trade organization? Corporate globalization and the erosion of democracy.* Washington, DC: Public Citizen.

Wolman, L. (1975). *The growth of American trade unions, 1880–1923.* New York: Arno Press.

Zulfacar, M. (1998). *Afghan immigrants in the USA and Germany. A comparative study of the use of ethnic social capital.* Münster, Lit Verlag.

CHAPTER 11

Accomplices to genocide. (1995, August 7). *The New Republic,* p. 7.

Allen, T. (Ed.). (1995). *Offerings at the wall.* Atlanta: Turner Publishing.

Anan, K. (2000). *We the peoples: The role of the United Nations in the 21st century: Millennium report of the Secretary-General of the United Nations.* New York: United Nations.

Burg, S. (1994). Why Yugoslavia fell apart. In M. Goldman (Ed.), *Russia, the Eurasian republics, and Central/Eastern Europe (*pp. 291–297). Sluice Dock, Guilford, CT: Dushkin Publishing Group.

Crossette, B. (2000, May 10). One more Africa mediating effort for UN traveling mission. *New York Times,* p. A1.

Goldman, M. (Ed.) (1988). *The Soviet Union and Eastern Europe* (2nd ed.). Sluice Dock, Guilford, CT: Dushkin Publishing Group.

Goldman, M. (Ed.) (1994). *Russia, the Eurasian republics, and Central/Eastern Europe.* Sluice Dock, Guilford, CT: Dushkin Publishing Group.

Human Rights Watch. (1999). A village destroyed: War crimes in Kosovo. *Human Rights Watch Report.* New York.

Human Rights Watch. (2000). Kosovo: Rape as a weapon of "ethnic cleansing." *Human Rights Watch Report.* New York.

Kaplan, R. (1993). *Balkan ghosts: A journey through history.* New York: Vintage.

Sivard, R. L. (1999). *World military and social expenditures 1999* (19th ed.). Washington, DC: World Priorities.

United Nations International Children's Emergency Fund. (1996). *Report on the impact of armed conflict on children.* New York: UNICEF.

United Nations International Children's Emergency Fund. (2000). *The progress of nations.* New York: UNICEF.

CHAPTER 12

Bellah, R., et al. (1985). *Habits of the heart: Individualism and commitment in American life.* Berkeley: University of California Press.

Boyett, J. P., & Conn, H. P. (1991). *Workplace 2000: The revolution shaping American business.* New York: Plume Books.

Carter, S. L. (1998). *Civility: Manners, morals, and etiquette of democracy.* New York: HarperPerennial.

Consumer Federation of America. (1998). *Card issuers hike fees and rates to bolster profits* [on-line]. Available: www.consumerfed.org.

Consumers Union. (2000). [On-line]. Available: www.consumersunion.org.

The downsizing of America. (1996). New York: NewYork Times Books.

The future of work: Career evolution. (2000, January 29). *The Economist,* 89–92.

Gans, H. (1988). *Middle American individualism: Political participation and liberal democracy.* Oxford: Oxford University Press.

Gordon, D. M. (1996). *Fat and mean: The corporate squeeze of working Americans and the myth of managerial downsizing.* New York: Free Press.

Kalleberg, A. L., Knoke, D., Marsden, P. V., & Spaeth, J.L. (1996). *Organizations in America: Analyzing their structures and human resource practices.* Thousand Oaks, CA: Sage.

Manning, R. (1999). *Credit card debt imposes huge costs on many college students* [on-line]. Available : www.consumerfed.org.

Organization of Economic Cooperation and Development. (2000). Table 6b. Annual number of hours worked per person. [On-line]. Available: www.ilo.org.

Phillips, K. (1991). *The politics of rich and poor: Wealth and the American electorate in the Reagan aftermath.* New York: HarperPerennial.

CHAPTER 13

American Automobile Manufacturers Association. (1996). *Motor vehicle facts and figures.* Washington, DC: AAMA.

Bell, M. M. (1998). *An invitation to environmental sociology.* Thousand Oaks, CA: Pine Forge Press.

Brower, M., & Leon W. (1999). *The consumer's guide to effective environmental choices.* Boston: Union of Concerned Scientists.

Brown, L., Renner, M., & Halweil, B. (1999). *Vital Signs 1999: The environmental trends that are shaping our future.* New York: Norton.

Bryant, D., Nielsen, D., & Tangley, L. (1997). *The last frontier: Forests: Ecosystems and economics on the edge.* Washington, DC: World Resources Institute.

Carbon Dioxide Information Analysis Center, Environmental Sciences Division, Oak Ridge National Laboratory. (November 1997). 1995 estimates of CO_2 emissions from fossil fuel burning and cement manufacturing based on the United Nations energy statistics and the U.S. Bureau of Mines cement manufacturing data. ORNL/DIAD-25, NDP-303, Oak Ridge, TN.

Cochrane, W. (1958). *Farm prices: Myth and reality.* Minnesota: University of Minnesota Press.

Food and Agricultural Organization of the United Nations. (1998). *State of the world's forests 1997.* Rome: FAO.

Hochschild, A. (1997). *The time bind: When work becomes home and home becomes work.* New York: Metropolitan Books.

Inglehart, R. (1995). Public support for environmental protection: Objective problems and subjective values in 43 societies. *PS: Political Science and Politics, 28*(1): 57–72.

Katz, P. (1994.) *The new urbanism: Toward an architecture of community.* New York: McGraw-Hill.

Korten, D. (1995). *When corporations rule the world.* West Hartford, CT: Kumarian.

MacKensie, J. J., Dower, R. C., & Chen, D.D.T., (1992). *The going rate: What it really costs to drive.* Washington, DC: World Resources Institute.

Meadows, D. (1999, April 15). The Dow passes ten thousand—hooray? *The Global Citizen.*

National Resources Conservation Service, U.S. Department of Agriculture (January 2000). *Percent changed in developed land area, 1982–1997.* Washington, DC: Government Printing Office.

Schor, J. (1998). *The overspent American: Upscaling, downshifting, and the new consumer.* New York: Basic Books.

Schor, J. (1992). *The overworked American: The unexpected decline of leisure.* New York: Basic Books.

Schnaiberg, A. (1980). *The environment: From surplus to scarcity.* New York and Oxford: Oxford University Press.

Stevenson, R. W. (2000, January 19). Fed reports family gains from economy. *New York Times.*

United Nations Development Program. (1999). *Human development report 1999.* New York: Oxford University Press.

United Nations Educational, Scientific, and Cultural Organization. (1999). Culture and communication. *UNESCO statistical yearbook 1999.* (Table IV.S.2). Geneva: United Nations. [On-line]. Available: unescostat.unesco.org/en/stats/stats0.htm.

United Nations Population Division. (1996). *1993 annual populations* (rev.) New York: United Nations.

Veblen, T. (1899/1967). *The theory of the leisure class.* New York: Funk and Wagnalls.

World Resources Institute. (2000). *Many of the Earth's forests have been cleared or degraded* [on-line]. Available: www.wri.org/powerpoints/trends/sld042.htm.

World Resources Institute. (2000). *Paper use is growing worldwide* [on-line]. Available: www.wri.org/wri/trends/paperwk.html.

World Resources Institute. (2000). *Per capita CO_2 emissions are small in developing countries* [on-line]. Available: www.wri.org/powerpoints/trends/sld030.htm.

World Resources Institute. (2000). *Motor vehicle use is highest in developed countries* [on-line]. Available: www.wri.org/powerpoints/trends/sld027.htm.

World Resources Institute. (2000, July 24). *Fragmenting forests: The loss of large frontier forests* [on-line]. Available: www.wri.org./wri/trends/fragment.html.

CHAPTER 14

Barlow, R. (1994). Population growth and economic growth: Some more correlations. *Population and Development Review, 20*: 153–165.

Bongaarts, J. (1992). Population growth and global warming. *Population and Development Review, 18*, 299–319.

Bongaarts, J. (1994). Population policy options in the developing world. *Science, 263*, 771–776.

Bongaarts, J. (1996a). Global trends in AIDS mortality. *Population and Development Review, 22*, 21–45.

Bongaarts, J. (1996b). Population pressure and the food supply system in the developing world. *Population and Development Review, 22,* 483–503.

Brown, L. R., et al. (1997). *State of the world.* New York: Norton.

Brown, L. R., et al. (2000). *State of the world.* New York: Norton.

Caldwell, J. C. (2000). Rethinking the African AIDS epidemic. *Population and Development Review, 26*, 117–135.

Coale, A. J. (1974). The history of the human population. *Scientific American, 231*, 40–51.

Coale, A. J., & Watkins, S. C. (Eds.). (1986). *The decline of fertility in Europe.* Princeton, NJ: Princeton University Press.

Dyson, T. (1994). Population growth and food production: Recent global and regional trends. *Population and Development Review, 20*, 397–411.

Ehrlich, P. R. (1968). *The population bomb.* New York: Ballantine Books.

Ehrlich, P. R., & Ehrlich, A. H. (1990). *The population explosion.* New York: Simon & Schuster.

Leach, M., & Fairhead, J. (2000). Challenging neo-Malthusian deforestation analyses in West Africa's dynamic forest landscapes. *Population and Development Review, 29*: 17–43.

National Academy of Sciences. (1986). *Population growth and economic development: Policy questions.* Washington DC: National Academy Press.

Preston, S. H. (1980). Causes and consequences of mortality declines in less developed countries during the twentieth century. In R. A. Easterlin (Ed.), *Population and economic change in developing countries,* pp. 289–360. Chicago: University of Chicago Press.

Preston, S. H., & Haines, M. R. (1991). *Fatal years: Child mortality in late nineteenth century America.* Princeton, NJ: Princeton University Press.

Scherr, S. J., & Yadav, S. (1996). *Land degradation in the developing world: Implications for food, agriculture, and the environment to 2020.* International Food Policy Research Institute Food Agriculture and the Environment Working Paper 14.

Schofield, R., Rehrer, D., & Bideau, A. (Eds.). (1991). *The decline of mortality in Europe.* New York: Oxford University Press.

Science summit on world population: A joint statement by 58 of the world's scientific academies. (1994). Reprinted in *Population and Development Review, 20,* 233–239.

Sen, A. (1981). *Poverty and famines: An essay on entitlement and deprivation.* New York: Oxford University Press.

Simon, J. L. (1981). *The ultimate resource.* Princeton, NJ: Princeton University Press.

Smil, V. (1994). How many people can the earth feed? *Population and Development Review, 20,* 255–292.

The Royal Society and the National Academy of Sciences. (1997). On sustainable consumption. Reprinted in *Population and Development Review, 23,* 683–686.

UNAIDS and WHO. (1999). *AIDS epidemic update: December 1999.* Geneva: Joint United Nations Programme on HIV/AIDS and World Health Organization.

United Nations. (1999). *World population prospects: The 1998 revision.* New York: United Nations.

United Nations. (1999a). *United Nations 1998 revision of the world population estimates and projections* [on-line]. Available: www.popin.org/pop1998/default. htm contents.

U.S. Census Bureau. (2000). [On-line]. Available: www.census.gov.

World Health Organization. (1991). *The world health report 1999: Making a difference.* Geneva: World Health Organization.

CHAPTER 15

Chege, S. (June 1999). Donors shift more aid to NGOs. In *Africa Recovery.* New York: UN Department of Public Information. [On-line]. Available: www.igc. org/globalpolicy/ngos/issues/chege.htm.

Cost effective HIV treatment. (1999). *International Journal of Public Health* [on-line]. Available: www.who.int/bulletin/news/vol.77no.9/hivtreatment.htm.

Daily Nation. (2000, May 11). MP's win motion on guns and bodyguards. [On-line]. Available: www.nationaudio.com/News/DailyNation/11052000/News/ News58.html.

Greenfield, K. T. (2000, April 17). Rwandan sorrow. *Time.*

Health agency says fake drugs killed 500. *Nando Times.* (1997). [On-line]. Available: www.techserver.com/newsroom/ntn/health/112897/health8_2589_ body.htm.

Lederberg, J. (1996). Infectious disease—A threat to global health and security. *Journal of the American Medical Association,* 417–419.

Randoli, M. (2000, June 28). Dutch to freeze aid to Kenya. *Daily Nation.* [On-line]. Available: www.nationaudio.com/News/DailyNation/28062000/ News/News73.html.

Strouse, J. (2000, April 16). How to give away $21.8 billion. *New York Times Magazine.*

UNAIDS. (2000a). *AIDS becoming Africa's top human security issue, UN warns.* Geneva: Joint United Nations Programme on HIV/AIDS (UNAIDS) press release, January 10, 2000. [On-line]. Available: www.unaids.org/whatsnew/press/eng/ny10100.html.

UNAIDS. (2000b). *UNAIDS/WHO hail consensus on use of cotrimoxazole for prevention of HIV-related infections in Africa.* Geneva: Joint United Nations Programme on HIV/AIDS (UNAIDS) press release, April 5, 2000. [On-line]. Available: www.unaids.org/whatsnew/press/eng/geneva050400.html.

UNAIDS. (2000c). *New public/private sector effort initiated to accelerate access to HIV/AIDS care and treatment in developing countries.* Geneva: Joint United Nations Programme on HIV/AIDS (UNAIDS) press release, May 11, 2000. [On-line]. Available: www.unaids.org/whatsnew/press/eng/geneva110500.html.

UNAIDS. (2000d). *New UN report estimates over one-third of today's 15 year-olds will die of AIDS in worst-affected countries.* Geneva: Joint United Nations Programme on HIV/AIDS (UNAIDS), press release, June 27, 2000. [On-line]. Available: www.unaids.org/whatsnew/press/eng/durban260600.html.

UNAIDS. (2000e). *AIDS epidemic threatens WSSD goals, UNAIDS says.* Geneva: Joint United Nations Programme on HIV/AIDS (UNAIDS) press release, June 29, 2000. [On-line]. Available: www.unaids.org/whatsnew/press/eng/geneva290600.html.

World Health Organization. (1998). *World Health Day highlights scandal of 600,000 maternal deaths each year.* New York: WHO/336 press release, April 1988. [On-line]. Available: www.who.int/inf-pr-1998/en/pr98-33.html.

World Health Organization. (1999a). *Removing obstacles to healthy development. WHO report on infectious diseases.* New York: WHO.

World Health Organization. (1999b). *Pasteur Merieux Connaught donates 50 million doses of polio vaccine for war-torn countries.* New York: WHO/55 press release, October 11, 1999. [On-line]. Available: www.who.int/inf-pr-1999/en/pr99-55.html.

World Health Organization. (2000). *Final push in campaign to eradicate polio. WHO and UNICEF issue year 2000 appeal to leaders of 30 affected nations.* New York: WHO/01 press release, January 6, 2000. [On-line]. Available: www.who.int/inf-pr-2000/en/pr2000-01.html.

World Health Organization. (2000a). *Drug resistance threatens to reverse medical progress.* New York: WHO/41 press release, June 12, 2000. [On-line]. Available: www.who.int/emc/WHO_docs/whoindex.html.

CHAPTER 16

Annan, K. (2000). *We the peoples: The role of the United Nations in the 21st century. Millennium report of the Secretary-General of the United Nations.* New York: United Nations.

Bornschier, V., & Chase-Dunn, C. (1985). *Transnational corporations and underdevelopment.* New York: Praeger.

Bradshaw, Y. W., & Wallace, M. (1996). *Global inequalities.* Thousand Oaks, CA: Pine Forge Press.

Covey, S. R. (1999). *Living the 7 habits: Stories of courage and inspiration.* New York: Simon & Schuster.

Lamb, D. (1988). *The Arabs: Journeys beyond the mirage.* New York: Vintage Books.

Ndegwa, S. (1996). *The two faces of civil society: NGOs and politics in Africa.* West Hartford, CT: Kumarian Press.

United Nations International Children's Emergency Fund. (1999). *The progress of nations.* New York: UNICEF.

APPENDIX

Schutt, R. K. (1999). *Investigating the social world: The process and practice of research* (2nd ed.). Thousand Oaks, CA: Pine Forge Press.

Smith, R. (1997). *Writing technical papers.* La Jolla, CA: UCSD Extension Corporate Education.

REFERENCES FOR TOPICAL ESSAYS

THE GLOBALIZATION OF TASTE

Beyond Beef Coalition (2000). [On-line]. Available: www.mcspotlight.org/campaigns/countries/usa/beyond_beef.html.

Braudel, F. (1974). *Capitalism and material life 1400–1800.* London: Fontana.

Elias, N. (1978). *The civilizing process: The history of manners.* New York: Arisen.

Fiddes, N. (1991). *Meat: A natural symbol.* London: Routledge.

Friedman, T. (2000). *The Lexus and the olive tree.* New York: Doubleday & Company.

Harris, M. (1986). *Good to eat.* London: Allen & Unwin.

Perkins Gilman, C. (1899/1966). *Women and economics: A study of the economic relation between men and women as a factor in social evolution.* New York: Harper & Row.

Ritzer, G. (1993). *The McDonaldization of society: An investigation into the changing character of contemporary social life.* Thousand Oaks, CA: Pine Forge Press.

Vidal, J. (1997). *McLibel: Burger culture on trial.* New York: Beacon Books.

HOW CULTURE SHAPES SCHOOLING

Bourdieu, P. (1988). *Homo academicus.* London: Polity Press.

Connolly, C. (1938/1973). *Enemies of promise.* London: Andre Deutsch.

Inkeles, A., & Sirowy, L. J. (1983). Convergent and divergent trends in national educational systems. *Social Forces, 62,* 303–333.

Jackson, P. W., Boostrom, R. E., & Hansen, D. T. (1993). *The moral life of schools.* San Francisco: Jossey-Bass.

Meyer, J. W., Nagel, J., & Snyder, C. W., Jr. (1993). The expansion of mass education in Botswana: Local and world society perspectives. *Comparative Education Review, 37,* 454–475.

Soares, J. A. (1999). *The decline of privilege: The modernization of Oxford University.* Stanford, CA: Stanford University Press.

Stevenson, H. W., & Stigler, J. W. (1992). *The learning gap: Why our schools are failing and what we can learn from Japanese and Chinese education.* New York: Summit.

Toure, S. (1965). Education and social progress. In L. G. Cowan, J. O'Connell, & D. G. Scanlon (Eds.), *Education and nation-building in Africa* (pp. 125–140). New York: Praeger.

BIOPIRACY AND GENE THEFT

ActionAid. (2000). *Crops and robbers. Biopiracy and the patenting of staple food crops* [on-line]. Available: www.actionaid.org.

Alvares, C. (1997). An Indian village bucks GATT over control of genetic resources. *Third World Resurgence, 84,* 11–12.

Center for International Environmental Law. (1999, November 4). U.S. Patent Office admits error, cancels patent on sacred 'Ayahuasca' plant. [On-line press release]. Available: www.biotechinfo.net/ayahuasca.html.

Rural Advancement Foundation International. (1999, December 1). Biopiracy project in Chiapas, Mexico denounced by Mayan indigenous groups. [On-line news release]. Available: www.rafi.org.

Shiva, V. (1997). *Biopiracy. The plunder of nature and knowledge.* Boston: South End Press.

SEX AS A GLOBAL COMMODITY

Bishop, R., & Robinson, L. S. (1998). *Night market: Sexual cultures and the Thai economic miracle.* New York: Routledge.

Davidson, J. O. (1998). *Prostitution, power, and freedom.* Ann Arbor: University of Michigan Press.

Larvie, P. (1999). Natural born targets: Male hustlers and AIDS prevention in urban Brazil. In P. Aggleton (Ed.), *Men who sell sex: International perspectives on male prostitution and HIV/AIDS* (pp. 159–177). Philadelphia: Temple University Press.

Once-hidden slave trade a growing U.S. problem. (2000, April 2). *New York Times.* [Obtained on-line through the listserve CISNEWS@cis.org, run by the Center for Immigration Studies, center@cis.org.]

Schein, L. (1997). The consumption of color and the politics of white skin in post-Mao China. In R. N. Lancaster & M. di Leonardo (Eds.), *The gender/sexuality reader: Culture, history, political economy* (pp. 473–486). New York: Routledge.

Tolentino, R. B. (1999). Bodies, letters, catalogs: Filipinas in transnational space. In S. Goek-Lin Lilm, L. E. Smith, & W. Dissanayake (Eds.), *Transnational Asia Pacific: Gender, culture, and the public sphere* (pp. 43–68). Urbana: University of Illinois Press.

Vargas, Z. (1998). Rank and file: Historical perspectives on Latino/a workers in the U.S. In *The Latino studies reader: Culture, economy, and society* (pp. 243–256). Malden, MA: Blackwell Publishers.

Watanabe, K. (1995). Trafficking in women's bodies, then and now: The issue of military comfort women. *Peace & Change, 20*, 501–514.

ACTIVISTS CRUSADE AGAINST SWEATSHOPS

Asher, M., & Barr, J. (2000, May 4). Three schools lose Nike millions: Michigan, Oregon, Brown punished over sweatshops. Reprinted from *Washington Post* in *The Capital Times* (Madison, WI), p1.

Bonacich, E., & Appelbaum, R. (2000). *Behind the label.* Berkeley: University of California Press.

Gereffi, G. (1994). The organization of buyer-driven global commodity chains: How U.S. retailers shape overseas production networks. In G. Gereffi & M. Korzeniewicz (Eds.), *Commodity chains and global capitalism* (pp. 95–122). Westport, CT: Praeger.

Greenhouse, S. (2000, April 29). Anti-sweatshop group invites input by apparel makers. *New York Times,* p. A9.

Greider, W. (1997). *One world, ready or not.* New York: Simon & Schuster.

Guidry, J., Kennedy, M., & Zald, M. (Eds.). *Social movements in the transnational public sphere.* University of Michigan Press, forthcoming.

Keck, M., & Sikkink, K. (1998). *Activists beyond borders.* Ithaca, NY: Cornell University Press.

Korzeniewicz, M. (1994). Commodity chains and marketing strategies: Nike and the global athletic footwear industry. In G. Gereffi & M. Korzeniewicz (Eds.), *Commodity chains and global capitalism* (pp. 247–266). Westport, CT: Praeger.

Ross, A. (Ed.). (1997). *No sweat: Fashion, free trade and the rights of garment workers.* Verso.

Sneider, J. (2000, May 16). Good propaganda, bad economics. *New York Times,* p. A23.

Photo Credits

Chapter 1

Page 1, AFP/CORBIS; page 5, John Coletti/Stock Boston; page 13, from top left: Mark Edwards/Still Pictures; Danny Lehman/CORBIS; Heldur Netocny/Panos Pictures; A. Ramey/Stock Boston; page 18, Adrian Arbib; page 22, Peter Menzel/Stock Boston; page 24, Earl Gritton/University of Wisconsin; page 26, top to bottom: David H. Wells/CORBIS; AFP/CORBIS; Reuters NewsMedia Inc./CORBIS; *Topical essay*, pages 37–38, Tracey Dawson.

Chapter 2

Page 41, Jean-Claude LeJeune/Stock Boston; page 44, from top: Bettmann/CORBIS; Schenectady Museum, Hall of Electrical History Foundation/CORBIS; Michael Hayman/Stock Boston; page 49, from top: Adam Woolfitt/CORBIS; Phyllis Picardi/Index Stock; page 53, both, Sean Sprague/Stock Boston; page 56, Jean-Claude LeJeune/Stock Boston; page 63, David Mangurian/Inter-American Development Bank; page 66, Susan Van Etten/Stock Boston; *Topical essay*, page 80, from top: George Bellerose/Stock Boston; Robert Fried/Stock Boston; AFP/CORBIS.

Chapter 3

Page 85, Michael Dwyer/Stock Boston; page 89, from top left: Hazel Hankin/Stock Boston; Bob Daemmrich/Stock Boston; Bob Daemmrich/Stock Boston; page 94, from top: Michael Dwyer/Stock Boston; Gale Zucker/Stock Boston; Michael Dwyer/Stock Boston; page 101, Spencer Grant/Stock Boston; page 105, Michael Dwyer/Stock Boston.

Chapter 4

Page 117, Claus Guglberger; page 118, Ionad an Bhlascaoid/Great Blasket Centre; page 120, from top: United Nations; Adrian Arbib; Rhoda Sidney/Stock Boston; page 124, Jan Halaska/Index Stock; page 129, from top: Lindsay Hebberd/CORBIS, both; Claus Guglberger; center; Bob Daemmrich/Stock Boston, bottom; page 133, from left: Library of Congress, Prints & Photographs Division, FSA/OWI Collection; SW Production/Index Stock; *Topical essays,* page 150, Don Stevenson/Index Stock; page 153, Elizabeth Crews; page 154, James L. Amos/CORBIS; page 155, Les Kurtz; page 159, Les Kurtz.

Chapter 5

Page 161, Al Seib/Los Angeles Times; page 164, from top: Laura Kleinhenz; Sergio Dorantes/CORBIS; CORBIS Photo Disk; page 167, Al Seib/Los Angeles Times; page 173, all: Library of Congress, Prints & Photographs Division, Detroit Publishing Company Collection; page 177, from left: Mike Mazzaschi/Stock Boston; Kirsten Stoller; page 178, Hulton Getty Picture Collection; page 182, Lionel Delevingne/Stock Boston; *Topical essay,* page 198, all: Adrian Arbib.

Chapter 6

Page 205, Michael Weisbrot/Stock Boston; page 206, Adrian Arbib; page 213, from top left: Susan J. Borges; Michael Weisbrot/Stock Boston; Spencer Grant/Stock Boston; Judy Gelles/Stock Boston; page 219, left, Hulton Getty Picture Collection; right, AP/Wide World Photos; page 221, from top: Bettmann/CORBIS; Marion Post Wolcott, Library of Congress, Prints & Photographs Division, FSA/OWI Collection; Oliver Pierce/Stock Boston; page 226, Elizabeth Crews/Stock Boston; page 232, Ellis Herwig/Stock Boston.

Chapter 7
Page 239, Stephanie Maze/CORBIS; page 240, both: Christine Osborne/CORBIS; page 245, both: Library of Congress Prints & Photographs Division, FSA/OWI Collection; page 246, from top: Hulton Deutsch Collection/CORBIS; Charles E. Rotkin/CORBIS; page 250, from top left: Library of Congress Prints & Photographs Division, FSA/OWI Collection; CORBIS; Stephanie Maze/CORBIS; page 253, Spencer Grant/Stock Boston; page 255, from top: The Purcell Team/CORBIS; Liba Taylor/CORBIS; *Topical essay,* page 276, Peter Turnley/CORBIS; page 279, AFP/CORBIS.

Chapter 8
Page 281, Stephanie Maze/CORBIS; page 284, Susi Speck Mayor/Alternistock; Russ Schlepman/CORBIS; Lawrence Migdale/Stock Boston; page 285, from left: Morton Beebe/CORBIS; Stephanie Maze/CORBIS; page 292, Liba Taylor/CORBIS; page 301, from top left: Dean Conger/CORBIS; Sean Sprague/Stock Boston; Hiram Ruiz/USCR; Harry Wilkes/Stock Boston; page 310, from left: Annie Griffiths Belt/CORBIS; United Nations.

Chapter 9
Page 319, Rodney White/AP/Wide World Photos; page 329, Fernando Llano/AP/Wide World Photos; page 332, Elwin Williamson/Index Stock; page 334, Ed Kashi/CORBIS; page 335, Jana Birchum; page 337, from top left: Daniel Portnoy/AP/Wide World Photos; Michael S. Yamashita/CORBIS; Saurabh Das/AP/Wide World Photos; Annie Griffiths Belt/CORBIS; page 243: Rodney White/AP/Wide World Photos.

Chapter 10
Page 353, AFP/CORBIS; page 355, Eric Draper/AP/Wide World Photos; page 362, top: Mike Mazzaschi/Stock Boston; bottom: Reed Saxon/AP/Wide World Photos; page 370, The Center for Commercial Free Public Education; page 375, from top: Gael Cornier/AP/Wide World Photos; Nati Harnik/AP/Wide World Photos; Judy Gelles/Stock Boston; page 382, Katherine Pope; page 387, from top: Dennis Cook/AP/Wide World Photos; AFP/CORBIS; *Topical essay,* page 394, left: Alison Wright/CORBIS; right: AFP/CORBIS; page 398, Harvey Finkle.

At Issue
Page 401, Sean Sprague/Stock Boston.

Chapter 11
Pages 402–403, AFP/CORBIS; page 409, from top: Andrew Testa/Panos Pictures; AFP/CORBIS; page 412, from left: Reuters LTD; Steve Raymer/CORBIS; page 417, from top: Reuters NewsMedia, Inc./CORBIS; AFP/CORBIS; page 418, AFP/CORBIS; page 419, from left: United Nations Photo, Reuters NewsMedia, Inc./CORBIS.

Chapter 12
Pages 420–421, Lawrence Manning/CORBIS; page 423, from top left: Dennis O'Clair/Index Stock; Catherine Karnow/CORBIS; Rob Crandall/Stock Boston; Matthew Borkoski/Stock Boston; page 425, from top: Rob Nelson/Stock Boston; Owen Franken/CORBIS; Bettmann/CORBIS; page 436, from left: Elizabeth Crews/Stock Boston; Spencer Grant/Stock Boston.

Chapter 13
Pages 440–441, (large photo) Michael Dwyer/Stock Boston; (inset) Peter Southwick/Stock Boston; page 448, from left, Martin Rogers/CORBIS, Jan Butchofsky-Houser/CORBIS; page 456, from top left, clockwise: CORBIS; Jonathan Blair/CORBIS; Vince Strano/CORBIS; Michael S. Yamashita/CORBIS.

Chapter 14

Pages 460–461, all: Jean-Claude LeJeune/Stock Boston; page 468, from top: Library of Congress Prints & Photographs Division, American Memory Collection, FSA/OWI; Howard Davies/CORBIS; Rick Strange/Index Stock; page 474, from top: AFP/CORBIS; AFP/CORBIS; Adrian Arbib; page 479, from top left: Paul Griffin/Stock Boston; David R. Austen/Stock Boston; Kevin R. Morris/CORBIS; Sean Sprague/Stock Boston.

Chapter 15

Pages 482–483, (large photo) Sean Sprague/Stock Boston; (inset) Anne Drobish/Moscow-Pullman Daily News, AP/Wide World Photos; page 489, from left: Bror Karlsson/Panos Pictures; Peter Turnley/CORBIS; page 490, Lenny Ignelzi/AP/Wide World Photos; page 495, Reuters NewsMedia/CORBIS; page 496, from top: Edmund Neil/Eye Ubiquitous/CORBIS, Paul Almasy/CORBIS; page 497, from left: Tim Page/CORBIS, Francene Keery/Stock Boston, Bob Daemmrich/Stock Boston.

Chapter 16

Page 502, from top: Sean Sprague/Stock Boston; Penny Tweedie/Panos Pictures; Judy Gelles/Stock Boston; page 503, left (top to bottom) Jim Sugar Photography/CORBIS; Peter Turnley/CORBIS; top right: D. Robert Franz/CORBIS.

Glossary/Index

acculturation, 136, 212
"Activists Crusade against Sweatshops" (Seidman), 393–399
affirmative action programs, 223
Afghanistan refugees, 363, 364
Africa
  civil wars in, 404, 411–412, 414–416
  conquest and colonization of, 215–218, 356
  economic development in, 15–16, 476, 509
  ethnic conflict in, 7, 205, 215–217, 403
  family size in, 478
  famine in, 472–473
  fertility rates in, 290
  healthcare issues in, 486, 488
  HIV/AIDS epidemic in, 309, 494–495
  income inequality in, 190–192
  life expectancy in, 467
  map of, 521
  perspective on traditional culture of, 24–25
  population growth in, 463, 464, 470
African Americans, 220
  child poverty of, 28
  criminal behavior of, 328
  impact of deindustrialization on, 222–224
  income inequality of, 221, 222, 260
  marriage patterns of, 288, 298, 307–308
  nonmarital childbearing of, 294
  residential segregation of, 224–225
  slavery and segregation of, 219–221
  status of contemporary race relations, 221–226
age
  and criminal behavior, 326–327, 340, 344
  and divorce, 297
  at first marriage, 286–288
age distribution, effects of changing, 103
agricultural societies, 169
  gender roles in, 244–246
  inequality in, 171–172
  role in evolution of global species, 209
  social cohesion in, 51–52
  See also low-income nations

AIDS epidemic. *See* HIV/AIDS epidemic
Albanian refugees, 410, 411
alternative causes, examining, 104–106
altruistic suicide, 54–55
American Association for Labor Legislation, 249
American Federation of Labor, 249
AmeriCares, 510
Amish, 127, 212
Amnesty International, 383, 386
Annan, Kofi, 414, 494, 506
anomic suicide, 55, 70
anomie: normlessness and moral drift, 53
  and crime, 332–333
anthropological studies, sociologists' use of, 121–122
antibiotics, misuse of, 384, 490
apartheid, 217–218
ASA Style Guide, 518
Asia
  economic crisis in, 4
  economic growth in, 15, 184–186, 189–190, 193
  impact on U.S. market, 424
  income inequality in, 189–190
  life expectancy in, 467
  map of, 522
  population growth in, 463, 464, 470
Asian Americans, 230
assimilation: process by which two or more formerly separate and distinct racial or ethnic groups merge into a single group, 212–214
  of African Americans, 219, 223
  of European immigrants in U.S., 226–229
  of present-day immigrants to U.S., 229–232
  segmented, 231–232
  in South Africa, 217–218
  See also race and ethnicity
AT&T, 2
attitudes, influence on behavior, 300–302
Audubon Society, 461

automobile
and credit card debt, 435
as environmental issue, 443, 450, 451, 453

baby boom, 467
Banda, Hastings, 12
Bangladesh
economic challenges of, 476
famine in, 473, 475
Becker, Gary, 304
behavior, influence on attitudes, 300–302
beliefs: statements about the nature of reality
that incorporate information accumu-
lated through the senses and the knowledge that comes from others and from
thinking about that information, 125–126
Bengal famine, 473
bibliography, preparing, 518
Bill and Melinda Gates Foundation, 495, 508
biochemical terrorism, 489
"Biopiracy and Gene Theft" (McMichael),
197–204
birth rates
in developed countries, 467
in developing countries, 469–471,
477–480
impact on population growth, 464–465
total fertility rates, 290–293
Blasket Islands, 117
"Body Ritual Among the Nacirema" (Miner),
130
Boehringer Ingelheim, 495
Boeing, 455
Bosnia-Herzegovina, 407, 410. *See also*
Yugoslavia
Botswana, HIV/AIDS epidemic in, 494
Brandeis, Louis, 249
Brazil, income inequality in, 189, 190
Brint, Steven, 149–154
Bristol-Myers Squibb, 495
Brown, Lester, 461, 471
Brundtland, Gro Harlem, 240
Buchanan, Patrick, 18
bureaucracy: large hierarchical organizations
governed by explicit rules and regulations,
63–64
burnout subculture, and suicide, 69–70
Bushnell, Prudence, 486
Byrd, James, 206

calculability, in rationalization, 65
Calvin, John, 48
Calvinism, 48–50

Cambodia, 403
Canada, political fragmentation in, 16
capital intensive: referring to modes of production that rely on machines that
require large investments of capital (i.e.,
lots of money) to develop and purchase,
172
capitalism: industrial economic system based
on private ownership of the means of production, 47
international, 58–63
religious foundations of, 48–50
Weber on, 48–51
See also industrialization
carbon dioxide emissions, 444, 543
CARE, 510
carrying capacity, Earth's, 471–472
Carter, Jimmy, 25
Caulder, Lauren, 161, 165, 180
causal relationship: relationship between
variables in which one causes the other,
97–98
causation, in scientific method, 88–90
Ceausescu, Nicolae, 27
Center for Democracy and Technology, 14
CFC production, decline in, 458–459
change
cultural, 139–141
factors involved in societal, 25–28
See also social change, positive
Chechnya, 488
childbearing
and cohabitation, 289, 294
and divorce, 297, 298
impact of economic conditions on, 307
impact of women's employment on,
304–306
nonmarital, 294–295
number of children, 290–293
timing of, 293–294
See also birth rates
child poverty, 24, 28–31, 187–188. *See also*
poverty
children
impact of mothers' employment on, 312
impact of war on, 411–412
in single-parent families, 311–312
street, 311
child soldiers, 411, 415
China
economic policies of, 378
family planning programs in, 290–292,
477, 478

famine in, 475
fertility rates in, 290–292
impact of global communication on, 11–12
impact of western culture on, 141, 142, 184
life expectancy in, 467
population growth in, 470
social movements in, 359
circumcision, as ritual, 128–130
citizen organizations, 386–387, 388
citizenship: membership in the community
of people subject to the authority of a
particular national state and, as such,
having certain rights and obligations, 357
civic engagement, study on decline in, 87–88
effects of changing age distribution on, 103
empirical evidence for, 93–95
examining alternative causes, 104–106
and geographic mobility, 90, 95
impact of comparison points on, 103–104
opposing views to, 99–103
role of television in, 96, 97–98, 105, 106,
107, 109–110
and voter turnout, 103–104, 105–106
See also social capital
civil rights movement, 133, 140, 167
civil unions, 281, 283, 295
Civil War, 219
civil war
increase in, 404–405
outside military intervention in, 413–414
See also ethnic conflict; war
class conflict: political and economic struggle
for dominance between social classes, 46,
174
class inequality, 165–166
and criminal behavior, 332–333, 345–346,
348
feminist perspective on, 242
in industrial societies, 172–174
Marx on, 45–48
and property, 166
See also inequality; social class; stratification
class structure, and economic development,
190, 191
clearance rates, for crimes, 342
Clinton, Bill, 58, 353, 372, 409, 495
Cloward, R. A., 335
Coca-Cola, 61
Cochrane, Walter, 455
cohabitation
and childbearing, 294
and divorce, 297, 298
increase in, 286–289

Coleman, James, 99
college students, credit card debt of, 435–437
colonization. *See* conquest and colonization
cosmetic surgery, 499
communication: use of signs and symbols to
convey meaning or thoughts from one
person to another; used to help people
coordinate their activities and transmit
their accumulated information and
knowledge to new members of the culture, 131–132
communism
creation of, 47
crime rates after fall of, 344
economic impact of fall of, 362
new states emerging from fall of, 367, 368
reasons for fall of, 27–28
Communist Manifesto, The (Marx, Engels), 47
community: group of people linked by shared
interests, common understandings,
shared identity, or shared place of residence, 122
and culture, 122–123
globalized, 123
impact of changing workplace on,
437–439
relational, 123
rituals for celebrating, 128
territorial, 122–123
community solutions, for social change,
510–511
comparison points, in scientific method,
103–104
computers, impact on labor force, 426–427.
See also Internet; technology
Comte, August, 45, 71
concentration camps, in former Yugoslavia,
407
conflict school: a type of sociological analysis
that is rooted in Marxism and that
stresses struggle, domination, and conflict between groups, 48
conflict subculture: a subculture in which
violence is valued for its own sake, 336
conquest and colonization
of Africa, 215–218, 356
American slavery, 219–221
as contact situation, 214–215
and contemporary U.S. race relations,
221–226
European, 59–61, 215–218, 356, 360–361
role in sexual division of labor, 260, 266
and world systems theory, 59–61

consolidation, of global species, 209–210. *See also* assimilation
conspicuous consumption, 445
Consumer Federation of America, 434
consumers, in culture industry, 137, 138
consumption
  ambivalence of individualized actions against, 452–453
  and change in family values, 300
  and credit card debt, 424, 434–437
  and cycle of work and spend, 434–437
  and desire for more, 442–443, 456–457
  dirty seven consumer activities, 449–451
  increase in competitive, 434–435, 445–446
  and increase in gross world product, 442, 443, 447
  of nonconsumption, 452
  overview of human, 443–447
  owning up to what we own, 447–449
  social organization of, 452–457
  social reorganization of, 457–459
  and treadmill of production, 455–457
  world map depicting purchasing power, 531
contact situation: conditions under which racial or ethnic groups first come together, 214
  conquest and colonization, 215–226
  immigration, 226–232
contraception, impact of, 467, 477, 478
contracting out, governmental, 369
control, in rationalization, 65
control group, 108–110
core nations, 58–59
corporations
  downsizing of, 1–3, 180, 424, 426–427
  gender differences in, 240, 257–258
  low-wage factories of, 252–254
  transnational, 61–63
  as treadmills of production, 455–457
  See also international trade; transnational corporations
correlation: association between variables that can be measured numerically, 97–98
countries, expanding numbers of, 16–17, 367–368. *See also* national states
credit card debt, 424, 434–437
crime: a violation of the formal norms or criminal laws, 320
  controlling, 338–348
  defining, 320–323
  and deviant subculture, 335–336

and differential association, 334–335
effect of modernization on, 330–332
globalization of, 328–330, 384
measuring rate of, 323–326
"official" statistics on, 323–324
organized, 329–330, 384
profile of typical offender, 326–328
self-reports on, 325
social control theory on, 336–338
structural strain as cause of, 332–333
theories on causes of, 330–338
victimization surveys on, 324–325
crime control, 338–348
  deterrence and incarceration for, 339–344
  social disorganization theory on, 345–346
  strengthening of social control mechanisms for, 344–345
crime rates
  and clearance rates, 342
  government reported, 323–324
  in U.S., 321–322, 339–340
criminal subculture: a type of deviant subculture in which the illegitimate means for pursuing success are well-organized and stable, 335–336
critical thinking, in scientific method, 92–95
Croatia, 407
Cuban immigrants, pluralism of, 212–214
cultural diffusion: the importing of both material and nonmaterial cultural objects from one society into another, 139–140
cultural lag: social strain resulting from a gap between the material and nonmaterial parts of culture, which arises from rapid culture change, 140–141
culture: set of tangible and intangible elements that give shape and meaning to the everyday lives of a particular group of people, 119
  beliefs, 125–126
  as center of globalization, 18–21
  change, 139–141
  and communication, 131–132
  and community, 122–123
  construction of, 132–139
  elements of, 123–132
  and ethnic identity, 21–23
  globalization of, 141–144
  local coexisting with global, 144–145
  material, 123–124
  nonmaterial, 125–130
  norms, 127–128

rituals, 128–130
role of technology in, 130–131
social production of, 137–139
sociological perspective on, 119–122
transmitting to individuals, 133–136
values, 126–127
culture industry system, 137–139
Currie, Elliot, 339, 343, 345–348, 349
cybercrimes, 328–329
Cyberspace Electronic Security Act, 12–14
Czechoslovakia
division of, 367, 368
fall of communism in, 27

data
careful interpretation of, 516–517
techniques for gathering, 107–113
See also scientific method; sociological
research
Davis, Kingsley, 168–169
Dawson, Tracey Jane, 35–39
DDT, exporting of, 487
death rates
child, 30–31, 487
in developed countries, 466
in developing countries, 467–469
impact on population growth, 464–465
maternal, 488
debate, in scientific inquiry, 106–107
debt reduction, for developing countries, 506,
507
definition issues, in scientific method, 99–103
deforestation, 444, 475–476, 542
deindustrialization: economic trend in
which well-paying, secure industrial jobs
are replaced by service jobs, many low
paying and insecure, due to a shift to a
postindustrial economy, 180–182
impact on African Americans, 222–224
impact on current U.S. immigrants,
230–231
and *maquiladora* phenomenon, 252–254
See also postindustrial societies
Delijaj, Imer, 411
Demery, Larry, 319–320, 339
democracy: a form of government that, at the
turn of the twenty-first century, social
scientists usually define as national states
in which (1) adult citizens have equal
rights, including the right of political
participation; (2) governments are bound
by rules that protect citizens, including

members of minorities, from arbitrary
actions; (3) all powerholders are either
elected by the citizens or appointed by
someone who is elected; and (4) citizens'
rights include rights of expression in
speech and writing and rights to form
organizations to advance their claims,
including political parties, 357
challenge of transnational power to,
381–388
growth of, 357, 358
in national state, 357–359
as threatened, 378–381
as universal model, 209
See also political and economic systems
demographic transition theory: theory of
population change asserting that population stability is achieved only after a society reaches a certain level of economic
prosperity and that once economic development has been attained, a society's
birth and death rates are approximately
equivalent, 290, 469
Dempsey, James, 14
Denton, Nancy, 224, 225, 336
dependent variable: in a causal relationship,
the variable that is taken to be the effect
or result, 90
deregulation, government, 369
description, in scientific method, 88–90
deterrence, impact on criminal behavior, 339,
342–343
de Tocqueville, Alexis, 99
developed countries
access to technology in, 10–11, 106, 107
child death rates in, 30–31
gap between rich and poor in, 29–30
measures of social capital in, 101–103
population growth in, 463, 464–467
suicide rates for, 67–70
See also high-income nations; industrial
societies
developing countries
access to technology in, 10–11 , 106, 107
child death rates in, 30–31
economic challenges of, 476–477
family change in, 309–311
family planning programs in, 477–480
fertility rates in, 290–292
foreign aid and investment in, 506
gender inequality in, 260–262, 264–267,
269

developing countries *(continued)*
   healthcare in, 469, 485–495
   income inequality in, 189–192
   low-wage factories in, 252–254
   maternal and natal care in, 496
   population growth in, 463–464, 465, 467–471
   reducing debt burden of, 506, 507
   statistical data from, 517
   structural adjustment programs in, 254–256, 308, 309–310, 485
deviance: any behavior that violates the norms of a culture, 320
deviant subculture: a subculture with many procriminal norms, values, and beliefs, 335–336
differential association: in Sutherland's theory, the extent to which people associate with deviant, procriminal norms, values, and beliefs, 334–335
differentiation, and species development, 207–209
diffusion, cultural, 139–140
DiIulio, John, 338, 339, 345
dirty seven consumer activities, 449–451
discrimination: unequal treatment of others based on their group membership, 211. *See also* race and ethnicity
disease
   controlling, in developing countries, 469
   drug resistant, 384, 489–491
   eradication of, 25–27
   globalization of, 5, 384, 500–501
   impact of international travel on, 491–493
   newly emerging, 486
   reemergence of, 485–486, 488–489, 490
   threat of infectious, 491–493, 500
   See also healthcare
disorderly work career, rise of, 424–426. *See also* workplace changes
dispersion, and species development, 207–209
division of labor, 52
   sexual, 243–247
divorce, 295–298
   children of, 311–312
   impact of economic conditions on, 307
   impact of legislation on, 302–303
   impact of women's employment on, 304–306
doctor-patient ratios, 497–498

Doctors Without Borders, 486, 510
domestic violence, 340
dominant group: more powerful and more privileged group in a society, regardless of numbers, 210–211
Donahue, Phil, 251
Dow Chemical Company, 25
downsizing, of labor force, 1–3, 180, 424, 426–427
downward reorganization, of state power, 366–369
drug trade, 329, 384
Durkheim, Emile, 51–55, 67, 70, 71, 91, 122, 168, 303, 331, 332, 344

East Africa, economic alliances in, 16
economic determinism, 46
economic development
   international comparisons of poverty, 532
   purchasing power per capita, 531
   world map of educated skilled labor, 533
   See also economic trends; global economy
economic development programs, impact on healthcare, 485–487. *See also* structural adjustment programs
economic entities, fifty richest, 61, 62
economic instability, threat of global, 384
economic policy, state as maker of, 360
economic systems
   and inequality, 169
   Marx on, 45–48, 58, 166
   See also political and economic systems
economic trends
   impact on family stability, 306–308
   impact on immigrant assimilation, 230–231
   impact on U.S. workplace, 424–426
   new international economic order, 505
   regional economic alliances, 14–16, 509
   See also global economy
economic underdevelopment, and population growth, 476–477
ecotourism, 5–6
education
   and decline in inequality, 174–175
   and divorce, 297
   gender differences in, 240, 262–267
   impact on birth rate, 293, 304, 478–480
   public expenditure on, 536
   racial differences in, 221, 222
   role in assimilation, 221–223, 228, 231
   and socialization, 134, 135

world-institutions perspective on, 262
world map of educated skilled labor, 533
Educational Amendment Act (1972), 263
efficiency, in rationalization, 65
egoistic suicide, 54, 70
Egypt
  gender inequality in, 239
  impact of globalization on, 141–143
Eheart, Brenda Krause, 511
Ehrlich, Anne, 471
Ehrlich, Paul, 461–462, 471
electoral systems, 359
employment. *See* workforce; workplace
  changes
Engels, Friedrich, 47
environment
  access to safe water, 544
  carbon dioxide emissions, 444, 543
  dirty seven consumer activities, 449–451
  as global concern, 384
  and human consumption, 443–447 (*see also*
    consumption)
  increasing demands on world ecosystems,
    443, 444
  rates of deforestation, 444, 475–476, 542
  sociology of inaction to, 449–452
  sustainable development of, 441–443
  and virtual environmentalism, 458–459
environmental degradation, and overpopulation, 461, 462, 475–476
Ethiopia, famine in, 472–473, 475
ethnic cleansing. *See* genocide
ethnic conflict
  in Africa, 7, 205, 215–217, 403
  in former Yugoslavia, 6–7, 406–410
  as global concern, 5, 210
  increase in, 404
  refugees of, 363–364
  See also war
ethnic diversity, world map depicting, 530
ethnic identity
  of European immigrants in U.S.,
    227–228
  impact of globalization on, 19–20
  influence on culture, 21–23
  new politics of, 372–376
  See also race and ethnicity
ethnocentrism: belief that one's own culture
  and derived beliefs are superior to other
  cultures and derived beliefs, 18
Europe
  dissatisfaction with democracy in, 380
  ethnic conflict in, 404
  fall of communism in, 7, 27–28, 344, 362
  gap between rich and poor in, 29–30
  immigration issues in, 374
  map of, 523
  political fragmentation in, 17
  population growth in, 463, 465–467
  refugees in, 363–364
  welfare states in, 187–189
European Coal and Steel Community, 382
European colonization, 356
  of Africa, 215–218
  and transnational trade, 360–361
  and world systems theory, 59–61
European Court of Human Rights, 366, 382
European immigrants, assimilation of U.S.,
  226–229
European Union (EU), 15, 17, 354, 509
  supranational authority of, 366, 381–383
Evans, R., 250
evidence, evaluating, in scientific method,
  95–96
experimental group, 108–110
experiments
  field, 110
  laboratory, 108–110
explanation, in scientific method, 88–90
extended family: a family group consisting of
  various relatives who live either in the
  same household or very close to each
  other and who are emotionally close,
  282–283
extractive sector, of workforce, 175, 176
Exxon, 61

F. Hoffmann-La Roche, 495
Falun Gong, 359
family: a group of individuals related to each
  other by blood, marriage, adoption, or
  some other mechanism that makes them
  a unit, although such units vary greatly
  according to region and generation, 282
changing patterns of marriage, 286–288
childbearing, 290–295
and crime prevention, 346–347
divorce and remarriage, 295–298
future of, 311–312
marriage vs. cohabitation, 288–289
postmodern, 285–286
recent trends in, 284–286
role in socialization, 134
single-parent, 28–29, 311–312, 347

family *(continued)*
  sociological approach to, 282–284
  structure in agricultural societies, 244–246
family change
  causes of, 298–309
  and changing economic conditions, 306–308
  consequences of, 309–312
  impact of AIDS epidemic on, 309
  impact of war on, 308–309
  and weakened family values, 299–303
  and women's increased employment,
    303–306
family planning programs, 462, 477–480
  cultural obstacles to, 480
family size
  decline in developed countries', 467
  in developing countries, 477–480
  impact of globalization on, 470
family values, 126–127
  recent changes in, 299–303
  survey on, 316
family wage: wage large enough for the wage
    earner to support a spouse and children,
    249–250, 258
  and family stability, 306–307
famine, 472–475. *See also* food production
fatalistic suicide, 55
Fay, Michael, 319, 320, 339
Federal Bureau of Investigation (FBI), 323
felony: a serious crime punishable by a prison
    term of more than a year, 321, 323, 324
female circumcision, 128
feminist perspective: set of theories that
    attempt to explain gender differences and
    inequalities by examining social institu-
    tions from the viewpoint of women and
    by attempting to change inequalities
    between women and men, 242–243
Ferraro, Geraldine, 251
fertility rates, variations in, 290–293. *See also*
    birth rates
field experiments, 110
field research, 112–113
film imports, 541
folkways, 127
food production
  declines in, 462
  as environmental issue, 450, 453–455
  and famine, 473
  and population growth, 471–472
  technological advances for, 471, 472
foreign aid, increasing, 506–508

foreign direct investment, 539
forests, human encroachment on, 444,
    475–476, 542
four Asian dragons, economic growth of,
    184–186, 189–190, 193
Fourth World Conference on Women, 239,
    252, 269
France
  family structures in, 281
  immigrants in, 365
free trade policies, 354, 378
Friedman, Thomas L., 141–143

Gaelic language, 117–118, 123
Gaines, Donna, 68–70, 112
Gates, Bill, 10
gender: social differences assigned to people
    of different sexes, 241
gender differences, 233
  in agricultural societies, 244–246
  in criminal behavior, 326–327
  in developing countries, 260–262,
    264–267, 269
  in education, 262–267
  in family roles, 283
  feminist perspective on, 242–243
  as global concern, 252–256, 269
  in hunting and gathering societies, 243–244
  impact of subsistence technology on,
    243–247
  impact of U.S. women's movement on,
    247–251
  and income inequality, 181–182, 246–247
  in industrial societies, 246–247
  and *maquiladora* phenomenon, 252–254
  in politics, 267–269
  positive changes in, 239–240
  social construction of, 241–242
  and structural adjustment programs,
    254–256
  and work, 257–262
gender empowerment measure, 535
General Electric, 1, 61
General Social Survey (GSS), 110–111
genocide, 403
  in former Yugoslavia, 407–410
  need to respond to, 417–418
Germany, anti-immigration movements in,
    374, 376
Ghana
  gender inequality in, 262
  structural adjustment programs in, 256

Glaxo Wellcome, 486, 495

global actions, for positive social change, 505–508

Global Alliance for Vaccines and Immunization (GAVI), 495, 508, 509

global economy, 3–4, 209

and corporate downsizing, 1–3, 180, 426–427

foreign direct investment, 539

global mobility of trade and investment, 362–363, 384, 427, 428

growth in global trade, 538

high-tech exports, 540

impact on labor force, 1–3, 426–427

impact on labor movement, 370–371

and *maquiladora* phenomenon, 252–254

regional economic alliances, 15–16

state management vs. market autonomy, 376–378

structural adjustment programs, 254–256, 485

and technology, 14–15

world systems theory, 58–63

and World Trade Organization, 353–355

See also globalization; international trade; transnational corporations

Global Fund for Children's Vaccines, 508

globalization: process by which societies become more similar with respect to economics, politics, culture, and other factors, thus affecting people's daily lives, 6

benefits of, 184–186

citizen organizations for controlling, 386–387

of consumerism, 434

of crime, 328–330, 384

of culture, 141–144

culture as center of, 18–21

of disease, 5, 384, 491–493, 500–501

and economic unification, 14–16

of education, 262

and ethnic and racial consolidation, 206

and film imports, 541

and gender inequality, 252–256, 260–262, 269

history of, 360–361

and income inequality among nations, 183–186

and inequality, 28–31

and interconnectedness of world events, 4–5

and mobility of people, 363–365

of political and economic systems, 360–365

and political fragmentation, 16–17

and technology, 10–14

and transnational governance, 366, 379–380, 381–385, 387–388

See also global economy; transnational organizations

"Globalization of Taste, The" (Hart), 75–83

global perspective, assumptions about, 7–9

global species consolidation: according to Wallace, elimination of the boundaries of race, ethnicity, and nationality that divide human beings, 207–210. *See also* race and ethnicity

Gompers, Samuel, 249

Gorbachev, Mikhail, 27–28, 140

Gordon, Milton, 212, 226

government. *See* national states; political and economic systems

government leadership, gender inequality in, 267–269

government organizations. *See* transnational organizations

grandparent, as new family role, 283

Great U-Turn: according to Bluestone and Harrison, reversal of the Kuznets curve in industrialized societies, which began in the United States in the 1970s, 178–180, 345

Green, Daniel, 319–320, 339

Greenbelt Movement, 510–511

greenhouse gasses, 476

guinea worm disease, eradication of, 25–27

Haitian immigrants, 232

Hart, Nicky, 75–83

Hawaii, separatist movement in, 17

healthcare

and bias of medical research, 499

elements of quality, 496–498

in era of drug resistance, 489–491

future challenges of, 500–501

as global concern, 5, 384

HIV/AIDS epidemic, 309, 494–495

impact of economic development programs on, 485–487

impact of international travel on, 491–493

impact of political turmoil on, 487–489

inequality in, 495–500

in low-income countries, 485–495

maternal and natal, 496

healthcare *(continued)*
   total healthcare expenditures, 546
   world map depicting life expectancy, 545
   world map depicting nutrition, 547
healthcare aid
   developing countries distrust of, 486–487
   use of nongovernmental agencies, 486
health insurance, unequal access to, 498
Health InterNetwork, 508
hierarchy, organizational, elimination of, 424,
      430–431
high-income nations, 183
   child death rates in, 30–31
   decentralized political structures in,
      367–369
   income inequality in, 187–189
   See also developed countries; industrial soci-
      eties
Hirschi, Travis, 336–338, 344
Hispanic Americans. *See* Latinos
Hitler, Adolph, 403
HIV/AIDS epidemic, 309, 494–495
Hochschild, Arlie, 458
Holbrooke, Richard C., 404
holocaust, 403. *See also* genocide
homicide, 321
   rates of intentional, 537
Hong Kong, economic growth in, 184–186,
      190
Hope for the Children Foundation, 511
Howard, P. E. N., 100, 113
"How Culture Shapes Schooling" (Brint),
      149–154
human capital: investments in people's liter-
      acy, education, and skill development,
      174
   in postindustrial economy, 181, 182
human development
   education expenditures, 536
   gender empowerment measure, 535
   human development index, 534
   rates of intentional homicide, 537
human resources, state's role in, 359. *See also*
      education
human rights organizations, 366, 383, 386
Human Rights Watch, 383, 386, 411, 516
hunting and gathering societies, 169, 170
   gender roles in, 243–244
   role in species development, 207–209
hypersegregation, 225
hypotheses: testable propositions derived
      from a more general theory, 90

Ileto, Joseph, 206
immigrant groups, in U.S., 365
   assimilation of European, 226–229
   status of present-day, 229–232
   See also minority groups; race and
      ethnicity
immigration
   as contact situation, 214, 226
   and new politics of ethnic identity,
      372–376, 379
   present-day, 364–365
   See also race and ethnicity
immunization programs, 469, 495, 508
   impact of war on, 488–489
incarceration
   impact on crime rate, 339–344
   and replacement effect, 343–344
   rising rate of U.S., 339–341
   See also crime
income inequality
   in Africa, 190–192
   in agricultural societies, 172
   between blacks and whites in U.S., 221,
      222, 260
   and consumption treadmill, 446–447
   and deinstitutionalization, 180–182
   in European welfare states, 187–189
   and gender differences, 181–182, 246–247,
      259–260
   and Great U-Turn, 178–180
   growth of worldwide, 162, 163
   in industrial societies, 172
   Kuznets curve on decline of, 174–175
   between nations, 183–186
   within nations, 186–192
   in newly industrialized countries, 189–190
   racial differences in, 221, 222, 260
   ratio of, 186, 187, 188
   in U.S., 177–182
   See also inequality
independent variable: in a causal relation-
      ship, the variable that is taken to be the
      cause, 90
India
   digital revolution in, 510
   family planning programs in, 477, 478
   life expectancy in, 467
   social stratification in, 163
   women's status in, 121
individualism
   as American value, 126–127
   vs. collectivism, 22–23, 143

and family change, 300
in industrial society, 52–53
individualistic perspective, vs. sociological
perspective, 56
individualized action, ambivalence of,
452–453
individuals
creating positive social change, 511–513
transmission of culture to, 133–136
industrialization: the process by which
machines and new forms of energy are
applied to economic production, transportation, and other tasks, 43
and class conflict, 45–48
cultural influences on, 48–51
and deindustrialization, 180–182
and deviance, 331
and ethnic and racial consolidation, 206
impact of, 42–45, 57
impact on life expectancy, 466
impact on social cohesion, 51–55
and population growth, 462
and suicide, 54–55, 67
industrial societies, 169
changing labor market in, 175–177
gender roles in, 246–247
inequality in, 172–177, 188
and Kuznets curve, 174–175
newly industrializing countries, 189–190
See also developed countries; high-income
nations
inequality
in access to technology, 10–11, 107,
183–184
within and across societies, 28–31
in agricultural societies, 171–172
amount of, in world, 503–504
class, Marx on, 45–48, 174
and class interests, 165–166
and consumption, 445, 446–447
and criminal behavior, 332–333, 345–346,
348
evolution of, 169–177
functions of, 168–169
in healthcare, 495–500
in hunting and gathering societies, 170
increase of, in U.S., 177–182
in industrial societies, 172–177
Kuznets curve on decline of, 174–175
between nations, 183–186
within nations, 186–192
sociological perspective on, 162–169

solutions to, 504–512 (*see also* social
changes)
three dimensions of, 166–168
and war, 404, 417
of world income, 162, 163
in world systems theory, 58–63
See also class inequality; gender differences;
income inequality; race and ethnicity
infant mortality rates, impact of war on, 487.
See also death rates
infectious disease
global burden of, 500
and international travel, 491–493
See also disease
influenza, 491
information technologies, 130–131, 426. *See
also* technology
Infosys Technologies, 510
infrastructure, state as provider of, 359
inner conflict, and socialization, 135
institutional subsystem, in culture industry,
137, 138
institutions: clusters of social structure
(groups, patterns of interaction, statuses,
and networks of relationships), culture
(both material and nonmaterial), and
technologies aimed at satisfying basic
human and social needs, 135
integration, in assimilation, 212
intermarriage
in assimilation, 212, 227
black-white, 225
international data, interpreting, 517
International Monetary Fund, 254, 381, 383,
387, 388, 485
international trade, 361, 362–363
film imports, 541
foreign direct investment, 539
free trade policies, 354, 378
growth in global trade, 538
high-tech exports, 540
See also global economy; transnational
corporations
International Tribunal for the Former
Yugoslavia, 408
Internet
citing sources from, 518
and community involvement, 100–101,
113
criminal activity on, 328–329
and globalization, 361
and global mobility of investment, 427, 428

Internet *(continued)*
    impact on repressive governments, 11–12
    inequality in access to, 10–11, 107, 184
    sociological research using, 515–516
    See also technology
investment, global mobility of, 362–363, 384,
        427, 428
    impact on labor movement, 371
    map of foreign direct investment, 539
    See also global economy
Irish potato famine, 473
Islamic culture, women in, 240
Italy, study of social solidarity in, 87,
        98–99

Japan
    economic growth in, 184–186
    ethnic identity in, 22–23
    impact on U.S. market, 424
    population growth in, 463, 464
Johnson Controls, 430
Jordan, James, 320
judicial systems, state's role in, 359–360
"just in time" delivery systems, 429–430

Karadzic, Radovan, 408
Kelley, Florence, 249
Kenya
    community organizations in, 510–511
    ethnic identity in, 20, 21–22
    family structures in, 281–282
    fertility rates in, 292
    healthcare in, 483–485, 486, 490–491
    political turmoil in, 487
Keynes, John Maynard, 377
kinship: an extended-family unit linked
        through blood ties, marriage, or adop-
        tion; generally closer physically and emo-
        tionally in developing countries, where
        extended families are important,
        282–283
Kosovo, 410, 411, 488
Krajisnik, Moncilo, 408
Kurtz, Lester R., 155–160
Kuznets, Simon, 174
Kuznets curve: according to Simon Kuznets,
        the decline in inequality in a society after
        the earliest stages of industrialization,
        174–175, 178
labor intensive: referring to modes of produc-
        tion that rely on hand labor or the aid of
        draft animals, 171

labor market
    changing structure of, 175–177
    and implied social contract, 422–424
    See also workforce; workplace changes
labor movement
    impact of changing U.S. workplace on,
        424, 431–432
    weakening of, 370–372, 373, 379
    and World Trade Organization, 354
Ladd, Everett, 101, 103
languages
    as cultural symbols, 131–132
    disappearance of, 117–118
    strengthening of ethnic, 21
Latin America
    drug cartels in, 329
    economic alliances in, 15
    life expectancy in, 467
    map of, 526
    population growth in, 463, 464
Latinos
    acculturation survey of, 237
    child poverty of, 28
    and income inequality, 260
    marriage patterns of, 288, 298, 308
    in U.S., 19, 229, 230
laws, as norms, 128
League of Nations, 381
leisure
    conspicuous, 445
    loss of, 446
Lenski, Gerhard, 169
liberal feminism, 243
life expectancy
    in developed countries, 465, 466
    in developing countries, 467–469, 494
    world map depicting, 545
lobbies, political, 359
local culture. *See* traditional culture
"Local Gods and Universal Faiths" (Kurtz),
        155–160
Loeb, J. J., 250
low-income nations, 183
    child death rates in, 30–31
    income inequality in, 186, 187, 190–192
    See also agricultural societies; developing
        countries

Maathi, Wangari, 511
McDonald's, 354
McDonaldization: the modern embodiment
        of the positive and negative consequences

of rationalization, as analyzed by George Ritzer, 64–67
as agent of globalization, 143
McMichael, Philip, 197–204
malaria, 469, 489, 490–491
Malawi
  gender differences in, 246
  impact of global communication on, 12
managerial subsystem, in culture industry, 137, 138
Mandela, Nelson, 217
Manpower Temporary Services, 3
manufacturing sector, of workforce, 176
maps, world
  access to safe water, 544
  annual rates of deforestation, 542
  carbon dioxide emissions, 543
  education expenditures, 536
  education of skilled labor, 533
  ethnic diversity, 530
  film imports, 541
  foreign direct investment, 539
  gender empowerment measure, 535
  growth in global trade, 538
  healthcare expenditure, 546
  high-tech exports, 540
  homicide, 537
  human development index, 534
  life expectancy, 545
  nutrition, 547
  population density, 528
  poverty, 532
  purchasing power, 531
  regions of world, 7–9, 520–527
  urbanization, 529
maquiladora **phenomenon:** movement among corporations in high-income countries to establish assembly plants in developing countries to take advantage of the lower wages and less restrictive labor and environmental laws (named after the Mexican term for such plants), 252–254
market autonomy: freedom of markets—for commodities, services, finance, land, and labor—to run themselves rather than being managed by the state, 376–378
marriage
  changing patterns of, 286–288
  and childbearing, 294–295
  civil unions, 281, 283, 295
  divorce and remarriage, 295–298
  impact of cohabitation on, 288–289

impact of economic conditions on, 306–308
impact of women's employment on, 304–306
intermarriage, 212, 225, 227
See also family
Marx, Karl, 45–48, 58, 71, 165–166, 174
Marxism, 45–48
  feminist, 242
  and modern capitalism, 58–63
Massey, Douglas, 224, 225, 228, 229, 230, 231, 232, 336
material culture: tangible elements of culture; the things you can see, touch, and hear, 123–124
  diffusion of, 139–140
maternal and natal healthcare, 496
matrilineal descent: method of determining inheritance based on the mother's side of the family, 244–246
Mbatia, Paul, 504
Mbeke, Thabo M., 217
measurement issues, in scientific method, 99–103
mechanical solidarity, 52, 331
media
  and culture industry system, 137
  and socialization, 135
medical research, 508
  economic bias in, 499
medical technology, impact on life expectancy, 466, 469
men's earnings, and family stability, 306–307
Mercator projection map, 7–9
Merck & Co., 495
Mercosur, 509
meritocracy, 169
Merton, Robert K., 332–333
Mexico
  immigration to U.S. from, 229, 230
  life expectancy in, 467
  low-wage factories in, 252–254
  political fragmentation in, 16–17
  population growth in, 470
Microsoft, 61
middle class
  African American, 223
  changing status of, 178–180, 181
  impact of deindustrialization on, 180–182
  in industrial societies, 172
Middle East
  economic alliance in, 509
  map of, 524

middle-income nations, 183
child death rates in, 30–31
income inequality in, 186, 187, 189–190
See also developing countries
military spending, vs. healthcare spending, 487, 488
Millennium Vaccine Initiative, 495
Millennium Survey, 300
Milosevic, Slobodan, 408, 410
Miner, Horace, 130
minority groups: less powerful and less privileged groups in a society, regardless of numbers, 210–211
assimilation model for, 212
impact of deindustrialization on, 222–224
income inequality of, 181–182
in U.S., 19
See also immigrant groups; race and ethnicity
misdemeanor: a less serious crime than a felony and punishable by less than a year in jail, 321
Mitchell, George, 417
Mladic, Ratko, 408
modernization, 57
and crime, 330–332
and organic solidarity, 52
perspective on, 24–25
and suicide, 54–55, 67
See also industrialization
Moi, Daniel, 483
monarchy, decline of, 43
Moore, Wilbert, 168–169
morality, in industrial society, 52–55, 331.
See also values
moral poverty, 345
mores, 127
mothers, working, impact on children, 312
Movement for Free and Fair Elections, 511
Moyer, Sean, 436–437
Mueller v. Oregon, 249
Mugabe, Robert, 404
multicultural feminism, 243
multiculturalism
challenges of, 19–21
in U.S. society, 4, 19, 212, 229–232
See also race and ethnicity
multinational corporations. *See* transnational corporations
Murphy Brown, 309
"My Personal Journey to a Global Perspective" (Dawson), 35–39
Myrdal, Gunnar, 206

Nagel, Joane, 275–280
Naisbitt, John, 17
national identity issues, 372–374, 379
national states: political and economic entities that exercise authoritative jurisdiction over some territory, 356
development of, 356
economics in, 359–360
emergence of new, 16–17, 367–368
female leadership in, 267–269
politics in, 356–359
potential for creating positive social changes, 509–510
professional economist power in, 379
reorganization of power in, 366–369
state management vs. market autonomy in, 376–378
vs. transnational structure of governance, 381–385
See also political and economic systems
nation-building, in peacekeeping efforts, 410, 418
"new consumerism," 445
new international economic order (NIEO), 505
newly industrializing countries (NICs), 189–190
new penology, 338–339
family assistance programs, 347
and importance of punishment, 339–344
and social control mechanisms, 344–345
nonconsumption, consuming, 451–452
nongovernmental organizations (NGOs)
as healthcare providers, 486
and positive social change, 509–511
nonmaterial culture: the intangibles that make one group of people different from another, such as beliefs, values, and norms, 125–130
diffusion of, 139–140
norms: a group's rule of conduct or code of behavior that outlines the means by which group members can legitimately pursue the ends suggested by their values, 127–128
folkways, 127
laws, 128
mores, 127
Norris, Pippa, 104–105, 106
North America, map of, 525
North American Free Trade Agreement (NAFTA), 15, 366, 509

North Atlantic Treaty Organization (NATO)
   peacekeeping of, 5, 414, 416
   and war in former Yugoslavia, 410
Northern Ireland, peace initiatives in, 417
North Korea, famine in, 473, 475
nuclear family: a family unit consisting of a
   mother, a father (or one of these), and
   dependent children, 283
nuclear proliferation, 383
nutrition, world map depicting, 547

O'Connor, Sandra Day, 251
observation, in scientific method, 112–113
Oceania
   map of, 527
   population growth in, 463
Ohlin, L. E., 335
one-child policy: government policy enacted
   in China to restrict each family to one
   child, 290–292
organic solidarity, 52, 54, 303, 331
Organization of Petroleum Exporting Countries (OPEC), 509
organizations
   bureaucratic, 63–64
   citizen, 386–387, 388
   elimination of hierarchies in, 424,
     430–431
   McDonaldization of, 64–67
   nongovernmental, 486, 510–511
   See also transnational organizations
organized crime, 329–330, 384
Ortega, Suzanne, 331
Otieno, S. M., 21–22, 127
outsourcing, corporate, 424, 429–430
outward reorganization, of state power, 369
overpopulation. *See* population growth
Overspent American, The (Schor), 445
OXFAM, 510

PACS *(Pacte civil de solidarité)*, 281, 283, 295
paper consumption, 444
Park, Robert, 206
Parsons, Talcott, 303–304
patriarchy: form of social organization in
   which decision-making positions are held
   primarily by men, 246
patrilineal descent: method of determining
   inheritance based on the father's side of
   the family, 246
peacekeeping
   arguments for and against, 413–414
   in former Yugoslavia, 410, 413

   global, 5, 415
   limitations of, 414–416
   in Sierra Leone, 415–416
   See also war
peers, and socialization, 134
people, global mobility of, 361, 363–365
periphery nations, 58
Peters projection map, 7–9
pharmaceutical companies, and medicine for
   poor, 494–495, 501
pharmaceuticals, fear of counterfeit, 487
plague, 466
Plains Indians
   and cultural diffusion, 139–140
   minimal inequality of, 170
pluralism: societal condition in which racial
   and ethnic groups are structurally separate and maintain a distinct identity and
   set of traditions, 212–214
pneumonic plague, 491
polio, 488–489
political and economic systems
   challenges to status quo of, 365–366
   citizen organizations impact on, 353–355,
     386–387
   democracy as threatened, 378–381
   economics in national state, 359–360
   gender differences in, 267–269
   globalization of, 360–365
   historical, 356
   and new politics of ethnic identity,
     372–376
   politics in national state, 356–359
   and professionalization of economic policy,
     379
   radical transformation of world, 504–505
   reorganization of national state power,
     366–369
   rise of modern state, 355–356
   state management vs. market autonomy,
     376–378
   structural adjustment programs, 254–256,
     308, 485
   transnational organizations, 353–355,
     361–363
   transnational structures of governance, 366,
     379–380, 381–385, 387–388
   weakening of labor movement in, 370–372,
     373, 379
   See also global economy
political fragmentation, worldwide increase
   in, 16–17, 209–210, 505
Pool, Mitzi, 437

Popenoe, David, 285
popular culture, influence on family values, 302
population: universe of all cases to which sample results can be generalized, 111–112
Population Action, 462
population density, map of, 528
population growth
    causes of, 464–465
    consequences of, 461–462
    cultural obstacles to slowing, 480
    in developed countries, 465–467
    in developing countries, 467–471
    and Earth's carrying capacity, 471–472
    and economic underdevelopment, 476–477
    and environmental degradation, 475–476
    and famine, 472–475
    historical and projected rates of, 461, 462–464
    programs for controlling, 462, 477–480
    slowing, 477–481
    total fertility rates, 290–293
postindustrial societies, 169–170
    income inequality in, 180–182
    See also deindustrialization
postmodern family, 285–286
poverty
    African American, 223, 225
    child, 28–31
    and criminal behavior, 345–346, 347
    increase of, in U.S., 28–30, 179–180
    international comparisons of, 532
    See also urban poverty
Poverty and Famines (Sen), 475
power: in Weber's theory of stratification, the ability to affect decision making to favor one's interests, 167
predestination, doctrine of, 48–50
predictability, in rationalization, 65
prejudice: tendency to think about other groups in negative ways, to attach negative emotions (contempt, disgust, hatred) to those groups, and to prejudge people based on their group membership, 211
prestige: in Weber's theory of stratification, the respect and honor accorded a person by others, 166, 167
primitive culture. *See* traditional culture
privatization: government turnover of its activities to the private sector, often to profit-seeking business enterprises, 369

probabilistic relationships, in scientific method, 96–97
process technologies, 131. *See also* technology
production, treadmill of, 455–457
production-of-culture model, 137–139
Progressive Movement, 249
property: in Weber's theory of stratification, class, or the distinction between people who own or control income-producing property and those who do not, 166, 167
    in agricultural societies, 171
property crime, 321
Protestants
    suicide rates of, 54
    work ethic of, 48–51
public and private sector partnerships, 508
public health issues, as global concern, 5, 384
public health programs
    decreased spending on, 485–486
    in developing countries, 469
    in industrial societies, 466
    See also healthcare
public opinion polls, 111
public policy, influence on family values, 302–303
punishment, increasing criminal, 339–344
purchasing power, world map depicting, 531
Putnam, Robert, 87–88, 93–97, 98–107, 112, 113–114, 344

Quayle, Dan, 309

race and ethnicity
    assimilation and pluralism, 212–214
    assimilation of European immigrants in U.S., 226–229
    and civil war, 404
    contemporary race relations in U.S., 221–226
    and criminal behavior, 328
    effect of European colonization on Africa, 215–218
    effect of slavery and segregation on African Americans, 219–221
    evolution of global species, 207–210
    impact of conquest and colonization on, 215–226
    impact of immigration on, 226–232
    and importance of contact situation, 214
    and income inequality, 260
    and lack of health insurance, 498
    minority and dominant groups, 210–211

and new politics of ethnic identity,
372–376
origins of, 207–209
prejudice and discrimination, 211
present-day immigrants in U.S., 229–232,
365
world map depicting ethnic diversity, 530
See also immigrant groups; minority groups
radical feminism, 242
rape
in former Yugoslavia, 407, 412
underreporting of, 323–325
as weapon of war, 412
rationalization: form of rational analysis inherent in capitalism that seeks to determine the single most efficient, cost-
effective way of accomplishing goals,
50–51, 63
bureaucracy in, 63–64
McDonaldization as, 64–67
Ravenstein, Ernest, 471
reality. *See* social construction of reality
recycling, 451
Red Cross, 510
redistributive policy: decision to divert economic resources toward poorer people,
regions, or countries, 377
refugees, 363–364, 410, 411
healthcare issues of, 487–488
regional economic alliances, 16–17,
508–509
relational community, 123
religion
connection with family, 283
and divorce, 295, 297
and family values, 299–300
impact of industrialization on, 48–50
remarriages, 297–298
replacement effect, in crime, 343–344
representative: referring to a sample that
reproduces the characteristics of the population from which it is drawn,
111–112
repressive governments, impact of global communication on, 11–12
research: disciplined, careful testing of a theory, 86
interaction with theory, 90–92
traditions of, 98–99
See also scientific method; sociological
research
residential segregation, 224–225

retreatist subculture: a subculture that
stresses disengagement and "dropping
out," often through the use of illegal
drugs, 336
Revolutionary United Front, 414–416
rituals: customary, often ceremonial, activities
that signify a culture's shared beliefs, values, and norms, 128–130
Ritzer, George, 64
Robinson projection maps, 519
Russia
incarceration in, 340, 341
organized crime in, 329, 344
suicide rates in, 67, 68
See also Soviet Union
Rwanda, ethnic conflict in, 205, 215–217,
403, 404, 411, 488

Sabanci, Guler, 161, 165
Sadisah, 162, 165
Salvation Army, 510
sample: subset of a population, 111–112
Sankoh, Foday, 414–416
Sarajevo, 407–408, 409–410. *See also*
Yugoslavia
Save the Children Foundation, 510
Scheibner, Megan, 299
Scheibner, Stephen, 299
Schnaiberg, Alan, 455
schools. *See* education
Schor, Juliet, 434, 442–443, 445
Schudson, Michael, 105
scientific method: system of conducting
research that stresses careful, self-critical,
disciplined, objective inquiry, 88
analyzing existing data in, 113
correlation and causation in, 97–98
description, explanation, and causation,
88–90
effects of changing age distribution on, 103
evaluation of evidence in, 95–96
examining alternative causes in, 104–106
experiments, 108–110
gathering data in, 107–113
importance of comparison points in,
103–104
interaction between theory and research,
90–92
issues of definition and measurement in,
99–103
observation, 112–113
probabilistic relationships in, 96–97

scientific method *(continued)*
skepticism and critical thinking in, 92–95
in sociology, 86–87
surveys, 110–112
traditions of research in, 98–99
value of debate in, 106–107
See also sociological research
segregation, African American, 219–221
residential, 224–225
Seidman, Gay W., 393–399
self-reports, on criminal behavior, 325
semiperiphery nations, 58
Semmelweis, Ignaz, 496
Sen, Amartya, 475
separatism: societal condition in which a
racial or ethnic group wishes to sever ties
with the dominant group and become
independent and autonomous, 212
Serbia
impact of global communication on, 12
and war in former Yugoslavia, 407–410
See also Yugoslavia
service sector, 176
growth of, 3, 176–177
and income inequality, 181–182
"Sex as a Global Commodity" (Nagel),
275–280
sexual division of labor: assignment of the
people in a society to certain types of
tasks based on their sex, 243–247
and family stability, 303–304
See also gender differences
sexual revolution, 251
Sierra Club, 461
Sierra Leone, civil war in, 411–412, 414–416
Simon, Julian, 471
simplicity movement, 451–452
Singapore
corporal punishment in, 319
economic growth in, 184–186, 190
single-parent families
children in, 311–312
and criminal behavior, 347
and poverty, 28–29
skepticism, in scientific method, 92–95
Skolnick, Jerome, 339
slavery, African American, 219–221, 361
Slovenia, 407
"Slow Food" movement, 143
smallpox, 466
social bonds: in Hirschi's social control theory, the attachments a person has with
other people, 336–338

social capital
defined, 99
measures of, in industrial nations,
101–102
See also civic engagement
social change, positive, 504
community-level solutions for, 510–511
economic cooperation between public and
private sector, 508
global solutions for, 505–508
increasing foreign aid, 506–508
individual solutions for, 512–513
national-level solutions for, 509–510
reducing poor countries' debt, 506, 507
regional solutions for, 508–509
world systems perspective on, 504–505
See also change
social class
impact on values and lifestyle, 196
and socialization process, 136
See also class inequality; stratification
social cohesion
impact of industrialization on, 51–53, 331
and suicide, 53–55
social conflict, and socialization, 135
social construction of gender, 241–242
and U.S. women's movement, 247–251
See also gender differences
social construction of reality: social
processes of developing a consensus
about what exists, in both a material and
a nonmaterial way, and what it all means
and then communicating that reality to
other people in the society, 132–139
acculturation, 136
socialization, 134–136
and social production of culture, 137–139
social contract, implied, in workplace, 422,
424
social control mechanisms, for controlling
crime, 344–345
social control theory, on criminal behavior,
336–338
social disorganization theory, on criminal
behavior, 338, 339, 345–346, 347
social inequality. *See* class inequality;
inequality
social institutions, and socialization, 135
socialism, 377–378
socialization: process of learning about and
adopting the nonmaterial elements of
one's culture and becoming familiar with
its material elements, 134–136

social mobility, 163–165, 168
  in agricultural societies, 171–172
social movements, in national state, 357–359
social organization of consumption, 452–457
  and treadmill of production, 455–457
  and virtual environmentalism, 457–459
social problems
  construction of, 143
  learning more about, 512
social production of culture, 137–139
sociological imagination: ability to see behaviors as the joint product of individual and societal forces, 56
sociological perspective: macro view of the social world that stresses the importance of the social context in which behavior takes place: groups, institutions, social processes, culture, society, and the relationships among societies, 55–57
sociological research, 515
  citing sources in, 518
  interpreting data for, 516–517
  reporting data responsibly in, 517–519
  using graphics in, 518
  using technology for, 515–516
  world maps useful for, 519–547 (*see also* maps)
sociology: study of human society, 6–7
  approach to families, 282–284
  creation of, 45
  and culture, 119–122
  Durkheim's contribution to, 51–55
  impact of industrialization on, 42–45, 57
  inequality as central concern of, 162–169
  Marx's contribution to, 45–48, 58
  perspective on, 55–57
  scientific inquiry in, 86–87 (*see also* scientific method)
  Weber's contribution to, 48–51
solutions. *See* social change, positive
Somalia, famine in, 475
South Africa, racial conflict in, 192, 217–218, 386
South America, map of, 526. *See also* Latin America
Southern African Development Community (SADC), 15, 509
South Korea, economic growth in, 184–186, 190
sovereign authority: exercise of final authority over some set of activities on some

territory, often believed to be lodged in national states, 356
Soviet Union
  collapse of, 7, 140, 344
  division of, 367, 368
  and fall of communism in Europe, 27–28, 362
  See also Russia
Srebrenica, 408, 416
Stacey, Judith, 285–286
Starbucks, 354
state intervention: government action for the purpose of having the economy behave in some desired fashion, 377–378
state power, reorganization of, 366–369. *See also* national states
stereotypes: rigid overgeneralizations about an entire group of people, 211
sterilization procedures, 496–497
stock market, and Asian economic crisis, 4
stratification: system by which valued goods and services are distributed in a society, 163–165
  and competitive consumption, 435, 445–446
  impact on socialization, 136
  and social mobility, 163
  three dimensions of, 166–168
  See also class inequality; inequality
street children: children who live and work primarily on the street because either their parents are no longer alive or they must earn money to help their impoverished families, 311
street crime: crimes that involve a personal confrontation between victim and offender and result in obvious loss or physical injury, 322
structural adjustment programs (SAPs): development programs implemented by a global funding agency that requires significant reform of a country's economy, 254–256, 308, 309–310, 485
structural-functionalism: type of sociological analysis rooted in Durkheim, Comte, and others that views society as a system consisting of different parts (structure) each of which plays a role, performs a function, or makes a contribution, 52
  and functions of inequality, 168–169
  and sexual division of labor, 303–304
structural pluralism, 214
structural strain, and crime, 332–333

subcontracting, corporate, 424, 429–430
subcultures, 122–123
 burnout, 69–70
 conflict, 336
 deviant, 335–336
 retreatist, 336
 and socialization process, 135
subsistence technology: manner in which a
 society's basic needs, such as food, shelter,
 and clothing, are satisfied, 169–170
 in agricultural societies, 171–172
 and gender roles, 243–247
 in hunting and gathering societies, 170
 in industrial societies, 172–177
 and inequality among nations, 183–186
suicide
 and credit card debt, 436–437
 Durkheim's study of, 53–55, 67, 70
 sociologic dimensions of, 92
 teenage, 41, 68–70
 worldwide, 67–68
supranational authority: exercise of authority beyond the level of the national states,
 366
surveys, 110–112, 122
Sutherland, Edwin, 334–335
Sweden
 immigrants in, 365
 marriage patterns in, 288–289
 women's status in, 119–121
symbols, in communication, 131–132

taboos, 127
Taiwan, economic growth in, 184–186, 190
technical subsystem, in culture industry, 137,
 138
technology: tools and methods for producing
 things, 130
 agricultural, 171, 471, 472
 and alienation, 24
 and cultural lag, 141
 cybercrimes, 328–329
 and Earth's carrying capacity, 471–472
 and global economy, 14–15
 impact on labor force, 426–427, 429–430
 impact on repressive governments, 11–12
 industrial, 169, 172
 inequality in access to, 10–11, 106, 107,
 183–184
 information, 130–131, 426
 initiatives to reduce unequal access to, 508
 map of high-tech exports, 540

and mobility of trade and investment, 363,
 427, 428
 and privacy issues, 12–14
 role in culture, 130–131
 role in decline in civic engagement, 88, 96,
 106, 107
 for sociological research, 515–516
 subsistence, 169–170 (*see also* subsistence
 technology)
teenage suicide, 41, 68–70
television
 role in decline in civic engagement, 88, 96,
 97–98, 105, 106, 109–110
 variation in access to, 106, 107
temporary workers, increase in, 424, 427–429
territorial community, 122–123
theory: explanation for the relationship
 between variables, 86
 interaction with research, 90–92
 sociology's use of, 6–7
 See also scientific method
Theory of the Leisure Class, The (Veblen), 445
Thompson, Warren S., 290
Thomson Consumer Electronics, 1
Thornton, Arland, 302
Tiananmen Square, 11–12
Tito, Marshal, 407
"tooth fairy" ritual, 130
total fertility rate (TFR): average number of
 children a woman of childbearing age can
 expect to bear given the prevailing birth
 rates, 290–293
trade, global mobility of, 361, 362–363. *See
 also* international trade
traditional culture
 coexisting with global culture, 144–145
 loss of, 117–119, 143–144
 perspective on, 24–25
transnational corporations (TNCs)
 early European, 360–361
 list of richest, 61, 62
 role in inequality between nations, 184
 and world systems theory, 61–63
 See also global economy; international trade
transnational organizations: organizations
 that maintain social relationships across
 national frontiers, 362
 citizen actions against, 386–387
 growth of, 361–363
 political authority of, 366, 379–380,
 381–383, 387–388
 role in managing global problems, 383–385

travel, international
increase in, 5–6, 491, 492
and infectious disease, 491–493
to obtain medicine, 491
tuberculosis, 384, 490, 491
Tuskegee Syphilis Study, 486–487
Tuzla, 408

U.S. Census Bureau, 95, 113
Uganda, 403
Ultimate Resource, The (Simon), 471
underclass, 180, 260
African American, 223, 336
UNICEF, 29, 308, 411, 506
Uniform Crime Report (UCR), 323, 324
union movement. *See* labor movement
Union of Concerned Scientists, 449
United Kingdom, political fragmentation in, 17
United Nations, 381, 383, 386, 414, 477, 494, 506, 516
peacekeeping efforts of, 414–416, 475
and war in former Yugoslavia, 408
United Nations Information Technology Services (UNITeS), 508
United Nations Security Council, 404
United Nations World Food Program, 472
United States
assimilation of European immigrants, 226–229
changing labor market in, 175–177
child poverty in, 28–31
contemporary race relations in, 221–226
crime rates in, 321–322, 339–340
declining union membership in, 370–371
dissatisfaction with democracy in, 380, 381
divorce rates in, 295, 296, 297
downward reorganization in, 369
ethnic and racial groups in, 19, 230, 365
fertility rates in, 292–293
government spending of, 187–188, 189
health insurance inequality in, 498
increasing income inequality in, 30, 177–182, 187, 188, 190, 221, 222
population growth in, 463, 464, 465–467
present-day immigrants to, 229–232
racial and ethnic hostility in, 206
rates of legal immigration to, 226, 227, 228
suicide rates in, 67–70
traditional values in, 126–127
wages lag in, 432–433

unmarried partner, as new family role, 283.
See also cohabitation
upward reorganization, of state power, 366
urbanization, 57, 172
and decline in inequality, 174–175
impact on social cohesion, 51, 52
and suicide, 54
world map depicting, 529
See also industrialization
urban poverty
of African Americans, 260
and current immigration, 232
and deindustrialization, 182, 223, 225
See also poverty
values: attitudes about what is desirable and moral, 126–127
change in family, 299–303
survey on family, 316
Vanderbilt, Cornelius, 445
variables: anything in the social world whose value or score can change, 88–89
correlation and causation of, 97–98
in experiments, 108–110
probabilistic relationships of, 96–97
See also scientific method
Veblen, Thorstein, 442–443, 445
venereal disease, 493
victimization survey: measurement of the crime rate based on interviews with representative samples of the population, 324–325
Vietnam war, 411–412
violence
and conflict subculture, 336
and differential association, 335
virtual environmentalism, 457–459
voter turnout
decline in, 105–106
study of, 103–104
voting rights, labor movement's support of, 370

Wallace, Walter, 207, 212, 214, 215, 232–233
Wal-Mart, 61
war
in former Yugoslavia, 6–7, 406–410
impact on family, 308–309
impact on healthcare, 487–489
increase in civil, 404–405
and limitations of peacekeeping, 414–416
outside military intervention in, 413–414
recommendations for ending, 416–419

war *(continued)*
refugees from, 363–364, 410, 411
voices of victims of, 411–413
See also ethnic conflict; peacekeeping
warmaker, national state as, 360
war tribunals, 408, 417
water, access to safe, 544
wealth
growing inequality of, 162, 163, 446–447
and prestige, 166–167
See also income inequality
Weber, Max, 48–51, 58, 63–64, 71,
166–168, 169
Web lifestyle, 10. *See also* Internet
WebMD Foundation, 508
Welfare Reform Act (1996), 376
welfare systems
European, 187–189
impact of immigration on, 374–376
labor movement's support of, 370
in national state, 357
western culture, domination of, 20, 118,
141–144, 262
white-collar crime: crime committed by
"respectable" people, often in the course
of their jobs, 322
Wilson, James Q., 338, 344–345, 346–348
Wilson, William Julius, 307
Witte, J. C., 100, 113
women
changing marriage age of, 286–288
and childbearing, 290–295, 478–480
college enrollment and degrees of,
263–264, 265
different cultural views of, 119–121
employment of, and family change,
303–306, 312, 478–480
gender empowerment measure, 535
and income inequality, 181–182, 189–190
in U.S. workforce, 247–251, 257–260
and work inequalities, 257–262
See also family; gender differences
women's movement, U.S., 247–251
Women's Technology Cluster, 240
Women's Trade Union League, 249
"Women 2000: Gender Equality, Development, and Peace for the 21st Century,"
252
workforce
early industrial, 43
gender inequality in developing countries',
260–262

impact of rationalization on, 63–64, 66–67
percentage of women in, 258, 260, 261
weakening of labor movement, 370–372,
373
world map of educated skilled labor, 533
workforce, U.S.
changing structure of, 175–177
disjunction between hours worked and pay,
432–434
and family wage, 249–250
gender differences in, 181–182, 257–260
impact of early women's movement on,
247–251
impact of global economy on, 1–3, 4
and implied social contract, 422–424
occupations expecting growth, 3, 257
temporary, 427–429
See also workplace changes
working class, in industrial societies,
172–174. *See also* class inequality
workplace, and socialization, 134
workplace changes
changing U.S. labor market, 175–177
cycle of work and spend, 434–437
and deindustrialization, 180–182
downsizing, 1–3, 180, 424, 426–427
elimination of organizational hierarchies,
424, 430–431
impact on community life, 437–439
and implied social contract, 422–424
increase in temporary workers, 424,
427–429
outsourcing and subcontracting, 424,
429–430
pros and cons of, 439
and rise of disorderly work career, 424–426
social consequences of, 432–439
weakening of labor movement, 370–372,
424, 431–432
See also workforce
World Bank, 254, 381, 383, 388, 485
World Health Organization (WHO), 485,
488, 490, 500, 508
world-institutions perspective: education
theory arguing that societies throughout
the world have adopted remarkably similar educational institutions based on
Western ideals, 262
world maps, 520–527. *See also* maps
world systems theory: modern version of
Marxism in which the globe is seen as a
single system dominated by core nations

(the "modern bourgeoisie"), 58–63, 166, 504–505
World Trade Organization (WTO), 353–355, 366, 381, 383, 387, 432
World War II, 178, 186, 228, 377, 381, 403
  impact on gender differences, 250–251
Worldwatch Institute, 461, 462
Wuthnow, Robert, 100

Yeltsin, Boris, 140
Yugoslavia, 403
  conflict in, 6–7, 12, 406–410
  and Dayton Accords, 410, 413
  division of, 16, 367, 368, 372, 407
  genocide in, 407–409

Zapatista National Liberation Army, 16

A Sociologist's Atlas

KATHLEEN M. FALLON

For students of sociology who are interested in society on a global scale, more information is available than ever before. Not only are all the usual printed resources available in libraries, but computers and the Internet have made it easier to find information both in print and in electronic form. Scholars and researchers around the world are sharing information via international conferences and the Internet as never before, and opportunities for you to speak with someone from another country or to travel there yourself are increasing as phone rates and airfares decrease.

There is not enough space in this atlas to provide exhaustive information on researching and reporting on societies around the world. Rather, we give you pointers on interpreting and using sociological data, especially international data, and bring together a selection of useful information in the form of maps to supplement the book's text and graphics and to give you a head start in researching topics of interest. (The maps included in the atlas are listed at the end of this introduction.) You can find additional information on researching and reporting on sociological topics at our Web site, www.pineforge.com/snc. But, first, check the quick tips offered here on using technology to find information, interpreting data carefully, and communicating your research findings responsibly.

Using Technology to Find Information

Sometimes browsing through traditional media like books and journals is the best way to find academic studies or information that doesn't clearly fall into the category you're researching or information in pre-1990s sources. You can supplement that form of research with computer-aided methods. Your school library, of course, can give you access to a number of electronic catalogs and databases, such as InfoTrac and Lexis-Nexis; most schools also have Web sites that allow you to search many databases online.

If you have access to the Web, you can also find a wealth of information through search engines and links from one useful site to associated sites. Be aware that search engines use slightly different procedures for selecting and presenting possibly relevant sites, so you may want to use more than one to find what you're looking for.

Other useful sources of electronic information are the many sites sponsored by governmental bodies (for example, the U.S. Department of Commerce), nongovernmental organizations (for example, Human Rights Watch), and international governing bodies (for example, the United Nations). They have Web sites full of data, reports, and graphics compiled by social scientists here and abroad. The URLs (Web addresses) for such sites often are intuitive: *www.un.org* is the address for the United Nations, and *www.hrw.org* is for Human Rights Watch. In any case, you can find a particular Web site by using a search engine.

Interpreting Data Carefully

Although information is plentiful, it is not all equally useful. For instance, some of the best sources of statistical and other hard data are tables, charts, and maps, which can be difficult to read if you are not familiar with the conventions of visual display. For some tips on interpreting those sorts of data, see the links at the Web site for this book at *www.pineforge.com/snc*.

Nor are data always reliable. Here are a few tips for dealing with information taken from Web sites (see also the links at www.pineforge.com/snc) and with international data.

Web data (Schutt, 1999, pp. 512–513):

- *Evaluate the quality of the source.* Many public and social service organizations publish data from research by qualified social scientists. Such information is far more reliable than information published on political, commercial, or special-interest sites. If you're not familiar with the source, check the home page for the site; most provide an "About Us . . ." page. That is not to say you should completely trust or distrust any site just because of who maintains it. You may glean some kernel of understanding or a useful link from a clearly subjective source, and even social scientists have their biases and blind spots. Just be aware of the underlying motivations of the source and evaluate whether the methods used to gather data were likely to yield valid and reliable results.

- *Anticipate change—and stagnation.* A Web site may have a short life, the sponsoring organization may change the URL, or the links from one site to another may be defunct. Look for copyright or publication dates on the Web site.

Some organizations put a lot of effort into establishing a site but don't update it.

- *Be concerned about the generalizability of data.* Keep in mind that the data you find on one site are about a particular situation at a particular time, compiled and reported by someone with a particular purpose. You can't necessarily use just one set of data to support your argument. One way to avoid shaky generalizations is to seek information from multiple sources.

International data:

- *Be aware of the difficulties of gathering statistical information in developing countries.* A number of developing countries do not have the resources to carry out regular statistical censuses. Therefore, their data may not be as up-to-date as those in more developed countries. In addition, individuals conducting surveys in developing countries may not have enough money to collect as many surveys as would be collected in developed countries, or they simply may not have the time or ability to reach some rural areas to collect needed information.

- *Be wary of "official" information.* Collecting data about politically repressive countries or countries in the midst of hostilities is difficult. The authorities may not collect certain types of information for political reasons, may misrepresent the results to serve their ends, or may withhold the results from outsiders.

- *Be careful when you generalize.* Even when data can be collected, the variables may not be comparable from country to country. For example, data compiled for labor force participation are not fully comparable across countries because of the different methods used to define work. Some countries may analyze labor force participation only between the ages of 15 and 64 years, while others include individuals who are younger or older. Analyzing sociological variables across societies shows general patterns, but comparisons remain problematic. When you are reporting comparative data, the best approach is to find out when and how the data were collected in each country, how the variables were defined, and what problems and unique situations may have influenced the results—and then to note those anomalies in your report and avoid unjustified generalizations.

Reporting Data Responsibly

Writing a report is not just a matter of describing the information you have collected from various sources. It also involves looking for interesting connections among the data and drawing your own conclusions about what they mean. Still, the foundation of any report is the facts that support your opinions. Given the constraints of time and money, most students will draw facts from other sources rather than gather the information firsthand.

As you write your report, be certain to cite the references you use in the paper, including electronic references—you don't want to be accused of plagiarism. It is unethical to "cut and paste" information from an electronic source and present it as your own, even if you make some slight adjustments in wording and appearance. If you use a direct quotation or paraphrase the original, make sure you cite not only the source and the year it was published but also the page number on which you found the information. Even if you simply refer to an argument or a line of thought presented in an article, book, or Web site, you need to cite the source and the year it was published.

At the end of your report, include a thorough bibliography or reference list of all the books, articles, and Internet resources you used. Be sure to list your sources in alphabetical order. For specific details on how to cite sources and how to prepare a bibliography, refer to the *ASA Style Guide* (the official guide of the American Sociological Association, which is based on the *Publication Manual of the American Psychological Association*), unless your professor specifies some other style guide. The system of citation recommended in the *ASA Style Guide* is generally referred to as the author-date system, because the name and date of each source is written in the text, usually in parentheses, and the full citations are in a bibliography or reference list at the end of the report. The ASA style is essentially the style used in this book.

Use special care in citing Web sources. One of your overall goals should be to enhance the credibility of your Web citation, which you can do by indicating the individual or organization responsible for the information, the date the information was published, and the date you accessed it. Another overall goal is to enable someone to find the original Web site, which is best accomplished by including the complete URL.

The bibliographic style for electronic documents continues to evolve. The *ASA Style Guide* and other style manuals have some recommendations. You can also find excerpts from the most current recommendations of the International Organization for Standardization (ISO) on the Web, at *www.nlc-bnc.ca/iso/tc46sc9/standard/690-2e.htm*. ISO has an ongoing project to develop a globally uniform style of citation for electronic sources.

You may want to present some of the information in your report in graphic form, either to emphasize certain points or to draw readers' attention to particular aspects of the data. Different types of graphics have different purposes. Tables are excellent for presenting large quantities of data in an organized way; charts, graphs, maps, and diagrams are best for highlighting trends, relationships, and processes. Here are some tips for the responsible use of graphics (Smith, 1997, p. 12).

- Use graphics to support the text of your report—to emphasize important points or provide necessary detail—not as a substitute for the text.

- Tie graphics into the text of your report by explaining their significant details and their significance to your topic.

- Label each graphic with a descriptive title and include important information such as the dates when the data were collected and peculiarities in the way variables were defined.

- Clearly and correctly label table columns. Clearly label the segments in pie charts and the axes (the horizontal and vertical framing lines) in line charts and bar graphs. Indicate the values of the data points, lines, and segments.

- Identify the source of the data and, if you are reproducing a graphic more or less as it was in the original source, credit its creator.

It is never wrong to credit someone for ideas or data you have taken from their work. In addition, citing other sources usually makes your report more credible, because you are showing that the ideas you present are shared by others and are supported by objective data.

Maps Included in This Atlas

The world maps in this book are based on the Robinson projection, which is often used for thematic maps to show how countries, regions, or continents compare on some variable. With the Robinson projection, shapes, areas, scales, and distances are somewhat distorted—least distorted toward the center and along the equator and most distorted along the north and south poles. Keep in mind that some distortion is inevitable no matter which projection is used.

In maps 9 through 28, the highest- and lowest-ranking nations on each variable are identified by name, along with their actual scores on the variable shown in the map.

Regions of the World
Map 1   The World
Map 2   Africa
Map 3   Asia
Map 4   Europe
Map 5   Middle East
Map 6   North America
Map 7   South America
Map 8   Oceania

Population and Culture
Map 9   Population Density
Map 10   Urbanization
Map 11   Ethnic Diversity

Economic Development
Map 12   Purchasing Power
Map 13   Poverty
Map 14   Education of Skilled Labor

Human Development
Map 15   Relative Human Development
Map 16   Empowerment of Women
Map 17   Education Expenditures
Map 18   Homicides

International Trade
Map 19   Growth in Global Trade
Map 20   Foreign Direct Investment
Map 21   High-Tech Exports
Map 22   Film Imports

Environment
Map 23   Deforestation
Map 24   Carbon Dioxide Emissions
Map 25   Access to Safe Water

Health
Map 26   Life Expectancy
Map 27   Health Expenditures
Map 28   Nutrition

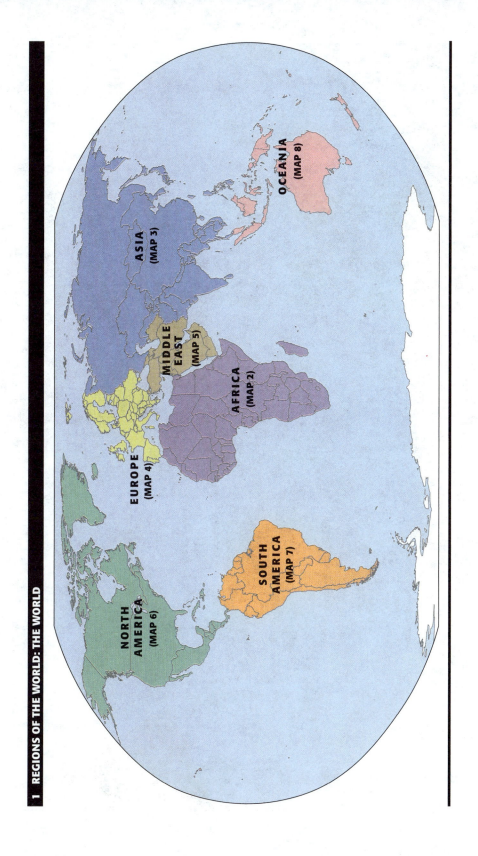

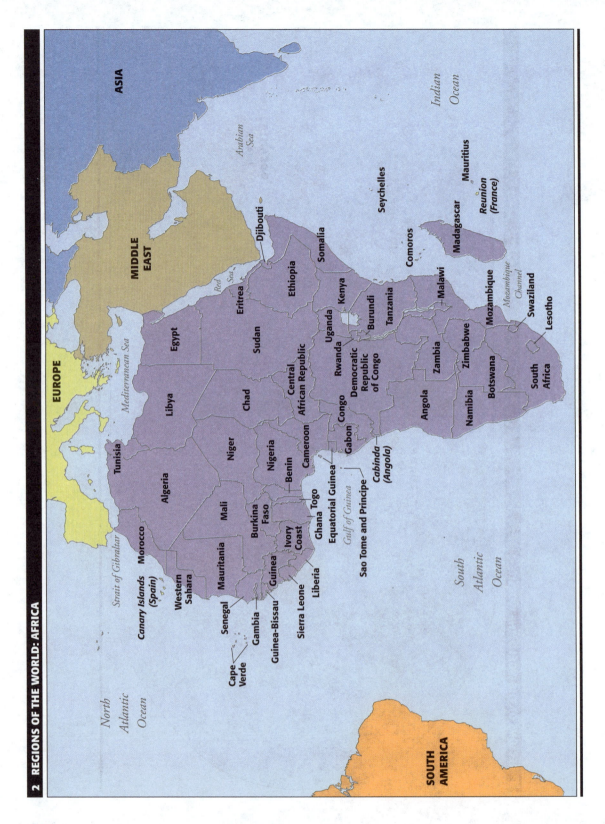

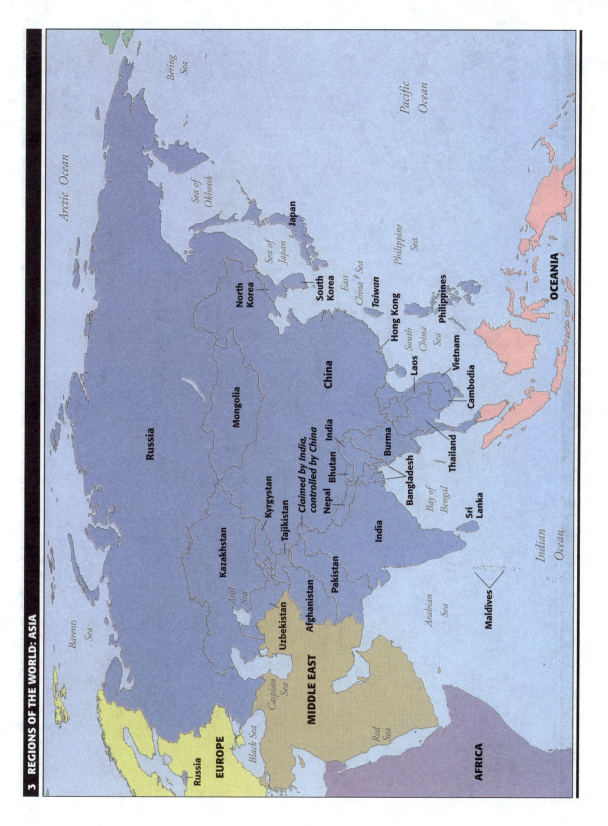

Arctic Ocean

Barents
Sea

Bering
Sea

Sea of
Okhotsk

Pacific
Ocean

EUROPE

Russia

Black Sea

Caspian
Sea

MIDDLE EAST

Red
Sea

AFRICA

Aral
Sea

Kazakhstan

Russia

Mongolia

Kyrgystan

Tajikistan

Uzbekistan

Afghanistan

Pakistan

Claimed by India,
controlled by China

Nepal Bhutan

India

India

Sri
Lanka

Maldives

Arabian
Sea

Bay of
Bengal

Bangladesh

Burma

Thailand

Indian
Ocean

Sea of Japan

Japan

North
Korea

South
Korea

East
China Sea

Taiwan

Hong Kong

South
China
Sea

Laos

Vietnam

Cambodia

Philippine
Sea

Philippines

OCEANIA

China

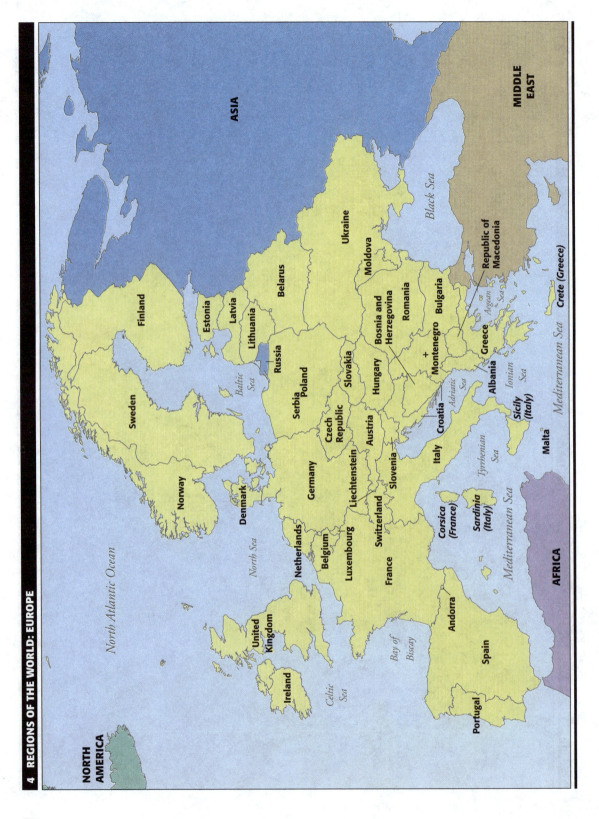

NORTH
AMERICA

North Atlantic Ocean

Ireland

United
Kingdom

Celtic
Sea

Bay of
Biscay

Portugal

Spain

Andorra

North Sea

Netherlands

Belgium

Luxembourg

France

Switzerland

Liechtenstein

Corsica
(France)

Sardinia
(Italy)

Mediterranean Sea

Denmark

Germany

Austria

Slovenia

Italy

Tyrrhenian
Sea

Malta

Norway

Sweden

Finland

Baltic
Sea

Estonia

Latvia

Lithuania

Russia

Poland

Czech
Republic

Serbia

Slovakia

Hungary

Croatia

Adriatic
Sea

Belarus

Ukraine

Moldova

Bosnia and
Herzegovina

Romania

Montenegro

Bulgaria

Albania

Greece

Ionian
Sea

Republic of
Macedonia

Aegean
Sea

Crete (Greece)

Mediterranean Sea

Black Sea

ASIA

MIDDLE
EAST

AFRICA

Sicily
(Italy)

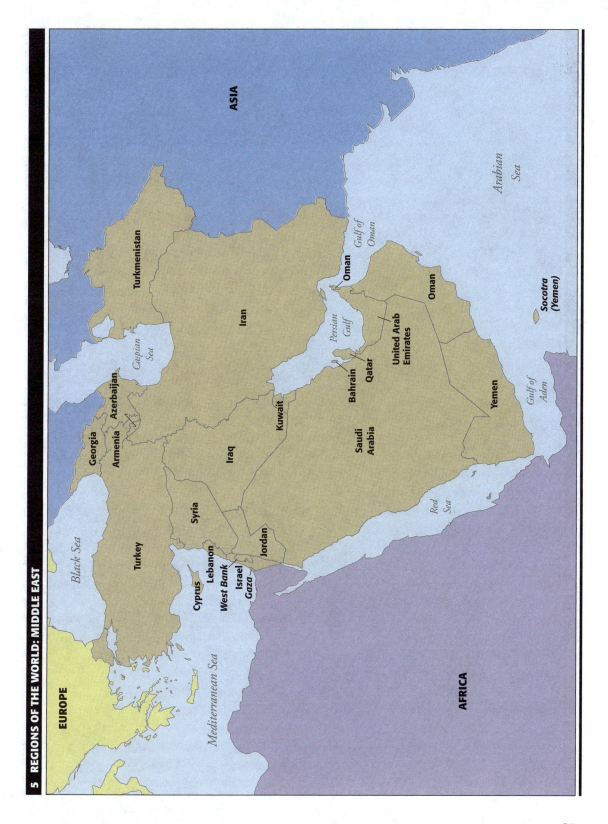

EUROPE

ASIA

AFRICA

Black Sea

Caspian Sea

Mediterranean Sea

Red Sea

Persian Gulf

Gulf of Oman

Gulf of Adem

Arabian Sea

Turkey

Cyprus

Lebanon

West Bank

Israel

Gaza

Jordan

Syria

Iraq

Kuwait

Saudi Arabia

Bahrain

Qatar

United Arab Emirates

Oman

Yemen

Oman

Iran

Turkmenistan

Azerbaijan

Armenia

Georgia

Socotra (Yemen)

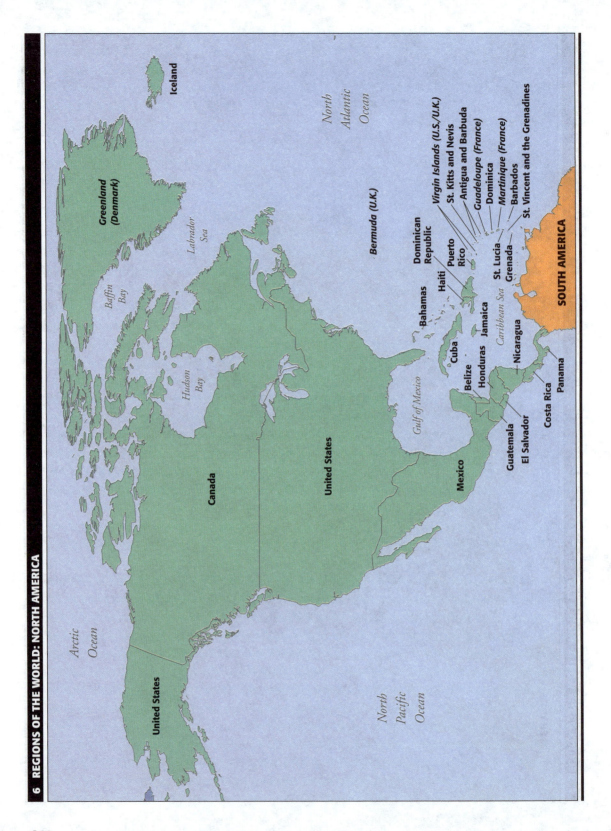

Iceland

Greenland
(Denmark)

North
Atlantic
Ocean

Labrador
Sea

Baffin
Bay

Bermuda (U.K.)

Virgin Islands (U.S./U.K.)
St. Kitts and Nevis
Antigua and Barbuda
Guadeloupe (France)
Dominica
Martinique (France)
Barbados
St. Vincent and the Grenadines

Dominican
Republic
Puerto
Rico
St. Lucia
Grenada

Haiti

Caribbean Sea

Bahamas

SOUTH AMERICA

Hudson
Bay

Cuba

Jamaica

Nicaragua

Belize
Honduras

Costa Rica
Panama

Gulf of Mexico

United States

Canada

Mexico

Guatemala
El Salvador

Arctic
Ocean

United States

North
Pacific
Ocean

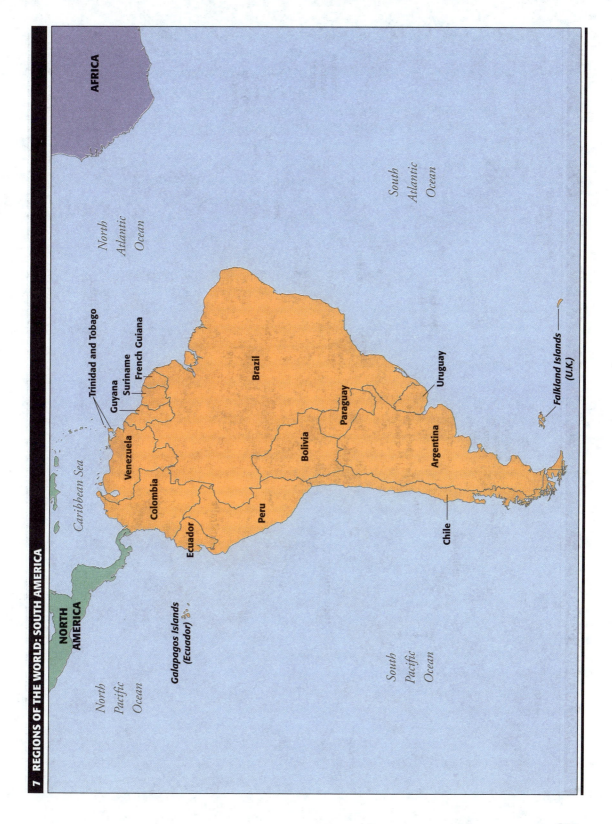

AFRICA

NORTH
AMERICA

North
Atlantic
Ocean

South
Atlantic
Ocean

Caribbean Sea

North
Pacific
Ocean

Trinidad and Tobago
Guyana
Suriname
French Guiana

Brazil

Venezuela

Colombia

Ecuador

Peru

Bolivia

Paraguay

Uruguay

Argentina

Chile

Galapagos Islands
(Ecuador)

South
Pacific
Ocean

Falkland Islands
(U.K.)

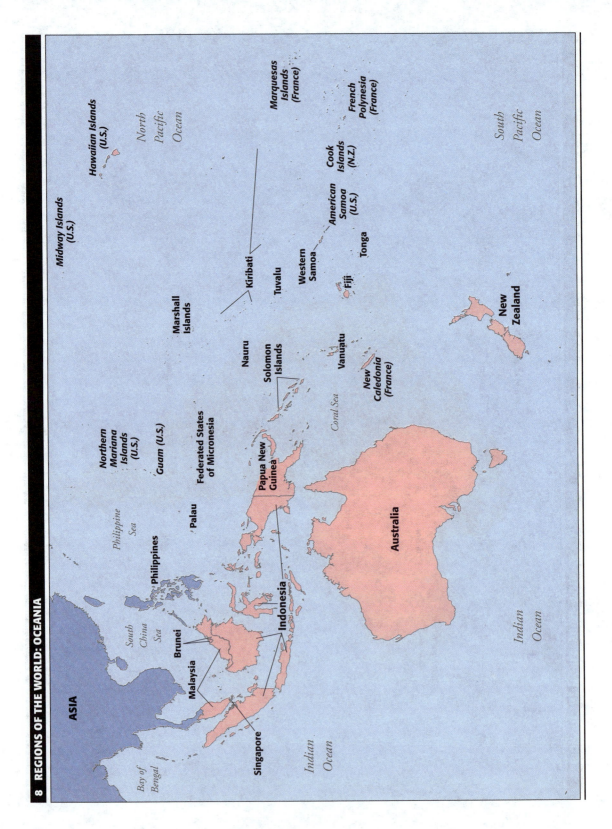

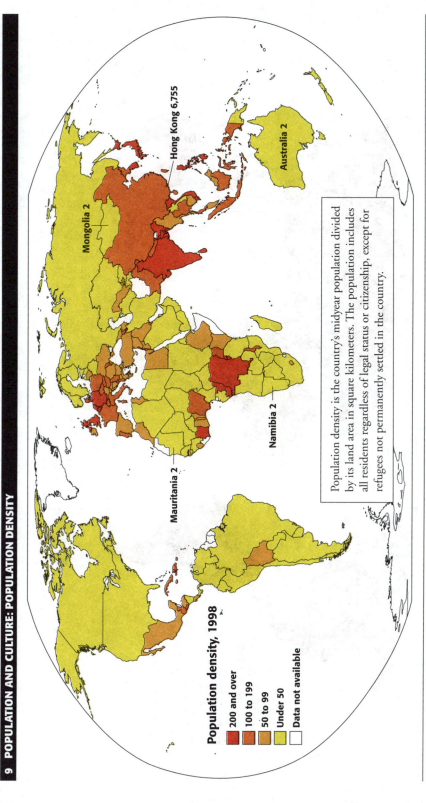

Hong Kong 6,755

Mongolia 2

Australia 2

Mauritania 2

Namibia 2

Population density is the country's midyear population divided by its land area in square kilometers. The population includes all residents regardless of legal status or citizenship, except for refugees not permanently settled in the country.

Population density, 1998

- 200 and over
- 100 to 199
- 50 to 99
- Under 50
- Data not available

Source: Data from "Size of the Economy," *World Development Indicators* (Table 1.1, pp. 10–13), 2000, Washington, DC: World Bank; available on-line at www.worldbank.org/data/wdi/pdfs/rab1_1.pdf.

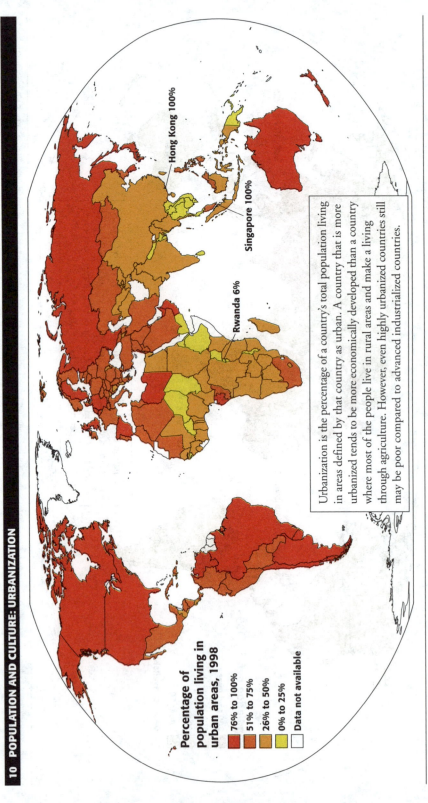

Percentage of
population living in
urban areas, 1998

76% to 100%
51% to 75%
26% to 50%
0% to 25%
Data not available

Hong Kong 100%

Singapore 100%

Rwanda 6%

Urbanization is the percentage of a country's total population living
in areas defined by that country as urban. A country that is more
urbanized tends to be more economically developed than a country
where most of the people live in rural areas and make a living
through agriculture. However, even highly urbanized countries still
may be poor compared to advanced industrialized countries.

Source: Data from "Urbanization," *World Development Indicators* (Table 3.10, pp. 150–153), 2000, Washington, DC: World Bank; available on-line at www.worldbank.org/data/wdi/pdfs/tab3_10.pdf.

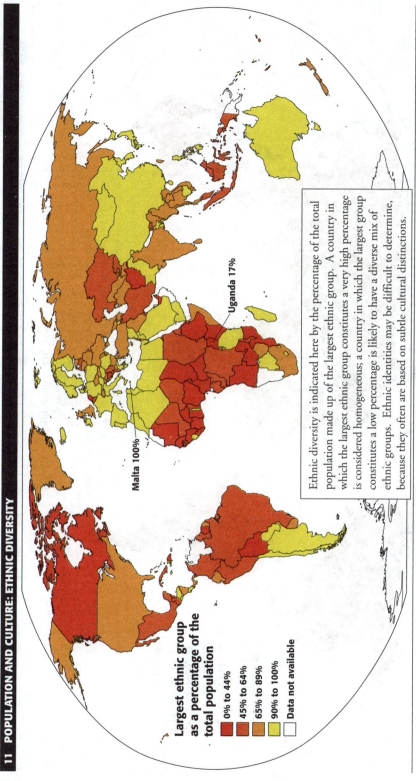

Largest ethnic group as a percentage of the total population

- 0% to 44%
- 45% to 64%
- 65% to 89%
- 90% to 100%
- Data not available

Malta 100%

Uganda 17%

Ethnic diversity is indicated here by the percentage of the total population made up of the largest ethnic group. A country in which the largest ethnic group constitutes a very high percentage is considered homogeneous; a country in which the largest ethnic group constitutes a low percentage is likely to have a diverse mix of ethnic groups. Ethnic identities may be difficult to determine, because they often are based on subtle cultural distinctions.

Source: Data from *The World Factbook*, 2000, Washington, DC: Central Intelligence Agency; available on-line at www.cia.gov/cia/publications/factbook/index.html. Additional data from *Understanding Black Africa*, by D. Morrison, 1989, New York: Paragon House.

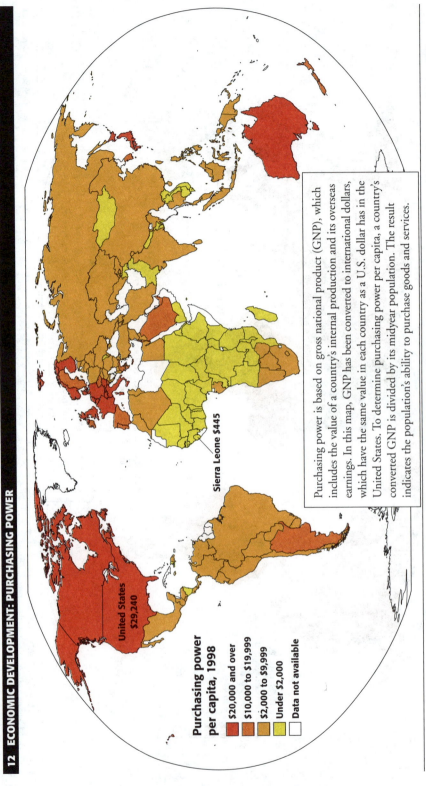

Purchasing power per capita, 1998

- $20,000 and over
- $10,000 to $19,999
- $2,000 to $9,999
- Under $2,000
- Data not available

United States $29,240

Sierra Leone $445

Purchasing power is based on gross national product (GNP), which includes the value of a country's internal production and its overseas earnings. In this map, GNP has been converted to international dollars, which have the same value in each country as a U.S. dollar has in the United States. To determine purchasing power per capita, a country's converted GNP is divided by its midyear population. The result indicates the population's ability to purchase goods and services.

Source: Data from "Size of the Economy," *World Development Indicators* (Table 1.1, pp. 10–13), 2000, Washington, DC: World Bank; available on-line at www.worldbank.org/data/wdi/pdfs/tab1_1.pdf.

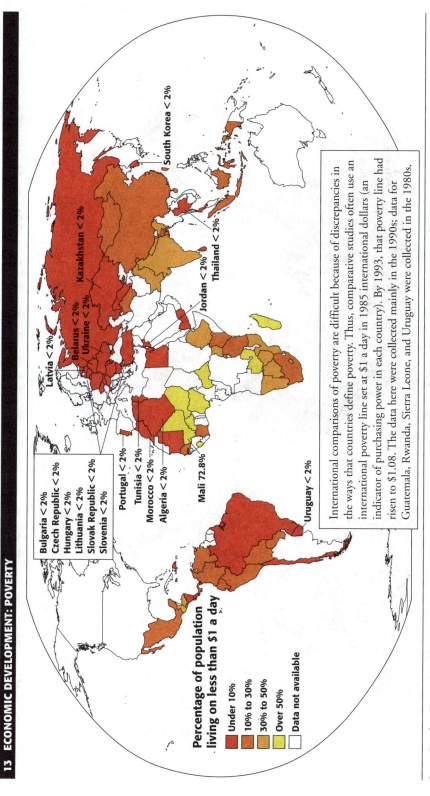

Percentage of population living on less than $1 a day

- Under 10%
- 10% to 30%
- 30% to 50%
- Over 50%
- Data not available

Bulgaria < 2%
Czech Republic < 2%
Hungary < 2%
Lithuania < 2%
Slovak Republic < 2%
Slovenia < 2%

Portugal < 2%
Tunisia < 2%
Morocco < 2%
Algeria < 2%
Mali 72.8%

Latvia < 2%
Belarus < 2%
Ukraine < 2%

Kazakhstan < 2%

South Korea < 2%

Jordan < 2%
Thailand < 2%

Uruguay < 2%

International comparisons of poverty are difficult because of discrepancies in the ways that countries define poverty. Thus, comparative studies often use an international poverty line set at $1 a day in 1985 international dollars (an indicator of purchasing power in each country). By 1993, that poverty line had risen to $1.08. The data here were collected mainly in the 1990s; data for Guatemala, Rwanda, Sierra Leone, and Uruguay were collected in the 1980s.

Source: Data from "Poverty," *World Development Indicators* (Table 2.7, pp. 62–65), 2000, Washington, DC: World Bank; available on-line at www.worldbank.org/data/wdi/pdfs/tab2_7.pdf.

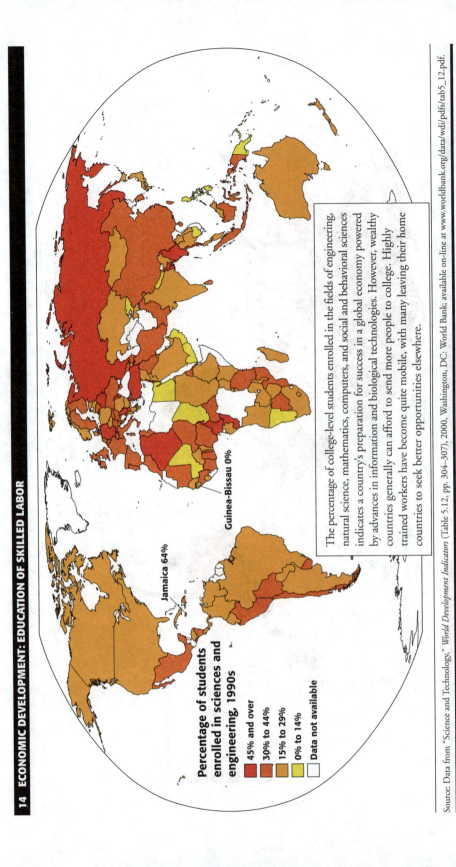

**Percentage of students
enrolled in sciences and
engineering, 1990s**

- 45% and over
- 30% to 44%
- 15% to 29%
- 0% to 14%
- Data not available

Jamaica 64%

Guinea-Bissau 0%

The percentage of college-level students enrolled in the fields of engineering, natural science, mathematics, computers, and social and behavioral sciences indicates a country's preparation for success in a global economy powered by advances in information and biological technologies. However, wealthy countries generally can afford to send more people to college. Highly trained workers have become quite mobile, with many leaving their home countries to seek better opportunities elsewhere.

Source: Data from "Science and Technology," *World Development Indicators* (Table 5.12, pp. 304–307), 2000, Washington, DC: World Bank; available on-line at www.worldbank.org/data/wdi/pdfs/tab5_12.pdf.

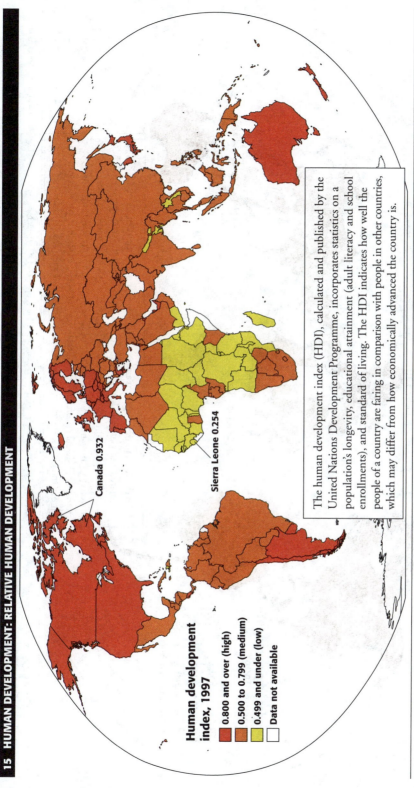

Human development index, 1997

- ■ 0.800 and over (high)
- ■ 0.500 to 0.799 (medium)
- ■ 0.499 and under (low)
- □ Data not available

Canada 0.932

Sierra Leone 0.254

The human development index (HDI), calculated and published by the United Nations Development Programme, incorporates statistics on a population's longevity, educational attainment (adult literacy and school enrollments), and standard of living. The HDI indicates how well the people of a country are faring in comparison with people in other countries, which may differ from how economically advanced the country is.

Source: Data from "Human development index," *Human Development Report 1999: Globalization with a Human Face* (Table 1, pp. 134–137), 1999, New York: United Nations Development Programme; available on-line at www.undp.org/hdro/Backmatter1.pdf.

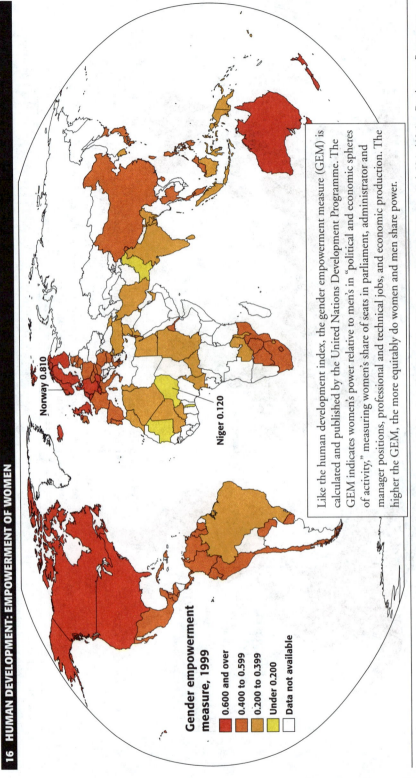

Gender empowerment
measure, 1999

- 0.600 and over
- 0.400 to 0.599
- 0.200 to 0.399
- Under 0.200
- Data not available

Norway 0.810

Niger 0.120

Like the human development index, the gender empowerment measure (GEM) is calculated and published by the United Nations Development Programme. The GEM indicates women's power relative to men's in "political and economic spheres of activity," measuring women's share of seats in parliament, administrator and manager positions, professional and technical jobs, and economic production. The higher the GEM, the more equitably do women and men share power.

Source: Data from "Gender empowerment measure," *Human Development Report 1999: Globalization with a Human Face* (Table 3, pp. 142–145), 1999, New York: United Nations Development Programme; available on-line at www.undp.org/hdro/Backmatter1.pdf.

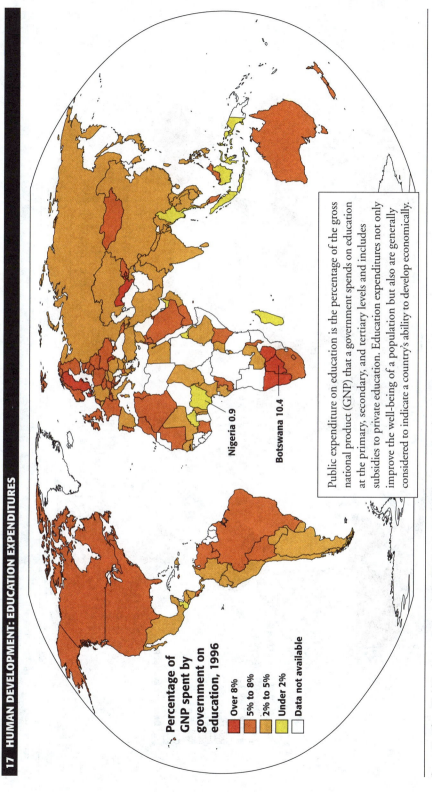

Percentage of GNP spent by government on education, 1996

- Over 8%
- 5% to 8%
- 2% to 5%
- Under 2%
- Data not available

Nigeria 0.9

Botswana 10.4

Public expenditure on education is the percentage of the gross national product (GNP) that a government spends on education at the primary, secondary, and tertiary levels and includes subsidies to private education. Education expenditures not only improve the well-being of a population but also are generally considered to indicate a country's ability to develop economically.

Source: Data from *World Development Indicators*, 1999, Washington DC: World Bank.

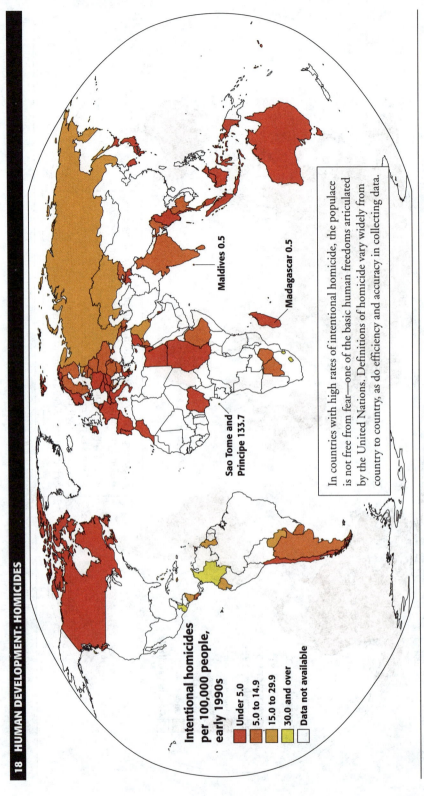

Intentional homicides
per 100,000 people,
early 1990s

- Under 5.0
- 5.0 to 14.9
- 15.0 to 29.9
- 30.0 and over
- Data not available

Maldives 0.5

Madagascar 0.5

Sao Tome and
Principe 133.7

In countries with high rates of intentional homicide, the populace is not free from fear—one of the basic human freedoms articulated by the United Nations. Definitions of homicide vary widely from country to country, as do efficiency and accuracy in collecting data.

Source: Data from "Crime," *Human Development Report 1999: Globalization with a Human Face* (Table 23, pp. 221–224), 1999, New York: United Nations Development Programme; available on-line at www.undp.org/hdro/Backmatter2.pdf.

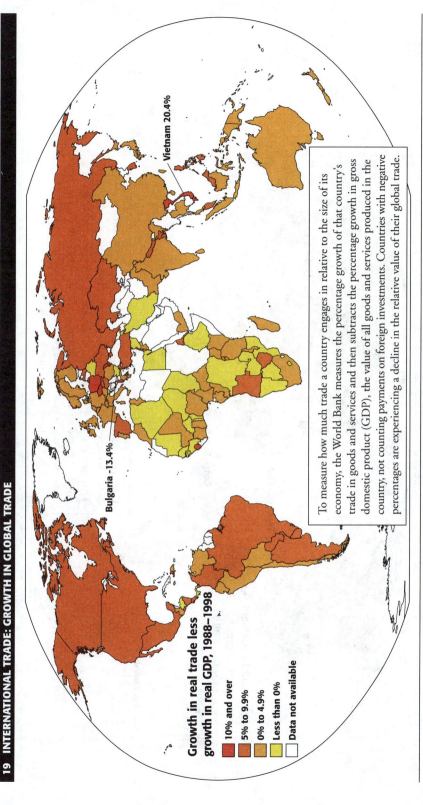

**Growth in real trade less
growth in real GDP, 1988–1998**

- 10% and over
- 5% to 9.9%
- 0% to 4.9%
- Less than 0%
- Data not available

Vietnam 20.4%

Bulgaria -13.4%

To measure how much trade a country engages in relative to the size of its economy, the World Bank measures the percentage growth of that country's trade in goods and services and then subtracts the percentage growth in gross domestic product (GDP), the value of all goods and services produced in the country, not counting payments on foreign investments. Countries with negative percentages are experiencing a decline in the relative value of their global trade.

Source: Data from "Integration with the global economy," *World Development Indicators* (Table 6.1, pp. 314–317), 2000, Washington, DC: World Bank; available on-line at www.worldbank.org/data/wdi2000/pdfs/tab6_1.pdf.

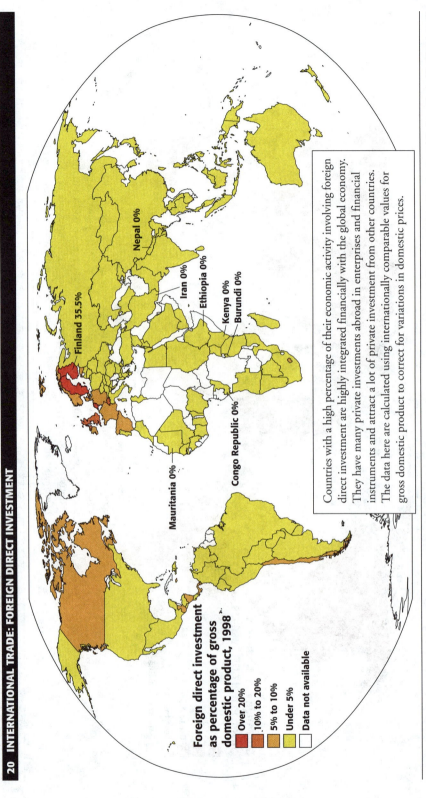

Foreign direct investment as percentage of gross domestic product, 1998

- Over 20%
- 10% to 20%
- 5% to 10%
- Under 5%
- Data not available

Finland 35.5%

Nepal 0%

Iran 0%

Ethiopia 0%

Kenya 0%
Burundi 0%

Mauritania 0%

Congo Republic 0%

Countries with a high percentage of their economic activity involving foreign direct investment are highly integrated financially with the global economy. They have many private investments abroad in enterprises and financial instruments and attract a lot of private investment from other countries. The data here are calculated using internationally comparable values for gross domestic product to correct for variations in domestic prices.

Source: Data from "Integration with the global economy," *World Development Indicators* (Table 6.1, pp. 314–317), 2000, Washington, DC: World Bank; available on-line at www.worldbank.org/data/wdi/pdfs/tab6_1.pdf.

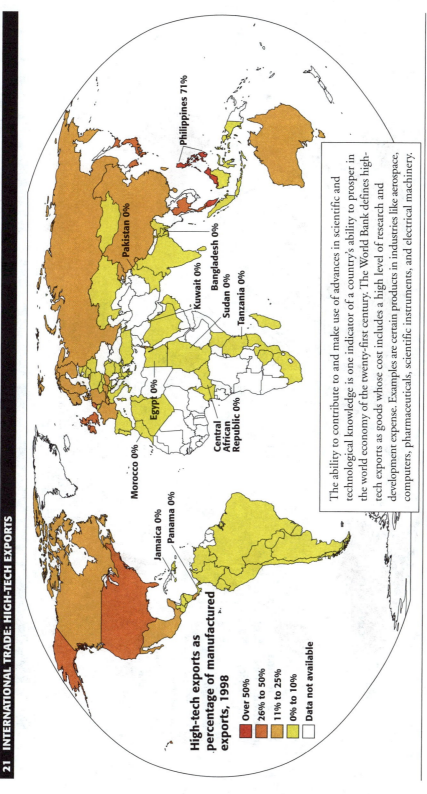

High-tech exports as percentage of manufactured exports, 1998

- Over 50%
- 26% to 50%
- 11% to 25%
- 0% to 10%
- Data not available

Philippines 71%

Pakistan 0%

Bangladesh 0%

Kuwait 0%

Sudan 0%

Tanzania 0%

Egypt 0%

Central African Republic 0%

Morocco 0%

Jamaica 0%

Panama 0%

The ability to contribute to and make use of advances in scientific and technological knowledge is one indicator of a country's ability to prosper in the world economy of the twenty-first century. The World Bank defines high-tech exports as goods whose cost includes a high level of research and development expense. Examples are certain products in industries like aerospace, computers, pharmaceuticals, scientific instruments, and electrical machinery.

Source: Data from "Science and technology," *World Development Indicators* (Table 5.12, pp. 304–307), 2000, Washington, DC: World Bank; available on-line at www.worldbank.org/data/wdi/pdfs/tab5_12.pdf.

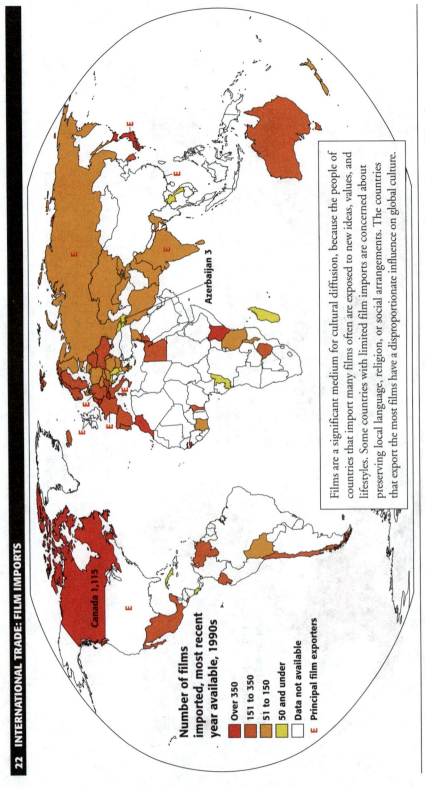

Number of films imported, most recent year available, 1990s

- Over 350
- 151 to 350
- 51 to 150
- 50 and under
- Data not available
- **E** Principal film exporters

Azerbaijan 3

Canada 1,115

Films are a significant medium for cultural diffusion, because the people of countries that import many films often are exposed to new ideas, values, and lifestyles. Some countries with limited film imports are concerned about preserving local language, religion, or social arrangements. The countries that export the most films have a disproportionate influence on global culture.

Source: Data from *UNESCO Statistical Yearbook* (Table IV-12), by United Nations Educational, Scientific, and Cultural Organization, 1999, Lanham, MD: Bernan Press; available on-line at unescostat.unesco.org/statsen/statistics/yearbook/tables\CultAndCom\Table_IV_12_Africa.html (and America.html, Asia.html, Europe.html, Oceania.html).

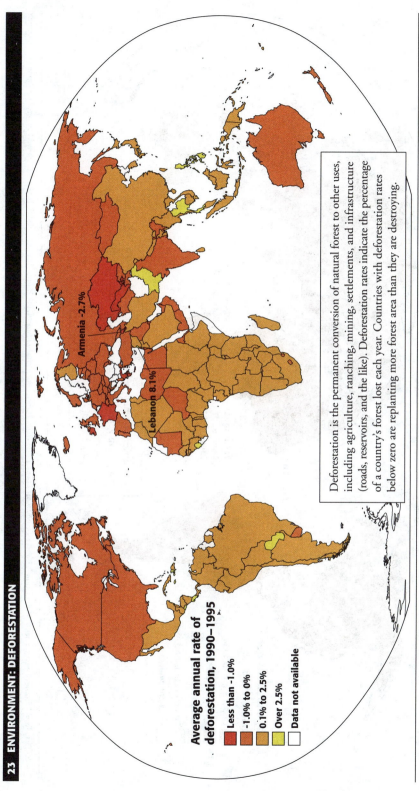

Average annual rate of deforestation, 1990–1995

- Less than -1.0%
- -1.0% to 0%
- 0.1% to 2.5%
- Over 2.5%
- Data not available

Armenia -2.7%

Lebanon 8.1%

Deforestation is the permanent conversion of natural forest to other uses, including agriculture, ranching, mining, settlements, and infrastructure (roads, reservoirs, and the like). Deforestation rates indicate the percentage of a country's forest lost each year. Countries with deforestation rates below zero are replanting more forest area than they are destroying.

Source: Data from *Human Development Report 1999: Globalization with a Human Face* (Table 18, pp. 205–208), 1999, New York: United Nations Development Programme; available on-line at www.undp.org/hdro/Backmatter2.pdf.

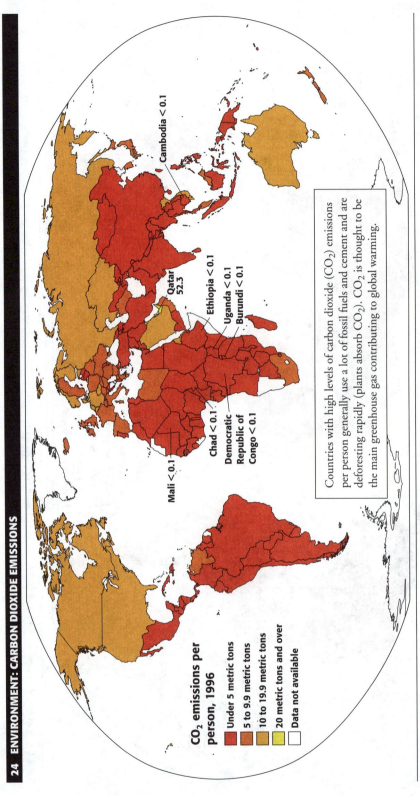

CO$_2$ emissions per person, 1996

- Under 5 metric tons
- 5 to 9.9 metric tons
- 10 to 19.9 metric tons
- 20 metric tons and over
- Data not available

Mali < 0.1

Chad < 0.1

Democratic Republic of Congo < 0.1

Ethiopia < 0.1

Uganda < 0.1

Burundi < 0.1

Qatar 52.3

Cambodia < 0.1

Countries with high levels of carbon dioxide (CO$_2$) emissions per person generally use a lot of fossil fuels and cement and are deforesting rapidly (plants absorb CO$_2$). CO$_2$ is thought to be the main greenhouse gas contributing to global warming.

Source: Data from "Profile of environmental degradation," *Human Development Report 1999: Globalization with a Human Face* (Table 18, pp. 221–224), 1999, New York: United Nations Development Programme; available on-line at www.undp.org/hdro/Backmatter2.pdf.

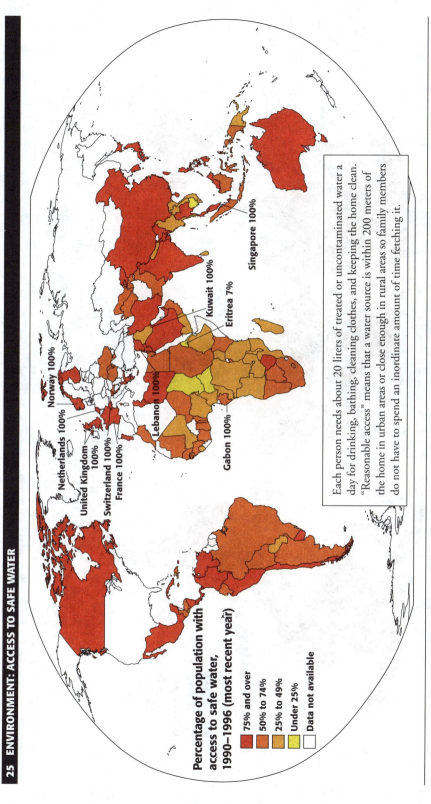

Percentage of population with access to safe water, 1990–1996 (most recent year)

- 75% and over
- 50% to 74%
- 25% to 49%
- Under 25%
- Data not available

Norway 100%

Netherlands 100%

United Kingdom 100%

Switzerland 100%

France 100%

Lebanon 100%

Gabon 100%

Kuwait 100%

Eritrea 7%

Singapore 100%

Each person needs about 20 liters of treated or uncontaminated water a day for drinking, bathing, cleaning clothes, and keeping the home clean. "Reasonable access" means that a water source is within 200 meters of the home in urban areas or close enough in rural areas so family members do not have to spend an inordinate amount of time fetching it.

Source: Data from "Development progress," *World Development Indicators* (Table 1.2, pp. 14–17), 2000, Washington, DC: World Bank; available on-line at www.worldbank.org/data/wdi2000/pdfs/tab1_2.pdf.

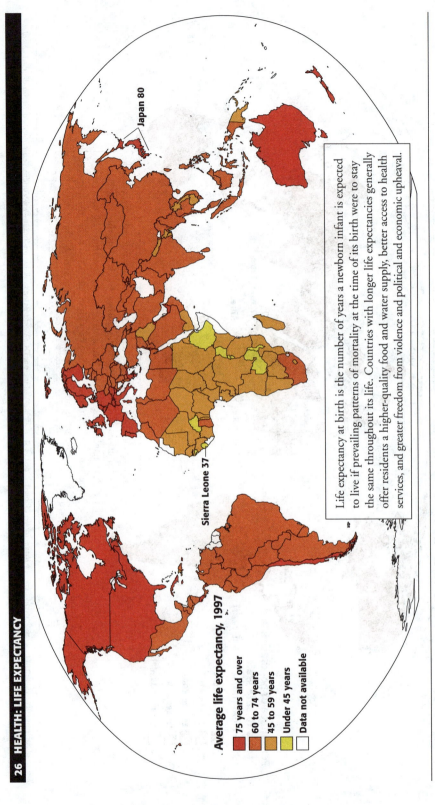

Average life expectancy, 1997

- 75 years and over
- 60 to 74 years
- 45 to 59 years
- Under 45 years
- Data not available

Japan 80

Sierra Leone 37

Life expectancy at birth is the number of years a newborn infant is expected to live if prevailing patterns of mortality at the time of its birth were to stay the same throughout its life. Countries with longer life expectancies generally offer residents a higher-quality food and water supply, better access to health services, and greater freedom from violence and political and economic upheaval.

Source: Data from *World Development Indicators*, 1999, Washington DC: World Bank.

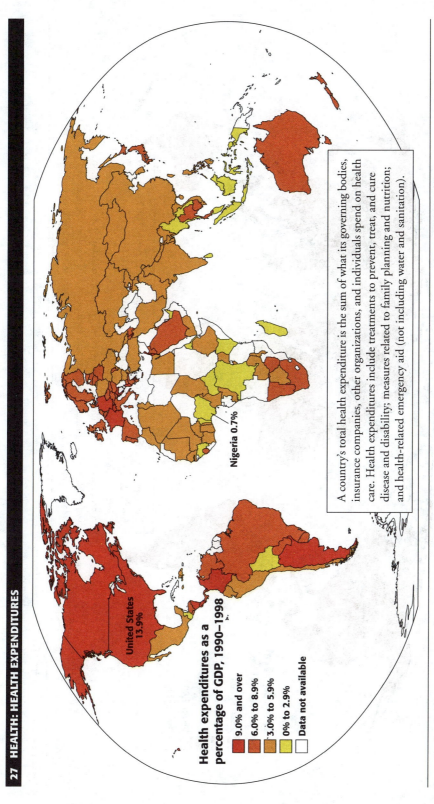

Health expenditures as a percentage of GDP, 1990–1998

- 9.0% and over
- 6.0% to 8.9%
- 3.0% to 5.9%
- 0% to 2.9%
- Data not available

United States 13.9%

Nigeria 0.7%

A country's total health expenditure is the sum of what its governing bodies, insurance companies, other organizations, and individuals spend on health care. Health expenditures include treatments to prevent, treat, and cure disease and disability; measures related to family planning and nutrition; and health-related emergency aid (not including water and sanitation).

Source: Data from "Health expenditure, services, and use," *World Development Indicators* (Table 2.14, pp. 90–93), 2000, Washington, DC: World Bank; available on-line at www.worldbank.org/data/wdi2000/pdfs/tab2_14.pdf.

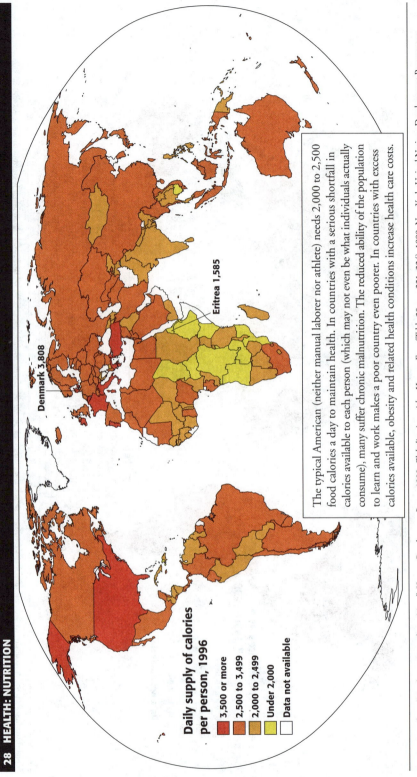

Daily supply of calories per person, 1996

- 3,500 or more
- 2,500 to 3,499
- 2,000 to 2,499
- Under 2,000
- Data not available

Denmark 3,808

Eritrea 1,585

The typical American (neither manual laborer nor athlete) needs 2,000 to 2,500 food calories a day to maintain health. In countries with a serious shortfall in calories available to each person (which may not even be what individuals actually consume), many suffer chronic malnutrition. The reduced ability of the population to learn and work makes a poor country even poorer. In countries with excess calories available, obesity and related health conditions increase health care costs.

Source: Data from "Food security and nutrition," *Human Development Report 1999: Globalization with a Human Face*. (Table 20, pp. 221–224), 1999. New York: United Nations Development Programme; available on-line at www.undp.org/hdro/Backmatter2.pdf.